ADVANCED TRENDS IN WIRELESS COMMUNICATIONS

Edited by **Mutamed Khatib**

Advanced Trends in Wireless Communications
Edited by Mutamed Khatib

Published by InTech

Janeza Trdine 9, 51000 Rijeka, Croatia

Publishing Process Manager Ivana Lorkovic

Technical Editor Teodora Smiljanic

Cover Designer InTech Design Team

Additional hard copies can be obtained from orders@intechopen.com

Advanced Trends in Wireless Communications, Edited by Mutamed Khatib
p. cm.
ISBN 978-953-307-183-1

For EU product safety concerns:
IN TECH d.o.o., Prolaz Marije Krucifikse Kozulić 3, 51000 Rijeka, Croatia,
info@intechopen.com or visit our website at intechopen.com.

Meet the editor

Dr. Mutamed Khatib was born in 1973. He received his B.Sc. degree in Telecommunication Engineering from Yarmouk University, Irbid, Jordan in 1996 and M.Sc. in Electrical & Electronic Engineering from Jordan University for Science and Technology, Irbid, Jordan in 2003. He received his PhD Degree in wireless and mobile systems from University Sains Malaysia (USM), Malaysia in 2009. From 1996 to 2005, he worked as Transmission, Outside Broadcasting and Studio Engineer in Palestinian Broadcasting Corporation (PBC). From 2005 to 2009 he worked as an Instructor in the Department of Electrical Engineering, Palestine Technical University (Kadoorie), Tul Karm, Palestine. Since September 2009, Dr. Mutamed Khatib is working as Assistant professor at the same university. Dr. Khatib has a number of publications to his credit in various international journals and conference proceedings. He is a member of IEEE, Palestinian Engineers Association and Arab Engineers Association.

Contents

Preface

Recently, mobile communication services are penetrating into our society at an explosive growth rate. All of the current communication systems have adopted digital technology. Nowadays, the demand for various wideband services such as high-speed Internet access and video/high-quality image transmission, is increasing. The third-generation mobile communication system has been, designed to support wideband services with the same quality as the fixed networks. The wireless communication systems are expected to play a more important role in providing portable access to future information services. The demand for new services to support Internet and advanced video applications presents the key technical challenges, i.e., multimedia access requires high-bandwidth and low-latency network connections for many users, mobility requires adaptation to time varying channel conditions and portability imposes severe constraints on receiver size and power consumption.

Physical limitations on wireless channels impose huge challenges on reliable communication. Bandwidth limitations, propagation loss, noise and interference make the wireless channel a narrow pipe that does not readily accommodate rapid flow of data. Thus, researchers aim to design systems that are suitable to operate in such channels, in order to have high performance quality of service. Also, the mobility of the communication systems requires further investigation to reduce the complexity and the power consumption of the receiver.

This book presents new techniques that improve the performance of the communication system used for transmission of digital data over time varying channels such as high frequency mobile channels. It aims to provide highlights of the current research in the field of wireless communication, and to offer a contribution to the recent advances in this field. The subjects discussed in this work are very valuable to any researcher in the communication field not only to researchers in the wireless related areas. The twenty-six chapters cover a wide range of topics in wireless communication starting with the channel characterization, the conventional and adaptive antenna design, networks coding, optical communication, Multi-Input Multi-Output (MIMO) systems, system fabrication and design, vehicular technologies, and communication protocols.

The editor would like to thank all of the authors for their valuable contributions in the area of wireless communications hoping that the book will be of great help to the readers.

February 2011

Dr. Mutamed Khatib
Department of Telecommunications and Technology
College of Engineering and Technology
Palestine Technical University – Kadoorie (PTU)
Tul Karm,
Palestine

Part 1

Channel Characterization and Applications

1

An Overview of the Physical Insight and the Various Performance Metrics of Fading Channels in Wireless Communication Systems

K.P. Peppas[1], H.E. Nistazakis[2] and G.S. Tombras[3]
[1]*National Center Of Scientific Research "Demokritos"*
[2,3]*Department of Electronics, Computers, Telecommunications and Control, Faculty of Physics*
National and Kapodistrian University of Athens
Greece

1. Introduction

In this chapter, we discuss on the physical insight and the various performance metrics of the wireless channels environment in today's communications schemes. The availability and reliability of such channels is closely related to the transmitted received signal fading conditions, a well known electromagnetic wave mitigation phenomenon due either to multipath wave propagation or to shadowing from physical or man made obstacles that affect wave propagation. In this respect, we first examine the various types of fading that the propagated signals may experience, being the multi path induced or fast fading and the shadow or slow fading, as well as flat fading and frequency selective fading. Then, we present the methodologies that have been suggested for evaluating fading channels and rely on different statistical distributions of the corresponding signal amplitude and phase variations. Such distributions have been concluded from the study of the physical phenomena and laws that govern wave propagation over different areas and under various conditions and most of them have been experimentally studied. Following the above, we consider the most of the main mathematical models that have been proposed and validated over time in describing the fading channels characteristics and concentrate on three important performance metrics being the average, or ergodic, capacity, the outage probability and the average bit error probability. Finally, by considering each of those fading channel models, we discuss their analytic convenience and accuracy with respect to the physical conditions implied.

2. Basic characteristics of fading channels

The propagation of energy in a mobile radio environment is characterized by various effects including multi path fading and shadowing. Such phenomena result in variations of the channel strength over both time and frequency, thus impairing the performance of wireless receivers. The above mentioned variations can be roughly classified into two categories:

- *Large Scale Fading*: This type of fading is due to path loss and shadowing. Path loss is the attenuation of the electromagnetic wave radiated by the transmitter as it propagates through space. It is noted that path loss is a major component in the analysis and design of the link budget of a telecommunication system. Shadowing occurs where a large obstacle between the transmitter and receiver obscures the main signal path between the transmitter and the receiver. Such obstacles attenuate signal power through absorption, reflection, scattering, and diffraction; when the attenuation is very strong, the signal is blocked.

- *Small Scale Fading*: In a wireless communication environment, the propagation of energy is characterized by waves that interact with physical obstacles via mechanisms such as reflection, scattering, diffraction and absorption. This interaction, results in the generation of a continuous distribution of partial waves (Braun & Dersch, 1991; Yacoub, 2007b). Each wave experiences differences in attenuation, delay and phase shift in accordance with the physical properties of the surface. The propagated signal arrives at the receiver through multiple paths, resulting in a rapidly fading combined signal. This phenomenon can have a constructive or destructive impact on the receiving signal, amplifying or attenuating the signal power seen at the receiver. Small Scale Fading typically occurs over very short distances, on the order of the carrier wavelength (Goldsmith, 2005).

Fading phenomena can also be classified to slow and fast fading. Such a classification is useful for the mathematical modeling of fading channels as well as for the performance assessment of communication systems operating over fading channels. The terms "slow" and "fast" refer to the rate at which the magnitude and phase of the received signal varies with respect to the channel changes. This classification is closely related to the coherence time T_c of the channel. The coherence time is a measure of the minimum time required for the magnitude change of the channel to become uncorrelated from its previous value, or equivalently, the period of time after which the correlation function of two samples of the channel response taken at the same frequency but different time instants drops below a predefined threshold. The coherence time is also related to the channel Doppler spread f_d as

$$T_c \simeq 1/f_d. \tag{1}$$

A wireless channel is called slow fading, when the coherence time of the channel, T_c, is large relative to the delay requirement of a specific application. In slow fading, the amplitude and phase change imposed by the channel can be considered roughly constant over the period of use. On the other hand, fast fading occurs when the coherence time of the channel, T_c is small relative to the delay requirement of the application (Simon & Alouini, 2005). In fast fading, the amplitude and phase change imposed by the channel varies considerably over the period of use. It should be noted that in a fast fading channel, coded symbols can be transmitted over multiple fades of the channel while in slow fading they cannot. Therefore, the characterization of a fading channel as slow or fast does not depend only on the environment but also on the application and the demanding bit rate (Tse & Viswanath, 2005). In practice, the characterization of a channel as fast or slow fading, depends strongly on the bit rate of the link. More specifically, as data rates increase, wireless communication channels become better described as slow fading. On the other hand, as the data rates decrease, the channel is better described as a fast fading one (Belmonte & Kahn, 2009).

Frequency selectivity is another important characteristic of fading channels. In flat fading, the coherence bandwidth of the channel is larger than the bandwidth of the signal. Therefore, all spectral components of the transmitted signal will experience the same magnitude of fading. This is the case for narrow-band systems, in which the transmitted signal bandwidth is much smaller than the channel's coherence bandwidth f_c. The coherence bandwidth is defined as the approximate maximum frequency interval over which two frequencies of a signal are likely to experience correlated amplitude fading and measures the frequency range over which the fading process is correlated. The coherence bandwidth is related to the maximum delay spread τ_{max} by

$$f_c \simeq 1/\tau_{max} \tag{2}$$

On the other hand, in frequency selective fading the spectral components of the transmitted signal are affected by different amplitude gains and phase shifts. This is the case for wide-band systems in which the channel's coherence bandwidth is smaller than the transmitted signal bandwidth.

3. Statistical modeling of flat fading channels

Depending on the nature of the propagation environment, the statistics of the mobile radio signal are well described by a great number of distributions available in the open technical literature. The short-term signal variation is described by several distributions, such as the Rayleigh, Rice (Nakagami-n), Nakagami-m, Hoyt (Nakagami-q), and Weibull distributions. The derivation of these well-known fading distributions is based on the assumption of a homogeneous diffuse scattering field, resulting from randomly distributed point scatterers. The assumption is however an approximation since the surfaces are spatially correlated in a realistic propagation environment (Braun & Dersch, 1991; Yacoub, 2007b). To address such non-homogeneities of the propagation medium more generic distributions have been proposed such as the generalized gamma, the κ-μ and the η-μ distributions.

Moreover, in addition to multi-path fading, the quality of the received signal is also affected by shadowing. The statistics of the path gain due to shadowing can be appropriately described by the log-normal distribution. In some environments, however, such as congested downtown areas and land-mobile satellite systems with urban shadowing, the receiver should react to the instantaneous composite multipath/shadow faded signal. In these cases, analysis of the channel model must take into account both multi-path and shadow fading.

In this section, we present an overview of the most popular distributions used for statistical fading models. Throughout this presentation, a narrow-band digital receiver is assumed. The fading amplitude at the input of the receiver, R is a random variable (RV) with mean-square value $\Omega = \mathbb{E}\langle R^2 \rangle$ with $\mathbb{E}\langle \cdot \rangle$ denoting expectation. We also define the probability density function (PDF) of R, $f_R(r)$ which depends on the nature of the propagation environment. The equivalent baseband received signal can be expressed as $z = sR + n$, where s is the transmitted symbol, and n is the additive white gaussian noise (AWGN) having one-sided power spectral density N_0 Watts/Hz. Typically, n is assumed to be statistically independent of R. The instantaneous signal-to-noise (SNR) per received symbol is $\gamma = R^2 E_s / N_0$, where $E_s = \mathbb{E}\langle |s|^2 \rangle$ is the energy per symbol. The corresponding average SNR per symbol is $\overline{\gamma} = \Omega E_s / N_0$. Performing a simple RV transformation, the PDF of γ is obtained as

$$f_\gamma(\gamma) = \frac{f_R\left(\sqrt{\frac{\Omega\gamma}{\overline{\gamma}}}\right)}{2\sqrt{\frac{\overline{\gamma}\gamma}{\Omega}}} \tag{3}$$

Finally, we define the moment generating function (MGF) $\mathcal{M}_\gamma(s)$ of γ as

$$\mathcal{M}_\gamma(s) \triangleq \mathbb{E}\langle \exp(-s\gamma) \rangle = \int_0^\infty \exp(-s\gamma) f_\gamma(\gamma) d\gamma. \tag{4}$$

In the following, the most commonly used fading distributions will be presented with respect to their PDFs and MGFs.

3.1 The Rayleigh fading model

The Rayleigh fading model agrees very well with experimental data when there are many objects in the environment that scatter the radio signal before it arrives at the receiver. It can also be applied to the propagation through the troposphere and ionosphere (Basu et al., 1987; James & Wells, 1955; Sugar, 1955) and to ship-to-ship radio links (Staley et al., 1996). According to the central limit theorem, if there is sufficiently much scatter, the channel impulse response will be well-modelled as a zero mean complex Gaussian process. In this case, the envelope of the channel impulse response will be Rayleigh distributed whereas the phase uniformly distributed between 0 and 2π radians. The probability density function of the channel fading amplitude R is given as

$$f_R(r) = \frac{2r}{\Omega}\exp\left(-\frac{r^2}{\Omega}\right), r \geq 0. \tag{5}$$

Using (3), the PDF of the equivalent instantaneous SNR per symbol, γ is given by

$$f_\gamma(\gamma) = \frac{1}{\overline{\gamma}}\exp\left(-\frac{\gamma}{\overline{\gamma}}\right), \gamma \geq 0. \tag{6}$$

As it can be observed, γ is exponentially distributed with parameter $1/\overline{\gamma}$. Finally, the MGF of γ is expressed in closed-form as follows

$$\mathcal{M}_\gamma(s) = \frac{1}{1+s\overline{\gamma}}. \tag{7}$$

3.2 The Rice fading model

The Rice fading model, also known as the Nakagami-n fading model, arises when there is a strong line-of-sight (LOS) component and many weaker components in the received signal (Rice, 1948). This model is common in micro-cellular urban and suburban land-mobile systems, pico-cellular indoor, satellite and ship-to-ship radio links (Bultitude et al., 1989; Munro, 1963; Rappaport & McGillem, 1989; Shaft, 1974). The probability distribution for the envelope of the received signal is given by:

$$f_R(r) = \frac{2(1+n^2)e^{-n^2}r}{\Omega}\exp\left[-\frac{(1+n^2)r^2}{\Omega}\right] I_0\left(2nr\sqrt{\frac{1+n^2}{\Omega}}\right), r \geq 0 \tag{8}$$

where $0 \leq n < \infty$ is the fading parameter and $I_0(\cdot)$ is the modified Bessel function of the first kind and zero order (Gradshteyn & Ryzhik, 2000b, Eq. (8.406)). The quantity $K = n^2$ is called the Rice factor. Note that setting $K = 0$ transforms this model into the Rayleigh fading model and setting $K = \infty$ would transform it into a simple AWGN model with no fading.
Using (3), the PDF of γ is given by

$$f_\gamma(\gamma) = \frac{(1+n^2)e^{-n^2}}{\overline{\gamma}}\exp\left[-\frac{(1+n^2)\gamma}{\overline{\gamma}}\right] I_0\left(2n\sqrt{\frac{(1+n^2)\gamma}{\overline{\gamma}}}\right), \gamma \geq 0. \tag{9}$$

As it can be observed, γ follows a non-central chi-square distribution. Finally, the MGF of γ is expressed in closed-form as follows

$$\mathcal{M}_\gamma(s) = \frac{1+n^2}{1+n^2+s\overline{\gamma}} \exp\left(-\frac{n^2 s\overline{\gamma}}{1+n^2+s\overline{\gamma}}\right). \tag{10}$$

3.3 The Hoyt fading model

The Hoyt fading model, also known as the Nakagami-q fading model (Hoyt, 1947), is common in satellite links subject to strong ionospheric scintillation (Bischoff & Chytil, 1969; Chytil, 1967). The probability distribution for the envelope of the received signal is given by:

$$f_R(r) = \frac{r(1+q^2)}{q\Omega} \exp\left[-\frac{(1+q^2)^2 r^2}{4q^2\Omega}\right] I_0\left(\frac{(1-q^4)r^2}{4q^2\Omega}\right), r \geq 0. \tag{11}$$

where $0 \leq q \leq 1$ is the fading parameter.
The PDF of γ is given by

$$f_\gamma(\gamma) = \frac{(1+q^2)}{2q\overline{\gamma}} \exp\left[-\frac{(1+q^2)^2\gamma}{4q^2\overline{\gamma}}\right] I_0\left(\frac{(1-q^4)\gamma}{4q^2\overline{\gamma}}\right), \gamma \geq 0. \tag{12}$$

Moreover, the MGF of γ is expressed in closed form as

$$\mathcal{M}_\gamma(s) = \left[1+2s\overline{\gamma} + \frac{(2s\overline{\gamma})^2 q^2}{(1+q^2)^2}\right]^{-1/2}. \tag{13}$$

3.4 The Weibull fading model

The Weibull fading, is a simple and flexible statistical model of fading used in wireless communications and based on the Weibull distribution. Empirical studies have shown it to be an effective model in both indoor and outdoor environments (Bertoni, 1988; Hashemi, 1993). Furthermore, this model has recently gained significant interest in the field of performance analysis of digital communications over fading channels (Karagiannidis et al., 2005; Sagias, Karagiannidis & Tombras, 2004; Sagias, Karagiannidis, Zogas, Mathiopoulos & Tombras, 2004; Sagias et al., 2003; Sagias & Tombras, 2007; Sagias, Zogas, Karagiannidis & Tombras, 2004; Zogas et al., 2005). The Weibull PDF is given by

$$f_R(r) = \frac{\beta}{(\Xi\Omega)^{\beta/2}} r^{\beta-1} \exp\left[-\left(\frac{r^2}{\Xi\Omega}\right)^{\beta/2}\right], r \geq 0. \tag{14}$$

where $\beta > 0$ is the fading parameter and $\Xi = 1/\Gamma(1+2/\beta)$, with $\Gamma(\cdot)$ being the Gamma function (Gradshteyn & Ryzhik, 2000b, Eq. (8.310/1)). For $\beta = 2$, (14) reduces to the Rayleigh fading model. The corresponding SNR per symbol has PDF given by

$$f_\gamma(\gamma) = \frac{\beta}{2(\Xi\overline{\gamma})^{\beta/2}} \gamma^{\beta/2-1} \exp\left[-\left(\frac{\gamma}{\Xi\overline{\gamma}}\right)^{\beta/2}\right], \gamma \geq 0. \tag{15}$$

One can observe that γ also follows a Weibull distribution with parameter $\beta/2$. For $\beta > 0$, the MGF of γ is expressed in closed form as (Yilmaz & Alouini, 2009)

$$\mathcal{M}_\gamma(s) = H_{1,1}^{1,1}\left[\frac{1}{\Xi\overline{\gamma}s} \middle| \begin{smallmatrix}(1,1)\\(1,2/\beta)\end{smallmatrix}\right]. \tag{16}$$

where $H^{m,n}_{p,q}(\cdot)$ is the H-Fox function (Cook, 1981). A computer program in Mathematica for the efficient implementation of the H-Fox function is given in (Yilmaz & Alouini, 2009, Appendix A). For the special case of $\beta = 2l/k$, where l, k are positive integers with $\mathrm{GCD}(l,k) = 1$, the MGF can be expressed in terms of the more familiar Meijer-G function as (Sagias & Karagiannidis, 2005)

$$\mathcal{M}_\gamma(s) = \frac{\beta}{2}\frac{1}{(\Xi\overline{\gamma}s)^{\beta/2}}\frac{l^{\beta/2}\sqrt{k/l}}{(\sqrt{2\pi})^{k+l-2}} G^{k,l}_{l,k}\left[\frac{l^l/k^k}{(\Xi\overline{\gamma}s)^{k\beta/2}}\middle|\begin{matrix}\Delta(l;1-\beta/2)\\ \Delta(k;0)\end{matrix}\right] \tag{17}$$

where $G^{m,n}_{p,q}(\cdot)$ is the Meijer-G function (Prudnikov et al., 1986) and $\Delta(k;x) \triangleq \{x/k, (x+1)/k, \cdots, (x+k-1)/k\}$. Note that the Meijer-G function is available in popular software mathematical packages such as Maple or Mathematica. Moreover, from (Gradshteyn & Ryzhik, 2000b), the Meijer-G function can be written in terms of the more familiar generalized hypergeometric functions.

3.5 The Nakagami-m fading model

The Nakagami-m fading model is a purely empirical model and is not based on results derived from physical consideration of radio propagation. It also often gives the best fit to land-mobile and indoor-mobile propagation experimental data (Aulin, 1981; Braun & Dersch, 1991). Moreover, is mathematically tractable because it leads to closed form analytical expressions for important wireless communication systems performance metrics (Simon & Alouini, 2005). The distribution of the received signal's envelope is given by (Nakagami, 1960)

$$f_R(r) = \frac{2m^m r^{2m-1}}{\Omega^m\Gamma(m)}\exp\left(-\frac{mr^2}{\Omega}\right), r \geq 0 \tag{18}$$

where $1/2 \leq m \leq \infty$ is the fading parameter. parameter. For $m = 1$ the model reduces to the Rayleigh fading model whereas for $m = 1/2$ to the one sided gaussian distribution. The PDF of the SNR per symbol, γ is distributed according to a gamma distribution given by

$$f_\gamma(\gamma) = \frac{m^m\gamma^{m-1}}{\overline{\gamma}^m\Gamma(m)}\exp\left(-\frac{m\gamma}{\overline{\gamma}}\right), \gamma \geq 0 \tag{19}$$

It can easily be shown that the MGF of γ is given by

$$\mathcal{M}_\gamma(s) = \left(1 + \frac{s\overline{\gamma}}{m}\right)^{-m}. \tag{20}$$

3.6 Generalized fading models: The generalized-gamma, η-μ and κ-μ distributions

In many practical cases, situations are encountered for which no distributions seem to adequately fit experimental data, though one or another may yield a moderate fitting. Some researches (Stein, 1987) even question the use of the Nakagami-m distribution because its tail does not seem to yield a good fitting to experimental data, better fitting being found around the mean or median. Recently the so called generalized-gamma, η-μ and κ-μ distributions have been proposed as alternative generic fading models. These distributions fit well experimental data and include as special cases the well known distributions presented above.

3.6.1 The generalized-gamma distribution

The generalized-gamma fading model, also known as the α-μ (Yacoub, 2007a) or Stacy fading model (Stacy, 1962), considers a signal composed of clusters of multi-path waves propagating in a non-homogeneous environment. Within any one cluster, the phases of the scattered waves are random and have similar delay times with delay-time spreads of different clusters being relatively large. The resulting envelope is obtained as a non-linear function of the modulus of the sum of the multipath components. The non-linearity is manifested in terms of a power parameter $\beta > 0$, such that the resulting signal intensity is obtained not simply as the modulus of the sum of the multipath components, but as this modulus to a certain given power (Yacoub, 2007a). The PDF of the fading envelope is given by

$$f_R(r) = \frac{\beta r^{m\beta-1}}{(\Omega\tau)^{m\beta/2}\Gamma(m)} \exp\left[-\left(\frac{r^2}{\Omega\tau}\right)^{\beta/2}\right], r \geq 0. \tag{21}$$

where $\beta > 0$ and $m > 1/2$ are parameters related to the fading severity and $\tau = \Gamma(m_i)/\Gamma(m_i + 2/\beta_i)$. This distribution is very generic as it includes the Rayleigh model ($\beta = 2, m = 1$), the Nakagami-m model ($\beta = 2$) and the Weibull model ($m = 1$). Moreover, for the limiting case ($\beta = 0, m = \infty$) it approaches the lognormal model. The PDF of the corresponding SNR is given by

$$f_\gamma(\gamma) = \frac{\beta\,\gamma^{m\,\beta/2-1}}{2\,\Gamma\,(m)\,(\tau\,\overline{\gamma})^{m\,\beta/2}} \exp\left[-\left(\frac{\gamma}{\tau\,\overline{\gamma}}\right)^{\beta/2}\right] \tag{22}$$

The MGF of γ is given by (Aalo et al., 2005; Yilmaz & Alouini, 2009)

$$\mathcal{M}_\gamma(s) = \frac{1}{\Gamma(m)} H^{1,1}_{1,1}\left[\frac{1}{\tau\overline{\gamma}s}\,\middle|\,\begin{matrix}(1,1)\\(m,2/\beta)\end{matrix}\right]. \tag{23}$$

For the special case of $\beta = 2l/k$, where l, k are positive integers with GCD$(l,k) = 1$, the MGF can be expressed in terms of the more familiar Meijer-G function as (Sagias & Mathiopoulos, 2005)

$$\mathcal{M}_\gamma(s) = \frac{\beta}{2\Gamma(m)}\frac{1}{(\tau\overline{\gamma}s)^{m\beta/2}}\frac{l^{m\beta/2}\sqrt{k/l}}{(\sqrt{2\pi})^{k+l-2}} G^{k,l}_{l,k}\left[\frac{l^l/k^k}{(\tau\overline{\gamma}s)^{k\beta/2}}\,\middle|\,\begin{matrix}\Delta(l;1-\beta m/2)\\ \Delta(k;0)\end{matrix}\right] \tag{24}$$

3.6.2 The η-μ distribution

The η-μ fading model is a generic fading distribution that provides an improved modeling of small-scale variations of the fading signal in a *non-line-of-sight condition*. This model considers a signal composed of clusters of multipath waves propagating in a non-homogeneous environment. The phases of the scattered waves within any one cluster are random and they have similar delay times. It is also assumed that the delay-time spreads of different clusters are relatively large (Yacoub, 2007b). The η-μ distribution uses two parameters η and μ to accurately model a variety of fading environments. More specifically, it comprises both Hoyt ($\mu = 0.5$) and Nakagami-m ($\eta \to 0, \eta \to \infty, \eta \to \pm 1$) distributions. Furthermore, it has been shown that it can accurately approximate the sum of independent non-identical Hoyt envelopes having arbitrary mean powers and arbitrary fading degrees (Filho & Yacoub, 2005). The η-μ fading model appears in two different formats: In Format 1, the in-phase and quadrature components of the fading signal within each cluster are assumed to be independent from each other and to have different powers, with the parameter $0 < \eta < \infty$ given by the ratio between them. In Format 2, $-1 < \eta < 1$ denotes the correlation between the powers of the in-phase and quadrature scattered waves in each multi-path cluster. In both formats, the parameter $\mu > 0$ denotes the number of multi-path clusters. The PDF of the fading envelope R is given by

$$f_R(r) = \frac{4\sqrt{\pi}\mu^{\mu+\frac{1}{2}}h^{\mu}}{\Gamma(\mu)H^{\mu-\frac{1}{2}}}\left(\frac{r}{\hat{r}}\right)^{2\mu}\exp\left[-2\mu h\left(\frac{r}{\hat{r}}\right)^2\right]I_{\mu-\frac{1}{2}}\left(2\mu H\left(\frac{r}{\hat{r}}\right)^2\right) \tag{25}$$

where $\hat{r} = \sqrt{\Omega}$. The PDF of the corresponding average SNR per symbol γ is obtained as

$$f_\gamma(\gamma) = \frac{2\sqrt{\pi}\mu^{\mu+\frac{1}{2}}h^{\mu}}{\Gamma(\mu)H^{\mu-\frac{1}{2}}}\frac{\gamma^{\mu-\frac{1}{2}}}{\overline{\gamma}^{\mu+\frac{1}{2}}}\exp\left(-\frac{2\mu\gamma h}{\overline{\gamma}}\right)I_{\mu-\frac{1}{2}}\left(\frac{2\mu H\gamma}{\overline{\gamma}}\right). \tag{26}$$

In Format 1, $h = (2+\eta^{-1}+\eta)/4$ and $H = (\eta^{-1}-\eta)/4$ whereas in Format 2, $h = 1/(1-\eta^2)$ and $H = \eta/(1-\eta^2)$. Finally, the MGF of γ, with the help of (Ermolova, 2008, Eq. (6)), (Peppas, Lazarakis et al., 2009, Eq. (2)) can be expressed as:

$$\mathcal{M}_\gamma(s) = (1+As)^{-\mu}(1+Bs)^{-\mu} \tag{27}$$

where $A = \frac{\overline{\gamma}}{2\mu(h-H)}$ and $B = \frac{\overline{\gamma}}{2\mu(h+H)}$.

3.6.3 The κ-μ distribution

The κ-μ fading model is a generic fading distribution that provides an improved modeling of small-scale variations of the fading signal in a *line-of-sight condition*. Similarly to the η-μ case, this model considers a signal composed of clusters of multipath waves propagating in a non-homogeneous environment. The phases of the scattered waves within any one cluster are random and they have similar delay times. It is also assumed that the delay-time spreads of different clusters are relatively large. The clusters of multipath waves are assumed to have scattered waves with identical powers, but within each cluster a dominant component is found (Yacoub, 2007b). As implied by its name, the κ-μ distribution uses two parameters κ and μ to accurately model a variety of fading enviromnents. More specifically, it comprises both Rice ($\mu = 1$) and Nakagami-m ($\kappa \to 0$) distributions. The parameter κ is defined as the ratio between the total power of the dominant components and the total power of the scattered waves, whereas the parameter μ denotes the number of multipath clusters. The PDF of the fading envelope R is given by

$$f_R(r) = \frac{2\mu(1+\kappa)^{\frac{\mu+1}{2}}}{\kappa^{\frac{\mu-1}{2}}\exp(\mu\kappa)}\left(\frac{r}{\hat{r}}\right)^{\mu}\exp\left[\mu(1+\kappa)\left(\frac{r}{\hat{r}}\right)^{\mu}\right]I_{\mu-1}\left(2\mu\sqrt{\kappa(1+\kappa)}\frac{r}{\hat{r}}\right) \tag{28}$$

where $\hat{r} = \sqrt{\Omega}$. The PDF of the corresponding average SNR per symbol, γ is easily obtained as

$$f_\gamma(\gamma) = \frac{\mu(1+\kappa)^{\frac{\mu+1}{2}}}{\kappa^{\frac{\mu-1}{2}}\exp(\mu\kappa)}\frac{\gamma^{\frac{\mu-1}{2}}}{\overline{\gamma}^{\frac{\mu+1}{2}}}\exp\left(-\frac{\mu(1+\kappa)\gamma}{\overline{\gamma}}\right)I_{\mu-1}\left(2\mu\sqrt{\frac{\kappa(1+\kappa)\gamma}{\overline{\gamma}}}\right) \tag{29}$$

Using (Ermolova, 2008) the MGF of γ is expressed in closed form as

$$\mathcal{M}_\gamma(s) = \frac{(1+\kappa)^{\mu}\mu^{\mu}}{[s\overline{\gamma}+(1+\kappa)\mu]^{\mu}}\exp\left(-\frac{\mu\kappa\overline{\gamma}s}{s\overline{\gamma}+\mu(1+\kappa)}\right) \tag{30}$$

3.7 Log-normal shadowing

The link quality of practical wireless communication systems is also affected by slow variation of the mean signal level due to shadowing. It is empirically confirmed that the log-normal distribution can accurately model the variation in received power in both outdoor and indoor radio propagation environments. The PDF of the instantaneous SNR per symbol γ is given by

$$f_\gamma(\gamma) = \frac{\xi}{\sqrt{2\pi}\sigma\gamma} \exp\left[-\frac{(10\log_{10}\gamma - \mu)^2}{2\sigma^2}\right] \tag{31}$$

where $\xi = 10/\ln 10 = 4.3429$, μ is the mean of $10\log_{10}\gamma$ expressed in dB and σ is the standard deviation of $10\log_{10}\gamma$, also in dB. The moment generating function of γ is given by

$$\mathcal{M}_\gamma(s) \simeq \frac{1}{\sqrt{\pi}} \sum_{n=1}^{N} w_{x_n} \exp\left(10^{(\sqrt{2}\sigma x_n + \mu)/10} s\right) \tag{32}$$

where x_n are the zeros of the N-order Hermite polynomial and w_{x_n} are the corresponding weight factors given by (Abramovitz & Stegun, 1964). Finally, it should be noted that the log-normal distribution is a very common and accurate model for wireless optical communication systems under weak atmospheric turbulence conditions (Kamalakis et al., 2006; Katsis et al., 2009; Laourine et al., 2007; Majumdar, 2005; Nistazakis, Tsiftsis & Tombras, 2009).

3.8 Generalized-K distribution

In a wireless propagation environment, multi-path fading and shadowing occur simultaneously in many practical cases. Such cases often appear in congested downtown areas with slow moving pedestrians and vehicles as well as in land-mobile satellite systems subject to vegetative and/or urban shadowing (Simon & Alouini, 2005). By averaging the signal power, which may follow one of the previously mentioned distributions, over the conditional density of the log-normally distributed mean signal power, various distributions may be obtained for modeling the composite environment, including the widely accepted Rayleigh- and Nakagami-log-normal (Simon & Alouini, 2005). However, these fading models are not widely used in the context of performance analysis of digital communication over fading channels due to their rather complicated mathematical expressions. The use of the gamma distribution as an alternative to the log-normal distribution, leads to other, mathematically more tractable, composite distributions such as the generalized-K (K_G) distribution which is a mixture of a Nakagami-m and a gamma distribution (Bithas et al., 2006; Peppas, 2009). Moreover, it has been proved that this alternative model has both theoretical and experimental support (Abdi & Kaveh, 1999; 2000). Furthermore, the K_G distribution includes the well known Double-Rayleigh model (Uysal, 2006). Therefore, it can be further employed to model the power statistics in so-called cascaded multi-path fading channels. Such channels occur in propagation through keyholes or in serial relaying communications systems employing fixed gain relays (Peppas et al., 2010; Yilmaz & Alouini, 2009). Consequently, the K_G distribution can accurately capture the effects of the combined multi-path fading and shadowing or cascaded multi-path fading, which are both frequently encountered in wireless systems. The squared K_G distribution, also known as the gamma-gamma distribution in optical communications theory, has been recently used in the performance analysis of free-space optical (FSO) communications systems over atmospheric turbulence channels (Al-Habash et al., 2001; Bayaki et al., 2009; Uysal et al., 2006). In FSO communications, the atmospheric turbulence results in rapid fluctuations at the received signal that severely degrade the optical link's performance. The gamma-gamma model in wireless optical communications theory is based on the assumption that small-scale irradiance fluctuations are modulated by large-scale irradiance fluctuations of the propagating wave, both modeled as independent gamma distributions. This distribution has become the dominant fading channel model for FSO links due to its excellent agreement with measurement data for a wide range of turbulence conditions (Al-Habash et al., 2001; Bayaki et al., 2009).

A closed form expression for the K_G PDF is obtained as follows: Let R be the instantaneous amplitude of a flat fading channel with PDF modeled by the Nakagami-m distribution, i.e.

$$f_{R|Y}(r) = \frac{2m^m r^{2m-1}}{Y^m \Gamma(m)} \exp\left(-\frac{mr^2}{Y}\right), r \geq 0 \tag{33}$$

When multi-path fading is superimposed on shadowing, the parameter Y, randomly varies, modeled in the following analysis with the gamma distribution. The PDF of Y is given by:

$$f_Y(y) = \frac{k^k y^{k-1} \exp(-ky/\Omega)}{\Gamma(k)\Omega^k}, y \geq 0 \tag{34}$$

where k is the shaping parameter and $\Omega = \mathbb{E}\langle Y \rangle$. The PDF of the K_G distribution, $f_R(r)$, is obtained by averaging (33) over (34), i.e.

$$f_R(r) = \int_0^\infty f_{R|Y}(r|y) f_Y(y) dy \tag{35}$$

Using (Gradshteyn & Ryzhik, 2000b, Eq. (3.471/9)) the analytical expression for the PDF of the corresponding fading envelope R is obtained as

$$f_R(r|m,k,\Omega) = \frac{4\Psi^{k+m}}{\Gamma(m)\Gamma(k)} r^{k+m-1} K_{k-m}(2\Psi r),\ r \geq 0 \tag{36}$$

where $K_a(\cdot)$ is the modified Bessel function of the second kind and order a and $\Psi = \sqrt{\frac{km}{\Omega}}$. For $k \to \infty$, (36) approximates the Nakagami-m distribution; for $m = 1$, it approximately models Rayleigh-lognormal fading conditions (Bithas et al., 2006); while for $m \to \infty$ and $k \to \infty$, it approaches the additive white Gaussian noise (AWGN) channel. The PDF of the average SNR per symbol, γ is given by

$$f_\gamma(\gamma) = \frac{2\Xi^{k+m}}{\Gamma(m)\Gamma(k)} \gamma^{(k+m)/2-1} K_{k-m}(2\Xi\sqrt{w}) \tag{37}$$

where $\Xi = \sqrt{\frac{km}{\bar{\gamma}}}$. The MGF of γ, can be obtained using (Bithas et al., 2006, Eq. (4)) as

$$\mathcal{M}_\gamma(s) = \left(\frac{\Xi^2}{s}\right)^{(k+m-1)/2} \exp\left(\frac{\Xi^2}{2s}\right) W_{-(k+m-1)/2,(k-m)/2}\left(\frac{\Xi^2}{s}\right) \tag{38}$$

where $W_{\lambda,\mu}(\cdot)$ is the Whittaker function (Gradshteyn & Ryzhik, 2000a, Eq. (9.220)).

4. Performance metrics of fading channels

4.1 Channel capacity

The huge growth of the number of the mobile subscribers world-wide, during the last decade, together with the increasing demand for higher information transmission rates and flexible access to diverse services, has raised demand for spectral efficiency in wireless communications systems. The pioneering work of Shannon established the significance of channel capacity as the maximum rate of communication for which arbitrarily small error probability can be achieved. Thus, the Shannon capacity provides a benchmark against which the spectral efficiency of practical transmission strategies can be compared.

Of particular interest is the study of the Shannon capacity of fading channels under different assumptions about transmitter and receiver channel knowledge. Shannon capacity results can be used to compare the effectiveness of both adaptive and nonadaptive transmission strategies in fading channels against their theoretical maximum performance. The main idea behind these transmission schemes is balancing of the link budget in real time, through adaptive variation of the transmitted power level, symbol rate constellation size, coding rate/scheme, or any combination of these parameters (Alouini & Goldsmith, 1999). Such schemes can provide a higher average spectral efficiency without sacrificing error rate performance. The disadvantage of these adaptive techniques is that they require an accurate channel estimate at the transmitter, additional hardware complexity to implement adaptive transmission, and buffering/delay of the input data since the transmission rate varies with channel conditions (Goldsmith & Varaiya, 1997).

Various works available in the open technical literature study the spectral efficiency of adaptive transmission techniques over fading channels. Representative past works can be found in (Alouini & Goldsmith, 1999; Laourine et al., 2008; Mallik et al., 2004; Peppas, 2010). For example in (Alouini & Goldsmith, 1999), an extensive analysis of the Shannon capacity of adaptive transmission techniques in conjunction with diversity combining over Rayleigh fading channels has been presented. Moreover in (Mallik et al., 2004), by assuming maximum ratio combining diversity (MRC) reception under correlated Rayleigh fading, closed-form expressions for the single-user capacity were presented. Finally, in (Laourine et al., 2008) the capacity of generalized-K fading channels under different adaptive transmission techniques was studied in detail.

The adaptive transmission schemes under consideration are optimal simultaneous power and rate adaptation (OPRA), optimal rate adaptation with constant transmit power (ORA), channel inversion with fixed rate (CIFR) and truncated channel inversion with fixed rate (TCIFR)(Biglieri et al., 1998; Goldsmith & Varaiya, 1997; Luo et al., 2003). The ORA scheme achieves the ergodic capacity by using variable-rate transmission relative to the channel conditions while the transmit power remains constant. The OPRA scheme also achieves the ergodic capacity of the system by varying the rate and power relative to the channel conditions, which, however, may not be appropriate for applications requiring a fixed rate. Finally, the CIFR and TCIFR schemes achieve the outage capacity of the system, defined as the maximum constant transmission rate that can be supported under all channel conditions with some outage probability (Biglieri et al., 1998; Luo et al., 2003).

4.1.1 Optimal rate adaptation with constant transmit power

Under the ORA policy, where channel state information (CSI) is available at the receiver only, the capacity is known to be given by (Alouini & Goldsmith, 1999; Lazarakis et al., 1994)

$$\langle C \rangle_{ORA} = \frac{1}{\ln 2} \int_0^{\infty} f_{\gamma}(\gamma) \ln(1+\gamma) d\gamma \tag{39}$$

It is noted that $\langle C \rangle_{ORA}$ was introduced by Lee in (Lee, 1990) as the average channel capacity of a flat-fading channel, since it is obtained by averaging the capacity of an AWGN channel $C_{awgn} = \log_2(1+\gamma)$ over the distribution of the received SNR γ. That is why capacity under the ORA scheme is also called ergodic capacity. Using Jensen's inequality we observe that

$$\langle C \rangle_{ORA} = \frac{1}{\ln 2} \mathbb{E}\langle \ln(1+\gamma) \rangle \leq \frac{1}{\ln 2} \ln(1+\mathbb{E}\langle \gamma \rangle) = \frac{1}{\ln 2} \ln(1+\overline{\gamma}) \tag{40}$$

where $\overline{\gamma}$ is the average SNR on the channel. Therefore we observe that the Shannon capacity under the ORA scheme is less than the Shannon capacity of an AWGN channel with the same average SNR. In other words, fading reduces Shannon capacity when only the receiver has CSI. Moreover, if the receiver CSI is not perfect, capacity can be significantly decreased (Goldsmith, 2005; Lapidoth & Shamai, 1997).

It is worth mentioning here, that the ergodic capacity is a very significant metric for the study of the wireless optical communication links, due to the strong influence of the atmospheric conditions in their performance, see e.g. (Andrews et al., 1999; Gappmair et al., 2010; Garcia-Zambrana, Castillo-Vasquez & Castillo-Vasquez, 2010; Garcia-Zambrana, Castillo-Vazquez & Castillo-Vazquez, 2010; Li & Uysal, 2003; Liu et al., 2010; Nistazakis, Karagianni, Tsigopoulos, Fafalios & Tombras, 2009; Nistazakis, Tombras, Tsigopoulos, Karagianni & Fafalios, 2009; Peppas & Datsikas, 2010; Popoola et al., 2008; Sandalidis & Tsiftsis, 2008; Tsiftsis, 2008; Vetelino et al., 2007; Zhu & Kahn, 2002). More specifically, the fast changes of the atmospheric turbulence conditions fades fast the transmitted signal and as a result, the estimation of the instantaneous channel capacity is nearly meaningless in this area of wireless communications.

4.1.2 Optimal simultaneous power and rate adaptation

For optimal power and rate adaptation (OPRA), the capacity is known to be given by (Alouini & Goldsmith, 1999, Eq. (7))

$$\langle C \rangle_{OPRA} = \int_{\gamma_0}^{\infty} \log_2\left(\frac{\gamma}{\gamma_0}\right) f_{\gamma}(\gamma)\, d\gamma \tag{41}$$

where γ_0 is the optimal cutoff SNR level below which data transmission is suspended. This optimal cutoff SNR must satisfy the equation (Alouini & Goldsmith, 1999, Eq. (8))

$$\int_{\gamma_0}^{\infty} \left(\frac{1}{\gamma_0} - \frac{1}{\gamma}\right) f_{\gamma}(\gamma)\, d\gamma = 1 \tag{42}$$

Since no data is sent when $\gamma < \gamma_0$, the optimal policy suffers a probability of outage P_{out}, equal to the probability of no transmission, given by

$$P_{\text{out}} = 1 - \int_{\gamma_0}^{\infty} f_{\gamma}(\gamma)\, d\gamma \tag{43}$$

4.1.3 Channel inversion with fixed rate

Channel inversion with fixed rate (CIFR) is a suboptimal transmitter adaptation scheme where the transmitter uses the CSI to maintain a constant received power, i.e., it inverts the channel fading. The channel then appears to the encoder and decoder as a time-invariant AWGN channel. CIFR is the least complex technique to implement, assuming good channel estimates are available at the transmitter and receiver. This technique uses fixed-rate modulation and a fixed code design, since the channel after channel inversion appears as a time-invariant AWGN channel. The channel capacity is given by

$$\langle C \rangle_{CIFR} = \frac{1}{\ln 2} \ln \left[1 + \frac{1}{\int_0^\infty \gamma^{-1} f_\gamma(\gamma)\, d\gamma} \right] \tag{44}$$

This technique has the advantage of maintaining a fixed data rate over the channel regardless of channel conditions. Therefore, the channel capacity given in (44) is called zero-outage capacity, since the data rate is fixed under all channel conditions and there is no channel outage. Practical coding techniques are available in the open technical literature that achieve near-capacity data rates on AWGN channels, so the zero-outage capacity can be approximately achieved in practice. It should be stressed that zero-outage capacity can exhibit a large data rate reduction relative to Shannon capacity in extreme fading environments. For example, in Rayleigh fading $\int_0^\infty \gamma^{-1} f_\gamma(\gamma)\, d\gamma$ diverges, and thus the zero-outage capacity given by (44) is zero. Channel inversion is also common in spread spectrum systems with near-far interference imbalances (Goldsmith, 2005).

4.1.4 Truncated channel inversion with fixed rate and outage capacity

The CIFR policy suffers a large capacity penalty relative to the other techniques, since a large amount of the transmitted power is required to compensate for the deep channel fades. By suspending transmission in particularly bad fading states (outage channel states), a higher constant data rate can be maintained in the other states and henceforth a significant increase in capacity. The outage capacity is defined as the maximum data rate that can be maintained in all nonoutage channel states times the probability of nonoutage. Outage capacity is achieved by using a modified inversion policy which inverts the channel fading only above a fixed cutoff fade depth γ_0, which we shall refer to as TCIFR. The capacity with this truncated channel inversion and fixed rate policy is given by

$$\langle C \rangle_{TCIFR} = \frac{1}{\ln 2} \ln \left[1 + \frac{1}{\int_{\gamma_0}^\infty \gamma^{-1} f_\gamma(\gamma)\, d\gamma} \right] (1 - P_{out}(\gamma_0)) \tag{45}$$

where P_{out} is the outage probability given by (43).

4.2 Outage probability

The outage probability is an important performance metric of wireless communications systems operating over fading channels. It is defined as the probability that the instantaneous SNR at the receiver output, γ, falls below a predefined outage threshold, γ_{th}. Based on this definition, the outage probability can be mathematically expressed as

$$P_{out} = \Pr\{\gamma < \gamma_{th}\} = \int_0^{\gamma_{th}} f_\gamma(\gamma) \mathrm{d}\gamma = F_\gamma(\gamma_{th}) \tag{46}$$

where $F_\gamma(\cdot)$ is the cumulative distribution of γ. For many of the well known fading distributions, the outage probability can be analytically evaluated using (46). An alternative method to numerically evaluate P_{out} can be obtained using the MGF of γ. More specifically, using the well known Laplace transform property $\mathcal{M}_\gamma(s) = s\mathbb{L}\{F_\gamma(\gamma)\}$, where $\mathbb{L}\{\cdot\}$ denotes Laplace transformation, P_{out} can be obtained as

$$P_{\text{out}} = \mathbb{L}^{-1}\left\{\frac{\mathcal{M}_\gamma(s)}{s};s;t\right\}\Bigg|_{t=\gamma_{\text{th}}} \tag{47}$$

Consequently, P_{out} can be evaluated using any of the well known methods for the numerical inversion of the Laplace transform, such as the Euler method, presented in (Abate & Whitt, 1995).

4.3 Average bit error probability

The last performance metric we deal with in this chapter, is the average bit error probability (ABEP). This performance metric is one of the most revealing regarding the wireless system behavior and the one most often illustrated in technical documents containing performance evaluation of wireless communications systems (Simon & Alouini, 2005). We present two methods to evaluate ABEP: A PDF-based approach and an MGF-based one.

4.3.1 PDF-based approach

Modulation Scheme	A	B	Λ
BPSK	$1/2$	1	-
BFSK	$1/2$	$1/2$	-
QPSK and MSK	1	$1/2$	-
Square M-QAM	$2\left(1-\frac{1}{\sqrt{M}}\right)$	$\frac{3}{2(M-1)}$	-
NBFSK	$1/2$	$1/2$	-
BDPSK	$1/2$	1	-
$\pi/4$-DQPSK	$\frac{1}{2\pi}$	$\frac{2}{2-\sqrt{2}\cos(\theta)}$	π
M-PSK	$\frac{1}{\pi}$	$\frac{\sin^2(\pi/M)}{\sin^2\theta}$	$\pi\left(1-\frac{1}{M}\right)$
M-DPSK	$\frac{1}{\pi}$	$\frac{\sin^2(\pi/M)}{1+\cos(\pi/M)\cos\theta}$	$\pi\left(1-\frac{1}{M}\right)$

Table 1. Parameters A, B and Λ for various coherent and non-coherent modulation schemes (PDF-based approach)

One common method we can use to determine the error performance of a digital communications system is to evaluate the decision variables and from these to determine the probability of error. For a fixed SNR, γ, analytical expressions for the error probability are well known for a variety of binary and M-ary modulation schemes (see for example (Proakis & Salehi, 2008)). When γ randomly varies, the ABEP can be obtained by averaging the conditional bit error probability, $P_e(E|\gamma)$, over the PDF of γ, namely

$$\overline{P}_{be}(E) = \int_0^\infty P_e(E|\gamma) f_\gamma(\gamma) \mathrm{d}\gamma \tag{48}$$

This yields:

Modulation Scheme	ABEP
BPSK	$\frac{1}{\pi}\int_0^{\pi/2}\mathcal{M}_\gamma\left(\frac{1}{\sin^2\theta}\right)\mathrm{d}\theta$
BFSK	$\frac{1}{\pi}\int_0^{\pi/2}\mathcal{M}_\gamma\left(\frac{1}{2\sin^2\theta}\right)\mathrm{d}\theta$
BFSK with minimum correlation	$\frac{1}{\pi}\int_0^{\pi/2}\mathcal{M}_\gamma\left(\frac{0.715}{\sin^2\theta}\right)\mathrm{d}\theta$
M-AM	$\frac{2(M-1)}{M\pi\log_2(M)}\int_0^{\pi/2}\mathcal{M}_\gamma\left(\frac{g_{AM}}{\sin^2\theta}\right)\mathrm{d}\theta, g_{AM}=\frac{3\log_2(M)}{M^2-1}$
Square M-QAM	$\frac{4}{\pi\log_2(M)}\left\{\left(1-\frac{1}{\sqrt{M}}\right)\int_0^{\pi/2}\mathcal{M}_\gamma\left(\frac{g_{QAM}}{\sin^2\theta}\right)\mathrm{d}\theta - \left(1-\frac{1}{\sqrt{M}}\right)^2\int_0^{\pi/4}\mathcal{M}_\gamma\left(\frac{g_{QAM}}{\sin^2\theta}\right)\mathrm{d}\theta\right\}, g_{QAM}=\frac{3\log_2(M)}{2(M-1)}$
NBFSK	$\frac{1}{2}\mathcal{M}_\gamma\left(\frac{1}{2}\right)$
BDPSK	$\frac{1}{2}\mathcal{M}_\gamma(1)$
M-PSK	$\frac{1}{\pi\log_2(M)}\int_0^{\pi-\pi/M}\mathcal{M}_\gamma\left(\frac{g_{PSK}}{\sin^2\theta}\right)\mathrm{d}\theta, g_{PSK}=\log_2(M)\sin^2\left(\frac{\pi}{M}\right)$
M-DPSK	$\frac{1}{\pi\log_2(M)}\int_0^{\pi-\pi/M}\mathcal{M}_\gamma\left(\frac{g_{PSK}}{1+\cos(\theta)\cos(\pi/M)}\right)\mathrm{d}\theta$

Table 2. Parameters A, B and Λ for various coherent and non-coherent modulation schemes (MGF-based approach)

- For non-coherent binary frequency shift keying (BFSK) and binary differential phase shift keying (BDPSK), $P_e(E|\gamma)$ can be expressed as

$$P_e(E|\gamma) = A\exp(-B\gamma) \tag{49}$$

where A,B constants depending on the specific modulation scheme.

- For binary phase shift keying (BPSK), square M-ary Quadrature Amplitude Modulation (M-QAM) and for high values of the average input SNR, $P_e(E|\gamma)$ is of the form

$$P_e(E|\gamma) = A\mathrm{erfc}(\sqrt{B\gamma}) \tag{50}$$

where $\mathrm{erfc}(\cdot)$ denotes the complementary error function (Gradshteyn & Ryzhik, 2000a, Eq. (8.250/1)).

- Finally, for Gray encoded $\pi/4$- Differential Quadrature Phase-Shift Keying ($\pi/4$-DQPSK), M-ary Phase-Shift Keying (M-PSK) and M-ary Differential Phase-Shift Keying (M-DPSK), $P_e(E|\gamma)$ is expressed as

$$P_e(E|\gamma) = \int_0^{\Lambda}\exp[-B(\theta)\gamma]\mathrm{d}\theta \tag{51}$$

The values of A, B and Λ for different modulation schemes are summarized in Table 1.

4.3.2 MGF-based approach

The MGF-based approach is useful in simplifying the mathematical analysis required for the evaluation of the average bit error probability and allows unification under a common framework in a large variety of digital communication systems, covering virtually all known modulation and detection techniques and practical fading channel models (Simon & Alouini, 2005). Using the MGF-based approach, the ABEP for non-coherent binary modulation signallings can be directly calculated (e.g. for BDPSK, $\overline{P}_{be}(E) = 0.5\mathcal{M}(1)$. For other types of modulation formats, such as M-PSK and M-QAM, single integrals with finite limits and integrands composed of elementary (exponential and trigonometric) functions have to be readily evaluated via numerical integration. Various ABEP expressions, evaluated using the MGF approach are presented in Table 2. For high-order modulation schemes, Gray coding is assumed.

5. References

Aalo, V., T.Piboongungon & Iskander, C.-D. (2005). Bit-error rate of binary digital modulation schemes in generalized gamma fading channels, *IEEE Communications Letters* 9(2): 139–141.

Abate, J. & Whitt, W. (1995). Numerical Inversion of Laplace Transforms of Probability Distributions, *ORSA Journal on Computing* 1(7): 36–43.

Abdi, A. & Kaveh, M. (1999). On the utility of the gamma PDF in modeling shadow fading (slow fading), *Proceedings of IEEE Vehicular Technology Conference*, Houston, TX, pp. 2308–2312.

Abdi, A. & Kaveh, M. (2000). Comparison of DPSK and MSK Bit Error Rates for K and Rayleigh-Lognormal Fading Distributions, *IEEE Commnunications Letters* 4(4): 122–124.

Abramovitz, M. & Stegun, I. (1964). *Handbook of Mathematical Functions with Formulas, Graphs, and Mathematical Tables*, Dover, New York.

Al-Habash, M. A., Andrews, L. C. & Phillips, R. L. (2001). Mathematical model for the irradiance PDF of a laser beam propagating through turbulent media, *Optical Engineering* 40(8): 1554–1562.

Alouini, M. S. & Goldsmith, A. J. (1999). Capacity of rayleigh fading channels under different adaptive transmission and diversity-combining techniques, *IEEE Transactions on Vehicular Technology* 48(4): 1165–1181.

Andrews, L. C., Phillips, R. L., Hopen, C. Y. & Al-Habash, M. A. (1999). Theory of optical scintillation, *Journal of Optical Society of America A* 16: 1417–1429.

Aulin, T. (1981). Characteristics of a digital mobile radio channel, *IEEE Transactions on Vehicular Technology* 30: 45–53.

Basu, S., MacKenzie, E. M., Basu, S., Costa, E., Fougere, P. F., Carlson, H. C. & Whitney, H. E. (1987). 250 MHz/GHz scintillation parameters in the equatorial, polar, and aural environments, *IEEE Journal on Selected Areas in Communications* 5: 102–115.

Bayaki, E., Schober, R. & Mallik, R. (2009). Performance analysis of MIMO free-space optical systems in gamma-gamma fading, *IEEE Transaction on Communications* 57(11): 3415–3424.

Belmonte, A. & Kahn, J. M. (2009). Capacity of coherent free space optical links using atmospheric compensation techniques, *Optics Express* 17(4): 2763–2773.

Bertoni, H. (1988). Coverage prediction for mobile radio systems operating in the 800 / 900 MHz frequency rangeŮreceived signal fading distributions, *IEEE Transactions on Vehicular Technology* 37(1): 57–60.

Biglieri, E., Proakis, J. & Shamai, S. (1998). Fading channels: Information theoretic and communications aspects, *IEEE Transactions on Information Theory* 44: 2619–2692.

Bischoff, K. & Chytil, B. (1969). A note on scintillation indices, *Planetary and Space Science* 17: 1059–1066.

Bithas, P. S., Sagias, N. C., Mathiopoulos, P. T., Karagiannidis, G. K. & Rontogiannis, A. A. (2006). On the performance analysis of digital comminications over generalized-K fading channels, *IEEE Communications Letters* 10(5): 353–355.

Braun, W. R. & Dersch, U. (1991). A physical mobile radio channel model, *IEEE Transactions on Vehicular Technology* 40(2): 472–482.

Bultitude, R. J. C., Mahmoud, S. A. & Sullivan, W. A. (1989). A comparison of indoor radio propagation characteristics at 910 MHz and 1.75 GHz, *IEEE Journal on Selected Areas in Communications* 7: 20–30.

Chytil, B. (1967). The distribution of amplitude scintillation and the conversion of scintillation indices, *Journal of Atmospheric and Solar-Terrestrial Physics* 29: 1175–1177.

Cook, I. D. (1981). *The H-function and probability density functions of certain algebraic combinations of independent random variables with H-function probability distribution*, PhD thesis, The University of Texas at Austin, Austin, TX.

Ermolova, N. (2008). Moment Generating Functions of the Generalized $\eta - \mu$ and $k - \mu$ Distributions and Their Applications to Performance Evaluations of Communication Systems, *IEEE Communications Letters* 12(7): 502 – 504.

Filho, J. C. S. S. & Yacoub, M. D. (2005). Highly accurate η-μ approximation to sum of m independent non-identical hoyt variates, *IEEE Antenna and Propagation Letters* 4: 436–438.

Gappmair, W., Hranilovic, S. & Leitgeb, E. (2010). Performance of ppm on terrestrial fso links with turbulence and pointing errors, *IEEE Communications Letters* 14(5): 468–470.

Garcia-Zambrana, A., Castillo-Vasquez, C. & Castillo-Vasquez, B. (2010). On the capacity of fso links over gamma gamma atmospheric turbulence channels using ook signaling, *Eurasip Journal on Wireless Communications and Networking, art. no. 127657, pages 9* .

Garcia-Zambrana, A., Castillo-Vazquez, B. & Castillo-Vazquez, C. (2010). Average capacity of fso links with transmit laser selection using non-uniform ook signaling over exponential atmospheric turbulence channels, *Optics Express* 18(19): 20445–20454.

Goldsmith, A. (2005). *Wireless Communications*, Cambridge University Press.

Goldsmith, A. J. & Varaiya, P. P. (1997). Capacity of fading channels with channel side information, *IEEE Transactions on Information Theory* 43(6): 1986–1992.

Gradshteyn, I. & Ryzhik, I. M. (2000a). *Tables of Integrals, Series, and Products*, 6 edn, Academic Press, New York.

Gradshteyn, I. S. & Ryzhik, I. M. (2000b). *Table of Integrals, Series, and Products*, 6 edn, ed. New York: Academic.

Hashemi, H. (1993). The indoor radio propagation channel, *Proceedings of the IEEE* 81(7): 943–967.

Hoyt, R. S. (1947). Probability functions for the modulus and angle of the normal complex variate, *Bell System Technical Journal* 26: 318–359.

James, H. B. & Wells, P. I. (1955). Some tropospheric scatter propagation measurements near the radio-horizon, *Proceedings of the IRE* pp. 1336–1340.

Kamalakis, T., Sphicopoulos, T., Muhammad, S. & Leitgeb, E. (2006). Estimation of the power scintillation probability density function in free-space optical links by use of multicanonical monte carlo sampling, *Optics Letters* 31(21): 3077–3079.

Karagiannidis, G., Zogas, D., Sagias, N., Kotsopoulos, S. & Tombras, G. (2005). Equal-gain and maximal-ratio combining over nonidentical Weibull fading channels, *IEEE Transactions on Wireless Communications* 4(3): 841–846.

Katsis, A., Nistazakis, H. E. & Tombras, G. S. (2009). Bayesian and frequentist estimation of the performance of free space optical channels under weak turbulence conditions, *Journal of the Franklin Institute* 346: 315–327.

Laourine, A., Alouini, M. S., Affes, S. & Stephenne, A. (2008). On the capacity of Generalized-K fading channels, *IEEE Transactions on Wireless Communications* 7(7): 2441–2445.

Laourine, A., Stephenne, A. & Affes, S. (2007). Estimating the ergodic capacity of log-normal channels, *IEEE communication Letters* 11(7): 568–570.

Lapidoth, A. & Shamai, S. (1997). Fading channels: how perfect need "perfect side information" be?, *IEEE Transactions on Information Theory* pp. 1118–1134.

Lazarakis, F., Tombras, G. S. & Dangakis, K. (1994). Average channel capacity in a mobile radio environment with rician statistics, *IEICE Trans. Commun.* E77-B(7): 971–977.

Lee, W. C. Y. (1990). Estimate of channel capacity in Rayleigh fading environment, *IEEE Transactions on Vehicular Technology* 39: 187–190.

Li, J. T. & Uysal, M. (2003). Optical wireless communications: system model, capacity and coding, *Proc. Vehic. Tech. Conf.* pp. 168–172.

Liu, C., Yao, Y., Sun, Y., Xiao, J. & Zhao, X. (2010). Average capacity optimization in free-space optical communication system over atmospheric turbulence channels with pointing errors, *Optics Letters* 35(19): 3171–3173.

Luo, J., Lin, L., Yates, R. & Spasojevic, P. (2003). Service outage based power and rate allocation, *IEEE Transactions on Information Theory* 49: 323–330.

Majumdar, A. K. (2005). Free-space laser communications performance in the atmospheric channel, *Journal of optical and fiber communications research* 2: 345–396.

Mallik, R. K., Win, M. Z., Shao, J. W., Alouini, M.-S. & Goldsmith, A. J. (2004). Channel Capacity of Adaptive Transmission With Maximal Ratio Combining in Correlated Rayleigh Fading, *IEEE Transactions on Wireless Communications* 3(4): 1124–1133.

Munro, G. H. (1963). Scintillation of radio signals from satellites, *Journal of Geophysical Research* 68.

Nakagami, M. (1960). The m-distribution: A general formula of intensity distribution of rapid fading, *Statistical Methods in Radio Wave Propagation*, Pergamon Press, Oxford, U.K., pp. 3–36.

Nistazakis, H. E., Karagianni, E. A., Tsigopoulos, A. D., Fafalios, M. E. & Tombras, G. S. (2009). Average capacity of optical wireless communication systems over atmospheric turbulence channels, *Journal of Lightwave Technology* 27(8): 974–979.

Nistazakis, H. E., Tombras, G. S., Tsigopoulos, A. D., Karagianni, E. A. & Fafalios, M. E. (2009). Capacity estimation of optical wireless communication systems over moderate to strong turbulence channels, *Journal of Communications and Networks* 11(4): 387–392.

Nistazakis, H. E., Tsiftsis, T. A. & Tombras, G. S. (2009). Performance analysis of free-space optical communication systems over atmospheric turbulence channels, *IET Communications* 3(8): 1402–1409.

Peppas, K. (2009). Performance evaluation of triple-branch GSC diversity receivers over generalized-K fading channels, *IEEE Communications Letters* 13(11): 829–831.

Peppas, K., Lazarakis, F., Alexandridis, A. & Dangakis, K. (2009). Error performance of digital modulation schemes with MRC diversity reception over η-μ fading channels, *IEEE Transactions on Wireless Communications* 8(10): 4974–4980.

Peppas, K., Lazarakis, F., Alexandridis, A. & Dangakis, K. (2010). Cascaded generalised-k fading channel, *IET Communications* 4(1): 116–124.

Peppas, K. P. (2010). Capacity of η-μ fading channels under different adaptive transmission techniques, *IET Communnications* 4: 532–539.

Peppas, K. P. & Datsikas, C. K. (2010). Average symbol error probability of general-order rectangular quadrature amplitude modulation of optical wireless communication systems over atmospheric turbulence channels, *IEEE/OSA Journal of Optical Communications and Networking* 2(1-3): 102–110.

Popoola, W. O., Ghassemlooy, Z. & Ahmadi, V. (2008). Performance of sub-carrier modulated free space optical communication link in negative exponential turbulence environment, *International Journal of Autonomous and Adaptive Communication Systems* 1(3): 342–355.

Proakis, J. & Salehi, M. (2008). *Digital Communications*, McGraw-Hill.

Prudnikov, A. P., Brychkov, Y. A. & Marichev, O. I. (1986). *Integrals and Series Volume 3: More Special Functions*, 1 edn, Gordon and Breach Science Publishers.

Rappaport, T. S. & McGillem, C. D. (1989). UHF fading in factories, *IEEE Journal on Selected Areas in Communications* 7: 40–48.

Rice, S. O. (1948). Statistical properties of a sine wave plus random noise, *Bell System Technical Journal* 27: 109–157.

Sagias, N. C. & Karagiannidis, G. K. (2005). Gaussian class multivariate weibull distributions: theory and applications in fading channels, *IEEE Transactions on Information Theory* 51(10): 3608–3619.

Sagias, N. C. & Mathiopoulos, P. T. (2005). Switched diversity receivers over generalized gamma fading channels, *IEEE Communications Letters* 9(10): 871–873.

Sagias, N., Karagiannidis, G. & Tombras, G. (2004). Error-rate analysis of switched diversity receivers in Weibull fading, *Electronics Letters* 40(11): 681–682.

Sagias, N., Karagiannidis, G., Zogas, D., Mathiopoulos, P. & Tombras, G. (2004). Performance analysis of dual selection diversity in correlated Weibull fading channels, *IEEE Transactions on Communications* 52(7): 1063–1067.

Sagias, N., Mathiopoulos, P. & Tombras, G. (2003). Selection diversity receivers in Weibull fading: Outage probability and average signal-to-noise ratio, *Electronics Letters* 39(25): 1859–1860.

Sagias, N. & Tombras, G. (2007). On the cascaded weibull fading channel model, *Journal of the Franklin Institute* 344(1): 1–11.

Sagias, N., Zogas, D., Karagiannidis, G. & Tombras, G. (2004). Channel capacity and second-order statistics in Weibull fading, *IEEE Communications Letters* 8(6): 377–379.

Sandalidis, H. G. & Tsiftsis, T. A. (2008). Outage probability and ergodic capacity of free-space optical links over strong turbulence, *Electronics Letters* 44(1): 46–47.

Shaft, P. D. (1974). On the relationship between scintillation index and Rician fading, *IEEE Transactions on Communications* 22: 731–732.

Simon, M. K. & Alouini, M. S. (2005). *Digital Communication over Fading Channels*, Wiley.

Stacy, E. (1962). A generalization of the gamma distribution, *The Annals of Mathematical Statistics* 3(33): 1187–1192.

Staley, T. L., North, R. C., Ku, W. H. & Zeidler, J. R. (1996). Performance of coherent MPSK on frequency selective slowly fading channels, *Proceedings of IEEE Vehicular Technology Conference (VTC 96)*, Atlanta, pp. 784–788.

Stein, S. (1987). Fading channel issues in system engineering, *IEEE Journal on Selected Areas in Communications* 5(2): 68–69.

Sugar, G. R. (1955). Some fading characteristics of regular VHF ionospheric propagation, *Proceedings of the IRE* pp. 1432–1436.

Tse, D. & Viswanath, P. (2005). *Fundamentals of Wireless Communication*, Cambridge University Press.

Tsiftsis, T. A. (2008). Performance of heterodyne wireless optical communication systems over gamma-gamma atmospheric turbulence channels, *Electronics Letters* 44: 373–375.

Uysal, M. (2006). Diversity analysis of space-time coding in cascaded rayleigh fading channels, *IEEE Commnunications Letters* 10(3): 165–167.

Uysal, M., Li, J. T. & Yu, M. (2006). Error rate performance analysis of coded free-space optical links over gamma-gamma atmospheric turbulence channels, *IEEE Transaction on Wireless Communications* 5(6): 1229–1233.

Vetelino, F. S., Young, S. & Andrews, L. (2007). Fade statistics and aperture averaging for gaussian beam waves in moderate to strong turbulence, *Applied Optics* 46(18): 3780–3789.

Yacoub, M. D. (2007a). The α-μ distribution: A physical fading model for the stacy distribution, *IEEE Transactions on Vehicular Technology* 56(1): 27–34.

Yacoub, M. D. (2007b). The κ-μ and the η-μ distribution, *IEEE Antennas and Propagations Magazine* 49(1): 68–81.

Yilmaz, F. & Alouini, M.-S. (2009). Product of the powers of generalized nakagami-m variates and performance of cascaded fading channels, *Proceedings of IEEE Global Telecommunications Conference*, pp. 1–8.

Zhu, X. & Kahn, J. M. (2002). Free-space optical communications through atmospheric turbulence channels, *IEEE Transaction on Communications* 50(8): 1293–1300.

Zogas, D., Sagias, N., Tombras, G. & Karagiannidis, G. (2005). Average output snr of equal-gain diversity receivers over correlative weibull fading channels, *European Transactions on Telecommunications* 16(6): 521–525.

2

Indoor Channel Characterization and Performance Analysis of a 60 GHz near Gigabit System for WPAN Applications

Ghaïs El Zein, Gheorghe Zaharia,
Lahatra Rakotondrainibe and Yvan Kokar
European University of Brittany (UEB)
INSA, IETR, UMR 6164
20 Avenue des Buttes de Coësmes, CS 70839, 35708 Rennes Cedex 7
France

1. Introduction

During the last decade, substantial knowledge about the 60 GHz millimeter-wave (MMW) channel has been accumulated and different architectures have been analyzed to develop MMW communication systems for commercial applications. The 60 GHz bandwidth is suitable for high data-rate and short-distance wireless communications. This interest is particularly due to the large bandwidth and the important power loss caused by the free space and walls attenuation which permits to reuse the same frequency bandwidth even in the next floor of the same building. A high frequency band leads to a small size of RF components including antennas. However, many challenges have to be overcome before designing the system, such as the cost, millimeter-wave circuits and millimeter-wave propagation. For any wireless system design, the selection of a modulation and coding scheme is a main consideration and has a large impact on the system complexity. Problems such as power amplifier (PA) non-linearity, oscillator phase noise, insertion loss and flatness are more important for these RF circuits. These effects should be taken into account in the overall communication system. It was shown in (U. H. Rizvi et al., 2008) that single carrier (SC) transmission has a lower tolerance to phase noise and is more resistant to the PA non-linearity than the multicarrier OFDM. Owing to these advantages, in (S. Kato et al., 2009), the authors proposed the single carrier (SC) transmission for multi-gigabit 60 GHz WPAN systems, as defined in IEEE 802.15.3C standard. Recently, the IEEE 802.15.3c, ECMA and Very High Throughput (VHT) groups were formed to normalize the future WPAN systems for the 60 GHz band (ECMA, 2008). Hence, different architectures have been analyzed to develop new MMW communication systems for commercial applications. Up to now, in the literature, several studies have considered propagation measurements, potential applications, circuit design issues and several modulation techniques at 60 GHz (P. Smulders, 2002). However, few efforts have been dedicated to the realization of a 60 GHz wireless system and the characterization of its performance in realistic environments.

This chapter presents an overview of several studies concerning the indoor wireless communications at 60 GHz performed by the IETR (Institute of Electronics and Telecommunications of Rennes). This work is a part of research Techim@ges, CPER Palmyre II and IGCYC projects financially supported by Region Bretagne and UEB. The characterization and the modeling of the indoor radio propagation channel are based on several measurement campaigns obtained for different configurations. Some typical residential environments were also simulated by ray tracing and Gaussian Beam Tracking. The obtained simulations are compared to the experimental results. This chapter also presents a full experimental implementation of a 60 GHz wireless Gigabit Ethernet (G.E.) communication system operating at near gigabit data rate. As the 60 GHz radio link operates only in a single room configuration, a hybrid technology with the Radio-over-Fiber (RoF) is used to ensure the communications in all the rooms of a residential environment. The single carrier architecture chosen for this system is presented. In the baseband (BB) processing block, an original method used for the byte/frame synchronization is also described. The proposed system provides a good trade-off between performance and complexity. Performance measurements of the realized system for different configurations and different indoor environments are presented.

The rest of this chapter is organized as follows: Section 2 presents an overview of several studies realized at IETR concerning the measurements and characterization of the 60 GHz radio propagation channel. Section 3 reports recent work concerning a 60 GHz radio communication system. In Section 4, recent measurement and simulation results are presented. Conclusions and perspectives are drawn in Section 5.

2. Channel measurements and characterization

2.1 Channel sounder

During the last decade, several research activities were carried out at IETR in the 60 GHz bandwidth: the realization of the channel sounder, the indoor radio channel measurements, simulation and characterization. A 60-GHz wideband channel sounder was developed at IETR, as shown in Fig. 1. This channel sounder has 500 MHz bandwidth, 40 dB relative dynamic and 2.3 ns effective time resolution, which means that two paths separated from by 69 cm, can be correctly discriminated. Based on the sliding correlation technique, this sounder is optimized to perform long term measurement campaigns. Some measurement results with Doppler analysis up to 20 kHz are presented in (S. Guillouard et al., 1999).

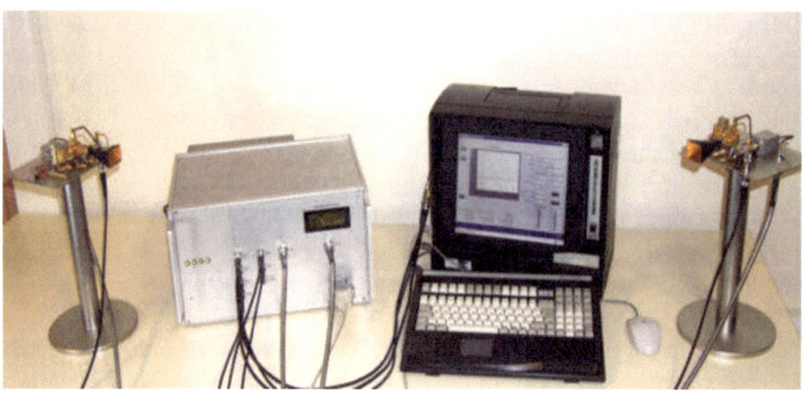

Fig. 1. Channel sounder at 60 GHz realized by IETR

2.2 Channel measurement and characterization

The study of wave propagation appears as an important task when developing a wireless system. The purpose of this chapter is to highlight different aspects concerning the wireless propagation channel at 60 GHz system (G. El Zein, 2009). In indoor environments, the radio propagation of electromagnetic waves between the transmitter (Tx) and the receiver (Rx), is characterized by the presence of multipath due to various phenomena such as reflection, refraction, scattering, and diffraction. In fact, the performance of communication systems is largely dependent on the propagation environment and on the structure of antennas. In this context, the space-time modeling of the channel is essential. For broadband systems, the analysis is usually made in the frequency domain and the time domain; this allows measuring the coherence bandwidth, the coherence time, the respective delay spread and Doppler spread values. Moreover, wave direction spread is used to highlight the link between propagation and system in the space domain. An accurate description of the spatial and temporal properties of the channel is necessary for the design of broadband systems and for the choice of the network topology. In (S. Collonge et al., 2004), the results of several studies concerning the radio propagation at 60 GHz in residential environments were published. These studies are based on several measurement campaigns realized with the IETR channel sounder (S. Guillouard et al., 1999). The measurements have been performed in residential furnished environments. The study of the angles-of-arrival (AoA) shows the importance of openings (such as doors, staircase, etc.) for the radio propagation between adjacent rooms (Fig. 2). In NLOS situation, the direct path is not available and the angular power distribution is more diffuse.

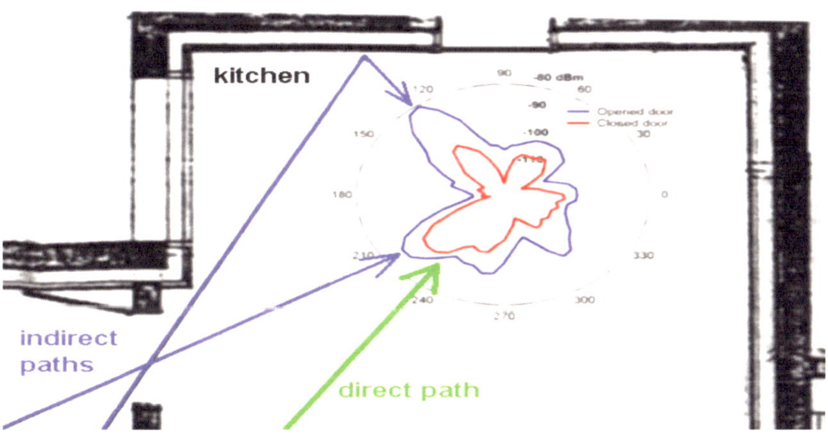

Fig. 2. Received power in the azimuthal plane (NLOS situation, with a horn antenna at Rx)

Radio propagation measurements between adjacent rooms show that the apertures (doors, windows, etc.) play a vital role in terms of power coverage. The wave propagation depends on antennas (beam-width, gain and polarization), physical environment (furniture, materials) and human activity. A particular attention is paid to the influence of the human activity on radio propagation, as shown in Fig. 3. The movements within the channel cause a severe shadowing effect; which can make the propagation channel not accessible during the shadowing event (S. Collonge et al., 2004). In this case, the angular diversity can be used; when a path is shadowed, another one, coming from another direction, can maintain the radio link.

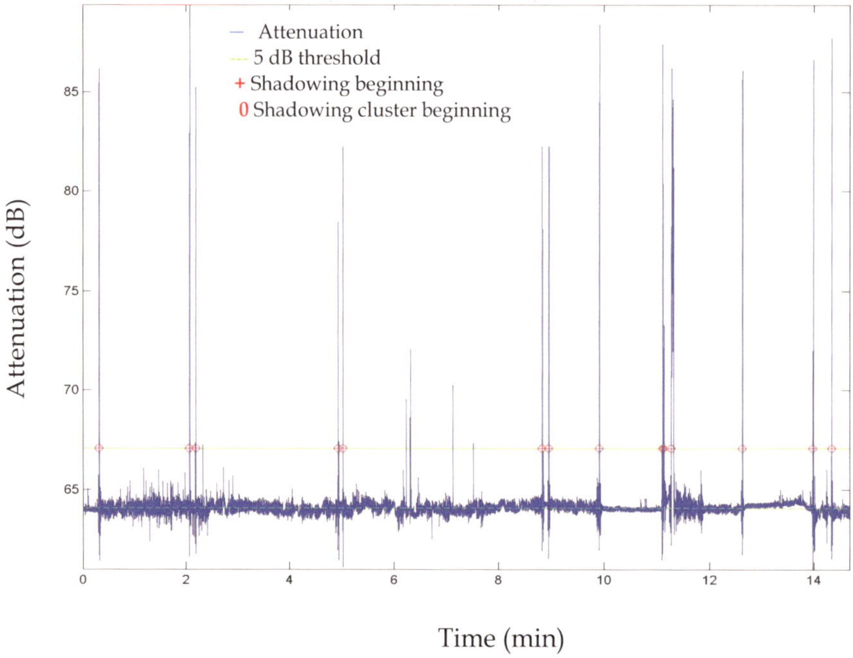

Fig. 3. Human activity measurement at 60 GHz (Rx antenna: horn, channel activity: 4 persons)

For the fading of the received signal, large-scale fading as well as small-scale effects are taken into consideration. Here, the large-scale fading at Tx-Rx distance, describes the average behavior of the channel, mainly caused by the free space path loss and the shadowing effect, while the small-scale fading characterizes the signal changes in a local area, only within a range of a few wavelengths (P. Smulders, 2009). From the database of impulse responses, several propagation characteristics are computed: attenuation, root mean square delay spread (τ_{RMS}), delay window, coherence bandwidth (B_{coh}) (S. Collonge et al., 2004). The use of directional antennas yield the benefits of reducing the number of multipath components (the channel frequency selectivity) and therefore to simplify the signal processing. Delay spread considerations reveal that RMS delay spread can be made very small (in the order of 1 ns when using narrow-beam antennas). This duration corresponds to the time symbol of 1 Gbps when using a simple BPSK modulation. Therefore, a data rate less than 1 Gbps can be achieved without further equalization. The coherence bandwidth $B_{coh,0.9}$ can be defined as the frequency shift where the correlation level falls below 0.9. As shown in (P. Smulders, 2009), the relationship between $B_{coh,0.9}$ and τ_{RMS} is obtained by:

$$B_{coh,0.9} = \frac{0.063}{\tau_{RMS}} \quad (1)$$

As shown in (N. Moraitis et al., 2004), when using directional antennas, the minimum observed coherence time was 32 ms (people walking at a speed of 1.7 m/s) which is much higher than the lower limit of 1 ms (omnidirectionnal antennas). The channel is considered invariant during the coherence time. Therefore, it can be estimated once per few thousands of data symbols for Gbps transmission rate. The Doppler effect, due mainly to the moving persons in the channel, depends also on the antenna beamwidth. In indoor environments, when using directional antennas (spatial filtering), this Doppler effect is considered not critical.

2.3 Deterministic simulations tool of the 60 GHz radio channel

Deterministic models are based on a fine description of a specific environment. Two approaches can be identified: the site-specific ray tracing and the techniques based on the processing and exploitation of measured data. Based on optical approximations, ray-tracing models need to complete geometrical and electromagnetic specifications of the simulated environment. They enable to estimate the channel characteristics with a good accuracy, if the modelled environment is not too complex. The ray-tracing is generally based on a 3D description of the environment. A simplified model is a necessity, in order to reduce the simulation time and the computational resources. Requiring much computational time, other models can be used based on the Maxwell's equations.

As described in (R. Tahri et al., 2005), two deterministic simulation tools have been used to complement the experimental characterization: a ray-tracing tool and a 3 D Gaussian Beam Tracking (GBT) technique. The GBT method based on Gabor frame approach is particularly well suited to high frequencies and permits a collective treatment of rays which offers significant computation time efficiency. Fig. 4 shows the power coverage obtained with GBT and X-Siradif ray tracing software.

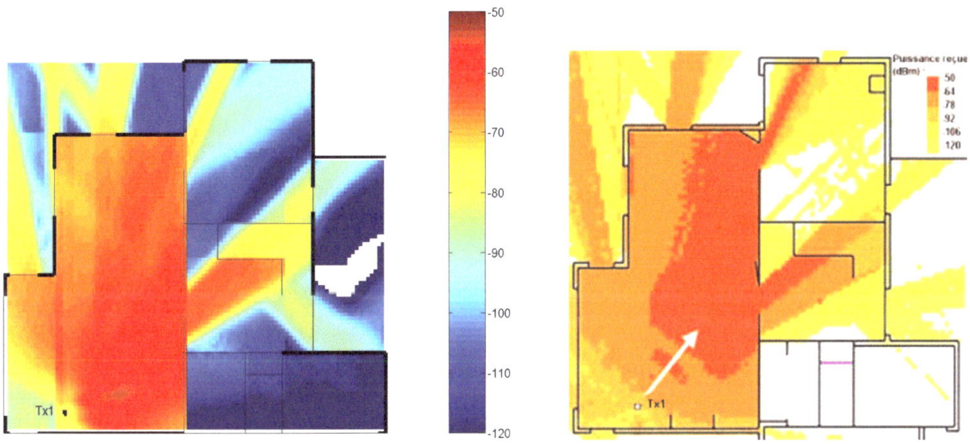

(a) Gaussian Beam Tracking (b) Ray tracing (X-Siradif)

Fig. 4. Power coverage map in the residential environment

The GBT algorithm and ray tracing technique are used for coverage simulations in an indoor environment (a house) at 60 GHz. The dimension of the house is 10.5×9.5×2.5 m^3. The building materials are mainly breeze blocks, plasterboards and bricks. The Tx (with patch antenna) is placed in a corner of the main room of the house, at a height of 2.2 m near the ceiling and slightly pointed toward the ground (15°). The azimuth angle is 50°. The receiving antenna (Rx) is a horn placed at a height of 1.2 m. At each location, the Rx antenna is pointing towards the Tx antenna. As one can observe in Fig. 4, the comparison of the power distribution in the environment, obtained with GBT and X-Siradif, is very satisfying. More details are given in (S. Collonge et al., 2004).

3. System design

A 60 GHz wireless Gigabit Ethernet (G.E.) communication system operating at near gigabit throughput has been developed at IETR. The realized system is shown in Fig. 5.

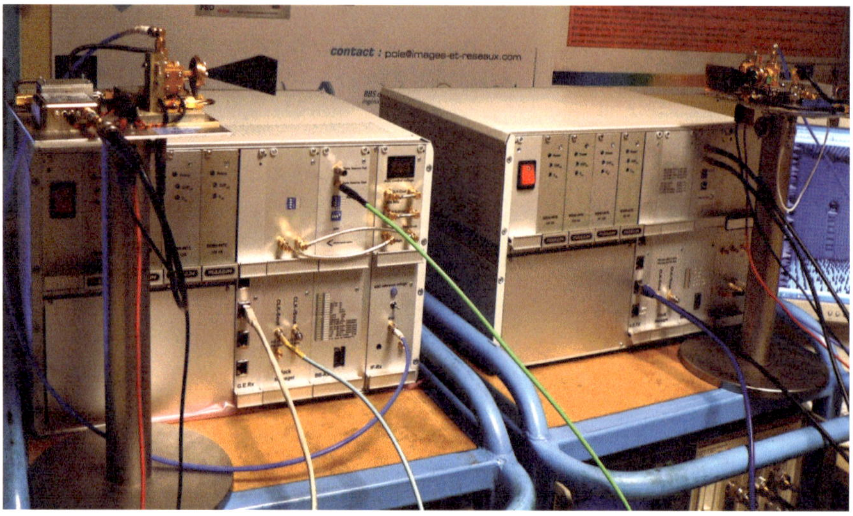

Fig. 5. Wireless Gigabit Ethernet at 60 GHz realized by the IETR

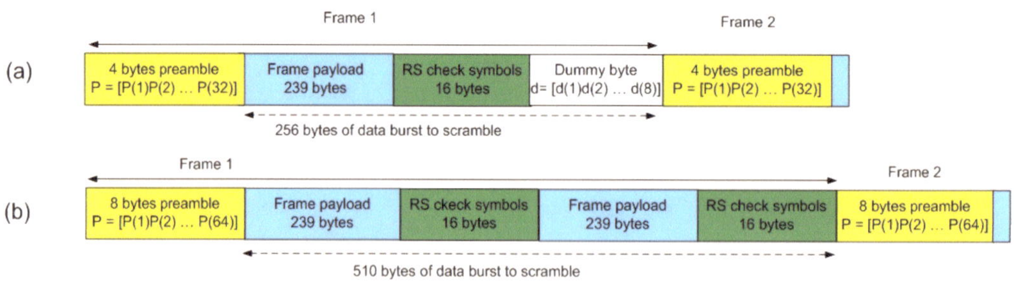

Fig. 6. Frame structure: a) 32-bits preamble; b) 64-bits preamble

This system covers 2 GHz available bandwidth. A differential binary shift keying (DBPSK) modulation and a differential demodulation are adopted at intermediate frequency (IF). In the baseband processing block, an original byte/frame synchronization technique is designed to provide a small value of the preamble false alarm and missing probabilities. Several measurements campaigns have been done for different configurations (LOS, NLOS, antenna depointing) and different environments (gym, hallways). In addition, bit error rate (BER) measurements have been performed for different configurations: with/without Reed Solomon RS (255, 239) coding and with byte/frame synchronization using 32/64 bits preambles. Our purpose is to compare the robustness of 32/64 bits preambles in terms of byte/frame synchronization at the receiver. The frame structure is shown in Fig. 6. The preambles are placed at the beginning of the frame payload of 239 bytes. As it will be shown later, when using the 32-bits preamble, the frame/byte synchronization is not reliable. Therefore, a 64-bits preamble was considered. In order to avoid the reduction of the code rate, each 64-bits preamble is followed by 2 RS frames, as shown in Fig. 6. In this case, the frame length is Lf = 255*2+8 = 518 bytes.

The design and realization of the overall system including the baseband, intermediate frequency and radiofrequency blocks, are described in this section.

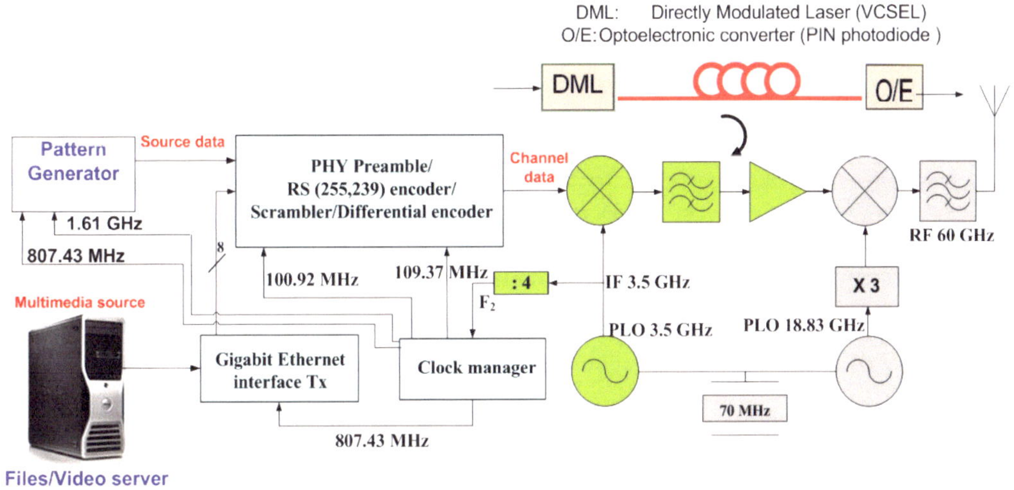

Fig. 7. 60 GHz wireless Gigabit Ethernet transmitter

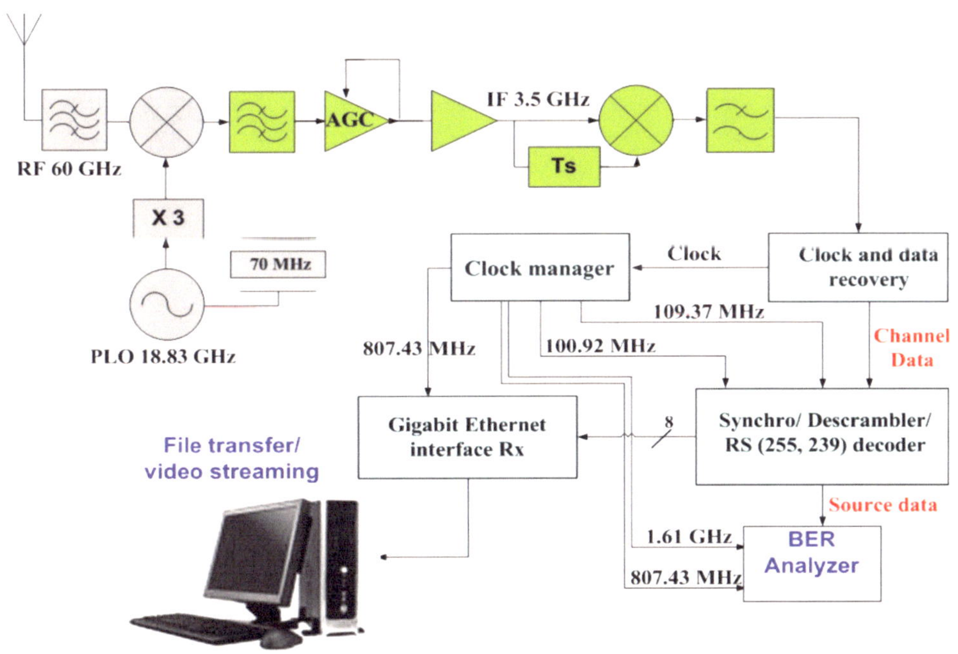

Fig. 8. 60 GHz wireless Gigabit Ethernet receiver

Fig. 7 and Fig. 8 show the block diagram of the Tx and Rx respectively. The realized system can operate with data received from a multimedia server using a G.E interface or from a pattern generator. As shown in Fig. 7, the clock of the encoded data is obtained from the intermediate frequency (IF = 3.5 GHz): F2 = IF/4 = 875 MHz. Using the frame structure with 64-bits preamble, the clock frequency for source data is:

$$f_1 = \frac{F_1}{8} = 100.929\,\text{MHz},$$
$$f_2 = \frac{F_2}{8} = 109.375\,\text{MHz}. \quad (2)$$

This frequency is obtained by the Clock manager block with a phase locked loop (PLL).
The transmitted signal must contain timing information that allows the clock recovery and the byte/frame synchronization at the receiver (Rx). Thus, scrambling and preamble must be considered. A differential encoder allows removing the phase ambiguity at the Rx (by a differential demodulator). Due to the hardware constraints, the first data rate was chosen at around 800 Mbps. Reed Solomon coding/decoding are used as a forward error correction.

3.1 Transmitter design

The G.E. interface of the transmitter is used to connect a home server to a wireless link with about 800 Mbps bit rate, as shown in Fig. 9.

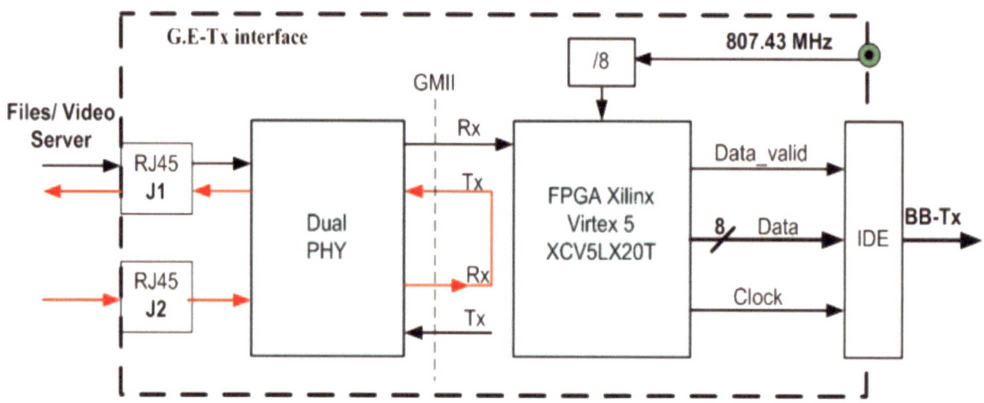

Fig. 9. Gigabit Ethernet interface of the transmitter

The gigabit media independent interface (GMII) is an interface between the media access control (MAC) device and the PHY layer. The GMII is an 8-bit parallel interface synchronized at a clock frequency of 125 MHz. However, this clock frequency is different from the source byte frequency f_1 = 807.43/8 =100.92 MHz generated by the clock manager in Fig. 7. Then, there is a risk of packet loss since the source is always faster than the destination. In order to avoid the packet loss, a programmable logic circuit (FPGA) is used. Therefore, the input byte stream is written into the dual port FIFO memory of the FPGA at a high frequency 125 MHz. The FIFO memory has been set up with two thresholds. When the upper threshold is attained, the dual PHY block (controlled by the

FPGA) sends a "stop signal" to the multimedia source in order to stop the byte transfer. Then, a frequency f_1 reads out continuously the data stored in the FIFO. In other hand, when the lower threshold is attained, the dual PHY block sends a "start signal" to begin a new Ethernet frame. Whatever the activity on the Ethernet access, the throughput at the output of the G.E. interface is constant. A header is inserted at the beginning of each Ethernet frame to locate the starting point of each received Ethernet frame at the receiver. Finally, the byte stream from the G.E. interface is transferred in the BB-Tx, as shown in Fig. 10.

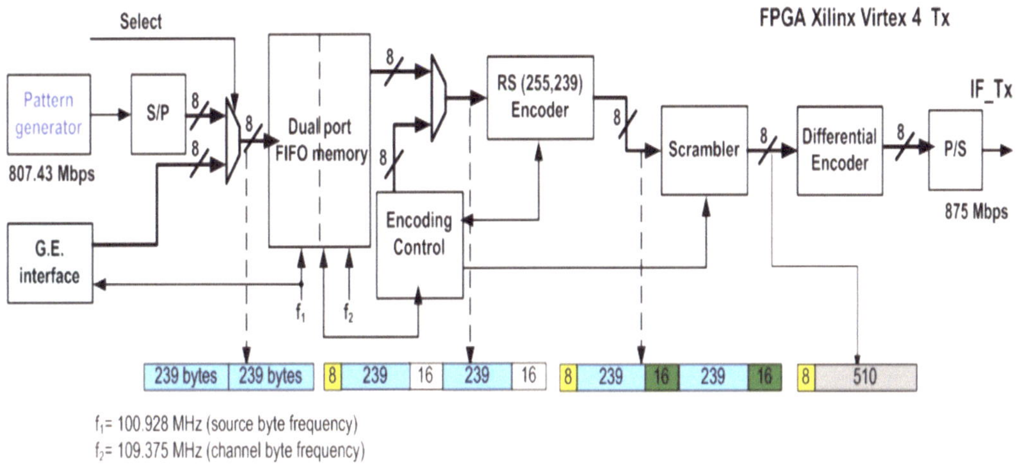

Fig. 10. Transmitter baseband architecture (BB-Tx)

A known pseudo-random sequence of 63 bits is completed with one more bit to obtain an 8 bytes preamble. This 8 bytes preamble is sent at the beginning of each frame to achieve good frame synchronization at the receiver. Due to the byte operation of a RS (255,239) coding, two clock frequencies f_1 and f_2 are used:

$$F_2 = \frac{3.5\,\text{GHz}}{4} = 875\,\text{MHz} \quad \text{and}$$
$$F_1 = \frac{2*239}{2*(239+16)+8} F_2. \tag{3}$$

The frame format is realized as follows: the input source byte stream is written into the dual port FIFO memory at a slow frequency f_1. When the FIFO memory is half-full, the encoding control reads out data stored in the register at a higher frequency f_2. The encoding control generates an 8 bytes preamble at the beginning of each frame, which is bypassed by the RS encoder and the scrambler. The RS encoder reads one byte every clock period. After 239 clock periods, the encoding control interrupts the bytes transfer during 16 clock periods, so 16 check bytes are added by the encoder. In all, two successive data words of 239 bytes are coded before creating a new frame. After coding, the obtained data are scrambled using an 8 bytes scrambling sequence. The scrambling sequence is chosen in order to provide at the receiver the lowest false detection of the preamble from the scrambled data. Then, the obtained scrambled byte stream is differentially encoded before the modulation. The differential encoder performs the delayed modulo-2 addition of the input data bit (b_k) with the output bit (d_{k-1}):

$$d_k = b_k \oplus d_{k-1} \tag{4}$$

The obtained data are used to modulate an IF carrier generated by a 3.5 GHz phase locked oscillator (PLO) with a 70 MHz external reference. The IF signal is fed into a band-pass filter (BPF) with 2 GHz bandwidth and transmitted through a RoF link, as shown in Fig. 11. The RoF link consists of a laser diode, an optical variable attenuator, an optical fiber of length 300 meters and a photoreceiver. Then, this IF signal is used to modulate directly the current of a laser diode operating at 850 nm. At the receiver, the optical signal is converted to an electrical signal by a PIN diode and amplified.

The overall RoF link is designed to offer a gain of 0 dB. The IF signal is sent to the RF block. This block is composed of a mixer, a frequency tripler, a PLO at 18.83 GHz and a band-pass filter (59-61 GHz). The local oscillator frequency is obtained using an 18.83 GHz PLO with the same 70 MHz reference and a frequency tripler. The phase noise of the 18.83 GHz PLO signal is about -110 dBc/Hz at 10 kHz off carrier. The BPF prevents the spill-over into adjacent channels and removes out-of-band spurious signals caused by the modulator operation. The 0 dBm obtained signal is fed into the horn antenna with a gain of 22.4 dBi and a half power beamwidth (HPBW) of 10°V and 12°H.

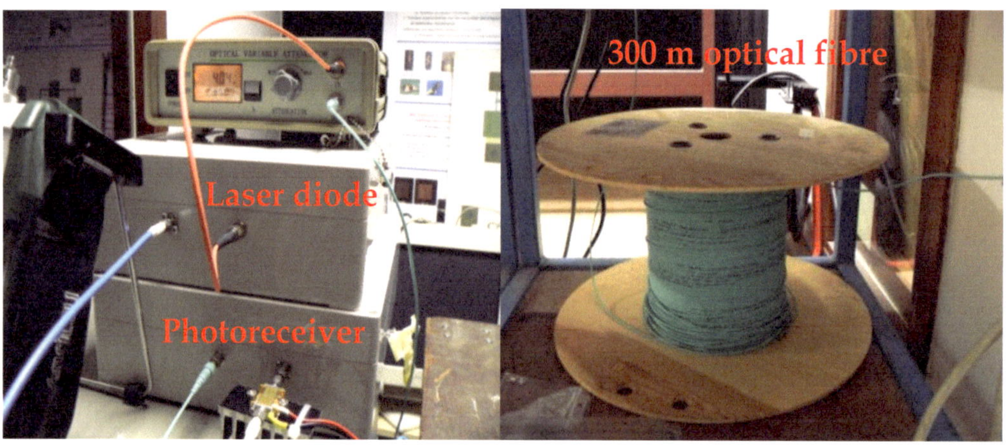

Fig. 11. Radio over Fibre link

3.2 Receiver design

The receive antenna, identical to the transmit horn antenna, is connected to a band-pass filter (59-61 GHz). The RF filtered signal is down-converted to an IF signal centered at 3.5 GHz and fed into a band-pass filter with a bandwidth of 2 GHz. An automatic gain control (AGC) with 20 dB dynamic ranges is used to ensure a quasi-constant signal level at the demodulator input when, for example, the Tx-Rx distance varies. The AGC loop consists of a variable gain amplifier, a power detector and a circuitry using a baseband amplifier to deliver the AGC voltage. This voltage is proportional to the power of the received signal. A low noise amplifier (LNA) with a gain of 40 dB is used to achieve sufficient gain. A simple differential demodulation enables the coded signal to be demodulated and decoded. In fact, the demodulation, based on a mixer and a delay line (delay equal to the symbol duration Ts = 1.14 ns), compares the signal phase of two consecutive symbols. A "1" is represented as a π-phase change and a "0" as no change. Owing to the product of two consecutive symbols, the ratio between the main lobe and the side lobes of the channel impulse response increases. This means that the differential demodulation is more resistant to intersymbol interference (ISI) effect compared to a coherent demodulation. Nevertheless, this differential demodulation is less performing in additive white Gaussian noise (AWGN) channel. Following the loop, a low-pass filter (LPF) with 1.8 GHz cut-off frequency removes the high frequency components of the obtained signal. For a reliable clock acquisition realized by the clock and data recovery (CDR) circuit, long sequences of '0' or '1' must be avoided. Thus, the use of a scrambler (and descrambler) is necessary.

A block diagram of the baseband architecture of the receiver is shown in Fig. 12. Owing to the RS (255, 239) decoder, the synchronized data from the CDR output are converted into a byte stream.

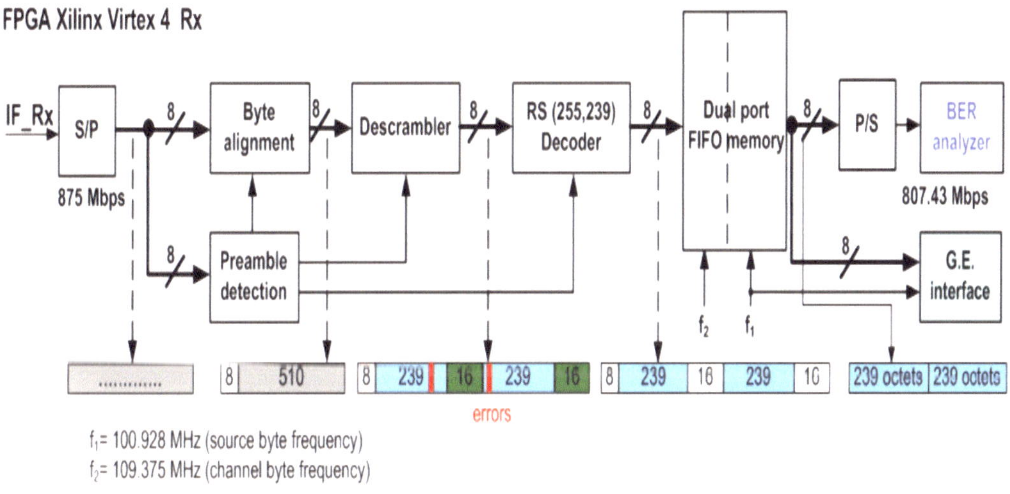

Fig. 12. Receiver baseband architecture (BB-Rx)

Fig. 13 shows the architecture of byte/frame synchronization using a 64 bits preamble.

The preamble detection is based on the cross-correlation of 64 successive received bits and the internal 64 bits preamble. Further, each C_k ($1 \leq k \leq 8$) correlator of 64 bits must analyze a 1-bit shifted sequence. Therefore, the preamble detection is performed with 64+7 = 71 bits, due to the different possible shifts of a byte. In all, there are 8 correlators in each bank of correlators. In addition, in order to improve the frame synchronization performance, two banks of correlators are used, taking into consideration the periodical repetition of the preamble: P1 (8 bytes) + D1 (510 bytes) + P2 (8 bytes) + D2 (510 bytes) + P3 (8 bytes). This process diminishes the false alarm probability (Pf) while the missing detection probability (Pm) is approximately multiplied by 2, as shown later. The preamble detection is obtained if the same C_k correlators in each bank of correlators indicate its presence. Therefore, the decision is made from 526 successive bytes (P1 + D1 + P2) of received data stored by the receiving shift register. In fact, the value of each correlation is compared to a threshold (S) to be determined. Setting the threshold at the maximum value (S = 64) is not practical, since a bit error in the preamble due to the channel impairments leads to a frame loss. A trade-off between Pm and Pf gives the threshold to be used. A false alarm is declared when the same C_k correlators in each bank of correlators detect the presence of the preamble within the scrambled data (D1 and D2).

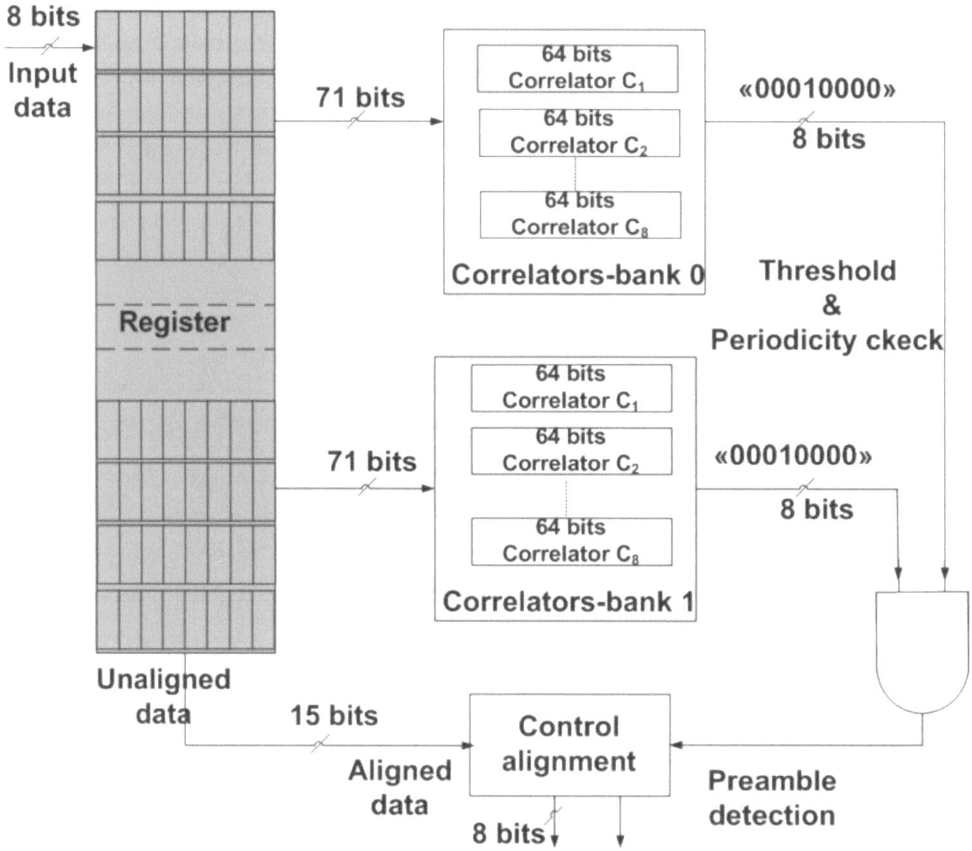

Fig. 13. The preamble detection and byte synchronization

The frame acquisition performance of the proposed 64 bits preamble was evaluated by simulations and compared to that of the 32 bits preamble (L. Rakotondrainibe et al., 2009). The frame structure with 32 bits preamble uses only a data word of 256 bytes (255 bytes + a "dummy byte"). Fig. 14a and Fig. 14b show the missing probability (Pm) versus channel error probability (p) for an AWGN channel, with 32 and 64 bits preamble, respectively. P_{m1} and P_{m2} are the missing detection probability using one bank and two banks of correlators, respectively.

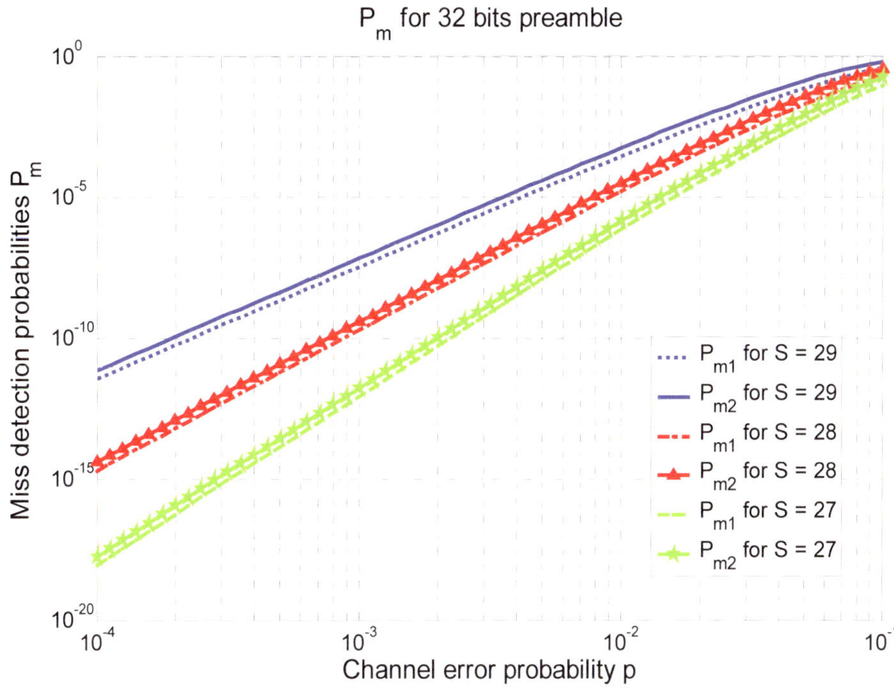

Fig. 14a. Miss detection probability with 32 bits preamble

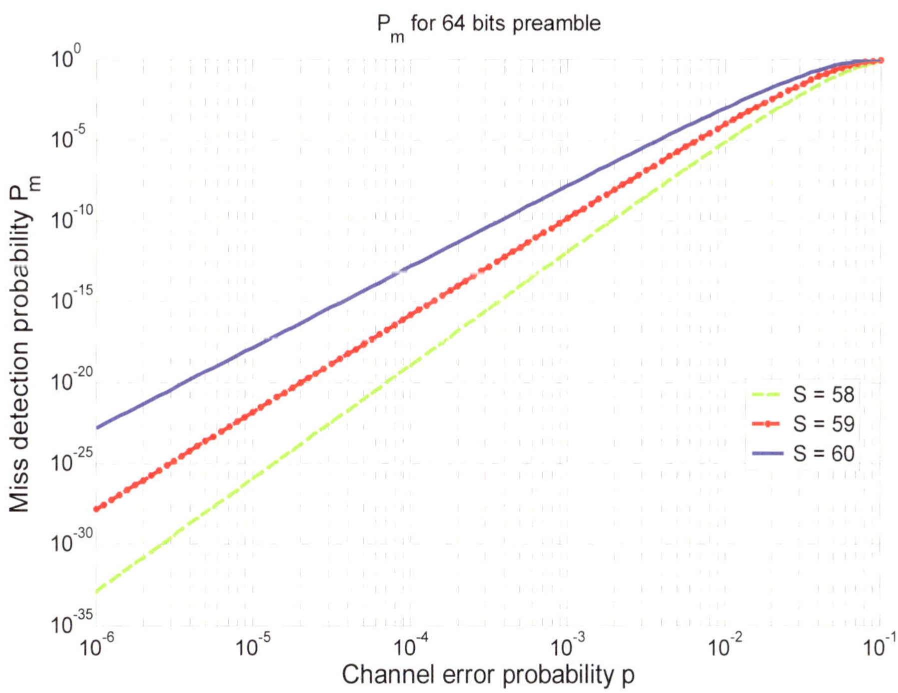

Fig. 14b. Miss detection probability with 64 bits preamble

Fig. 15a and Fig. 15b show the false alarm probability versus threshold S, with 32 and 64 bits preamble, respectively.

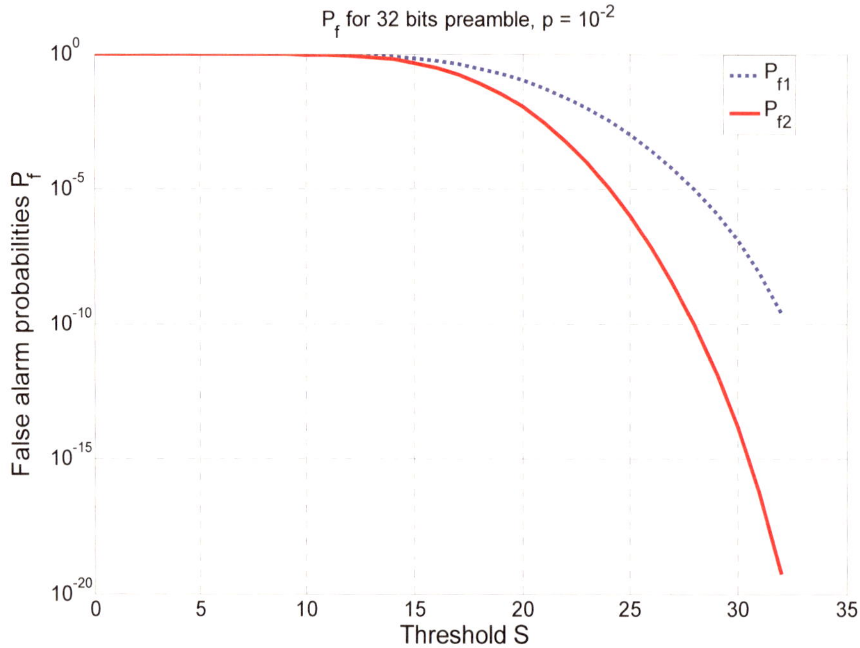

Fig. 15a. False alarm probability with 32 bits preamble

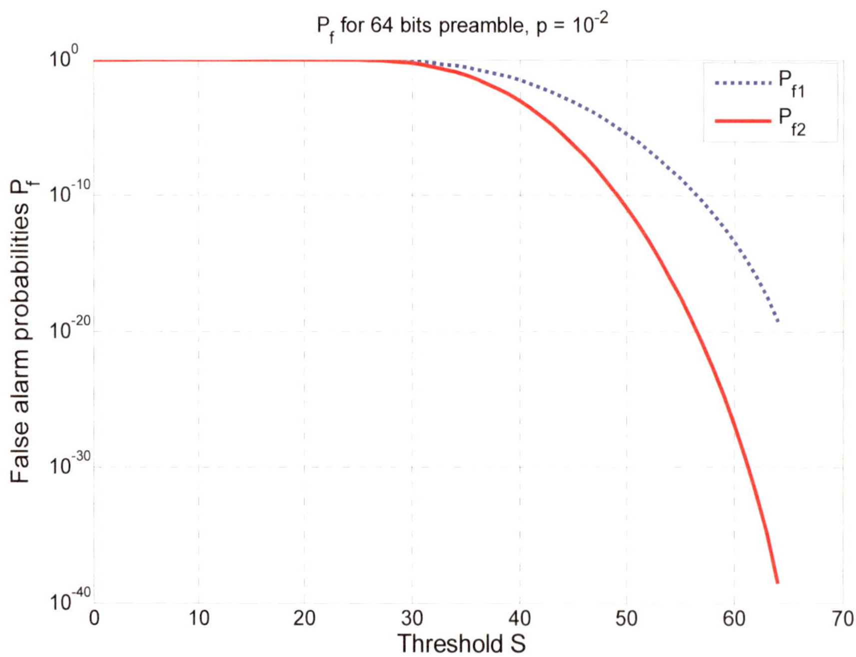

Fig. 15b. False alarm probability with 64 bits preamble

In these figures, P_{f1} and P_{f2} indicate the false alarm probabilities using one and two banks of correlators, respectively. The effect of p on the false alarm probability is insignificant since the random data bits "0" and "1" are assumed to be equiprobable. With the 64 bits preamble, for p = 10^{-3}, the result indicate that $P_m = 10^{-10}$ and $P_{f2} = 10^{-24}$ for S = 59. However, with the 32 bits preamble, we obtain $P_m = 10^{-7}$, $P_{f2} = 10^{-13}$ for S = 29. This means that, for a data rate about 1 Gbps, the preamble can be lost several times per second because $P_m = 10^{-7}$ (S = 29) with 32 bits preamble. We can notice that, for given values of p and P_{F2}, the 64 bits preamble shows a smaller false alarm probability compared to that obtained with the 32 bits preamble.

After the synchronization, the descrambler performs the modulo-2 addition between 8 successive received bytes and the descrambling sequence of 8 bytes. At the receiver, the baseband processing block regenerates the transmitted byte stream, which is then decoded by the RS decoder. The RS (255, 239) decoder can correct up to 8 erroneous bytes and operates at a fast clock frequency f_2 = 109.37 MHz. The byte stream is written discontinuously into the dual port FIFO memory at a fast clock frequency f_2. A slow clock frequency f_1 = 100.92 MHz reads out continuously the byte stream stored by the register, since all redundant information is removed. Afterwards, the byte stream is transferred to the receiver Gigabit Ethernet interface, as shown in Fig. 16. The feedback signal can be transmitted via a wired Ethernet connection or a Wi-Fi radio link due to its low throughput.

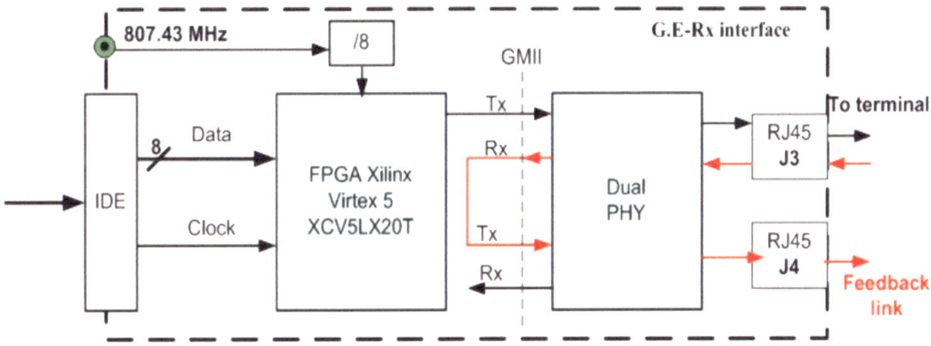

Fig. 16. Receiver Gigabit Ethernet interface

4. System performance analysis

4.1 System bandwidth

A vector network analyzer (HP 8753D) is used to measure the frequency response and impulse response figures of RF blocks including the LOS propagation channel by the parameter S_{21}. The objective was to determine the system bandwidth and to estimate the multipath channel effects, when using directional horn antennas. Measurements were performed in a corridor where the major part of the transmitted power is focused in the direction of the receiver. The RF-Tx and RF-Rx were placed at a height of 1.5 m. After measurement set-up and calibration, we obtain 2 GHz available bandwidth from the frequency response figure (Fig. 17). However, the RF blocks present some ripples in the band of flatness around 2 dB.

A perfect system must have an impulse response with only one lobe. Fig. 18 presents the result of an impulse response of the RF Tx-Rx blocks at 10 m Tx-Rx distance. A back-to-back test was realized using a 45 dB fixed attenuator at 60 GHz but similar results were obtained. Therefore, few side lobes were obtained which are mainly due to RF components imperfections.

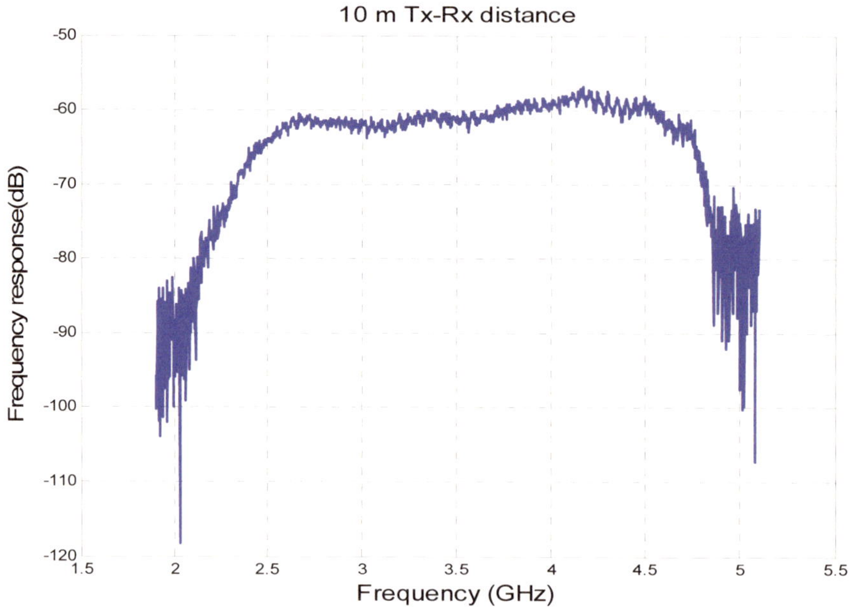

Fig. 17. Frequency response of RF blocks (Tx & Rx) using horn antennas

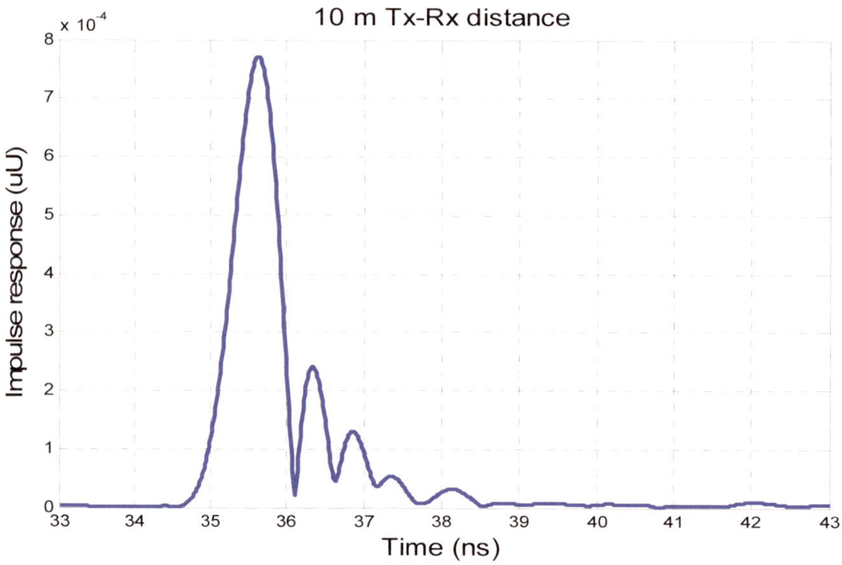

Fig. 18. Impulse response of RF blocks (Tx & Rx) using horn antennas

4.2 IF back-to-back performance results

The objective is to determine the signal to noise ratio (SNR) degradation of the realized DBPSK system with an ideal DBPSK system at a same bit error rate (BER).

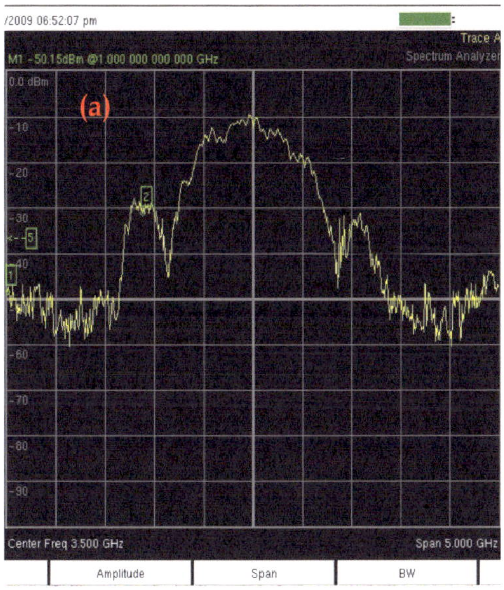

Fig. 19a. IF-Rx spectrum without noise

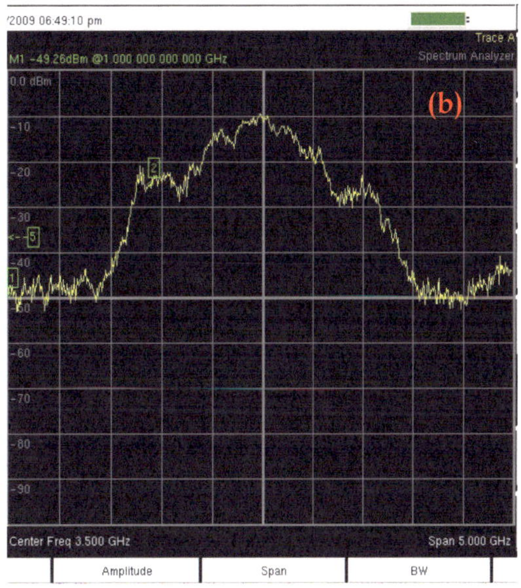

Fig. 19b. IF-Rx spectrum with noise

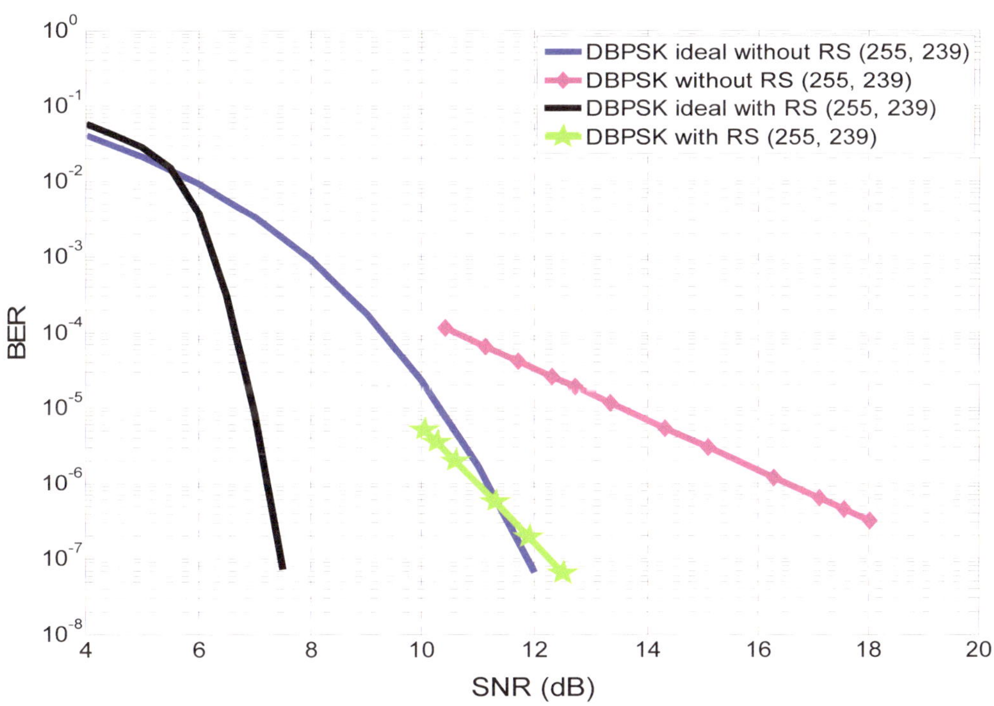

Fig. 20. BER versus SNR in the presence of AWGN

Back-to-back test of the realized DBPSK system (without RF blocks and AGC loop) was carried out at IF. The goal is to evaluate the BER versus SNR at the demodulator input. Hence, an external AWGN is added to the IF modulated signal (before the IF-Rx band pass filter). The external AWGN is a thermal noise generated and amplified by successive amplifiers. This noise feeds a band pass filter and a variable attenuator so that the SNR is varied by changing the noise power. Fig. 19a and Fig. 19b show the spectrum at IF, without and with extra AWGN respectively. The measured BER versus SNR is shown in Fig. 20. Compared to an ideal system, at a BER of 10^{-5}, the SNR degradation of the realized system is about 3.5 and 3 dB for uncoded and coded data, respectively. Indeed, at the receiver, the 2 GHz bandwidth of the filter is too wide for a throughput of 875 Mbps. In order to avoid the increased power noise in the band, the filter bandwidth could be reduced to 1.1 GHz, for example.

4.3 Link budget

Using the free space model, Fig. 21 shows the estimated IF received power versus the Tx-Rx distance. This result takes into account the 0 dBm transmitted power, the antenna gains (horn or patch), the path loss (free space model) and the implementation losses of RF blocks. Two types of antennas were used: horn antenna and patch antenna. The patch antenna has a gain of 8 dBi and a HPBW of 30°. The IF receiver noise power is:

$$N_L = -174\,(\text{dBm}/\text{Hz}) + NF + 10\log(B) = -71.98\,\text{dBm}. \quad (5)$$

where NF = 9 dB is the total noise figure and B = $2{*}10^9$ Hz is the receiver bandwidth. As shown in Fig. 20, the minimum SNR needed for BER = 10^{-4} is about 10.5 dB. Thus, the receiver sensitivity is about P_S = - 61.5 dBm. Therefore, the demodulator input power must be greater than 0 dBm.

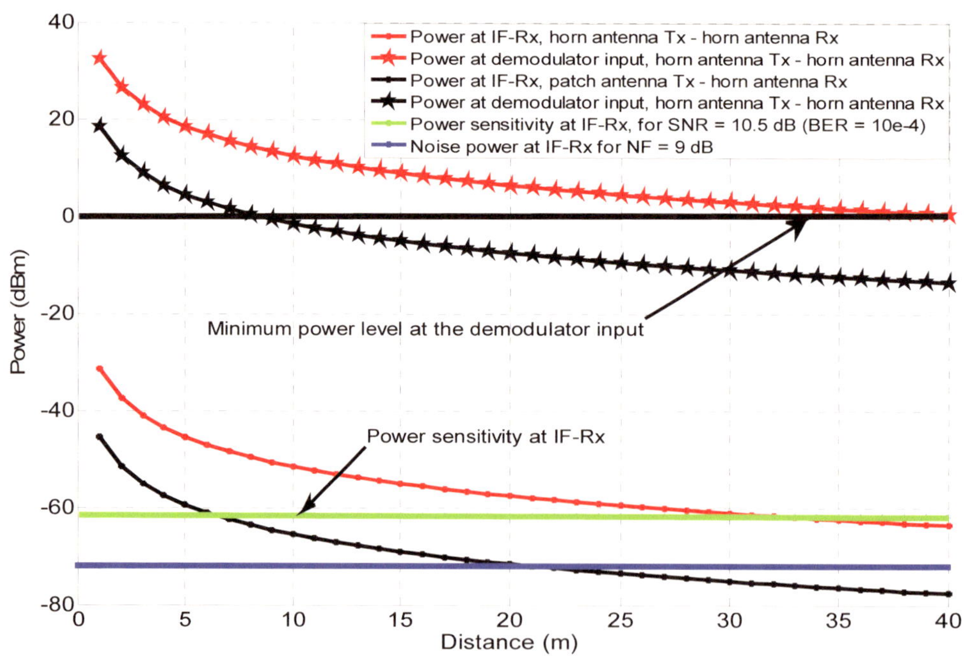

Fig. 21. The IF received power versus Tx-Rx distance

We can see that, a Tx-Rx distance of around 30 m can be achieved when using horn antennas at the transmitter and receiver, but only with 7 meters when using a patch antenna at Rx.

4.4 Indoor system performance

Based on the realized 60 GHz system, several measurements have been performed in a large gym and hallways, over distances ranging from 1 to 40 meters. At each distance, the BER was recorded during 5 minutes. The Tx and Rx horn antennas were situated at a height of 1.35 m above the floor. These measurements were conducted under LOS conditions with a fixed Rx and the Tx placed on a trolley pushed in a horizontal plane to various points about the environment. Also, during the measurements, the Tx and Rx were kept stationary, without movement of persons.

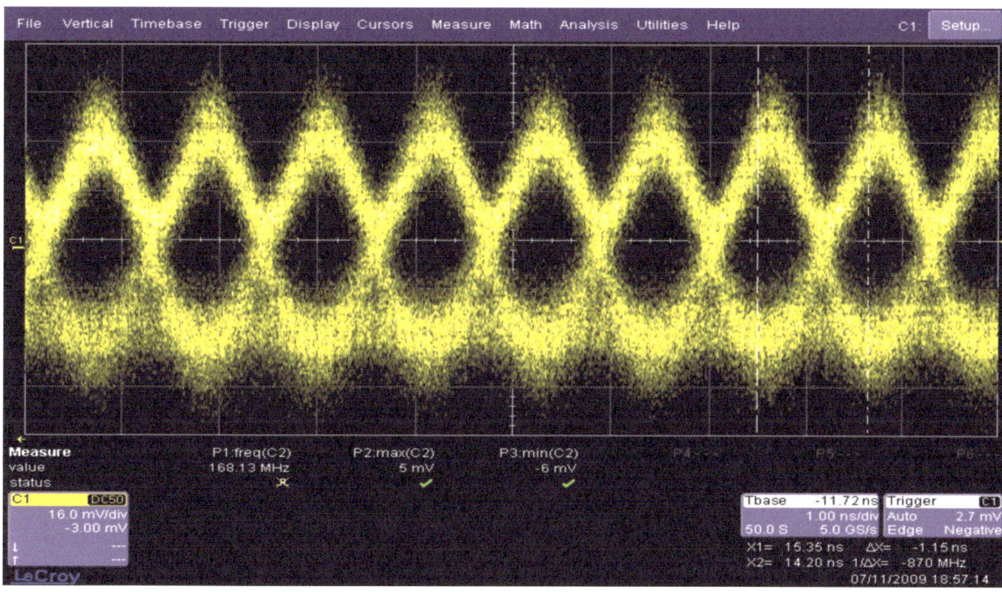

Fig. 22. Eye diagram for a 30 m Tx-Rx distance (in a large gym)

A pseudo-random sequence of 127 bits provided by a pattern generator was used as data source. Fig. 22 shows the eye diagram observed for a 30 m Tx-Rx distance (in a large gym). This suggests that a good communication link quality could be achieved at this distance.

We seek to evaluate the maximum distance attained between Tx-Rx for two possible configurations of an AGC amplifier, at minimum or maximum gain. Fig. 23 shows the measured BER results, with or without the AGC loop.

For a BER = 10^{-4}, when the amplifier gain is set at 8 dB, the upper limit of the Tx-Rx distance is about 7 m. However, the Tx-Rx distance can be increased at 35 m when the AGC gain amplifier is set at 28 dB.

As shown in Fig. 23, for the same BER = 10^{-6}, the Tx-Rx distance is around 27 m without channel coding and around 36 m with RS coding. This result proves the RS coding efficiency. Compared to the result in Fig. 21, a good agreement of a Tx-Rx maximum distance was obtained. This means that the multipath components are greatly reduced by the spatial filtering of the horn antennas (pencil beam).

However, the main problem of using directional antennas is the human obstruction. The signal reaching the Rx is randomly affected by people moving in the area and can lead to frequent outages of the radio link. For properly aligned antennas, it is confirmed that the communication is entirely interrupted when the direct path is blocked by a human body (synchronization loss). Therefore, an attenuation of around 20 dB was obtained when the direct path is blocked (as indicated in the power detector at the receiver). High gain antennas are needed for the 60 GHz radio propagation but to overcome this major problem, it is possible to exploit the angular diversity obtained by switching antennas or by beamforming (S. Kato et al., 2009). To improve the system reliability, a Tx mounted on the ceiling, preferably placed in the middle of the room can mitigate the radio beam blockage caused by people or furniture (S. Collonge et al., 2004). In real applications, the Tx antenna should have a large beamwidth to cover all the devices operating at 60 GHz in a room and the Rx antenna placed within the room should be directive so that the LOS components are amplified and the reflected components are attenuated by the antenna pattern.

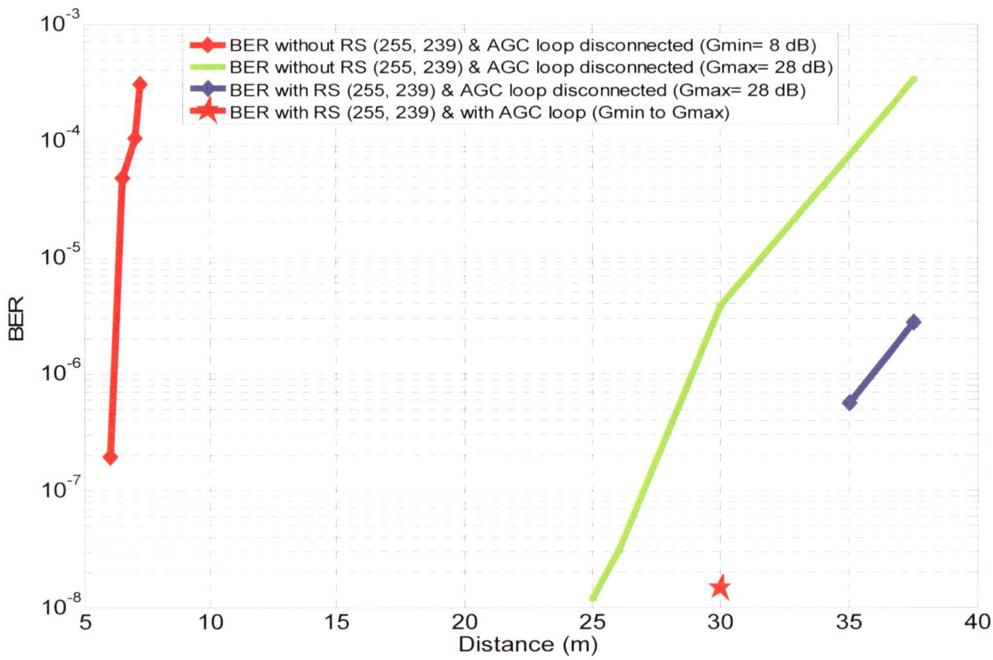

Fig. 23. BER versus the Tx-Rx distance in a large gym, using 32 bits preamble and S = 29

In order to examine the effects of the antenna directivity and the multipath fading, BER measurements were also conducted within a hallway over distances ranging from 1 to 40 meters. As shown in Fig. 24, the door of a 4 cm thickness (agglomerated wood), was opened during the BER measurements. The hallway has concrete walls and wooden doors on both sides. The Tx-Rx antennas (placed in the middle of the hallway) were positioned at a height of 1.35 m. The idea was to analyze the results of BER measurements with and without RS coding in a hallway separated by a door.

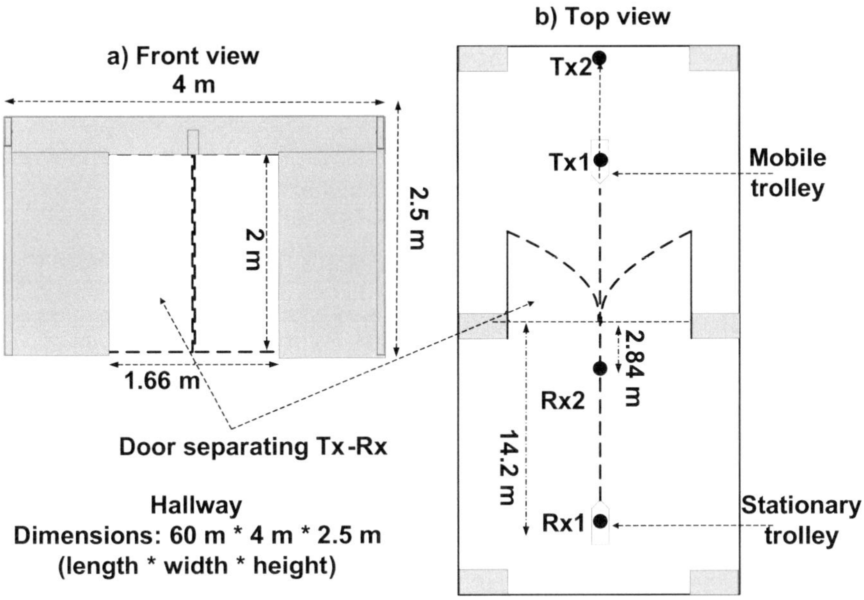

Fig. 24. The hallway: a) Front view; b) Top view

Due to the guided nature of the radio propagation along the hallway, the major part of the transmitted power is focused in the direction of the receiver. This means that in hallway the path loss exponent is considered less than 2 (as in a free space model). In the hallway, the door and walls can cause reflections and diffractions of the transmitted signal, in particular when the Rx position is far away from the opening door (as Rx1 position shown in Fig. 24). We found that for the same 32 m Tx-Rx distance, the received signal power was similar for both positions Tx1-Rx1 and Tx2-Rx2. However, the BER without coding is equal to $2.8*10^{-2}$ (due to some synchronization losses) and $2.8*10^{-5}$ for Tx1-Rx1 and Tx2-Rx2 positions, respectively. In the case of Tx1-Rx1 position, diffractions and reflections from the borders of the opening door can be the dominant contributors to the significant BER degradation.

BER measurements versus Tx-Rx distance using 64 bits preamble ($\gamma = 58$) were also carried out (in the case of Rx2 position). We found that for a Tx-Rx2 distance less than 32 m, all transmitted bits are received without errors (with RS coding) during 5 minutes measurement. Compared to the result obtained with the 32 bits preamble, as shown in Fig. 23, our investigation revealed that the frame structure using 64 bits preamble is better than 32 bits preamble in terms of byte/frame synchronization.

We also evaluate the BER performance when the door is closed. We observed that the attenuation increases of about 15 dB. A similar value was obtained in (S. Collonge et al., 2004). In this situation, the propagation channel is also unavailable during the "shadowing events" and lead to permanent synchronization loss. Therefore, radio electric openings (windows ...) are necessary.

We seek to determine also the BER degradation in function of Rx antenna depointing, as shown in Fig. 25. Measurement was done in a large gym and each BER result is recorded during 5 minutes. The distance between Tx-Rx is fixed but only the antenna Rx is slightly turned at right or at left. We found that the synchronization loss can be obtained at a BER of around 10^{-4} which corresponds to the Rx beam depointing of around 12°. This means that the Rx horn antenna needs to be properly well aligned in the direction of the Tx beam antenna. In a hallway environment, the misalignment of beam antennas (of a few degrees) can seriously influence the BER performance due to the multipath components caused by the sides of walls and the door borders. In the worst case, the misalignment errors can lead to occasional synchronization losses, giving a BER higher than 10^{-4}.

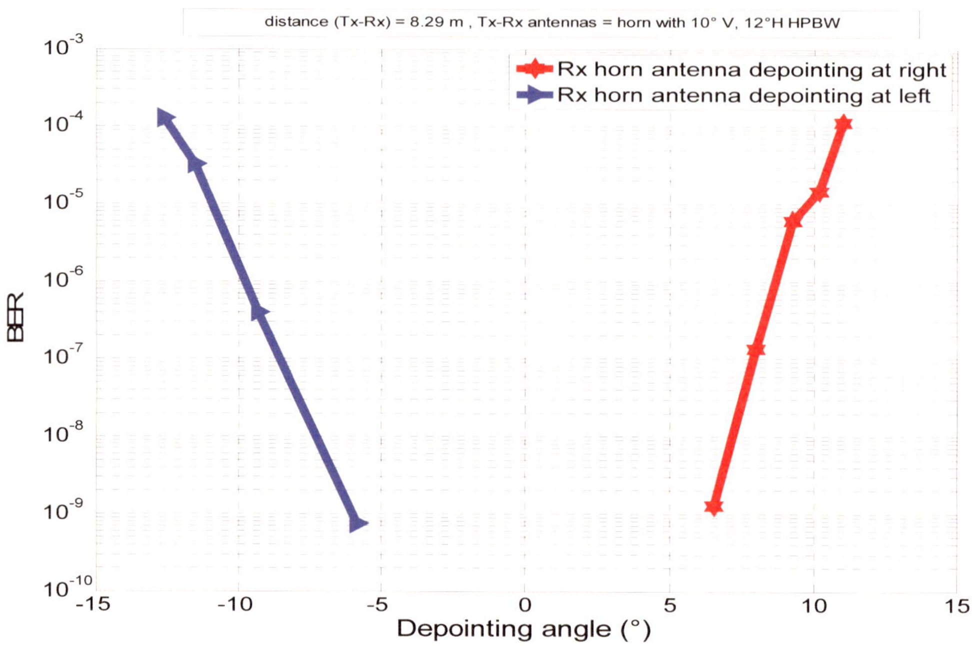

Fig. 25. BER as a function of an Rx antenna misalignment

5. Conclusion

In this chapter, a brief overview of several studies performed at IETR on 60 GHz indoor wireless communications is presented. The characterization of the radio propagation channel is based on several measurement campaigns realized with the channel sounder of IETR. Some typical residential environments were also simulated by ray tracing and Gaussian Beam Tracking. The obtained results show a good agreement with the experimental results. Recently, the IETR developed a single carrier wireless communication system operating at 60 GHz. The realized system provides a good trade-off between performance and complexity. An original method used for the byte/frame synchronization is also described. The numerical results show that the proposed 64 bits preamble allows obtaining better BER results comparing to the previously proposed 32 bits preamble. This new frame structure allows obtaining a high preamble detection probability and a very small false alarm probability. As a result, a Tx-Rx distance greater than 30 meters was attained with low BER using high gain horn antennas. In order to support a Gbps reliable transmission within a large room and severe multipath dispersion, a convenient solution is to use high gain antennas. However, our investigation revealed that the high gain antenna directivity stresses the importance of the antennas pointing precision. In addition, the use of directional antennas for 60 GHz WPAN applications is very sensitive to objects blocking the LOS path. Due to the hardware constraints, the first data rate was chosen at 875 Mbps. Using a new CDR circuit limited at 2.7 Gbps, a data rate of 1.75 Gbps can be achieved with the same DBPSK architecture or with DQPSK architecture. For suitable quality requirements in Gbps throughput, an adaptive equalizer should be added to counteract the ISI influence. The demonstrator will be further enhanced to prove the feasibility of wireless communications at data rates of several Gbps in different environments, especially in non line-of-sight (NLOS) configurations.

6. References

ECMA (2008) . Rate 60 GHz PHY, MAC and HDMI PAL, Standard ECMA-387, December 2008. *[online]: http : // www.ecma-international.org/publications/standards/Ecma-387.htm.*

P. F. M. Smulders (2002). Exploiting the 60 GHz Band for Local Wireless Multimedia Access: Prospects and Future Directions, *IEEE Communications Magazine*, Vol. 40, No. 1: 140-147.

C. C. Chong, K. Hamaguchi, P. F. M. Smulders and S. K. Yong (2007). Millimeter-Wave Wireless Communication Systems: Theory and Applications, *EURASIP Journal on Wireless Communications and Networking*, Vol. 2007, article ID 72831, 89 pages.

G. El Zein (2009). Propagation Channel Modeling for Emerging Wireless Communication Systems, *IEEE ACTEA 2009*: 457 - 462, Zouk Mosbeh, Lebanon.

S. Guillouard, G. El Zein and J. Citerne (1999). Wideband Propagation Measurements and Doppler Analysis for the 60 GHz Indoor Channel. *in Proc. IEEE MTT-S International Microwave Symposium* , 1751-1754, Anaheim - CA, USA.

S. Collonge, G. Zaharia and G. EL Zein (2004). Influence of Human Acitivity on Wideband Characteristics of the 60 GHz Indoor Radio Channel, *IEEE Transactions on Wireless Communications*, Vol. 3, No. 6: 2396-2406.

P. F. M. Smulders (2009). Statistical Characterization of 60 GHz Indoor Radio Channels, *IEEE Transactions on Antennas and Propagation*, Vol. 57, No. 10 (October 2009): 2820-2829.

N. Moraitis and P. Constantinou (2004). Indoor Channel Measurements and Characterization at 60 GHz for Wireless Local Area Network Applications, *IEEE Transactions on Antennas and Propagation,* Vol. 52, No. 12: 3180–3189.

R. Tahri, D. Fournier, S. Collonge, G. Zaharia and G. El Zein (2005). Efficient and fast gaussian beam-tracking approach for indoor-propagation modeling, *Microwave and Optical Technology Letters,* Vol. 45, No. 5: 378-381.

S. Kato, H. Harada, R. Funada, T. Baykas, C. Sean Sum, J. Wang and M. A. Rahman (2009). Single Carrier Transmission for Multi-Gigabit 60-GHz WPAN Systems, *IEEE Journal on Selected Areas in Communications,* vol. 27, No. 8: 1466-1478, ISSN: 0733-8716.

L. Rakotondrainibe, Y. Kokar, G. Zaharia, G. Grunfelder and G. EL Zein (2009). Toward a Gigabit Wireless Communications System, *International Journal of Communication Networks and Information Security (IJCNIS)*, Vol. 1, No. 2: 36-42.

K. C. Huang and D. J. Edwards (2008). Millimeter Wave Antennas for Gigabit Wireless Communications: A Practical Guide to Design and Analysis in a System Context, in *book chapter, a John Wiley and Sons Ltd*, 291 pages, ISBN 978-0-470-51598-3 (HB).
U. H. Rizvi, G. J. M. Janssen and J. H. Weber (2008). Impact of RF Circuit Imperfections on Multi-carrier and Single-carrier based Transmissions at 60 GHz, *in Proc. IEEE Radio and Wireless Symposium*, 691–694, ISBN: 978-1-4244-1463-5.

3

Performance Analysis of Maximal Ratio Diversity Receivers over Generalized Fading Channels

Kostas Peppas
National Center Of Scientific Research "Demokritos"
Greece

1. Introduction

Diversity reception, is an efficient communication receiver technique for mitigating the detrimental effects of multi-path fading in wireless mobile channels at relatively low cost. Diversity combining is the technique applied to combine the multiple received copies of the same information bearing signal into a single improved signal, in order to increase the overall signal-to-noise ratio (SNR) and improve the radio link performance. The most important diversity reception methods employed in digital communication receivers are maximal ratio combining (MRC), equal gain combining (EGC), selection combining (SC) and switch and stay combining (SSC) (Simon & Alouini, 2005). Among these well-known diversity techniques, MRC is the optimal technique in the sense that it attains the highest SNR of any combining scheme, independent of the distribution of the branch signals since it results in a maximum-likelihood receiver (Simon & Alouini, 2005).

Of particular interest is the performance analysis of MRC diversity receivers operating over generalized fading channels, as shown by the large number of publications available in the open technical literature. The performance of MRC diversity receivers depends strongly on the characteristics of the multipath fading envelopes. Recently, the so-called η-μ fading distribution that includes as special cases the Nakagami-m and the Hoyt distribution, has been proposed as a more flexible model for practical fading radio channels (Yacoub, 2007). The η-μ distribution fits well to experimental data and can accurately approximate the sum of independent non-identical Hoyt envelopes having arbitrary mean powers and arbitrary fading degrees (Filho & Yacoub, 2005).

In the context of performance evaluation of digital communications over fading channels this distribution has been used only recently. Representative past works can be found in (Asghari et al., 2010; da Costa & Yacoub, 2007; 2008; Ermolova, 2008; 2009; Morales-Jimenez & Paris, 2010; Peppas et al., 2009; 2010). For example, in (da Costa & Yacoub, 2007), the average channel capacity of single branch receivers operating over η-μ channels was derived. In (da Costa & Yacoub, 2008), expressions for the moment generating function (MGF) of the above mentioned channel were provided. Based on these results, the average bit error probability (ABEP) of coherent binary phase shift keying (BPSK) receivers operating over η-μ fading channels was obtained. Furthermore, in (da Costa & Yacoub, 2009), using an approximate yet highly accurate expression for the sum of identical η-μ random variables, infinite series representations for the Outage Probability and ABEP of coherent and non

coherent digital modulations for MRC and EGC receivers are presented. The derived infinite series were given in terms of Meijer-G functions (Prudnikov et al., 1986, Eq. (9.301)).
In this chapter we present a thorough performance analysis of MRC diversity receivers operating over non-identically distributed η-μ fading channels. The performance metrics of interest is the average symbol error probability (ASEP) for a variety of M-ary modulation schemes, the outage probability (OP) and the average channel capacity. The well known MGF approach (Simon & Alouini, 2005) is used to derive novel closed-form expressions for the ASEP of M-ary phase shift keying (M-PSK), M-ary differential phase shift keying (M-DPSK) and general order rectangular quadrature amplitude modulation (QAM) using MRC diversity in independent, non identically distributed (i.n.i.d) fading channels. The derived ASEP expressions are given in terms of Lauricella and Appell hypergeometric functions which can be easily evaluated numerically using their integral or converging series representation (Exton, 1976). Furthermore, in order to offer insights as to what parameters determine the performance of the considered modulation schemes under the presence of η-μ fading, a thorough asymptotic performance analysis at high SNR is performed. A probability density function (PDF) -based approach is used to derive useful performance metrics such as the OP and the channel capacity. To obtain these results, we provide new expressions for the PDF of the sum of i.n.i.d squared η-μ random variables. The PDF is given in three different formats: An infinite series representation, an integral representation as well as an accurate closed form expression. It is shown that our newly derived expressions incorporate as special cases several others available in the literature, namely those for Nakagami-m and Hoyt fading.

2. System and Channel model

We consider an L-branch MRC receiver operating in an η-μ fading environment. Assuming that signals are transmitted through independently distributed branches, the instantaneous SNR at the combiner output is given by

$$\gamma = \sum_{\ell=1}^{L} \gamma_\ell \tag{1}$$

where γ_ℓ is the instantaneous SNR of the ℓ-th branch.
The moment generating function (MGF) of γ, defined as $\mathcal{M}_\gamma(s) = \mathbb{E}\langle \exp(-s\gamma) \rangle$, with the help of (Ermolova, 2008, Eq. (6)) can be expressed as :

$$\mathcal{M}_\gamma(s) = \prod_{i=1}^{L} \int_0^\infty \exp(-s\gamma_i) f_{\gamma_i}(\gamma_i) d\gamma_i = \prod_{i=1}^{L} (1 + A_i s)^{-\mu_i} (1 + B_i s)^{-\mu_i} \tag{2}$$

where $A_i = \frac{\overline{\gamma}_i}{2\mu_i(h_i - H_i)}$ and $B_i = \frac{\overline{\gamma}_i}{2\mu_i(h_i + H_i)}$, $i = 1 \cdots L$.
In the following analysis, we first address the error performance of the considered system using an MGF-based approach. Moreover, the outage probability and the average channel capacity will be addressed using a PDF-based approach.

3. Error rate performance analysis

In this Section, we make use of the MGF-based approach for the performance evaluation of digital communication over generalized fading channels (Alouini & Goldsmith, 1999b; Simon & Alouini, 1999; 2005) to derive the ASEP of a wide variety of modulation schemes when used in conjunction with MRC.

3.1 M-ary PSK

The ASEP of M-ary PSK signals is given by (Simon & Alouini, 2005, Eq. (5.78))

$$P_s(e) = \mathcal{I}_1 + \mathcal{I}_2 \tag{3}$$

where

$$\mathcal{I}_1 = \frac{1}{\pi}\int_{\pi/2}^{\pi-\pi/M} \mathcal{M}_\gamma\left(\frac{g_{PSK}}{\sin^2\theta}\right)d\theta,\ \ \mathcal{I}_2 = \frac{1}{\pi}\int_0^{\pi/2}\mathcal{M}_\gamma\left(\frac{g_{PSK}}{\sin^2\theta}\right)d\theta \tag{4}$$

and $g_{PSK} = \sin^2(\pi/M)$. For the integral $\mathcal{I}_1$ by performing the change of variable $x = \cos^2\theta/\cos^2(\pi/M)$ and after some necessary manipulations, one obtains:

$$\begin{aligned}\mathcal{I}_1 &= \frac{\cos\left(\frac{\pi}{M}\right)}{2\pi}\int_0^1 x^{-\frac{1}{2}}\left(1-x\cos^2\frac{\pi}{M}\right)^{-\frac{1}{2}}\prod_{i=1}^{L}\left(1+\frac{A_i g_{PSK}}{1-x\cos^2\frac{\pi}{M}}\right)^{-\mu_i}\left(1+\frac{B_i g_{PSK}}{1-x\cos^2\frac{\pi}{M}}\right)^{-\mu_i}dx\\
&= \frac{1}{2\pi}\cos\left(\frac{\pi}{M}\right)\mathcal{M}_\gamma(g_{PSK})\int_0^1 x^{-1/2}\left(1-x\cos^2\frac{\pi}{M}\right)^{2\sum_{i=1}^{L}\mu_i-1/2}\\
&\times\prod_{i=1}^{L}\left(1-\frac{\cos^2\frac{\pi}{M}}{1+A_i g_{PSK}}x\right)^{-\mu_i}\prod_{i=1}^{L}\left(1-\frac{\cos^2\frac{\pi}{M}}{1+B_i g_{PSK}}x\right)^{-\mu_i}dx\\
&= \frac{1}{\pi}\cos\left(\frac{\pi}{M}\right)\mathcal{M}_\gamma(g_{PSK})F_D^{(2L+1)}\left(\frac{1}{2},\frac{1}{2}-2\sum_{i=1}^{L}\mu_i,\mu_1,\cdots\mu_L,\mu_1,\cdots\mu_L;\frac{3}{2};\cos^2\frac{\pi}{M}\right.\\
&\left.,\frac{\cos^2\frac{\pi}{M}}{1+A_1 g_{PSK}},\cdots,\frac{\cos^2\frac{\pi}{M}}{1+A_L g_{PSK}},\frac{\cos^2\frac{\pi}{M}}{1+B_1 g_{PSK}}\cdots\frac{\cos^2\frac{\pi}{M}}{1+B_L g_{PSK}}\right)\end{aligned} \tag{5}$$

where $F_D^{(n)}(v,k_1,\cdots,k_n;c;z_1,\cdots,z_n)$ is the Lauricella multiple hypergeometric function of n variables defined as (Prudnikov et al., 1986, Eq. (7.2.4.57)), (Prudnikov et al., 1986, Eq. (7.2.4.15)):

$$\begin{aligned}F_D^{(n)}(v,k_1,\cdots,k_n;c;z_1,\cdots,z_n) &= \frac{\Gamma(c)}{\Gamma(c-v)\Gamma(v)}\int_0^1 x^{v-1}(1-x)^{c-v-1}\prod_{i=1}^{n}(1-z_i x)^{-k_i}dx\\
&= \sum_{l_1,l_2,\cdots,l_n=0}^{\infty}\frac{(v)_{l_T}}{(c)_{l_T}}\prod_{i=1}^{n}\frac{(k_i)_{l_i}}{\Gamma(l_i+1)}z_i^{l_i},\ |z_i|<1\end{aligned} \tag{6}$$

where $l_T = \sum_{i=1}^{n} l_i$, $(\alpha)_\beta = \Gamma(\alpha+\beta)/\Gamma(\alpha)$ is the Pochhammer symbol. The integral in (6) exists for $\Re\{c-v\} > 0$ and $\Re\{v\} > 0$ where $\Re\{\cdot\}$ denotes the real part. If $n = 2$, this function reduces to the Appell hypergeometric function F_1 (Prudnikov et al., 1986, Eq. (7.2.1.41)) whereas if $n = 1$, it reduces to the Gauss hypergeometric function ${}_2F_1$. It is seen from (5) that the conditions for series convergence and integral existence of $F_D^{(2L+1)}$ are satisfied.

For the integral $\mathcal{I}_2$ by performing the change of variable $x = \cos^2\theta$ and after some manipulations we obtain:

$$\mathcal{I}_2 = \frac{\mathcal{M}_\gamma(g_{PSK})}{2\pi} \int_0^1 x^{-\frac{1}{2}} (1-x)^{2\sum_{i=1}^L \mu_i - \frac{1}{2}} \prod_{i=1}^L \left(1 - \frac{1}{1+A_i g_{PSK}} x\right)^{-\mu_i} \left(1 - \frac{1}{1+B_i g_{PSK}} x\right)^{-\mu_i} dx$$
$$= \frac{\Gamma\left(2\sum_{i=1}^L \mu_i + 1/2\right)}{2\sqrt{\pi}\Gamma(2\sum_{i=1}^L \mu_i + 1)} \mathcal{M}_\gamma(g_{PSK}) F_D^{(2L)} \left(\frac{1}{2}, \mu_1, \cdots \mu_L, \mu_1, \cdots \mu_L; 2\sum_{i=1}^L \mu_i + 1; \frac{1}{1+A_1 g_{PSK}}, \right.$$
$$\left. \ldots, \frac{1}{1+A_L g_{PSK}}, \frac{1}{1+B_1 g_{PSK}}, \ldots, \frac{1}{1+B_L g_{PSK}}\right) \tag{7}$$

For the case of BPSK ($M = 2, g_{PSK} = 1$), it can be observed that $\mathcal{I}_1 = 0$ and therefore the expression for the ASEP is reduced to the following compact form:

$$P_s(e) = \frac{\Gamma\left(2\sum_{i=1}^L \mu_i + 1/2\right)}{2\sqrt{\pi}\Gamma(2\sum_{i=1}^L \mu_i + 1)} \mathcal{M}_\gamma(1) F_D^{(2L)} \left(\frac{1}{2}, \mu_1, \cdots \mu_L, \mu_1, \cdots \mu_L; 2\sum_{i=1}^L \mu_i + 1; \frac{1}{1+A_1}, \ldots, \frac{1}{1+A_L}, \frac{1}{1+B_1}, \ldots, \frac{1}{1+B_L}\right) \tag{8}$$

For independent and identically distributed (i.i.d.) fading channels, where $h_i = h$, $H_i = H$, $\mu_i = \mu$, $A_i = A$ and $B_i = B$, using the integral representation of $F_D^{(2L+1)}$ and $F_D^{(2L)}$, the following simplified forms are obtained:

$$\mathcal{I}_{1_{iid}} = \frac{1}{\pi} \cos\left(\frac{\pi}{M}\right) \mathcal{M}_\gamma(g_{PSK}) F_D^{(3)} \left(\frac{1}{2}, \frac{1}{2} - 2L\mu, L\mu, L\mu; \frac{3}{2}; \cos^2\frac{\pi}{M}, \frac{\cos^2\frac{\pi}{M}}{1+Ag_{PSK}}, \frac{\cos^2\frac{\pi}{M}}{1+Bg_{PSK}}\right) \tag{9}$$

$$\mathcal{I}_{2_{iid}} = \frac{\Gamma(2L\mu + 1/2)}{2\sqrt{\pi}\Gamma(2L\mu+1)} \mathcal{M}_\gamma(g_{PSK}) F_1 \left(\frac{1}{2}, L\mu, L\mu; 2L\mu + 1; \frac{1}{1+Ag_{PSK}}, \frac{1}{1+Bg_{PSK}}\right) \tag{10}$$

For the special case of Hoyt fading channels ($\mu = 0.5$) and no diversity ($L = 1$), the expression for the ASEP of M-ary PSK is reduced to a previously known result (Radaydeh, 2007, Eq. (18)). Finally, for Nakagami-m fading channels and i.i.d. branches, using (10) and (Prudnikov et al., 1986, Eq. (7.2.4.60)), a previously known result may be obtained (Adinoyi & Al-Semari, 2002, Eq. (6)).

3.2 M-ary DPSK

The ASEP of M-ary DPSK signals is given by (Simon & Alouini, 2005, Eq. (8.200))

$$P_s(e) = \frac{2}{\pi} \int_0^{\pi/2 - \pi/2M} \mathcal{M}_\gamma\left(\zeta \sin^2\frac{\pi}{M}\right) d\theta \tag{11}$$

where $\zeta = \left(1 + \cos\frac{\pi}{M} - 2\cos\frac{\pi}{M}\sin^2\theta\right)^{-1}$. Applying the transformation $x = \sin^2\theta / \cos^2(\pi/2M)$ and after some algebraic manipulations the ASEP of M-ary DPSK can be expressed as:

$$P_s(e) = \frac{1}{\pi}\cos\left(\frac{\pi}{2M}\right)\mathcal{M}_\gamma(f(M))\int_0^1 x^{-1/2}\left(1 - x\cos^2\frac{\pi}{2M}\right)^{-1/2}\left(1 - x\cos\frac{\pi}{M}\right)^{2\sum_{i=1}^{L}\mu_i}$$
$$\times\prod_{i=1}^{L}\left(1 - \frac{\cos\frac{\pi}{M}}{1+A_i f(M)}x\right)^{-\mu_i}\left(1 - \frac{\cos\frac{\pi}{M}}{1+B_i f(M)}x\right)^{-\mu_i} dx$$
$$= \frac{2}{\pi}\cos\left(\frac{\pi}{2M}\right)\mathcal{M}_\gamma(f(M))F_D^{(2L+2)}\left(\frac{1}{2},\frac{1}{2},-2\sum_{i=1}^{L}\mu_i,\mu_1,\mu_1,\cdots,\mu_L,\mu_L;\frac{3}{2};\cos^2\frac{\pi}{2M},\right.$$
$$\left.\cos\frac{\pi}{M},\frac{\cos\frac{\pi}{M}}{1+A_1 f(M)},\frac{\cos\frac{\pi}{M}}{1+B_1 f(M)},\cdots,\frac{\cos\frac{\pi}{M}}{1+A_L f(M)},\frac{\cos\frac{\pi}{M}}{1+B_L f(M)}\right) \tag{12}$$

where $f(M) = \frac{\sin^2(\pi/M)}{2\cos^2(\pi/2M)}$.
For binary DPSK signals ($M = 2$), using $F_D^{(N)}(v, k_1, k_2, \cdots, k_N; c; z, 0, \cdots, 0) = {}_2F_1(v, k_1; c; z)$ and ${}_2F_1\left(\frac{1}{2}, \frac{1}{2}; \frac{3}{2}; z\right) = \arcsin(\sqrt{z})/\sqrt{z}$ (Prudnikov et al., 1986, Eq. (7.3.2.76)), the derived result is reduced to the well known expression for the error probability of binary DPSK signals over generalized fading channels, i.e. $P_{M=2}(e) = \frac{1}{2}\mathcal{M}_\gamma(1)$.
For the i.i.d. case, using the integral representation of the Lauricella function, a simplified expression of $P_s(e)$ may be obtained as:

$$P_s(e) = \frac{2\cos\left(\frac{\pi}{2M}\right)\mathcal{M}_\gamma(f(M))}{\pi}F_D^{(4)}\left(\frac{1}{2},\frac{1}{2},-2L\mu,L\mu,L\mu;\frac{3}{2};\right.$$
$$\left.\cos^2\frac{\pi}{2M},\cos\frac{\pi}{M},\frac{\cos\frac{\pi}{M}}{1+Af(M)},\frac{\cos\frac{\pi}{M}}{1+Bf(M)}\right) \tag{13}$$

3.3 General order rectangular QAM

We consider a general order rectangular QAM signal which may be viewed as two separate Pulse Amplitude Modulation (PAM) signals impressed on phase-quadrature carriers. Let also M_I and M_Q be the dimensions of the in-phase and the quadrature signal respectively and $r = d_Q/d_I$ the quadrature-to-in-phase decision distance ratio, with d_I and d_Q being the in-phase and the quadrature decision distance respectively. For general order rectangular QAM, the ASEP is given by (Lei et al., 2007, Eq. (4))

$$P_s(e) = 2p\mathcal{J}(a) + 2q\mathcal{J}(b) - 4pq[\mathcal{K}(a,b) + \mathcal{K}(b,a)] \tag{14}$$

where

$$\mathcal{J}(t) = \frac{1}{\pi}\int_0^{\pi/2}\mathcal{M}_\gamma\left(\frac{t^2}{2\sin^2\theta}\right)d\theta,\ \ \mathcal{K}(u,v) = \frac{1}{2\pi}\int_0^{\pi/2-\arctan(v/u)}\mathcal{M}_\gamma\left(\frac{u^2}{2\sin^2\theta}\right)d\theta \tag{15}$$

and $p = 1 - 1/M_I$, $q = 1 - 1/M_Q$, $a = \sqrt{\frac{6}{(M_I^2-1)+r^2(M_Q^2-1)}}$, $b = \sqrt{\frac{6r^2}{(M_I^2-1)+r^2(M_Q^2-1)}}$. Using the result in (7), the integral $\mathcal{J}(t)$ can be easily evaluated in terms of the Lauricella functions as:

$$\mathcal{J}(t) = \frac{\Gamma\left(2\sum_{i=1}^{L}\mu_i + 1/2\right)}{2\sqrt{\pi}\Gamma(2\sum_{i=1}^{L}\mu_i + 1)}\mathcal{M}_\gamma(t^2/2)F_D^{(2L)}\left(\frac{1}{2},\mu_1,\cdots\mu_L,\mu_1,\cdots\mu_L;2\sum_{i=1}^{L}\mu_i+1;\frac{2}{2+A_1t^2},\right.$$
$$\left.\cdots,\frac{2}{2+A_Lt^2},\frac{2}{2+B_1t^2},\cdots,\frac{2}{2+B_Lt^2}\right) \tag{16}$$

To evaluate $\mathcal{K}(u,v)$ in (15), applying the transformation $x = 1 - (v^2/u^2)\tan^2\theta$ and after performing some algebraic and trigonometric manipulations, we obtain:

$$\mathcal{K}(u,v) = \frac{uv\mathcal{M}_\gamma(\frac{u^2+v^2}{2})}{4\pi(u^2+v^2)}\int_0^1(1-x)^{2\sum_{i=1}^{L}\mu_1-\frac{1}{2}}\left(1-\frac{u^2}{u^2+v^2}x\right)^{-1}$$
$$\times\prod_{i=1}^{L}\left(1-x\frac{2+A_iu^2}{2+A_iu^2+A_iv^2}\right)^{-\mu_i}\left(1-x\frac{2+B_iu^2}{2+B_iu^2+B_iv^2}\right)^{-\mu_i}dx$$
$$=\frac{uv\mathcal{M}_\gamma(\frac{u^2+v^2}{2})}{2\pi(u^2+v^2)\left(4\sum_{i=1}^{L}\mu_i+1\right)}F_D^{(2L+1)}\left(1,1,\mu_1,\cdots,\mu_L,\mu_1,\cdots,\mu_L;2\sum_{i=1}^{L}\mu_i+\frac{3}{2};\right.$$
$$\left.\frac{u^2}{u^2+v^2},\frac{2+A_1u^2}{2+A_1u^2+A_1v^2},\cdots\frac{2+A_Lu^2}{2+A_Lu^2+A_Lv^2},\frac{2+B_1u^2}{2+B_1u^2+B_1v^2},\cdots,\frac{2+B_Lu^2}{2+B_Lu^2+B_Lv^2}\right) \tag{17}$$

For i.i.d. branches (16) reduces to:

$$\mathcal{J}_{iid}(t) = \frac{\Gamma(2L\mu+1/2)}{2\sqrt{\pi}\Gamma(2L\mu+1)}\mathcal{M}_\gamma(t^2/2)F_1\left(\frac{1}{2},L\mu,L\mu;2L\mu+1;\frac{2}{2+At^2},\frac{2}{2+Bt^2}\right) \tag{18}$$

whereas (17) is reduced to:

$$\mathcal{K}_{iid}(u,v) = \frac{uv\mathcal{M}_\gamma(\frac{u^2+v^2}{2})}{2\pi(u^2+v^2)(4L\mu+1)}F_D^{(3)}\left(1,1,L\mu,L\mu;2L\mu+\frac{3}{2};\frac{u^2}{u^2+v^2},\frac{2+Au^2}{2+Au^2+Av^2},\right.$$
$$\left.\frac{2+Bu^2}{2+Bu^2+Bv^2}\right) \tag{19}$$

For the special case of Nakagami-m channels, using (Prudnikov et al., 1986, Eq. (7.2.4.60)), (18) is reduced to a previously known result (Lei et al., 2007, Eq. 11). Moreover, using the infinite series representation of the Lauricella function (6), (Prudnikov et al., 1986, Eq. (7.2.4.60)) and after some necessary manipulations, (19) is reduced to a previously known result (Lei et al., 2007, Eq. 15).

3.4 Asymptotic error rate analysis at high SNR

The asymptotic performance analysis of a diversity system at high SNR region allows one to gain useful insights regarding the parameters determining the error performance. At high SNR, the ASEP of a digital communications system has been observed in certain cases to be approximated as (Simon & Alouini, 2005; Wang & Yannakis, 2003)

$$P_s(e) \simeq C_d\overline{\gamma}^{-d} \tag{20}$$

where C_d is referred to as the coding gain, and d as the diversity gain. The diversity gain determines the slope of the ASEP versus average SNR curve, at high SNR, in a log-log scale. Moreover, C_d (expressed in decibels) represents the horizontal shift of the curve in SNR relative to a benchmark ASEP curve of $P_s(e) \simeq \overline{\gamma}^{-d}$.

In (Wang & Yannakis, 2003), the authors developed a simple and general method to quantify the asymptotic performance of wireless transmission in fading channels at high SNR values. In this work, it was shown that the asymptotic performance depends on the behavior of the PDF of the instantaneous channel power gain denoted by β, $p(\beta)$. Moreover, it was shown that if the MGF of $p(\beta)$ can be expressed for $s \to \infty$ as $|\mathcal{M}_\beta(s)| = C|s|^{-d} + o(|s|^{-d})$, a diversity gain equal to d may be obtained. It is noted that we write $f(x) = o[g(x)]$ as $x \to x_0$ if $\lim_{x\to x_0} \frac{f(x)}{g(x)} = 0$. We observe that (2) can be expressed as:

$$\mathcal{M}_\gamma(s) = \prod_{i=1}^{L} \left[s^{-2} A_i B_i \left(1 + \frac{1}{A_i s}\right)\left(1 + \frac{1}{B_i s}\right)\right]^{-\mu_i} = Cs^{-d} + o(s^{-d}) \tag{21}$$

for $s \to \infty$, where $C = \prod_{i=1}^{L} (A_i B_i)^{-\mu_i} = \prod_{i=1}^{L} h_i^{\mu_i} \left(\frac{\overline{\gamma}_i}{2\mu_i}\right)^{-2\mu_i}$ and $d = 2\sum_{i=1}^{L} \mu_i$. This interesting result shows that the diversity gain of the considered system depends on the number of the receive antennas L as well as on the parameters μ_i. For the special case of i.i.d. branches, it is obvious that a diversity gain equal to $2\mu L$ may be obtained.

3.4.1 Asymptotic ASEP of M-PSK

At high SNR, using the previously derived asymptotic expression for the MGF, $\mathcal{I}_1$ can be computed as:

$$\mathcal{I}_{1_{asym}} = \frac{C \cos\frac{\pi}{M}}{2 g_{PSK}^d \pi} \int_0^1 x^{-1/2} \left(1 - x\cos^2\frac{\pi}{M}\right)^{-1/2+d} dx = \frac{C\cos\frac{\pi}{M}}{\pi g_{PSK}^d} {}_2F_1\left(\frac{1}{2} - d, \frac{1}{2}; \frac{3}{2}; \cos^2\frac{\pi}{M}\right) \tag{22}$$

Also, a simplified asymptotic expression of $\mathcal{I}_2$ may be obtained as:

$$\mathcal{I}_{2_{asym}} = \frac{C}{g_{PSK}^d \pi} \int_0^{\pi/2} \sin^{2d}\theta d\theta = \frac{C\Gamma(d + 1/2)}{2\sqrt{\pi}\Gamma(d+1) g_{PSK}^d} \tag{23}$$

In Figure 1 the ASEP for BPSK modulation is plotted as a function of $\overline{\gamma}_1$ for constant η equal to 2 and for various values of μ and L. An exponential power decay profile is considered, that is the average input SNR of the l-th branch is given by $\overline{\gamma}_l = \overline{\gamma}_1 \exp[-\delta(l-1)]$ where δ is the decay factor. We also assume $\delta = 0.5$. As expected, by keeping η constant, an increase in μ and/or L results in an improvement of the system performance. For comparison purposes, for $L = 1, 2$ and 3, the ASEP of the BPSK modulation for the Hoyt fading channel ($\mu = 0.5$) has also been plotted versus the average input SNR per branch. It is obvious that the Hoyt channel results in the worst symbol error performance. The asymptotic performance of the BPSK ASEP expressions is also investigated and as it can be observed, for no diversity ($L = 1$) and small values of μ, the high SNR asymptotic expressions yield accurate results even for low to medium SNR values. Moreover in Figure 2 the ASEP of M-PSK modulation is plotted as a function of the first branch average input SNR $\overline{\gamma}_1$, for the η-μ fading channel, Format 1 and for different values of M and L, with $\eta_\ell = \eta = 2$ and $\mu_\ell = \mu = 1.5$, $\ell = 1, 2, 3$. As one can observe, an increase in the number of diversity branches from $L = 1$ to $L = 3$ significantly enhances the system's error performance. In the same figure, the exact and the asymptotic

ASEP results are also compared. As it is evident, the asymptotic results correctly predict the diversity gain, however for large M and L, the predicted asymptotic behavior of the ASEP curves shows up at relatively high SNR (e.g. for $M = 16$, $L = 3$ we need $\overline{\gamma}_1 > 30$dB).

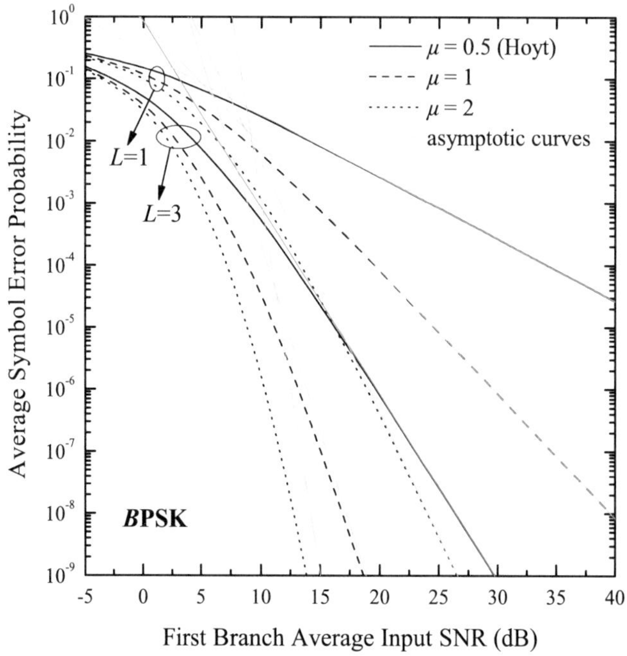

Fig. 1. Average Symbol Error Probability of BPSK receivers with MRC diversity $(L = 1, 3)$ operating over n.i.d. η-μ fading channels (Format 1), for $\eta = 2$ and for different values of μ, as a function of the First Branch Average Input SNR ($\delta = 0.5$)

3.4.2 Asymptotic ASEP of M-DPSK

For M-DPSK, by substituting (21) to (11) and using the same methodology for the evaluation of the corresponding integral, the following asymptotic expression of $P_s(e)$ may be obtained as:

$$\begin{aligned} P_s(e) &= \frac{C[f(M)]^{-d}}{\pi} \cos\left(\frac{\pi}{2M}\right) \int_0^1 x^{-1/2} \left(1 - x\cos^2\frac{\pi}{2M}\right)^{-1/2} \left(1 - x\cos\frac{\pi}{M}\right)^d dx \\ &= \frac{2C[f(M)]^{-d}}{\pi} \cos\left(\frac{\pi}{2M}\right) F_1\left(\frac{1}{2}, \frac{1}{2}, -d; \frac{3}{2}; \cos^2\frac{\pi}{2M}, \cos\frac{\pi}{M}\right) \end{aligned} \quad (24)$$

In Fig. 3 similar results for M-DPSK signal constellations are given with $\eta_\ell = \eta = 2$, $\mu_\ell = \mu = 1.5$ and $L = 1, 3$, $\delta = 0.5$. As in the case of coherent modulation, the performance of the considered system significantly improves as the number of diversity branches increases. Asymptotic results are also included and as it can be observed, the asymptotic approximation predicts the diversity gain correctly and provides good approximation to the exact error performance in the high SNR region, especially when L and/or μ are small.

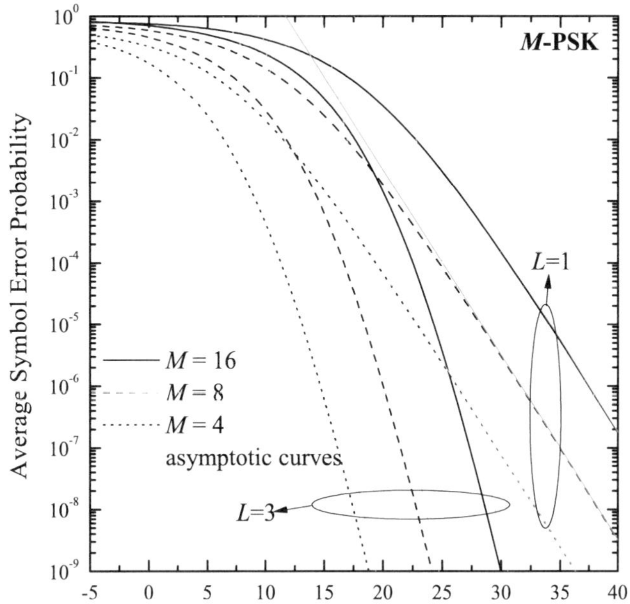

Fig. 2. Average Symbol Error Probability of M-PSK receivers with MRC diversity $(L = 1, 3)$ operating over n.i.d. η-μ fading channels (Format 1), for different values of M, as a function of the First Branch Average Input SNR ($\eta = 2$, $\mu = 1.5$, $\delta = 0.5$)

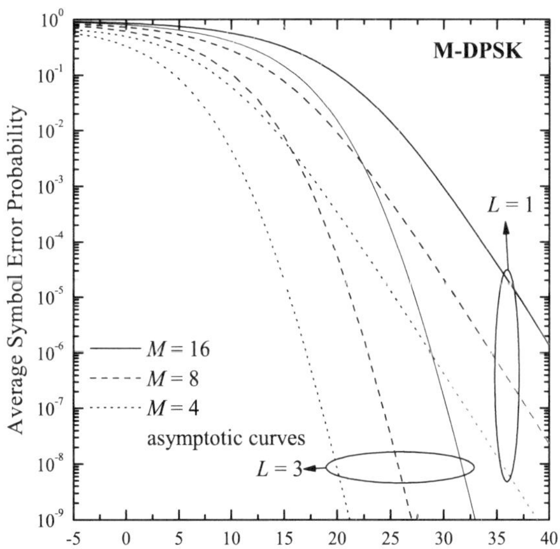

Fig. 3. Average Symbol Error Probability of M-DPSK receivers with MRC diversity $(L = 1, 3)$ operating over n.i.d. η-μ fading channels (Format 1), for different values of M, as a function of the First Branch Average Input SNR ($\eta = 2$, $\mu = 1.5$, $\delta = 0.5$)

3.4.3 Asymptotic ASEP of general order rectangular QAM

For general order rectangular QAM and at high SNR values, the following asymptotic form for $\mathcal{J}(t)$ may be obtained:

$$\mathcal{J}_{asym}(t) = \frac{2^d C}{t^{2d}\pi}\int_0^{\pi/2} \sin^{2d}\theta d\theta = \frac{2^{d-1}C\Gamma(d+1/2)}{\sqrt{\pi}\Gamma(d+1)t^{2d}} \tag{25}$$

Moreover, using the integral representation of the ${}_2F_1$ function, a simplified asymptotic expression for $\mathcal{K}(u,v)$ may be obtained, as:

$$\begin{aligned}\mathcal{K}_{asym}(u,v) &= \frac{2^{d-2}Cuv}{\pi(u^2+v^2)^{d+1}}\int_0^1 (1-x)^{d-1/2}\left(1-\frac{u^2}{u^2+v^2}x\right)^{-d-1} dx \\ &= \frac{2^{d-1}Cuv}{\pi(u^2+v^2)^{d+1}(2d+1)}\,{}_2F_1\left(1,d+1;d+\frac{3}{2};\frac{u^2}{u^2+v^2}\right)\end{aligned} \tag{26}$$

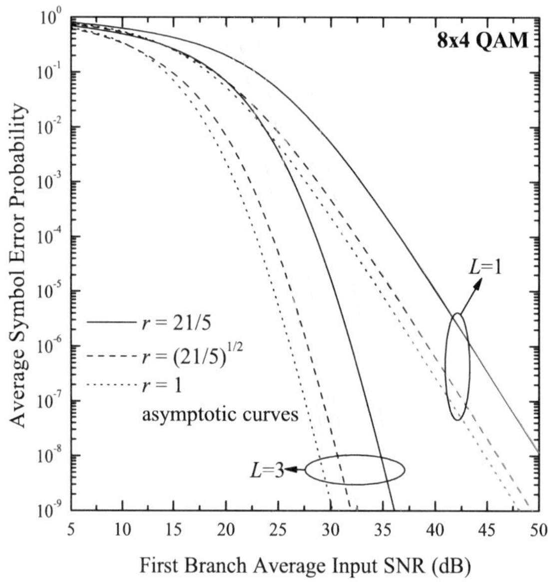

Fig. 4. Average Symbol Error Probability of 8 × 4 QAM receivers with MRC diversity ($L = 1,2,3$) operating over η-μ fading channels (Format 1), for different values of r, as a function of the Average Input SNR per Branch ($\eta = 2$, $\mu = 1.5$, $\delta = 0.5$)

In Figure 4 the error performance of a 8 × 4 QAM system is illustrated for $\eta = 2$, and $\mu = 1.5$ with $\delta = 0.5$. The ASEP is plotted for different values of L and r and as it is obvious, the error performance significantly increases as L increases. Also, it can be observed that the ASEP deteriorates substantially as r increases, for all values of μ. Moreover, asymptotic results have been included and as it is evident, the simplified asymptotic expressions yield accurate results at high SNR values, especially when L and/or r are small.

4. A PDF-based approach for outage probability and channel capacity evaluation

The PDF of γ in (1) may be obtained by taking the inverse Laplace transform of $\mathcal{M}_\gamma(s)$, i.e.

$$f_\gamma(\gamma) = \mathbb{L}^{-1}\{\mathcal{M}_\gamma(s);s;\gamma\} \tag{27}$$

where $\mathbb{L}^{-1}\{\cdot;s;t\}$ denotes inverse Laplace transform. It is noted that the PDF of L i.i.d. η-μ channels is an η-μ distribution with parameters η, $L\mu$ and $L\overline{\gamma}$ (Yacoub, 2007). In the following analysis analytical expressions for $f_\gamma(\gamma)$ will be obtained. This statistical result is then applied to the evaluation of the outage probability and channel capacity of MRC receivers operating over η-μ channels.

4.1 Infinite series representation of the PDF of the sum of independent η-μ variates

We may observe that in (2), each factor of the form $(1+sA_\ell)^{-\mu_\ell}$ is the MGF of a gamma-distributed random variable with parameters μ_ℓ and A_ℓ. Similarly, each factor of the form $(1+sB_\ell)^{-\mu_\ell}$ is the MGF of a gamma-distributed random variable with parameters μ_ℓ and B_ℓ. Hence, the PDF of the sum of L independent squared η-μ variates may be obtained as the PDF of the sum of $2L$ independent gamma variates with suitably defined parameters. Using Moschopoulos (1985) and (Alouini et al., 2001, eq. (2)), the PDF of γ may be expressed as

$$f_\gamma(\gamma) = \prod_{j=1}^{L}(A_jB_j)^{-\mu_j}\sum_{k=0}^{\infty}\xi_k\frac{\gamma^{2\sum_{\ell=1}^{L}\mu_\ell+k-1}e^{-\frac{\gamma}{C_m}}}{C_m^k\Gamma\left(k+2\sum_{\ell=1}^{L}\mu_\ell\right)}, \tag{28}$$

where $C_m = \min\{A_\ell, B_\ell\}$ and the coefficients ξ_k may be recursively obtained as

$$\xi_{k+1} = \frac{1}{k+1}\sum_{i=1}^{k+1}\left[\sum_{j=1}^{L}\mu_j\left(1-\frac{C_m}{A_j}\right)^i+\sum_{j=1}^{L}\mu_j\left(1-\frac{C_m}{B_j}\right)^i\right]\xi_{k+1-i},\ k=0,1,2,\ldots, \tag{29}$$

with $\xi_0 = 1$.

4.2 Integral representation of the PDF of the sum of independent η-μ variates

An alternative expression for the PDF of γ may be obtained by using the Gil-Pelaez result (Gil-Pelaez, 1951) to obtain the inverse Laplace transform of (2). The cumulative distribution function (CDF) of γ may be obtained as

$$F_\gamma(\gamma) = \mathbb{L}^{-1}\left\{\frac{\mathcal{M}_\gamma(s)}{s};s;\gamma\right\} = \frac{1}{2}-\frac{1}{\pi}\int_0^\infty\frac{\Im\{\mathcal{M}_\gamma(\jmath t)e^{-\jmath\gamma t}\}}{t}dt, \tag{30}$$

where $\jmath = \sqrt{-1}$, and $\Im\{\cdot\}$ is the imaginary part. By expressing $\mathcal{M}_\gamma(\jmath t)$ in polar form and substituting in (30), the CDF of γ may be expressed as

$$F_\gamma(\gamma) = \frac{1}{2}-\frac{1}{\pi}\int_0^\infty\frac{\sin\left\{\sum_{\ell=1}^{L}\mu_\ell[\arctan(A_\ell t)+\arctan(B_\ell t)]-t\gamma\right\}}{t\prod_{\ell=1}^{L}[(1+t^2A_\ell^2)\,(1+t^2B_\ell^2)]^{\frac{\mu_\ell}{2}}}dt, \tag{31}$$

The corresponding PDF may be obtained by taking the derivative of (31) with respect to γ, yielding

$$f_\gamma(\gamma) = \int_0^\infty\frac{\cos\left\{\sum_{\ell=1}^{L}\mu_\ell[\arctan(A_\ell t)+\arctan(B_\ell t)]-t\gamma\right\}dt}{\pi\prod_{\ell=1}^{L}[(1+t^2A_\ell^2)\,(1+t^2B_\ell^2)]^{\frac{\mu_\ell}{2}}}. \tag{32}$$

Both integrals can be numerically evaluated in an efficient way, for example by using the Gauss-Legendre quadrature rule (Abramovitz & Stegun, 1964, eq. (25.4.29)) over (32) or (31) (Efthymoglou et al., 1997). Another fast and computationally efficient means to evaluate such integrals is symbolic integration, using any of the well known software mathematical packages such as Maple or Mathematica.

4.3 A Closed-Form expression of the PDF of the sum of independent η-μ variates

A closed-form expression of the PDF of γ may be obtained by making use of the following Laplace transform pair (Srivastava & L.Manocha, 1984, p. 259)

$$\mathbb{L}\{t^{\alpha-1}\Phi_2^{(n)}\left(b_1,\ldots b_n;\alpha;x_1t,\ldots,x_nt\right);s;t\} = \frac{\Gamma(\alpha)}{s^{\alpha}}\prod_{j=1}^{n}\left(1-\frac{x_j}{s}\right)^{-b_j}, \; \alpha>0, \tag{33}$$

where $\Phi_2^{(L)}(\cdot)$ is the confluent Lauricella hypergeometric function defined in (Srivastava & L.Manocha, 1984, eq. 10, p. 62)

$$\Phi_2^{(n)}\left(b_1,\ldots b_n;\alpha;x_1,\ldots x_n\right) = \sum_{l_1,l_2,\cdots,l_n=0}^{\infty}\frac{(b_1)_{l_1}\cdots(b_n)_{l_n}}{(\alpha)_{l_1+\ldots+l_n}}\frac{x_1^{l_1}}{l_1!}\cdots\frac{x_n^{l_n}}{l_n!}, \tag{34}$$

with $(\alpha)_\beta = \Gamma(\alpha+\beta)/\Gamma(\alpha)$ being the Pochhammer symbol. By comparing (33) and (2), the PDF of γ may be obtained as

$$\begin{aligned} f_\gamma(\gamma) = & \frac{\prod_{\ell=1}^{L}(A_\ell B_\ell)^{-\mu_\ell}\gamma^{2\sum_{j=1}^{L}\mu_\ell-1}}{\Gamma\left(2\sum_{\ell=1}^{L}\mu_\ell\right)}\Phi_2^{(2L)}\left(\mu_1,\mu_1,\cdots,\right. \\ & \left.\mu_L,\mu_L,2\sum_{\ell=1}^{L}\mu_\ell,-\frac{\gamma}{A_1},-\frac{\gamma}{B_1}\cdots,-\frac{\gamma}{A_L},-\frac{\gamma}{B_L}\right). \end{aligned} \tag{35}$$

It is noted that the both the integral and infinite series representations for the pdf of Y are much more convenient for accurate and efficient numerical evaluation than this accurate closed form, especially for large values of L, i.e. $L>6$. (Efthymoglou et al., 2006). However, accurate results may be obtained by expressing the series in (34) as multiple integrals (Saigo & Tuan, 1992) that can be easily evaluated numerically (Efthymoglou et al., 2006).

5. Applications to the performance analysis of MRC diversity systems

In this section, based on our previously derived results the outage probability and the average channel capacity of MRC diversity systems will be derived. Moreover, an analytical expression for the average error probability for binary modulation schemes will be derived in closed-form using the PDF-based approach. As it will become evident both the PDF and the MGF-based approach yield the same results.

5.1 Outage probability

The outage probability is defined as the probability that the instantaneous SNR at the combiner output, γ, falls below a specified threshold γ_{th}, i.e. $P_{out}(\gamma_{\text{th}}) = Pr(\gamma<\gamma_{\text{th}}) = F_\gamma(\gamma_{\text{th}})$. Using (28) and with the help of (Gradshteyn & Ryzhik, 2000, eq. (8.356.3)), an infinite series representation of the outage probability may be obtained as

$$P_{out}(\gamma_{\text{th}}) = C_m^U\prod_{\ell=1}^{L}(A_\ell B_\ell)^{-\mu_\ell}\sum_{k=0}^{\infty}\xi_k\left[1-\frac{\Gamma\left(k+U,\frac{\gamma_{\text{th}}}{C_m}\right)}{\Gamma(k+U)}\right], \tag{36}$$

where $U \triangleq 2\sum_{\ell=1}^{L} \mu_\ell$. and $\Gamma(\cdot,\cdot)$ is the incomplete gamma function (Gradshteyn & Ryzhik, 2000, eq. 8.350.2). Moreover, using (31), an integral representation of the outage probability may readily be obtained as

$$P_{out}(\gamma_{\text{th}}) = \frac{1}{2} - \frac{1}{\pi}\int_0^\infty \frac{\sin[V(t) - t\gamma_{\text{th}}]}{W(t)} dt, \tag{37}$$

where

$$V(t) \triangleq \sum_{\ell=1}^{L} \mu_\ell[\arctan(A_\ell t) + \arctan(B_\ell t)], \tag{38a}$$

$$W(t) \triangleq t\prod_{\ell=1}^{L}[\left(1+t^2A_\ell^2\right)\left(1+t^2B_\ell^2\right)]^{\frac{\mu_\ell}{2}}, \tag{38b}$$

Finally, by integrating (35) term-by-term, a closed form expression for $P_{out}(\gamma_{\text{th}})$ may be obtained as

$$P_{out}(\gamma_{\text{th}}) = \frac{\prod_{j=1}^{L}(A_\ell B_\ell)^{-\mu_\ell}\gamma_{\text{th}}^{U}}{\Gamma(1+U)}\Phi_2^{(2L)}\left(\mu_1,\ \mu_1,\cdots,\mu_L,\mu_L,1+U,-\frac{\gamma_{\text{th}}}{A_1},-\frac{\gamma_{\text{th}}}{B_1}\cdots,\right. \\ \left. -\frac{\gamma_{\text{th}}}{A_L},-\frac{\gamma_{\text{th}}}{B_L}\right). \tag{39}$$

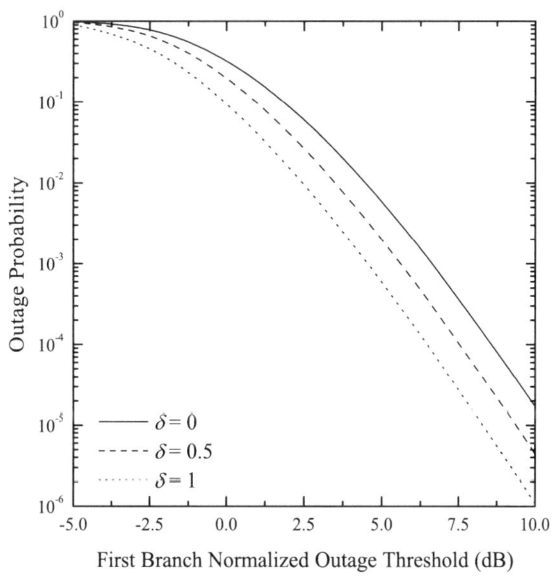

Fig. 5. Outage Probability of dual-branch MRC diversity receivers ($L = 2$) operating over η-μ fading channels (Format 1, $\eta = 2$, $\mu = 1.5$) , for different values of δ, as a function of the First Branch Normalized Outage Threshold

In Figure 5 the outage performance of a dual-branch MRC diversity system versus the first branch normalized outage threshold $\overline{\gamma_1}/\gamma_{\text{th}}$ illustrated for $\eta = 2$, and $\mu = 1.5$. An exponentially power decay profile with $\delta = 0, 0.5, 1$ is considered. The outage probability is plotted for different values of δ and as it is obvious, the outage performance increases as δ decreases. Note that both the integral representation, given by (36) and the infinite series representation, given by (37) yield identical results.

5.2 Channel capacity

For fading channels, the ergodic channel capacity characterizes the long-term achievable rate averaged over the fading distribution and depends on the amount of available channel state information (CSI) at the receiver and transmitter Alouini & Goldsmith (1999a). Two adaptive transmission schemes are considered: Optimal rate adaptation with constant transmit power (ORA) and optimal simultaneous power and rate adaptation (OPRA). Under the ORA scheme that requires only receiver CSI, the capacity is known to be given by Alouini & Goldsmith (1999a)

$$\langle C\rangle_{ORA} = \frac{1}{\ln 2}\int_0^{\infty} f_\gamma(\gamma)\ln(1+\gamma)d\gamma \tag{40}$$

In order to obtain an analytical expression of $\langle C\rangle_{ORA}$ for the considered DS-CDMA system, we first make use of the infinite series representations of the PDF of γ given by (28). Then, by expressing the exponential and the logarithm in terms of Meijer-G functions (Prudnikov et al., 1986, Eq.(8.4.6.5)), (Prudnikov et al., 1986, Eq. (8.4.6.2)) and applying the result given in (Prudnikov et al., 1986, Eq. (2.24.1.1)), the following expression for the capacity may be obtained:

$$\langle C\rangle_{ORA} = \frac{C_m^U}{\ln 2}\prod_{\ell=1}^{L}(A_\ell B_\ell)^{-\mu_\ell}\sum_{k=0}^{\infty}\xi_k\frac{G_{3,2}^{1,3}\left[C_m\left|\begin{matrix}1,1,1-U-k\\1,0\end{matrix}\right.\right]}{\Gamma(k+U)}, \tag{41}$$

where $G_{p,q}^{m,n}[\cdot]$ is the Meijer-G function (Gradshteyn & Ryzhik, 2000, Eq. (9.301)). For the OPRA scheme, the capacity is known to be given by (Alouini & Goldsmith, 1999a, Eq. (7))

$$\langle C\rangle_{OPRA} = \int_{\gamma_0}^{\infty}\log_2\left(\frac{\gamma}{\gamma_0}\right)f_\gamma(\gamma)\,d\gamma, \tag{42}$$

where γ_0 is the cutoff SNR below which transmission is suspended. By substituting (28) to (42), expressing the logarithm and the exponential in terms of Meijer-G functions (Prudnikov et al., 1986, Eq.(8.4.6.5)), (Prudnikov et al., 1986, Eq. (8.4.3.1)) and with the help of (Prudnikov et al., 1986, Eq. (2.24.1.1)), $\langle C\rangle_{OPRA}$ may be obtained as

$$\langle C\rangle_{OPRA} = \frac{C_m^U}{\ln 2}\prod_{l=1}^{L}(A_l B_l)^{-\mu_l}\sum_{k=0}^{\infty}\xi_k\frac{G_{3,2}^{0,3}\left[\frac{C_m}{\gamma_0}\left|\begin{matrix}1,1,1-U-k\\0,0\end{matrix}\right.\right]}{\Gamma(k+U)}. \tag{43}$$

In Figure 6 the average of a triple-branch MRC diversity system under the ORA transmission scheme, is illustrated versus $\overline{\gamma_1}$ for $\eta = 2$, and $\mu = 1.5$. An exponentially power decay profile with $\delta = 0, 0.5, 1$ is considered. The average channel capacity is plotted for different values of δ and as it is obvious, the capacity improves as δ decreases.

5.3 Average bit error probability

The conditional bit error probability $P_e(\gamma)$ in an AWGN channel may be expressed in unified form as

$$P_e(\gamma) = \frac{\Gamma(b, a\gamma)}{2\Gamma(b)} \tag{44}$$

where a and b are parameters that depend on the specific modulation scheme. For example, $a = 1$ for binary phase shift keying (BPSK) and $1/2$ for binary frequency shift keying (BFSK). Also, $b = 1$ for non-coherent BFSK and binary differential PSK (BDPSK) and $1/2$ for coherent

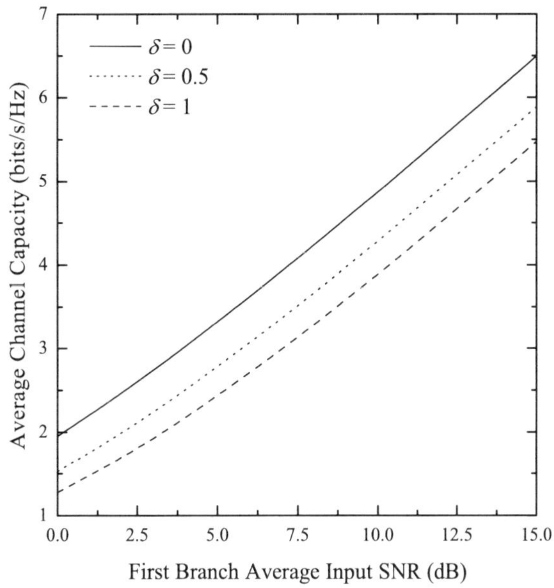

Fig. 6. Average Channel Capacity of triple-branch MRC diversity receivers ($L = 3$) operating over η-μ fading channels, (Format 1, $\eta = 2$, $\mu = 1.5$), under ORA policy, for different values of δ, as a function of the First Branch Average Input SNR

BFSK/BPSK. The average bit error probability (ABEP) for the considered system may be obtained by averaging $P_e(\gamma)$ over the PDF of γ i.e.,

$$\overline{P}_{be} = \int_0^{\infty} P_e(\gamma) f_\gamma(\gamma) d\gamma. \tag{45}$$

Using (28) in conjunction with (45) and with the help of (Gradshteyn & Ryzhik, 2000, eq. 6.455) the ABEP may be obtained as

$$\begin{aligned}\overline{P}_{be} = \frac{a^b C_m^{U+b}}{2\Gamma(b)} \prod_{\ell=1}^{L} (A_\ell B_\ell)^{-\mu_\ell} \sum_{k=0}^{\infty} {}_2F_1\left(1, k+U+b; k+U+1; \frac{1}{1+aC_m}\right) \\ \times \xi_k \frac{\Gamma(k+U+b)}{(1+aC_m)^{k+U+b}\Gamma(k+U+1)}\end{aligned}, \tag{46}$$

where ${}_2F_1(\cdot)$ is the Gauss hypergeometric function (Prudnikov et al., 1986, eq. (7.2.1.1)). Also, by substituting (32) to (45), the ABEP is expressed as a two-fold integral. This expression may be simplified by performing integration by parts and after some algebraic manipulations as follows

$$\begin{aligned}\overline{P}_{be} = \frac{1}{2\pi} \int_0^{\infty} \Bigg\{ \cos[V(t)] \frac{a^b \sin(b \arctan(t/a))}{(t^2+a^2)^{b/2}} + \sin[V(t)] \\ \left[1 - \frac{a^b \cos(b \arctan(t/a))}{(t^2+a^2)^{b/2}}\right] \Bigg\} \frac{dt}{W(t)}\end{aligned}. \tag{47}$$

This integral can be efficiently evaluated by means of the Gauss-Legendre quadrature integration rule or by symbolic integration. Finally, an alternative ABEP expression may be obtained by substituting (35) to (45). By integrating the corresponding infinite series term-by-term and with the help of (Abramovitz & Stegun, 1964, eq. (6.5.37)), the ABEP may be obtained in closed form as

$$\overline{P}_{be} = \frac{\Gamma(U+b)\prod_{\ell=1}^{L}(A_\ell B_\ell)^{-\mu_\ell}}{2a^U\Gamma(b)\Gamma(U+1)} F_D^{(2L)}\left(U+b,\mu_1,\mu_1,\cdots,\mu_L,\mu_L;U+1;\right. \\ \left. -\frac{1}{aA_1},-\frac{1}{aB_1}\cdots,-\frac{1}{aA_{M_L}},-\frac{1}{aB_{M_L}}\right). \tag{48}$$

This expression can be easily evaluated using the integral representation of the Lauricella function. This representation converges if $\left|\frac{1}{aA_\ell}\right| < 1$ and $\left|\frac{1}{aB_\ell}\right| < 1, \forall \ell = 1,\dots L$. To guarantee that these conditions are always be fulfilled, we may use the following identity (Exton, 1976, p. 286)

$$F_D^{(n)}(a,b_1,\cdots,b_n;c;x_1,\cdots,x_n) = \left[\prod_{\ell=1}^{L}(1-x_\ell)^{-b_\ell}\right] \\ \times F_D^{(n)}\left(c-a,b_1,\cdots,b_n;c;\frac{x_1}{x_1-1},\cdots,\frac{x_n}{x_n-1}\right). \tag{49}$$

Thus, (48) can be written as

$$P_s(e) = \frac{\Gamma\left(2\sum_{i=1}^{L}\mu_i+b\right)}{2\Gamma(b)\Gamma(2\sum_{i=1}^{L}\mu_i+1)}\mathcal{M}_\gamma(a)F_D^{(2L)}\left(b-1,\mu_1,\cdots\mu_L,\mu_1,\cdots\mu_L;2\sum_{i=1}^{L}\mu_i+1;\frac{1}{1+aA_1},\right. \\ \left.\cdots,\frac{1}{1+aA_L},\frac{1}{1+aB_1},\cdots,\frac{1}{1+aB_L}\right) \tag{50}$$

As it can easily be observed, for BPSK modulation ($a = 1$, $b = 1/2$), (50) reduces to (8), thus verifying the correctness of our analysis. Finally, it is worth mentioning that in Moschopoulos (1985), a proof for the uniform convergence of the series in (28) is provided and a bound for the truncation error is presented. Our conducted numerical experiments confirmed this bound on the truncation error and showed that infinite series converge steadily for all the scenarios of interest, a fact that was also established in Alouini et al. (2001).

6. Conclusions

In this chapter, a thorough performance analysis of MRC diversity receivers operating over η-μ fading channel was provided. Using the MGF-based approach, we derived closed-form expressions for a variety of M-ary modulation schemes. Moreover, in order to provide more insight as to which parameters affect the error performance, asymptotic expressions for the ASEP were derived. Based on these formulas, we proved that the diversity gain depends only on the parameter μ in each branch whereas η affects only the coding gain. Furthermore, we provided three new analytical expressions for the PDF of the sum of non-identical η-μ variates. Such expressions are useful to assess the outage performance and the average channel capacity of MRC diversity receivers under different adaptive transmission schemes. Finally, based on this PDF-based analysis, alternative expressions for the error performance of MRC receivers are provided. Various numerically evaluating results are presented that illustrate the analysis proposed in this chapter.

7. References

Abramovitz, M. & Stegun, I. (1964). *Handbook of Mathematical Functions with Formulas, Graphs, and Mathematical Tables*, Dover, New York, ISBN 0-486-61272-4.

Adinoyi, A. & Al-Semari, S. (2002). Expression for evaluating performance of BPSK with MRC in Nakagami fading, *IEE Electronics Letters* 38(23): 1428–1429.

Alouini, M.-S., Abdi, A. & Kaveh, M. (2001). Sum of gamma variates and performance of wireless communication systems over Nakagami-fading channels, *IEEE Transactions on Vehicular Technology* 50(6): 1471–1480.

Alouini, M.-S. & Goldsmith, A. J. (1999a). Capacity of Rayleigh fading channels under different adaptive transmission and diversity-combining techniques, *IEEE Transactions on Vehicular Technology* 48(4): 1165–1181.

Alouini, M.-S. & Goldsmith, A. J. (1999b). A unified approach for calculating the error rates of linearly modulated signals over generalized fading channels, *IEEE Transactions on Communications* 47: 1324–1334.

Asghari, V., da Costa, D. B. & Aissa, S. (2010). Symbol error probability of rectangular QAM in MRC systems with correlated η-μ fading channels, *IEEE Transactions on Vehicular Technology* 59(3): 1497–1497.

da Costa, D. B. & Yacoub, M. D. (2007). Average Channel Capacity for Generalized Fading Scenarios, *IEEE Communications Letters* 11(12): 949–951.

da Costa, D. B. & Yacoub, M. D. (2008). Moment Generating Functions of Generalized Fading Distributions and Applications, *IEEE Communications Letters* 12(2): 112–114.

da Costa, D. B. & Yacoub, M. D. (2009). Accurate approximations to the sum of generalized random variables and applications in the performance analysis of diversity systems, *IEEE Communications Letters* 57(5): 1271–1274.

Efthymoglou, G. P., Aalo, V. A. & Helmken, H. (1997). Performance analysis of coherent DS-CDMA systems in a Nakagami fading channel with arbitrary parameters, *IEEE Transactions on Vehicular Technology* 46(2): 289–297.

Efthymoglou, G. P., Piboongungon, T. & Aalo, V. A. (2006). Performance analysis of coherent DS-CDMA systems with MRC in Nakagami-m fading channels with arbitrary parameters, *IEEE Transactions on Vehicular Technology* 55(1): 104–114.

Ermolova, N. (2008). Moment Generating Functions of the Generalized $\eta - \mu$ and $k - \mu$ Distributions and Their Applications to Performance Evaluations of Communication Systems, *IEEE Communications Letters* 12(7): 502 – 504.

Ermolova, N. (2009). Useful integrals for performance evaluation of communication systems in generalized η- μ and κ-μ fading channels, *IET Communnications* pp. 303–308.

Exton, H. (1976). *Multiple Hypergeometric Functions and Applications*, Wiley, New York.

Filho, J. C. S. S. & Yacoub, M. D. (2005). Highly accurate η-μ approximation to sum of M independent non-identical Hoyt variates, *IEEE Antenna and Propagation Letters* 4: 436–438.

Gil-Pelaez, J. (1951). Note on the inversion theorem, *Biometrika* 38: 481–482.

Gradshteyn, I. & Ryzhik, I. M. (2000). *Tables of Integrals, Series, and Products*, 6 edn, Academic Press, New York.

Lei, X., Fan, P. & Hao, L. (2007). Exact Symbol Error Probability of General Order Rectangular QAM with MRC Diversity Reception over Nakagami-m Fading Channels, *IEEE Communications Letters* 11(12): 958 – 960.

Morales-Jimenez, D. & Paris, J. F. (2010). Outage probability analysis for η-μ fading channels, *IEEE Communications Letters* 14(6): 521–523.

Moschopoulos, P. G. (1985). The distribution of the sum of independent gamma random variables, *Ann. Inst. Statist. Math. (Part A)* 37: 541–544.

Peppas, K., Lazarakis, F., Alexandridis, A. & Dangakis, K. (2009). Error performance of digital modulation schemes with MRC diversity reception over η-μ fading channels, *IEEE Transactions on Wireless Communications* 8(10): 4974–4980.

Peppas, K. P., Lazarakis, F., Zervos, T., Alexandridis, A. & Dangakis, K. (2010). Sum of non-identical independent squared η-μ variates and applications in the performance analysis of DS-CDMA systems, *IEEE Transactions on Wireless Communications* 9(9): 2718–2723.

Prudnikov, A. P., Brychkov, Y. A. & Marichev, O. I. (1986). *Integrals and Series Volume 3: More Special Functions*, 1 edn, Gordon and Breach Science Publishers.

Radaydeh, R. M. (2007). Average Error Performance of M-ary Modulation Schemes in Nakagami-q (Hoyt) Fading Channels, *IEEE Communications Letters* 11(3): 255 – 257.

Saigo, M. & Tuan, V. K. (1992). Some integral representations of multivariate hypergeometric functions, *Rendicoti der Circolo Matematico Di Palermo* 61(2): 69–80.

Simon, M. K. & Alouini, M.-S. (1999). A unified approach to the probability of error for noncoherent and differentially coherent modulations over generalized fading channels, *IEEE Transactions on Communications* 46: 1625–1638.

Simon, M. K. & Alouini, M. S. (2005). *Digital Communication over Fading Channels*, Wiley.

Srivastava, H. M. & L.Manocha, H. (1984). *A Treatise on Generating Functions*, Wiley, New York.

Wang, Z. & Yannakis, G. (2003). A simple and general parametrization quantifying performance in fading channels, *IEEE Transactions on Communications* 51(8): 1389–1398.

Yacoub, M. D. (2007). The κ-μ and the η-μ distribution, *IEEE Antennas and Propagations Magazine* 49(1): 68–81.

4

Humidity Measurements using Commercial Microwave Links

Noam David, Pinhas Alpert and Hagit Messer
Tel Aviv University
Israel

1. Introduction

Atmospheric humidity strongly affects the economy of nature and has a cardinal part in a variety of environmental processes (e.g. Allan et al., 1999). As the most influential of greenhouse gases, it absorbs long-wave terrestrial radiation. Through the water vapour evaporation and recondensation cycle, it plays a central part in the Earth's energy redistribution mechanism by transferring heat energy from the surface to the atmosphere. Meteorological decision-support for weather forecasting is based on atmospheric model results, the accuracy of which is determined by the quality of its initial conditions or forcing data. Humidity, in particular, is a critical variable in the initialization of these models. The Mesoscale Alpine Programme (MAP) which set out to improve prediction of the regional weather, and specifically rainfall and flooding, concluded that accurate moisture fields for initialization were of great importance in achieving improved results (Ducrocq et al., 2002).

Humidity measurements are predominantly obtained by either surface stations, radiosondes or satellite systems. The typical surface station instruments commonly provide only very local, point, observations, and therefore suffer from low spatial resolution. Moisture though, is a field with an unusually high variability in the mesoscale as demonstrated, for instance, by structure functions (Lilly & Gal-Chen, 1983). Compounding this problem is the limited accessibility to position humidity gauges in heterogeneous terrain, or areas with complex topography. Satellites allow for a large area to be covered, but are frequently not accurate enough in measuring surface level moisture while this near-surface moisture is, in most cases, the important variable for convection. Radiosondes, which are typically launched only 2-4 times a day, also provide very limited information. Additionally, these monitoring methods are costly for implementation, deployment and maintenance.

Because of surface perturbation a point measurement close to the surface (for example 2m from the ground as in a standard meteorological surface station) is not satisfactory for model initialization. What is ideally required for meteorological modeling purposes is an area average measurement of near-surface moisture over a box with the scale of the model's grid and at an altitude of a few tens of meters. Current measuring tools cannot effectively provide this type of data. The method we present in this chapter provides a unique way of obtaining precisely this type of measurement. We introduce a technique, originally published by David et al. (2009), to measure atmospheric humidity using data collected by wireless communication networks.

2. Humidity monitoring using commercial microwave networks

2.1 Microwave links measurements as a basis for environmental monitoring

The propagation of the electromagnetic beam in the lower atmosphere, at centimeter and shorter wavelengths, is impaired by various weather phenomena (primarily precipitation, oxygen, water vapour, snow, mist and fog). The presence of line of sight and Fresnel zone clearance, propagation phenomena - diffraction, refraction, absorption and scattering - all affect the electromagnetic channel, causing attenuations to the radio signals (Raghavan, 2003). Thus, wireless communication networks provide built-in environmental monitoring tools, as was demonstrated for rainfall observations (Messer et al., 2006; Messer, 2007; Leijnse et al., 2007).

The attenuation of an electromagnetic wave, at requencies of tens of GHz, due to the interaction with rain droplets is well studied. The common approach relating the attenuation A [dB km^{-1}] with the rain rate R [mm $hour^{-1}$] is the power law model (Olsen at al., 1978):

$$A = aR^b \tag{1}$$

Where the constants a and b are, in general, functions of wave- frequency, its polarization and the drop size distribution (Jameson, 1991) . Given measurements of the Received Signal Level (RSL), the rain induced attenuation A can be estimated and in turn the average rainfall rate R.

Several works have shown that based on this technique, further applications, concerning rainfall monitoring, can be achieved (e.g. Zinevich et al., 2008-2009; Goldstein et al., 2009). Additionally, microwave links have been shown to be applicable for the identification of melting snow (Upton et al., 2007). An extensive study, concerning the hydrometeorological application of microwave links, was conducted, where in addition to the ability to measure precipitation, a Radio Wave Scintillometry-Energy Budget Method (RWS-EBM) to estimate areal evaporation using a microwave link (radio wave scintillometer) in combination with an energy budget constraint, was demonstrated (Leijnse, 2007). Zinevich et al. (2010) have recently discussed the prediction of rainfall measurement errors based on commercial wireless communication data.

2.2 Wireless communication networks as a water vapour monitoring system

Wireless communication, and in particular cellular networks, are widely distributed, operating in real time with minimum supervision, and therefore can be considered as continuous, high resolution humidity observation apparatus.

Environmental monitoring using data from wireless communication networks offers a completely new approach to quantifying ground level humidity. Since cellular networks already exist over large regions of the land, including complex topography such as steep slopes and since the method only requires standard data (saved by the communication system anyway), the costs are minimal.

Of the various wireless communication systems, we focus on the microwave point-to-point links which are used for backhaul communication in cellular networks, as they seem to have the most suitable properties for our purposes: they are static, line-of-sight links, built close to the ground, and operate in a frequency range of tens of GHz. Built-in facilities enable RSL measurements to be recorded at different time resolutions according to the different equipment types (typically, measurements are taken between once per minute to once per

24 hours). Some systems store only minimum and maximum RSL measurements per 15 minutes intervals. The magnitude resolution also varies for different types of equipment, it typically ranges between 0.1 dB to a few dB per link. Some of the microwave networks are equipped with automatic power control systems (however, not the ones used during the current study), in these cases, the transmitted signal level records should be taken into account in addition to the RSL measurements. In this research, the wireless system used for humidity observations has a magnitude resolution of 0.1 dB per link. This communication network provides attenuation data every few seconds, but only stores one data point per 24 hours (at 03:00 a.m.).The system can be configured to store data at shorter time intervals; it is a matter of technical definition by the cellular companies. Therefore, it has the potential of providing moisture observations at high temporal resolution. The length of an average microwave link is on the order of a few km and tends to be shorter in urban areas and longer in rural regions. In typical conditions of 1013 hPa pressure, 15 °C temperature and water vapour density of 7.5 g/m^3, the attenuation caused to a microwave beam interacting with the water vapour molecules at a frequency of ~ 22 GHz is roughly around 0.2 dB/km (Rec. ITU-R P.676-6, 2005, Liebe, 1985). Therefore, perturbations caused by humidity can be detected.

3. Theory and methods

At frequencies of tens of GHz, the main absorbing gases in the lower atmosphere are oxygen and water vapour. While oxygen has an absorption band around 60 GHz, water vapour has a resonance line at 22.235 GHz. The information concerning the attenuation and absorption by atmospheric water vapour and oxygen is based on the pioneering work of Van Vleck from 1947 (see also Gunn & East, 1954; Bean & Dutton, 1968). Although other atmospheric molecules have spectral lines in this frequency region, their expected strength is too small to affect propagation significantly (Raghavan, 2003; Meeks, 1976). As a consequence, an incident microwave signal, interacting with an H_2O molecule is attenuated, particularly if its frequency is close to the molecule's resonant one. Since backhaul links in cellular networks often operate around frequencies of 22 to 23 GHz, we focus on the 22.235 GHz absorbing line to monitor the water vapour.

3.1 The refractive index

In case of a homogeneous medium, the velocity of propagation, v, is given by (Raghavan, 2003):

$$v = (\varepsilon'\mu')^{-1/2} \tag{2}$$

ε' [Farads/m]- The permittivity of the medium through which the wave propagates.
μ' [Henries/m]- The magnetic inductive capacity of the medium.
In free space, the velocity of light, *c*, is known as follows:

$$c = (\varepsilon_0\mu_0)^{-1/2} \tag{3}$$

$\varepsilon_0 = 8.85\times10^{-12}$ [Farads/m]- The permittivity of free space.
$\mu_0 = 4\pi\times10^{-7}$ [Henries/m] - The magnetic inductive capacity of free space.
The dielectric constant of the medium, ε, which expresses the extent to which a material concentrates electric flux, is defined as the following ratio: $\varepsilon'/\varepsilon_0 = \varepsilon$.

$\mu'/\mu_0 = \mu$ - The magnetic permeability of the medium.
The refractive index of the medium, n, is defined as the ratio of the velocity in free space to that in the medium:

$$n \equiv \frac{c}{v} = (\varepsilon\mu)^{1/2} \tag{4}$$

Thus, for the propagation medium considered here, the value of μ can be taken as unity and therefore:

$$n^2 = \varepsilon \tag{5}$$

In our case, the dielectric is not perfect (due to absorption) and hence the refractive index $\tilde{n}$ is a complex quantity of which $n = \mathrm{Re}(\tilde{n})$ is the real part. The imaginary part, $\mathrm{Im}(\tilde{n})$, represents the absorption.

3.2 The absorption coefficient - γ

An electromagnetic wave propagating through a medium in the +z direction can be described as follows (Jackson, 1999):

$$\vec{E}(z,t) = E_0 e^{i(\tilde{k}z - \omega t)}\hat{\eta} \tag{6}$$

$$\vec{B}(z,t) = B_0 e^{i(\tilde{k}z - \omega t)}(\hat{z} \times \hat{\eta}) \tag{7}$$

The complex amplitudes of the electric field, $\vec{E}$, and the magnetic field , $\vec{B}$, are denoted by E_0 and B_0 , respectively.

$\hat{\eta}$ - Unit vector (in the x-y plane).

$\tilde{k}$ - The complex wave-number [rad/m].

ω - The angular frequency [rad/sec].

As the electromagnetic wave propagates, it carries energy along with it. The energy flux density (energy per unit area, per unit time) transported by the fields is given by the complex Poynting vector $\vec{S}$. The average in time, S_a, of the magnitude of the Poynting vector, is expressed as (Kerr, 1951; Raghavan, 2003):

$$S_a = \frac{1}{2}\mathrm{Re}(\vec{E} \times \vec{H}^*) \tag{8}$$

The asterisk signifies the complex conjugate while the vector $\vec{H}$, associated with the magnetic field $\vec{B}$, is given in equation (9):

$$\vec{B} = \mu'\vec{H} \tag{9}$$

The intensity, I, of an electromagnetic wave is proportional to S_a (Jackson, 1999). Therefore, by substituting equations (6), (7) and (9) into equation (8):

$$I(z) \propto \left| e^{i(\tilde{k}z - \omega t)} \right|^2 = e^{-2Im(\tilde{k})z} \tag{10}$$

Hence:

$$I(z) = I_0 e^{-2Im(\tilde{k})z} \tag{11}$$

Where I_0 and I are the intensity of the incident electromagnetic radiation and that after the material, respectively.
On the other hand, according to Beer-Lambert law:

$$I(z) = I_0 e^{-\gamma z} \tag{12}$$

While γ [m^{-1}] is the absorption coefficient.
Hence:

$$\gamma = 2Im(\tilde{k}) \tag{13}$$

The connection between the complex refractive index and the complex wave number is known to be (Raghavan, 2003):

$$\tilde{n} = Re(\tilde{n}) + iIm(\tilde{n}) = \frac{c\tilde{k}}{\omega} = \frac{cRe(\tilde{k})}{\omega} + i\frac{cIm(\tilde{k})}{\omega} \tag{14}$$

Therefore, from equations (13) and (14):

$$\gamma = \frac{2\omega}{c} Im(\tilde{n}) = \frac{4\pi f}{c} Im(\tilde{n}) \tag{15}$$

Finally, in order to obtain γ in dB/km:

$$\gamma_{[dB/km]} = \left[\frac{10}{\ln 10}\right]_{[dB]} \frac{4\pi \left[f_{[GHz]} \cdot 10^9\right] \cdot \left[N''_{[N\ units]} \cdot 10^{-6}\right]}{3 \cdot 10^5_{[km/s]}} = 0.1820 f_{[GHz]} N''_{[N\ units]} \tag{16}$$

While N'' is the imaginary part of the refractive index in N units (the index of refraction, n, is equivalent to (n-1)·106 N units).

3.3 Estimating humidity through wireless communication networks measurements

The attenuation γ [dB km^{-1}] due to dry air and water vapour is well studied and can be evaluated (Rec. ITU-R P.676-6, 2005, Liebe 1985) using:

$$\gamma = A_w + A_o \ [dB\ km^{-1}] \tag{17}$$

Hence, according to equations (16) and (17):

$$A_W + A_O = 0.1820fN'' \quad [\text{dB km}^{-1}] \tag{18}$$

Where:

A_w: The specific attenuation due to water vapour [dB km^{-1}].

A_o: The specific attenuation due to dry air [dB km^{-1}]

Assuming moist air A_o, is one order of magnitude lower comparing to A_w, since at frequencies of ~22 GHz, the signal loss is caused predominantly by the water vapour (assuming no precipitation, fog or other hydrometeors found along the propagation path).

f: The link's frequency [GHz].

N''= N''(p,T,ρ): The imaginary part of the complex refractivity measured in N units, a function of the pressure p[hPa], temperature T[°C] and the water vapour density ρ[g m^{-3}].

While:

$$N'' = \sum_i S_i F_i + N''_D \tag{19}$$

Si= Si (p,T): The strength of the i-th line [KHz].

Fi= Fi (p,T,ρ,f): Line shape factor [GHz^{-1}].

N''_D= N''_D(p,T,f): The dry continuum due to pressure-induced nitrogen absorption and the Debye spectrum.

The summation is of the individual resonance lines from oxygen and water vapour, the sum extends over all lines up to 1000 GHz. The detailed expression of the functions of N'' is described in the literature (Rec. ITU-R P.676-6, 2005; Liebe, 1985).

3.4 Estimating humidity through surface station data

Since meteorological surface stations normally do not provide the absolute moisture ρ, it was derived using the known relations (Rec. ITU-R P.676-6, 2005; Liebe 1985; Bolton, 1980):

$$e_S = 6.112\exp\left(\frac{17.67T}{T + 243.5}\right) \tag{20}$$

$$e = \rho\frac{T + 273.15}{216.7} \tag{21}$$

$$\frac{e}{e_S}100\% \equiv RH \tag{22}$$

e_s- The saturation water vapour pressure [hPa].

e- The water vapour partial pressure [hPa].

T- The temperature [°C].

ρ- The water vapour density [g/m^3].

RH- The relative humidity [%].

Hence:

$$\rho = 1324.45 \times \frac{RH}{100\%} \times \frac{\exp\left(\frac{17.67T}{T + 243.5}\right)}{T + 273.15} \tag{23}$$

3.5 Statistical tests

We investigated the correlation between absolute humidity values calculated using the method described, and those measured using a regular humidity gauge. The correlation analysis was performed using the Pearson's correlation test with the level of significance at 0.05 (Neter, 1996).

The Root Mean Square Difference (RMSD) was used according to the following definition:

$$\mathrm{RMSD}\ [g/m^3] = \sqrt{\frac{\sum_{i=1}^{N} (\rho_{mi} - \rho_{gi})^2}{N}} \tag{24}$$

ρ_{mi} - The i-th water vapour density measurement as measured using the microwave link $[g/m^3]$.

ρ_{gi} - The i-th water vapour density measurement as measured using the humidity gauge $[g/m^3]$.

N - Number of samples.

The humidity measurements taken via the microwave link were calculated from a signal instantaneously sampled at 03:00 a.m. Humidity measurements with the regular humidity gauge were taken at the surface stations every half hour, and from these measurements, the ones relating to the same hour were selected.

4. Results

Humidity observations, based on commercial microwave links data, were made in several different locations in Israel (Figure 1), and at several different times. The results presented here (Figure 2) are for Haifa Bay area, northern Israel and Ramla region, central Israel (four study cases are demonstrated here, two for each area). The observations of these four microwave links were made during November 2005, May 2008 and September 2007, April-May 2007, respectively.

Figures 2(a)-2(d) present the water vapour density ρ (g/m^3) as estimated using RSL measurements from the microwave link data (dark) vs. conventional humidity gauge data (bright).

The results, presented here, show very good match between the conventional technique and the novel method. The calculated correlation coefficients, in these cases, were between 0.82 to 0.9. The RMSD were found to be 1.8 $[g/m^3]$ and 2 $[g/m^3]$ for the links located by Harduf and Kfar Bialik, respectively. The RMSD of the central site measurements (Ramla area) were 3.4 $[g/m^3]$ (for both cases in this region). Similar comparisons were performed for other links and other time slots showing correlations in the range of 0.5-0.9. The system from which the data were collected captures a single signal every 24 hours at 03:00 a.m. The surface station observations used were taken from the vicinity of the link's area at the same hour. Since rainfall causes additional signal-attenuation, days when showers occurred approximately at 03:00 a.m. till 04:00 a.m. (according to close by surface stations), were excluded.

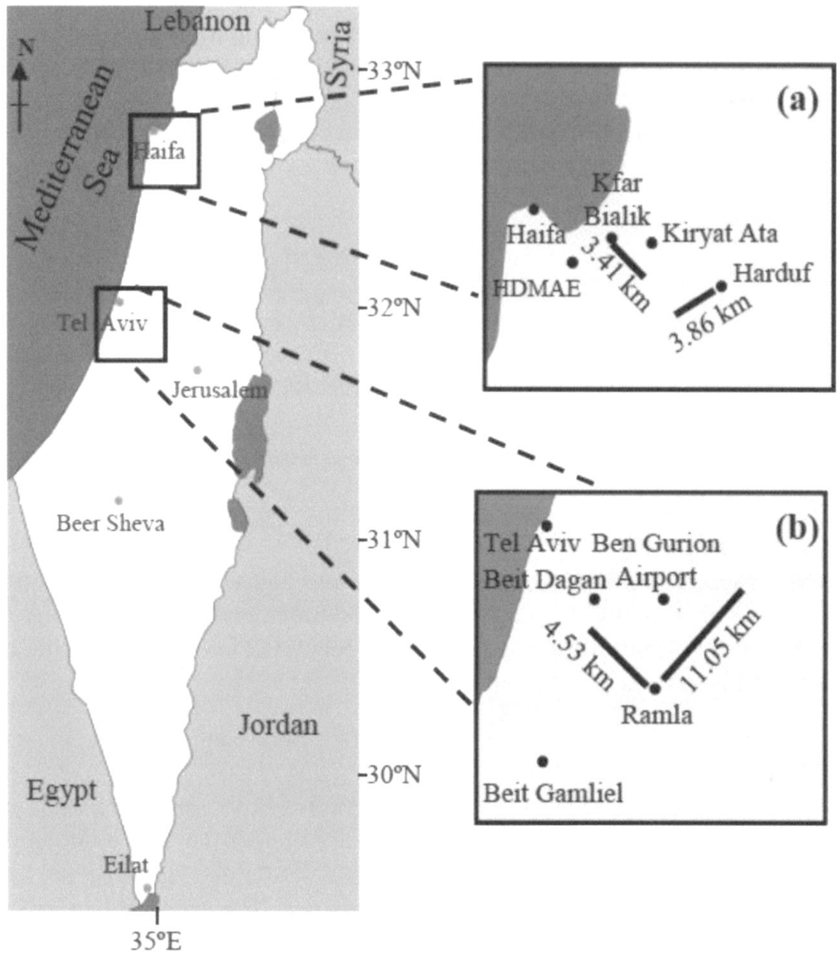

Fig. 1. The examined regions (taken from David et al., 2009).
1(a) North Israel: Two microwave links are presented (marked as lines) in front of Kiryat Ata, Haifa bay (where the humidity gauge is located). The first link (3.86 km long) is located on two hills, its transmiter and receiver are found at heights of 265 and 233 m Above Sea Level (ASL). The distance from the surface station to a point located in the middle of this wireless link is 7.5 km. The transmiting and receiving units of the second radio link (3.41 km) are situated 25 and 41 m ASL while the surface station- link distance is 3 km in this case. The Kiryat Ata surface station is situated 45 m ASL.
1(b) Central Israel: The two microwave links in front of Ben-Gurion airport meteorological station (humidity gauge's location). The distance from the surface station to a point located in the middle of the 4.53 km link is 6.5 km. This link's transmitter and receiver are located at heights of 95 and 63 m ASL. The longer link (11.05 km) is located 5 km from the surface satation while its transmitting and receiving units are situated 116 and 98 m ASL. The airport surface station is situated at 41 m ASL

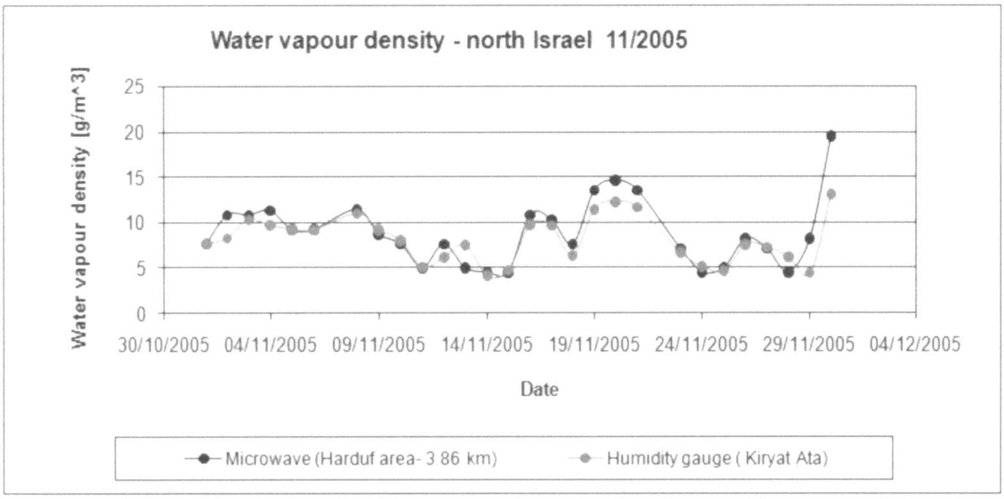

Fig. 2(a). Northern Israel (taken from David et al., 2009) - The observations were made, by the 3.86 km wireless link, during the month of November 2005, where 2 rainy days were excluded (7 and 22 November). The rainfall data were taken from two different surface stations situated in the Haifa District Municipal Association for the Environment (HDMAE) and in Kiryat Ata, about 12.5 km and 7 km, respectively, from Harduf (see Fig. 1a). The link's frequency is 22.725 GHz. The calculated correlation between the two curves is 0.9 while the RMSD is 1.8 [g/m^3]

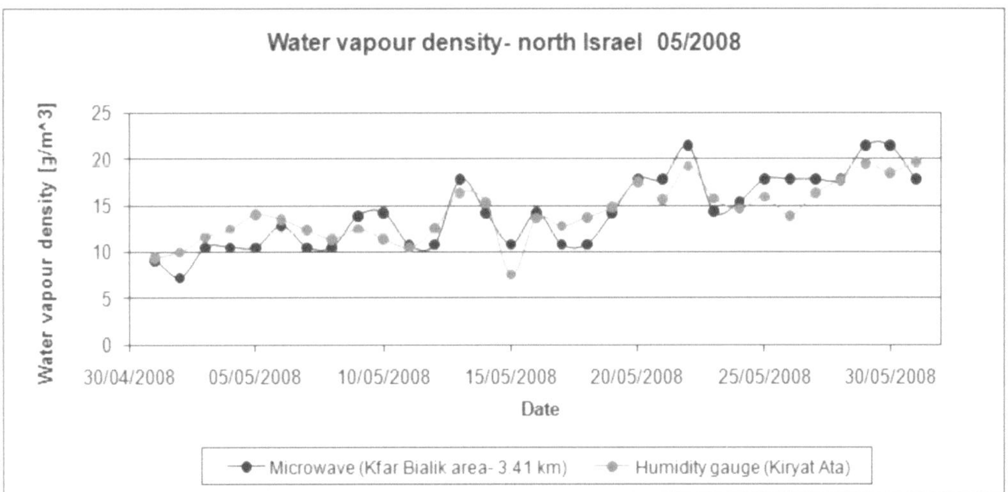

Fig. 2(b). Northern Israel - The humidity measurements were made, by the 3.41 km microwave link, during May 2008. The correlation between the two measurements is 0.87 with RMSD of 2 [g/m^3]. Link's frequency: 22.05 GHz

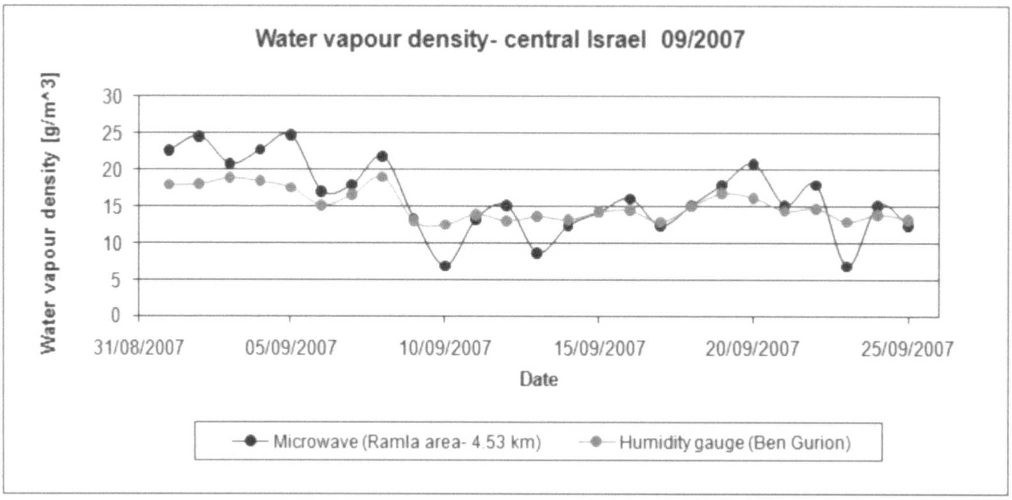

Fig. 2(c). Central Israel - The measurements were taken during the month of September 2007 (25 days). The link's frequency is 22.525 GHz and the calculated correlation between the time series is 0.89 with RMSD of 3.4 [g/m^3]

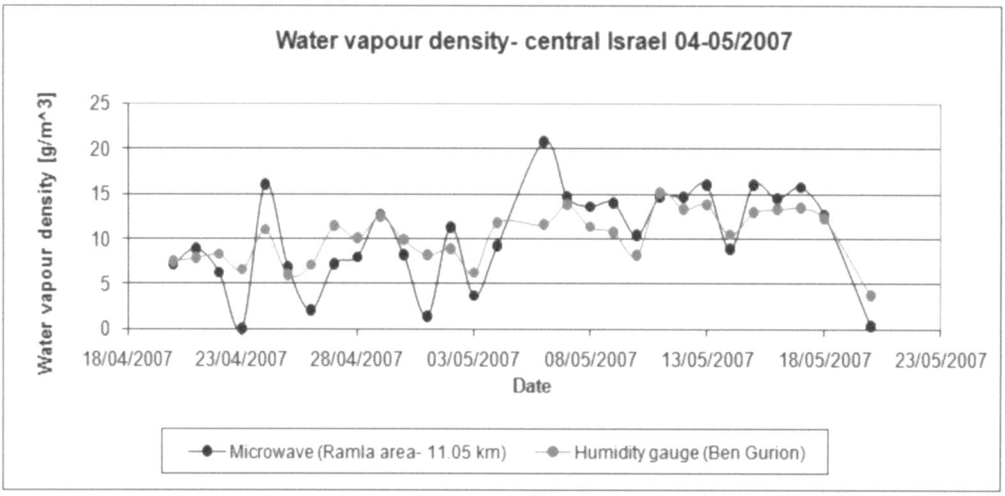

Fig. 2(d). Central Israel (taken from David et al., 2009) - The measurements were taken between 20 April and 20 May 2007, excluding 2 days when showers occurred (5 and 19 May). The precipitation data were taken from Beit Gamliel surface station which is located about 13 km from Ramla (see Fig. 1b). It should be noted that it is possible that the increased attenuation in this case that is greater than the typical moist air attenuation, was caused as a result of other interference such as wind moving the transmitter or receiver (Leijnse et al., 2007). As there was a surface station that recorded precipitation in the area, the increased attenuation was ascribed to precipitation. Further investigation is required to identify the sources of these perturbations. The link's frequency is 21.325 GHz and the calculated correlation between the time series is 0.82 with RMSD of 3.4 [g/m^3]

The largest difference between the traditional and the novel measurement methods (Figure 2d) appears on the night of 6 May 2007. This night was a holiday in Israel ("Lag Ba'omer"), where hundreds of bonfires were lit all across the country. As a result, many particles were released into the low atmosphere speeding up the creation of smog and possibly fog (the measured relative humidity by a radiosonde launched at 03:00 a.m. from Beit Dagan (Fig. 1b), a few km away from the microwave link, at an altitude of 95 m ASL was 97%). The reason for the additional attenuation observed by the microwave link (expressed by a higher moisture level) might be due to local fog (Raghavan, 2003), implying that the system may provide the ability to monitor this phenomenon through the use of wireless communication data. When excluding the 6 May measurement, the correlation increases to 0.85 and the RMSD decreases to 2.9 [g/m^3]. Further investigation is needed concerning this point.

5. Uncertainties

Commercial microwave links are designed for efficient data transmission and high communication performance rather than measuring the water vapour density. Hence, estimation of the uncertainties for observations that are non-optimal in the first place is fundamental in order to assure usability of the data. The uncertainty in measuring temperature and pressure are of the magnitude 0.1 degrees Celsius, and 1 mb, respectively. However, changes of this magnitude in pressure or temperature do not create a significant change in the absolute humidity calculation based on this model (Rec. ITU-R P.676-6, 2005; Liebe, 1985). The dominant uncertainty affecting the absolute humidity calculation is that of the attenuation quantization error. The uncertainty depends on the path length. Since the quantization error of the wireless system used is 0.1 dB per link, the uncertainty in evaluating attenuation is ± 0.025 dB/km for a typical 4 km long link (a length which is of the order of magnitude of three out of the four links used in the cases presented here). As a result we get that the error in calculating absolute humidity for this link length is of the magnitude of ± 1 g/m^3. In the case of an 11.05 km link, the uncertainty in evaluating the attenuation is ± 0.01 dB/km, hence the corresponding error in calculating the absolute humidity is of the magnitude of ± 0.5 g/m^3. The estimated uncertainty in measuring humidity with regular humidity gauges is about 0.2 to 0.5 g/m^3 (depending on the relative humidity and the temperature), while the error in measuring relative humidity was taken to be 3%.

Dry air effect on attenuation is one order of magnitude lower than that of water vapour in this case. Quantitatively it is about 0.01 dB/km for dry air and 0.19 dB/km as a result of humidity (for a 1 km link, operating near 22 GHz, temperature of 15 °C, humidity of 7.5 g/m^3 and a sea level pressure). However, the algorithm takes into account the effects of dry air, and corrects for them. Another atmospheric parameter which can be estimated based on the model is the imaginary part of the refractive index- N", as aforementioned, this variable represents the absorption. Under the same atmospheric conditions as mentioned previously and for a link operating near 22 GHz, a typical value which was obtained for this variable, based on the model, is: 0.044 [N units] while the uncertainty is ± 0.006 [N units] for a 4 km link and ± 0.003 [N units] for an 11 km link.

Rain, fog, snow and clouds create additional attenuation in relation to that caused by water vapour. One of the research challenges we are faced with is separating the effects of different attenuation sources. As we aim to prove feasibility, at this stage, the technique is limited to periods where none of the aforementioned phenomena exist along the link line-of-sight. The microwave links are sensitive to mechanical oscillations. Therefore, strong winds, that may cause movement of either the receiver or the transmitter (or both), may also be considered as a source of error (Leijnse et al., 2007).

6. Conclusions and future plan

Our results show very good agreement between the conventional way to measure water vapour over the low troposphere and our proposed, novel method based on wireless communication networks measurements. However, some disparities are expected of course. That is since measurements from the microwave links are line integrated data, where in-situ measurements as made by a typical humidity gauge are point measurements. In addition, the difference in location between the measurement sites and particularly the difference in the moisture level with altitude which can be significant at night hours, introduces additional disparities between the microwave measurements and those made by the conventional humidity gauges.

The measurements from the northern links present a better correspondence with the humidity gauge readings, compared to the measurements which were made by the microwave links located in central Israel. Additionally, it is possible to note that the Harduf area link presents, in general, a better agreement with the humidity gauge data as compared to that of the other three links. While it will need to be further investigated, we can suggest several reasons for the observed discrepancy: The representativeness of the spot humidity gauges is a factor. It is possible that the humidity gauge in the northern area better represents the average humidity in the region than the Ben Gurion airport humidity gauge does. Thus, it is possible that, the measurements of the central area humidity gauge do not correspond as well to the measurements of the microwave link that represent the average humidity along the paths (distances of 4.5 km and 11.05 km). Moreover, it is important to note that the transmitting and receiving units of the Harduf link are located on hilltops, and are higher off the ground, so that the microwave beam travels over a valley. On the other hand, while the other three links are located between 25 to 95 m ASL, their masts heights (where the transmitters and receivers are installed) are only between 15 to 33 m above the surface itself. It is possible then, that those links are more prone to reflection and surface interference (Leijnse et al., 2007).

The wireless measurement technique can thus either replace existing techniques or preferably be used in conjunction with them in order to obtain more accurate moisture fields.

Given the newly available data provided by the wireless communication facilities, improved initialization of atmospheric models can be achieved, thus enhancing prediction and hazards warning skills as well as providing a better understanding of the global climate system.

7. Acknowledgements

We wish to acknowledge and thank Y. Dagan, Y. Eisenberg (Cellcom), N. Dvela, A. Shilo (Pelephone) for their cooperation and for providing the microwave data for our research.

We also thank B. Goldman (Haifa District Municipal Association for the Environment) and A. Arie (Meteo-tech) for humidity gauge data.

In addition, we would like to thank our research team members: A. Zinevich, Y. Ostromtzky, Dr. R. Samuels, D. Charkasky, O. Auslender and R. Radian (Tel Aviv University) for their advice and assistance throughout this research.
This work was supported by a grant from the Yeshaya Horowitz Association, Jerusalem. Additional support was given by the PROCEMA-BMBF project and by the GLOWA-JR BMBF project.

8. References

Allan, R. P.; Shine, K. P.; Slingo, A. & Pamment, J. A. (1999). The dependence of clear-sky outgoing long-wave radiation on surface temperature and relative humidity. *Q. J. Roy. Meteor. Soc.*, 125, pp.2103-2126.

Bolton, D (1980). The computation of equivalent potential temperature. *Mon. Weather. Rev.*, 108, pp.1046-1053.

Bean, BR.; Dutton, EJ. & Central Radio Propagation Laboratory. (1968). *Radio meteorology*, Dover Publications, New York

Ducrocq, V.; Ricard, D.; Lafore, J. P. & Orain, F. (2002). Storm-scale numerical rainfall prediction for five precipitating events over France: On the importance of the initial humidity field. *Weather Forecast.*, 17, pp.1236-1256.

David, N.; Alpert, P.; & Messer, H. (2009). Technical Note: Novel method for water vapour monitoring using wireless communication networks measurements. *Atmos. Chem. Phys.*, 9, pp.2413-2418, doi:10.5194/acp.9.2413.2009.

Goldshtein, O. ; Messer, H. & Zinevich, A. (2009). Rain rate estimation using measurements from commercial telecommunications links. *IEEE T. Signal Proces.*, 57(4), pp.1616-1625, doi:10.1109/TSP.2009.2012554.

Gunn, KLS. & East TWR. (1954). The microwave properties of precipitation particles. *Quart. J.Roy. Meteor.Soc.*, 80, pp.522-545.

Jackson, JD. (1999). *Cssical electrodynamics. 3rd ed*. Wiley, New York.

Jameson, A. (1991). A comparison of microwave techniques for measuring rainfall. *J. Appl. Meteorol.*, 30, pp.32-54.

Kerr, DE. (1951). The propagation of short radio waves, MIT Radiation Laboratory Series 13, McGraw-Hill, New York.

Leijnse, H.; Uijlenhoet, R. & Stricker, J. N. M. (2007). Rainfall measurement using radio links from cellular communication networks. *Water Resour. Res.*, 43, W03201, doi:10.1029/2006WR005631.

Leijnse, H.; Uijlenhoet, R. & Stricker, J. N. M. (2007). Hydrometeorological application of a microwave link: 1. Evaporation. *Water Resour. Res.*, 43, W04416, doi:10.1029/2006WR004988.

Leijnse, H.; Uijlenhoet, R. & Stricker, J. N. M. (2007). Hydrometeorological application of a microwave link: 2. Precipitation. *Water Resour. Res.*, 43, W04417, doi:10.1029/2006WR004989.

Leijnse, H. (2007). Hydrometeorological application of a microwave links: measurement of evaporation and precipitation. Ph.D. thesis, Wageningen University.

Lilly, D. K. & Gal-Chen, T. (1983). *North Atlantic Treaty Organization & Scientific Affairs Division. Mesoscale meteorology-theories, observations, and models*, Reidel, Dordrecht, Netherlands.

Liebe, HJ. (1985). An updated model for millimeter wave propagation in moist air. *Radio Science*, 20, pp.1069-1089.

Meeks, M. L. (1976). *Methods of experimental physics: Astrophysics*, Academic Press. New York.

Messer, H.; Zinevich, A. & Alpert, P. (2006). Environmental monitoring by wireless communication networks, *Science*, 312, pp.713.

Messer, H. (2007). Rainfall monitoring using cellular networks, *IEEE Signal Proc. Mag.*, 24, pp.142-144.

Neter, J.; Kutner, M. H.; Nachtsheim, C. & Wasserman, W. (1996). *Applied Linear Statistical Models, 4th Edition,* McGraw Hill, Inc., 640–645.

Olsen R.; Rogers, D. & Hodge, D. (1978). The aR^b relation in the calculation of rain attenuation, *IEEE Trans. Antennas Propagat.*, AP-26, pp. 318-329.

Raghavan, S. (2003). *Radar Meteorology.* Kluwer Academic Publishers, Dordrecht.

Rec. ITU-R P.676-6. (2005). Attenuation by atmospheric gases, *ITU-R Recommendations.*

Upton, G.; Cummings, R. & Holt, A. (2007). Identification of melting snow using data from dual-frequency microwave links. *IEEE Proc. Microwaves Antennas Propag.*, 1(2), pp.282-288.

Van Vleck, JH. (1947). Absorption of microwaves by uncondensed water vapor, *Phys. Rev.*, 71, pp.425-433.

Zinevich, A.; Alpert, P. & Messer, H. (2008). Estimation of rainfall fields using commercial microwave communication networks of variable density. *Adv. Water Resour.*, 31(11), pp.1470-1480, doi:10.1016/j.advwatres.2008.03.003.

Zinevich, A. ; Messer, H. & Alpert, P. (2009). Frontal rainfall observation by a commercial microwave communication network. *J. Appl. Meteorol. Clim.*, 48(7), pp.1317-1334, doi: 10.1175/2008jamc2014.1.

Zinevich, A.; Messer, H. & Alpert, P. (2010). Prediction of rainfall intensity measurement errors using commercial microwave communication links. *Atmos. Meas. Tech.*, 3, pp.1385-1402..

Part 2

Antenna Design and Performance

5

Assessment of Indoor Propagation and Antenna Performance for Bluetooth Wireless Communication Links

Tommy Hult[1] and Abbas Mohammed[2]
[1]*Department of Electrical and Information Technology, Lund University*
[2]*School of Engineering, Blekinge Institute of Technology*
Sweden

Over the last decade the world has witnessed explosive growth in the use of wireless mobile communications. Looking around we find users with mobile phones, wireless PDAs, MP3 players, keyboards etc. and wireless headphones to connect to these devices - a small testament of the impact of wireless communications on our daily lives. In addition the burst of new technologies such as Bluetooth and other short-range wireless communications are encouraging the further development of a wide variety of distributed wireless devices (Mohammed, 2002).

Bluetooth is one of those short range wireless communication technology systems which aims at replacing many proprietary cables that connect one device with another with one universal short-range radio link. Recently, many mobile devices (e.g., mobile phones, PDAs, computer mice) with integrated Bluetooth modules have been introduced. Their wireless technology is used to transfer any kind of data onto these devices.

Propagation of radio waves inside buildings is a very complicated issue, and it depends significantly on the indoor environment (home, office, factory) and the topography (LOS: line of sight and NLOS: non-line of sight). The statistics of the indoor channel varies with time due to movements of people and equipment (Obayashi & Zander, 1998). A survey of indoor propagation measurement and models can be found in (Hashemi, 1993), and electromagnetic propagation effects in (Sander & Reed, 1978). There are limited investigations in the open literature on the measurements and simulations of multipath wave propagation effects on the performance of live Bluetooth links.

In this chapter we present measurement campaigns (signal power, bit error rate and data rate) in an indoor office building for LOS and NLOS propagation scenarios and assess their effects on the Bluetooth link. These measurements were carried out using various antennas (omni-directional and directive antennas), and we will present comparative analysis to access the potential improvement in system performance gained from the use of directive antennas. We will also show the effect of antenna parameters (gain and efficiency) on the results and the overall impact on the quality and coverage of the Bluetooth link.

The organization of this chapter is as follows. In section 2 we provide a brief description of the building in the tested indoor office environment and the various types of antennas used in the measurement trials and their related parameters. In section 3 we present the results of these measurements. Finally, section 4 concludes the chapter.

1. Bluetooth

Bluetooth devices operate in the unlicensed industrial, scientific and medical (ISM) band at 2.4 GHz, and with a total bandwidth of 83.5 MHz (Bisdikian, 2001; Bluetooth, 2002; Haartsen, 2000). According to the IEEE 802.11 standard, this band is globally available, license-free and follow a basic set of power, spectral emission and interference specifications.
There are two types of connections depending on the number and functions of the Bluetooth system. These connections form a piconet topology which is either point-to-point or point-to-multipoint networks. In the point-to-point connection, only two Bluetooth devices are involved, while several Blutooth devices are connected in the point-to-multipoint connection. In these configurations the Bluetooth device that first creates a connection is designated as the *master* device and the others would then become *slave* devices. The maximum number of eight Bluetooth devices can be connected into a piconet, (i.e.,1 master and 7 slaves).
The topology of the connection can be extended to involve more piconets depending on the function of each Bluetooth device. This extended net is called a scatternet, in which a Bluetooth device could be active in more than one piconet.
The Bluetooth radio utilize spectrum spreading through the use of frequency hopping between 79 channels displaced by 1 MHz, from 2.402 GHz to 2.481 GHz, although in some countries the frequency hopping range is reduced to 23 hops (McDermott-Wells, 2004). The frequency hopping provides a redcution of interference from other devices in the busy ISM band. Even though the Bluetooth technology includes a retransmission scheme for lost data packets, the frequency hopping will minimize the possibility of data blocking when there are many Bluetooth devices within range of each other. The gross data rate of the Bluetooth technology is 1 Mbps (Bisdikian, 2001; Bluetooth, 2002; Miller & Bisdikian, 2001).
Each Bluetooth device is classified into 3 power classes,

- class 1 with a maximum transmit power of 20 dBm.
- class 2 with a maximum transmit power of 4 dBm.
- class 3, with a maximum transmit power of 0 dBm.

To obtain the most efficient use of the bandwidth within a channel while maintaining an acceptable bit error rate, the digital bit stream is modulated using Gaussian Frequency Shift Keying (GFSK).
The power emission is controlled at the receiver side by monitoring the Received Signal Strength Indicator (RSSI) and sending Link Manager Protocol (LMP) control commands to the transmitter asking for the transmit power to be reduced if the RSSI value is higher than the necessary threshold required to maintain a better link quality. If the RSSI value is too low, then the receiver may request the power to be increased (Bisdikian, 2001; Bluetooth, 2002; Miller & Bisdikian, 2001).
The Bluetooth protocol uses a combination of circuit and packet switching. Slots can be reserved for three supported synchronous voice channels and one asynchronous data channel. In addition there is a supported channel for both asynchronous data and synchronous voice.

2. The tested indoor office environment

The measurement trials were performed indoors in typical office environments. In this section we will describe the building structure and material where the measurements took place and later in the results section we show the sensitivity of the Bluetooth link, employing different

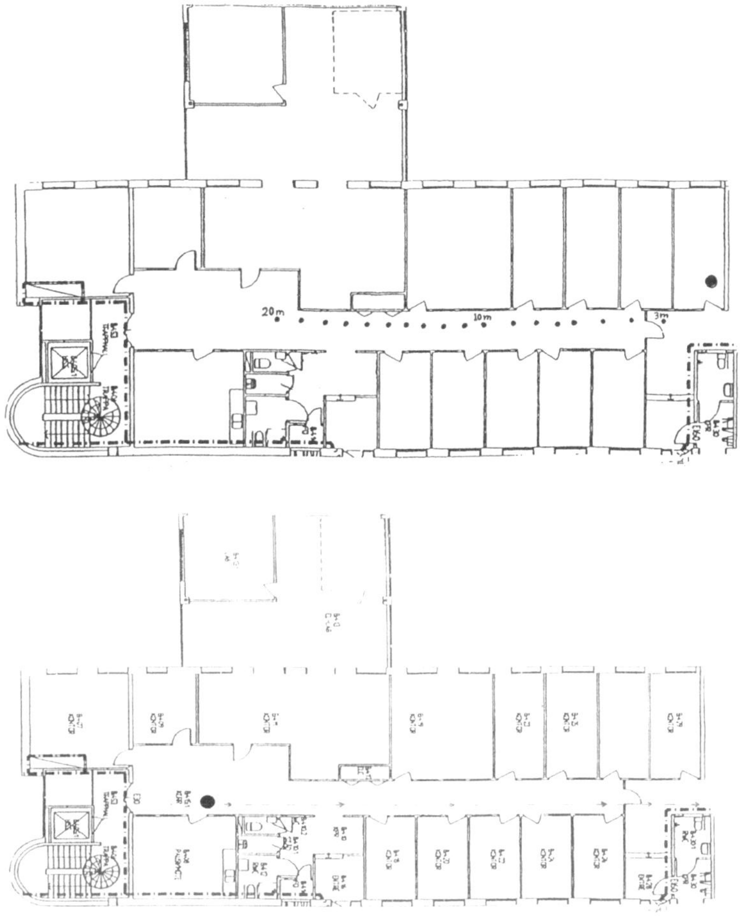

Fig. 1. Description of the indoor office environment used in the measurement scenarios for: NLOS (top figure) and LOS (bottom figure).

antenna types, in these indoor environments. Figure 1 shows a typical example of office environment which is quite common all over the world. The dimensions of the hallway of the building in this figure are (45 x 1.85 x 2.30) meters. Most doors are mainly made of wood except of the two outer doors, one at each end of the hallway, which are made of metal. The inner walls in the hallway consists of a large single pane window in a wooden frame. The walls between the rooms consists of two plasterboards supported by two vertical steel crossbars and the plasterboards are nailed to vertical wooden crossbars that are situated at regular intervals inside the wall. Mostly all the furniture in the office are made of wood and plastic. The outer walls of the building are made of concrete isolated with thermal material and dual pane windows surrounded by wooden/metal frames.

2.1 The used antennas

The antenna is the interface between the transmitter/receiver and the propagation medium, and it therefore is a deciding factor in the performance of a radio communication system.

To improve and develop the design of Bluetooth antenna, the Bluetooth Special Interest Group (SIG) has left the antenna part as an open door for the antenna manufacturers. In the past few years, the designs of Bluetooth antennas have been developed significantly and since then many companies have entered the Bluetooth antenna market and others have already left it. The Bluetooth radio module has to be connected to an antenna to transport the electromagnetic energy from the radio module to the antenna (transmitter), or from the antenna to the radio module (receiver). In addition, there are three important parameters concerning both the propagation of electromagnetic waves and the definition of the coverage of the wireless devices. These parameters are the receiver sensitivity, output power and antenn a gain.

The radiation pattern of an antenna could be *omnidirectional* (a circular pattern with the same radiation in every direction in one plane) or *directional*. Therefore the radiation pattern in a particular direction determines if the antenna has a directive gain or not. Fixed network devices such as LAN Access Points (LAP) could use antennas that are directed as they are installed. Conversely, mobile devices such as cellular phones, laptops, cameras, etc. need to transmit and receive at any direction and angel. As a consequence, in the choice of an antenna for a product, its position as well as its parameters (gain, efficiency and radiation pattern) should be taken into account and investigated properly.

In this chapter, both omnidirectional and directive antenna types have been used and tested. The range of the Bluetooth antenna is much different in practical measurements than the theoretically anticipated range especially in an office environment; this observation will also be revealed in the measurement results section. The popular antenna types for Bluetooth devices are the external dipole, microstrip and *planar inverted-F antenna* (PIFA). In this chapter the Bluetooth Application Tool Kit has been used in the measurements as we have mentioned above. In order to connect and measure with different antennas by using the Bluetooth Application Tool Kit module which has an originally microstrip PIFA antenna printed on a Printed Circuit Board (PCB), a cable with SMA connector has been connected to a feeding point with impedance of 50 ohm as a requirement for each Bluetooth antenna when it would be mounted on the board. The different antenna types used in these tests are presented below; the operational frequency range for all antennas is 2.4-2.5 GHz and their nominal feeding impedance is 50 ohm. It is worth mentioning at this point that generic names have been given to the different antennas used in these measurements rather than their specific names. The various tested antennas and their radiation patterns are presented in the appendix. The PIFA antenna used in the Master Bluetooth device has two galvanic contacts, one to the earth and the other as a feeding point with impedance of 50 ohm. The structure of the PIFA antenna is optimized for small size requirements, large bandwidth and efficient gain. The size of the PIFA antenna is (25 x 7) mm.

The *Half Wave Model 1* antenna (Appendix figure 5) relies on a reflection formed wave between the active element and a conductive plane. The gain value of this antenna is 9.2 dBi and its efficiency is 95%. Because of its large size, this antenna can be used as an external antenna for some applications like a printer server and measuring instruments. The return loss, which has been measured with a network analyzer, is 14.4 dB.

The *Half Wave Model 2* antenna (Appendix figure 6) is an external antenna which was supplied with an adjustable radiator angle. This antenna could take different positions (vertical, horizontal, etc.). The *Half Wave Model 2* antenna is characterized by a radiation pattern which is almost the same in all directions (omnidirectional). The gain value of this antenna is 1.6 dBi, the efficiency is 75% and the return loss is 15 dB.

The *Quart Wave Model 1* antenna (Appendix figure 9) has a small size of (18.2 x 3.9 x 1.6) mm, and it is a surface-mounted embedded antenna. It can be integrated into PC cards, mobile phones, access points and Bluetooth enabled devices. It is a linearly polarized antenna with a peak gain of 2 dBi.

The *Quart Wave Model 2* antenna (Appendix figure 8) is also small in size (21 x 4 x 3) mm and can be used as an embedded antenna for Bluetooth enabled devices. The gain value of this antenna is 4.1 dBi, its efficiency value is 68% and the return loss is 10.784 dB. The radiation pattern of the *Quart Wave Model 2* antenna is not omnidirectional.

The *Half Wave Model 3* antenna (Appendix figure 7) has relatively small size (27 x 8 x 3) mm and can be used both as an embedded antenna and an external antenna for Bluetooth enabled devices. The radiation pattern of this antenna indicates that the *Half Wave Model 3* antenna is not an omnidirectional antenna. The gain value of this antenna is 4.0 dBi, its efficiency is 62% and the return loss is 13.46 dB.

2.2 The measurements setup

Measurement campaigns were conducted so that we can get an understanding of how the signal power, BER and the data rate are affected by NLOS and LOS propagation scenarios for the different Bluetooth antennas that have been used in the indoor office environment. The antennas used in these measurement trials and their parameters have been described in the previous section.

One room (back room marked with a dot) and part of the hallway were used in the measurements to provide NLOS and LOS scenarios between the two Bluetooth devices/antennas, respectively, as shown in figure 1. A PC is connected to a Bluetooth device with PIFA antenna, have been used as a stationary Bluetooth device (Master). Another PC with a Bluetooth device (Slave), was rolled along the hallway in 1 m interval following the dotted line in figure 1. The various used antennas, which are described in the previous section, were replaced alternately on the Slave side. In this chapter, the Receiver Signal Strength Indicator (RSSI) is used in the measurements; this term and signal power has been used interchangeably here. The Bluetooth RSSI measurement compares the received signal power with two threshold levels, which define the Golden Receive Power Range (Bisdikian, 2001). Note that all the results for signal power measurements were registered after measuring it 10 times to ensure that a stable signal is being measured. For the fast fading dip identification, the measured return value of RSSI was flickering (or hopping) from 0 dB to -20 dB and back again to 0 dB and so on (i.e., a stable result couldn't be measured).

Note that the door in the back room, where the master was placed for NLOS scenario, was open and other doors in the hallway were also open during the measurements. In addition, people in the office were allowed to move freely during the measurements, and the results of these measurements were registered after a successful data transmission. For the NLOS measurement scenario all the measurements have been started at the range of 3 meters (see figure 1) in order to avoid the direct LOS path.

3. Results of the measurements

Antennas that are able to direct the transmitted and received signals' energy are of great interest for future wireless communication systems. The directivity implies reduced transmit power and interference and hence potential for increased capacity, quality and range. In this section we present the measurement trials using different directive antennas and compare with isotropic antenna for NLOS and LOS propagation scenarios described in the previous section. The results of three types of measurement trials (signal power, bit error rate and data rate) will be presented in this section.

The RSSI or signal power measurement results are shown in figure 2. It is evident from this figure that a significant reduction in signal power is achieved with the gradual increase of both the distance and the number of the obstacles between the Master and the Slave along the dotted line in figure 1. Increasing the distance even further will ultimately produce a break in transmission; that is a disconnection between the radio modules at different distances depending on the parameters (gain and efficiency) of the different used antennas and the propagation scenario. This is the reason why the *Half Wave Model 1* antenna (9.2 dBi, 95%) has the highest signal power and best range (19 meters) while the *Half Wave Model 3* antenna (4 dBi, 62%) has the lowest signal power and range (9 meters). The results of the other antennas are intermediate between the results of the above two mentioned antennas.

Note that a successful data transmission was impossible after the coverage range of each antenna as shown in figure 2. The most important distance in this scenario is at 10 meters which is the anticipated range of the Bluetooth class 3 modules used in these measurements.

An interesting observation in NLOS scenario is the reception of stable (or constant) signal power level (in some distances for all the used antennas) in spite of increasing the distance between the Master and the Slave. This can be clearly seen from the RSSI results in figure 2 for example at the distance from 9-12 meters.

An important observation that can be made from figure 2 regarding LOS scenario is that the signal still exists in the hallway much farther beyond the operating range of 10 meters (see for example *Half Wave Model 1*). This phenomenon could be explained by the tunnelling effect where the hallway acts as a waveguide to the reflected radio waves from the walls along the hallway. Hence the increased coverage ranges as compared to NLOS scenario.

In figure 3 we show the results of BER measurements for the different antennas. BER is defined as the number of errors in the system that occurs within a given sequence of bits. For example, a BER of 0.001% means that in average one bit out of 10000 bits is corrupted. Generally, the BER becomes higher by increasing the distance between the transmitter and the receiver, and by increasing the number of obstacles in the communications path. However, the effect of fast fading on the measurement results is evident from the rapid fluctuation of the measured BER values for all antennas as shown in figure 3. Again, the *Half Wave Model 1* antenna provided the best results (lowest BER values) among the used antennas, which is clearly related to its high gain and efficiency parameters.

For NLOS scenario in figure 3 (top plot), the highest BER value of 1.964% was obtained by the *Half Wave Model 3* antenna at a distance of 12 m, while the lowest BER value of 0.378% (at the same distance) was obtained by the *Half Wave Model 1* antenna. The BER results of the other antennas were in between the above mentioned values. On the other hand, for LOS scenario in figure 3 (bottom plot), the results of BER measurements show a minimum value of 0.0% (no errors) and a maximum value of 0.905%. In other words, the BER is lower in LOS as compared to NLOS scenario as expected. Again, the *Half Wave Model 1* antenna has the best results (lowest BER values) among the used antennas, which is clearly related to its high gain and efficiency parameters.

Finally, the results of the data rate measurements are plotted in figure 4. From these plots we notice only a very slight reduction of the Bluetooth link data rates with increasing the distance. The data rate results are also in agreement with the pattern of the BER results in figure 3; that is the higher the BER value, the lower the data rate that can be achieved and vice versa. This can be clearly seen in the distance of 12 m for NLOS scenario, where the highest data rate value

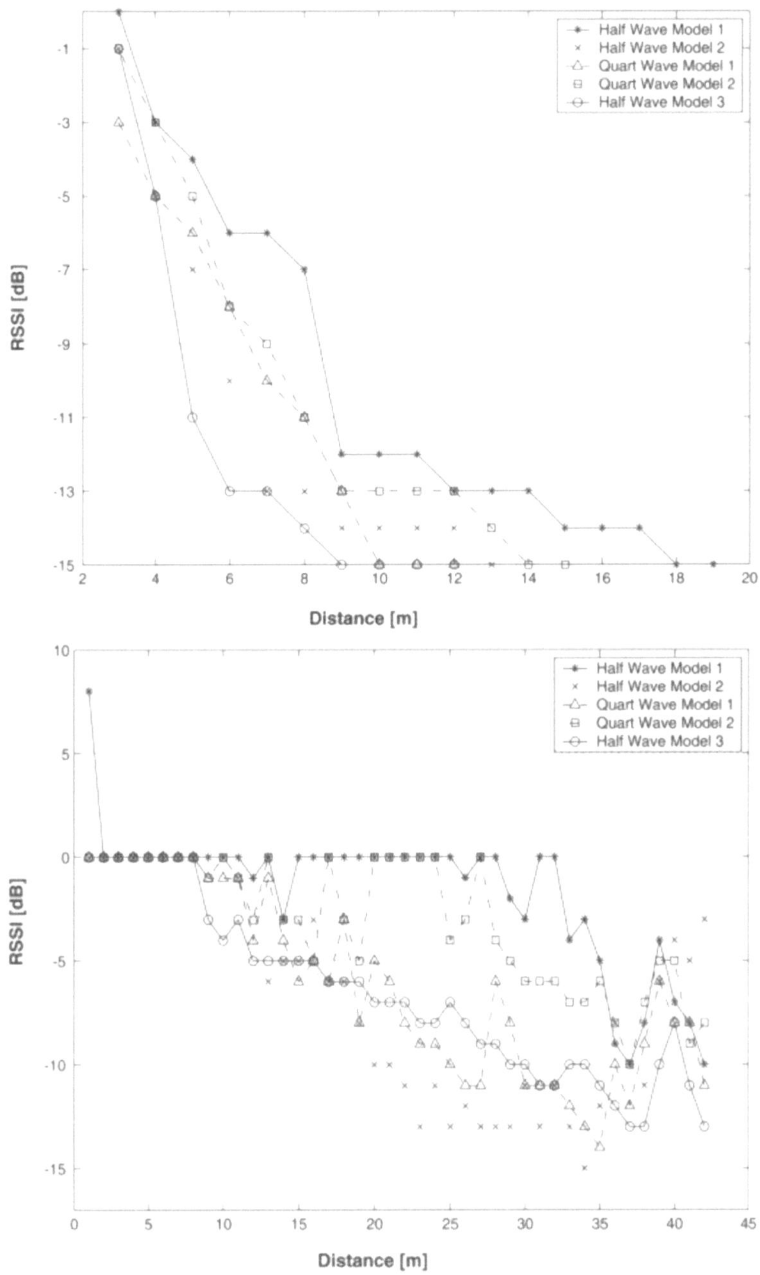

Fig. 2. The signal power measurements results for: NLOS (top figure) and LOS (bottom figure). The RSSI generally drops with increasing the distance between the Master and the Slave.

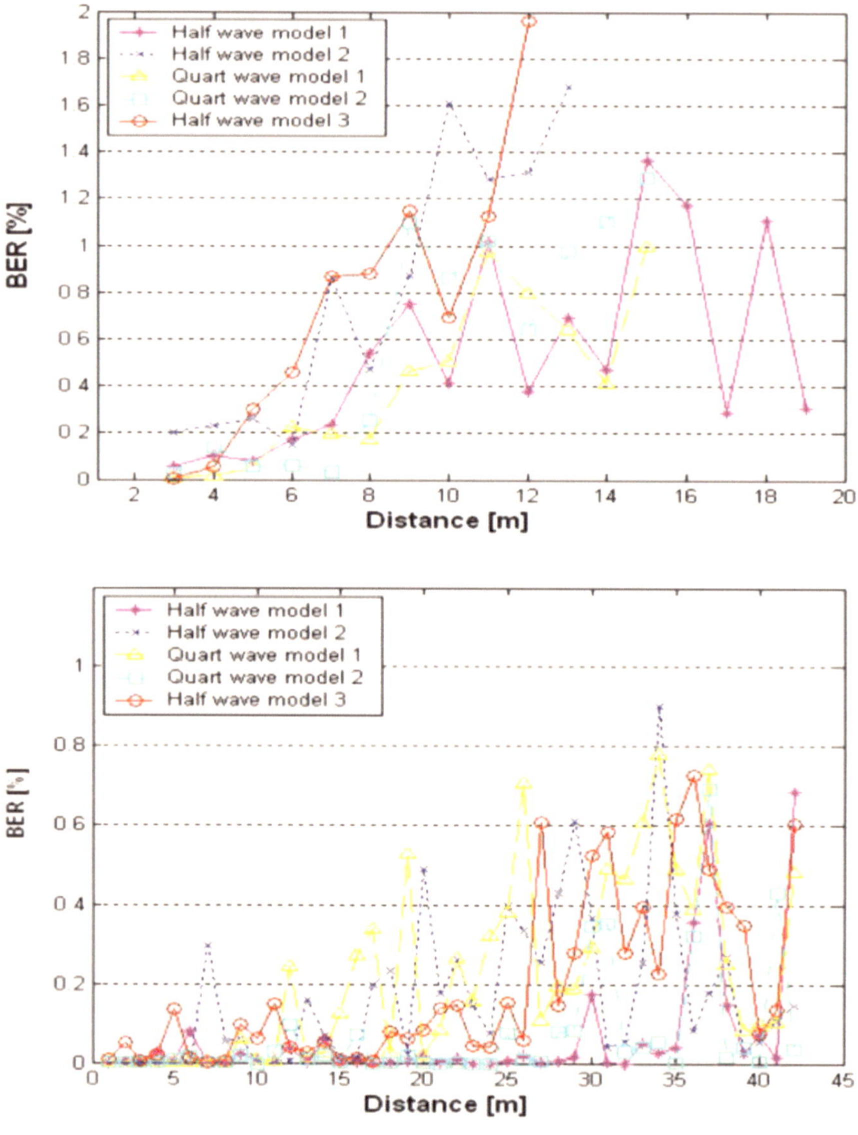

Fig. 3. The BER measurement results for: NLOS (top figure) and LOS (bottom figure). The BER increases with distance and the rapid fluctuations are due to fast fading.

of about 172.2 kbps was obtained by the *Half Wave Model 1* antenna and the lowest data rate value of 169.4 kbps was obtained by the *Half Wave Model 3* antenna. The results of the *Quart Wave Model 2, Quart Wave Model 1* and *Half Wave Model 3* antennas has followed a similar pattern by giving intermediate data rate values as was the case for RSSI and BER scenarios. A similar pattern of results (not shown) were obtained from LOS scenario.

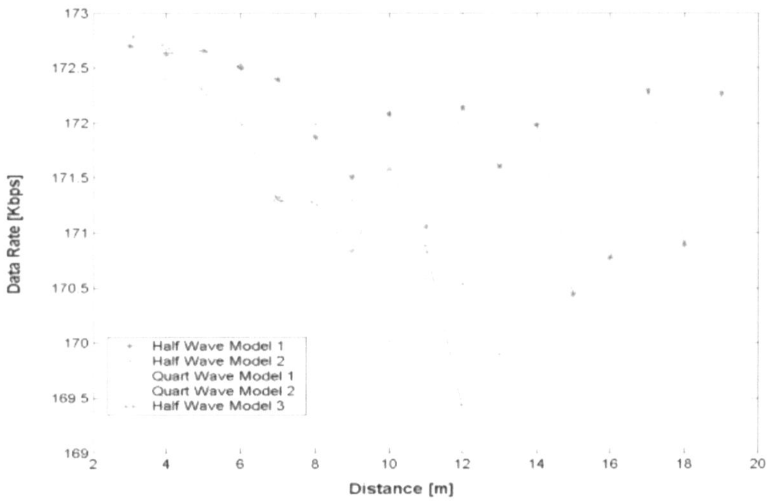

Fig. 4. The data rate measurement results for NLOS. Only a slight drop in data rates is obtained with increasing distance between the transmitter and receiver.

4. Conclusions

In this chapter we have presented the results of measurement trials of the Bluetooth link employing different antennas operating at 2.4 GHz in NLOS and LOS propagation scenarios for indoor office environments. The measurement results have shown a noticeable degradation in performance by increasing the distance between the Master and the Slave. It was also shown that a disconnection in the Bluetooth transmission link was obtained at different distances for each antenna, which in turn was dependent on the antenna parameters (gain and the efficiency). We have also explored the effect of the antenna parameters and the relation between BER, signal power and data rate. The indoor trials have revealed that a link with lower BER values provide higher capacity (data rate), less power requirements and better coverage.

5. Appendix: Antenna types

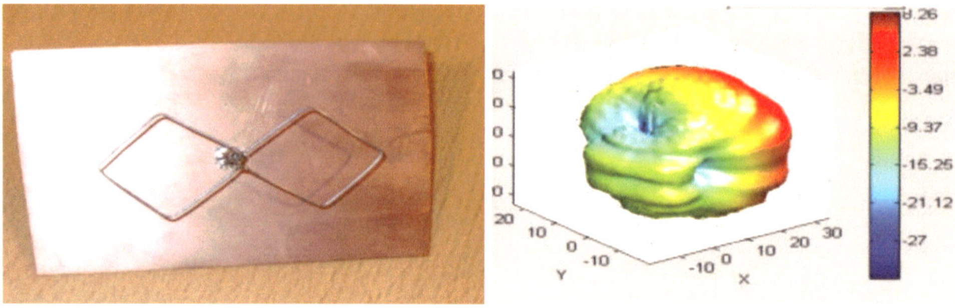

Fig. 5. Antenna type: *Half wave model 1*

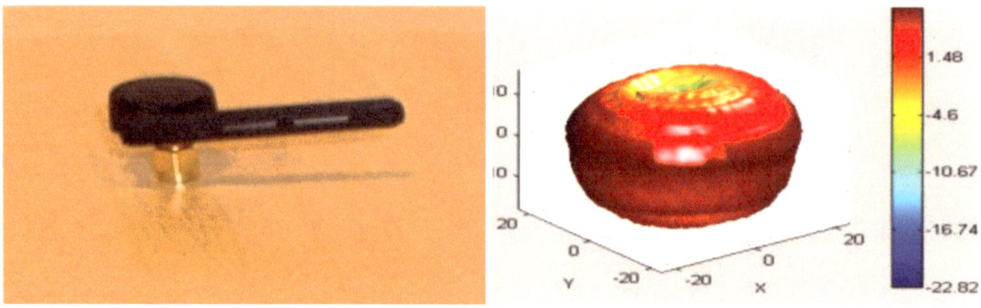

Fig. 6. Antenna type: *Half wave model 2*

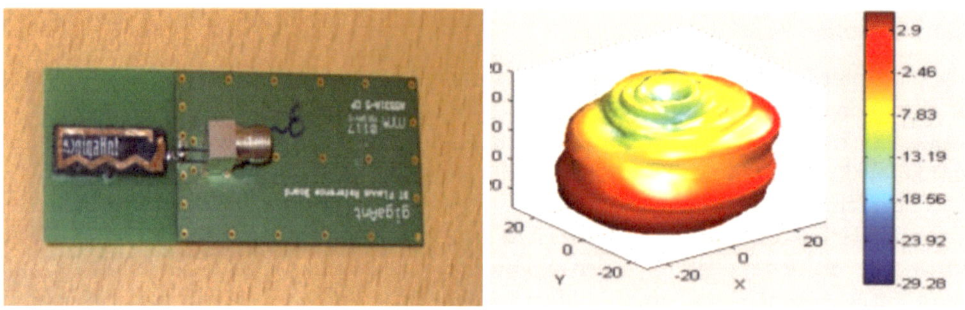

Fig. 7. Antenna type: *Half wave model 3*

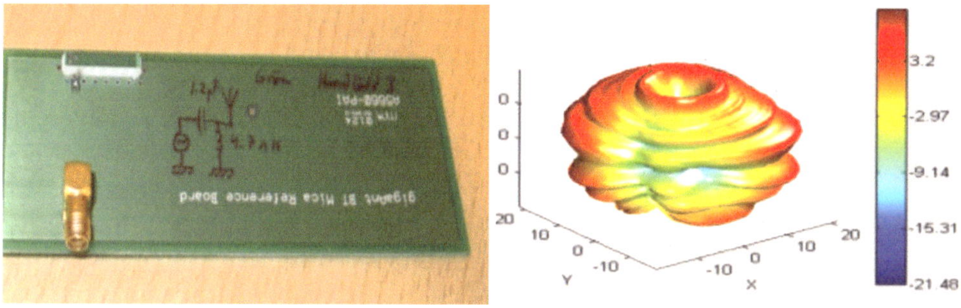

Fig. 8. Antenna type: *Quarter wave model 2*

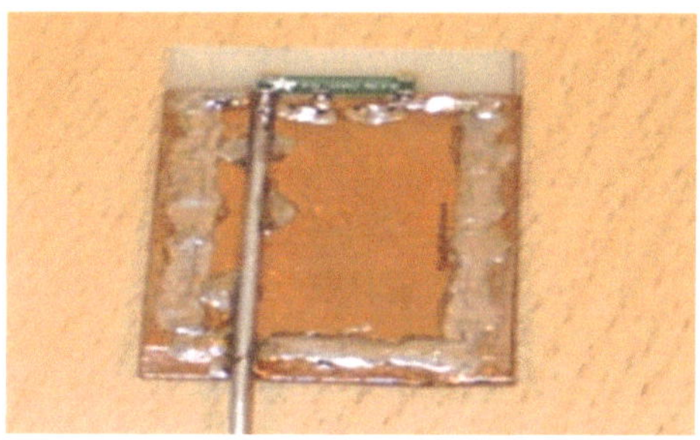

Fig. 9. Antenna type: *Quarter wave model 1*

6. References

Bisdikian, C. (2001). An overview of the bluetooth wireless technology, *IEEE Communications Magazine* Vol. 39(No. 12): 86–94.

Bluetooth (2002). http://www.bluetooth.com, *Bluetooth SIG* .

Haartsen, J. (2000). The bluetooth radio system, *IEEE Personal Communications* Vol. 7(No. 1): 28–36.

Hashemi, H. (1993). The indoor radio propagation channel, *Proceedings of the IEEE* Vol. 81(No. 7): 943–968.

McDermott-Wells, P. (2004). What is bluetooth?, *IEEE Potentials* Vol. 23(No. 5): 33–35.

Miller, B. A. & Bisdikian, C. (2001). *Bluetooth Revealed*, Prentice Hall PTR, Upper Saddle River, NJ.

Mohammed, A. (2002). Advances in signal processing for mobile communication systems, *Special Issue of Wiley's International Journal of Adaptive Control and Signal Processing* Vol. 16(No. 8): 539–540.

Obayashi, S. & Zander, J. (1998). A body-shadowing model for indoor radio communication environments, *IEEE Transactions on Antenna and Propagation* Vol. 46(No. 6): 920–927.

Sander, K. F. & Reed, G. A. (1978). *Transmission and Propagation of Electromagnetic Waves*, Cambridge University Press.

6

Adaptive Antenna Arrays for Ad-Hoc Millimetre-Wave Wireless Communications

Val Dyadyuk, Xiaojing Huang, Leigh Stokes, Joseph Pathikulangara, Andrew R. Weily, Nasiha Nikolic, John D. Bunton and Y. Jay Guo
CSIRO ICT Centre
Australia

1. Introduction

New technologies that employ millimetre-wave frequency bands to achieve high speed wireless links are gaining more attention (Dyadyuk et. al., 2007, 2009b, 2010a; Hirata et. al., 2006; Lockie & Peck, 2009; Kasugi et. al., 2009; Wells, 2009) due to increasing demand for wideband wireless communications. Very wide uncongested spectrum is available in the E—bands (71-76 GHz and 81-86 GHz) recently allocated for wireless communications in USA, Europe, Korea, Russia and Australia. The E-band provides an opportunity for line-of - sight (LOS) links with higher data rates, well suited for fibre replacement and backhaul applications.

Future mobile and ad-hoc communications networks will require higher bandwidth and longer range. An ad-hoc or mobile (e.g. inter-aircraft) network that relies on high gain antennas also requires beam scanning. Adaptive antenna arrays have found a wide rage of applications and are becoming essential parts of wireless communications systems (Abbaspour-Tamijani & Sarabandi, 2003; Do-Hong & Russer, 2004; Gross, 2005; Guo, 2004; Krim & Viberg, 1996; Mailloux, 2005, 2007; Rogstad et al., 2003; Singh et al., 2008). While the spectrum available in the millimetre-wave frequency bands enables multi-gigabit-per second data rates, the practically achievable communication range is limited by several factors. These include the higher atmospheric attenuation at these frequencies and limited output power of monolithic microwave integrated circuits (MMIC) (Doan et al., 2004; Dyadyuk et al., 2008a; Kasper et al., 2009; Floyd et al., 2007; Reynolds et. al., 2006; Vamsi et. al., 2005, Zirath et al., 2004) due to physical constraints. Therefore, the performance of the ad-hoc or mobile millimetre-wave networks requires enhancement by using spatial power combining antenna arrays.

Advantages of spatial power combining arrays for long-range high-speed millimetre-wave LOS links are discussed in Section 2. Combining multiple antennas, each of which has its own low noise amplifier (LNA) or power amplifier (PA), to form an antenna array not only increases the communications range but also enables smart antenna technology to be applied to optimize the system performance. The increased transmission power of an antenna array provides an opportunity to realize longer range point-to-point LOS links, such as those providing wireless connectivity between aircraft and/or between aircraft and ground vehicles or control stations.

A proposed hybrid antenna array concept (Guo et. al., 2009; Dyadyuk & Guo, 2009a; Huang et al., 2009) for high-speed long-range millimeter-wave mobile and ad hoc wireless networks is described in Section 3. The hybrid array consists of a number of analogue sub-arrays and a digital beamformer to overcome the space constraint and digital implementation complexity problem for a large array at mm-wave frequencies.

Section 4 formulates the time- and frequency-domain digital beamforming algorithms proposed for the hybrid antenna arrays (Huang et al., 2010a, 2010b) and discusses their relative merits.

Section 5 describes a small-scale prototype that implements an analogue-beam-formed phased antenna array. The prototype (Dyadyuk & Stokes, 2010a) was developed to demonstrate a communications system with gigabit per second data rates in the E-band using an electronically steerable array as an initial step towards fully ad-hoc communications systems that implement hybrid antenna arrays. The steerable beam receiver and a fixed beam transmitter form a prototype of the E-band communication system that implements an adaptive antenna array. The prototype configuration is flexible and can be used for experimental verification of both analogue and digital beam forming algorithms. The main functional block of the prototype is a four-channel receive RF module integrated with a linear end-fire Quasi-Yagi antenna array.

Section 6 describes the design, EM simulations and tests results of a Quasi-Yagi antenna array (Deal et al. 2000; Nikolic & Weily, 2009, 2010) used in the receive RF module described above. Array element spacing was 2 mm (or 0.48 wavelengths at the carrier frequency) to suppress the appearance of grating lobes for scanning angles up to ± 42 degrees.

The test results of the E-band prototype that implements a phased antenna array are given in Section 7. Measured radiation patterns for the analogue beamformed array are presented and compared with EM simulation predictions. Beam steering accuracy of 1 degree has been achieved with 6-bit digital phase shift and magnitude control at IF. A small ad-hoc point-to-point link has also been tested with reasonable Bit Error Rate (BER) measured for selected angles using 8PSK modulation at 1.5Gbps data rate with the receive array beam formed in the direction of arrival of the transmitted signal. Digital beamforming experiments have also been conducted on this prototype using a wideband frequency-domain algorithm showing antenna array patterns very close to those obtained with analogue beamforming and simulations. A quantitative analysis of the digital beam forming results is beyond the scope of this chapter and can be found in Dyadyuk et al., 2010c; Huang et al., 2010b.

Finally, conclusions are drawn in Section 8. Analytical results were experimentally verified using a steerable receive array demonstrator in the E-band.

The future research objectives and challenges of practical implementation of large adaptive millimetre-wave antenna arrays have also been addressed. This work represents a stepping stone towards realisation of high-data rate millimetre-wave communication systems employing hybrid antenna arrays.

2. Spatial power combining arrays at mm-wave frequencies

With the advance in digital signal processing techniques, the adaptive antenna array is becoming an essential part of wireless communications systems (Guo, 2004; Mailoux, 2005). The use of adaptive antenna arrays for long range millimeter wave ad-hoc communication networks is particularly critical due to increased free space loss and reduced level of practically achievable output power relative to those available in lower frequency bands. An ad-hoc or mobile network that relies on high gain antennas also requires beam scanning. The antenna beam can be steered to a desired direction with appropriate beam forming. Passive phased arrays generally suffer from losses in combining networks that are very high at the mm-wave frequencies.

In a spatial power-combining phased array transmitter, each individual element has a power amplifier (PA). To generate a pencil beam in a particular direction, the signal radiated from each element is delayed electronically in order to compensate for differences in the free-space propagation time from the different elements. In a spatial power-combining transmitter with multiple radiating elements, this coherent addition increases the Effective Isotropic Radiated Power (EIRP) in two ways: firstly via the increase in directivity due to the increased electrical aperture; and secondly, via the increase in total radiated power through the increased number of power amplifiers. So if we take the efficiency of the spatial power combining transmitter to be η, for an array of N elements, each generating an EIRP of P watts, the EIRP of the transmitter is $\eta N^2 P$ watts. Assuming an efficiency of 100%, the increase in EIRP in going from 1 to N elements is 20 $log(N)$ dB. These results are plotted in Figure 1, where the equivalent EIRP of passive and active arrays is plotted versus number of array elements.

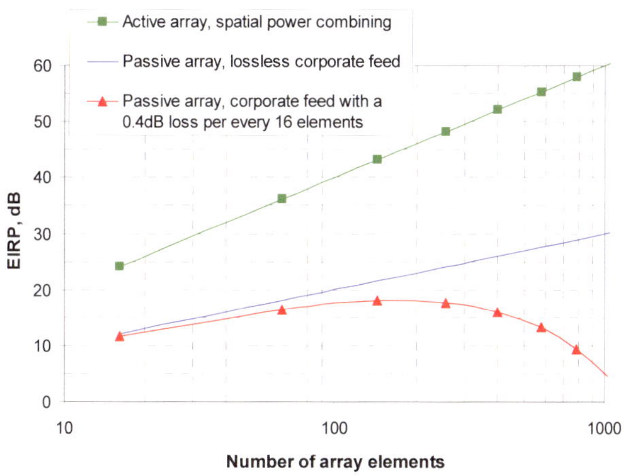

Fig. 1. Active versus passive phased array transmitters

It should be noted that the data for a lossless corporate feed plotted in Fig. 1 is a theoretical assumption only. It does not take into account the power combining loss for the passive array with a single PA. The combining loss is hard to predict as it largely depends on number of elements, operating frequency and other parameters of a specific design, and could be in the order of several dB. An example shown in Fig. 1 that uses an optimistic assumption of only 0.4dB loss per every 16-element block (e.g., 0.1 dB per stage using a binary combining structure) illustrates a low efficiency of passive power combining. Thus, EIRP is rapidly reduced for a moderate-size array (when the number of element is more that 300), and larger passive arrays would be impractical.

Where the receive terminal is equipped with an identical antenna array having a low noise amplifier associated with each element, the effective SNR increases proportionally to N^3 or more (due to reduction of the effective receiver noise dependent on the degree of the correlation).

To achieve wide bandwidth with a phased array requires detailed calculation of mutual coupling between elements, since this determines the impedance match at each element and the radiation pattern of the complete array, and these two are interrelated. The apparent impedance match at each element can vary widely as the main beam is scanned. In general, the array bandwidth is limited by array considerations that are directly related to the array element size, and the impedance bandwidth of an isolated array element, which is also related to the element size by basic electromagnetic considerations.
For a directly-radiating phased array, the element spacing is determined by the need to suppress grating lobes, that is, additional main lobes in the radiation pattern of the array. For a linear phased array with the main beam scanned at an angle θ_0 from broadside, the equation for grating lobes is easily determined (Mailloux, 2005) as:

$$\frac{d}{\lambda} = \frac{k}{\sin\theta_0 - \sin\theta_{gl}} \tag{1}$$

where d_s is the array spacing, λ is the wavelength, θ_{gl} is the angle of the grating lobe and k is the order of the grating lobe. If the maximum scan angle is taken to be θ_0, then we can suppress the appearance of grating lobes so long as the array element spacing satisfies the condition for the smallest operating wavelength λ_{min}:

$$\frac{d_s}{\lambda_{\min}} \leq \frac{1}{1+\sin\theta_0} \tag{2}$$

For a uniform square lattice array with element size equal to the element spacing d_s, the ratio of upper to lower operating frequency is related to the maximum scan angle by:

$$\frac{f_{\max}}{f_{\min}} = \frac{d_s}{1+\sin\theta_0} \tag{3}$$

Thus for larger, wideband elements the bandwidth is limited by array effects, whereas for small, resonant elements, the element bandwidth typically restricts the overall array bandwidth. In an ideal broadband phased array, a high-gain pencil beam is generated by a true time delay at each element that compensates exactly for the free-space propagation delay. Developing a low-loss, linear delay line directly at mm-wave frequencies is very challenging. Equivalent delay can also be implemented by delay/phase-shift in the IF and LO channels, or implemented digitally. For a relatively narrow-band system, implementing the delay as an equivalent phase shift at the centre frequency is a simple option, and then many of the problems of mm-wave phase shifters can be avoided by implementing the phase shift directly on the IF or LO. When an array is scanned with phase shift instead of true time delay, the position of the main beam varies with frequency, and this effect becomes more pronounced the further the beam is scanned from the array normal. To calculate the array bandwidth, a common definition used is to define the upper and lower frequencies of the band as the frequencies where the main beam has moved from the desired scan angle to the 3dB points of the beam. Then, for a large uniform array, the fractional bandwidth B is given by:

$$B \approx \frac{0.866\,\lambda}{D\sin\theta_0} \tag{5}$$

where D is the array diameter, and θ_0 is the maximum scan angle. The corresponding gain G at the maximum scan angle is related to the physical area A by:

$$G \approx \eta \frac{4\pi}{\lambda^2} A \cos\theta_0 \tag{6}$$

where η is the efficiency.

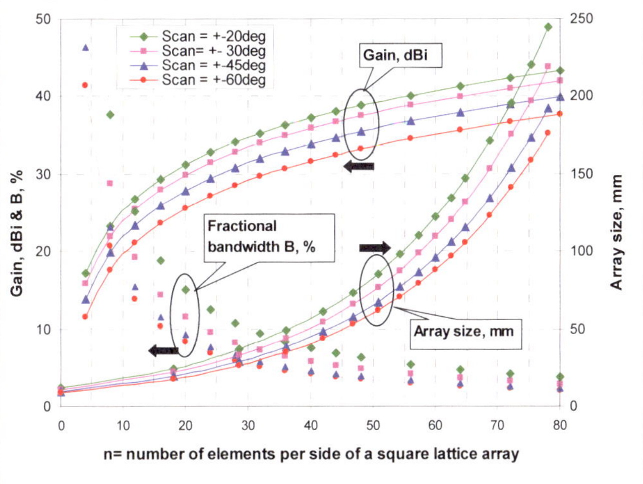

Fig. 2. Array gain, size and fractional bandwidth calculated for selected scan angles at for a centre frequency of 73GHz

At the mm-wave frequencies, phase-only beam steering becomes practical for this type of transmitting array since the size of a high EIRP array remains moderate. This is illustrated in Fig. 2 where the square lattice array gain, size and fractional bandwidth are calculated at the centre frequency of 73 GHz using equations (1 - 6) and assuming a maximum scan angle of 60 degrees, and an efficiency of 1. It can be noted that for a 1000-element array, the fractional bandwidth exceeds 7% at the scan angles within ±45°. This allows for a phase-only beam steering over the full 5 GHz wide RF channels available in the E-band.

3. Hybrid antenna array

Small size, high EIRP active antenna arrays would be suitable for long range inter-aircraft communications as atmospheric attenuation at millimeter-wave frequencies is low at elevated altitudes (above the rain height). Figure 3a shows the predicted communication range for a point-to-point link (Dyadyuk et al., 2010a) equipped with active square lattice $N=n^2$ element arrays. Operating frequency is 73GHz, transmit power is 15 dBm per array element, reference atmospheres and other link specification details are available in Dyadyuk et al., 2010a.

There are two major technical problems to be solved for practical realisation of such systems: the tight space constraints and beamforming complexity. As antenna elements must be spaced closely together to prevent grating lobes, array element spacing is extremely small (about 2 mm in the E-band) as illustrated in Fig. 3b.

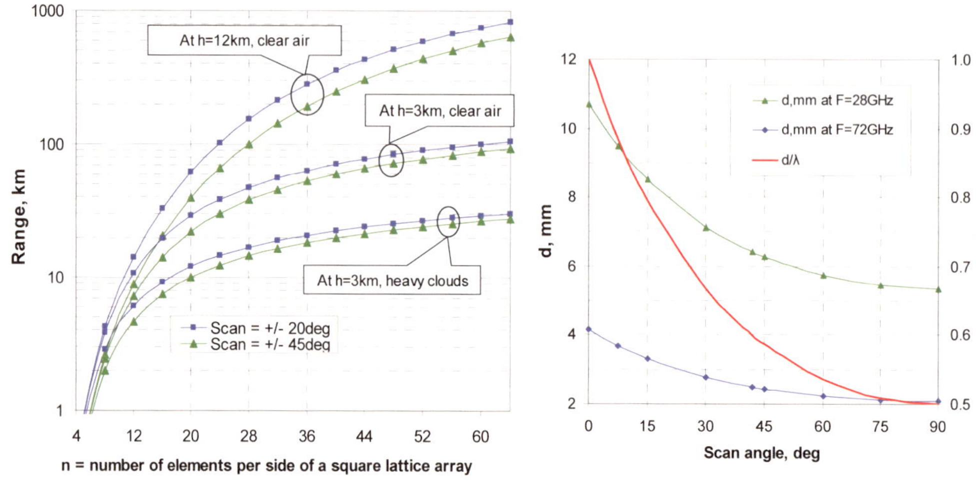

a) b)

Fig. 3. a) Predicted range of a PTP link equipped with active antenna arrays calculated for 1GHz bandwidth, centre frequency of 73GHz and transmitted power of 15 dBm per element; b) Theoretical maximum array element spacing

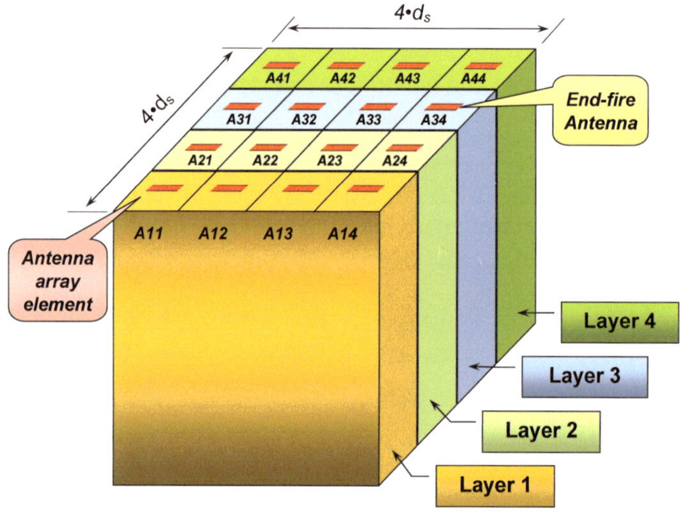

Fig. 4. Configuration of a 4x4 element square lattice sub-array. Each "layer" represents a four-element sub-module integrated on a common printed circuit board

The RF front end components, such as the low noise amplifier (or power amplifier), frequency converter, local oscillator (LO), as well as the intermediate frequency (IF) or baseband circuitry in the analogue signal chain should be tightly packed behind the antenna elements. Difficulties of integration of the RF front end components can be illustrated on a simple example of a commercial GaAs low noise amplifier ALH459 available from Hittite Microwave (Velocium product line). While the width of a bare die is 1.6mm, an additional space needed to accommodate the DC bias circuitry (using single-layer ceramic capacitors

and resistors) increases the width to 3.5-3.7 mm, which is greater than the maximum antenna element spacing required. Although there has been a rapid progress in the CMOS and SiGe technology for the mm-wave applications (Cathelin et al., 2007; Floyd et al., 2007; Grass et al., (2007); Laskin et al., 2007; Pfeiffer et al., 2008; Reynolds et al., 2007) and advanced multi-chip module integration technologies (Posada et al., 2007), GaAs MMIC are likely to be a preferable technology for the E-band low noise and power amplifiers for some years to come.
A schematic representation of a configuration of a 4 by 4 element sub-array with element spacing d_s is shown in Fig. 4. End-fire antenna array elements are preferable to broadside elements for a planar integration of the antenna elements with the RF chains.

Thus, the area of a 4 by 4 sub-array with IF beam forming implemented in the E-band is about 100 mm^2 (d_s =2.5mm) and it would provide a tight, but feasible accommodation for each the IF, LO, power and control circuits. An arrangement shown in Fig. 4 allows for staggered placement of the adjacent MMICs within each layer. A number of such analogue sub-arrays can be controlled by a digital beam former to form a hybrid antenna array.

4. Beamforming algorithms for a hybrid adaptive array

Since the antenna elements in an array must be placed close together to prevent grating lobes, the analogue components, such as the LNA or PA and the down or up converter associated with each antenna element, must be tightly packed behind the antenna element. This space constraint appears to be a major engineering challenge at mm-wave frequencies. For example, at 74 GHz frequency, the required element spacing is only about 2 mm. With the current MMIC technology, the practical implementation of such a digital antenna array remains very difficult (Doan et al., 2004; Rogstad et al., 2003). Another issue with pure digital beamformers is the excessive demand on real time signal processing for high gain antennas. To achieve an antenna gain of over 30 dBi, for instance, one may need more than 1000 antenna elements. This makes most beamforming algorithms impractical for commercial applications. Furthermore, to perform wideband digital beamforming, each signal from/to an antenna element is normally divided into a number of narrow-band signals and processed separately, which also adds to the cost of digital signal processing significantly. Therefore, a full digital implementation of large, wideband antenna arrays at mm-wave frequencies is simply unrealistic (Gross, 2005). Finally, although multipath is not a major concern for the above mentioned LOS applications, the relative movement between transmitters and receivers will bring other technical challenges such as fast Doppler frequency shift and time-varying angle-of-arrival (AoA) of the incident beam.
A novel hybrid adaptive receive antenna array is proposed using a time-domain (Huang et al., 2009) and frequency-domain (Huang et al., 20010b; Dyadyuk et al., 2010c) approaches to solve the digital implementation complexity problem in large arrays for long range high data rate mm-wave communications. In this hybrid antenna array, a large number of antenna elements are grouped into analogue sub-arrays. Each sub-array uses an analogue beamformer to produce a beamformed sub-array signal, and all sub-array signals are combined using a digital beamformer to produce the final beamformed signal (Guo et al., 2009). Each element in a sub-array has its own radio frequency (RF) chain and employs an analogue phase shifting device at the intermediate frequency (IF) stage. Signals received by all elements in a sub-array are combined after analogue phase shifting, and the analogue

beamformed signal is down-converted to baseband and then converted into the digital domain. In this way, the complexity of the digital beamformer is reduced by a factor equal to the number of elements in a sub-array. For example, for a 1024 element hybrid array of 64 sub-arrays each having 16 elements, only 64 inputs to the digital beamformer are necessary, and the complexity is reduced to one sixteenth for algorithms of linear complexity, such as the least mean square (LMS) algorithm. The cost of the digital hardware is also significantly reduced.

The digital beamformer estimates the AoA information to control the phases of the phase shifters in the analogue sub-arrays and also adjusts the digital weights applied to the sub-array output signals to form a beam. Sub-array technology has been used over the past decades (Abbaspour-Tamijani & Sarabandi, 2003; Goffer et al., 1994; Haupt, 2007; Mailloux, 2005, 2007). Prior ideas include employing a time delay unit to each phased sub-array for bandwidth enhancement, and eliminating phase shifters in the sub-array for applications requiring only limited-field-of-view.

The proposed hybrid antenna array concept differs in that it is a new architecture allowing the analogue sub-arrays and the low complexity digital beamformer to interact with each other to accommodate the current digital signal processing capability and MMIC technology, thus enabling the implementation of a large adaptive antenna array. Two time-domain Doppler-resilient adaptive angle-of-arrival estimation and beamforming algorithms were proposed (Huang et al., 2009) for two configurations of sub-arrays: the interleaved and the side-by-side sub-array. The formulated differential beam tracking (DBT) and the differential beam search (DBS) algorithms have been evaluated. Simulations based on a 64 element hybrid planar array of four 4 by 4 element subarrays were used to evaluate the DBT and DBSD algorithms performance. Recursive mean square error (MSE) bounds of the developed algorithms were also analyzed.

The DBT algorithm was proposed for the hybrid array of interleaved sub-arrays. It does not have a phase ambiguity problem and converges quickly. The DBS algorithm was proposed for the side-by-side sub-arrays. It scans all the possible beams to solve the phase ambiguity problem, but it converges slowly. Both the DBT and DBS algorithms require the computation of sub-array cross-correlations in the time-domain. For practical implementation reasons, a hybrid antenna array of side-by-side sub-arrays is preferable.

Performing AoA estimation and beam forming in the frequency-domain would significantly reduce the implementation complexity and also mitigate the wideband effects on the hybrid array. A frequency-domain beamforming algorithm has been proposed and successfully evaluated on a small-scale linear array demonstrator. Simulation results show that the performance of the proposed algorithms is dependent on the fractional bandwidth of the hybrid array. Detailed description of the digital beamforming algorithms can be found in Dyadyuk et al., 1010c; Huang et al., 2010b. The remainder of this chapter will focus on the analogue sub-array as a part of a hybrid array.

5. Ad-hoc communication system prototype

5.1 System block diagram

The prototype has been developed to demonstrate a communications system with gigabit per second data rates using an electronically steerable array as an initial step towards fully ad-hoc communications systems. The prototype configuration is flexible and can be used for experimental verification of both analogue and digital beam forming algorithms. The scannable beam receiver and a fixed beam transmitter form a prototype of the E-band communication system that implements an adaptive antenna array. Block diagram Fig. 5 shows the configuration for analogue beam forming experiments.

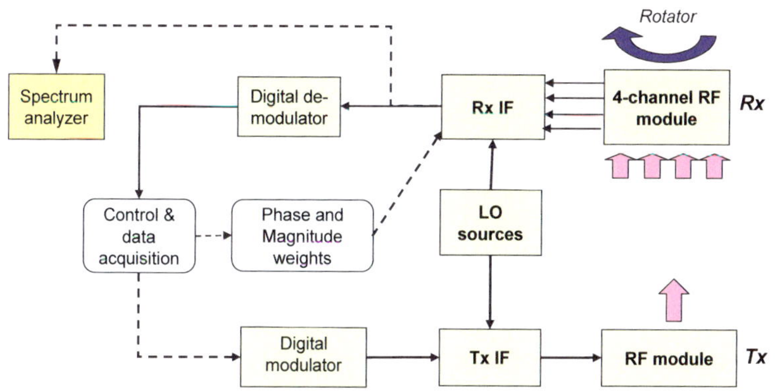

Fig. 5. Block diagram of the E-band communication system that implements a steerable receive antenna array

The receive RF module is mounted on a rotator providing mechanical steering in the azimuth plane for the array pattern measurement. Both the receiver and transmitter use dual frequency conversion with the baseband (IF2) frequency 1 – 2 GHz that enables re-use of the digital modulator and demodulator reported earlier in Dyadyuk et al., 2007.

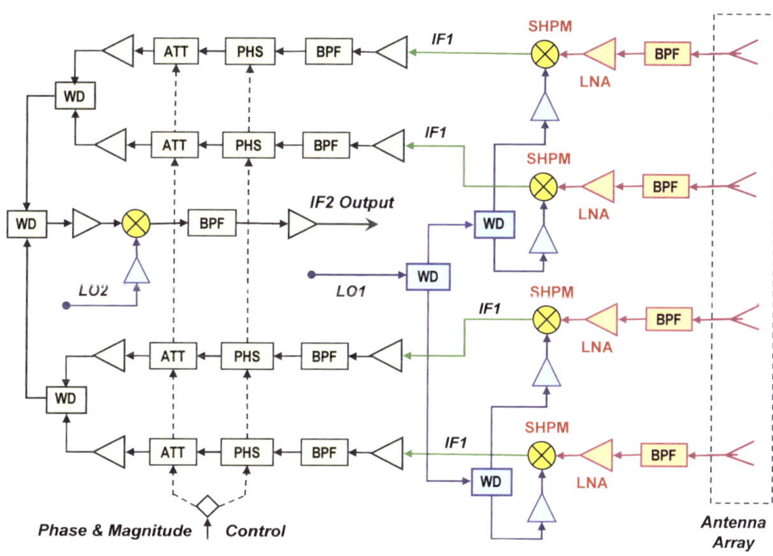

Fig. 6. Simplified schematic of the E-band steerable receive array configured for analogue beam-forming

The receive IF module (Rx IF) has been developed in two versions. In the digital beam forming configuration, each of the IF channels is connected to a digital beam former that replaces the de-modulator. For the analogue beam forming configuration all IF outputs are combined before de-modulation as shown in Fig. 6 where BPF, LNA, SHPM, WD, PHS and

ATT denotes a band-pass filter, low noise amplifier, sub-harmonically pumped mixer, Wilkinson divider, phase shifter and attenuator respectively.
Phase and magnitude controls for each channel are implemented at IF using 6-bit digital phase shifters HMC649LP6 and attenuators HMC4214LP3 available from Hittite Microwave Corporation. They are used to equalize the channels frequency responses (initial calibration) and to apply required beam forming weights.
A single channel transmit module has been built using the up-converter (Dyadyuk et al., 2008a) that uses a sub-harmonically pumped (SHPM) GaAs Schottky diode mixer (Dyadyuk et al., 2008b) with an addition of a commercial band-pass filter and a medium power amplifier, and a corrugated horn antenna with the gain of 22.5 dBi. Measured to the antenna input of the RF transmitter (Dyadyuk & Guo, 2009), the small signal conversion gain and the output power at -1 dB gain compression was 35±1 dB and +15±1 dBm respectively over the operating frequency range of 71.5 - 72.5 GHz.

5.2 RF module of a steerable receive array

The main functional block of the prototype is a four-channel dual-conversion receive RF module integrated with a four-element linear end-fire quasi-Yagi antenna array described below in Section 6. Figure 7 shows a photograph of the assembled RF module (a) and typical measured conversion gain for each channel (b).

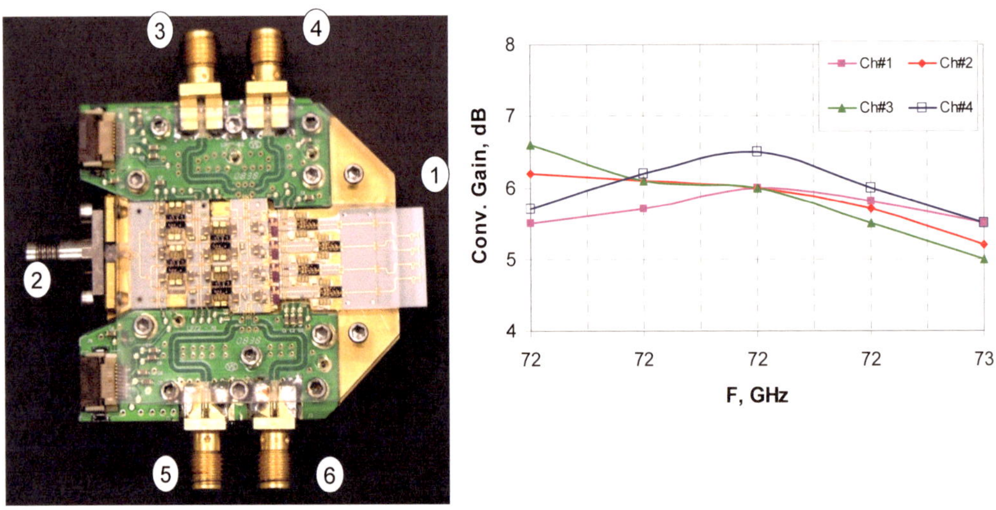

a) b)

Fig. 7. a) Photograph of the RF module assembly where: 1 is the antenna array; 2 is the LO input; 3-6 are IF outputs; b) Typical measured conversion gain (RF to IF1) for each channel

The RF module uses sub-harmonic frequency converters (Dyadyuk et al., 2008b) at the LO frequency of 38 GHz. For each channel we have used a combination of CSIRO and commercial-off the-shelf MMICs similar to those reported earlier for a single-channel receiver (Dyadyuk et al., 2008a). The IF pre-amplifiers, interconnect, matching, and group delay equalization circuits have been developed using a standard commercial thin-film process on ceramic substrate. It includes 16 MMICs, 12 types of microwave boards (on 127um Alumina substrate), 140 microwave passives, and about 400 wire-bond connections.

The receiver is usable over the frequency range of 71 to 76 GHz at the sub-harmonic LO of 38 to 39 GHz and intermediate frequency 1 to 7 GHz. Typical conversion gain was 6 ± 1 dB over the operating RF and IF frequency range of 71.5 -72.5 GHz and 3.5 -4.5 GHz respectively. The maximum magnitude imbalance between each of four channels was below ± 1.5 dB.

6. Quasi-Yagi antenna and linear array for E-band applications

This section of the chapter describes a single quasi-Yagi antenna element and four-element linear arrays designed to operate in the 71-76 GHz band, using planar microstrip technology. Four linear arrays, each containing four elements and having a different beamforming network are designed, fabricated and tested. For testing of the arrays, a suitable microstrip-to-waveguide transition was designed and its calculated reflection coefficient and transmission loss are included. The simulated results for a single element and the measured and simulated reflection coefficient, radiation patterns and gain for each array are presented.

6.1 Quasi-Yagi element

The element used to design the array is based on the antenna presented in Kaneda et al., 1998; Deal et al., 2000; Kaneda et al., 2002. As reported by Deal et al., 2000, a quasi-Yagi antenna is a compact and simple planar antenna that can operate over an extremely wide frequency bandwidth (of the order of 50%) with good radiation characteristics in terms of beam pattern, front-to-back ratio and cross-polarization. The compact size of the single element ($<\lambda_0/2$ by $\lambda_0/2$ for entire substrate) and low mutual coupling between the elements make it ideal for use in an array. The antenna is compatible for integration with microstrip-based monolithic-microwave-integrated circuits (MMICs).

The quasi-Yagi antenna is fabricated on a single dielectric substrate with metallization on both sides, as shown in Fig. 8. The top metallization consists of a microstrip feed, a broad-band microstrip-to-coplanar stripline (CPS) balun and two dipoles. One dipole is the driver element fed directly by the CPS and the second dipole (the director) is parasitically fed. The metallization on the bottom plane forms the microstrip ground, and is truncated to create the reflector element for the antenna. The driver on the top plane simultaneously directs the antenna propagation toward the endfire direction, and acts as an impedance-matching parasitic element. The driver element may also be implemented using a folded dipole to give greater flexibility in the design of the driver impedance value and to enable use on a liquid crystal polymer substrate (Nikolic et al., 2009; Nikolic et al, 2010).

For this application, the quasi-Yagi antenna is fabricated on an Alumina substrate with following specifications: dielectric thickness 127μm, metallization thickness 3μm, dielectric permittivity ε_r=9.9 and loss tangent, tan δ = 0.0003.

The single element is optimized using CST Microwave Studio to improve the return loss over a wide frequency bandwidth centred at 72 GHz. The antenna dimensions and schematic configuration are shown in Fig. 8. The total area of the substrate is approximately 2.5 mm by 3 mm.

The impedance bandwidth (defined as return loss greater than 10 dB) of the single element shown in Fig. 9a, calculated using CST Microwave Studio, extends from 50.1 - 81.4 GHz.

The co- and cross-polar radiation pattern for two principle planes at 72 GHz is shown in Fig. 9b. The realized gain of the single element is 5.4 dBi from 71 - 76 GHz.

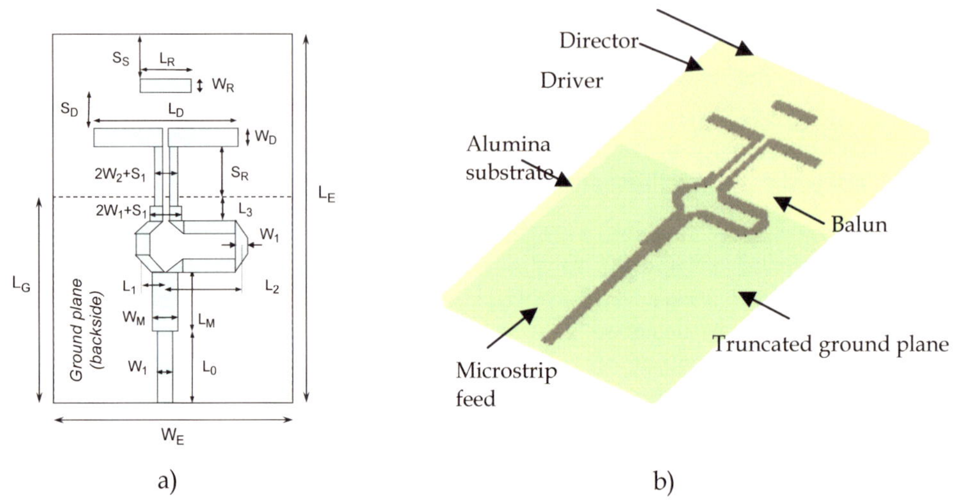

Fig. 8. Schematic of the quasi-Yagi antenna array element. L_E=3, W_E=2.5, W_1=0.12, L_0=0.45, L_G=1.54, L_M=0.54, W_M=0.205, L_1=0.22, L_2=0.7, L_3=0.1, S_1=0.06, W_2=0.06, L_D=1.29, L_R=0.488, W_D=0.12, W_R=0.12, S_R=0.516, S_D=0.323, S_S=0.383 (all dimensions in mm), substrate 127 um Alumina (ε_r=9.9, $tan\delta$=0.0003). b) Perspective view of a quasi-Yagi antenna

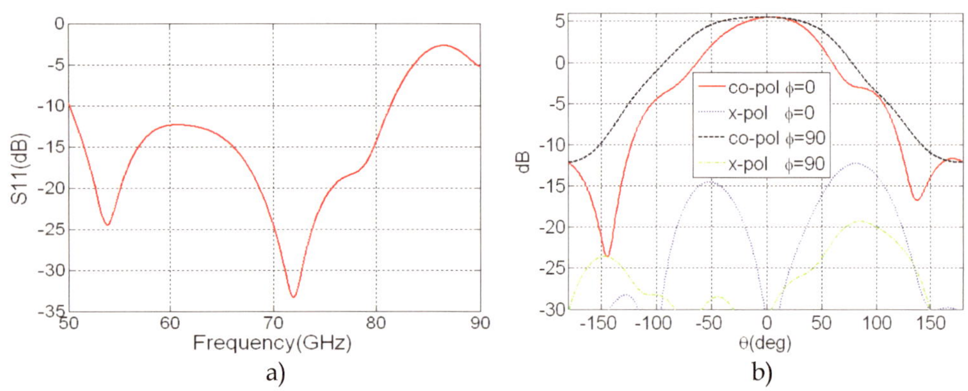

Fig. 9. a) Predicted reflection coefficient and b) radiation pattern at 72 GHz of the quasi-Yagi antenna shown in Fig. 8

6.2 Design of the arrays of quasi-Yagi antenna

The initial design of the four-element linear array was completed using the results for the radiation pattern of a single quasi-Yagi antenna multiplied by the array factor. The array factor is calculated assuming a linear array of equally spaced and uniformly excited elements. The spacing between the elements of $d=0.48\lambda_0$, shown in Fig. 10, was selected to minimise the appearance of grating lobes. The mutual coupling between the elements is presented in Fig. 11a.

The array factor for a uniformly excited four-element linear array with equal phase shift between each two consecutive elements is calculated from (Stutzman & Thiele, 1981)

$$AF = \frac{\sin(2\psi)}{\sin\left(\frac{1}{2}\psi\right)}; \text{ where } \psi = kd\cos\theta + \beta; \; k = \frac{2\pi}{\lambda_0}; \qquad 7)$$

The maximum of the array factor AF occurs for $\psi=0$. Let θ_m be the angle for which the array factor is maximal. Then, for the angle θ_m, measured from the line along which the array elements are placed, the required element-to-element phase shift β in the excitations is given by

$$\beta = -kd\cos\theta_m \qquad (8)$$

Assuming that the spacing between the elements is $d=0.48\lambda_0$, the required phase shift β is calculated using (2) and the results are summarized in Table 1.

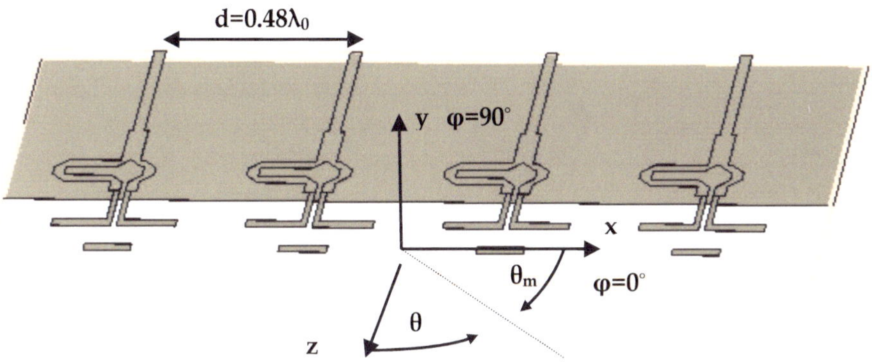

Fig. 10. Four-element linear array of quasi-Yagi antennas

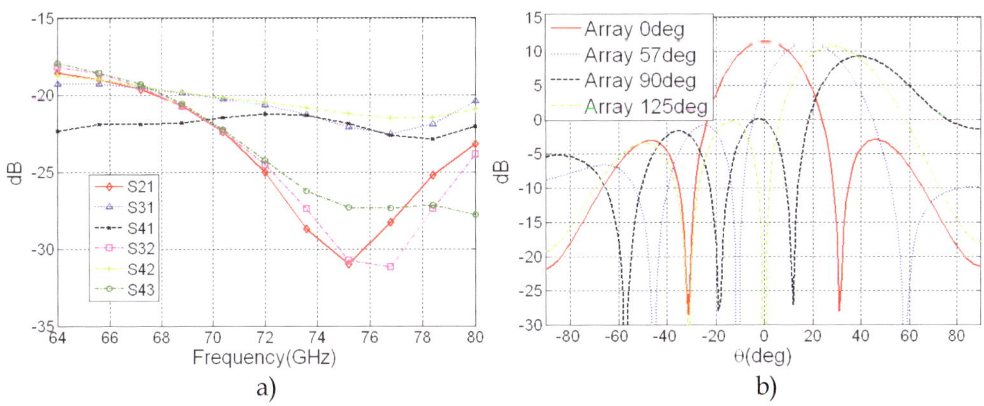

Fig. 11. a) Calculated mutual coupling between elements of the four-element linear array shown in Fig. 10. b) Calculated radiation pattern of the four-element linear array for the φ=0° plane assuming different scanning angles

Array Description	θ	θ_m=90°- θ	β
Array 0deg	0°	90°	0°
Array 57deg	~20°	~70°	-57°
Array 90deg	~30°	~60°	-90°
Array 125deg	~40°	~50°	-125°

Table 1. The phase shift β between the array elements calculated using (2) and different angles θ_m

Using the values of the phase shift β, presented in Table 1, the radiation pattern of the four-element linear array is calculated in CST MWS and the results are shown in Fig. 11b. The next step was to design the microstrip feed networks to produce the required inter-element phase difference β, given in Table 1. Four microstrip feed networks were designed using simple T-junction power dividers and quarter-wavelength matching sections, as shown in Fig. 12.

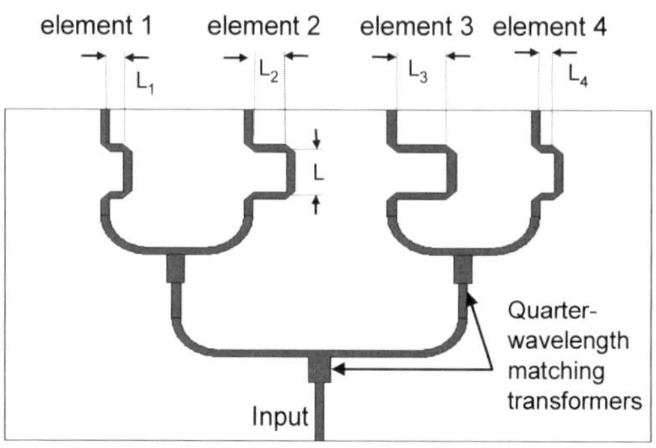

Fig. 12. Plan view of the microstrip feed network with equal amplitude and phase shift between the outputs

Three feed networks were designed to provide equal amplitudes at all elements and the element to element phase shift of β=57°, β=90° and β=125°. The required phase shift was achieved using microstrip lines L_1, L_2, L_3 and L_4, shown in Fig. 12 and for each array these lengths were optimized at 72 GHz. L=0.65 mm was selected for all arrays. For the array with the main beam pointing in the z-direction the feed network is designed using $L_1 = L_2 = L_3 = L_4 = 0$.

6.3 Microstrip-to-waveguide transition

In order to measure the network parameters and the radiation pattern of the array a suitable transition between the microstrip line and WR-15 waveguide has been optimized at 72 GHz. The configuration of the microstrip-to-waveguide transition is shown in Fig. 13a. Inner dimensions of the WR-15 waveguide are 3.76 mm by 1.88 mm, and its recommended operating frequency is from 50 GHz to 75 GHz. The important design parameters of the transition are the slot size in the waveguide wall, distance from the probe to the waveguide short-circuit, the length of the probe and the size of the rectangular cap at the end of the probe. Calculated results for the reflection and transmission coefficients are presented in Fig. 13b. Predicted return loss is better that 10 dB over the 60-80 GHz band and the transmission loss is less than 0.15 dB over the same band.

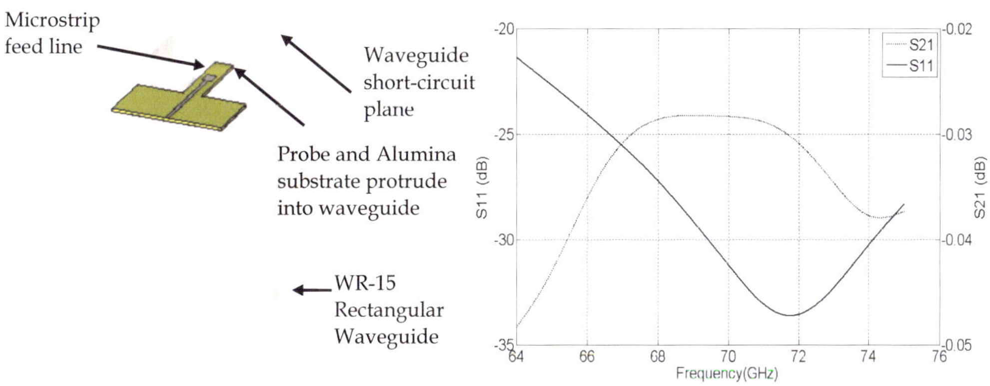

Fig. 13. a) Waveguide-to-microstrip transition b) Predicted reflection and transmission coefficients of the waveguide-to-microstrip transition

6.4 Measured results

Four separate linear quasi-Yagi arrays with integrated microstrip feed networks and microstrip-to-waveguide transitions were fabricated and tested. The layouts of two arrays are shown in Fig. 14.

The arrays were fabricated and bonded to the brass fixture blocks using conductive epoxy by the CSIRO Gigahertz Packaging Laboratory. The mechanical fixture design for the arrays is shown in Fig. 15a. Network measurements were undertaken from 68-76 GHz in the CSIRO Gigahertz Testing Laboratory using a HP 8510C VNA.

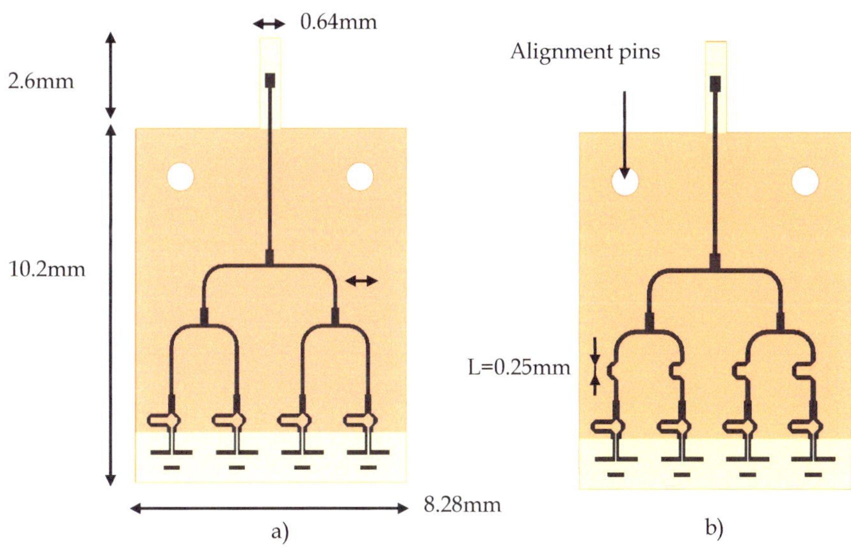

Fig. 14. Layouts of: a) Array-0°, and b) Array-57°

The measured reflection coefficients of the arrays are shown in Fig. 15b. For all arrays, the measured reflection coefficient was lower than -10 dB in the frequency bandwidth of 70.2-76 GHz.

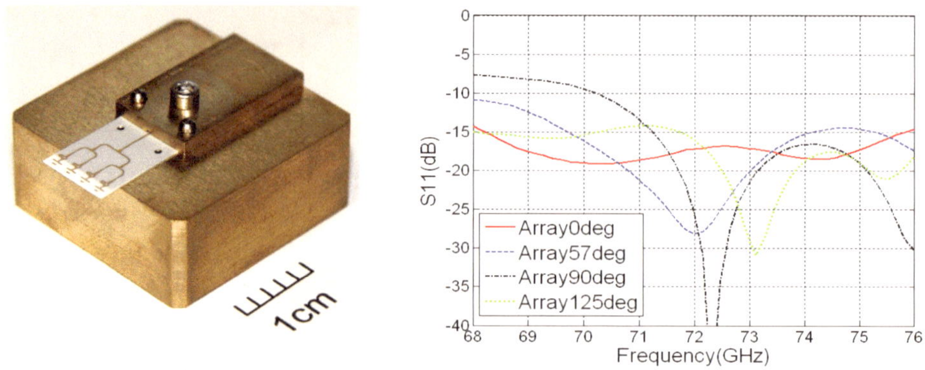

a) b)

Fig. 15. a) Photograph of a four-element linear array prototype integrated with a microstrip-to-waveguide transition. b) Measured reflection coefficients for all arrays

Radiation patterns and gain were measured in an anechoic chamber in CSIRO at 71.5 GHz, 72 GHz and 72.5 GHz. The radiation patterns were measured using a linearly polarized horn antenna at the transmitter. The simulated and measured co- and cross-polar radiation patterns of the array with the main beam in the broadside direction are shown in Fig. 16. Similar agreement between the simulated and measured results was achieved for the other three arrays and also at the other two frequencies.

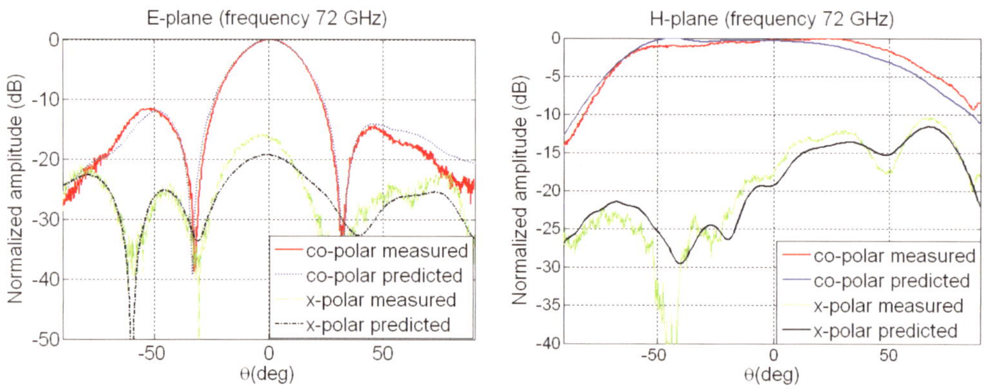

a) b)

Fig. 16. Measured radiation patterns of the Array-0deg at 72 GHz: a) E-plane and b) H-plane

Fig. 17 shows the measured normalized radiation patterns of the four arrays in the xz-plane. The side lobe levels may be improved by using a tapered excitation of the elements instead of the simple equal-amplitude excitation.

Computed and measured gain is compared in Fig. 18. The measured gain for all arrays is 8-9 dBi at 72 GHz, and the scan loss is about 1 dB. The measured gain for all arrays is about 1dB lower than the simulated results and this may be due to some additional losses in the microstrip-to-waveguide transition or higher losses in the dielectric material used for fabrication of the antennas.

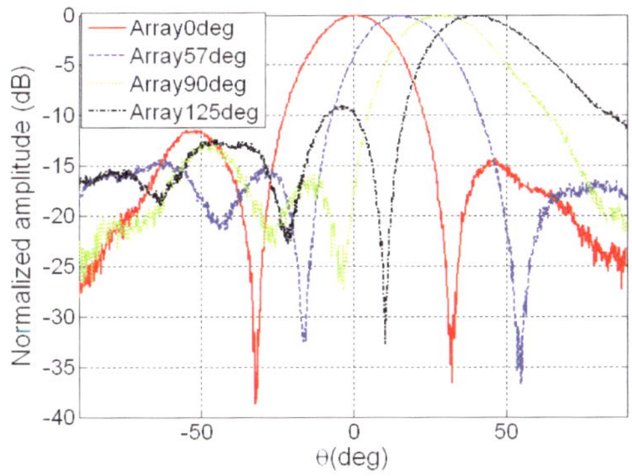

Fig. 17. Measured co-polar E-plane radiation patterns for all arrays at 72 GHz.

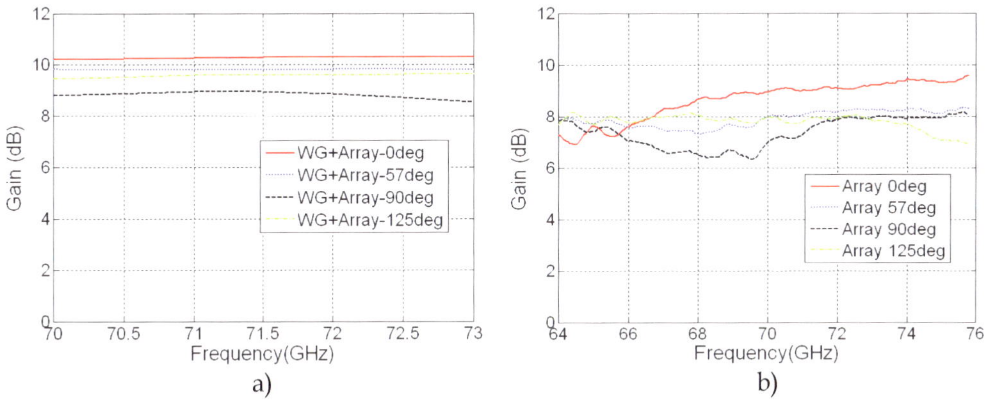

Fig. 18. a) Calculated and b) measured gain for the four-element linear arrays

7. E-Band prototype test results

The analogue beam forming measurements were conducted in the CSIRO 12m far field anechoic chamber as shown in Fig. 19a where 1 is the receive array masked with absorbers, 2 is a rotator, 3 is the transmit antenna aperture and 4 is the de-modulator and power supply modules. Transmitter, digital modulator and control equipment were located on the outside of the chamber.

The available signal to noise ratio was above 33 dB for the measurement distance up to 6m, but most of the tests were conducted at the distance of 2.2m to minimize unwanted reflections from the walls and ceiling of the chamber.

The receive array has been calibrated by cancelling the main beam to obtain a null at zero degree azimuth angle. The calibration procedure was as follows. With one channel at a time active, magnitudes of all channel outputs were set equal. Then, with channel pairs active in the sequence 2-3, 1-2 and 3-4, phase weights were adjusted to null each pair. Then a 180 degree phase shift was applied to the null calibration reference settings to peak the main beam at 0° azimuth. Fig. 19b shows the E-plane array patterns measured for the null reference and the main beam steered to a 0° azimuth. Simulated data from CST Microwave Studio is shown for an array packaged in a waveguide test fixture depicted in Fig. 15a.

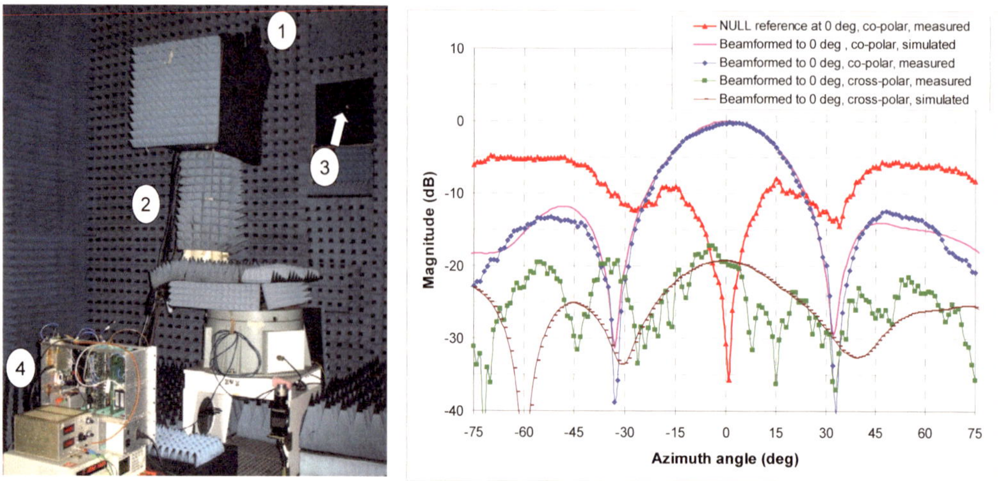

a) b)

Fig. 19. a) System test setup in the 12m far field anechoic chamber; b) Measured and simulated E-plane array co-polar and cross-polar patterns for the main beam formed at 0° azimuth and the measured pattern for the null calibration

Experiments were conducted to validate obtained phase and magnitude weights by cancelling the main beam at a selection of azimuth angles as shown in Fig. 20.

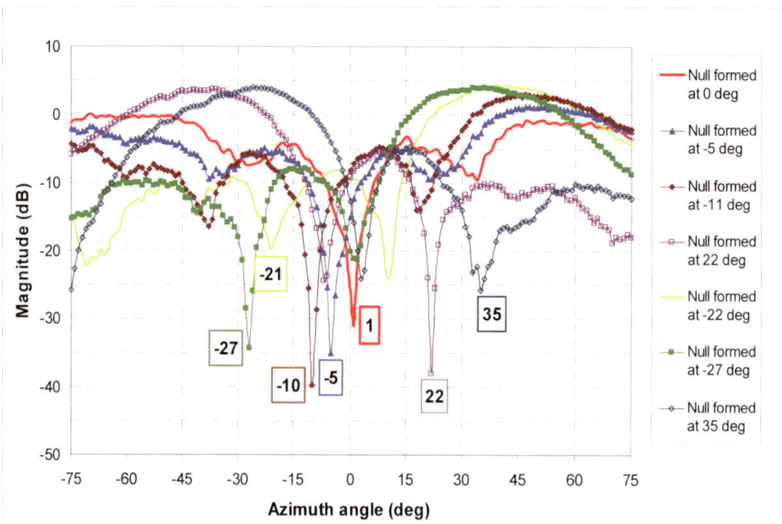

Fig. 20. Measured E-plane co-polar patterns for the array beam formed to cancel the main beam (form a null) at selected azimuth angle

Labels appended to each pattern show actual measured null positions. Experimental results were in a very close agreement with analytical estimates (≈ 1 degree). The array was steered to a selection of other positive and negative azimuth angles and E-plane antenna patterns were measured at each of the selected angles. The theoretical phase weights were applied to the null calibration reference settings to steer the beam to the non-zero azimuths. These weights were calculated using the array factor formula for an uniformly excited array. Examples of measured E-plane co-polar antenna patterns are shown in Fig. 21 and Fig. 22.

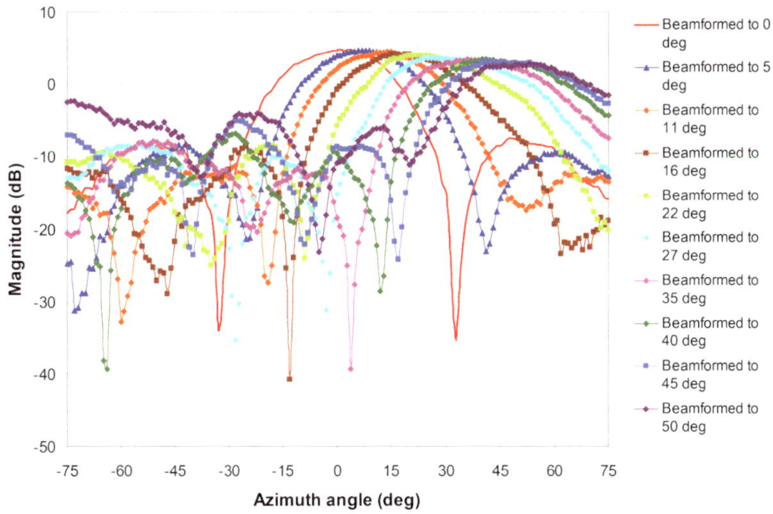

Fig. 21. Measured E-plane co-polar patterns for the array beam formed to a selection of positive azimuth angles

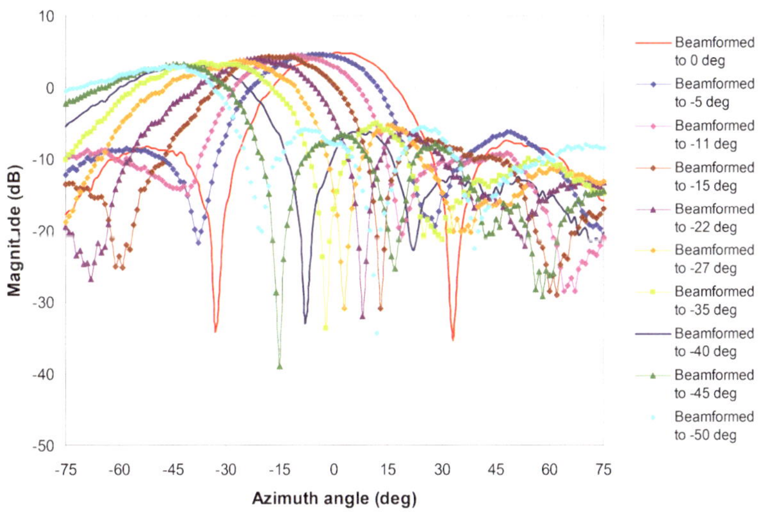

Fig. 22. Measured E-plane co-polar patterns for the array beam formed to a selection of negative azimuth angles

Cross-polar patterns have also been measured. A summary of the E-plane measurements is shown in Fig. 23. Measured antenna array patterns were very close to those predicted by the electromagnetic simulations (as described in Section 6) for steering angles ± 40°.

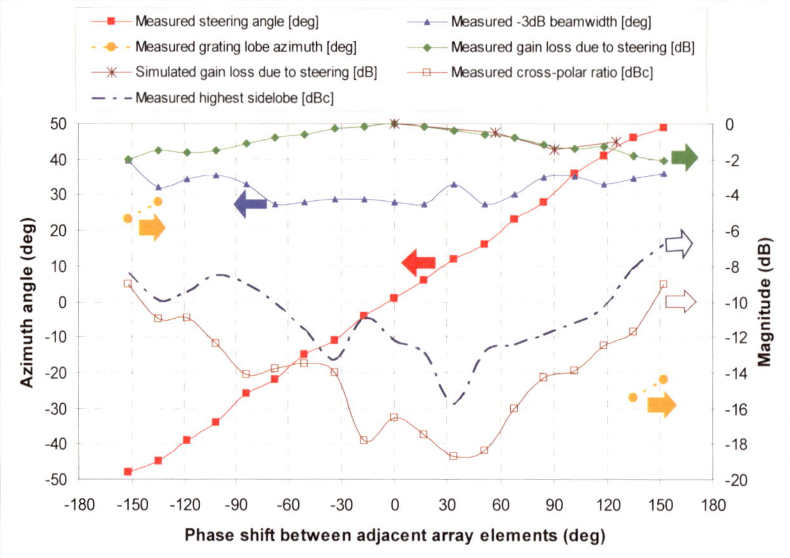

Fig. 23. Summary of the measurements

Measured array gain was 9.5dBi for steering angles below 22° and reduced to approximately 7.5dBi at the maximum steering angle of ± 42°. Grating lobes were observed only at the steering angles beyond ± 43°. Beam steering accuracy of 1 degree has been achieved with 6-bit digital phase shift and magnitude control at IF.

A small ad-hoc point-to-point link has also been tested with reasonable Bit Error Rate (BER) measured for selected angles using 8PSK modulation at 1.5 Gbps data rate. A single channel of the digital modem (Dyadyuk et al., 2007) was used for this experiment. The IF channel was centered at 1.5 GHz with the 625 MHz bandwidth and carried 1.5 Gbps Grey-coded 8-PSK pseudo- random noise sequences. Although pre-compensation (Dyadyuk et. al, 2007) reduces the residual BER, a dynamic pre-compensation would be required at different steering angles.

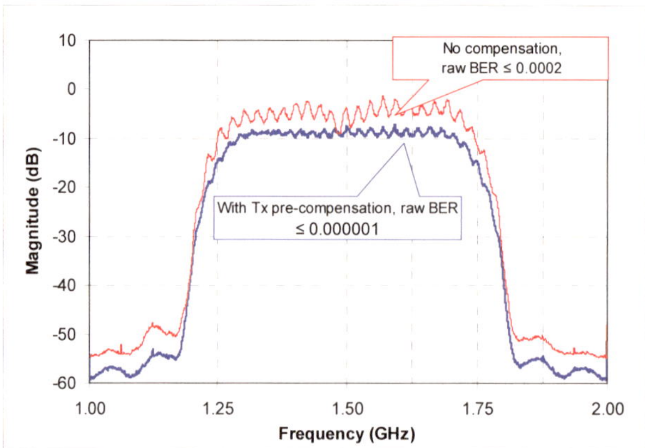

Fig. 24. Received signal at the output of A/D converter and measured BER for pre-compensated and un-compensated pseudo-random 8PSK symbols transmitted at 1.5 Gbps

Uncompensated transmit symbols used in this experiment for simplicity provided a reasonably low BER of 10^{-4}. In Fig. 24 the frequency response without signal pre-distortion (the upper trace) has a clear 3 dB ripple due largely to: a) mismatches between the Rx antenna outputs and the RF pre-amp inputs, and b) mutual coupling between the Rx antenna elements. Rx antenna s-parameters measurements indicated a return loss of 10 dB was to be expected with a 50 Ohm termination. Pre-distortion of the transmitted IF signal to cancel the distortion introduced by the RF transmission channels can be seen (the lower trace in Fig. 24) to reduce the ripples to 1.5 dB, and consequently reduce the 0-degree azimuth BER by a factor of 100.

Further improvement in BER would require better matching of the Rx antenna array and enhancement of the pre-compensation algorithm to better cancel the effects of mutual coupling.

A sample of measured raw BER at a selection of physical positions of the array and electronic steering angles is given in Table 2.

Array position (deg)	Scan angle, (deg)	Measured BER	Scan angle (deg)	Measured BER
-11	0	0.006	-11	0.0003
11	0	0.005	11	0.0002
-22	0	0.02	-22	0.0006
22	0	0.015	22	0.0005
-33	0	0.999	-33	0.001
33	0	0.99	33	0.009

Table 2. Measured raw BER at selected azimuth steering angles

8. Conclusion

In this chapter, we have presented a novel hybrid adaptive antenna array system for high data rate millimeter-wave ad-hoc wireless communications, and described hybrid digital beamforming algorithms.

The design of a single quasi-Yagi antenna element and four linear arrays has also been presented. The impedance bandwidth (return loss greater than 10 dB) of the single extends from 50.1 - 81.4 GHz and the realized gain is 5.4 dBi from 71 - 76 GHz. The arrays were designed and fabricated using quasi-Yagi antennas integrated with microstrip feed networks and suitable microstrip-to-waveguide transitions for testing. The feed networks were optimized to provide the required element-to-element phase shift between the antenna elements in order to point the main beam to the angles of 0°, 20°, 30° and 40°. The radiation patterns for all arrays were measured and excellent agreement between the simulated and measured results was achieved for the co- and cross-polar radiation patterns. The measured gain for all arrays is 8-9 dBi at 72 GHz, which is about 1 dB lower than the simulated results. For all arrays, the measured reflection coefficient is lower than -10dB in the frequency bandwidth of 70.2-76 GHz.

A steerable E-band receive array demonstrator that implements a four-element linear antenna array has been tested using analogue phase-only beam forming at IF. Measured array patterns were close to EM simulated estimates for steering angles up to ± 40 degree. Beam steering accuracy of 1 degree has been achieved with 6-bit digital phase shift at IF.

An ad-hoc wireless communication system has also been demonstrated. Reasonable BER was measured for an 8PSK data stream at 1.5 Gbps with the receive array beam formed in the direction of arrival of the transmit signal. To our knowledge, this work represents the first experimental results on a steerable antenna array in the E-band.

The developed demonstrator has also been used for experimental verification of the proposed wideband digital beam forming algorithms. Quantities analysis of the digital beamforming experiments is out of the scope of this chapter and can be found in (Dyadyuk et al., 20019c and Huang et al., 2010b).

Further work is focused on development of advanced multi-chip-module integration techniques for practical realization of tightly spaced mm-wave active antenna arrays and development of a larger 2D array prototype for experimental verification of the proposed hybrid beamforming algorithms.

9. References

Abbaspour-Tamijani, A. & Sarabandi, K. (2003). An affordable millimeter-wave beam-steerable antenna using interleaved planar sub-arrays. *IEEE Trans. Antennas & Propagation,* vol. 51, no. 9, Sept. 2003, pp. 2193-2202, ISSN: 0018-9480.

Deal, W. R; Kaneda, N.; Sor, J.; Qian Q.Y. & Itoh, T. (2000). A new quasi-Yagi antenna for planar active antenna arrays, *IEEE Trans. on Microwave Theory and Techniques,* Vol. 48, No. 6, June 2000, pp. 910-918, ISSN: 0018-9480.

Doan, C. H.; Emami, S.; Sobel, D. A.; Niknejad, A. M. & Brodersen, R. W. (2004). Design considerations for 60 GHz CMOS radios. *IEEE Communications Mag.,* vol. 42, no. 12, Dec. 2004, pp. 132-140, ISSN: 0163-6804.

Do-Hong, T. & Russer, P. (2004). Signal processing for wideband smart antenna array applications," *IEEE Microwave Magazine,* March 2004, pp. 57–67, ISSN: 1527-3342.

Dyadyuk, V.; Bunton, J. D.; Pathikulangara, J.; Kendall, R.; Sevimli, O.; Stokes, L. & Abbott, D. (2007). A multi-Gigabit mm-wave communication system with improved spectral efficiency," *IEEE Transactions on Microwave Theory and Techniques,* Vol. 55, No. 12, December 2007, pp. 2813–2821, ISSN: 0018-9480.

Dyadyuk, V.; Stokes, L. & Shen, M. (2008a). Integrated W-band GaAs MMIC Modules for Multi-Gigabit Wireless Communication Systems. *Proceedings of the 2008 Global Symposium on Millimeter Waves (GSMM 2008),* April 2008, pp. 25-28, Nanjing, China ISBN: 978-1-4244-1885-5.

Dyadyuk, V.; Archer, J. W. & Stokes L. (2008b). W-Band GaAs Schottky Diode [MMIC Mixers for Multi-Gigabit Wireless Communications. *In: Advances in Broadband Communication and Networks, Agbinya, J. I. et al (Ed.),* 2008; Chapt. 4, pp. 73-103, River Publishers, ISBN: 978-87-92329-00-4, Denmark.

Dyadyuk, V. & Guo Y. J. (2009a). Towards multi-Gigabit ad-hoc wireless networks in the E-band. *Proceedings of Global Symposium on Millimeter Waves (GSMM 2009),* April 2009, pp.1-4, Sendai, Japan.

Dyadyuk, V.; Guo, Y. J. & Bunton, J. D. (2009b). Study on High Rate Long Range Wireless Communications in the 71-76 and 81-86 GHz bands. *Proceedings of the 39th European Microwave Conference (EuMC2009), Proceedings,* Sep. 2009, pp.1315-1318, Rome, Italy.

Dyadyuk, V.; Guo, Y. J. & Bunton J. D. (2010a). Enabling Technologies for Multi-Gigabit Wireless Communications in the E-band. *In: Fares, S. A & Adachi, F., eds. Mobile and*

Wireless Communications: Network layer and circuit layer design, In-TECH, 2010, Chapt. 13, pp. 263-280. ISBN: 978-953-307-042-01.

Dyadyuk, V. & Stokes L. (2010b). Wideband adaptive beam forming in the E-band: Towards a hybrid array. *Proceedings of Global Symposium on Millimeter Waves (GSMM 2010)*, April 2010, Incheon, Korea.

Dyadyuk, V.; Huang, X.; Stokes L. & Pathikulangara J. (2010c). Implementation of Wideband Digital Beam Forming in the E-band: Towards a Hybrid Array. *Proceedings of the 40th European Microwave Conference (EuMC2010)*, Sep. 2010, pp. 914 - 917, Paris, France.

Floyd, B.; Reynolds, S.; Valdes-Garcia, A.; Gaucher, B.; Liu, D.; Beukema, T. & Natarajan, A. (2007). Silicon technology, circuits, packages, and systems for 60-100 GHz, *IEEE MTT-S Intern. Microwave Symp. (IMS2007), Workshop WSN*, Honolulu, Hawaii, June 2007.

Goffer, A. P.; Kam, M. & Herczfeld, P. R. (1994). Design of phased arrays in terms of random sub-arrays. *IEEE Trans. Antennas Propagation*, vol. 42, no. 6, June 1994, pp. 820-826.

Gross, F. B. (2005). Smart *Antennas for Wireless Communications*, McGraw-Hill.

Guo, Y. Jay. (2004). *Advances in Mobile Radio Access Networks*, Artech House, Inc.

Guo, Y. J.; Bunton, J. D.; Dyadyuk, V. & Huang, X. (2009). Hybrid Adaptive Antenna Array. *Australian provisional patent*, AU2009900371, 2 Feb 2009.

Haupt, R. L. (2007). Optimized weighting of uniform sub-arrays of unequal sizes. *IEEE Trans. Antennas Propagation*, vol. 55, no. 4, Apr. 2007, pp.1207–1210.

Hirata, A.; Kosugi, T.; Takahashi, H.; Yamaguchi, R.; Nakajima, F.; Furuta, T.; Ito, H.; Sugahara, H.; Sato, Y. & Nagatsuma, T. (2006). 120-GHz-band millimeter-wave photonic wireless link for 10-Gb/s data transmission. *IEEE Trans. Microwave Theory Tech.*, vol. 54, no. 5, May 2006, pp. 1937–1044.

Huang, X.; Guo, Y. J. & Bunton, J. D. (2009). Adaptive AoA estimation and beamforming with hybrid antenna array of sub-arrays. *2009 IEEE Vehicular Technologies Conference (VTC 2009-Fall)*, Sep 2009, Anchorage, Alaska, USA.

Huang, X.; Guo, Y. J. & Bunton, J. D. (2010a). A hybrid adaptive antenna array. *IEEE Transactions on Wireless Communications*, vol. 9, no. 5, 2010, pp. 1770-1779.

Huang, X.; Dyadyuk, V.; Guo Y. J.; Stokes, L. & Pathikulangara, J. (2010b). Frequency-Domain Digital Calibration and Beamforming with Wideband Antenna Array. *Globecom 2010*, Dec 2010, Miami, FL, USA.

Kaneda, N.; Qian, Q. Y. & Itoh, T. (1998). A novel Yagi-Uda dipole array fed by a microstrip-to-CPS transition, *Proceedings of Asia-Pacific Microwave Conf.*, Dec. 1998, pp. 1413-1416, Yokohama, Japan.

Kaneda, N.; Deal, W. R; Qian, Q. Y.; Waterhouse, R. & Itoh, T. (2002). A broad-band planar quasi-Yagi antenna, *IEEE Trans. on Antennas and Propagation*, Vol. 50, No. 8, August 2002, pp. 1158-1160, ISSN: 0018-926X.

Kasper, E.; Kissinger, D.; Russer P. & Weigel, R. (2009). High Speeds in a Single Chip. *IEEE Microwave Magazine*, Vol. 10, No. 7, Dec. 2009, pp. S28-S33, ISSN: 1527-3342.

Kosugi, T.; Hirata, A.; Nagatsuma, T. & Kado, Y. (2009). MM-Wave Long-Range Wireless Systems. *IEEE Microwave Magazine*, Vol. 10, No. 5, Apr. 2009, pp. 68-76, ISSN: 1527-3342.

Krim, H. & Viberg, M. (1996). Two decades of array signal processing research. *IEEE Signal Process. Mag.*, July 1996, pp. 67-94.

Lockie, D. & Peck, D. (2009). High-Data-Rate Millimeter-Wave Radios. *IEEE Microwave Magazine*, Vol. 10, No. 5, Aug. 2009, pp. 75-83, ISSN: 1527-3342.

Mailloux, R. J. (2005). *Phased Array Antenna Handbook,* Artech House, Inc.

Mailloux, R. J. (2007). *Sub-array technology for large scanning arrays. In Second European Conf. Antennas Propagation (EuCAP2007),* Nov. 2007.

Nikolic, N. & Weily, A. R. (2009). Printed quasi-Yagi antenna with folded dipole driver, *Proceedings of IEEE Antennas and Propagation Society (AP-S) International Symposium*, June 2009, Charleston, SC, USA.

Nikolic, N. & Weily, A. R. (2010). E-band planar quasi-Yagi antenna with folded dipole driver, *accepted for publication in IET Proceedings on Microwaves, Antennas and Propagation,* 2010, ISSN: 1751-8725.

Reynolds, S. K.; Floyd, B. A.; Pfeiffer, U. R.; Beukema, T.; Grzyb, J.; Haymes, C.; Gaucher, B. & Soyuer, M. (2006). A Silicon 60-GHz Receiver and Transmitter Chipset for Broadband Communications, *IEEE Journal of Solid-State Circuits*, Vol.41, Issue 12, Dec. 2006, pp.2820 - 2831.

Rogstad, D.; Mileant, A. & Pham, T. (2003). *Antenna Arraying Techniques in the Deep Space Network*. Wiley-IEEE.

Singh, H.; Oh, J.; Kweon, C. Y.; Qin, X.; Shao, H.-R. & Ngo, C. (2008). A 60 GHz wireless network for enabling uncompressed video communication. *IEEE Communications Magazine,* De. 2008, pp. 71–78, ISSN: 0163-6804.

Stutzman, W. L & Thiele, G. A. (1981). *Antenna Theory and Design*, John Wiley & Sons Inc., ISBN 0-471-04458-X, New York.

Vamsi, K.; Paidi, Griffith, Z.; Wei, Y.; Dahlstrom, M.; Urteaga, M.; Parthasarathy, N.; Seo, M.; Samoska, L.; Fung, A. & Rodwell, M. J. W. (2005). G-Band (140–220 GHz) and W-Band (75–110 GHz) InP DHBT Medium Power Amplifiers", *IEEE Transactions on Microwave Theory and Techniques*, Vol. 52, No. 2, Feb. 2005, pp. 598-605.

Wells, J. (2009). Faster than fiber: the future of multi-Gb/s wireless. *IEEE Microwave Magazine*, Vol. 10, No. 3, May 2009, pp. 104–112, ISSN: 1527-3342.

Xia, T.; Zheng, Y.; Wan, Q. & Wang, X. (2007). Decoupled estimation of 2-D angles of arrival using two parallel uniform linear arrays. *IEEE Trans. Antennas & Propagation*, vol. 55, no. 9, Sep. 2007, pp. 2627-2632.

Zirath, H.; Masuda, T.; Kozhuharov, R. & Ferndahl, M. (2004). Development of 60-GHz front-end circuits for a high-data-rate communication system. *IEEE J. Solid-State Circuits*, vol. 39, no. 10, Oct. 2004, pp. 1640-1649.

Part 3

Network Coding and Design

7

Flexible Network Codes Design for Cooperative Diversity

Michela Iezzi[1], Marco Di Renzo[2] and Fabio Graziosi[1]
[1]*University of L'Aquila*
Department of Electrical and Information Engineering
Center of Excellence for Research DEWS,
Via G. Gronchi 18, Nucleo Industriale di Pile, 67100 L'Aquila
[2]*L2S, UMR 8506 CNRS – SUPELEC – Univ Paris–Sud*
Laboratory of Signals and Systems (L2S)
French National Center for Scientific Research (CNRS)
École Supérieure d'Électricité (SUPÉLEC)
University of Paris-Sud XI (UPS),
3 rue Joliot-Curie, 91192 Gif-sur-Yvette (Paris)
[1] *Italy*
[2]*France*

1. Introduction

Wireless networked systems arise in various communication contexts, and are becoming a bigger and integral part of our everyday life. In today practical networked systems, information delivery is accomplished through routing: network nodes simply store-and-forward data, and processing is accomplished only at the end nodes. Network Coding (NC) is a recent field in electrical engineering and computer science that breaks with this assumption: instead of simply forwarding data, intermediate network nodes may recombine several input packets into one or several output packets (Ahlswede et al., 2000). NC offers the promise of improved performance over conventional network routing techniques. In particular, NC principles can significantly impact the next-generation of wireless *ad hoc*, sensor, and cellular networks, in terms of both energy efficiency and throughput (Ho et al., 2003).

However, besides the many potential advantages and applications of NC over classical routing, the NC principle is not without its drawbacks. A fundamental problem that NC needs to face over lossy (*e.g.*, wireless) networks is the so-called error propagation problem: corrupted packets injected by some intermediate nodes might propagate through the network until the destination, and might render impossible to decode the original information (Cai & Yeung, 2002). As a matter of fact, the application of NC to a wireless context needs to take into account that the wireless medium is highly unpredictable and inhospitable for adopting the existing NC algorithms, which have mostly been designed by assuming wired (*i.e.*, error-free) networks as the blueprint. Furthermore, in contrast to routing, this problem is crucial in NC due to the algebraic operations performed by the internal nodes of the network: the mixing of packets within the network makes every packet flowing through it statistically dependent on other packets, so that even a single erroneous packet might affect the correct detection of all the other packets (Koetter & Kschischang, 2008). On the contrary, the same error in networks using just routing would affect only a single source-to-destination path. An up-to-date overview of recent results and open problems related to the application of NC to a wireless context can be found in (Di Renzo et al., 2010a), (Di Renzo et al., 2010b).

NC finds successful application in wireless cooperative networks (Pabst, 2004), (Scaglione et al., 2006), since it offers an efficient way for overcoming their limitations in terms of achievable throughput (Katti et al., 2008b). More specifically, in wireless cooperative networks multiple radios are deployed in a neighborhood. The radios connect to each other via wireless links to form a multi-hop wireless network, with a few nodes acting as gateways that connect the wireless network to, *e.g.*, the Internet. Packets traverse multiple wireless links before reaching the gateway and finally the wired network (and, thus, the destination). Multi-hop networks extend the coverage area without expensive wiring, thus offering cheap and moderately fast connectivity, which is often sufficient for accessing the Internet assuming normal browsing habits (Pabst, 2004). However, the price to be paid for this improved robustness in the transmission of data is the reduction of the achievable data rate, which is due to two main reasons: i) the transmission of redundant information to achieve the benefits of spatial diversity, and ii) the practical need to adopt the half-duplex constraint, which precludes the nodes to transmit and receive data simultaneously (Wang et al., 2009). In this context, NC offers an intelligent solution to boost the channel capacity of multi-hop wireless networks by combining information from different packets at the packet (Katti et al., 2008a), (Chachulski et al., 2007), symbol (Katti et al., 2008c), or signal (Katti et al., 2007) level: data mixing allows the system to offset the throughput limitations set by the half-duplex constraint and to reduce the amount of redundant data to be transmitted. For example, the inherent capability offered by NC to recover the throughput of cooperative networking has been clearly assessed for the so-called two-way relay channel (Zhang et al., 2006).

Moving from the considerations above, it is evident that the design of efficient and robust protocols and algorithms to exploit the properties of NC in a cooperative networking scenario will play an important role for the next generation of wireless networks that require high data transmission rates. In particular, to take full advantage of the benefits of NC in a cooperative scenario, the network codes have to be properly designed in order to: i) maximize the probability of correct decoding at the destination nodes in order to minimize the effects of the error propagation problem, ii) reduce the energy consumptions of the overall cooperative network with the aim to prolong its operational life, and iii) keep the complexity of the relay nodes performing NC at a low level. Originally, the design of network codes has mainly been concerned with methods to achieve the maximum information flow (Ahlswede et al., 2000), (Li et al., 2003), (Koetter & Medard, 2003), (Ho et al., 2006). However, in the recent period considerable effort has been devoted to the design of efficient network codes to attain the maximum diversity gain (Xiao & Skoglund, 2009a), (Xiao & Skoglund, 2009b), Rebelatto et al. (2010a), (Rebelatto et al., 2010b), (Topakkaya & Wang, 2010), which is known to determine the Bit Error Probability (BEP) for high Signal-to-Noise-Ratios (SNRs) (Wang & Giannakis, 2003). More specifically, as far as a multi-source multi-relay cooperative scenario is concerned, in (Xiao & Skoglund, 2009a) it has been shown that binary NC is sub-optimal for achieving full-diversity, and in (Rebelatto et al., 2010b) it has been pointed out that max-diversity-achieving network codes can be obtained by resorting to the theory of non-binary linear block codes. For example, as far as the canonical two-source two-relay cooperative network is concerned, the methods proposed in (Xiao & Skoglund, 2009a), (Xiao & Skoglund, 2009b), (Rebelatto et al., 2010a), (Rebelatto et al., 2010b) can achieve full-diversity, when, instead, XOR-based binary NC (Katti et al., 2008a) cannot. The solution proposed by all these papers to overcome the limitation in the achievable diversity is based on using network codes in a non-binary Galois field. However, the price to be paid for this performance improvement is the additional complexity required at the relay nodes, which must network-code the received packets by using non-binary arithmetic. Also, longer decoding delays are, in general, required to design full-diversity-achieving network codes (Rebelatto et al., 2010b). Furthermore, the solutions available in (Xiao & Skoglund, 2009a), (Xiao & Skoglund, 2009b), Rebelatto et al. (2010a), (Rebelatto et al., 2010b) aim at guaranteeing the same diversity gain for all the active sources of the network, which, in general, leads to an inflexible network code design as multiple sources might have different Quality-of-Service (QoS) requirements, and, so, might need different diversity gains. In conclusion, the solutions available so far seem to be still inflexible to accommodate the needs of the multi-source multi-relay scenario, as well as to keep the computational complexity of the relay nodes at a low level.

Motivated by these design challenges, the aim of this book chapter is to propose a new and flexible method to design network codes for cooperative wireless networks with the objectives of: i) improving the diversity gain of conventional relay-only (Scaglione et al., 2006) and XOR-based binary NC (Katti et al., 2008a), ii) keeping at a low level the complexity of the relays, and iii) having the flexibility of assigning to each source a different diversity gain according to the desired QoS. In this book chapter, we show that these design goals can be simultaneously achieved by exploiting the theory of Unequal Error Protection (UEP) linear block codes for the flexible and robust design of network codes for multi-source multi-relay networks (Masnick & Wolf, 1967), (Boyarinov & Katsman, 1981). In particular, by focusing on the canonical two-source two-relay network scenario we prove that, by adopting a simple (4,2,2) UEP code (Van Gils, 1983, Table I) as a network code, at least one source can achieve a better diversity gain than conventional relay-only or XOR-only NC protocols without the need to either use non-binary operations or require additional time-slots. The adoption of UEP coding theory for wireless relay networks (Nguyen et al., 2010) and for random NC with application to multimedia content distribution (Thomos & Frossard, 2004) is receiving a growing interest. However, to the best of the authors knowledge, none of the available works have exploited UEP coding theory for the flexible design of distributed network codes for diversity purposes.

The reminder of this book chapter is organized as follows. In Section 2 and Section 3, system model and network code design are introduced, respectively. In Section 4, a low-complexity detector based on the Maximum-Likelihood (ML) principle for demodulation and network decoding at the destination node is derived. In Section 5, an analytical framework to compute the Average BEP (ABEP) and the diversity gain of various network codes is proposed. In Section 6, numerical results are shown to substantiate our claims and compare the UEP-based network code design with conventional relay and NC methods. Finally, Section 7 concludes the book chapter.

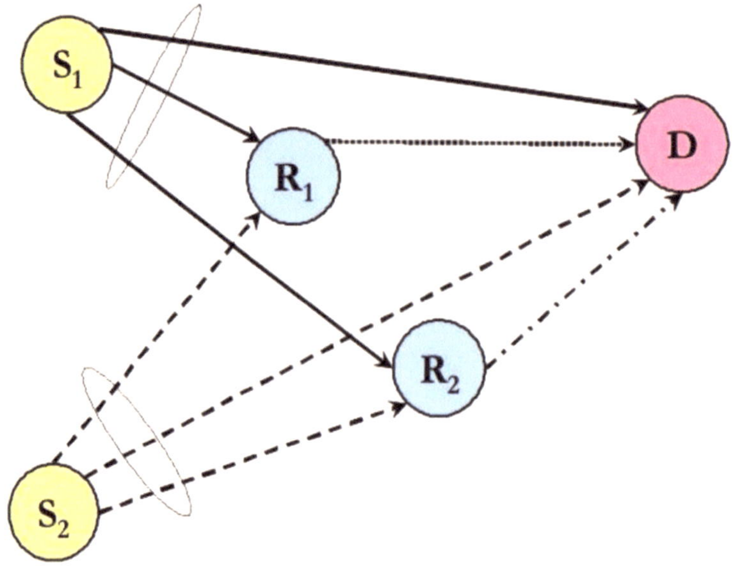

Fig. 1. Two-source two-relay network topology. Different line-styles denote transmission over orthogonal channels (*e.g.*, time-slots (Scaglione et al., 2006)) to avoid mutual interference: S_1 transmits in time-slot 1 (solid lines), S_2 in time-slot 2 (dashed lines), R_1 in time-slot 3 (dotted lines), and R_2 in time-slot 4 (dashed-dotted lines).

2. System model

Let us consider the canonical two-source two-relay cooperative network shown in Figure 1. Generalization to multi-source multi-relay networks is possible, but it is not considered in this book chapter due to space constraints. The working principle of the network in Figure 1 is as follows. In time-slots $t = 1, 2$, source node S_t broadcasts a modulated symbol, x_{S_t}, with average energy E_m. For analytical tractability, Binary Phase Shift Keying (BPSK) modulation is considered, *i.e.*:

$$x_{S_t} = \sqrt{E_m}(1 - 2b_{S_t}) \tag{1}$$

where $b_{S_t} = \{0, 1\}$ is the bit emitted by S_t.

Accordingly, the signals received at relays R_1, R_2, and destination D are:

$$\begin{cases} y_{S_tR_1} = h_{S_tR_1}x_{S_t} + n_{S_tR_1} \\ y_{S_tR_2} = h_{S_tR_2}x_{S_t} + n_{S_tR_2} \\ y_{S_tD} = h_{S_tD}x_{S_t} + n_{S_tD} \end{cases} \tag{2}$$

where h_{XY} is the fading coefficient from node X to node Y, which is a circular symmetric complex Gaussian random variable with zero mean and variance σ^2_{XY} per dimension (*i.e.*, a Rayleigh fading channel model is considered). For analytical tractability, independent and identically distributed (i.i.d.) fading over all the wireless links is considered, *i.e.*, $\sigma_0^2 = \sigma^2_{XY}$ for any X and Y. Furthermore, n_{XY} denotes the complex Additive White Gaussian Noise (AWGN) at the input of node Y and related to the transmission from node X to node Y. The

AWGNs in different time-slots are independent and identically distributed with zero mean and variance $N_0/2$ per dimension.
Upon reception of $y_{S_1R_1}$, $y_{S_1R_2}$, $y_{S_2R_1}$, and $y_{S_2R_2}$, the relays R_1 and R_2 attempt to decode the symbols transmitted by S_1 and S_2 in a similar fashion as in a Decode-and-Forward (DF) cooperative protocol (Scaglione et al., 2006). Unlike other solutions available in the literature for network code design for cooperative networks (Xiao & Skoglund, 2009a) (Xiao & Skoglund, 2009b), (Rebelatto et al., 2010a), (Rebelatto et al., 2010b), we do not rely on powerful (*i.e.*, Shannon-like) channel codes at the physical layer, which allow each relay to detect correct and wrong packets, and enable them to forward only the former ones. We consider a very simple implementation in which the relays demodulate-network-code-and-forward (D-NC-F) each received symbol without checking whether the symbol is correct or wrong. The main aim of this assumption is to keep the complexity of the relays at a very low level (Koetter & Kschischang, 2008), and to understand the robustness, in terms of coding and diversity gain, of the error propagation problem (Di Renzo et al., 2010a), (Di Renzo et al., 2010b) on various network codes.
In particular, we consider ML-optimum demodulation that exploits Channel State Information (CSI) about the source-to-relay channels at each relay node, as follows ($t = 1, 2$):

$$\begin{cases} \hat{b}_{S_tR_1} = \underset{\tilde{b}_{S_t}\epsilon\{0,1\}}{\operatorname{argmin}}\{|y_{S_tR_1} - \sqrt{E_m}h_{S_tR_1}(1-2\tilde{b}_{S_t})|^2\} \\ \hat{b}_{S_tR_2} = \underset{\tilde{b}_{S_t}\epsilon\{0,1\}}{\operatorname{argmin}}\{|y_{S_tR_2} - \sqrt{E_m}h_{S_tR_2}(1-2\tilde{b}_{S_t})|^2\} \end{cases} \tag{3}$$

where ˆ denotes the estimated symbol, and ˜ denotes the trial symbol used in the hypothesis-detection problem.
After demodulating $\hat{b}_{S_tR_q}$ for $t = 1, 2$ and $q = 1, 2$, each relay, R_q, executes the following operations: i) it performs NC on these symbols, ii) it re-modulates the network-coded symbol, and iii) it transmits the modulated symbol to the destination during the third (if $q = 1$) and fourth (if $q = 2$) time-slot. By denoting with $f_{R_q}(\cdot,\cdot)$ the NC operation performed by relay R_q, and with b_{R_q} the network-coded symbol, *i.e.*, $b_{R_q} = f_{R_q}(\hat{b}_{S_1R_q}, \hat{b}_{S_2R_q})$, the signal received at the destination, D, is:

$$y_{R_qD} = h_{R_qD}x_{R_q} + n_{R_qD} \tag{4}$$

where $x_{R_q} = \sqrt{E_m}(1-2b_{R_q})$.

After four time-slots, the destination has four received signals, *i.e.*, $y_{S_1D}, y_{S_2D}, y_{R_1D}, y_{R_2D}$, from which it tries to infer the pair of symbols b_{S_1} and b_{S_2} transmitted by S_1 and S_2, respectively. The derivation of the detector used by the destination, D, can be found in Section 4, and its performance analysis in Section 5.

3. UEP–based network code design

In (4), we have implicitly described the network code used by relay R_q with $b_{R_q} = f_{R_q}(\cdot,\cdot)$. In this book chapter, four network codes (or NC scenarios) are investigated:

- *Scenario 1*: $b_{R_1} = \hat{b}_{S_1R_1}$ and $b_{R_2} = \hat{b}_{S_2R_2}$. This network code corresponds to the working scenario in which relays R_1 and R_2 only decode-and-forward the signals received from sources S_1 and S_2, respectively (relay-only scenario) (Scaglione et al., 2006).

- *Scenario 2*: $b_{R_1} = \hat{b}_{S_1R_1} \oplus \hat{b}_{S_2R_1}$ and $b_{R_2} = \hat{b}_{S_1R_2} \oplus \hat{b}_{S_2R_2}$, where $\oplus$ denotes bit-wise XOR operation. This network code corresponds to the working scenario in which relays R_1 and R_2 demodulate-network-code-and-forward the signals received from sources S_1 and S_2, respectively. Furthermore, they use conventional binary NC (XOR-only scenario) (Katti et al., 2008a).
- *Scenario 3*: $b_{R_1} = \hat{b}_{S_1R_1} \oplus \hat{b}_{S_2R_1}$ and $b_{R_2} = \hat{b}_{S_2R_2}$. This scenario corresponds to using a distributed network code obtained from a $(4, 2, 2)$ UEP code (Van Gils, 1983, Table I), where a higher diversity gain has to be assigned to source S_2.
- *Scenario 4*: $b_{R_1} = \hat{b}_{S_1R_1}$ and $b_{R_2} = \hat{b}_{S_1R_2} \oplus \hat{b}_{S_2R_2}$. This scenario corresponds to using a distributed network code obtained from a $(4, 2, 2)$ UEP code (Van Gils, 1983, Table I), where a higher diversity gain has to be assigned to source S_1.

Scenario 1 and *Scenario 2* correspond to state-of-the-art distributed coding techniques (Rebelatto et al., 2010b), while *Scenario 3* and *Scenario 4* are the flexible network codes we are interested in studying in this book chapter. The reason why UEP coding theory can be a suitable tool to design distributed network codes for application scenarios in which different sources require a different diversity gain (see also Section 1) has its information-theoretic foundation in (Zhang, 2008). In fact, in (Zhang, 2008) it is shown that the minimum distance of a network code plays the same role as it plays in classical coding theory. Furthermore, from classical coding theory we know that the minimum distance of a linear block code directly determines the diversity gain over fully-interleaved fading channels (Proakis, 2000, Ch. 8), (Simon & Alouini, 2000, Ch. 12). In UEP linear codes, each systematic bit has its own minimum distance, and the set of these distances is known as *separation vector* (Masnick & Wolf, 1967), (Boyarinov & Katsman, 1981). From (Van Gils, 1983, Table I), the network code of *Scenario 3* is a UEP distributed code with separation vector $[2, 3]$, which means that the minimum distance for the bits sent by S_1 and S_2 is equal to 2 and 3, respectively. Likewise, the network code of *Scenario 4* is a UEP distributed code with separation vector $[3, 2]$, which means that the minimum distance for the bits sent by S_1 and S_2 is equal to 3 and 2, respectively. Thus, from (Zhang, 2008) it follows that by using a network code constructed from UEP coding theory we can individually assign different diversity gains to different sources. Also, note that, unlike (Xiao & Skoglund, 2009a), (Rebelatto et al., 2010b), this is obtained by neither using a non-binary Galois field nor introducing extra delays. The complexity and decoding latency of all the network codes studied in this book chapter are, on the other hand, the same. The downside is that only one source can achieve full-diversity. To the best of the authors knowledge, the adoption of UEP coding theory to design distributed network codes for multi-hop/cooperative networks with noisy and faded source-to-relay channels has never been addressed in the literature. Finally, we note that although, for analytical tractability and space constraints, only the two–source two-relay network topology is here investigated, UEP coding theory can be applied to generic multi-source multi-relay networks, by using, *e.g.*, the codes available in (Van Gils, 1983, Table I).

4. Receiver design

We consider that the destination, D, uses a detector based on a low–complexity implementation of the Maximum Likelihood Sequence Estimation (MLSE) criterion. In particular, according to the MLSE criterion, given y_{S_1D}, y_{S_2D}, y_{R_1D}, and y_{R_2D} introduced in Section 2, the proposed receiver estimates the distributed codeword that has most probably

been transmitted (Proakis, 2000). However, in order to keep the complexity of the detector at a low level, we introduce some simplifications in the analytical development with the aim of reducing the computational complexity and the *a priori* CSI required at the destination for optimal decoding. Of course, this leads to a sub–optimal receiver design, but allows the destination not to estimate the wireless channel over all the wireless links of the network.
Before proceeding with the development of the detector, we need to identify the codebook, *i.e.*, the set of distributed codewords that can be received by the destination in a noise-less and fading-less scenario. The codebook is denoted by $\mathcal{C} = \{\mathbf{c}^{(1)}, \mathbf{c}^{(2)}, \mathbf{c}^{(3)}, \mathbf{c}^{(4)}\}$, where $\mathbf{c}^{(j)}$ is the j-th codeword of $\mathcal{C}$, and $c_i^{(j)}$ is the i-th element of $\mathbf{c}^{(j)}$ for $i = 1, 2, 3, 4$. More specifically, in a noise-less and fading-less scenario we have: $c_1^{(j)} = b_{S_1}$, $c_2^{(j)} = b_{S_2}$, $c_3^{(j)} = b_{R_1}$, and $c_4^{(j)} = b_{R_2}$. As far as the NC scenarios described in Section 3 are concerned, the following codebooks can be obtained:

- $\mathcal{C} = \{0000, 0101, 1010, 1111\}$ for *Scenario 1*
- $\mathcal{C} = \{0000, 0111, 1011, 1100\}$ for *Scenario 2*
- $\mathcal{C} = \{0000, 0111, 1010, 1101\}$ for *Scenario 3*
- $\mathcal{C} = \{0000, 0101, 1011, 1110\}$ for *Scenario 4*

Detection at the destination encompasses two main steps, which involve physical and network layers, respectively.

1. *Step 1 (Physical Layer)*: From the received signals, y_{S_1D}, y_{S_2D}, y_{R_1D}, and y_{R_2D}, hard-decision estimates of $[b_{S_1}, b_{S_2}, b_{R_1}, b_{R_2}]$ are provided by using a ML-optimum receiver, which exploits channel information on the source-to-destination and relay-to-destination wireless links ($t = 1, 2$ and $q = 1, 2$):

$$\begin{cases} \hat{b}_{S_tD} = \underset{\tilde{b}_{S_t} \in \{0,1\}}{\operatorname{argmin}} \{|y_{S_tD} - \sqrt{E_m} h_{S_tD}(1 - 2\tilde{b}_{S_t})|^2\} \\ \hat{b}_{R_qD} = \underset{\tilde{b}_{R_q} \in \{0,1\}}{\operatorname{argmin}} \{|y_{R_qD} - \sqrt{E_m} h_{R_qD}(1 - 2\tilde{b}_{R_q})|^2\} \end{cases} \tag{5}$$

2. *Step 2 (Network Layer)*: The hard-decision estimates $\hat{\mathbf{c}} = [\hat{c}_1, \hat{c}_2, \hat{c}_3, \hat{c}_4] = [\hat{b}_{S_1D}, \hat{b}_{S_2D}, \hat{b}_{R_1D}, \hat{b}_{R_2D}]$ are input to the network layer, which uses a MLSE–optimum criterion to jointly estimate the bits emitted by the sources S_1 and S_2, as follows (Proakis, 2000), (Simon & Alouini, 2000):

$$\left[\hat{b}_{S_1}, \hat{b}_{S_2}\right] = \underset{\tilde{b}_{S_1} \in \{0,1\},\, \tilde{b}_{S_2} \in \{0,1\}}{\arg\max} \left\{\Pr\left\{ \tilde{b}_{S_1}, \tilde{b}_{S_2} \middle| \hat{b}_{S_1D}, \hat{b}_{S_2D}, \hat{b}_{R_1D}, \hat{b}_{R_2D} \right\}\right\} \tag{6}$$

where $\Pr\{\cdot\}$ denotes probability.
Since the network codes studied in Section 3 can be regarded as systematic linear block codes (Proakis, 2000), (6) can be re-written as follows:

$$\left[\hat{b}_{S_1}, \hat{b}_{S_2}\right] = \left[c_1^{(\hat{j})}, c_2^{(\hat{j})}\right] = \underset{\left\{c_1^{(j)}, c_2^{(j)}\right\} \in \mathcal{C}}{\arg\max} \left\{\Pr\left\{ c_1^{(j)}, c_2^{(j)} \middle| \hat{c}_1, \hat{c}_2, \hat{c}_3, \hat{c}_4 \right\}\right\} \tag{7}$$

Finally, by applying the Bayes theorem, by taking into account that the symbols emitted by the sources (and, thus, the codewords) are equiprobable, and by noticing that the hard-decisions $\hat{\mathbf{c}} = [\hat{c}_1, \hat{c}_2, \hat{c}_3, \hat{c}_4] = [\hat{b}_{S_1D}, \hat{b}_{S_2D}, \hat{b}_{R_1D}, \hat{b}_{R_2D}]$ are independently computed, (7) simplifies as follows:

$$\left[\hat{b}_{S_1}, \hat{b}_{S_2}\right] = \left[c_1^{(\tilde{j})}, c_2^{(\tilde{j})}\right] = \underset{\left\{c_1^{(\tilde{j})}, c_2^{(\tilde{j})}\right\} \in C}{\arg\max} \left\{ \prod_{i=1}^{4} \left[\Pr\left\{ \hat{c}_i \middle| c_i^{(\tilde{j})} \right\} \right] \right\} \tag{8}$$

where, according to Section 3, we have: $c_3^{(\tilde{j})} = f_{R_1}\left(c_1^{(\tilde{j})}, c_2^{(\tilde{j})}\right)$ and $c_4^{(\tilde{j})} = f_{R_2}\left(c_1^{(\tilde{j})}, c_2^{(\tilde{j})}\right)$.

By carefully looking at (8), we notice that the computation of $\Pr\left\{ \hat{c}_i \middle| c_i^{(\tilde{j})} \right\}$ for $i = 1,2,3,4$ and $\tilde{j} = 1,2,3,4$ requires the knowledge of the channel gains over all the wireless links of the network, including the source-to-relay links to which the destination has not direct access. The availability of this information typically requires some cross-layer interactions between physical and network layers, along with the design of a so-called channel-aware detector (Chamberland & Veeravalli, 2007), (Di Renzo et al., 2009). With the aim to simplify the complexity of the detector, we retain two main assumptions (A) in this book chapter: A1) we consider that the destination has no knowledge of the channels over the source-to-relay links, and A2) we consider that the network layer only knows the fading distribution of the source-to-destination and relay-to-destination wireless links, but it does not know the exact realization of the channel gains.

From A1), it can be readily proved that $\Pr\left\{ \hat{c}_i \middle| c_i^{(\tilde{j})} \right\}$ for $i = 1,2,3,4$ and $\tilde{j} = 1,2,3,4$ follows a Bernoulli distribution (Proakis, 2000) that does not depend on the source-to-relay links, as shown below:

$$\begin{cases} \Pr\left\{ \hat{c}_1 \middle| c_1^{(\tilde{j})} \right\} = \left(1 - P_{S_1D}\right)^{1-d_1(\tilde{j})} P_{S_1D}^{d_1(\tilde{j})} \\ \Pr\left\{ \hat{c}_2 \middle| c_2^{(\tilde{j})} \right\} = \left(1 - P_{S_2D}\right)^{1-d_2(\tilde{j})} P_{S_2D}^{d_2(\tilde{j})} \\ \Pr\left\{ \hat{c}_3 \middle| c_3^{(\tilde{j})} \right\} = \left(1 - P_{R_1D}\right)^{1-d_3(\tilde{j})} P_{R_1D}^{d_3(\tilde{j})} \\ \Pr\left\{ \hat{c}_4 \middle| c_4^{(\tilde{j})} \right\} = \left(1 - P_{R_2D}\right)^{1-d_4(\tilde{j})} P_{R_2D}^{d_4(\tilde{j})} \end{cases} \tag{9}$$

where: i) $P_{XD} = Q\left(\sqrt{\bar{\gamma}\,|h_{XD}|^2}\right)$ with $X = \{S_1, S_2, R_1, R_2\}$ is the error probability over the link from node X to node D, ii) $\bar{\gamma} = 2E_m/N_0$, iii) $Q(x) = \left(1/\sqrt{2\pi}\right)\int_0^{+\infty} \exp(-t^2/2)dt$ is the Gaussian Q-function, and iv) $d_i\left(\tilde{j}\right) = d_H\left(\hat{c}_i, c_i^{(\tilde{j})}\right) = \left|\hat{c}_i - c_i^{(\tilde{j})}\right|$ for $i = 1,2,3,4$, where $d_H(a,b)$ denotes the Hamming distance between two bits a and b (Proakis, 2000). From A2), as the network layer has no access to the actual fading gains but only knows their distribution, we need to replace P_{XD} in (9) with its average value, as follows:

$$\bar{P}_{XD} = \mathrm{E}\{P_{XD}\} = \int_0^{+\infty} Q\left(\sqrt{\bar{\gamma}\xi}\right) g_{|h_{XD}|^2}(\xi)\, d\xi \tag{10}$$

where $\mathrm{E}\{\cdot\}$ denotes the expectation operator computed over fading channel statistics, and $g_{|h_{XD}|^2}(\cdot)$ is the Probability Density Function (PDF) of the fading power gain $|h_{XD}|^2$.

Since, according to Section 2, we consider i.i.d. Rayleigh fading channels, $\bar{P}_{XD}$ can be readily computed in closed–form as follows (Simon & Alouini, 2000) (for $X = \{S_1, S_2, R_1, R_2\}$):

$$\bar{P} = \bar{P}_{XD} = \frac{1}{2}\left(1 - \sqrt{\frac{2\sigma_0^2\bar{\gamma}}{1 + 2\sigma_0^2\bar{\gamma}}}\right) \tag{11}$$

Finally, by substituting (9) and (11) into (8), and computing the logarithm, we obtain, after some algebra, the result as follows:

$$\begin{aligned}\left[\hat{b}_{S_1}, \hat{b}_{S_2}\right] = \left[c_1^{(\hat{j})}, c_2^{(\hat{j})}\right] &= \underset{\left\{c_1^{(j)}, c_2^{(j)}\right\} \in C}{\arg\max} \left\{ \ln\left(\frac{\bar{P}}{1-\bar{P}}\right) \sum_{i=1}^{4} d_i(\tilde{j}) \right\} \\ &= \underset{\left\{c_1^{(j)}, c_2^{(j)}\right\} \in C}{\arg\max} \left\{ \ln\left(\frac{\bar{P}}{1-\bar{P}}\right) \sum_{i=1}^{4} \left|\hat{c}_i - c_i^{(\tilde{j})}\right| \right\}\end{aligned} \tag{12}$$

By taking into account that $\ln\left(\bar{P}/(1-\bar{P})\right)$ is a negative (for $\bar{P} \in [0, 1/2]$) factor that does not effect the outcome of the detector, (12) simplifies as follows:

$$\left[\hat{b}_{S_1}, \hat{b}_{S_2}\right] = \left[c_1^{(\hat{j})}, c_2^{(\hat{j})}\right] = \underset{\left\{c_1^{(\tilde{j})}, c_2^{(\tilde{j})}\right\} \in C}{\arg\min} \left\{ \sum_{i=1}^{4} \left|\hat{c}_i - c_i^{(\tilde{j})}\right| \right\} \tag{13}$$

which turns out to be a (distributed) Minimum Distance Decoder (MDD) receiver for network decoding.

In (13), it is important to note that multiple codewords of a codebook might have the same Hamming distance from the hard-decisions $\hat{\mathbf{c}} = [\hat{c}_1, \hat{c}_2, \hat{c}_3, \hat{c}_4] = [\hat{b}_{S_1D}, \hat{b}_{S_2D}, \hat{b}_{R_1D}, \hat{b}_{R_2D}]$ provided by the physical layer. In this case, we simply assume that the detector randomly chooses one of them with equal probability.

5. Performance analysis

The objective of this section is to develop an accurate analytical framework to compute the ABEP of the MDD receiver in (13) for the four NC scenarios described in Section 3. To this end, we compute first the BEP conditioned upon fading channel statistics, and then the average over the wireless channel.

5.1 Conditional bit error probability (BEP)

To compute the BEP, we take into account that:

1. For analytical tractability, we use union bound methods that require the estimation of the Pairwise Error Probability (PEP) for each pair of codewords of the codebook (Proakis, 2000).
2. We assume that the codewords of the distributed network code are equiprobable.
3. We separately compute the BEP of sources S_1 and S_2, since, as mentioned in Section 1 and Section 3, we are interested in showing that UEP-based distributed network codes provide different performance for different sources, according to the specified separation vector.

Accordingly, the BEP of source S_t for $t = 1, 2$ can be upper-bounded as follows ($t = 1, 2$)[1]:

$$\mathrm{BEP}^{(S_t)} = \frac{1}{4} \sum_{j_1=1}^{4} \sum_{j_2 \neq j_1 = 1}^{4} \mathrm{PEP}^{(S_t)}\left(j_1 \to j_2\right) \tag{14}$$

where $\mathrm{PEP}^{(S_t)}\left(j_1 \to j_2\right)$ is defined as:

$$\mathrm{PEP}^{(S_t)}\left(j_1 \to j_2\right) = \Pr\left\{\mathbf{c}^{(j_1)} \to \mathbf{c}^{(j_2)} \left| c_t^{(j_1)} \neq c_t^{(j_2)} \right.\right\} \tag{15}$$

where $\Pr\left\{\mathbf{c}^{(j_1)} \to \mathbf{c}^{(j_2)} \left| c_t^{(j_1)} \neq c_t^{(j_2)} \right.\right\} = \Pr\left\{\mathbf{c}^{(j_1)} \to \mathbf{c}^{(j_2)}\right\}$ if $c_t^{(j_1)} \neq c_t^{(j_2)}$ and $\Pr\left\{\mathbf{c}^{(j_1)} \to \mathbf{c}^{(j_2)} \left| c_t^{(j_1)} \neq c_t^{(j_2)} \right.\right\} = 0$ if $c_t^{(j_1)} = c_t^{(j_2)}$, and it allows us to compute the BEP of each source individually. As a matter of fact, the detector might be wrong in estimating the transmitted codeword, but this does not necessarily lead to a decoding error in the bits transmitted by *both* sources. As an example, let us consider *Scenario* 3 and the transmission of $\mathbf{c}^{(2)} = 0111$. If the receiver (wrongly) decodes $\hat{\mathbf{c}}^{(2)} = \mathbf{c}^{(4)} = 1101$, then this results in an error only for the bit emitted by S_1, while there is no error for S_2.

From (15) and by grouping together common PEPs, it can be shown that the BEP of S_1 and S_2 in (14) simplifies as follows:

$$\begin{cases} \mathrm{BEP}^{(S_1)} = \mathrm{PEP}^{(S_1)}\left(1 \to 3\right) + \mathrm{PEP}^{(S_1)}\left(1 \to 4\right) \\ \mathrm{BEP}^{(S_2)} = \mathrm{PEP}^{(S_2)}\left(1 \to 2\right) + \mathrm{PEP}^{(S_2)}\left(1 \to 4\right) \end{cases} \tag{16}$$

where we conclude that only three PEPs need to be computed to estimate the error performance, as it can be shown that: $\mathrm{PEP}\left(1 \to 2\right) = \mathrm{PEP}^{(S_1)}\left(1 \to 2\right) = \mathrm{PEP}^{(S_2)}\left(1 \to 2\right)$, $\mathrm{PEP}\left(1 \to 3\right) = \mathrm{PEP}^{(S_1)}\left(1 \to 3\right) = \mathrm{PEP}^{(S_2)}\left(1 \to 3\right)$, and $\mathrm{PEP}\left(1 \to 4\right) = \mathrm{PEP}^{(S_1)}\left(1 \to 4\right) = \mathrm{PEP}^{(S_2)}\left(1 \to 4\right)$.

[1] Note that, to simplify the notation, we avoid to emphasize that BEP and PEP are conditioned upon the fading channel. Instead, we use ABEP and APEP to denote the same functions when averaged over fading channel statistics.

The PEPs in (16) can be computed from (13). In particular, by direct inspection of (13), the generic PEP can be explicitly written as follows:

$$\begin{aligned}\mathrm{PEP}^{(S_t)}(j_1 \to j_2) &= \Pr\left\{\mathbf{c}^{(j_1)} \to \mathbf{c}^{(j_2)} \left| c_t^{(j_1)} \neq c_t^{(j_2)} \right.\right\} \\ &= \Pr\left\{D_{j_1} > D_{j_2} \left| c_t^{(j_1)} \neq c_t^{(j_2)} \right.\right\} + \frac{1}{2}\Pr\left\{D_{j_1} = D_{j_2} \left| c_t^{(j_1)} \neq c_t^{(j_2)} \right.\right\}\end{aligned} \quad (17)$$

where we have defined $D_j = \sum_{i=1}^{4} \left| \hat{c}_i - c_i^{(j)} \right|$ for $j = 1, 2, 3, 4$. Note that the second addend in the second line of (17) is due to the closing comment made in Section 4, where we have remarked that the detector randomly chooses with equal probability (*i.e.*, 1/2) one of the two decision metrics D_{j_1} and D_{j_2} in (17) if they are exactly the same.

Let us now introduce the random variable:

$$D_{j_1,j_2} = D_{j_1} - D_{j_2} = \sum_{i=1}^{4} \left[\left| \hat{c}_i - c_i^{(j_1)} \right| - \left| \hat{c}_i - c_i^{(j_2)} \right| \right] \quad (18)$$

Then, by denoting the probability density function of D_{j_1,j_2} conditioned upon $c_t^{(j_1)} \neq c_t^{(j_2)}$ in (18) by $g_{D_{j_1,j_2}}\left(\cdot \left| c_t^{(j_1)} \neq c_t^{(j_2)} \right.\right)$, the PEP in (17) can be formally re-written as follows:

$$\mathrm{PEP}^{(S_t)}(j_1 \to j_2) = \int_{0^+}^{+\infty} g_{D_{j_1,j_2}}\left(\xi \left| c_t^{(j_1)} \neq c_t^{(j_2)} \right.\right) d\xi + \frac{1}{2}\int_{0^-}^{0^+} g_{D_{j_1,j_2}}\left(\xi \left| c_t^{(j_1)} \neq c_t^{(j_2)} \right.\right) d\xi \quad (19)$$

Closed-form expressions of $\mathrm{PEP}^{(S_t)}(j_1 \to j_2)$ are computed in Section 5.3.

5.2 Average bit error probability (ABEP)

The ABEP can be readily computed from (14) by exploiting the linearity property of the expectation operator. In formulas, we have:

$$\mathrm{ABEP}^{(S_t)} = \mathrm{E}\left\{\mathrm{BEP}^{(S_t)}\right\} = \frac{1}{4}\sum_{j_1=1}^{4}\sum_{j_2 \neq j_1 = 1}^{4} \mathrm{APEP}^{(S_t)}(j_1 \to j_2) \quad (20)$$

where $\mathrm{APEP}^{(S_t)}(j_1 \to j_2) = \mathrm{E}\left\{\mathrm{PEP}^{(S_t)}(j_1 \to j_2)\right\}$.

The APEPs in (20) can be computed by taking the expectation of (19) after computing the integrals. Closed-form expressions of these APEPs are given in Section 5.3.

5.3 Average pairwise error probability (APEP)

The closed-form computation of the APEPs in (20) requires the knowledge of the probability density function $g_{D_{j_1,j_2}}\left(\cdot \left| c_t^{(j_1)} \neq c_t^{(j_2)} \right.\right)$ in (19). In Section 2, we have mentioned that, as opposed to many state-of-the-art research works, our system setup accounts for errors over the source-to-relay links. More specifically, (3) shows that the relays might incorrectly demodulate the bits transmitted by the sources. Even though the MDD receiver in (13) is unaware of these decoding errors, as explained in Section 4, they affect its performance and need to be carefully taken into account for computing the APEPs.

More specifically, in Section 4 we have shown that the relays operate in a D-NC-F mode, which means that they perform two error-prone operations: i) they use the DF protocol for relaying the received symbols, and ii) they combine the symbols received from the sources by using NC. The accurate computation of the APEPs in (20) requires that the error propagation caused by DF and NC operations at the relays are accurately quantified.

5.3.1 DF and NC operations: The effect of realistic source-to-relay channels

As far as DF is concerned, the error propagation of this relay protocol in two-hop relay networks has already been quantified in the literature. In particular, in (Hasna & Alouini, 2003) the following result is available.

Given a two-hop, source-to-relay-to-destination (S-R-D), wireless network, the end-to-end (*i.e.*, at destination D) probability of error, P_{SRD}, is given by:

$$P_{SRD} = P_{SR} + P_{RD} - 2P_{SR}P_{RD} \tag{21}$$

where P_{SR} and P_{RD} are the error probabilities over the source-to-relay and relay-to-destination links, respectively.

By taking into account the analysis in Section 4, it can be readily proved that $P_{\text{SR}} = Q\left(\sqrt{\bar{\gamma}\,|h_{\text{SR}}|^2}\right)$ and $P_{\text{RD}} = Q\left(\sqrt{\bar{\gamma}\,|h_{\text{RD}}|^2}\right)$. The average end-to-end probability of error, $\bar{P}_{SRD}$, can be computed from (10) and (11), and by taking into account that channel fading over the two links is uncorrelated. The final result from (21) is:

$$\bar{P}_{SRD} = \text{E}\{P_{SRD}\} = \bar{P}_{SR} + \bar{P}_{RD} - 2\bar{P}_{SR}\bar{P}_{RD} = 2\bar{P} - 2\bar{P}^2 \tag{22}$$

Let us now consider the error propagation effect due to NC operations and caused by errors over the source-to-relay channels. In this book chapter, NC, when performed by the relays, only foresees binary XOR operations (see Section 3). Thus, we analyze the error propagation effect in this case only. The result is summarized in Proposition 1.

Proposition 1. *Let b_{S_1} and b_{S_2} be the bits emitted by two sources S_1 and S_2 (see, e.g., (1)). Furthermore, let $\hat{b}_{S_1}$ and $\hat{b}_{S_2}$ be the bits estimated at relay R (see, e.g., (3)) after propagation through the wireless links S_1-to-R and S_2-to-R, respectively. Finally, let $b_R = \hat{b}_{S_1} \oplus \hat{b}_{S_2}$ be the network-coded bit computed by the relay R. Then, the probability, P_R, that the network-coded bit, b_R, is wrong due to fading and noise over the source-to-relay channels is as follows:*

$$P_R = \Pr\left\{\left(\hat{b}_{S_1} \oplus \hat{b}_{S_2}\right) \neq \left(b_{S_1} \oplus b_{S_2}\right)\right\} = P_{S_1R} + P_{S_2R} - 2P_{S_1R}P_{S_2R} \tag{23}$$

where P_{S_1R} and P_{S_2R} are the error probabilities over the S_1-to-R and S_2-to-R wireless links, respectively. Similar to the analysis of the DF relay protocol, it can be readily proved that $P_{\text{S}_1\text{R}} = Q\left(\sqrt{\bar{\gamma}\,|h_{\text{S}_1\text{R}}|^2}\right)$ and $P_{\text{S}_2\text{R}} = Q\left(\sqrt{\bar{\gamma}\,|h_{\text{S}_2\text{R}}|^2}\right)$.

Proof: The result in (23) can be proved by analyzing all the error events related to the estimation of $\hat{b}_{S_1}$ and $\hat{b}_{S_2}$ at relay R. In particular, four events have to be analyzed: (a) no decoding errors over the S_1-to-R and S_2-to-R links, *i.e.*, $\hat{b}_{S_1} = b_{S_1}$ and $\hat{b}_{S_2} = b_{S_2}$; (b) decoding

(a) No decoding errors

b_{S_1}	b_{S_2}	$b_{S_1} \oplus b_{S_2}$	$\hat{b}_{S_1}$	$\hat{b}_{S_2}$	b_R
0	0	0	0	0	0
0	1	1	0	1	1
1	0	1	1	0	1
1	1	0	1	1	0

(b) Decoding errors over the $S_1 - R$ link

b_{S_1}	b_{S_2}	$b_{S_1} \oplus b_{S_2}$	$\hat{b}_{S_1}$	$\hat{b}_{S_2}$	b_R
0	0	0	1	0	1
0	1	1	1	1	0
1	0	1	0	0	0
1	1	0	0	1	1

(c) Decoding errors over the $S_2 - R$ link

b_{S_1}	b_{S_2}	$b_{S_1} \oplus b_{S_2}$	$\hat{b}_{S_1}$	$\hat{b}_{S_2}$	b_R
0	0	0	0	1	1
0	1	1	0	0	0
1	0	1	1	1	0
1	1	0	1	0	1

(d) Decoding errors over both links

b_{S_1}	b_{S_2}	$b_{S_1} \oplus b_{S_2}$	$\hat{b}_{S_1}$	$\hat{b}_{S_2}$	b_R
0	0	0	1	1	0
0	1	1	1	0	1
1	0	1	0	1	1
1	1	0	0	0	0

Table 1. Error propagation effect due to NC at the relays for realistic source-to-relay channels.

errors only over the S_1-to-R link, *i.e.*, $\hat{b}_{S_1} \neq b_{S_1}$ and $\hat{b}_{S_2} = b_{S_2}$; (c) decoding errors only over the S_2-to-R link, *i.e.*, $\hat{b}_{S_1} = b_{S_1}$ and $\hat{b}_{S_2} \neq b_{S_2}$; and (d) decoding error over both S_1-to-R and S_2-to-R links, *i.e.*, $\hat{b}_{S_1} \neq b_{S_1}$ and $\hat{b}_{S_2} \neq b_{S_2}$. These events are summarized in Table 1. In particular, we notice that errors occur if and only if there is a decoding error over a single wireless link. On the other hand, if errors occur in both links they cancel out and there is no error in the network-coded bit. Accordingly, P_R can be formally written as follows:

$$\begin{aligned} P_R &= \Pr\left\{\hat{b}_{S_1} \neq b_{S_1}\right\} + \Pr\left\{\hat{b}_{S_2} \neq b_{S_2}\right\} - 2\Pr\left\{\hat{b}_{S_1} \neq b_{S_1} \text{ and } \hat{b}_{S_2} \neq b_{S_2}\right\} \\ &= \Pr\left\{\hat{b}_{S_1} \neq b_{S_1}\right\} + \Pr\left\{\hat{b}_{S_2} \neq b_{S_2}\right\} - 2\Pr\left\{\hat{b}_{S_1} \neq b_{S_1}\right\}\Pr\left\{\hat{b}_{S_2} \neq b_{S_2}\right\} \end{aligned} \quad (24)$$

which leads to the final result in (23). This concludes the proof of Proposition 1. □

Finally, we note that, from (23), the average probability of error at the relay with NC, $\bar{P}_R$, can be computed from (10) and (11), and by taking into account that the fading over two links is uncorrelated. The final result from (23) is:

$$\bar{P}_R = \mathrm{E}\{P_R\} = \bar{P}_{S_1 R} + \bar{P}_{S_2 R} - 2\bar{P}_{S_1 R}\bar{P}_{S_2 R} = 2\bar{P} - 2\bar{P}^2 \quad (25)$$

Very interestingly, by comparing (22) and (25) we notice that DF and NC produce the same error propagation effect. Thus, by combining them, as the network codes in Section 3 foresee, we can expect an error concatenation problem. In particular, by combining the results in (22) and (25), the end-to-end error probability of the bits emitted by sources S_1 and S_2 and received by destination D (denoted by $P_{S_1(R_1R_2)D}$ and $P_{S_2(R_1R_2)D}$, respectively) can be computed as shown in (26)-(29) for *Scenario 1*, *Scenario 2*, *Scenario 3*, and *Scenario 4*, respectively:

$$\begin{cases} P_{S_1(R_1R_2)D} = P_{S_1R_1} + P_{R_1D} - 2P_{S_1R_1}P_{R_1D} \\ P_{S_2(R_1R_2)D} = P_{S_1R_2} + P_{R_2D} - 2P_{S_1R_2}P_{R_2D} \end{cases} \quad (26)$$

$$\begin{cases} P_{S_1(R_1R_2)D} = [P_{S_1R_1} + P_{S_2R_1} - 2P_{S_1R_1}P_{S_2R_1}] + P_{R_1D} - 2[P_{S_1R_1} + P_{S_2R_1} - 2P_{S_1R_1}P_{S_2R_1}]P_{R_1D} \\ P_{S_2(R_1R_2)D} = [P_{S_1R_2} + P_{S_2R_2} - 2P_{S_1R_2}P_{S_2R_2}] + P_{R_2D} - 2[P_{S_1R_2} + P_{S_2R_2} - 2P_{S_1R_2}P_{S_2R_2}]P_{R_2D} \end{cases} \tag{27}$$

$$\begin{cases} P_{S_1(R_1R_2)D} = [P_{S_1R_1} + P_{S_2R_1} - 2P_{S_1R_1}P_{S_2R_1}] + P_{R_1D} - 2[P_{S_1R_1} + P_{S_2R_1} - 2P_{S_1R_1}P_{S_2R_1}]P_{R_1D} \\ P_{S_2(R_1R_2)D} = P_{S_1R_2} + P_{R_2D} - 2P_{S_1R_2}P_{R_2D} \end{cases} \tag{28}$$

$$\begin{cases} P_{S_1(R_1R_2)D} = P_{S_1R_1} + P_{R_1D} - 2P_{S_1R_1}P_{R_1D} \\ P_{S_2(R_1R_2)D} = [P_{S_1R_2} + P_{S_2R_2} - 2P_{S_1R_2}P_{S_2R_2}] + P_{R_2D} - 2[P_{S_1R_2} + P_{S_2R_2} - 2P_{S_1R_2}P_{S_2R_2}]P_{R_2D} \end{cases} \tag{29}$$

The average values of $P_{S_1(R_1R_2)D}$ and $P_{S_2(R_1R_2)D}$, *i.e.*, $\bar{P}_{S_1(R_1R_2)D} = \mathrm{E}\left\{P_{S_1(R_1R_2)D}\right\}$ and $\bar{P}_{S_2(R_1R_2)D} = \mathrm{E}\left\{P_{S_2(R_1R_2)D}\right\}$ can be computed by using arguments similar to (22) and (25). The final result is here omitted due to space constraints and to avoid redundancy.

5.3.2 Closed–form expressions of APEPs

From (16) and (20), it follows that only three APEPs need to be computed, for each NC scenario in Section 3, to estimate the ABEP of both sources. Due to space constraints, we avoid to report the details of the derivation of each APEP for all the NC scenarios. However, since the derivations are very similar, we summarize in Appendix A the detailed computation of a generic APEP. All the other APEPs can be derived by following the same procedure.

In particular, by using the development in Appendix A the following results can be obtained:

Scenario 1:

$$\begin{cases} \mathrm{APEP}\,(1 \to 2) &=& \bar{P}_{S_2D}\bar{P}_{S_2(R_1R_2)D} + (1/2)\,(1 - \bar{P}_{S_2D})\,\bar{P}_{S_2(R_1R_2)D} \\ &+& (1/2)\left(1 - \bar{P}_{S_2(R_1R_2)D}\right)\bar{P}_{S_2D} \\ \\ \mathrm{APEP}\,(1 \to 3) &=& \bar{P}_{S_1D}\bar{P}_{S_1(R_1R_2)D} + (1/2)\,(1 - \bar{P}_{S_1D})\,\bar{P}_{S_1(R_1R_2)D} \\ &+& (1/2)\left(1 - \bar{P}_{S_1(R_1R_2)D}\right)\bar{P}_{S_1D} \\ \\ \mathrm{APEP}\,(1 \to 4) &=& (1/2)\,(1 - \bar{P}_{S_1D})\,(1 - \bar{P}_{S_2D})\,\bar{P}_{S_1(R_1R_2)D}\bar{P}_{S_2(R_1R_2)D} \\ &+& (1/2)\,(1 - \bar{P}_{S_1D})\left(1 - \bar{P}_{S_1(R_1R_2)D}\right)\bar{P}_{S_2D}\bar{P}_{S_2(R_1R_2)D} \\ &+& (1/2)\,(1 - \bar{P}_{S_1D})\left(1 - \bar{P}_{S_2(R_1R_2)D}\right)\bar{P}_{S_2D}\bar{P}_{S_1(R_1R_2)D} \\ &+& (1/2)\,(1 - \bar{P}_{S_2D})\left(1 - \bar{P}_{S_1(R_1R_2)D}\right)\bar{P}_{S_1D}\bar{P}_{S_2(R_1R_2)D} \\ &+& (1/2)\,(1 - \bar{P}_{S_2D})\left(1 - \bar{P}_{S_2(R_1R_2)D}\right)\bar{P}_{S_1D}\bar{P}_{S_1(R_1R_2)D} \\ &+& (1/2)\left(1 - \bar{P}_{S_1(R_1R_2)D}\right)\left(1 - \bar{P}_{S_2(R_1R_2)D}\right)\bar{P}_{S_1D}\bar{P}_{S_2D} \\ &+& (1 - \bar{P}_{S_1D})\,\bar{P}_{S_2D}\bar{P}_{S_1(R_1R_2)D}\bar{P}_{S_2(R_1R_2)D} \\ &+& (1 - \bar{P}_{S_2D})\,\bar{P}_{S_1D}\bar{P}_{S_1(R_1R_2)D}\bar{P}_{S_2(R_1R_2)D} \\ &+& \left(1 - \bar{P}_{S_1(R_1R_2)D}\right)\bar{P}_{S_1D}\bar{P}_{S_2D}\bar{P}_{S_2(R_1R_2)D} \\ &+& \left(1 - \bar{P}_{S_2(R_1R_2)D}\right)\bar{P}_{S_1D}\bar{P}_{S_2D}\bar{P}_{S_1(R_1R_2)D} \\ &+& \bar{P}_{S_1D}\bar{P}_{S_2D}\bar{P}_{S_1(R_1R_2)D}\bar{P}_{S_2(R_1R_2)D} \end{cases} \tag{30}$$

Scenario 2:

$$\left\{ \begin{aligned} \mathrm{APEP}\,(1 \to 2) &= (1 - \bar{P}_{S_2D})\,\bar{P}_{S_1(R_1R_2)D}\bar{P}_{S_2(R_1R_2)D} \\ &+ \left(1 - \bar{P}_{S_1(R_1R_2)D}\right)\bar{P}_{S_2D}\bar{P}_{S_2(R_1R_2)D} \\ &+ \left(1 - \bar{P}_{S_2(R_1R_2)D}\right)\bar{P}_{S_2D}\bar{P}_{S_1(R_1R_2)D} \\ &+ \bar{P}_{S_2D}\bar{P}_{S_1(R_1R_2)D}\bar{P}_{S_2(R_1R_2)D} \\ \mathrm{APEP}\,(1 \to 3) &= (1 - \bar{P}_{S_1D})\,\bar{P}_{S_1(R_1R_2)D}\bar{P}_{S_2(R_1R_2)D} \\ &+ \left(1 - \bar{P}_{S_1(R_1R_2)D}\right)\bar{P}_{S_1D}\bar{P}_{S_2(R_1R_2)D} \\ &+ \left(1 - \bar{P}_{S_2(R_1R_2)D}\right)\bar{P}_{S_1D}\bar{P}_{S_1(R_1R_2)D} \\ &+ \bar{P}_{S_1D}\bar{P}_{S_1(R_1R_2)D}\bar{P}_{S_2(R_1R_2)D} \\ \mathrm{APEP}\,(1 \to 4) &= (1/2)\,(1 - \bar{P}_{S_1D})\,\bar{P}_{S_2D} + (1/2)\,(1 - \bar{P}_{S_2D})\,\bar{P}_{S_1D} \\ &+ \bar{P}_{S_1D}\bar{P}_{S_2D} \end{aligned} \right. \tag{31}$$

Scenario 3:

$$\left\{ \begin{aligned} \mathrm{APEP}\,(1 \to 2) &= (1 - \bar{P}_{S_2D})\,\bar{P}_{S_1(R_1R_2)D}\bar{P}_{S_2(R_1R_2)D} \\ &+ \left(1 - \bar{P}_{S_1(R_1R_2)D}\right)\bar{P}_{S_2D}\bar{P}_{S_2(R_1R_2)D} \\ &+ \left(1 - \bar{P}_{S_2(R_1R_2)D}\right)\bar{P}_{S_2D}\bar{P}_{S_1(R_1R_2)D} \\ &+ \bar{P}_{S_2D}\bar{P}_{S_1(R_1R_2)D}\bar{P}_{S_2(R_1R_2)D} \\ \mathrm{APEP}\,(1 \to 3) &= \bar{P}_{S_1D}\bar{P}_{S_1(R_1R_2)D} + (1/2)\,(1 - P_{S_1D})\,\bar{P}_{S_1(R_1R_2)D} \\ &+ (1/2)\left(1 - \bar{P}_{S_1(R_1R_2)D}\right)\bar{P}_{S_1D} \\ \mathrm{APEP}\,(1 \to 4) &= (1 - \bar{P}_{S_1D})\,\bar{P}_{S_1(R_1R_2)D}\bar{P}_{S_2(R_1R_2)D} \\ &+ \left(1 - \bar{P}_{S_1(R_1R_2)D}\right)\bar{P}_{S_1D}\bar{P}_{S_2(R_1R_2)D} \\ &+ \left(1 - \bar{P}_{S_2(R_1R_2)D}\right)\bar{P}_{S_1D}\bar{P}_{S_1(R_1R_2)D} \\ &+ \bar{P}_{S_1D}\bar{P}_{S_1(R_1R_2)D}\bar{P}_{S_2(R_1R_2)D} \end{aligned} \right. \tag{32}$$

Scenario 4:

$$\begin{cases} \text{APEP}\,(1 \to 2) & = & (1/2)\,(1-\bar{P}_{S_2D})\,\bar{P}_{S_2(R_1R_2)D} + \bar{P}_{S_2D}\bar{P}_{S_2(R_1R_2)D} \\ & + & (1/2)\left(1-\bar{P}_{S_2(R_1R_2)D}\right)\bar{P}_{S_2D} \\ \text{APEP}\,(1 \to 3) & = & (1-\bar{P}_{S_1D})\,\bar{P}_{S_1(R_1R_2)D}\bar{P}_{S_2(R_1R_2)D} \\ & + & \left(1-\bar{P}_{S_1(R_1R_2)D}\right)\bar{P}_{S_1D}\bar{P}_{S_2(R_1R_2)D} \\ & + & \left(1-\bar{P}_{S_2(R_1R_2)D}\right)\bar{P}_{S_1D}\bar{P}_{S_1(R_1R_2)D} \\ & + & \bar{P}_{S_1D}\bar{P}_{S_1(R_1R_2)D}\bar{P}_{S_2(R_1R_2)D} \\ \text{APEP}\,(1 \to 4) & = & (1-\bar{P}_{S_1D})\,\bar{P}_{S_2D}\bar{P}_{S_1(R_1R_2)D} \\ & + & (1-\bar{P}_{S_2D})\,\bar{P}_{S_1D}\bar{P}_{S_1(R_1R_2)D} \\ & + & \left(1-\bar{P}_{S_1(R_1R_2)D}\right)\bar{P}_{S_1D}\bar{P}_{S_2D} \\ & + & \bar{P}_{S_1D}\bar{P}_{S_2D}\bar{P}_{S_1(R_1R_2)D} \end{cases} \quad (33)$$

5.4 Diversity analysis

Let us now study the performance (ABEP_∞) of the MDD receiver for high SNRs, which allows us to understand the diversity gain provided by the network codes described in Section 3 (Wang & Giannakis, 2003). To this end, we need to first provide a closed-form expression of the ABEP of S_1 and S_2 from the APEPs computed in Section 5.3.2. By taking into account that the wireless links are i.i.d. and that the average error probability over a single-hop link is given by $\bar{P}$ in (11), from (20), (30)-(33), and some algebra, the ABEPs for *Scenario 1*, *Scenario 2*, *Scenario 3*, and *Scenario 4* are as follows, respectively:

Scenario 1: $\text{ABEP}^{(S_1)} = \text{ABEP}^{(S_2)} = (1/2)\bar{P}_1 + (1/2)\bar{P}_3 + (1/2)\bar{P}_1\bar{P}_2 + (1/2)\bar{P}_1\bar{P}_3 + (1/2)\bar{P}_1\bar{P}_4 + (1/2)\bar{P}_2\bar{P}_3 + (1/2)\bar{P}_3\bar{P}_4 - (1/2)\bar{P}_1\bar{P}_2\bar{P}_3 - (1/2)\bar{P}_1\bar{P}_2\bar{P}_4 - (1/2)\bar{P}_1\bar{P}_3\bar{P}_4 - (1/2)\bar{P}_2\bar{P}_3\bar{P}_4 - (1/2)\bar{P}_1\bar{P}_2\bar{P}_3\bar{P}_4$, where we have defined $\bar{P}_1 = \bar{P}_2 = \bar{P}$ and $\bar{P}_3 = \bar{P}_4 = 2\bar{P} - 2\bar{P}^2$.

Scenario 2: $\text{ABEP}^{(S_1)} = \text{ABEP}^{(S_2)} = (1/2)\bar{P}_1 + (1/2)\bar{P}_2 + \bar{P}_1\bar{P}_3 + \bar{P}_1\bar{P}_4 + \bar{P}_3\bar{P}_4 - \bar{P}_1\bar{P}_2\bar{P}_4 - \bar{P}_1\bar{P}_3\bar{P}_4$, where we have defined $\bar{P}_1 = \bar{P}_2 = \bar{P}$ and $\bar{P}_3 = \bar{P}_4 = 3\bar{P} - 6\bar{P}^2 + 4\bar{P}^3$.

Scenario 3: $\text{ABEP}^{(S_1)} = (1/2)\bar{P}_1 + (1/2)\bar{P}_3 + \bar{P}_1\bar{P}_2 + \bar{P}_1\bar{P}_4 + \bar{P}_2\bar{P}_4 - \bar{P}_1\bar{P}_2\bar{P}_4$ and $\text{ABEP}^{(S_2)} = \bar{P}_1\bar{P}_2 + \bar{P}_1\bar{P}_3 + \bar{P}_1\bar{P}_4 + 2\bar{P}_2\bar{P}_4 + \bar{P}_3\bar{P}_4 - 2\bar{P}_1\bar{P}_2\bar{P}_4 - 2\bar{P}_2\bar{P}_3\bar{P}_4$, where we have defined $\bar{P}_1 = \bar{P}_2 = \bar{P}$, $\bar{P}_3 = 3\bar{P} - 6\bar{P}^2 + 4\bar{P}^3$, and $\bar{P}_4 = 2\bar{P} - 2\bar{P}^2$.

Scenario 4: $\text{ABEP}^{(S_1)} = \bar{P}_1\bar{P}_2 + 2\bar{P}_1\bar{P}_3 + \bar{P}_1\bar{P}_4 + \bar{P}_2\bar{P}_3 + \bar{P}_3\bar{P}_4 - 2\bar{P}_1\bar{P}_2\bar{P}_3 - 2\bar{P}_1\bar{P}_3\bar{P}_4$ and $\text{ABEP}^{(S_2)} = (1/2)\bar{P}_2 + (1/2)\bar{P}_4 + \bar{P}_1\bar{P}_2 + \bar{P}_1\bar{P}_3 + 2\bar{P}_2\bar{P}_3 - \bar{P}_2\bar{P}_4 - 2\bar{P}_1\bar{P}_2\bar{P}_3$, where we have defined $\bar{P}_1 = \bar{P}_2 = \bar{P}$, $\bar{P}_3 = 2\bar{P} - 2\bar{P}^2$, and $\bar{P}_4 = 3\bar{P} - 6\bar{P}^2 + 4\bar{P}^3$.

From the results above, we notice that in *Scenario 1* and *Scenario 2* both sources have the same ABEP. Furthermore, for all the NC scenarios we can easily compute ABEP_∞ and the diversity gain (Div) of S_1 and S_2, as shown in Table 2. In particular, from Table 2 we observe that, by using UEP coding theory for network code design (*i.e.*, *Scenario 3* and *Scenario 4*), at least one source can achieve a diversity gain greater than that obtained by using relay–only or XOR–only network codes (*i.e.*, *Scenario 1* and *Scenario 2*). Furthermore, this performance improvement is obtained by increasing neither the Galois field nor the number of time-slots

	$\text{ABEP}_\infty^{(S_1)}$	$\text{ABEP}_\infty^{(S_2)}$	Div_{S_1}	Div_{S_2}
Scenario 1	$(3/2)\bar{P}$	$(3/2)\bar{P}$	1	1
Scenario 2	$\bar{P}$	$\bar{P}$	1	1
Scenario 3	$2\bar{P}$	$16\bar{P}^2$	1	2
Scenario 4	$16\bar{P}^2$	$2\bar{P}$	2	1

Table 2. ABEP_∞ of S_1 and S_2 and diversity gain.

	$\text{ABEP}_\infty^{(S_1)}$	$\text{ABEP}_\infty^{(S_2)}$	Div_{S_1}	Div_{S_2}
Scenario 1	$\bar{P}$	$\bar{P}$	1	1
Scenario 2	$\bar{P}$	$\bar{P}$	1	1
Scenario 3	$\bar{P}$	$6\bar{P}^2$	1	2
Scenario 4	$6\bar{P}^2$	$\bar{P}$	2	1

Table 3. ABEP_∞ of S_1 and S_2 and diversity gain with ideal source-to-relay channels.

(Rebelatto et al., 2010b). Finally, by studying the diversity gain provided by the network codes obtained from UEP coding theory in terms of separation vector (SP), we observe that the achievable diversity gain is equal to $\text{Div} = \text{SP} - 1$. From the theory of linear block codes, we know that this is the best achievable diversity for a (4,2,2) UEP-based code that uses a MDD receiver design at the destination (Proakis, 2000), (Simon & Alouini, 2000). Better performance can only be achieved by using a more complicated receiver design, which, *e.g.*, exploits CSI at the network layer.

5.5 Effect of realistic source-to-relay channels

In Section 2, we have mentioned that the relays simply D-NC-F the received bits even though the source-to-relay channels are error-prone, and so the transmission is affected by the error propagation problem. Thus, it is worth being analyzed whether this error propagation effect can decrease the diversity gain achieved by the MDD receiver or whether only a worse coding gain can be expected. To understand this issue, in this section we study the performance of an idealized working scenario in which it is assumed that there are no decoding errors at the relays. In other words, we assume $\hat{b}_{S_tR_q} = b_{S_t}$ for $t = 1, 2$ and $q = 1, 2$ in (3). In this case, the expression of the ABEP for high SNRs can still be computed from (20) and (30)-(33), but by taking into account that $\bar{P} = \bar{P}_{S_1D} = \bar{P}_{S_2D} = \bar{P}_{S_1(R_1R_2)D} = \bar{P}_{S_2(R_1R_2)D}$. The final result of ABEP_∞ for S_1 and S_2 is summarized in Table 3.

By carefully comparing Table 2 and Table 3, we notice that there is no loss in the diversity gain due to decoding errors at the relay. However, for realistic source-to-relay channels the ABEP is, in general, slightly worse. Interestingly, we notice that *Scenario 2* is the most robust to error propagation, and, asymptotically, there is no performance degradation.

6. Numerical examples

In this section, we show some numerical results to substantiate claims and analytical derivations. A detailed description of the simulation setup can be found in Section 2. In particular, we assume: i) BPSK modulation, ii) $\sigma_0^2 = 1$, and iii) according to Section 5.5, both scenarios with and without errors on the source-to-relay wireless links are studied.

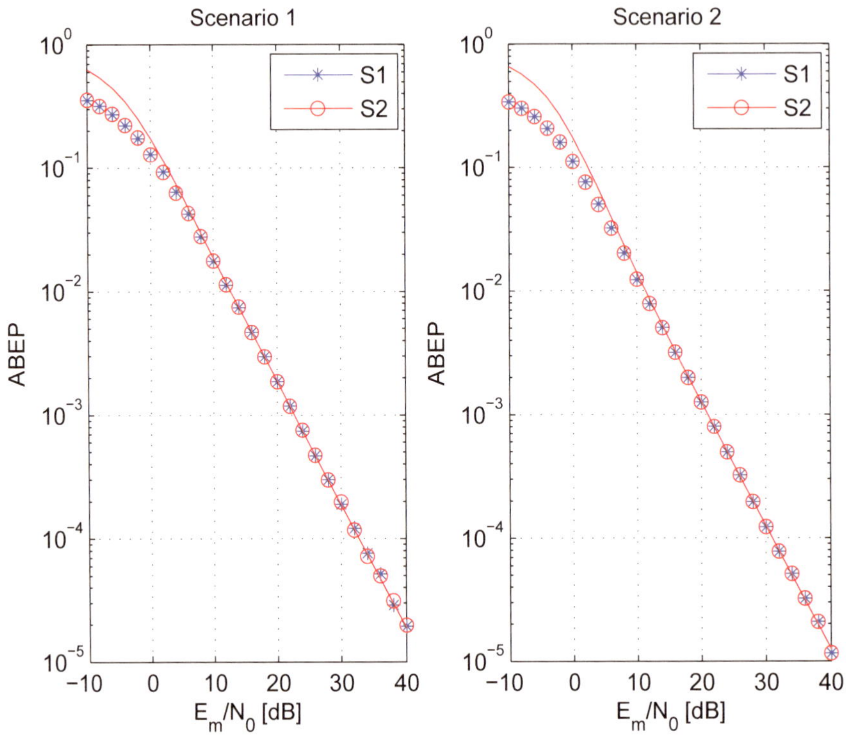

Fig. 2. ABEP against E_m/N_0. Solid lines show the analytical model and markers Monte Carlo simulations ($\sigma_0^2 = 1$).

The results are shown in Figure 2 and Figure 3 for realistic source-to-relay links, and in Figure 4 and Figure 5 for ideal source-to-relay links, respectively. By carefully analyzing these numerical examples, the following conclusions can be drawn: i) our analytical model overlaps with Monte Carlo simulations, thus confirming our findings in terms of achievable performance and diversity analysis; ii) as expected, it can be noticed that the ABEP gets slighlty worse in the presence of errors on the source-to-relay wireless links for *Scenario 1*, *Scenario 3*, and *Scenario 4*, while, as predicted in Table 3, the XOR–only network code (*Scenario 2*) is very robust to error propagation and there is no performance difference between Figure 2 and Figure 4; and iii) the network code design based on UEP coding theory allows the MDD receiver to achieve, for at least one source, a higher diversity gain than conventional relaying and NC methods, and without the need to use either additional time-slots or non-binary operations.

More specifically, the complexity of UEP–based network code design is the same as relay–only and XOR–only cooperative methods. For example, by looking at the results in Figure 3 and Figure 5, we observe that the network code in *Scenario 3* is the best choice when the data sent by S_2 needs to be delivered i) either with the same transmit power but with better QoS or ii) with the same QoS but with less transmit power if compared to S_1. The working principle of the network code in *Scenario 3* has a simple interpretation: if S_2 is the "golden user", then we should dedicate one relay to only forward its data without performing NC on the data of S_1. A similar comment can be made about *Scenario 4* if S_1 is the "golden user". This result

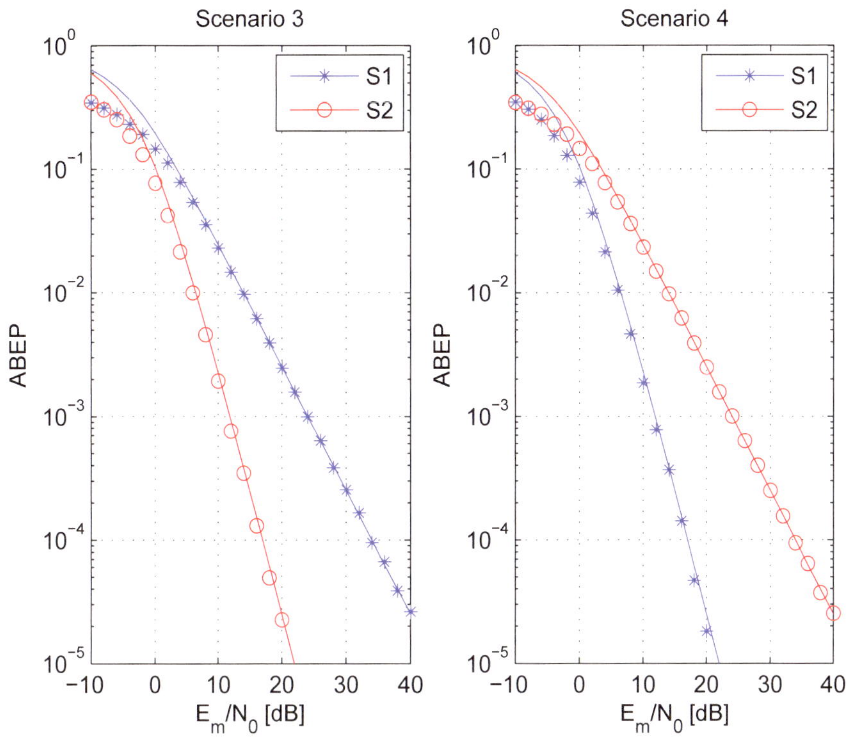

Fig. 3. ABEP against E_m/N_0. Solid lines show the analytical model and markers Monte Carlo simulations ($\sigma_0^2 = 1$).

highlights that, from the network optimization point of view, there might be an optimal choice of the relay nodes that should perform relay-only and NC coding operations. By constraining the relays to perform simple operations (*e.g.*, to work in a binary Galois field), this hybrid solution might provide better performance than scenarios where all the nodes perform NC. However, analysis and numerical results shown in this book chapter have also highlighted some important limitations of the MDD receiver. As a matter of fact, with conventional relaying and NC methods only diversity equal to one can be obtained, while with UEP-based NC at least one user can achieve diversity gain equal to two. However, the network topology studied in Figure 1 would allow each source to achieve a diversity gain equal to three, as three copies of the messages sent by both sources are available at the destination after four time-slots. This limitation is mainly due to the adopted detector, which does not exploit channel knowledge at the network layer and does not account for the error propagation caused by realistic source-to-relay wireless links. The development of more advanced channel-aware receiver designs is our ongoing research activity.

7. Conclusion

In this book chapter, we have proposed UEP coding theory for the flexible design of network codes for multi-source multi-relay cooperative networks. The main advantage of the proposed method with respect to state-of-the-art solutions is the possibility of assigning the diversity

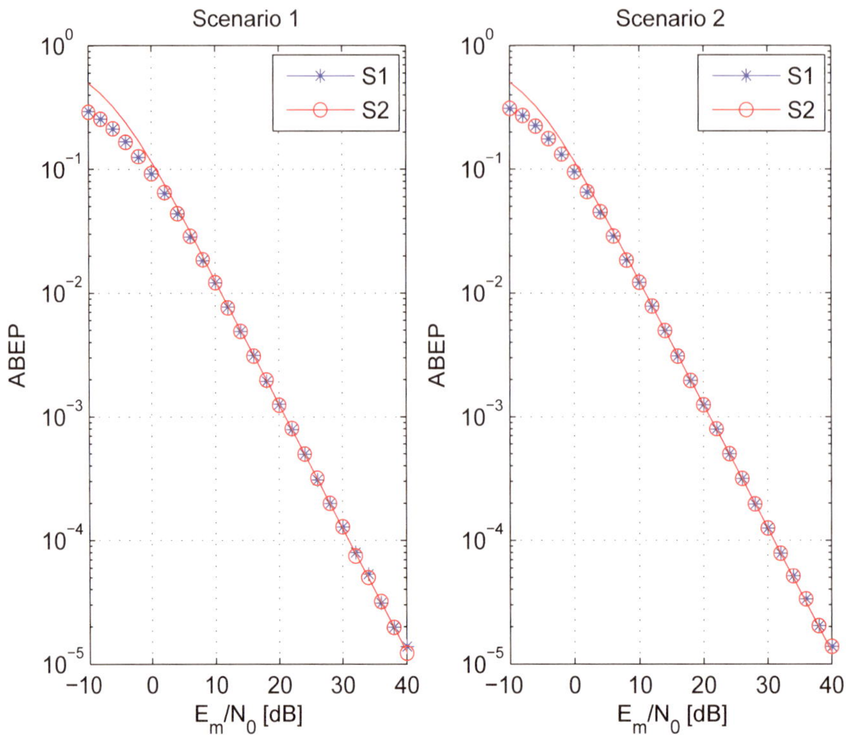

Fig. 4. ABEP against E_m / N_0. Solid lines show the analytical model and markers Monte Carlo simulations ($\sigma_0^2 = 1$). Ideal source-to-relay channels.

gain of each user individually. This offers a great flexibility for the efficient design of network codes for cooperative networks, as energy consumption, performance, number of time-slots required to achieve the desired diversity gain, and complexity at the relay nodes for performing NC can be traded-off by taking into account the specific and actual needs of each source, and without the constraint of over-engineering (*e.g.*, working in a larger Galois field or using more time-slots than actually required) the system according to the needs of the source requesting the highest diversity gain.

Ongoing research is now concerned with the development of more robust receiver schemes at the destination, with the aim of better exploiting the diversity gain provided by the UEP-based network code design.

8. Acknowledgment

This work is supported, in part, by the research projects "GREENET" (PITN–GA–2010–264759), "JNCD4CoopNets" (CNRS – GDR 720 ISIS, France), and "Re.C.O.Te.S.S.C." (PORAbruzzo, Italy).

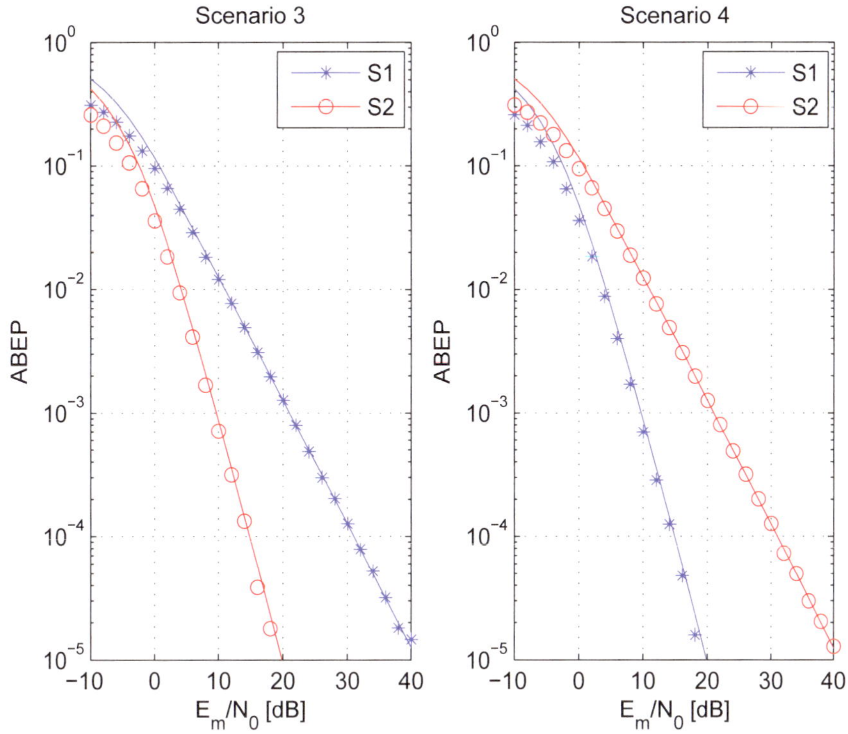

Fig. 5. ABEP against E_m / N_0. Solid lines show the analytical model and markers Monte Carlo simulations ($\sigma_0^2 = 1$). Ideal source-to-relay channels.

9. References

Ahlswede R. et al. (year 2000), Network information flow, *IEEE Trans. Inform. Theory*, Vol. 46(No. 4), 1204-1216.

Boyarinov I. M. and Katsman G. L. (year 1981), Linear unequal error protection codes, *IEEE Trans. Inform. Theory*, Vol. IT-27(No. 2), 168-175.

Cai N. and Yeung R. W. (2002), Network coding and error correction, *Proceedings of IEEE ITW*, Bangalore, India, pp. 119-122.

Chachulski S. et al. (2007), Trading structure for randomness in wireless opportunistic routing, *Proceedings of ACM SIGCOMM*, Kyoto, Japan, pp. 169-180.

Chamberland J.-F. and Veeravalli V. V. (year 2007), Wireless sensors in distributed detection applications - An alternative theoretical framework tailored to decentralized detection, *IEEE Signal Process. Mag.*, Vol. 24(No. 3), 16-25.

Di Renzo M. et al. (year 2009), Distributed data fusion over correlated log-normal sensing and reporting channels: Application to cognitive radio networks, *IEEE Trans. Wireless Commun.*, Vol. 8(No. 12), 5813-5821.

Di Renzo M., Iezzi M., and Graziosi F. (2010a), Beyond routing via network coding: An overview of fundamental information-theoretic results, *Proceedings of IEEE PIMRC*, Istanbul, Turkey, pp. 1-6.

Di Renzo M. et al. (2010b), Robust wireless network coding - An overview, *Springer Lecture Notes*, Vol. 45, pp. 685–698.

Hasna M. O. and Alouini M.-S. (year 2003), End-to-end performance of transmission systems with relays over Rayleigh-fading channels, *IEEE Trans. Wireless Commun.*, Vol. 2(No. 6), 1126-1131.

Ho T. et al. (2003), The benefits of coding over routing in a randomized setting, *Proceedings of IEEE ISIT*, Yokohama, Japan, p. 442.

Ho T. et al. (year 2006), A random linear network coding approach to multicast, *IEEE Trans. Inform. Theory*, Vol. 52(No. 10), 4413-4430.

Katti S., Gollakota S., and Katabi D. (2007), Embracing wireless interference: Analog network coding, *Proceedings of ACM SIGCOMM*, Kyoto, Japan, pp. 397-408.

Katti S. et al. (year 2008a), XORs in the air: Practical wireless network coding, *IEEE/ACM Trans. Networking*, Vol. 16(No. 3), 497-510.

Katti S. (2008b), Network coded wireless architecture, *Ph.D. Dissertation*, Massachusetts Institute of Technology.

Katti S. et al. (2008c), Symbol-level network coding for wireless mesh networks, *Proceedings of ACM SIGCOMM*, Seattle, USA, pp. 401-412.

Koetter R. and Medard M. (year 2003), An algebraic approach to network coding, *IEEE/ACM Trans. Networking*, Vol. 11(No. 5), 782-795.

Koetter R. and Kschischang F. (year 2008), Coding for errors and erasures in random network coding, *IEEE Trans. Inform. Theory*, Vol. 54(No. 8), 3579-3591.

Li S.-Y. R., Yeung R. W., and Cai N. (year 2003), Linear network coding, *IEEE Trans. Inform. Theory*, Vol. 49(No. 2), 371-381.

Masnick B. and Wolf J. (year 1967), On linear unequal error protection codes, *IEEE Trans. Inform. Theory*, Vol. IT-3(No. 4), 600-607.

Nguyen H. X., Nguyen H. H., and Le-Ngoc T. (year 2010), Signal transmission with unequal error protection in wireless relay networks, *IEEE Trans. Veh. Technol.*, Vol. 59(No. 5), 2166-2178.

Pabst R. et al. (year 2004), Relay-based deployment concepts for wireless and mobile broadband radio, *IEEE Commun. Mag.*, Vol. 42(No. 9), 80-89.

Proakis J. J. (2000), *Digital Communications*, McGraw-Hill, 4th ed.

Rebelatto J., Uchoa-Filho B., Li Y., and Vucetic B. (2010a), Generalized distributed network coding based on nonbinary linear block codes for multi-user cooperative communications, submitted. Available at: http://arxiv.org/abs/1003.3501.

Rebelatto J., Uchoa-Filho B., Li Y., and Vucetic B. (2010b), Multi-user cooperative diversity through network coding based on classical coding theory, submitted. Available at: http://arxiv.org/abs/1004.2757.

Scaglione A., Goeckel D., Laneman N. (year 2006), Cooperative wireless communications in mobile ad hoc networks, *IEEE Signal Process. Mag.*, Vol. 24(No. 9), 18-29.

Simon M. K. and Alouini M.-S. (2000), Digital Communication over Fading Channels, *John Wiley and Sons*, 1st ed.

Thomos N. and Frossard P. (year 2009), Network coding and media streaming, *J. Commun.*, Vol. 4(No. 8), 628-639.

Topakkaya H. and Wang Z. (2010), Wireless network code design and performance analysis using diversity-multiplexing tradeoff, submitted. Available at: http://arxiv.org/abs/1004.3282.

Van Gils W. J. (year 1983), Two topics on linear unequal error protection codes, *IEEE Trans. Inform. Theory*, Vol. IT-29(No. 6), 866-876.

Wang Z. and Giannakis G. (year 2003), A simple and general parameterization quantifying performance in fading channels, *IEEE Trans. Commun.*, Vol. 51(No. 8), 1389-1398.

Wang C., Fan Y., and Thompson J. (year 2009), Recovering multiplexing loss through concurrent decode-and-forward (DF) relaying, *Wireless Pers. Commun.*, Vol. 48, 193-213.

Xiao M. and Skoglund M. (2009a), M-user cooperative wireless communications based on nonbinary network codes, *Proceedings of IEEE ITW*, Taormina, Italy, pp. 316-320.

Xiao M. and Skoglund M. (2009b), Design of network codes for multiple-user multiple-relay wireless networks, *Proceedings of IEEE ISIT*, Seoul, Korea, pp. 2562-2566.

Zhang S., Liew S., and Lam P. (2006), Hot topic: Physical layer network coding, *Proceedings of ACM MobiHoc*, Florence, Italy, pp. 358-365.

Zhang Z.(year 2008), Linear network error correction codes in packet networks, *IEEE Trans. Inform. Theory*, Vol. 54(No. 1), 209-218.

A. Appendix: Proof of (30)–(33)

To understand how (30)-(33) are computed, in this section we provide a step-by-step derivation of the computation of $\text{APEP}(1 \to 3)$ for source S_1 and *Scenario 1, i.e.*, $\text{APEP}^{(S_1)}(1 \to 3) = \Pr\{0000 \to 1010\}$. Note that since $c_1^{(1)} = 0 \neq c_1^{(3)} = 1$, we avoid to emphasize, for the sake of simplicity, this conditioning in what follows. Other APEPs, for all the other scenarios, can be obtained with a similar analytical derivation.
From (19), the PEP can be computed as follows:

$$\text{PEP}^{(1)}(1 \to 3) = \int_{0^+}^{+\infty} g_{D_{1,3}}(\xi)\, d\xi + \frac{1}{2}\int_{0^-}^{0^+} g_{D_{1,3}}(\xi)\, d\xi \tag{34}$$

where $g_{D_{1,3}}(\cdot)$ is the probability density function of random variable $D_{1,3}$:

$$D_{1,3} = \sum_{i=1}^{4}\left[\left|\hat{c}_i - c_i^{(1)}\right| - \left|\hat{c}_i - c_i^{(3)}\right|\right] = \sum_{i=1}^{4} \beta_i^{(1,3)} \tag{35}$$

where $\beta_i^{(1,3)} = \left|\hat{c}_i - c_i^{(1)}\right| - \left|\hat{c}_i - c_i^{(3)}\right|$ for $i = 1,2,3,4$.

By direct inspection, it is possible to show that $\beta_i^{(1,3)}$ for $i = 1,2,3,4$ are independent Bernoulli distributed random variables with probability density function as follows:

$$\begin{cases} g_{\beta_1}(\xi) = (1 - P_{S_1 D})\,\delta(\xi + 1) + P_{S_1 D}\,\delta(\xi - 1) \\ g_{\beta_2}(\xi) = \delta(\xi) \\ g_{\beta_3}(\xi) = \left(1 - P_{S_1(R_1 R_2)D}\right)\delta(\xi + 1) + P_{S_1(R_1 R_2)D}\,\delta(\xi - 1) \\ g_{\beta_4}(\xi) = \delta(\xi) \end{cases} \tag{36}$$

where $\delta(\cdot)$ is the Dirac delta function.

It is relevant to notice that $g_{\beta_2}(\xi) = g_{\beta_4}(\xi) = \delta(\xi)$, *i.e.*, $\beta_2 = \beta_4 = 0$ with unit probability, because $c_2^{(1)} = c_2^{(3)}$ and $c_4^{(1)} = c_4^{(3)}$, and, so, regardless of the estimates $\hat{c}_2$ and $\hat{c}_4$ provided by the physical layer, we always have $\left|\hat{c}_2 - c_2^{(1)}\right| - \left|\hat{c}_2 - c_2^{(3)}\right| = 0$ and $\left|\hat{c}_4 - c_4^{(1)}\right| - \left|\hat{c}_4 - c_4^{(3)}\right| = 0$. Since $\beta_i^{(1,3)}$ for $i = 1, 2, 3, 4$ are independent random variables, the probability density function of $D_{1,3}$ in (35) can be computed via the convolution operator:

$$\begin{aligned} g_{D_{1,3}}(\xi) &= \left(g_{\beta_1} \otimes g_{\beta_2} \otimes g_{\beta_3} \otimes g_{\beta_4}\right)(\xi) = \left(g_{\beta_1} \otimes g_{\beta_3}\right)(\xi) \\ &= \left[\left(1 - P_{S_1 D}\right) P_{S_1(R_1 R_2)D} + \left(1 - P_{S_1(R_1 R_2)D}\right) P_{S_1 D}\right] \delta(\xi) \\ &+ \left(1 - P_{S_1 D}\right)\left(1 - P_{S_1(R_1 R_2)D}\right) \delta(\xi + 2) + P_{S_1 D} P_{S_1(R_1 R_2)D} \delta(\xi - 2) \end{aligned} \tag{37}$$

where $\otimes$ denotes convolution.
Furthermore, by substituting (37) into (34) we can get the final result for the PEP:

$$\begin{aligned} \text{PEP}^{(1)}(1 \to 3) &= (1/2)\left(1 - P_{S_1 D}\right) P_{S_1(R_1 R_2)D} + (1/2)\left(1 - P_{S_1(R_1 R_2)D}\right) P_{S_1 D} \\ &+ P_{S_1 D} P_{S_1(R_1 R_2)D} \end{aligned} \tag{38}$$

Finally, the APEP can be computed by simply taking the expectation of (38) and by considering that fading over all the wireless links is independent distributed:

$$\begin{aligned} \text{APEP}^{(1)}(1 \to 3) &= \text{E}\left\{\text{PEP}^{(1)}(1 \to 3)\right\} \\ &= (1/2)\left(1 - \bar{P}_{S_1 D}\right) \bar{P}_{S_1(R_1 R_2)D} + (1/2)\left(1 - \bar{P}_{S_1(R_1 R_2)D}\right) \bar{P}_{S_1 D} \\ &+ \bar{P}_{S_1 D} \bar{P}_{S_1(R_1 R_2)D} \end{aligned} \tag{39}$$

We observe that (39) coincides with (30), and this concludes our proof.

8

Diversity and Decoding in Non-Ideal Conditions

(Chun-Ye) Susan Vasana, Ph.D.
University of North Florida
United States

1. Introduction

Nowadays, there are many products that provide personal wireless services to users who are on the move. Multiple antenna diversity is usually required to make a wireless link more reliable. User terminals have to be small enough to consume and emit low power. As a result, antennas cannot be spaced far apart enough to have independent and diverse branches for the received signals. Another issue affecting diversity gain is the unbalanced branches due to different locations or different polarizations of the antennas. The average signal power received from those unbalanced branches is different. Both the branch correlation and power imbalance degrade the benefits of diversity reception. Therefore, it is very important to investigate such effects before applying diversity reception to practical mobile or wireless radio systems.

There have been a significant numbers of theoretical researches reported in the area of diversity systems and combining techniques. Some papers considered diversity systems with the correlated branches as in the references. The problems of correlated and unbalanced branches are addressed in (Dietze et al., 2002) and (Mallik et al., 2002) for the two-branch diversity system and for the Rayleigh fading channel. This chapter will address both the effects of branch correlation and power imbalance for generic L branches diversity system. The diagonalization transformation is used in the performance analysis for diversity reception with the correlated Rayleigh-fading signals in (Fang et al., 2000)-(Chang & McLane, 1997). Here, the diagonalization transformer is introduced as a linear transformer implemented before the diversity branches are being combined, which can transform the correlated and balanced branches to the uncorrelated and unbalanced ones, and vice versa. A real world simulation system is included in the chapter, which has the extended result of the paper (Vasana & McLane, 2004).

Most analyses assume that the fading signal components are correlated in diversity branches but the noise components are independent in the branches. However, the external noise and interference that come with the fading signals are correlated. Plus, the coupling of diversity branches has the same effect on both signal and noise components. Some paper assumes that the dominant noise and interference have the same correlation distribution as the fading signals (Chang & McLane, 1997). This chapter assumes a generic case, in which the noise components are correlated with a correlation equal or smaller than the correlation between signal components. If the transmitted signal is u(t), the received signal from the kth branch can be expressed as:

$$r_k(t) = A_k\, u(t) + n_k(t)= s_k(t) + n_k(t) \qquad k=1, 2, \ldots, L \tag{1}$$

where:

$$A_k = R_k\, e^{-j\Phi k}, \quad k=1, 2, \ldots, L \tag{2}$$

is the complex, fading phasor of $r_k(t)$. And $n_k(t)$ is the additive white Gaussian noise and interference component. For the Rayleigh or Rician fading channels, the envelope of the received signal, R_k, in the first term of equation (1) can be approximately described by the Rayleigh or Rician distribution, depending on if there is or not a major stable line-of-sight (LOS) path between the transmitter and the receiver. In both cases, the complex fading phasor, A_k, k=1, 2, …, L, are complex correlated Gaussian random variables. So is the first term, $A_k u(t)$, in equation (1) as u(t) is a deterministic transmitted signal.
With the fading model in equations (1) and (2), the fading signal components received in k^{th} antennas, $s_k(t)$, k=1, 2, …, L, are complex Gaussian processes with real and imaginary components, X_k and Y_k, both with zero mean for the Rayleigh fading, and non-zero mean for the Rician fading. For the simplicity of analysis, assume that the L branches have identical correlation coefficient and there is no cross correlation between any in-phase and quadrature-phase components. There are only correlation coefficients between any two diversity branches, ρ, which is related to the antenna distance and coupling effects.

2. The conversion between correlation and imbalance among diversity branches

The same effect to the diversity gain was measured with either correlation between diversity branches or power imbalance among the branches. A linear transformation can transform one situation to another.

2.1 Diagonalization transformation

The diagonalization technique has been used successfully in the error performance analysis for diversity with correlated branches (Fang, etc. 2000) and (Chang & McLane, 1997). Here the diagonalization technique is used as a transformer at the diversity reception. The intent is to develop a simple linear system to deal with the correlated or unbalanced branches in diversity systems, and maximize diversity gain by combining methods under different situations (Vasana, 2008).
Assuming the correlation coefficients among the L branches is identical, and the average power of the received signal components for each branch is identical to $2\sigma_s^2$. Furthermore, the correlation distribution between in-phase components is the same as the correlation between quadrature-phase components. Under the above assumption, the covariance matrix C_X or C_Y for the signal components, X_k and Y_k, is symmetric as:

$$C_X = C_Y = \sigma_s^2 \begin{pmatrix} 1 & \rho_s & \rho_s & \cdots & \rho_s \\ \rho_s & 1 & \rho_s & \cdots & \rho_s \\ & & \cdots & & \\ \rho_s & \rho_s & \rho_s & \cdots & 1 \end{pmatrix} \tag{3}$$

The linear transformation between the received signal vector $R = [r_1, r_2, \ldots, r_L]$ and transformed signal vector $Z = [z_1, z_2, \ldots, z_L]$ is:

$$\begin{cases} z_1 = \xi_1^{(1)} r_1 + \xi_2^{(1)} r_2 + \ \dots \ + \xi_L^{(1)} r_L \\ z_2 = \xi_1^{(2)} r_1 + \xi_2^{(2)} r_2 + \ \dots \ + \xi_L^{(2)} r_L \\ \dots \\ \dots \\ z_{L-1} = \xi_1^{(L-1)} r_1 + \xi_2^{(L-1)} r_2 + \ \dots \ + \xi_L^{(L-1)} r_L \\ z_L = (r_1 + r_2 + \ \dots \ + r_L)/\sqrt{L} \end{cases} \tag{4}$$

where $[\xi_1^{(i)}, \xi_2^{(i)}, \dots, \xi_L^{(i)}]$ for i=1, 2, ..., L-1 are eigenvectors of the covariance matrix in equation (3). As an example of L=3 diversity systems, the transformation in equation (4) was given in (Vasana, 2008).

After the transformation as in equation (4), the the covariance matrix C_{Zr} or C_{Zi} for the real and imaginary signal components, Z_r and Z_i, of the trnasformed signal vector Z, is diagnoalized as follow:

$$C_{Zr} = C_{Zi} = \sigma_s^2 \begin{pmatrix} 1-\rho_S & 0 & 0 & \dots & 0 & 0 \\ 0 & 1-\rho_S & 0 & \dots & 0 & 0 \\ & & \dots & & & \\ 0 & 0 & 0 & \dots & 1-\rho_S & 0 \\ 0 & 0 & 0 & 0 & \dots & 1+(L-1)\rho_S \end{pmatrix} \tag{5}$$

The diagnoalized covariance matrix above indicates there are no corrleation between L transformed branches. The values in the diagnoal of the matrix (5) are the eigenvalues of the covariance matrix (3) of the signal vector before the transformation, which indicates the average signal power in each branches. Equation (5) shows that after the transformation the first (L-1) branches have the same average power but the Lth branch has the different average power from the others. The diagonalization transformation can be expressed in the following blockdiagram. The diagonalizer transformer in the Fig. 1 is a linear transformation between vector R and Z by equation (4), using the eigenvector derived from the convariance matrix in (3).

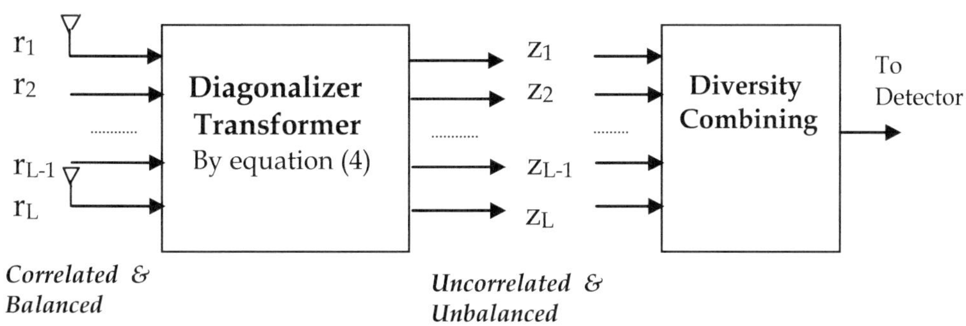

Fig. 1. Diagonalizer (Transformer) Block Diagram

The outputs of the transformer are a set of uncorrelated complex Gaussian random processes with λ_i as their variance values. That is, using the diagonalizer, the L branch correlated random processes have been transformed to the L branch uncorrelated random processes. However, the average signal power of each branch will not be the same, but are the twice of the values in the diagnoal position of the matrix in (5) as follow:

$$\begin{cases} (P_s)_i = (P_X)_i + (P_Y)_i = 2\sigma_s^2(1 - \rho_s), & i = 1, 2, \ldots, L-1 \\ (P_s)_L = (P_X)_i + (P_Y)_i = 2\sigma_s^2\left[1 + (L-1)\rho_s\right] \end{cases} \tag{6}$$

The noise and interference components, $n_k(t)$, k=1, 2, ..., L, of the received signal $r_k(t)$, k=1, 2, ..., L, in equation (1) have the same correlation distribution as in equation (3) but with smaller correlation coefficient ρ_n and average noise power σ_n^2. At the outputs of the transformer, the noise components will be similarly de-correlated. Hence, the average signal-to-noise ratios (SNR) in the L branches at the output of the transformer will be:

$$\begin{cases} (P_s / P_n)_i = \dfrac{\sigma_s^2(1 - \rho_s)}{\sigma_n^2(1 - \rho_n)} & i = 1, 2, \ldots, L-1 \\ (P_s / P_n)_L = \dfrac{\sigma_s^2\left[1 + (L-1)\rho_s\right]}{\sigma_n^2\left[1 + (L-1)\rho_n\right]} \end{cases} \tag{7}$$

From the above equations, the followings can be concluded:

1. Before the transformation the signal-to-noise ratios (P_s/ P_n) are the same for all L branches, which is σ_s^2 / σ_n^2 for the power balanced L branches.
2. After the transformation the signal-to-noise ratio (P_s/ P_n) of the Lth branch is enhanced usually as $\rho_s > \rho_n$. The Lth branch is the combinational branch just as what the equal-gain combining method does.
3. After the transformation the signal-to-noise ratios $(P_s/ P_n)_i$ of the 1st to $(L-1)^{th}$ branches are reduced as $\rho_s > \rho_n$. They can provide (L-1) balanced diversity branches as the SNR are the same in all the (L-1) branches.

2.2 Discussion of different diversity conditions

This section illustrates the magic transformation between correlation and power imbalance of diversity branches. The diagonalizer is derived and is introduced here before the diversity branches are combined, which can transform the correlated and balanced branches to the uncorrelated and unbalanced ones, and vice versa. This section assumes a generic model, in which noise and interference components are correlated with a correlation equal to or less than the correlation of signal components. Modeling and simulation of an example and the performance can be found for various dual diversity scenarios in (Vasana, 2008). Discussions on how to maximize diversity gains are made in various signal and noise conditions, and with different combining methods as following cases.

Case 1: $\rho_s = \rho_n$

Resulted from the system analysis and simulation, this technology is especially effective when the noise/interference components have the same correlation as the signal components, i.e, $\rho_s = \rho_n$. This is the case when interferences, which come along with the desired signal, are the main source of noise, such as the cases in CDMA (Code Division Multiple Access) systems and wireless networks, etc. In such as the diagonalizer described in this section can be viewed as a "decorrelator" - to totally straighten the correlation effect and resulted balanced signal-to-noise ratio among diversity branches in those practical non-ideal scenarios. The equation (7) with $\rho_s = \rho_n$ becomes

$$\begin{cases} (P_s / P_n)_i = \sigma_s^2 / \sigma_n^2, & i = 1, 2, \ldots, L-1 \\ (P_s / P_n)_L = \sigma_s^2 / \sigma_n^2 \end{cases} \tag{8}$$

The outputs at the transformer will have unequal signal or noise power distribution as in (6) but balanced signal-to-noise ratio among the diversity branches as in (8). It is the ideal situation to use the diagonalizer. The diversity gain will be maximized with the use of the diagonalizer. The average signal-to-noise ratio in each diversity branch at both inputs and outputs of the transformer are the same, $(P_s / P_n)_i = \sigma_s^2 / \sigma_n^2$, for i =1, 2, …, L.

Case 2: $\rho_s >> \rho_n$

If the correlation between signal components is much greater than the correlation between noise components among the diversity branches, i.e. $\rho_s >> \rho_n$, the average signal-to-noise ratio (P_s / P_n) at the output of the transformer will be enhanced in the Lth branch z_L. This last branch at the output of the transformer, z_L, alone can be used as the combined diversity branch. It can be seen in (9) by substituting $\rho_s >> \rho_n$ in the equation (7):

$$\begin{cases} (P_s / P_n)_i \approx \dfrac{\sigma_s^2 (1 - \rho_s)}{\sigma_n^2} & i = 1, 2, \ldots, L-1 \\ (P_s / P_n)_L \approx \dfrac{\sigma_s^2 \left[1 + (L-1)\rho_s\right]}{\sigma_n^2} \end{cases} \tag{9}$$

Case 3: $\rho_n = 0$

There is extreme case when the noise components are uncorrelated and balanced among the branches. Substituting $\rho_n = 0$ to equation (7) it becomes:

$$\begin{cases} (P_s / P_n)_i = \dfrac{\sigma_s^2 (1 - \rho_s)}{\sigma_n^2} & i = 1, 2, \ldots, L-1 \\ (P_s / P_n)_L = \dfrac{\sigma_s^2 \left[1 + (L-1)\rho_s\right]}{\sigma_n^2} \end{cases} \tag{10}$$

In such case, the diagonalization transformation has no effect on the noise components. The signal components will become unbalanced after the transformation, but the noise components are still independent and balanced. If the correlation is evenly distributed among the L diversity branches, the (L-1) branches will still be balanced after the transformation as in (6). Diversity gain can be achieved by using these (L-1) uncorrelated and balanced branches at the output of the diagonalizer transformer, practically when L is at least greater than 3. However, it can be seen from equation (10) that the reduced signal-to-noise ratio needs to be considered in these (L-1) transformed branches, while the last Lth transformed branch has an increased signal-to-noise ratio.

Case 4: $\rho_s = \rho_n = 0$, but unbalanced branches ($\sigma_{r1}^2 = q\, \sigma_{r2}^2$)

The transformation in equation (4) is a two-way transformation. It is meant that it can transform not only a set of correlated & balanced branches to a set of uncorrelated & unbalanced ones, but also a set of unequal power branches (unbalanced) & uncorrelated branches to a set of balanced & correlated branches. With the revised condition of uncorrelated but unbalanced diversity branches to be transformed, the block diagram in Fig.1 becomes Fig. 2.

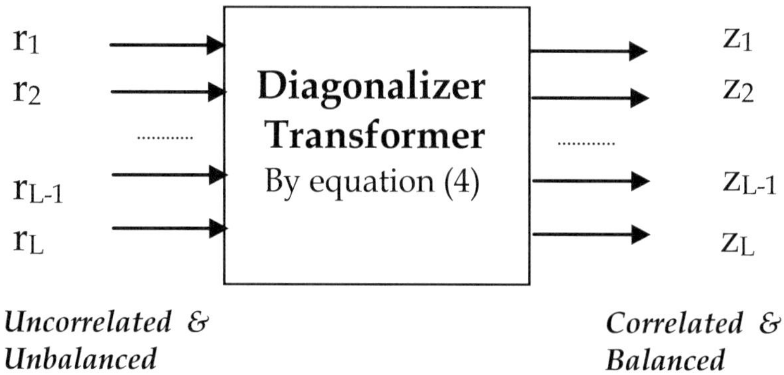

Fig. 2. Diagonalizer (Transformer) Block Diagram (w/. revised condition)

To illustrate this point by using an example of dual diversity (L=2), let r_1 and r_2 be the uncorrelated but unbalanced diversity branches, and the average power of r_1 is q times that of r_2, where $0< q <1$. After the transformation for dual diversity (L=2) z_1 and z_2 in equation (4) is as simple as:

$$\begin{cases} z_1 = (r_1 + r_2)/\sqrt{2} \\ z_2 = (r_1 - r_2)/\sqrt{2} \end{cases} \tag{11}$$

z_1 and z_2 are correlated but with equally average power as:

$$\begin{cases} \sigma_{z1}^2 = \left(\sigma_{r1}^2 + \sigma_{r2}^2\right)/2 \\ \sigma_{z2}^2 = \left(\sigma_{r1}^2 + \sigma_{r2}^2\right)/2 \end{cases} \tag{12}$$

and the correlation coefficient as:

$$\rho_{z1z2}(\%) = \frac{E(z_1 z_2)}{\sigma_{z1}\sigma_{z2}} = \frac{\sigma_{r1}^2 - \sigma_{r2}^2}{\sigma_{r1}^2 + \sigma_{r2}^2} = \frac{1-q}{1+q} \tag{13}$$

where the power imbalance ratio q between r_1 and r_2 can be expressed in decible:

$$q(\text{dB}) = 10 \log (q) \tag{14}$$

Thus, the diversity system with unequal average signal power can be transformed to the correlated diversity system with balanced diversity branches.

For maximal-ratio combining, the performance of the diversity system with or without the diagonalizer is the same, as in (Fang et al., 2000), (Loyka et al., 2003) and (Bi et al., 2003). The Lth branch at the output of the transformer gives an equal-gain combining of the original correlated branches. For square-law combining, the performance analysis using diagonalization technique is illustrated in detail in (Chang & McLane, 1997).

2.3 The simulation results

A switch algorithm, which is discussed in Section 4, is simulated to combine two diversity branches in various cases. The Rayleigh fading channel is considered in the simulation. The envelopes of faded signals in two diversity branches are shown as the first two signals in the Fig 3 (Vasana, 2008). This is the case when there is 90% correlation between two diversity branches. The combined signal envelop is shown in the 3rd signal in the Fig 3, in which many deep fading dips are avoided.

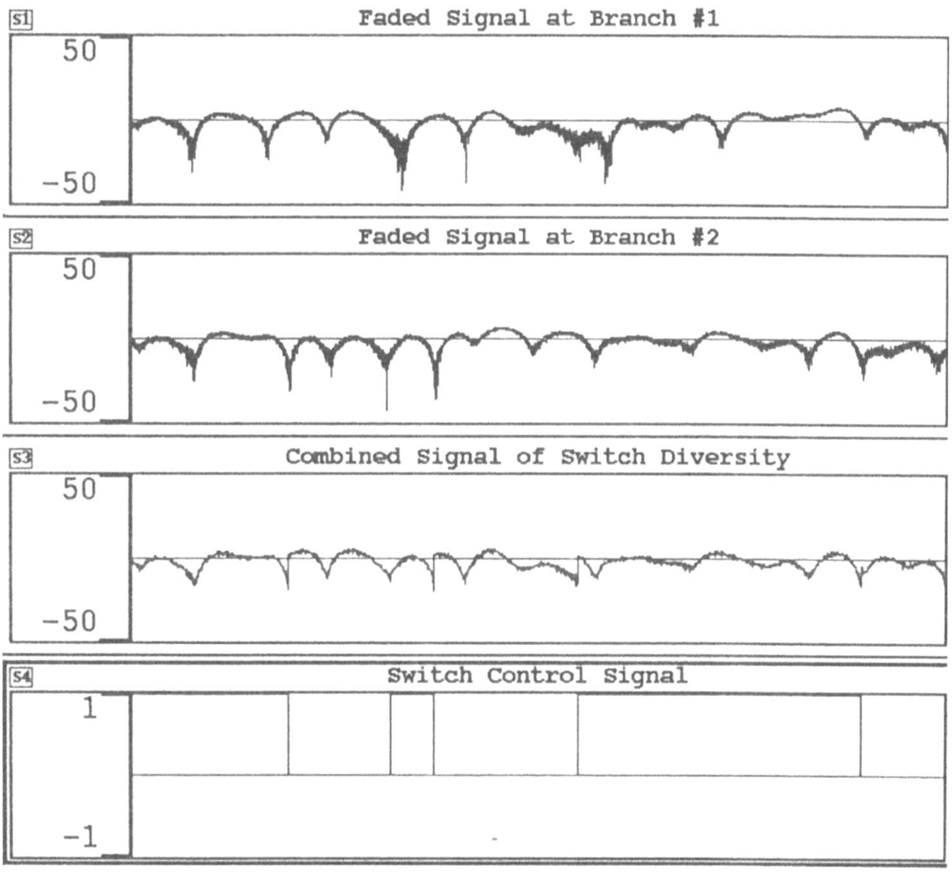

Fig. 3. Fading Signal Envelopes in Diversity Branches (L=2)

From the other simulation results of symbol-error-rate (SER) or the average bit-error-rate (BER) listed in the Table of (Vasana, 2008), the following comparison and conclusions can be obtained:

1. Dual antenna diversity is better than no diversity, even with high correlation (ρ_s =90%) or high power imbalance (5dB) between the diversity branches.
2. Correlation or imbalance issues between branches degrade the diversity gain in a similar manner, e.g. 50% correlation case has the same performance as 3dB imbalance case.

In summary, a linear transformer, which diagonalizes the covariance matrix of the diversity branches, is presented and investigated in this section. Not only this diagonalizer can transfer the correlated and balanced diversity branches to the uncorrelated and unbalanced branches, but also can transfer the unbalanced and uncorrelated diversity branches to the balanced and correlated branches. The combining method can be chosen, depending on which situation gives the best performance. Simulation results and the intuitive explaination of switch diversity with dual antenna branches are shown here. This tranformation technology is especially effective when the noise components have the same correlation as the signal components. This is the cases when interferences which come along with the desired signal are the main source of noise, such as the cases in CDMA systems and wireless networks, etc. The method described in this section can act like a "filter" - to totally filter out the correlation among diversity branches in these cases.

3. The soft-decision decoding in correlated diversity combining

This section adds another mechanism in combating wireless channel fading - combining convolutional coding with antenna diversity. The method and its performance of the combination of convolutional decoding and antenna diversity with square-law combining on a Rayleigh fading channel are presented here. The diversity branches are correlated or power imbalanced; and the Viterbi soft-decision decoding is performed at the receiver detection. The upper bound performance of the non-coherent detection systems has been determined with the above conditions. Our analysis holds for any number of diversity branches but the computations presented here are for dual diversity. The performance shows the combining of error-correction coding and diversity is very effective even in non-ideal diversity conditions.

3.1 The soft-decision detection

The encoder accepts k binary digits at a time and puts out n binary digits in the same time interval. Thus the code rate is $R_c = k/n$. When the Viterbi decoding algorithm is used, the optimum decoding algorithm for a convolutional encoded sequence transmitted over a memoryless channel is used in the paper (Viterbi & Omura, 1979).

In the system block diagram of Fig. 4, the diversity transformer is the diagonalizaiton transformation discussed in Section 2 to transform correlated & balanced diversity branches to uncorrelated & unbalanced diversity branches. In addition, soft-decision decoding with non-coherent detection is used in this section, which uses square-law combining to provide the decoding variables from the transformed uncorrelated signals received original from L correlated antennas. The notations here can also be found in (Modestino & Mui, 1976, Gradshteyn & Ryzhik, 1980) .

From (Chang & McLane, 1997) the normalized fading signals at the receiver front-end with matched filters at kth diversity branch are:

$$\begin{cases} r_{0k} = 2\bar{E}_b R_k e^{-j\Phi k} + N_{0k} \\ r_{1k} = N_{1k} \end{cases} \tag{15}$$

where binary bit 0 is assumed to be transmitted. The r_{0k} are the outputs from the filters matched to the transmitted signal and r_{1k} are the outputs that only include AWGN components.

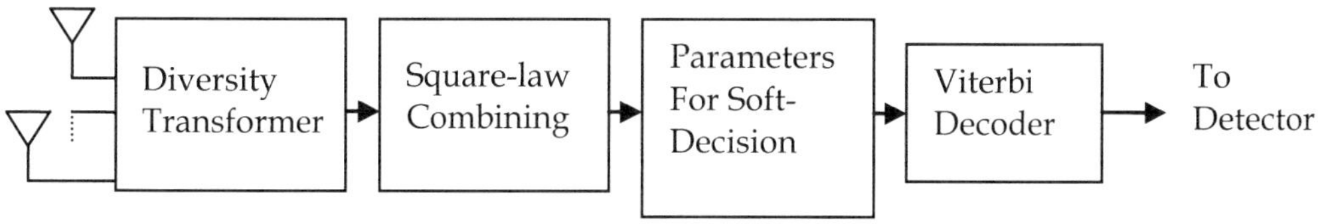

Fig. 4. Soft-Decision Detection Block Diagram

For non-coherent orthogonal demodulation, the output of the square-law combiner with L diversity branches is given by following equaiton:

$$\begin{cases} y_{0jm} = \sum_{k=1}^{L} \left| 2\bar{E}_b R_k e^{-j\Phi k} + N_{0jmk} \right|^2 = \sum_{k=1}^{L} |r_{0k}|^2 = \sum_{k=1}^{L} |z_{0k}|^2 \\ y_{1jm} = \sum_{k=1}^{L} |N_{1jmk}|^2 = \sum_{k=1}^{L} |r_{1k}|^2 = \sum_{k=1}^{L} |z_{1k}|^2 \end{cases} \tag{16}$$

where z_{0k} and z_{1k} are the diagonalized random variables as in (4) that have been transformed from the correlated diversity branches r_{0k} and r_{1k} for k = 1,2,…,L for respective matched filter outputs. It can be proven that the square-law combining gives the same output for combining the branches whether at the input or the output of the diagnoalizer transformer using the transformation of (4). In equation (16) the z_{0k} and z_{1k} are uncorrelated Gaussian random variables with zero mean and variances equal to the eigenvalues of the covariance matrix as in (3), and so are the values of the signal power in each branches after the diagnoalization tranformation as in (6). In equation (6) ρ_s is the correlation between L diversity antennas in the receiver.

The input sequence to the Viterbi decoder, which is the output from the square-law combining, are $\{y_{jm}$, m=1,2,…,n; j=1,2,…} for the j-th trellis branch and the m-th bit in that branch. The coded binary digits are denoted by $\{c_{jm}$, m=1, 2,. . ., n; j = 1, 2,…} for the j-th trellis branch and the m-th bit in that branch. The Viterbi soft-decision decoder (Viterbi & Omura, 1979) with non-coherent detection forms the branch metrics as

$$\mu_j^{(r)} = \sum_{m=1}^{n} \left[c_{jm}^{(r)} y_{1jm} + \left(1 - c_{jm}^{(r)}\right) y_{0jm} \right] \tag{17}$$

Furthermore, a metric for the r-th path consisting of B branches through the trellis is defined as:

$$U^{(r)} = \sum_{j=1}^{B} \mu_j^{(r)} \tag{18}$$

where r denotes any one of the competing paths at each node. For example, the all-zero path, denoted as r=0, has a path metric

$$U^{(0)} = \sum_{j=1}^{B} \sum_{m=1}^{n} y_{0jm} \tag{19}$$

3.2 The error performance upper bound

Assume that perfect interleaving is used so that there is no fading correlation between consecutive coded symbols. The probability of error in the pairwise comparison of the metrics $U^{(0)}$ and $U^{(r)}$ is

$$P_2(d) = \Pr\left[\sum_{i=1}^{d} y_{1i} > \sum_{i=1}^{d} y_{0i}\right] = \Pr\left[\mu_r \geq \mu_0\right], \tag{20}$$

where d is the Hamming distance for error events in the code trellis. The bit error probability of binary codes is upper-bounded for k=1 (no diversity) as

$$\bar{P}_b < \sum_{d=d_{free}}^{\infty} \beta_d P_2(d) \tag{21}$$

where β_d is given in (Chang & McLane, 1995) .
On making use of (16),

$$\mu_0 = \sum_{i=1}^{d} y_{0i} = \sum_{i=1}^{d} \sum_{k=1}^{L} \left| 2\bar{E}_b R_k e^{-j\Phi k} + N_{0ik} \right|^2 \tag{22}$$

and

$$\mu_r = \sum_{i=1}^{d} y_{1i} = \sum_{i=1}^{d} \sum_{k=1}^{L} \left| N_{1ik} \right|^2 \tag{23}$$

$$P_2(d) = \int_0^{\infty} f_{\mu 0}(\mu_0) \left[\int_0^{\mu_0} f_{\mu r}(\mu_r)\, d\mu_r \right] d\mu_0 \tag{24}$$

For Rayleigh fading, the probability density function of μ_0 and μ_r in equation (24), $f_{\mu 0}(\mu_0)$ and $f_{\mu r}(\mu_r)$, can be found in (Chang & McLane, 1995).

3.3 The numerical results

Consider a simple convolutional code with constraint length K_c =3, code rate R_c =1/2, and perfect interleaving is assumed. For a fair comparison with uncoded system, the average signal energy per information bit for the coding system is used, which is denoted as $\bar{E}_b$. The average SNR corresponding to an information bit, γ_b, is related with the average SNR used through the analysis as (Proakis, 1989) $\gamma_b = \gamma_c / R_c$.
The union bound has been calculated for this K_c=3, R_c=1/2 convolutional code plus dual diversity with correlation by using the equations (21) – (24) as detailed in (Chang & McLane,

1995) . The performance of the K_c=3, R_c=1/2 convolutional code plus a dual diversity system is comparied with the coding system alone.

Numerical calculation of the performance of a K_c=3, R_c=1/2 convolutional code plus correlated diversity with L=2, 4 and 6 and various correlation coefficient as well as the comparison with coding alone system or the diversity alone system are presented in the plots in (Chang & McLane, 1995). The following conclusion can be drawn from the plots:

1. The Viterbi soft-decision decoding plus correlated diversity system is more effective relative to a coding alone system, even with dual diversity with correlation coefficient as high as $\rho_s = 0.9$. It can be seen that the performance with correlation coefficient as ρ_s = 0.5 does not lose much diversity gain corresponding to the performance with independent diversity ($\rho_s = 0$).
2. Combining a convolutional coding with a diversity system is more effective than using diversity alone within a practical SNR range with L=2, 4, and 6.
3. Combining coding and diversity technique is significant in the conditions where diversity branches are correlated. The gain of combining coding with diversity relative to a diversity alone system seems bigger with branch correlation as $\rho_s = 0.5$ than $\rho_s = 0$.
4. It is found that convolutional coding plus diversity is more effective than block coding plus diversity, which is also discussed in (Chang & McLane, 1995) .

In summary, the performance of soft-decision Viterbi decoding, non-coherent demodulator can be upper-bounded when the diversity branches are correlated. Such correlation does not strongly degrade the performance of the coding plus diversity system. The correlation coefficients must be above 0.5 to get appreciable losses. In other words, the convolutional coding and diversity perform effectively when they are used together. This detection method can be used in Multiple-Input and Multiple Output (MIMO) system where multiple antennas are used for diversity at receivers.

4. Antenna switch diversity for practical situations

For antenna diversity, the multiple RF (Radio Frequency) front-end paths associated with multiple antennas are costly in terms of size, power and complexity. Antenna selection is a scheme to reduce the unnecessary RF front-end paths and to capture many of the advantages of diversity systems. This section of the chapter presents an antenna switch algorithm as one kind of selection diversity methods. This algorithm minimizes the unnecessary frequent switches because the switches between diversity branches could bring extra noise and errors to the detector. This algorithm is robust in non-ideal antenna situations where correlation and average power imbalance among antennas are unavoidable. The performance of this antenna switch algorithm is shown with sizable gain in those situations.

4.1 The switch diversity strategy

Optimum selection diversity is defined to choose the antenna/RF path with the highest SNR, and to perform detection based on the signal from the selected path (Simon & Alouini, 2002). Theoretically this leads the optimal results. However, a suboptimal version of selection diversity, known as scan diversity, tests the paths one by one until one is found with SNR above a predetermined threshold. This path is used for detection (Sanayei & Nosratinia, 2004).

However, some practical issues are overlooked in those antenna selection algorithms. The RF switches available with current technologies are far from ideal, which may offset some of the advantage of antenna selection if the antenna switching is frequently performed. Another important shortcoming of the practical switches is their transfer attenuation, which must be compensated by more power from the output stage amplifier of the transmitter and/or by a more sensitive low noise amplifier at the receiver (Sanayei & Nosratinia, 2004). The antenna switch algorithm presented in this section will reduce the unnecessary switches and maximize the overall diversity gain under non-ideal conditions.

This antenna switch algorithm is developed and inspired by a philosophy of selection and switching positions. For example, "Should you always monitor the job market and switch to the best job available to you?", "Is the grass always greener on the other side of the fence?", "Is the *best* performing position you found at the switching moment going to last long?" Since switching incurs some transition difficulties and losses as well as the cost and price for monitoring multiple positions/branches, constantly switching to the currently measured *best* position/branch may not be the best strategy. When should the switch be performed then? The answer is when the current position/branch is *bad* enough. Now, only one position/branch, which is the currently working position/branch, needs to be monitored. Switching to an available position/branch occurs only when the current position/branch is found to be unacceptable. The above strategy has been put into the antenna diversity algorithm in wireless communication and was simulated to be a better practical switch method not only in our life situations, but also in diversity systems.

4.2 The switch diversity algorithm

Fig. 8 shows this antenna switch scheme. Multiple receiver antennas are used to receive the signals from possible multiple transmitter antennas. Here only one of the RF paths is selected to be used in signal detection for the simplicity of illustration. And only the selected RF path is monitored and measured in terms of signal strength.

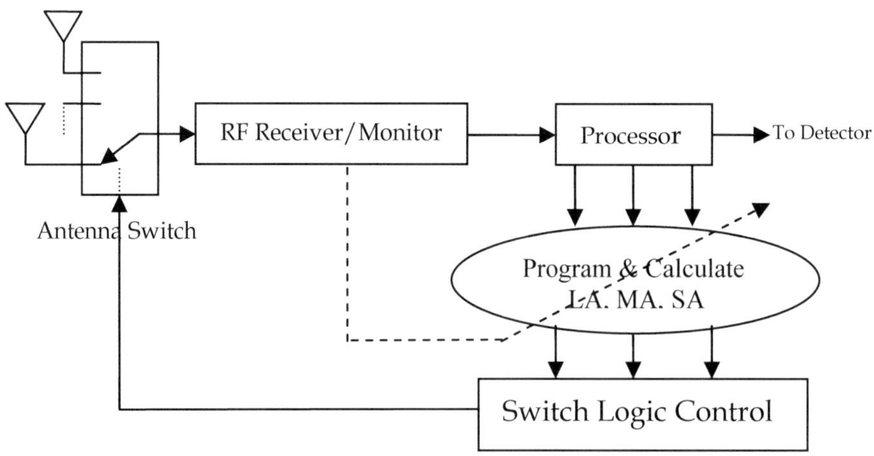

Fig. 5. Antenna Switch Diversity for Wireless Channel

The switch threshold is determined in real-time by moving averages of the measured signal power in long-term, medium-term and short term. In mobile wireless communications, there are fading, Doppler effect, and multipath effect, etc. The long-term average of signal power (LA) characterizes the average signal quality in recent environment. The short-term average of signal power (SA) gives the instantaneous signal strength and the depth of fading at the instance. The medium-term average of signal power (MA) tries to quickly assess the overall signal strength. Comparing MA and LA, the knowledge of the speed of the wireless fading channel can be gained. The periods of long-term, short-term and medium-term can be programmed depending on the speed of mobile and channel condition, the modulation schemes, and the transmission bit/symbol rate.

The switch decision can be designed based on the algorithm that is patented in a US patent (Chang, 1997). The switch decision or threshold can be also made at the signal processor and switch logic control unit of the receiver, which is programmable through the RF path monitor as in Fig. 5. The decoding information and BER measure, which indicate the wireless channel conditions, can be utilized in program the terms used in calculating the LA, MA and SA.

4.3 Practical situations discussion

The switch algorithm presented here is preferable to the theoretically optimal selection diversity due to several reasons. 1) The optimal selection algorithm needs monitoring all the diversity branches at all time, which results in needing multiple RF-front receiver/monitor paths. And it leads to increase the cost and size of the reciever. 2) The optimal selection introduces a lot of switch transitions. The transitions can cause amplitude discontinuous and phase distortion, which then will bring noise and errors to the signal detection. Switch only at deep fades as in the presented switch algorithm reduces the unnecessary switches but keeps the most of the diversity gain.

This switch algorithm is suitable for the practical situation where diversity correlation and power imbalance are unavoidable. This kinds of non-ideal antenna condition impact on diversity gains of selection diversity has been discussed in many published papers (Simon & Alouini, 2002, Dietze et al., 2002, Chang & McLane, 1997, Zhang, 2002, Mallik et al., 2000). The switch algorithm presented here is designed in removing the deep fades which are the causes of the major detection errors. As discussed in Section 2 these deep fades are comparatively rare events in probabilistic terms. Therefore, even when two receiver diversity branches have a fairly high overall correlation and large average power imbalance, there is a low probability that both branches will be suffering this rare event (i.e. deep fading) simultaneously. An example is shown in Fig. 3. That is why the switch algorithm which only switches at deep fades is insensitive to diversity correlation and power imbalance. This intuitive prediction becomes convincing by the simulation results presented in (Vasana, 2005).

This switch algorithm is also workable for the practical situation where channel conditions are unknown. The monitoring and comparing of LA, MA and SA can be made to estimate the channel conditions of fast fading and Doppler effects, etc. Therefore, this switch diversity can be self adjusting and adopting to the transmission environment chang.

In summary, this antenna switch diversity presented here is cost-effective and robust. The antenna selection at the front of the receiver reduces the unnecessary RF front-end paths but captures the diversity effect of the multiple antennas. This scheme is designed to switch only when it is necessary and therefore minimizes the switch noise and transition errors. The switch control decisions are made based on a few measured parameters to capture the real-time dynamic channel conditions. Those parameters are easy to be cooperated with BER and soft-decision decoding information to make more sophisticated switch control decisions. The algorithm is robust in practical situations, such as non-ideal diversity situations, no channel knowledge, and fast fading, etc. This is demonstrated in system simulations in (Vasana, 2005).

5. Conclusion

This chapter has discussed the diversity and coding methods to combat fading in wireless communication. The fading models which are used in the analysis are Rayleigh fading with non-LOS and Rician fading with LOS. The diversity branches are considered with non-ideal conditions such as correlation and power imbalance. In spite of all these non-ideal diversity conditions, there is still significant diversity gain when applying antenna diversity reception to practical mobile or wireless radio systems.

An intuitive explanation for many of the diversity non-ideal conditions so they can have acceptable reception is given here. The diversity gain is only achieved when there is deep fading, which does not occur at all-time moments. The overall time correlation and power imbalance will affect, but will not totally eliminate, the diversity gain at those deep fading moments. Section 2 discussed the effect of diversity with various non-ideal conditions - correlated or unbalanced diversity branches for Rayleigh fading signals both in theory and in simulation results.

A linear diagonalization transformation is illustrated in Section 2 & 3. This transformer not only can transfer the correlated and balanced diversity branches to the uncorrelated and unbalanced branches, but also can transfer the unbalanced and uncorrelated diversity branches to the balanced and correlated branches. This tranformation technology is especially effective when the noise components have the similar correlation as the signal components.

In Section 3 the performance upper-bound of soft-decision Viterbi decoding, non-coherent demodulator is derived when the diversity branches are correlated. Numerical calculation shows that such correlation does not strongly degrade the performance of the soft-decision decoding system. The correlation coefficients must be above 0.5 to get noticable losses in the coding & diversity gain. In other words, the combination of the convolutional coding and diversity performs effectively to combat fading in wireless communication with practical non-ideal diversity conditions.

The antenna switch diversity, presented in Section 4, is a practical and cost-effective modification to the optimal selection diversity. The antenna selection at the front-end of the receiver reduces the unnecessary RF paths but captures the diversity gain of multiple antennas. This algorithm is designed to switch only when the current path is in *bad* conditions (e.g. deep fading), and therefore minimizes the extensive switch noise and transition errors. One algorithm shows how the switch control decisions are made based on the real-time dynamic channel conditions. The algorithm is robust in practical conditions, such as non-ideal antenna diversity, no channel knowledge and fast fading, etc. The performance improvements are demonstrated in the system simulations.

6. References

Bi, G.; Yang, C. & Fang, L. (2003). Reply to "Comments on 'New method of performance analysis for diversity reception with correlated Rayleigh-fading signals'', *IEEE transactions on vehicular technology,* vol.52, no.3, May 2003.

Chang, S. et al. (1997). Communication Device Having Antenna Switch Diversity and Method Therefore, *US Patent PN# 5,692,019,* Issued in 1997.

Chang, C-Y. S. & McLane, P. J. (1997). Bit-Error-Probability for Noncoherent Orthogonal Signals in Fading with Optimum Combining for Correlated Branch Diversity, *IEEE transactions on information theory,* vol.43, no.1, January 1997.

Chang, C. S. & McLane, P. J. (1995). Convolutional Codes with Correlated Diversity and Non-Coherent Orthogonal Modulation, *IEEE International Conference on Communications,* Seattle, June 1995.

Chang, C. S. & McLane, P. J. (1994). Bit-error-probability for non-coherent orthogonal signals in fading with optimum combining for correlated branch diversity, *IEEE Trans. on Information Theory,* Vol. 43, No.1, January 1994.

Dietze, K.; Dietrich, C. B. & Stutzman, W. L. (2002). Analysis of a two-branch maximal ratio and selection diversity system with unequal (SNR)s and correlated inputs for a Rayleigh fading channel, *IEEE transactions on wireless communications,* vol.1, no.2, April 2002.

Fang, L.; Bi, G. & Kot, A. C. (2000). New method of performance analysis for diversity reception with correlated Rayleigh-fading signals, *IEEE transactions on vehicular technology,* vol.49, no.5, September 2000.

Gradshteyn, I. S. & Ryzhik, I. M. (1980). *Table of Integral Series and Products,* New York, Academic Press Inc., 1980.

Loyka, S. & Tellambura, C. & Kouki, A. etc. (2003). Comments on 'New method of performance analysis for diversity reception with correlated Rayleigh-fading signals', *IEEE transactions on vehicular technology,* vol.52, no.3, May 2003.

Mallik, R. K., Win, M. Z., & Winters, J. H. (2002). Performance of dual-diversity predetection EGC in correlated Rayleigh fading with unequal branch SNR, *IEEE transactions on communications,* vol.50, no.7, July 2002

Mallik, R. K.; Win, M. Z. & Winters, J. H. (2000). Performance of predetection dual diversity in correlated Rayleigh fading: EGC and SD, *GLOBECOM '00, IEEE Global Telecommunications Conference,* San Francisco, 27 November-1 December, 2000.

Modestino, J. W. & Mui, S. Y. (1979). Convolutional code performance in the Rician fading channel, *IEEE Trans. on Commun.,* Vol. 24, June 1976

Proakis, J. (1989). *Communications,* 2nd Edition, McGraw-Hill, New York , 1989.

Sanayei, S. & Nosratinia, A. (2004). Antenna Selection in MIMO Systems, *IEEE Communications Magazine, vol.42, no.10,* October 2004.

Simon, M. K. & Alouini, M. (2002). A Compact Performance Analysis of Generalized Selection Combining with Independent but Non-identically Distributed Rayleigh Fading Paths, *IEEE Trans. Commun., vol.50, no.9,* Sept. 2002.

Vasana, S. (2008). Modeling and Simulation of the Conversion of Correlated and Unbalanced Antenna Diversity Systems, *International Journal of Modeling and Simulation,* Vol.28, No.1, 2008.

Vasana, S. (2005). Antenna Switch Algorithm in MIMO Systems, *Proceedings of IASTED International Conference on Communication Systems and Applications (CSA),* July 2005.

Viterbi, A. & Omura, J. (1979). *Principles of Communications,* McGraw-Hill, New York, 1979.

Zhang, Q. T. (2002). Generic SER formulas for noncoherent MFSK with L diversity on various correlated fading channels, *ICC 2002, IEEE International Conference on Communications,* April-2 May, 2002, New York, NY, USA.

9

Block Transmission Systems in Wireless Communications

Mutamed Khatib
Palestine Technical University
Palestine

1. Introduction

In block transmission systems, the data symbols are grouped in the form of blocks of certain length separated by blocks of known symbols (Kaleh 1995). The receiver for this kind of systems is the Non-linear Data Directed Estimator (NDDE) introduced in (Perl et al. 1987; Crozier et al. 1992).

Block transmission systems are based on the assumption that the channel should be constant within the block, which means that the block duration must be sufficiently short in comparison with the channel profile (Kaleh 1995).

Block Linear Equalizer (BLE) has been proposed in (Crozier et al. 1992; Kaleh 1995; Ghani 2003; Hayashi & Sakai 2006) for transmitting digital data over time varying and time dispersive channels. The system is a synchronous serial data transmission system that employs transmission of alternating blocks of data and training symbols (Kaleh 1995). In contrast to the recursive symbol-by-symbol detection approach usually employed, each data block is detected as a unit (Ghani 2003). This system requires an estimate of the channel impulse response and assumes that it remains unchanged during the transmission of a block of data symbols.

BLE system has advantages over the conventional linear and nonlinear equalizer in that the channel is always equalized exactly and there are no error extension effects. Although the transmission efficiency is reduced due to the addition of training symbol blocks between consecutive data blocks, this disadvantage is more than offset in comparison to the advantages offered by the system (Ghani 2003).

In this chapter, some block linear equalizers are introduced, where each impulse at the input to the transmitter is the corresponding input signal element and it may be either binary or multilevel. The signal elements are assumed to be antipodal and statistically independent. The linear baseband channel has an impulse response $y(t)$ and includes all transmitter and receiver filters used for pulse shaping and linear modulation and demodulation. The impulse response $h(t)$ of the transmitter and receiver filters in cascade is assumed to be such that:

$$h(t) = \begin{cases} 1 & t = 0 \\ 0 & t \neq 0 \end{cases} \tag{1}$$

2. Block linear equalizer

The main block diagram of the BLE is shown in Fig.1. White Gaussian noise with zero mean and a two sided power spectral density of σ^2 is added at the output of the transmission path, giving the zero mean Gaussian waveform $w(t)$ at the output of the receiver filter, hence the received signal is:

$$r(t) = \sum_i s_i y(t - iT) + w(t) \tag{2}$$

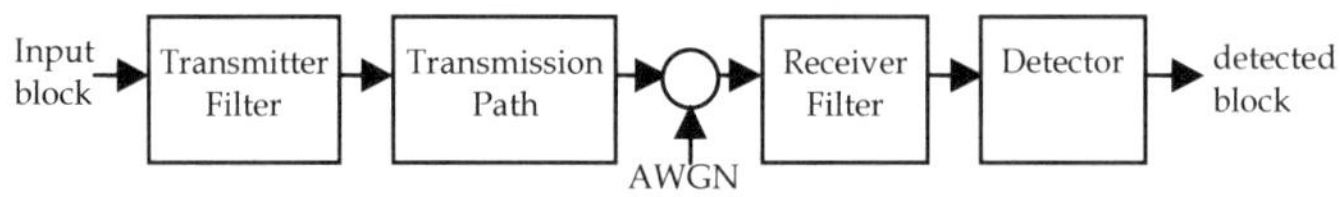

Fig. 1. Model of the Block transmission system (Ghani 2003)

The received signal at the output of the receiver filter is sampled at time instant $t = iT$, where T is the symbol interval. In this block transmission system, consecutive blocks of m information symbols at the input to the transmitter filter are separated by blocks of g zero level symbols as shown in Fig. 2, where g is the largest memory length of the channel $y(t)$, and $y = \begin{bmatrix} y_o & y_1 & \dots & y_g \end{bmatrix}$ is the sampled impulse response (Ghani 2003).

$$\underbrace{0 \;\; 0 \;\; \dots \;\; 0}_{g \text{ zero-level elements}} \;\Big|\; \underbrace{s_1 \;\; s_2 \;\; \dots \;\; s_m}_{m \text{ signal elements}} \;\Big|\; \underbrace{0 \;\; 0 \;\; \dots \;\; 0}_{g \text{ zero-level elements}} \;\Big|\; \underbrace{s_1 \;\; s_2 \;\; \dots \;\; s_m}_{m \text{ signal elements}}$$

Fig. 2. Structure of transmitted signal elements in Block System (Ghani 2003)

For each received group of m signal-elements there are $n = m + g$ sample values at the detector input that are dependent only on the m elements and independent of all other elements. The detector uses these n values in the detection of the symbol block. The detected values are then used for the estimation of the channel sampled impulse response using the same equipment (Ghani 2003; Ghani 2004).
If only the ith signal-element in a group is transmitted, in the absence of noise and with s_i set to unity, the corresponding received n sample values used for the detection of m elements of a group are given by the n-component row vector:

$$\mathbf{Y}_i = \overbrace{0 \;\; \dots \;\; 0}^{i-1} \;\; \overbrace{y_0 \;\; y_1 \;\; \dots \;\; y_g}^{g+1} \;\; \overbrace{0 \;\; \dots \;\; 0}^{m-i} \tag{3}$$

Where y_h must be non-zero for at least one element in the range 0 to g. The sum of the m received signal elements in a group and in the absence of noise is therefore, given by:

$$\mathbf{R} = \sum_{i=1}^{m} s_i \mathbf{Y}_i = \mathbf{SY} \tag{4}$$

Where $\mathbf{S}$ is the m-component row vector whose i^{th} component is s_i and represents the transmitted signal block. $\mathbf{Y}$ is an $m \times n$ matrix whose i^{th} row $\mathbf{Y}_i$ is given by Eq. 3. Since at least one of the y_h is non -zero, the rank of the matrix $\mathbf{Y}$ is always m, and hence, the m rows

of the matrix **Y** are linearly independent. Note that the sampled impulse response of the channel completely determines the matrix **Y** (Ghani 2004).
In the presence of noise, the sample values corresponding to a received signal block at the detector input is given by the vector **R** where (Ghani 2003; Ghani 2004):

$$\mathbf{R} = \mathbf{SY} + \mathbf{W} \tag{5}$$

Where **W** is the n-component noise vector whose components are sample values of statistically independent Gaussian random variable with zero mean and variance σ^2.
The vectors **R**, **SY** and **W** can be represented as points in the n-dimensional Euclidean signal space. Assume that the detector has prior knowledge of $\mathbf{Y}_i$, but has no prior knowledge of the s_i or σ^2. A knowledge of the $\mathbf{Y}_i$ of course implies a knowledge of the channel impulse response. Since the detector knows **Y**, it knows the m-dimensional subspace spanned by $\mathbf{Y}_i$ and hence the subspace containing the vector **SY**, for all s_i. Since the detector has no prior knowledge of s_i, it must assume that any value of **S** is as likely to be received as any other, and in particular, as far as the detector is concerned, s_i need not be ± 1. For a given vector **R** the most likely value of **SY** is now at the minimum distance from **R**. Clearly, if **R** lies in the subspace spanned by the $\mathbf{Y}_i$, then the most likely value of **SY** is **R**. In general, **R** will not lie in this sub-space. In this case, the best estimate the detector can make of **S** is the m-component vector **X**, whose components may have any real values, and are such that **XY** is at the minimum distance from **R**. By the projection theorem (Varga 1962), **XY** is the orthogonal projection of **R** onto the m-dimensional subspace spanned by the $\mathbf{Y}_i$. It follows that $\mathbf{R} - \mathbf{XY}$ is orthogonal to each of the $\mathbf{Y}_i$, so that (Ghani 2003; Ghani 2004):

$$(\mathbf{R} - \mathbf{XY})\mathbf{Y}^T = 0 \tag{6}$$

In other words,

$$\mathbf{X} = \mathbf{RY}^T\left(\mathbf{YY}^T\right)^{-1} \tag{7}$$

Thus, if the received signal vector **R** is fed to the n input terminals of the linear network $\mathbf{Y}^T\left(\mathbf{YY}^T\right)^{-1}$, the signals at the m output terminals are the components x_i of the vector **X**, where **X** is the best linear estimate the detector can make of **S**. Thus:

$$\mathbf{X} = \mathbf{RY}^T\left(\mathbf{YY}^T\right)^{-1} = \mathbf{S} + \mathbf{U} \tag{8}$$

The m vector **U** is the noise vector at the output of the network $\mathbf{Y}^T\left(\mathbf{YY}^T\right)^{-1}$. Each component u_i of the noise vector **U** is a sample value of a Gaussian random variable with a variance not equal to σ^2, and which differ from one component to another (Ghani 2003; Ghani 2004).
In the final stage of the detection process, the receiver examines the signs of the x_i and allocates the appropriate binary values to the corresponding signal elements, to give the detected value of **S**. The detector requires no prior knowledge of the received signal level and is linear up to the decision process just mentioned. It can be seen that in the linear $n \times m$ network $\mathbf{Y}^T\left(\mathbf{YY}^T\right)^{-1}$, $\mathbf{Y}^T$ represents a set of m matched filters or correlation detectors tuned

to the m $\mathbf{Y}_i$ whose m outputs feed the inverse network represented by the matrix $\left(\mathbf{Y}\mathbf{Y}^T\right)^{-1}$ (Ghani 2003). The probability of error for the block linear equalizer is: (Hsu 1985; Perl et al. 1987; Crozier et al. 1992):

$$P_e = \frac{1}{2} erfc\left(\frac{1}{\eta}\sqrt{\frac{E_b}{N_o}}\right) \tag{9}$$

where η^2 is the effect of the linear matrix $\mathbf{Y}^T\left(\mathbf{Y}\mathbf{Y}^T\right)^{-1}$ on the AWGN vector.

3. Channel Impulse Response (CIR)

Table 1 shows some FIR channels with their normalized vectors, and norm values (Kaleh 1995; Proakis 1995; Ghani 2003). Channels usually normalized when studying transmission systems, especially when there is comparison between different transmission systems. This will not affect the behavior of the channel, but prevent any possible bias in the results.
The vector $\begin{bmatrix}0.235 & 0.667 & 1 & 0.667 & 0.235\end{bmatrix}$ represents the sampled impulse response for a channel with moderate amplitude distortion as shown in Fig. 3 (b) (Ghani 2003). It is preferred to be used in this chapter because its length as it is useful to compare long channels with shorter ones. Channel vector $\begin{bmatrix}0.707 & 1 & 0.707\end{bmatrix}$ represents a channel with severe distortions as shown in Fig. 3 (d). It is used here because it has the same norm as the vector $\begin{bmatrix}0.235 & 0.667 & 1 & 0.667 & 0.235\end{bmatrix}$, but with less length. This makes it good choice to be compared with $\begin{bmatrix}0.235 & 0.667 & 1 & 0.667 & 0.235\end{bmatrix}$ without worrying about the norm effect.

Channel vector	Channel after normalization	Norm
$\begin{bmatrix}0.235 & 0.667 & 1 & 0.667 & 0.235\end{bmatrix}$	$\begin{bmatrix}0.166 & 0.472 & 0.707 & 0.472 & 0.166\end{bmatrix}$	1.4143
$\begin{bmatrix}0.707 & 1 & 0.707\end{bmatrix}$	$\begin{bmatrix}0.5 & 0.707 & 0.5\end{bmatrix}$	1.4141
$\begin{bmatrix}0.5 & 1 & -0.5\end{bmatrix}$	$\begin{bmatrix}0.408 & 0.816 & -0.408\end{bmatrix}$	1.2247
$\begin{bmatrix}0.5 & 1 & 0.5\end{bmatrix}$	$\begin{bmatrix}0.408 & 0.816 & 0.408\end{bmatrix}$	1.2247
$\begin{bmatrix}1 & 2 & 1\end{bmatrix}$	$\begin{bmatrix}0.408 & 0.816 & 0.408\end{bmatrix}$	2.4495
$\begin{bmatrix}0.707 & 2.234 & 0.707\end{bmatrix}$	$\begin{bmatrix}0.289 & 0.913 & 0.289\end{bmatrix}$	2.4494

Table 1. Wireless channel models (Kaleh 1995; Proakis 1995; Ghani 2003)

The channel given by the vector $\begin{bmatrix}1 & 2 & 1\end{bmatrix}$ is one of worst channels that may affect the transmitted signal because it has second order null in frequency domain, and introduces severe signal distortion (Kaleh 1995). This channel characteristics are shown in Fig. 3 (j). Channel vector $\begin{bmatrix}0.5 & 1 & 0.5\end{bmatrix}$ is used as it has the same normalized vector as $\begin{bmatrix}1 & 2 & 1\end{bmatrix}$, the difference is in the amplitude. So, it is suitable to study the effect of the channel amplitude.
Also, $\begin{bmatrix}0.5 & 1 & -0.5\end{bmatrix}$ is a useful channel in comparison as it is the same like $\begin{bmatrix}0.5 & 1 & 0.5\end{bmatrix}$, but with a reversed sign at one of the elements. So, it is suitable for the symmetry test.

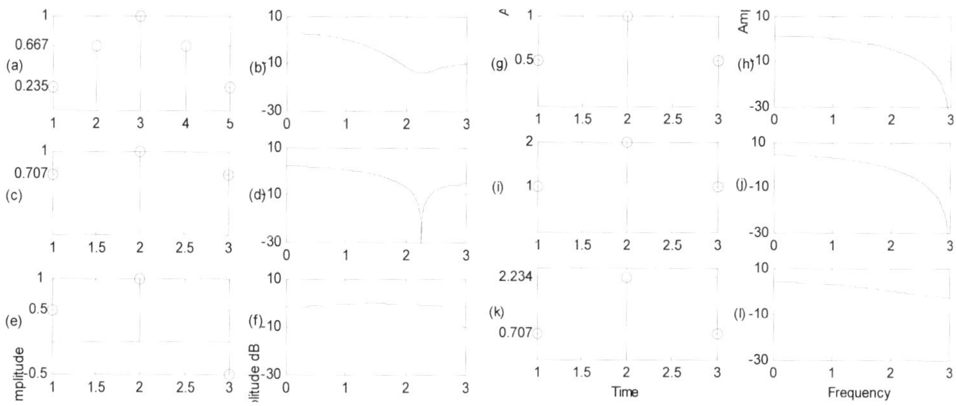

Fig. 3. Impulse responses and amplitude spectrums for channels in Table 1

4. Precoding of transmitted signal

A new technique is developed in this section, which is suitable for downlink band-limited ISI channels. This technique reduces the complexity of the receiver in which the detection process needs only a threshold decision to retrieve the transmitted data, no match filtering or any other processing is needed. In the base station, a precoder is used to generate a code from the transmitted signal that makes it immune to the channel, so, there is no need for any further equalization process in the receiver that reduces the mobile unit receiver to a decision process due to a certain threshold testing. It depends on the channel's prior knowledge at the base station, so, the channel characteristics are assumed to be known both at the transmitter and the receiver. When comparing the process of adding a coder at the base station with the simplicity gained at the receiver units, it will be acceptable because few base stations serve many receiver units in the downlink.

4.1 System model

The system considered is shown in Fig. 4. The signal at the input to the transmitter is a sequence of k-level element values $\{s_i\}$, where k = 2, 4, 8,... and the $\{s_i\}$ being statistically independent and equally likely to have any of the possible values. The buffer-store at the input to the transmitter holds m successive element values $\{s_i\}$. In the coder, the m $\{s_i\}$ are converted into the corresponding m coded signal-elements. The coder performs a linear transformation on the m $\{s_i\}$ to generate the corresponding sequence of impulses that is fed to the baseband channel $y(t)$ which is assumed that it is either time invariant or varies slowly with time.

White Gaussian noise, with zero mean and variance σ^2, is assumed to be added to the data signal at the output of the transmission path, giving the Gaussian waveform $w(t)$ added to the data signal.

The sampled impulse-response of the baseband channel is given by the $(g+1)$ component row vector as explained in Section 2.

The received waveform $r(t)$ at the output of the baseband channel is sampled at the time instants $\{iT\}$, for all integers $\{i\}$. The $\{r_i\}$ are fed to the buffer store which contains two separate stores. While one of these stores holds a set of the received $\{r_i\}$ for a detection process, the other store is receiving the next set of $\{r_i\}$ in preparation for the next detection. A group of m elements are detected simultaneously in a single detection process, from the set of $\{r_i\}$ that depends only on these elements. The receiver uses the knowledge of the $\{y_i\}$ and the possible values of $\{s_i\}$ in the detection of the m element values $\{s_i\}$ from the received samples $\{r_i\}$. A period of nT is available for the detection process, n is given by:

$$n = m + g \tag{10}$$

where m is the block length, and g is the channel length -1.

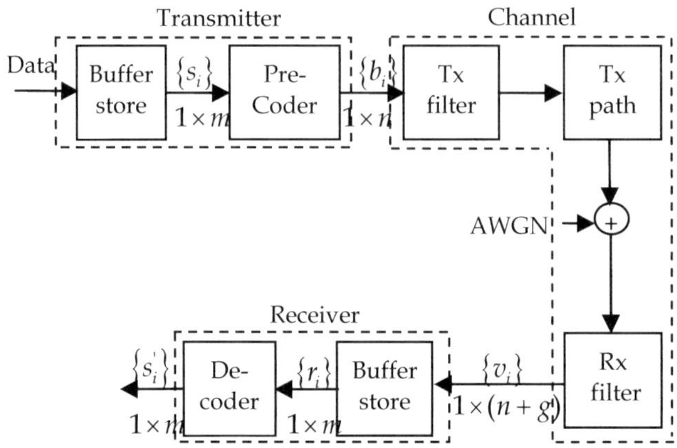

Fig. 4. The downlink of the precoding system

Except where otherwise stated, the decoder in Fig. 4 determines from the appropriate set of received $\{r_i\}$ the m estimated $\{x_i\}$ of the m element-values $\{s_i\}$ in a received group of elements. Each x_i is an unbiased estimate of the corresponding s_i such that:

$$x_i = s_i + u_i \tag{11}$$

where u_i is a zero mean Gaussian random variable. The detector detects each s_i by testing the corresponding x_i against a threshold. The detected value of s_i is designated as s_i'.

4.2 Design and analysis of the precoder

In this system, using buffer store, an $1\times m$ vector $\mathbf{S} = [s_1 \quad s_2 \quad \cdots \quad s_m]$ is formed from the symbols to be transmitted. This vector is coded at the transmitter. The coder accepts the input vector **S** and codes it to form the $1\times n$ signal vector **B**, which is the convolution between the input vector **S** and the $m\times n$ coder matrix **F**, i.e.:

$$\mathbf{B} = \sum_{i=1}^{m} \mathbf{s_i F_i} = \mathbf{SF} \tag{12}$$

where $\mathbf{F_i}$ is the n component row vector.

This convolution process will add a time gap of gT seconds between each pair of adjacent groups of m signal-elements. Then, the output values from the coder multiplexer are fed to the baseband channel. At the receiver, the sample values of the received signal, corresponding to a single group of m signal elements, will normally be a sequence of $n+g$ non-zero sample values. The sequence of these $n+g$ values in the absence of noise is:

$$v_i = \sum_{j=1}^{n} b_j y_{i-j} \qquad i = 1,\ 2,\ \ldots,\ n+g \tag{13}$$

Taking a practical example to clarify the convolution here, if $m=2$, and $g=1$, so $n=3$ and $n+g=4$. The output of the channel will be the 1×4 vector $\mathbf{V}$ whose elements are:

$$\mathbf{V} = \left[b_1 y_o + b_2 y_{-1} + b_3 y_{-2} \quad b_1 y_1 + b_2 y_o + b_3 y_{-1} \quad b_1 y_2 + b_2 y_1 + b_3 y_o \quad b_1 y_3 + b_2 y_2 + b_3 y_1\right] \tag{14}$$

Applying the limitations on the channel impulse response, $\mathbf{V}$ may be written as:

$$\mathbf{V} = \left[b_1 y_o + b_2 0 + b_3 0 \quad b_1 y_1 + b_2 y_o + b_3 0 \quad b_1 0 + b_2 y_1 + b_3 y_o \quad b_1 0 + b_2 0 + b_3 y_1\right] \tag{15}$$

So, this result is multiplication of **B** by a 3×4 matrix **C** that depends on:

$$\mathbf{C} = \begin{bmatrix} y_o & y_1 & 0 & 0 \\ 0 & y_o & y_1 & 0 \\ 0 & 0 & y_o & y_1 \end{bmatrix} \tag{16}$$

In vector form, it may be written as:

$$\mathbf{V} = \mathbf{BC} \tag{17}$$

where $\mathbf{V}$ is the $1\times(n+g)$ received signal, and **C** is the $n\times(n+g)$ channel with i^th^ row is:

$$\mathbf{C_i} = \overbrace{0 \;\ldots\; 0}^{i-1}\ \overbrace{y_o \;\; y_1 \;\; \ldots \;\; y_g}^{g+1}\ \overbrace{0 \;\ldots\; 0}^{n-i} \tag{18}$$

Assume now that successive groups of signal-elements are transmitted, and one of these groups is that just considered. The first transmitted impulse of the group occurs at time T seconds. Fig. 5 shows the $n+g$ received samples which are the components of **V**.

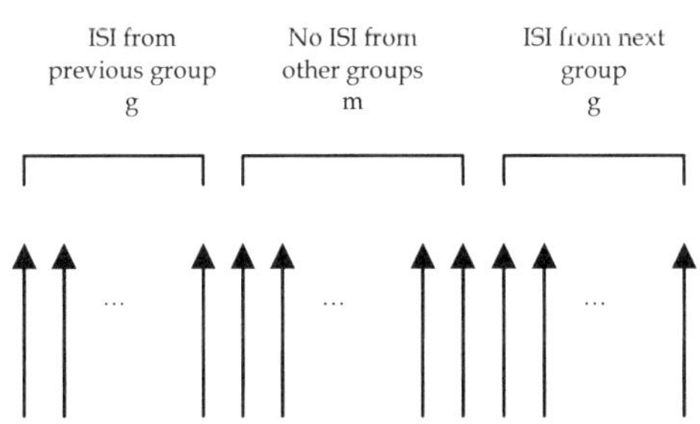

Fig. 5. Sequence of $n+g$ samples for one received block

Due to the Inter Block Interference (IBI), the first elements of the block (g components) of V are affected in part on the preceding received group of m signal-elements. Also, the last g components of **V** are dependent in part on the following received group of m elements. Thus there is Intersymbol Interference (ISI) from adjacent received groups of elements in both the first and the last g components of **V**. However, the central m components of **V** depend only on the corresponding transmitted group of m elements, and can therefore be used for the detection of these elements without ISI from adjacent groups.

Returning back to the same example of $m=2$ and $g=1$, the central m components of **V** are:

$$\mathbf{V}_{central} = \left[b_1 y_1 + b_2 y_o + b_3 0 \quad b_1 0 + b_2 y_1 + b_3 y_o \right] \tag{19}$$

which is the multiplication of **B** by a 3×2 matrix that depends on the channel, and equal to:

$$\frac{\mathbf{V}_{central}}{\mathbf{B}} = \begin{bmatrix} y_1 & 0 \\ y_o & y_1 \\ 0 & y_o \end{bmatrix} \tag{20}$$

Mathematically, if only the central m components of **V** are wanted, this matrix now represents the channel (mathematically only). To make this matrix somehow looks like the matrix **C**, this matrix is the transpose of a new 2×3 matrix **D** that is equal to:

$$\mathbf{D} = \begin{bmatrix} y_1 & y_o & 0 \\ 0 & y_1 & y_o \end{bmatrix} \tag{21}$$

In general, the central m components of the vector **V**, $\left[v_{g+1} \quad v_{g+2} \quad \dots \quad v_{g+m} \right]$, can be obtained by introducing a new matrix $\mathbf{BD}^{\mathrm{T}}$ where **D** is the $m \times n$ matrix of rank m whose i^th^ row is:

$$\mathbf{D}_{\mathrm{i}} = \overbrace{0 \quad \dots \quad 0}^{i-1} \quad \overbrace{y_g \quad y_{g-1} \quad \dots \quad y_o}^{g+1} \quad \overbrace{0 \quad \dots \quad 0}^{m-i} \tag{22}$$

Thus, $\mathbf{BD}^{\mathrm{T}}$ is a $1 \times m$ vector where each row of it gives information about the received symbols at that row:

$$\mathbf{BD}^{\mathrm{T}} = \left[v_{g+1} \quad v_{g+2} \quad \dots \quad v_{g+m} \right] \tag{23}$$

When noise is present, the received vector is:

$$\mathbf{R} = \mathbf{BD}^{\mathrm{T}} + \mathbf{W} \tag{24}$$

It may be easily shown that the coder matrix **F** has to be:

$$\mathbf{F} = \left(\mathbf{DD}^{T} \right)^{-1} \mathbf{D} \tag{25}$$

Thus, under the assumed conditions, the linear network **F** representing the transformation performed by the coder is such that it makes the m signal elements of a group orthogonal at the input of the detector and also maximizes the tolerance to additive white Gaussian noise in the detection of these signal elements.

Now the block diagram of the precoding system, using the new assumptions about the precoder and the channel matrix, may be re-drawn as in Fig. 6.

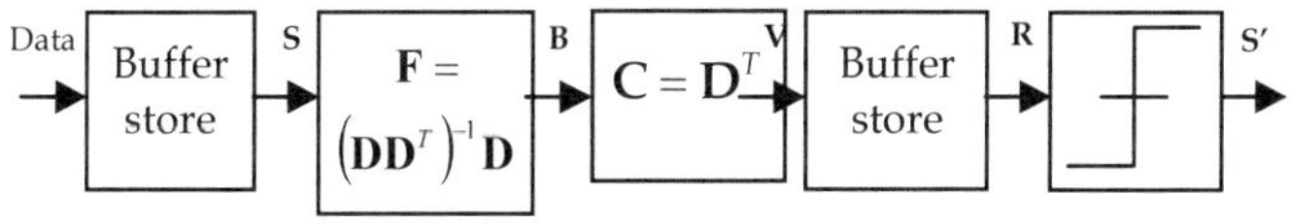

Fig. 6. Block diagram of the precoding system in vector form

4.3 Performance evaluation of the precoding system

Assume that the possible values of s_i are equally likely and that the mean square value of **S** is equal to the number of bits per element. Suppose that the m vectors $\{\mathbf{D}_i\}$ have unit length. Since there are m k-level signal elements in a group, the vector **S** has k^m possible values each corresponding to a different combination of the m k-level signal-elements. So, the vector **B** whose components are the values of the corresponding impulses fed to the baseband channel, has k^m possible values. If e is the total energy of all the k^m values of the vector **B**, then in order to make the transmitted signal energy per bit equal to unity, the transmitted signal must be divided by:

$$\ell = \sqrt{\frac{e}{nk^m}} \tag{26}$$

The m samples of the received signal from which the corresponding $\{s_i\}$ are detected, are:

$$\mathbf{R}' = \frac{1}{\ell}\mathbf{BD}^T + \mathbf{W} \tag{27}$$

Then, the m sample values which are the components of the vector **V** (after taking only the central m components), must first be multiplied by the factor ℓ to give the m vector:

$$\mathbf{R} = \ell\mathbf{V} = \mathbf{BD}^T + \ell\mathbf{W} = \mathbf{S} + \mathbf{U} \tag{28}$$

where **U** is an m vector that represents the AWGN vector after being multiplied by ℓ.
The mean of the new noise vector **U** is zero and its variance is:

$$\eta_T^2 = \ell^2\sigma^2 \tag{29}$$

Thus, the tolerance to noise of the system is determined by the value of η_T^2. When there is no signal distortion from the channel, $(\mathbf{DD}^T)^{-1}$ is an identity matrix. Under these conditions, $\ell = 1$, so that $\eta_T^2 = \sigma^2$.
Now, the block diagram can be finally drawn as:

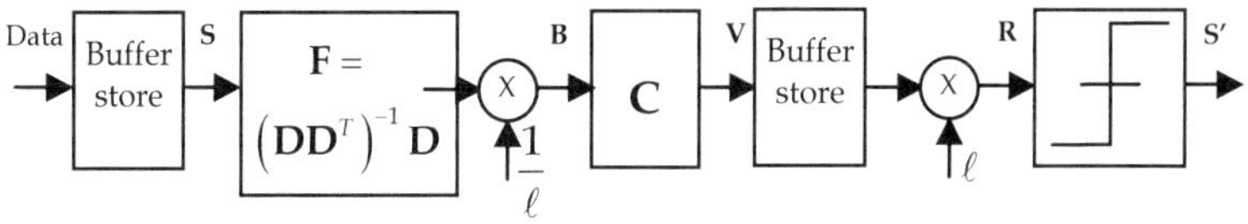

Fig. 7. Final block diagram of the precoding system

Note that the $m \times n$ network transforms the transmitted signal such that the corresponding sample values at the receiver are the best linear estimates of the $\{s_i\}$. The variance now is η_T instead of σ. So, the bit error rate equation may be written as:

$$P_e = \frac{1}{2} erfc\left[\frac{\sqrt{\xi_b}}{\sqrt{2\eta_T}}\right] = \frac{1}{2} erfc\left[\frac{1}{\ell}\sqrt{\frac{\xi_b}{N_o}}\right] \tag{30}$$

4.4 Numerical results of the precoding system

The bit error rate curves for the precoding system is shown in Fig. 8 (a). The signal elements are binary antipodal having possible values as +1 or −1. There are four elements in a group (block length $m = 4$) and these are equally likely to have any of the two values. The sampled impulse response of the channel is $\{y_i\} = [0.408 \quad 0.817 \quad 0.408]$. This channel has a second order null in the frequency domain and introduces severe signal (amplitude) distortion.

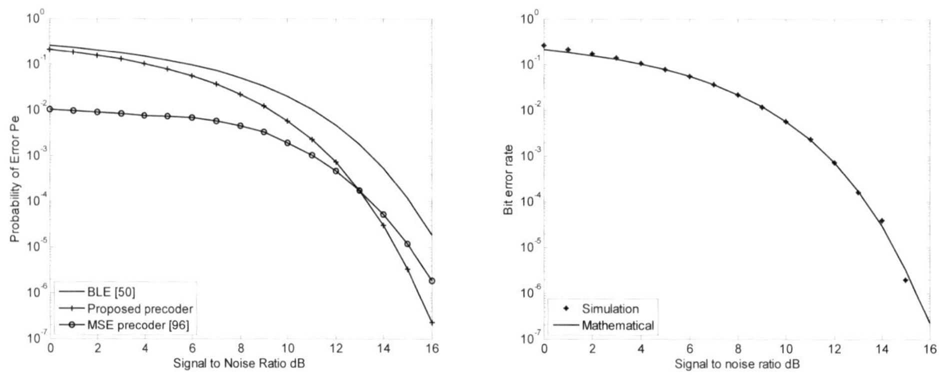

Fig. 8. (a) Probability of bit error versus SNR for the precoding system,
(b) Mathematical and simulation results for the precoding system

The curves in Fig. 8 (a) were obtained by plotting the results of Eq. 30 for the proposed precoding system, Eq. 9 for the BLE and simulating the MSE precoder. In proposed precoder and the BLE, the same block length, and channel impulse response (CIR) were assumed. CIR was normalized to avoid any possible bias. From Fig. 5.1, it is clear that the proposed precoding system returns in about 2 dB enhancement in comparison with the BLE. The MSE linear precoder is simulated using 4 transmitted antennas and 2 receivers with 8 bits per user. The performance of the MSE precoder is better than the proposed precoder because 2 receivers are used. For high SNRs, the performance of the proposed precoder starts to be better than the MSE precoder because the MSE precoder uses a built in estimator. This estimator depends on pilot symbols, which will be affected by noise, and will return some inaccuracy in the channel estimation.

The precoding system has better performance than the block linear equalizer, each one of them provides the best linear estimate of a received group of m signal elements. In the block linear equalizer, all the signal processing is carried out at the receiver, while in the proposed precoding system, all the processing is done at transmitter, and leaves the receiver simple.

The proposed system depends on transmitting the data in blocks. The source of these data may be serial, i.e. from the same source, or even parallel from different sources. So, the length on the block is expected to have a great effect on the performance.
Simulation program is developed by Matlab. It is assumed that the channel characteristics are known, and fixed for all the transmission procedure. Channel impulse response may vary through the transmission, but it must be fixed within the block, and it should be known all the time. A certain estimation method is not suggested, but literature is rich with many methods, and any adaptive one may be used.
In order to make a comparison between the mathematical results for the precoding system presented in Fig. 8 (a), and the simulation program results, Fig. 8 (b) is introduced, which clarify that the behavior is the same.
Fig. 9 (a) shows the probability of error of the system for different values of SNR using four different lengths of the block, i.e. $m=1$, $m=2$, $m=4$ and $m=8$, the channel here is assumed to have impulse response $Y=[0.408 \quad 0.817 \quad 0.408]$.
It is clear from the figure that increasing the block length will reduce the performance of the system and the probability of error becomes worse. This result is expected because increasing the block length will increase the value of the transmitted vector energy ℓ, which maximizes the variance of the noise **U** at the output of the system as given in Eq. 29.

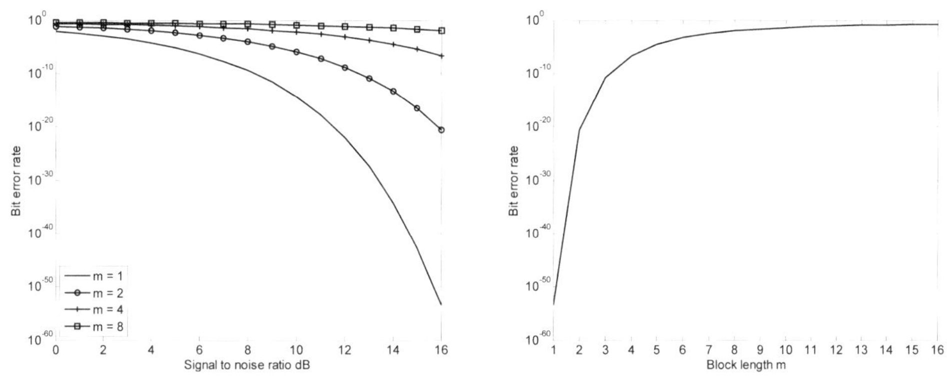

Fig. 9. (a) Effect of block length on the precoding system performance,
(b) Behavior of the precoding system of different block lengths

Also, increasing the block length will increase the intersymbol interference inside the block itself (IBI between the blocks is removed by using guard band). Theoretically, the best result will be for $m=1$, which means transmitting each bit separately, and this is practically not accepted because in this case, each bit will use g bits as a guard band, and this is a great loss in the bandwidth. So, one must find an optimum solution for the block length.
In order to show the effect of various block lengths on the performance of the system, in Fig. 9 (b), there is a plot for continuous values of m under the same channel for different signal to noise ratios. From the curve, it is clear, not only that the system has better performance for short blocks, but also that the behavior will be almost stable for long codes, and the block length will not affect too much on the system.
There is no way to control the channel characteristics in the atmosphere, but at least, it is possible to decide whether to recommend the system in this area or not. So, some further tests are made to show the effect of the channel parameters on the system performance.

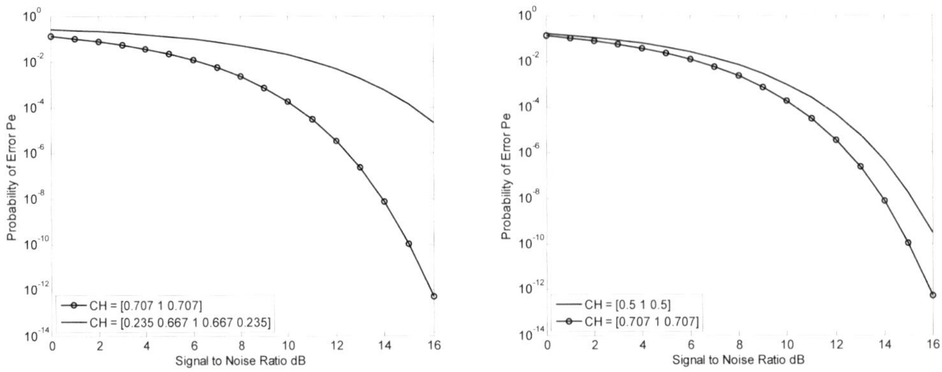

Fig. 10. (a) Effect of channel length on the precoding system,
(b) Effect of channel variance on the precoding system

In Fig. 10 (a), the effect of the channel length on the performance of the system is studied. Here, two different channels are used with different lengths, the first channel is $[0.707 \quad 1 \quad 0.707]$ with $g=2$ while the second channel has $g=4$, i.e. $[0.235 \quad 0.667 \quad 1 \quad 0.667 \quad 0.235]$, both of them have the same norm values, as shown in Table 1, and they both have a bad amplitude spectrum as given in Fig. 3 (b),(d).

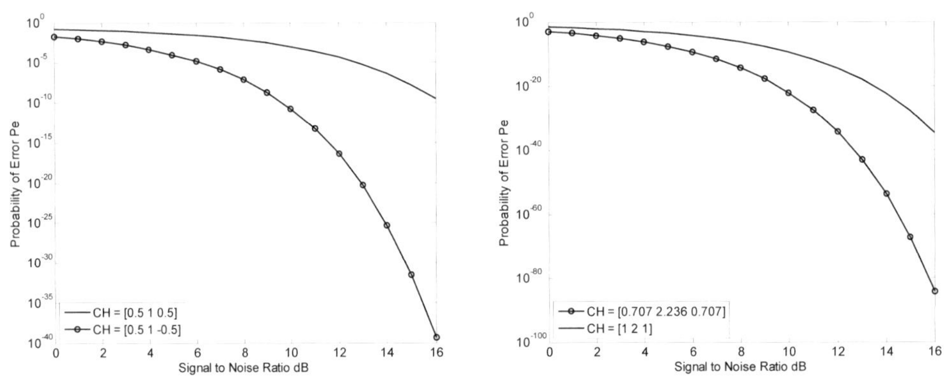

Fig. 11. (a) Effect of channel symmetry on the precoding system,
(b) Effect of channel amplitude on the precoding system

Although increasing the channel length will give the system more guard band to reduce IBI, and despite of the fact that the amplitude spectrum for the longer channel is better than shorter one, it is noticed that the shorter channel is better than the longer one.
This is because increasing the channel length will increase the variance ℓ of the $m \times n$ precoder matrix **F** too, affecting an increase in the noise variance η_T^2 at the receiver.
Note that the channel itself has no direct effect on the system as shown in Eq. 28.
It is clear from Table 2 that the value of ℓ is much higher for the long channel than the short one, which gives a good explanation for the better performance of the shorter one because the noise variance will be high for the long channel in comparison with the short channel.

Channel vector	ℓ^2			
	$m=1$	$m=2$	$m=4$	$m=8$
$[0.235 \quad 0.667 \quad 1 \quad 0.667 \quad 0.235]$	0.1	0.5182	4.7725	15.5051
$[0.707 \quad 1 \quad 0.707]$	0.1667	0.5001	1.5694	3.0711
$[0.5 \quad 1 \quad -0.5]$	0.2222	0.3333	0.4571	0.5571
$[0.5 \quad 1 \quad 0.5]$	0.2222	0.6000	2.0825	9.6000
$[1 \quad 2 \quad 1]$	0.0556	0.1500	0.5206	2.4000
$[0.707 \quad 2.234 \quad 0.707]$	0.0556	0.1154	0.2090	0.2970

Table 2. The normalization factors for channels in the precoding system

Then, the effect of the channel norm value on the performance of the system is tested, as shown in Fig. 10 (b). Here, two channels that differ in variance are used, but similar in length, i.e. $\mathbf{CH}_1 = [0.707 \quad 1 \quad 0.707]$ with variance 1.4141, and $\mathbf{CH}_2 = [0.5 \quad 1 \quad 0.5]$ with variance 1.2247 as given in Table 1. It is clear that the channel with high variance (norm) has better performance than that with low variance. The channel will not affect the received data directly, it affects the matrix **D** which depends on the channel parameters as given in Eq. 22. So, ℓ will differ as shown in Table 2 giving more noise in the channel with low norm.

Making a look on the effect of the channel symmetry, as in Fig. 11 (a), typical channels, with the same length g and the same norm, are used as given in Table 1, but the sign of one of them is reversed at one side, i.e. $[0.5 \quad 1 \quad 0.5]$ and $[0.5 \quad 1 \quad -0.5]$. Asymmetric channels gave better performance than symmetric one. It is not strange because the symmetric channel increases the energy of the transmitted signal with a great ratio more than the asymmetric. Also, Fig. 3 (f) shows that the asymmetric one has a good amplitude spectrum too.

The amplitude of the channel will has its effect too. Fig. 11 (b) is an example, two channels are used : $\mathbf{CH}_1 = [0.707 \quad 2.234 \quad 0.707]$, and $\mathbf{CH}_2 = [1 \quad 2 \quad 1]$, both of them have the same length, the same variance, but with different amplitude. The first channel gave better performance because it results in a lower value of ℓ^2 as in Table 2.

5. Sharing system with guard band

In some application, where the transmitted signal faces a badly scattering channel, or in systems that need very high signal to noise ratio, receiver simplicity is not a place of concern. In these systems, one can accept some processing in the receiver in order to increase the performance of the system. A sharing strategy between the transmitter and the receiver for the downlink of the communication system in band-limited ISI channels has been developed. The sharing is such that some equalization is done at the transmitter, while the rest of the process is done at the receiver. This results in an enhancement in comparison with the precoding system, where all the equalization process is done at the transmitter and leaves the receiver quite simple. Also, as in the precoding case, it is assumed that the transmitter has prior knowledge of the channel impulse responce.

5.1 System model of the sharing system with guard band

Figure 12 shows the basic model of the sharing system considered. The Transmitter of the system will no differ from the precoding system described in Section 4. The difference between the two models can be seen obviously in the receiver. The receiver buffer store chooses the central m component of the vector **V** to form the vector **R**, which will be fed to the receiver's processor matrix $\mathbf{F_2}$. This block is new, it was not mentioned in the precoding system, and this is the main difference between the two systems.

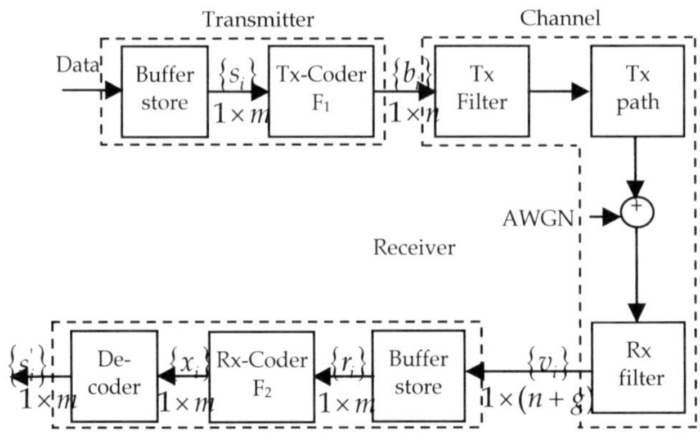

Fig. 12. Basic model of the sharing system with guard band

In the sharing process, the transmitter's processor operates as a precoding scheme on the transmitted signal, and the receiver's processor completes the detection process on the received vector to obtain the detected value of **S**. In each case, it has an exact prior knowledge of the channel characteristics **Y**, derived from the knowledge of the sampled impulse response of the channel. In the case of a time-varying channel, the rate of change in **Y** is assumed to be negligible over the duration of a received group of m signal elements, and sufficiently slow to enable **Y** to be correctly estimated from the received data signal.

5.2 Design and analysis of the sharing system with guard band

The main goal from this system is to present a system with better performance than the precoding system. The channel characteristics have no effect on the behavior of the precoding system. The only effected element is the AWGN as shown in Eq. 28. So, let us look on the variance distribution of the precoding system to see how it could be improved. The variance at the output of the system is shown in Fig. 13 and given in the Eq. 29 In order to reduce the power of the noise at the output of the system, η_T^2 should be reduced.

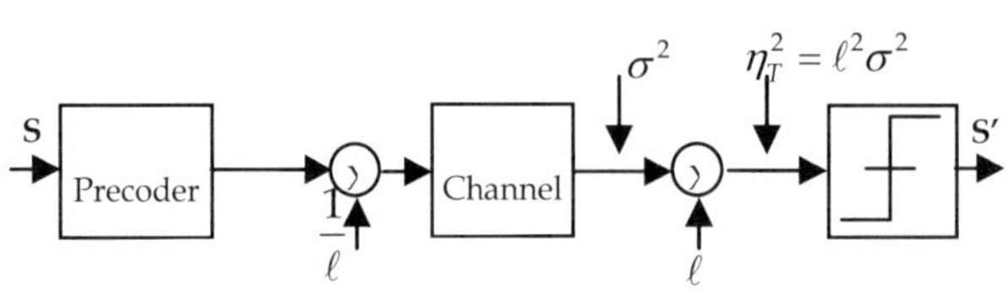

Fig. 13. Variance distribution in the precoding system

The main idea proposed here is to split the precoding process given in Section 4 between the transmitter and the receiver. The full precoder is given in Eq. 25. Here, the full precoder equation should be divided between the transmitter and the receiver by taking part of the $(.)^{-1}$ to the receiver, so that the transmitter's share of the process is the $m \times n$ matrix:

$$\mathbf{F}_1 = \left(\mathbf{D}\mathbf{D}^T\right)^{-p}\mathbf{D} \tag{31}$$

where:

$$0 \le p \le 1 \tag{32}$$

and the receiver's share of the process is the $m \times m$ matrix:

$$\mathbf{F}_2 = \left(\mathbf{D}\mathbf{D}^T\right)^{-q} \tag{33}$$

where:

$$q = p - 1 \tag{34}$$

So, the total equation of the system from the input to the output is:

$$\mathbf{X} = \mathbf{S}\mathbf{F}_1\mathbf{C}\mathbf{F}_2 = \mathbf{S} \tag{35}$$

As mentioned earlier, the assumption that $\mathbf{C} = \mathbf{D}^T$ is because that only the central m components of the vector **V**, i.e., $\begin{bmatrix} v_{g+1} & v_{g+2} & \dots & v_{g+m} \end{bmatrix}$, will be taken into consideration because they give information about the transmitted data without ISI.
In absence of AWGN, it is clear from the Eq. 36 above that there is no need for any further processing after the receiver's share of the equalization process, but when noise is present,

$$\mathbf{X} = \left(\mathbf{S}\mathbf{F}_1\mathbf{C} + \mathbf{W}\right)\mathbf{F}_2 = \mathbf{S} + \tilde{\mathbf{W}} \tag{36}$$

The variance distribution of the sharing system is shown in Fig. 14. The effect of this change in the variance distribution through the system block diagram will be explained later in the next subsection.

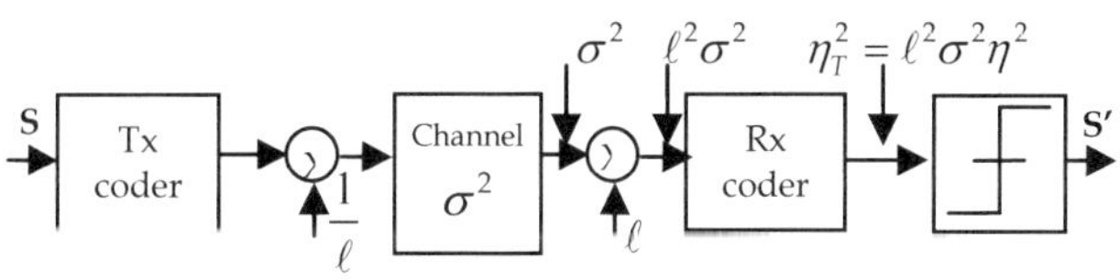

Fig. 14. Variance distribution in the sharing system with guard band

5.3 Performance evaluation of the sharing system with guard band

Using the same assumptions as in the precoding system, the tolerance to noise of the transmitter's share is the same as the precoding system, and is determined by $\ell^2\sigma^2$.
In the receiver, it is clear that the tolerance to noise can be calculated by:

$$\eta^2 = \frac{1}{m}\sum_{j=1}^{m}\sum_{i=1}^{m}\left(f_2\right)_{ij}^2 \tag{37}$$

and, the total tolerance to noise from both the transmitter's and the receiver's shares is

$$\eta_T = \sqrt{\ell^2\eta^2\sigma^2} = \ell\,\eta\,\sigma \tag{38}$$

In case of no distortion, the signal to noise ratio $(SNR)_{ND}$ is given by:

$$SNR_{ND} = \frac{\xi_b}{\sigma^2} \tag{39}$$

while the signal to noise ratio in the real channel (with noise) is:

$$SNR_C = \frac{\xi_b}{\eta_T^2} = \frac{\xi_b}{\ell^2\eta^2\sigma^2} \tag{40}$$

In order to understand the behavior of the system, the signal to noise ratio relative to no distortion channel is calculated as follows:

$$SNR_{relative} = \frac{SNR_C}{SNR_{ND}} = \frac{1}{\ell^2\eta^2} \tag{41}$$

or in dB:

$$SNR_{relative} = 10\log_{10}\left(\frac{1}{\ell^2\eta^2}\right) \text{dB} \tag{42}$$

The bit error rate equation may be written as:

$$P_e = \frac{1}{2}erfc\left[\frac{\sqrt{\xi_b}}{\sqrt{2}\eta_T}\right] = \frac{1}{2}erfc\left[\frac{1}{\ell\eta}\sqrt{\frac{\xi_b}{N_o}}\right] \tag{43}$$

5.4 Numerical results for sharing system with guard band

The equations of the transmitter coder and the receiver coder are given in Eq. 31 and Eq. 33 respectively. From the mentioned equations, the most effective part is the sharing ratio factors p and q. The relation between p and q is linear, so, the factor p is taken as the main factor to test the system and find the optimum solution that gives the best performance.

Table 3 shows the numerical results of the variables: the energy of the transmitted vector ℓ given in Eq. 26, the effect on noise variance from the receiver share of the equalization process η^2 given in Eq. 37 and the total variance of the vector at the output of the system η_T^2 and its square root η_T given in Eq. 38 All the readings were taken for the channel $[1 \quad 2 \quad 1]$ after being normalized, i.e., $[0.408 \quad 0.816 \quad 0.408]$, with block length $m = 4$ and $m = 8$. Taking the case for $m = 8$, it is clear from Table 3 that the minimum relative signal to noise ratio is -7.65 dB, which is obtained when the sharing factor p is 0.75, which means that the optimum solution for this system is obtained for $p = 0.75$. So, the coders equations may be finally written as in the following equations:

$$\mathbf{F}_1 = \left(\mathbf{DD}^T\right)^{-0.75}\mathbf{D} \tag{44}$$

$$\mathbf{F}_2 = \left(\mathbf{DD}^T\right)^{-0.25} \tag{45}$$

The value of $SNR_{relative}$ when $p = 1$ (all the process is done in the transmitter and leaves the receiver empty, i.e., precoding system) is -11.58 dB. Comparing those two values of

$SNR_{relative}$ shows that the effect of the sharing on the total performance of the system is around 4 dB enhancement for $m = 8$, and 2 dB for $m = 4$.

	$m = 4$					$m = 8$				
p	ℓ	η^2	η_T^2	η_T	SNR relative	ℓ	η^2	η_T^2	η_T	SNR relative
0.00	0.82	59.37	39.58	6.29	-15.98	0.89	1798.70	1438.90	37.93	-31.58
0.10	0.79	34.90	21.74	4.66	-13.37	0.86	699.40	514.71	22.69	-27.12
0.20	0.77	20.66	12.30	3.51	-10.90	0.83	273.63	189.78	13.78	-22.78
0.30	0.77	12.36	7.27	2.70	-8.62	0.82	108.14	73.34	8.56	-18.65
0.40	0.78	7.52	4.57	2.14	-6.60	0.84	43.47	30.56	5.53	-14.85
0.50	0.82	4.69	3.12	1.77	-4.95	0.89	18.00	14.40	3.79	-11.58
0.60	0.89	3.03	2.38	1.54	-3.76	1.02	7.85	8.20	2.86	-9.14
0.70	1.00	2.06	2.06	1.44	-3.14	1.27	3.73	6.05	2.46	-7.82
0.75	1.08	1.74	2.03	1.42	-3.07	1.47	2.70	5.82	2.41	-7.65
0.80	1.17	1.50	2.06	1.44	-3.14	1.73	2.03	6.05	2.46	-7.82
0.90	1.42	1.18	2.38	1.54	-3.76	2.51	1.31	8.20	2.86	-9.14
1.00	1.77	1.00	3.12	1.77	-4.95	3.79	1.00	14.40	3.79	-11.58

Table 3. Numerical results of the sharing system with guard band

In order to give more details about the performance of the system in figures, Fig. 15 (a) shows the effect of the p on the signal to $SNR_{relative}$ for $m = 4$. It is clear that the system has the best performance at $p = 0.75$, with about 2 dB gain more than the case where $p = 1$.

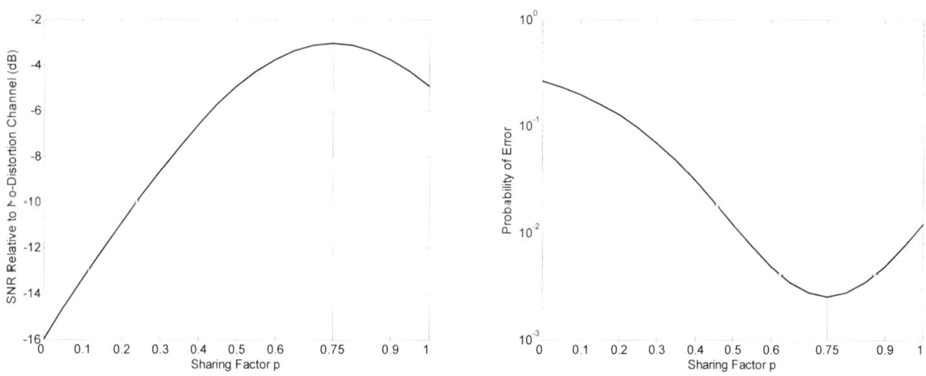

Fig. 15. (a)Effect of sharing factor p on the SNR in the sharing system with guard band, (b) Effect of sharing factor p on the BER in the sharing system with guard band

Then, Fig. 15 (b) shows the effect of bit error rate for all values of p for $m = 4$, also, $p = 0.75$ is the best. In both cases, the channel impulse response was limited to $[0.408 \quad 0.816 \quad 0.408]$, while the SNR was chosen to be 9 dB. Now, after determining the optimum solution of the system that gives the best performance, the total behavior of the system is observed, in terms of the probability of error for different values of SNR, and to compare that curve with other previously introduced systems such as the precoding system and the BLE.

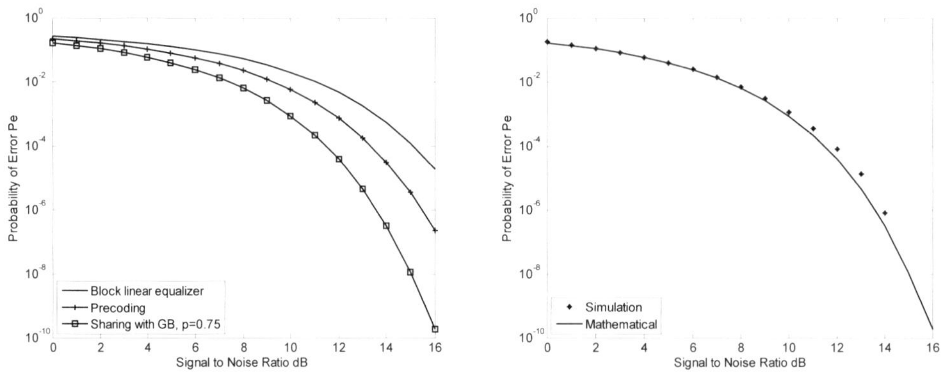

Fig. 16. (a) Probability of error for the sharing system with guard band,
(b) Mathematical and simulation results in sharing system with guard band

The BER for this is shown in Fig. 16 (a). It improved the performance with about 2 dB which is a good improvement in badly scattered channels. For the sake of comparison the bit error rate for the block linear equalizer and the precoding system are also given. Figure 20 (b) shows a comparison between the mathematical results, and the output of the Matlab simulation program for $m = 4$ and $Y = [0.408 \quad 0.816 \quad 0.408]$. The results were similar, so, now it is proved that the model presented earlier is correct.

When testing the effect of the block length m on the behavior of the system, and taking into consideration the points discussed while testing this variable for the precoding system, one can easily expect that the performance will become better by reducing the block length, because of the effect of the coders on the variances, and the IBI problem.

Before start testing this variable, the behavior of the most effective elements that almost control everything should be understood. When the effect of the variables on the precoding system is tested, there was one main variable which is the energy of the transmitted code ℓ. This factor (ℓ) depends only on the transmitted energy, and has no relationship with the receiver side, because the receiver was empty there. But here, another complicated element η_T appeared, as given in Eq. 38, and its components: ℓ and η as in Eq. 26 and Eq. 37.

The noise will be affected by both transmitter and receiver. This change may be constructive some times if the value of ℓ or η is less than 1. In case of getting a value of 1 for either ℓ and η, this means that this element is neutral, and will not affect the system. It is also expected, in special cases, that one stage will cancel the effect of the other if the multiplication of ℓ and η is equal to 1. The way that how those variables change by changing the block length will have an important role in performance.

Figure 21 (a) gives an idea about their behavior for $Y = [1 \quad 2 \quad 1]$. It is clear that all the variables are increasing rapidly by increasing the block length, which means that the performance of the system will be worse for long blocks.

Here, ℓ and η will be stable for very long codes, but the effective variable η_T will continue increasing. So, the behavior of the block length is not expected to take a stable region as in precoding, and will take another shape, but when plotting the BER vs. block length in Fig. 17 (b) for $Y = [1 \quad 2 \quad 1]$, the behavior is the same (only the performance is better), and this is because of the nonlinearity of the error complementary function used to calculate the BER.

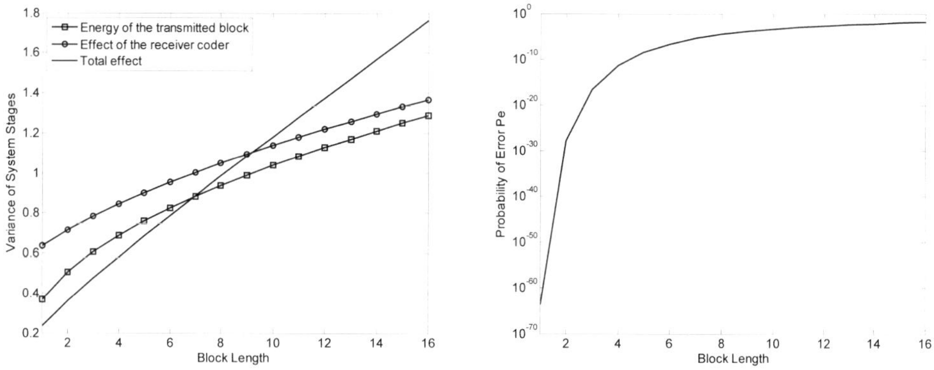

Fig. 17. (a) The behavior of the system variance in sharing system with guard band, (b) Effect of the block length m on the BER in sharing system with guard band

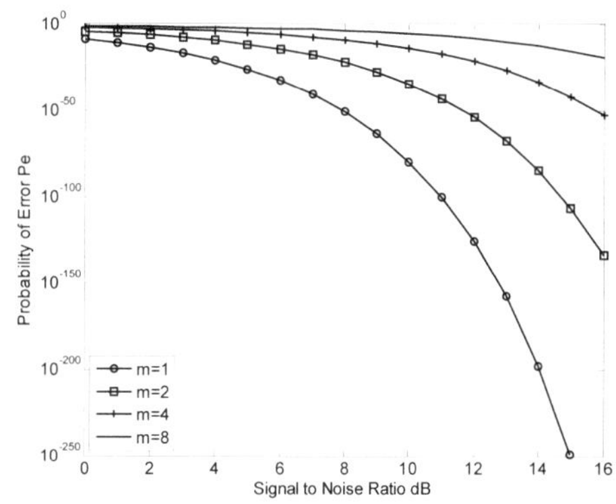

Fig. 18. Effect of block length on sharing system with guard band

Figure 22 shows the BER of the system versus SNR for four block lengths. The channel here is assumed to be $Y = [1 \quad 2 \quad 1]$. It is clear that increasing the block length will reduce the performance of the system rapidly. Now, let us test different channel characteristics to see which channels are suitable for this system, but before doing that, and referring to the effect of the block length results, one can say that it will take the same behavior as the precoding system because it depends mainly on the major players in this system, which are the factors that affect variances of the noise vector, as given in Table 4. Also, the amplitude spectrum of the channel will have an effect too. So, in order to focus only on the variables of the system, channels that have identical amplitude spectrum will be taken in each case of comparison.

In Fig. 19 (a), the effect of the channel length on the performance of the system is studied, for $m = 4$, using two different channels with different lengths: $g = 2$ and $g = 4$, but with the same norm values, as shown in Table 1. The channels used here are: $[0.235 \quad 0.667 \quad 1 \quad 0.667 \quad 0.235]$ and $[0.707 \quad 1 \quad 0.707]$. From Table 4, it is clear that both ℓ^2 and η^2 for the long channel are higher than the short one (in the studied case of $m = 4$) causing and increase in the noise variance. The results show better performance for the channel with less noise (the short one).

Channel vector	$m=1$		$m=2$		$m=4$		$m=8$	
	ℓ^2	η^2	ℓ^2	η^2	ℓ^2	η^2	ℓ^2	η^2
$[0.235 \quad 0.667 \quad 1 \quad 0.667 \quad 0.235]$	0.14	0.71	0.37	1.10	1.09	2.18	2.20	3.29
$[0.707 \quad 1 \quad 0.707]$	0.24	0.71	0.46	0.92	0.84	1.26	1.23	1.53
$[0.5 \quad 1 \quad -0.5]$	0.27	0.82	0.41	0.82	0.55	0.83	0.66	0.83
$[0.5 \quad 1 \quad 0.5]$	0.27	0.82	0.51	1.02	0.95	1.42	1.76	2.20
$[1 \quad 2 \quad 1]$	0.14	0.41	0.26	0.51	0.47	0.71	0.88	1.10
$[0.707 \quad 2.234 \quad 0.707]$	0.14	0.41	0.23	0.46	0.34	0.51	0.44	0.55

Table 4. The effective parameters on the sharing system with guard band

Then, the effect of the channel norm value of the performance of the system is tested, as shown in Fig. 19 (b). Two channels that differ in variance are used, but similar in length, i.e., $[0.707 \quad 1 \quad 0.707]$ and $[1 \quad 2 \quad 1]$. The channel with higher variance (norm) has better performance than the one with lower variance. Again, one look on Table 4 will make it a logic result because $[0.707 \quad 1 \quad 0.707]$ will face more noise.

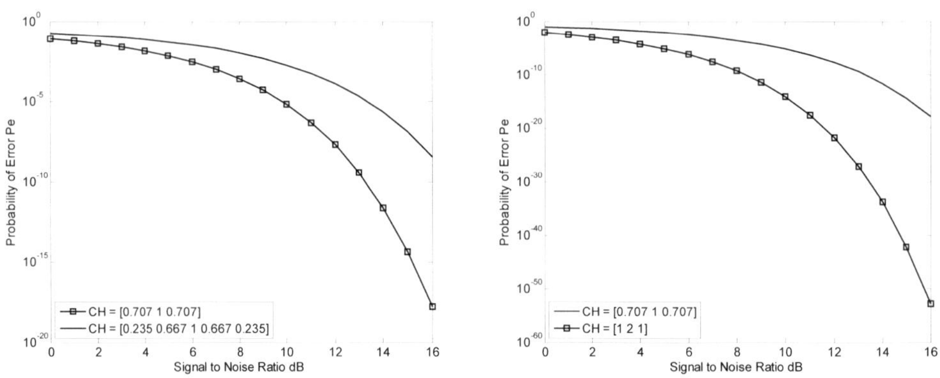

Fig. 19. (a) Effect of channel length on sharing system with guard band,
(b) Effect of channel variance on sharing system with guard band

Also, taking any other case from the tested channels will give the same results for any block length, but the case of $m=4$ is taken to make it easy to compare different figures.

In Fig. 20 (a), typical channels are used, but the sign of one of them is reversed at one side, also, asymmetric channels gave much better performance than symmetric one as expected. Many factors helped the asymmetric channel to have better performance such as the noise level due to the values of ℓ and η given in Table 4, and the great amplitude spectrum as shown in Fig. 3 (f). At last, the effect of amplitude of the impulse response is tested in Fig. 20 (b), Although the length, the symmetry and the norm were typical, but the amplitude affects the values of ℓ and η in a way that helps $[0.707 \quad 2.234 \quad 0.707]$ to have better performance.

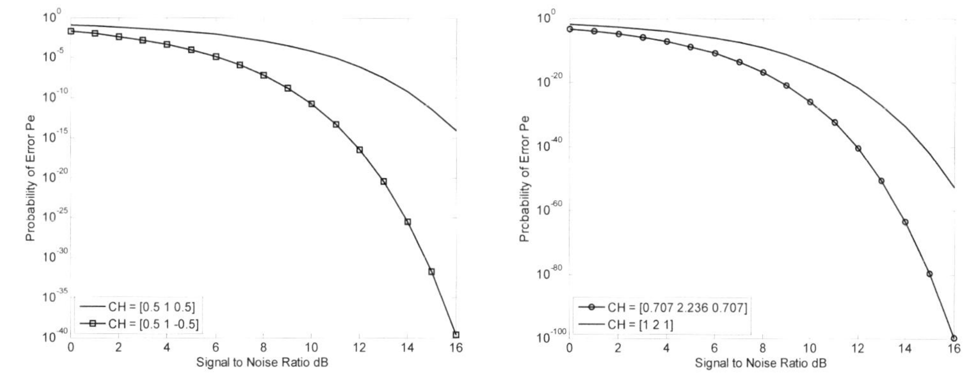

Fig. 20. (a) Effect of channel symmetry on sharing system with guard band, (b) Effect of channel amplitude on sharing system with guard band

6. Sharing system without guard band

The main difference between this system and the sharing system with GB is length of the transmitted vector. Both of them may transmit the same vector at the input of the transmitter, but after coding, the previous system generates a longer code than this one. This will give that system two guard band areas after and before the transmitted block, which will be useful in environments with many obstacles that usually cause duplicate versions of the transmitted signal, and finally cause Inter Symbol Interference (ISI).

Unfortunately, all the advantages can not be available in one system. The immunity against ISI will cause increase in bandwidth in an unaccepted ratios in some applications where the bandwidth is very narrow, or in crowded environments that result in long channel impulse response. For example, transmission in codes of 4 elements in an environment with a baseband channel of length 5 ($g = 4$), will cause a transmitted block of length 12 at the previous system and of length 8 at this one.

So, this system is introduced as a bandwidth efficient system, if the ISI may be accepted in certain ratios.

6.1 System model of the sharing system without guard band

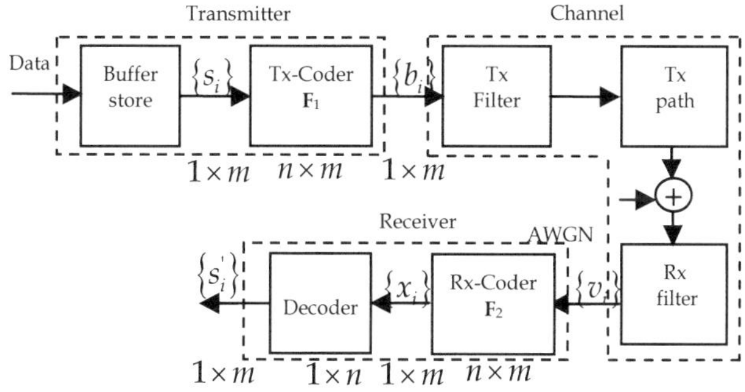

Fig. 21. Basic model of sharing system without guard band

Figure 21 shows the sharing system without guard band considered. The signal at the input to the transmitter will not differ from the two previous systems. Here, the buffer-store at the input to the transmitter holds m successive element values $\{s_i\}$ to form the $1 \times m$ data vector **S**. The difference is the size of the transmitter's processor, $\mathbf{F}_1$, in this case, it is an $m \times m$ matrix instead of $m \times n$, so, in this processor, **S** is converted into the m vector **B**.
Note that channel vector **Y** is arranged in the same manner as done for **C** in the previous sections, but here, because the transmitted block contains only m elements instead of n elements, the size of the channel matrix is $m \times n$ instead of $n \times n + g$.
The output of the channel is the $1 \times n$ vector **V** which will be fed to the receiver's processor $\mathbf{F}_2$ to complete the detection process on the received vector to obtain the detected value of **S**.

6.2 Design and analysis of the sharing system without guard band

As it was done in the sharing system with GB, the equalization process, between the transmitter and the receiver, will be split. Here, the size of the channel output vector is $1 \times n$, and the size of the receiver's coder is $n \times m$, which means that all the vector elements are needed for the coding process. Here, no way to choose only the central components. So, no need to introduce a new matrix to represent the channel in the coders design. The transmitter's share of the process will be the $m \times m$ matrix:

$$\mathbf{F}_1 = \left(\mathbf{Y}\mathbf{Y}^T\right)^{-p} \tag{46}$$

and the receiver's share of the process is the $n \times m$ matrix:

$$\mathbf{F}_2 = \mathbf{Y}^T\left(\mathbf{Y}\mathbf{Y}^T\right)^{-q} \tag{47}$$

The rest of the analysis will not differ from the other two systems.

6.3 Performance evaluation of the sharing system without guard band

In order to study the performance of the system, the tolerance to noise, from the transmitter's and the receiver's shares, should be found. Assume that the possible values of **S** are equally likely and that the mean square value of **S** is equal to the number of bits per element. Suppose that the m vectors $\{\mathbf{Y}_i\}$ have unit length. Since there are m k-level signal elements in a group, the vector **S** has k^m possible values each corresponding to a different combination of the m k-level signal-elements. So, the vector **B** whose components are the values of the corresponding impulses fed to the baseband channel, has k^m possible values. If e is the total energy of all the k^m values of the input data vector **S**, then in order to make the transmitted signal energy per bit is unity, the transmitted signal must be divided by:

$$\ell = \sqrt{\frac{e}{mk^m}} \tag{48}$$

Note here that the difference between this equation and Eq. 26 is the length of the transmitted vector (it was n in Eq. 26). The n sample values which are the components of the vector $\mathbf{V}'$, must first be multiplied by the factor ℓ to give the m-component vector

$$\mathbf{V} = \ell\mathbf{V}' = \mathbf{B}\mathbf{Y} + \ell\mathbf{W} = \mathbf{S} + \mathbf{U} \tag{49}$$

where **U** is an m vector whose components are sample independent Gaussian random variables with zero mean and variance $\ell^2\sigma^2$. Thus, the tolerance to noise of the transmitter's share is determined by the value of $\ell^2\sigma^2$. In the receiver, the tolerance to noise is:

$$\eta^2 = \frac{1}{m}\sum_{j=1}^{m}\sum_{i=1}^{n}(f_2)_{ij}^2 \tag{50}$$

So, the total tolerance to noise from both the transmitter's and the receiver's shares is:

$$\eta_T = \sqrt{\ell^2\eta^2\sigma^2} = \ell\eta\sigma \tag{51}$$

The signal to noise ratio, relative to no distortion channel, is:

$$SNR_{relative} = 10\log_{10}\left(\frac{1}{\ell^2\eta^2}\right)\text{dB} \tag{52}$$

The bit error rate may be written as:

$$P_e = \frac{1}{2}erfc\left[\frac{\sqrt{\xi_b}}{\sqrt{2}\eta_T}\right] = \frac{1}{2}erfc\left[\frac{1}{\ell\eta}\sqrt{\frac{\xi_b}{N_o}}\right] \tag{53}$$

From Eq. 53 above, it is clear that the performance is affected by both the transmitter and reciver share. This came from the effect on the AWGN variance. The effect of the transmitter share comes from the fact that the transmitter equalizer will change the average energy (energy per bit) of the transmitted vector, causing a change in the signal power, so, SNR will be changed.

6.4 Numerical analysis of the sharing system without guard band

From Table 5.4, the minimum $SNR_{relative}$ is -8.62 dB, which is obtained when p is 0.25, which means that the best performance will be obtained using the equations below.

$$\mathbf{F}_1 = \left(\mathbf{YY}^T\right)^{-0.25} \tag{54}$$

$$\mathbf{F}_2 = \mathbf{Y}^T\left(\mathbf{YY}^T\right)^{-075} \tag{55}$$

For the case of $m = 8$, the value of $SNR_{relative}$ when $p = 0$ is -12.55 dB, which means that the sharing system without guard band gives 4 dB enhancement in comparison with the block linear equalizer. Referring to Table 3, the best value for the sharing system with guard band was -7.65dB, so, the system discussed here is not better than the one discussed before. The sharing system with guard band BER is better than this one, but the benefit here is the bandwidth saving because less added bits are used in the transmitted code. It is not strange to discover that the difference between the sharing systems (in performance) is the same as the full systems (the precoding and the block linear equalizer). Each one of the sharing systems have a special case, when removing the sharing by using full (or null) factor, that returns to the full case. The results in Table 5 were calculated for the normalized channel $Y = [0.408 \quad 0.816 \quad 0.408]$ and block lengths $m = 4$ and $m = 8$.

	$m=4$					$m=8$				
p	ℓ	η^2	η_T^2	η_T	SNR relative	ℓ	η^2	η_T^2	η_T	SNR relative
0.00	1.00	4.69	4.69	2.16	-6.71	1.00	18.00	18.00	4.24	-12.55
0.10	1.09	3.03	3.57	1.89	-5.52	1.14	7.85	10.25	3.20	-10.11
0.20	1.22	2.06	3.09	1.76	-4.91	1.42	3.73	7.56	2.75	-8.79
0.25	1.32	1.74	3.04	1.74	-4.83	1.64	2.70	7.27	2.70	-8.62
0.30	1.44	1.50	3.09	1.76	-4.91	1.93	2.03	7.56	2.75	-8.79
0.40	1.74	1.18	3.57	1.89	-5.52	2.80	1.31	10.25	3.20	-10.11
0.50	2.16	1.00	4.69	2.16	-6.71	4.24	1.00	18.00	4.24	-12.55
0.60	2.74	0.91	6.86	2.62	-8.36	6.59	0.88	38.21	6.18	-15.82
0.70	3.52	0.88	10.91	3.30	-10.38	10.40	0.85	91.67	9.57	-19.62
0.80	4.54	0.89	18.46	4.30	-12.66	16.54	0.87	237.22	15.40	-23.75
0.90	5.91	0.93	32.60	5.71	-15.13	26.45	0.92	643.38	25.37	-28.09
1.00	7.71	1.00	59.37	7.71	-17.74	42.41	1.00	1798.70	42.41	-32.55

Table 5. Numerical results of the sharing system without guard band

Fig. 22 (a) shows the effect of p on $SNR_{relative}$. It is clear that the best performance is at $p = 0.25$. In Fig. 5.22 (b), the effect of BER for all values of p is plotted. In both cases, the channel impulse response was limited to $Y = [0.408 \quad 0.816 \quad 0.408]$, while the SNR was chose to be 9 dB and the block length $m = 4$. The bit error rate for the system described here is shown in Fig. 23 (a) with comparison with other systems discussed through this chapter. Although its performance is not the best of all, but it still better than the block linear equalizer by 2 dB, and, almost, the same as the precoding system. Figure 23 (b) shows a comparison between the mathematical results obtained and the output of the Matlab simulation program for $m = 4$ and $Y = [0.408 \quad 0.816 \quad 0.408]$. The results were similar.

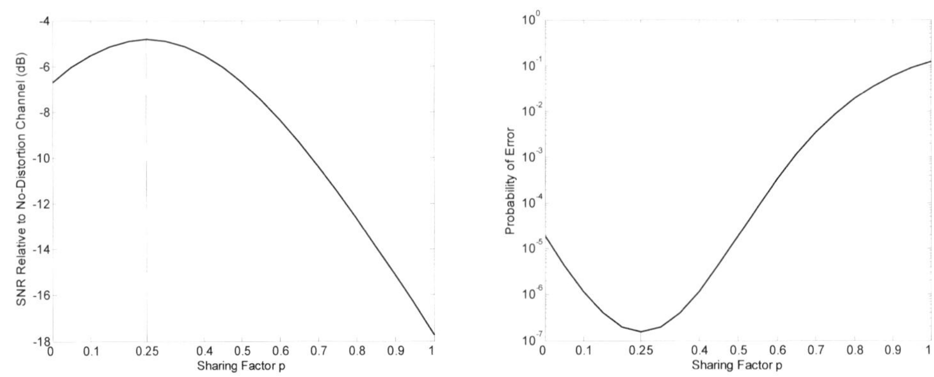

Fig. 22. (a) Effect of the factor p on the SNR in sharing system without guard band, (b) Effect of the factor p on the BER in sharing system without guard band

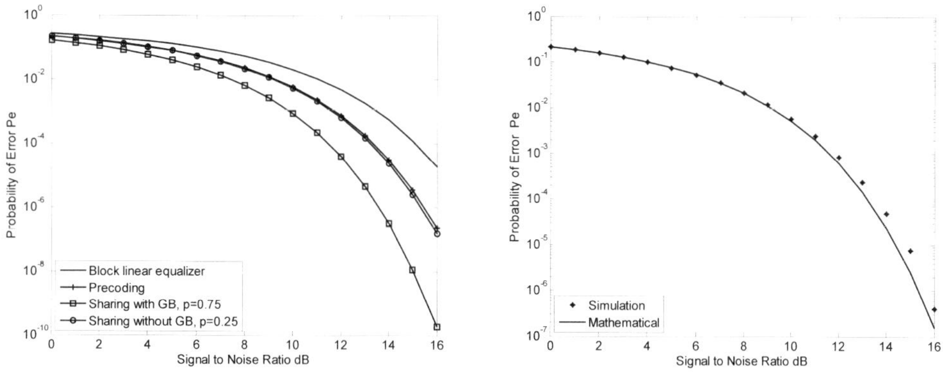

Fig. 23. (a) Probability of error for the sharing system without guard band,
(b) Mathematical & simulation results in sharing system without guard band

Figure 24 (a) shows BER of the system for different values of SNR using different block lengths. Increasing the block length will reduce the performance. In Fig. 24 (b), the effect of the channel length on the performance of the system is tested. Here, two different channels are used with different lengths, but with the same norm.

	$m=1$		$m=2$		$m=4$		$m=8$	
Channel vector	ℓ^2	η^2	ℓ^2	η^2	ℓ^2	η^2	ℓ^2	η^2
$[0.235 \quad 0.667 \quad 1 \quad 0.667 \quad 0.235]$	0.71	0.71	1.10	1.10	2.18	2.18	3.29	3.29
$[0.707 \quad 1 \quad 0.707]$	0.71	0.71	0.92	0.92	1.26	1.26	1.53	1.53
$[0.5 \quad 1 \quad -0.5]$	0.82	0.82	0.82	0.82	0.83	0.83	0.83	0.83
$[0.5 \quad 1 \quad 0.5]$	0.82	0.82	1.02	1.02	1.42	1.42	2.20	2.20
$[1 \quad 2 \quad 1]$	0.41	0.41	0.51	0.51	0.71	0.71	1.10	1.10
$[0.707 \quad 2.234 \quad 0.707]$	0.41	0.41	0.46	0.46	0.51	0.51	0.55	0.55

Table 6. The effective parameters on the sharing system without guard band

The short channel, as in the two previously discussed systems, will give better performance because it will face less noise as shown in Table 6.

Then, the effect of the channel norm value of the performance of the system is tested, as shown in Fig. 25 (a). Here, two channels that differ in variance are used, but similar in length. The channels with higher variance (norm) have better performance than those with lower variance.

In Fig. 25 (b), typical channels are the sign of one of them is reversed at one side. The effect was great. Asymmetric channels gave much better performance than symmetric one. It is not strange because the symmetric channel increases the coder variance four times more than the asymmetric one.

The amplitude of the channel has the same effect like the previous two systems because of the values of the energy of the transmitted signal and the effect of the receiver share given in Table 6. Fig. 26 is an example.

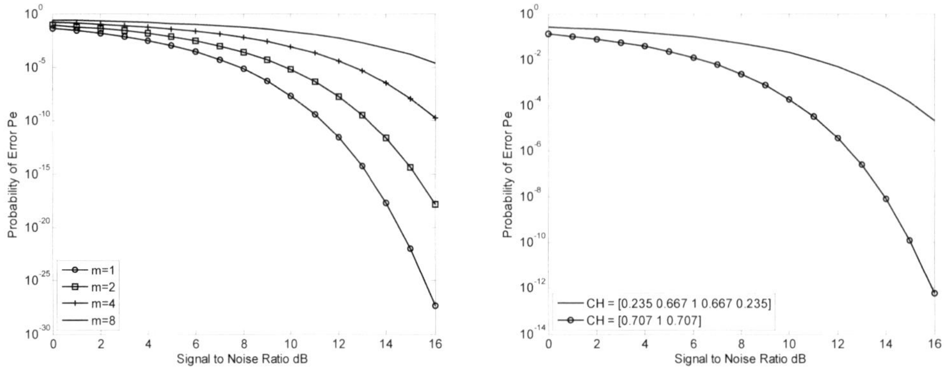

Fig. 24. (a) Effect of block length *m* on sharing system without guard band, (b) Effect of channel length *g* on sharing system without guard band

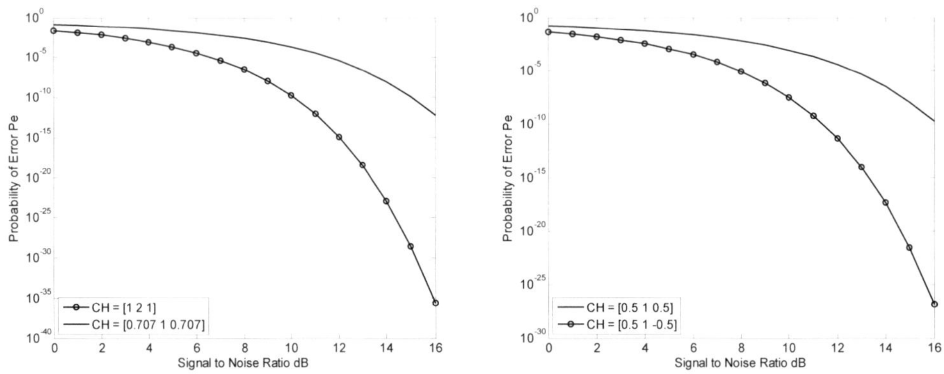

Fig. 25. (a) Effect of channel norm on sharing system without guard band, (b) Effect of channel symmetry on sharing system without GB

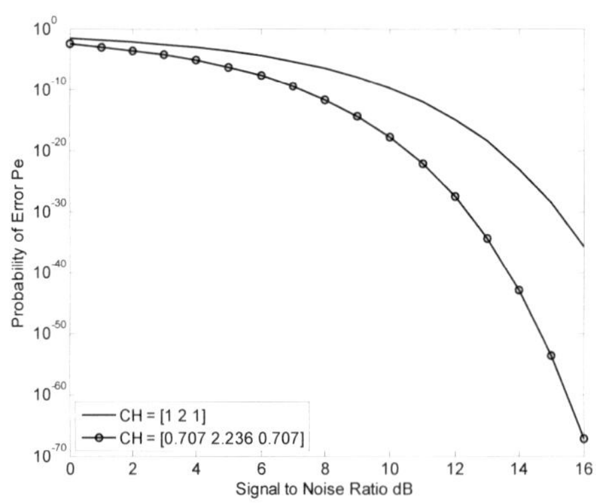

Fig. 26. Effect of channel amplitude on sharing system without GB

7. Conclusion

Here, the three proposed systems in this chapter will be summarized, taking the block linear equalizer as a reference, and all the systems have been evaluated based on a transmitted data block of length $m=4$ and $m=8$ in a channel with $Y=[0.408 \quad 0.816 \quad 0.408]$. The information given in this comparison may vary when changing the channel, but it will stay relatively constant.

Table 7 shows a comparison between the systems. From the point-view of the bit error rate at $m=4$, the block linear equalizer (BLE) is taken as a reference system with 0 dB improvement. The precoding system gives improvement for about 1.75 dB in comparison with the BLE, while the sharing system results in 1.9 dB enhancement more than the precoding one (3.65 dB more than the BLE). The sharing system without GB was worse than the one with GB, but it still better than the BLE by 1.9 dB and almost the same as the precoding (0.15 dB enhancement).

	Block linear equalizer	Precoding system	Sharing with GB	Sharing without GB
BER ($m=4$)	0 dB (reference)	1.75 dB	3.65 dB	1.9 dB
BER ($m=8$)	0 dB (reference)	1 dB	4.9 dB	4 dB
extra bits (GB)	g	$2g$	$2g$	g
ISI immunity	No	Yes	Yes	No
Transmitter Processing	0%	100%	75%	25%
Receiver Processing	100%	0%	25%	75%

Table 7. Comparison between the systems

Now, from the point-view of the extra bits in the transmitted vector, the BLE will use n bits for each m data signal ($n=m+g$, where $g+1$ is the channel length), and the same value of n for the sharing system without guard band. While the precoding system and the sharing system with GB are generating $n+g$ vector in order to transmit an m data bits, with increase of g bits.

Those extra used bits are useful from the point-view of immunity toward intersymbol interference. Removing the extra bits at the receiver side will remove the bits that faced the intersymbol interference in the channel. So, it is expected that the precoding system and the sharing system with GB are immune to ISI, while the BLE and the sharing system without GB will face ISI.

Form the point-view of the receiver complexity, all the processing will be done in the receiver in the BLE, while it all will be done in the transmitter in the precoding system, leaving the receiver quite simple. The other two systems will share the processing between the transmitter and the receiver in different ratios.

8. Acknowledgment

Author would like to thank Palestinian Technical University-Khadoorie (PTU-K) for supporting the publication of this chapter.

9. References

Crozier, S., Falconer, D. & Mahmoud, S. (1992). Reduced Complexity Short-Block Data Detection Techniques for Fading Time-Dispersive Channels. *IEEE Transactions on Vehicular Technology* Vol. 41,No. 3: 255-265.

Ghani, F. (2003). Block Data Communication System for Fading Time Dispersive Channels. *Proceedings of 4th National Conference on Telecommunication Technology*, Malaysia.

Ghani, F. (2004). Performance Bounds for Block Transmission System. *Proceedings of 2004 IEEE Asia-Pacific Conference on Circuits and Systems*, USA.

Hayashi, K. & Sakai, H. (2006). Single Carrier Block Transmission without Guard Interval. *Proceedings of 17th Annual IEEE International Symposium on Personal, Indoor and Mobile Radio Communications*, Finland.

Hsu, F. (1985). Data Directed Estimation Techniques for Single-Tone HF Modems. *Proceedings of IEEE military communication conference*, USA.

Kaleh, G. (1995). Channel Equalization for Block Transmission Systems. *IEEE Journal on Selected Areas in Communications* Vol. 13,No. 1: 110-121.

Perl, J., Shpigel, A. & Reichman, A. (1987). Adaptive Receiver for Digital Communication over HF Channels. *IEEE Journal on Selected Areas in Communications* Vol. 5,No. 2: 304-308.

Proakis, J. (1995). *Digital Communications*. New York, McGraw Hill.

Varga, R. (1962). *Matrix Iterative Analysis*. Englewood Cliffs , New Jersey, Prentice Hall.

10

Frequency Hopping Spread Spectrum: An Effective Way to Improve Wireless Communication Performance

Yang Liu
Department of Information Technology, Vaasa University of Applied Sciences
Finland

1. Introduction

To improve the performance of short-range wireless communications, channel quality must be improved by avoiding interference and multi-path fading. Frequency hopping spread spectrum (FHSS) is a transmission technique where the carrier hops from frequency to frequency. For frequency hopping a mechanism must be designed so that the data can be transmitted in a clear channel and avoid congested channels. Adaptive frequency hopping is a system which is used to improve immunity toward frequency interference by avoiding using congested frequency channels in hopping sequence. Mathematical modelling is used to simulate and analyze the performance improvement by using frequency hopping spread spectrum with popular modulation schemes, and also the hopping channel situations are investigated.

In this chapter the focus is to improve wireless communication performance by adaptive frequency hopping which is implemented by selecting sets of communication channels and adaptively hopping sender's and receiver's frequency channels and determining the channel numbers with less interference. Also the work investigates whether the selected channels are congested or clear then a list of good channels can be generated and in practice to use detected frequency channels as hopping sequence to improve the performance of communication and finally the quality of service.

The Fourier transform mathematical modules are used to convert signals from time domain to frequency domain and vice versa. The mathematical modules are applied to represent the frequency and simulate them in MATLAB and as result the simulated spectrums are analysed. Then a simple two-state Gilbert-Elliot Channel Model (Gilbert, 1960; Elliott, 1963) in which a two-state Markov chain with states named "Good" and "Bad" is used to check if the channels are congested or clear in case of interference. Finally, a solution to improve the performance of wireless communications by choosing and using "Good" channels as the next frequency hopping sequence channel is proposed.

2. Review of related theories

2.1 Spread spectrum

Spread spectrum is a digital modulation technology and a technique based on principals of spreading a signal among many frequencies to prevent interference and signal detection. As the name shows it is a technique to spread the transmitted spectrum over a wide range of frequencies. It started to be employed by military applications because of its Low Probability of Intercept (LPI) or demodulation, interference and anti-jamming (AJ) from enemy side. The idea of Spreading spectrum is to spread a signal over a large frequency band to use greater bandwidth than the Data bandwidth while the power remains the same. And as far as the spread signal looks like the noise signal in the same frequency band it will be difficult to recognize the signal which this feature of spreading provides security to the transmission.

Compared to a narrowband signal, spread spectrum spreads the signal power over a wideband and the overall SNR is improved because only a small part of spread spectrum signal will be affected by interference (Liu, 2008). In a communication system in sender and receiver sides' one spreading generator has located which based on the spreading technique they synchronize the received modulated spectrum.

2.2 Shannon capacity and theoretical justification for spread spectrum

Claude Shannon published the fundamental limits on communication over noisy channels in 1948 in the classic paper "A Mathematical Theory of Communication". Shannon showed that error-free communication is possible on a noisy channel provided that the data rate is less than the channel capacity. Shannon capacity (data rate) equation is the basis for spread spectrum systems, which typically operate at a very low SNR, but use a very large bandwidth in order to provide an acceptable data rate per user. Applying spread spectrum principles to the multiple access environments is a development occurring over the last decade (Bates & Gregory, 2001).

The Shannon equation states that the channel capacity "C" (error free bps) is directly proportional to the bandwidth "B" and is proportional to the log of SNR. Shannon capacity applies only to the additive white Gaussian noise (AWGN) channel. The channel capacity is a theoretical limit only; it describes the best that can possibly be done with any code and modulation method.

The basis for understanding the operation of spread spectrum technology begins with Shannon/Hartley channel capacity theorem:

$$C = B \times \log_2(1 + S / N) \tag{1}$$

In this equation, C is the channel capacity in bits per second (bps), which is the maximum data rate for a theoretical bit error rate (BER). B is the required bandwidth in Hz and S/N is the signal to noise ratio. Assume that C which represents the amount of information allowed by communication channel, also represent the desired performance. S/N ratio expresses the environmental conditions such as obstacles, presence of jammers, interferences, etc.

There is another explanation of this equation is applicable for difficult environments, for example when a low SNR caused by noise and interference. This approach says that one can maintain or even increase communication performance by allowing more bandwidth (high B), even when signal power is below the noise. In Shannon formula by changing the log base from 2 to e (the Napierian number) and noting that $\ln = \log_e$ Therefore:

$$C / B = (1 / \ln 2) \times \ln(1 + S / N) = 1.443 \times \ln(1 + S / N) \tag{2}$$

Applying the Maclaurin series development for

$$\ln(1+x) = x - x^2/2 + x^3/3 - x^4/4 + \dots + (-1)^{k+1}x^k/k + \dots \tag{3}$$

$$C/B = 1.443 \times (S/N - (S/N)^2/2 + (S/N)^3/3 - (S/N)^4/4 + \dots \tag{4}$$

S/N is usually low for spread spectrum applications, considering that the signal power density can even be below the noise level. Assuming a noise level such that $S/N << 1$, Shannon's expression becomes simply:

$$C/B \approx 1.443 \times S/N \tag{5}$$

And very roughly:

$$C/B \approx S/N \text{ or } N/S \approx B/C \tag{6}$$

To send error free information for a given noise to signal ratio in the channel, therefore, one need only perform the fundamental spread spectrum signal spreading operation: increase the transmitted bandwidth.

2.3 Frequency hopping spread spectrum

Frequency hopping spread spectrum is a transmission technology used in wireless networks and a technique to generate spread spectrum by hopping the carrier frequency. FHSS uses narrow band signal which is less than 1 MHz, In this method data signal is modulated with a narrowband carrier signal that "hops" in random and hopping happens in pseudo-random "predictable" sequence in a regular time from frequency to frequency which is synchronized at both ends. Using FHSS technology improves privacy, it is a powerful solution to avoid interference and multi path fading (distortion), it decreases narrowband interference, increases signal capacity, improve the signal to noise ratio, efficiency of bandwidth is high and difficult to intercept also this transmission can share a frequency band with many types of conventional transmissions with minimal interference. For frequency hopping a mechanism must be defined to transmit data in a clear channel and to avoid the congested channels. Frequency hopping is the periodic change of transmission frequency and hopping happens over a frequency bandwidth which consists of numbers of channels. Channel which is used as a hopped channel is instantaneous bandwidth while the hopping spectrum is called total hopping bandwidth. Frequency hopping categorized into slow hopping and fast hopping which by slow hopping more than one data symbol is transmitted in same channel and by fast hopping frequency changes several times during one symbol. Hopping sequence means which next channel to hop; there are two types of hopping sequence: random hopping sequence and deterministic hopping sequence.

The focus of this work is on slow and deterministic frequency hopping sequence. In a frequency hopping network, there can be different number of receivers which one sender is designed as Base that is responsible to transmit the synchronization data to the receivers.

2.4 Adaptive frequency hopping

Adaptive frequency hopping (AFH) is a system in which devices constantly change their operating frequency to avoid interference from other devices and maintain security. AFH classifies channels as 'Good' or 'Bad' and adaptively selects from the pool of Good channels. 'Bad channels' means the channels with interference. The Idea of using AFH is to hop only over Good and clear channels it means to choose the frequency channels that they have less interferences. For using AFH there must be a mechanism to choose 'Good' and 'Bad' channels. Using AFH has some advantages which they are:

- Active avoidance to narrowband interference and frequency fading
- Avoids crowded frequencies in hopping sequence
- Performance of BER is high
- Reduces transmission power
- Working with adaptive channel will further enhance system performance

RSSI (Received Signal Strength Indication) tells each channel quality to generate a list for 'bad channels'. As for using AFH there must be a mechanism to choose 'Good' and 'Bad' channels, this mechanism can be done by functionalizing one of the duplex channel as the feedback channel. The feedback information contains the channel numbers which are in use. In a duplex communication system as shown in Figure 1 there is a transmitter A and a receiver B to define as uplink and downlink from the sender to receiver and for the selection of frequency channel as the next hop to use the feedback from uplink. Also a system must be proposed to generate a hopping sequence number as the channel number which uplink "receiver" sends this number by the feedback to downlink "sender". Transmitter A baste on predefined frequency or control channel sends the data to receiver B, the RSSI value of downlink which is equivalent as SIR is measured at the end B. The receiver B analysis the data and sends a number to sender A over the uplink and if the measured data is below the criterion then LQA determines that channel needs to be switched. Sender A uses this number as a variable in a predefined algorithm which calculates the sequence of frequencies that must be used and sends a synchronization signal over downlink by the first frequency based on the calculated sequence to acknowledge the receiver side B that it has correctly calculated the sequence number. Finally communication starts between sender and receiver and both end receiver and sender change their frequencies based on the calculated order.

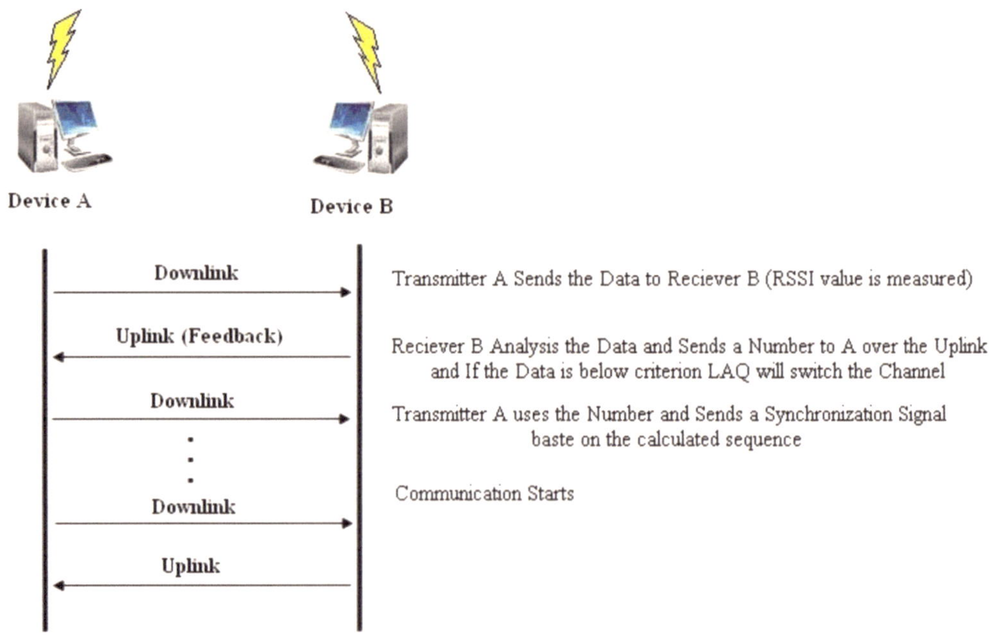

Fig. 1. Shows the communication scheme

To illustrate the system and principles of a proposed AFH scheme more, assume that there is a duplex transceiver system as shown in Figure 2. The system is an ordinary Frequency hopping system which uses a number of narrowband channels (Zander & Malmgren, 1995). As in Figure 2 HS is called Hope Sequence Generator, it generates pseudo-random symbols out of alphabet of size **Na**. The generated sequence **Na** is fed to the Mapping function that Maps incoming symbols onto a symbol alphabet of size **N**. And then these symbols are fed to the Frequency Hopper-Dehopper. The effect of these operations is that the system will use only **Na** out of **N** available frequency at any time. The selection of which frequency to be used is made by LQA on the receiver side and since a duplex system is used the selected frequency is fed back to the transmitter side in the shape of a frequency map on the return channel.

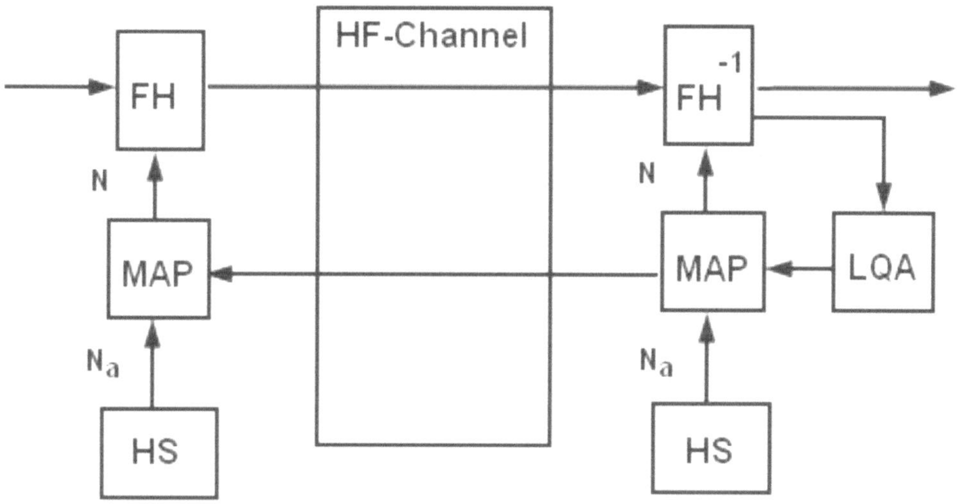

Fig. 2. Duplex transceiver system

To simplify the understanding of the AFH proposed system, assume a block-oriented transmission scheme is under use as shown in Figure 3.

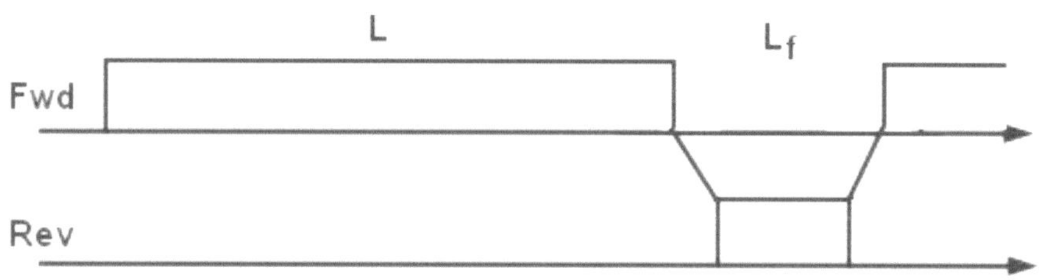

Fig. 3. Block-oriented transmission scheme

According to Figure 3, the transmitter transmits a frame of **L** chips which each contains one channel symbol. After the transmission of the block, the receiver performs its LQA and replies by transmitting the new frequency map **Lf** as a feedback block to be used in the subsequent (Forward) block transmission. It is important to mention that the proposed scheme the entire frequency map is transmitted at every updating instant and since the feedback channel is not perfectly reliable this procedure assures a high reliability. To generate a hopping sequence number as the channel number that uplink "receiver" sends this number by the feedback to downlink "sender" can be shown in a linear equation (Zander & Malmgren, 1995) and assuming binary transmission the size of the feedback block is:

$$C_f = N_a \log_2 N + C_{OH} + R_x$$
$$N = TotalAvailableChannels$$
$$N_a = ActiveChannels$$
$$C_f = ChipsOnFeedback$$
$$C_{OH} = FeedbackOverhead$$
$$R = ChipRate$$
$$\tau = propogationTime + LOADelay$$

LOH is feedback overhead which includes error detection symbols.

2.5 Channel and interference

Compared to the other kinds of wireless communications, high frequency (HF) communication is selectively fading because of the multipath propagation and abundance of interference from the others. Interference always exists in any wireless system. In the improved system bit error rate is highly important for the improvement of the communication systems. Every frequency channel due to interferences and fading shows different signal to noise ratio. In some of the frequency channels there are stronger SNR and these channels are more suitable for the transmission. Adaptive Frequency Hopping is a powerful solution and a technique that deals with different kind of interferences, noise sources and fading. For the simplicity of the work the focus will be only on the interference as the main disturbance in achieving a desired and suitable transmission quality and neglect all the other disturbance resources such as other noises and fading.

3. Markov chain

A Markov Chain process is a random process with the Markov property which means that given the present state the coming future states are independent from the past. Also the future states will be reached by probabilistic process and in every step the system may change its state from current state to another or remain in the same state, these changes in the states are called transitions and the probabilities are called transition probabilities.
Markov chain is formally presented as:

$$\Pr(X_{n+1} = x \mid X_n = x_n, \ldots, X_1 = x_1) = \Pr(X_{n+1} = x \mid X_n = x_n) \tag{7}$$

A discrete time Markov Chains is a stochastic dynamical system in which the probability of arriving in a particular state at a particular time moment depends only on the state at the previous moment. That is:

1. States are discrete: i = 0, 1, 2,...
2. Time is discrete: t = 1, 2,...
3. Probabilities Pij of transition from state i to state j in one time step are constant, i.e., they do not depend on time and do not depend on how the system got in state i "Markov property".

3.1 Gilbert-Elliot channel model

Bit error Models generate a sequence of noise bits (where 0's represent good bits and 1's represent bit errors) which to produce output bits modulo 2 to the input bits must be added. Models are grouped into two classes (Lemmon, 2002):

1. Memoryless Models
2. Models with Memories

In Memoryless Models the noise bits are produced by a sequence of independent trials that each trial has the same probability $P(0)$ of producing a correct bit and probability $P(1) = 1 - P(0)$ of producing a bit error.

The actual measurement from the communication channels indicate that these channels are with memories, for example the probability of 100's bit is errorous is dependent on the 99's bit. For modelling of these kinds of probabilistic situations a commonly technique is used that is called Markov Chain, This technique helps to make the bit error probability depend on the states. The use of Markov Chain technique in bit error models was introduced by Gilbert-Elliot for the first time. Gilbert model based on Markov Chain has two states G (Good) and B (Bad or for Burst). In state G, transmission is error-free and in sate B the link has probability **h** of transmitting a bit correctly. Figure 4 shows a transition diagram and bit error probabilities for Markov Chain. The situation of small **p** is where transition jumps from **B to G** and the capital **P** is where the probability of jumping from **G to B**. Also the states B and G tend to persist and the model simulates bursts of errors.

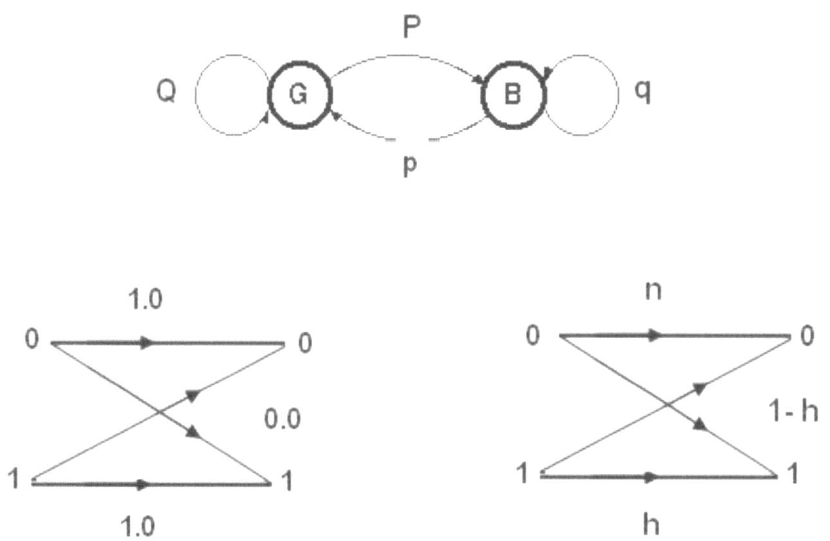

Fig. 4. Transition diagram and bit error probabilities model

The model has shown above is the transition diagram and bit error probability for Gilbert-Elliot Model and simply has three independent parameters (**p, P** and **h**) and also describes the error performance of wireless links.
The parameters p, P and h are not directly observable and must therefore be determined from statistic measurements of the error process and also important to note that Runs of G alternates with runs of B. The run length has geometric distributions, with mean 1/P for the G-runs and 1/p for the B-runs.

3.2 Geometric distribution

A Bernoulli process is a discrete time stochastic process consisting of sequence of independent random variables which take the values over two symbols, the general example for Bernoulli is coin tossing that's why it's said a Bernoulli process is coin flipping several times and also a variable in such a sequence called Bernoulli variable. Bernoulli distribution has two possible outcomes labeled by **n = 0** and **n = 1**, in which **n = 1** is 'Success' with probability p and **n = 0** is 'Failure' occurs with probability **q = 1 - p**, where **1 < p < 1**. The performance of a fixed number of trials with fixed probability of success on each trial is known as a Bernoulli trial. The distribution of heads and tails in coin tossing is an example of Bernoulli distribution with **p = q = 1/2.**
Geometric distribution is number of Failures before the first success on sequence of independent Bernoulli trials. The geometric distribution is a district distribution for
n = 0, 1, 2 ... having probability density function:

$$\Pr(X = x) = (1 - p)^{x-1} p \tag{8}$$

Also the mean value of x will be calculated as:

$$E[x] = \sum_{x=1}^{\infty} x \Pr(X = x) \tag{9}$$

Which is equal to **1/p**, also the Runs length of Good and Bad states can be expressed by geometric distribution in which for the Good runs, mean value of **1/P** and for the Bad runs, the mean value of **1/p** is used. Also the time fraction in both of Good and Bad states based on persistence in each state can be calculated for example the fraction of time spent in B state is:

$$P(B) = \frac{P}{P + p} \tag{10}$$

The sequence of states cannot be reconstructed from the sequence of bits in the error process, because both of 0's and 1's (The Good bits and bit errors) are produced in the B state and since bit errors happen only in state B with probability of **1-h** then the probability of error is:

$$P(1) = P(1, B) = P(B)P(1 \mid B) = (1 - h)\frac{P}{P + p} \tag{11}$$

However the bits of the error process (Runs of 0's and 1's) and the distribution of run lengths of 0's (error Gaps) and 1's (error Bursts) are observable to determine model parameters.

3.3 Parameter estimation

The determination of the three parameters p, P, and h from measurements of the error process requires that parameters be expressed as functions of three other parameters that are directly observable and for Markov Chain parameter estimation the functions which have been proved formerly (Lemmon, 2002), that those are:

$$\mu_{EB} = \frac{1}{1-q(1-h)} \tag{12}$$

$$\mu_{EG} = \frac{h(1-Q)+(1-q)}{(1-h)(1-Q)[1-q(1-h)]} \tag{13}$$

$$\sigma_{EB}^2 = \frac{\sqrt{q(1-h)}}{1-q(1-h)} \tag{14}$$

$$\sigma_{EG}^2 = \frac{(1-h)(qJ+p-Q)J(J+1)}{[1-q(1-h)](J-L)(1-J)^3} + [J \leftrightarrow L] - \mu_{EG}^2 \tag{15}$$

In the equations μ_{EB} is the mean error bust length and μ_{EG} is the mean error gap length, σ_{EB}^2 is the variance of the error burst distribution and σ_{EG}^2 is the variance of error gap distribution. J and L are defined as:

$$2J = Q + hq + \sqrt{(Q+hq)^2 + 4h(p-Q)} \tag{16}$$

$$2L = Q + hq - \sqrt{(Q+hq)^2 + 4h(p-Q)} \tag{17}$$

4. Matlab modelling

4.1 Gilbert-Elliot modelling

Gilbert-Elliot channel model is used for modelling a telecommunication channel. For obtaining the parameters of this model, first a sequence of data bit is given to the transmitter and then from the receiver side the transmitted data is received as output data. With the input sequence and output sequence, bit error sequence can be calculated easily. By having this bit error sequence and the method of parameter estimation in Lemmon (2002) the model parameters can be calculated.

For this reason channel simulation is done with Simulink. To obtain the bit sequence of input and output, two variables with names "in" and "out" are used. With XORing the input and output bit sequences the bit error sequence is calculated. By setting bit error sequence at argument of function marcov, Markov parameters can be achieved from the output of function marcov. In function marcov by using the function coef, the sequence of error burst and error gap can be calculated. After calculation of statistical parameters of these two sequences, Markov parameters can be then calculated by function fsolve which solves nonlinear equations.

4.2 Defining Markov chain parameters

To obtain Markov parameters in Matlab, a function of marcov is created as follow.

```
error_seq= xor(in,out);
z=marcov(error_seq);
z=fsolve(@solv,[.1 .1 .1],[],meb,meg,veg);
```

In this function the error sequence is first inputted to the function of coef then the output of sequence is obtained as 0's and 1's.

For example assume there is a sequence of:

error_seq = [0 1 0 0 0 1 1 1 0 1 1 0 1 0 1 1 1 1 0 0 0]

Then at the output of function coef will obtain:

error_burst_seq = [1 3 2 1 4]

error_gap_seq = [1 3 1 1 1 3]

Now from the output error_burst_seq and error_gap_seq which is the sequence of error runs it can be seen that the length of the run of the errors has come in order of their happenings. Next step is to calculate the mean value and the variance of the sequence.

4.3 Channel performance evaluation

100 communication channels are evaluated and channel performances are categorized based on Gilbert-Elliot channel model. Gilbert-Elliot model is used for modelling a real communication channel and evaluating the performance of the channels, in which first a bit sequence is sent through a channel and then its bit error sequence is computed. Using bit error sequence helps to find out the parameters of the model. Markov parameters can be used to find following two functions: Fraction of time spent in state B (Bad) from equation (10) and probability of the error from equation (11).

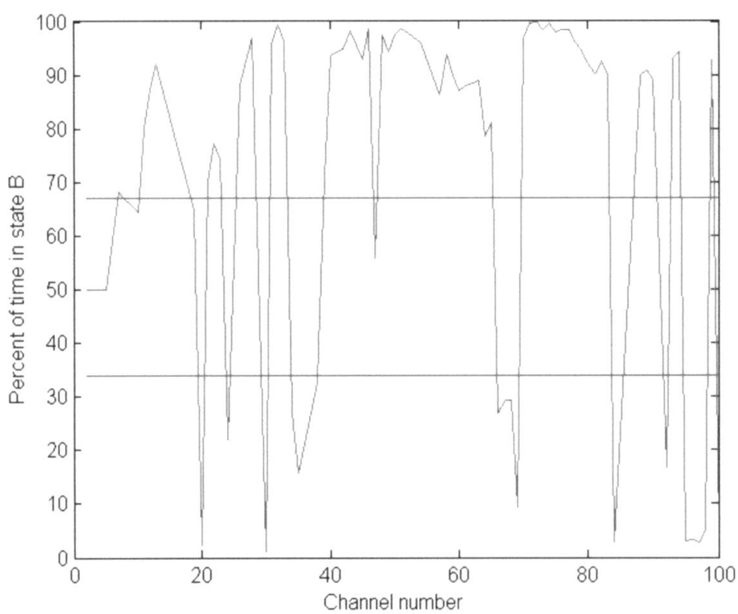

Fig. 5. Percent of time that each channel spends in state B

To evaluate the channel performance based on Gilbert-Elliot Markov chain model the information about bit error sequence is collected to simulate the channel model with Matlab. Additive white Gaussian noise (AWGN) channels with 100 random input powers are used in simulation.

First the percent of time is computed which each channel spends in state B or in the other word the probability of being in state B that multiplied by 100. Figure 5 shows the result of each channel being in Bad state.

The achieved result from Figure 2 helps to categorize the Channels based on three different groups as "Bad Channels", "Good Channels" and "Very Good Channels" by identifying two threshold values and categorizing those decides to transmit data over "Very Good" and "Good" channels then by such transmission the performance of the communication system can be improved. Then the error probability in Bad state for each channel is computed. Figure 6 shows these probabilities for 100 different channels.

4.4 Testing

Gilbert-Elliot channel model is used to simulate the error process and correctly reproduce all of its statistical properties. To validate the model, the error process generated by the model must be compared to the measured error process. For testing, the program bit error sequence is generated using Markov chain model. Two programs are made as follow: marcov_gen is a bit error sequence generator for Markov parameters and marcov_test tests the bit error sequence and the output is displayed in workspace.

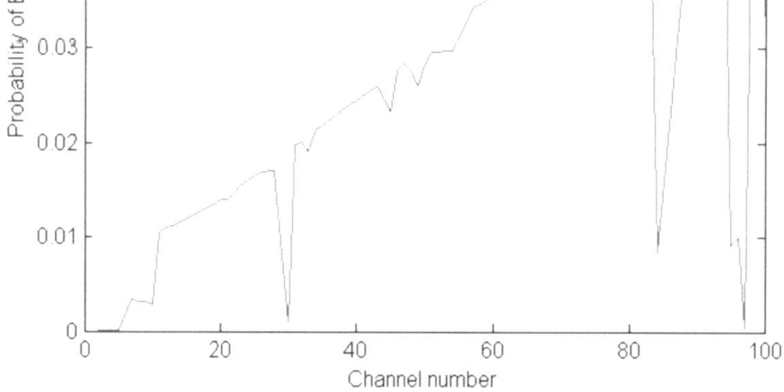

Fig. 6. Error probability being in Bad state for each channel

The objective of the parameter estimation is to choose values of the model parameters that generate error burst and error gap distributions that reassembles the corresponding measured distributions as close as possible. Therefore for testing the mean and variance of error burst and error gap of regenerated error sequence are calculated and compared by statistical parameters of channel bit error sequence, where the result is shown in Table 1.

	error burst mean	error gap mean	error gap variance	
SNR = 3dB Input power = 1	1.0568	18.1134	319.4516	A
	1.0492	18.4713	319.3184	B
SNR = 3dB Input power = 2	1.1456	7.7868	48.9981	A
	1.1500	8.0421	55.0026	B
SNR = 3dB Input power = 3	1.2201	5.6570	25.5754	A
	1.2271	5.5166	24.5044	B

A: Statistical parameters channel error sequence.
B: Statistical parameters of regenerated error sequence.

Table 1. Statistical parameters of channel error and regenerated error sequence

For testing, first Markov model parameters of a channel error sequence are computed, then a sequence of the model is generated and statistical parameters are computed. The statistical parameters must be as equal as channel error sequence. It is important to mention that first state of the Markov model in function marcov_gen chooses the probability 0.5, so sometimes two different answers can be seen and that the nearest one to the error sequence statistic is the correct one.

5. Evaluation of frequency hopping

To design the frequency hopping (FH) model, MATLAB Simulink has been used. The spreader at transmitter section is an M-FSK modulation but the input of the modulator is hopping index. This section consists of a PN Sequence Generator, an Assemble Packets block and a Goto block as shown in Figure 7.

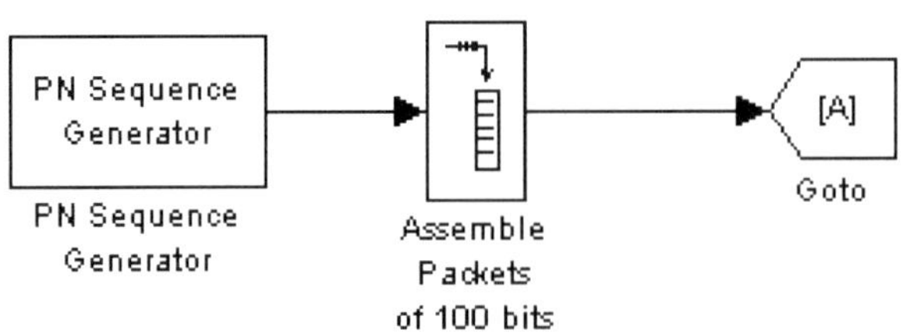

Fig. 7. Model of frequency hopping in Simulink

The design of frequency hopping spreader is shown in Figure 8. The spreader part consists of M-FSK modulator base (with M equal to 64), a From block (Hop index that is created in previous step), a To Frame block and a Multiplication block. The block parameter of FSK modulator is 64 in M-FSK number and it means that there are 64 hopping sections. These sub-bands are selected by the hop indexes.

The design of frequency hopping despreader, is the same as spreader section but the output of M-FSK modulator block is complex conjugated as shown Figure 9.

This frequency hopping model is used for evaluation of three different modulations: QAM, QPSK, GFSK, and compares the performance with the situation without frequency hopping. Performance evaluation is based on BER values under two situations (with and without FH) versus normalized signal-to-noise ratio (SNR) measured by E_b/N_0 values of the channel, as shown in Figure 10, 11, 12.

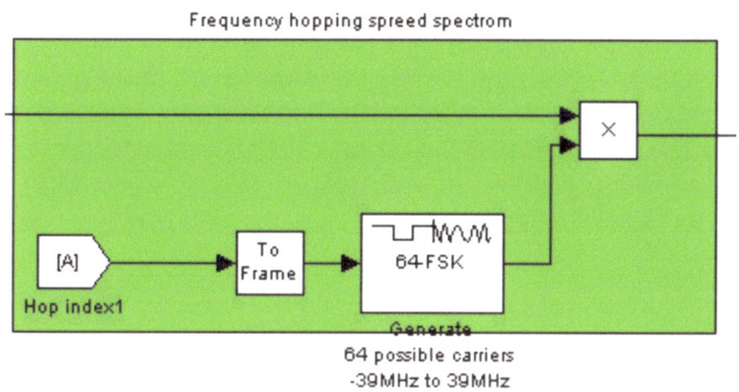

Fig. 8. Design of frequency hopping spreader

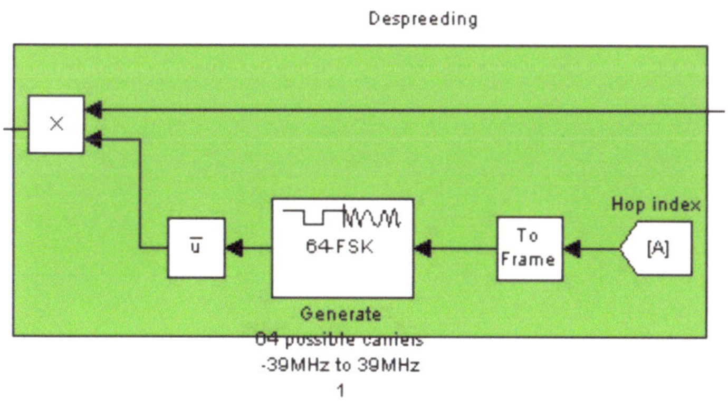

Fig. 9. Design of frequency hopping despreader

From Figure 10 it can be seen that applying FH with QAM modulation does not lead to a sensible improvement in performance or significant reduction of BER. From Figure 11 it can be seen that applying FH with QPSK modulation gives a good result and reduces significantly BER compared to without FH at same level of SNR. From Figure 12 it can be seen that applying FH with GFSK modulation reduces dramatically BER compared to without FH at same level of SNR and lead to a much higher performance.

In overall, based on the evaluation results it can be concluded that applying the designed FH schemes with certain modulations can improve their communication performances, especially at weak SNR levels as most cases of short range wireless communications have.

6. Conclusion

As a result of the work it can be concluded that adaptive frequency hopping is a powerful technique to deal with interference and Gilbert-Elliot channel model is a good technique to analyze the situations of channels by categorizing the channel conditions based on their performance as Good or Bad, and then apply adaptive frequency hopping which hops frequencies adaptively by analyzing the state of the channel in case of environmental problems such as interferences and noises to improve the communication performance.

Frequency hopping spread spectrum is modelled with MATLAB and three different modulations i.e. QAM, QPSK and GFSK are studied to investigate which of these modulations are good to apply with FHSS model. The simulation results show that applying FHSS with QAM modulation dose not lead to a remarkable reduction of BER, but with QPSK modulation gives a good result and reduces BER at lower SNR, while in GFSK modulation shows a significant reduction of BER and lead to a high performance.

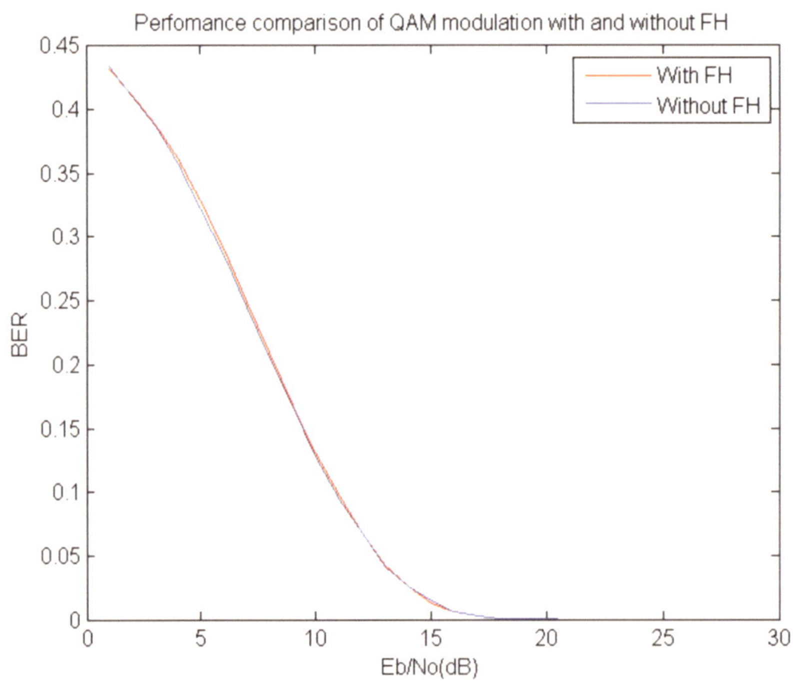

Fig. 10. QAM modulation

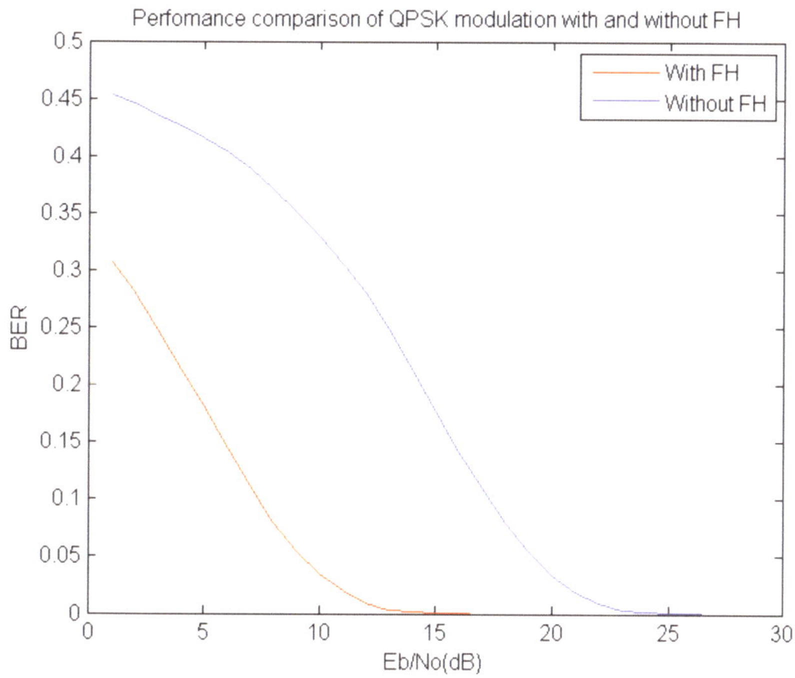

Fig. 11. QPSK modulation

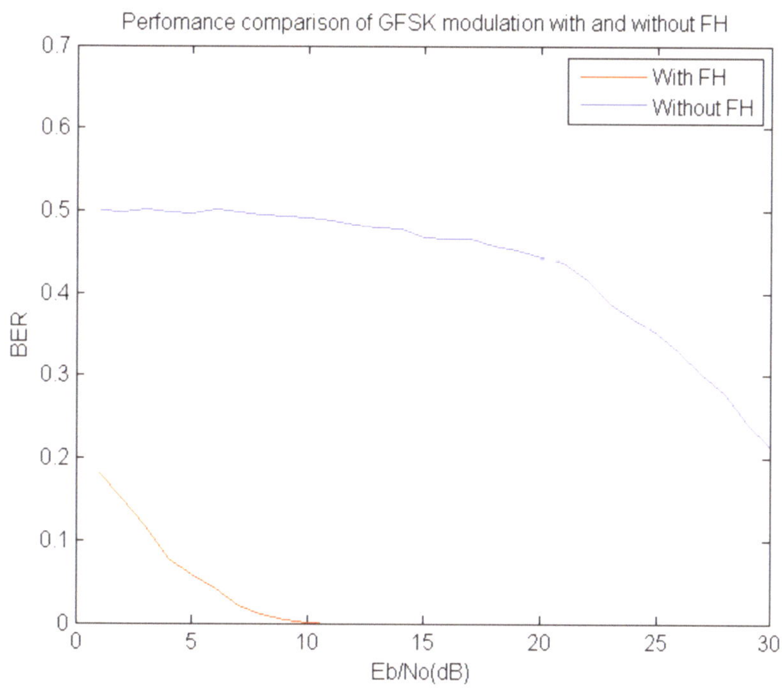

Fig. 12. GFSK modulation

7. References

Bates, R. J. & Gregory, D. W. (2001). *Voice & Data Communications Handbook*, McGraw-Hill Osborne Media

Elliott, E. O. (1963). Estimates of error rates for codes on burst-noise channels, *Bell System Technical Journal*, Vol. 42, pp. 1977-1997

Gilbert, E. N. (1960). Capacity of burst-noise channels, *Bell System Technical Journal*, Vol. 39, pp. 1253-1265

Lemmon, J. J. (2002). Wireless link statistical bit error model, *Institute for Telecommunication Sciences*

Liu, Y. (2008). Enhancement of short range wireless communication performance using adaptive frequency hopping, *Proceeding of 4th IEEE International Conference on Wireless Communications, Networking and Mobile Computing*, Dalian, China, Oct. 2008

Zander, J. & Malmgren, G. (1995). Adaptive frequency hopping in HF communications, *IEE Proceedings Communications*, Vol. 142, pp. 99-105

Ziemer, R.; Peterson, E. R. L. & Borth, D. E, (1995). *Introduction to Spread Spectrum Communications*, Prentice Hall

Part 4

Multi-Input Multi-Output Models

11

Wireless Communication: Trend and Technical Issues for MIMO-OFDM System

Yoon Hyun Kim[1], Bong Youl Cho[2] and Jin Young Kim[3]
[1,3]Kwangwoon University,
[2]Nokia-Siemens Networks,
Seoul
Korea

1. Introduction

High-performance 4th generation (4G) broadband wireless communication system can be enabled by the use of multiple antennas not only at transmitter but also at receiver ends. A multiple input multiple output (MIMO) system provides multiple independent transmission channels, thus, under certain conditions, leading to a channel capacity that increases linearly with the number of antennas. Orthogonal frequency division multiplexing (OFDM) is known as an effective technique for high data rate wireless mobile communication. By combining these two promising techniques, the MIMO and OFDM techniques, we can significantly increase data rate, which is justified by improving bit error rate (BER) performance. In this section, we briefly describe the concept of MIMO system. Through comparison with CDMA system, its key benefits are discussed.

1.1 Concept of MIMO system

The idea of using multiple receive and multiple transmit antennas has emerged as one of the most significant technical breakthroughs in modern wireless communications. Theoretical studies and initial prototyping of these MIMO systems have shown order of magnitude spectral efficiency improvements in communications. As a result, MIMO is considered a key technology for improving the throughput of future wireless broadband data systems

MIMO is the use of multiple antennas at both the transmitter and receiver to improve communication performance. It is one of several forms of smart antenna technology. MIMO technology has attracted attention in wireless communications, because it offers significant increases in data throughput and link range without requiring additional bandwidth or transmit power. This is achieved by higher spectral efficiency and link reliability or diversity (reduced fading). Because of these properties, MIMO is an important part of modern wireless communication standards such as IEEE 802.11n (Wifi), IEEE 802.16e (WiMAX), 3GPP Long Term Evolution (LTE), 3GPP HSPA+, and 4G systems to come.

Radio communication using MIMO systems enables increased spectral efficiency for a given total transmit power by introducing additional spatial channels which can be made available by using space-time coding. In this section, we survey the environmental factors that affect MIMO performance. These factors include channel complexity, external interference, and channel estimation error. The 'multichannel' term indicates that the receiver incorporates multiple antennas by using space-time-frequency adaptive processing. Single-input single-output (SISO) is the well-known wireless configuration, single-input multiple-output (SIMO) uses a single transmit antenna and multiple receive antennas, multiple-input single-output (MISO) has multiple transmit antennas and one receive antenna. And multiuser-MIMO (MU-MIMO) refers to a configuration that comprises a base station with multiple transmit/receive antennas interacting with multiple users, each with one or more antennas.

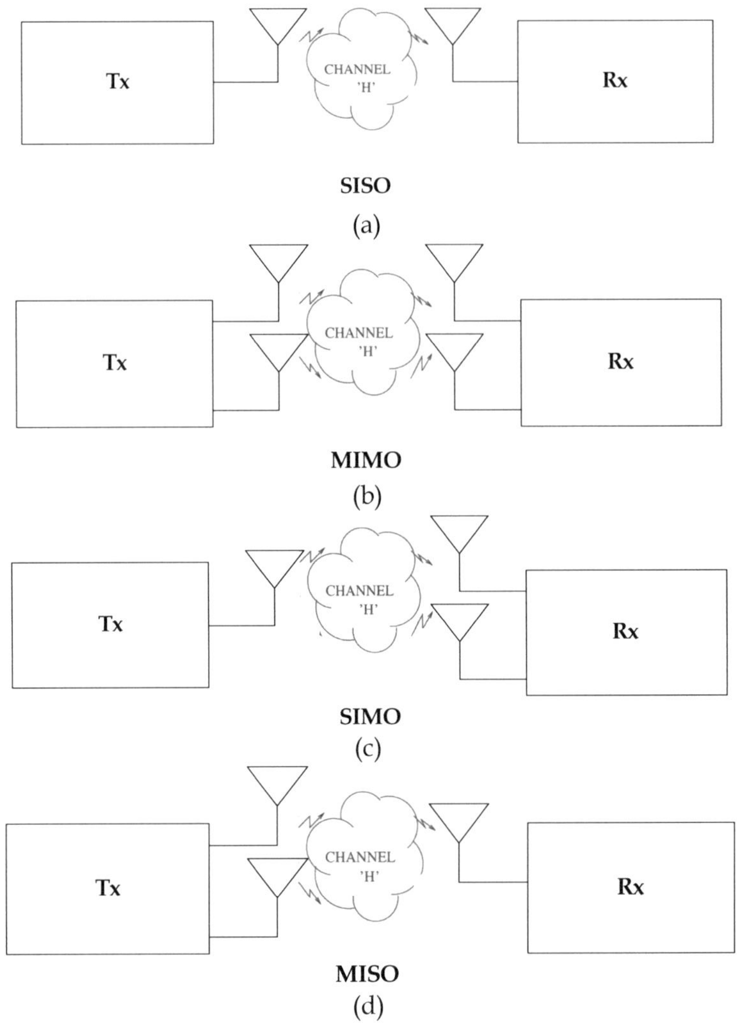

Fig. 1.1. Different antenna system
(a) SISO mode (b) MIMO mode (c) SIMO mode (d) MISO mode

1.2 Key benefits

1.2.1 Array gain

Array gain can be made available through processing at the transmitter and/or the receiver, and results in an increase in average received signal-to-noise ratio (SNR) due to a coherent combining effect. Transmit-receive array gain requires channel knowledge at the transmitter and receiver, respectively, and depends on the number of transmit and receive antennas. Channel knowledge at the receiver is typically available whereas channel state information at the transmitter is in general more difficult to obtain.

Array gain means a power gain of signals that is achieved by using multiple-antennas at transmitter and/or receiver. It is the average increase in the SNR at the receiver that arises from the coherent combining effect of multiple antennas at the receiver or transmitter or both. If the channel is known to the transmitter with multiple antennas, the transmitter can apply appropriate weight to the transmission, so that there is coherent combining at the receiver. The array gain in this case is called transmitter array gain. Alternately, if we have only one antenna at the transmitter and no knowledge of the channel, then the receiver can suitably weight the incoming signals so that they coherently add up at the output, thereby enhancing the signal. This is called receiver array gain which can be exploited in SIMO case. Essentially, multiple antenna systems require some level of channel knowledge either at the transmitter or receiver or both to achieve this array gain.

1.2.2 Diversity gain

In a wireless channel, signals can experience fadings. When the signal power drops significantly, the channel is said to be in a fade and this gives rise to high BER. Diversity is a powerful technique to mitigate fading in wireless links, so diversity is often used to combat fading. Diversity techniques rely on transmitting the signal over multiple (ideally) independently fading paths over time, frequency, space, or others. Spatial (or antenna) diversity is preferred over time/frequency diversity as it does not incur expenditure in transmission time or bandwidth.

A diversity scheme refers to a method for improving the reliability of a message signal by using two or more communication channels with different characteristics. Diversity plays an important role in combating fading and co-channel interference and avoiding error bursts. It is based on the fact that individual channels experience different levels of fading and interference. Multiple versions of the same signal may be transmitted and/or received and combined in the receiver. Alternatively, a redundant forward error correction code may be added and different parts of the message transmitted over different channels. Diversity techniques may exploit the multipath propagation, resulting in a diversity gain, often measured in decibels.

The following classes of diversity schemes can be identified

- Time diversity: Multiple versions of the same signal are transmitted at different time instants. Alternatively, a redundant forward error correction code is added and the message is spread in time by means of bit-interleaving before it is transmitted. Thus, error bursts are avoided, which simplifies the error correction.
- Frequency diversity: This type of diversity provides replicas of the original signal in the frequency domain. The signals are transmitted using several frequency channels or the signals are spread over a wide spectrum that is affected by frequency-selective fading. The former method can be found in coded-OFDM systems such as IEEE 802.11agn, WiMAX, and LTE, and the latter method can be found in CDMA systems such as 3GPP WCDMA.
- Multiuser diversity: Multiuser diversity is obtained by opportunistic user scheduling at either the transmitter or the receiver. Opportunistic user scheduling is as follows: the

transmitter selects the best user among candidate receivers according to the qualities of each channel between the transmitter and each receiver. In FDD systems, a receiver typically feedback the channel quality information to the transmitter with the limited level of resolution.

- Space diversity (antenna diversity): The signal is transmitted over several different propagation paths. In the case of wired transmission, this can be achieved by transmitting via multiple wires. In the case of wireless transmission, it can be achieved by antenna diversity using multiple transmit antennas (transmit diversity) and/or multiple receive antennas (receive diversity). In the latter case, a diversity combining technique is applied before further signal processing takes place. If the antennas are far apart, for example at different cellular base station sites or WLAN access points, this is called macrodiversity or site diversity. If the antennas are at a distance in the order of one wavelength, this is called microdiversity. A special case is phased antenna arrays, which also can be used for beamforming, MIMO channels and Space-time coding (STC). Space diversity can be further classified as follows.

- Receive diversity: Maximum ratio combining is a frequently applied diversity scheme in receivers to improve signal quality
- Transmit diversity: In this case we introduce controlled redundancies at the transmitter, which can be then exploited by appropriate signal processing techniques at the receiver. There are open loop transmit diversity where transmitter does not require channel information and closed loop transmit diversity where transmitter requires channel information to make this possible. Closed loop transmit diversity is sometimes regarded as a Beamforming. Space-time codes for MIMO exploit both transmit as well as receive diversity schemes, yielding a high quality of reception.
- Polarization diversity: Multiple versions of a signal are transmitted and/or received via antennas with different polarization. A diversity combining technique is applied on the receiver side.
- Cooperative diversity: Achieves antenna diversity gain by using the cooperation of distributed antennas belonging to each node.

1.2.3 Multiplexing gain

Spatial multiplexing gain is achieved when a system is transmitting different streams of data from the same radio resource in separate spatial dimensions. Data is hence sent and received over multiple channels - linked to different pilot signals, over multiple antennas. This results in capacity gain at no additional power or bandwidth.

Spatial multiplexing is transmission techniques in MIMO wireless communication to transmit multiple data signals from each of the multiple transmit antennas. Therefore, the space dimension is reused, or multiplexed, more than one time.

If the transmitter is equipped with N_T antennas and the receiver has N_R antennas, the maximum spatial multiplexing order is

$$N_s = \min(N_T, N_R). \tag{1-1}$$

If a linear receiver is used, this means that N_s streams can be transmitted in parallel, ideally leading to an N_s increase of the spectral efficiency. The practical multiplexing gain can be limited by spatial correlation and the rank property of the channel, which means that some of the parallel streams may have very weak or no channel gains.

1.2.4 Interference reduction

Fig. 1.2 presents a K-user MIMO interference channel with K transmitter and receiver pairs. The k-th transmitter and its corresponding receiver are equipped with M_k and N_k antennas respectively. The k-th transmitter generates interference at all $l \neq k$ receivers. Assuming the communication channel to be frequency-flat, the $C^{N_k \times 1}$ received signal y_k at the k-th receiver, can be represented as

$$y_k = H_{kk}x_k + \sum_{\substack{l=1 \\ l \neq k}}^{K} H_{kl}x_l + n_k, \tag{1-2}$$

where $H_{kl} \in C^{N_k \times M_l}$ represents the channel matrix between the l-th transmitter and k-th receiver, x_k is the $C^{M_k \times 1}$ transmit signal vector of the k-th transmitter and the $C^{N_k \times 1}$ vector n_k represents AWGN with zero mean and covariance matrix $R_{n_k n_k}$. Each entry of the channel matrix is a complex random variable drawn form a continuous distribution. It is assumed that each transmitter has complete knowledge of all channel matrices corresponding to its direct link and all the other cross-links in addition to the transmitter power constraints and the receiver noise covariances.

We denote by G_k, the $C^{M_k \times d_k}$ precoding matrix of the k-th transmitter. Thus $x_k = G_k s_k$, where s_k is a $d_k \times 1$ vector representing the d_k independent symbol streams for the k-th user pair. We assume s_k to have a spatiotemporally white Gaussian distribution with zero

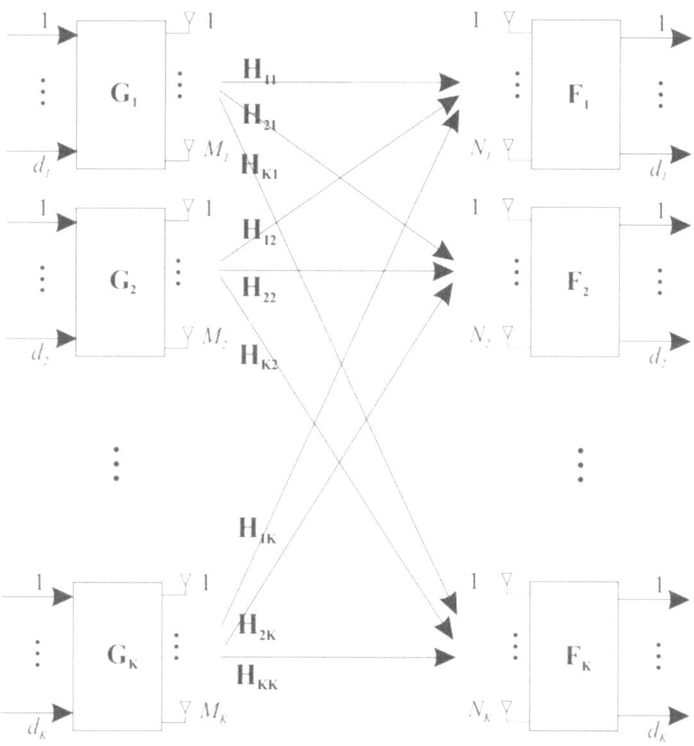

Fig. 1.2. MIMO Interference Channel

mean and unit variance, $s_k \sim N(0, I_{dk})$. The k-th receiver applies $F_k \in C^{d_k \times N_k}$ to suppress interference and retrieve its d_k desired streams. The output of such a receive filter is then given by

$$r_k = F_k H_{kk} G_k s_k + \sum_{\substack{l=1 \\ l \neq k}}^{K} F_k H_{kl} G_l s_l + F_k n_k \tag{1-3}$$

Note that F_k does not represent the whole receiver but only the reduction from a N_k-dimensional received signal y_k to a d_k-dimensional r_k, to which further receive processing is applied.

Co-channel interference arises due to frequency reuse in MIMO wireless channels. When multiple antennas are used, the differentiation between the spatial signatures of the desired signal and co-channel signals can be exploited to reduce interference. Interference reduction requires knowledge of the desired signal's channel. Exact knowledge of the interferer's channel may not be necessary. Interference reduction can also be implemented at the transmitter, where the goal is to minimize the interference energy sent toward the co-channel users while delivering the signal to the desired user. Interference reduction allows aggressive frequency reuse and thereby increases multicell capacity. We note that in general it is not possible to exploit all the leverages of MIMO technology simultaneously due to conflicting demands on the spatial degrees of or number of antennas. The degree to which these conflicts are resolved depends upon the signalling scheme and transceiver design.

2. MIMO system

In this section, the MIMO channel model is discussed first, which are deterministic, and frequency flat or selective fading channels. This study will be carried out mathematical derivation of the capacity in each MIMO channel. We begin with basic system capacities which compare SISO, SIMO and MIMO, and then we explore to general case that the system has M_T transmit antennas and N_R receive antennas. Finally, fundamental capacity limits for transmission over MIMO channels is discussed

Many kinds of signal encoding schemes that support multiple antenna systems have well been studied [2]. Among them, the primary ones include Bell Labs Layered Space Time (BLAST), space-time trellis codes (STTC), space-time block codes (STBC) and cyclic delay diversity (CDD) and so on. So, the latter part in this chapter, we introduce STBC and STTC signal models for transmitter / receiver structure in MIMO system.

2.1 MIMO channel model

We consider MIMO channels with N_T transmit and N_R receive antennas. The block diagram of such a MIMO channel model is shown in Figure 2.1.

The channel matrix $\mathbf{H}$ is a $N_R \times N_T$ complex matrix with

$$\mathbf{H} = \begin{bmatrix} h_{1,1} & h_{1,2} & \cdots & h_{1,N_T} \\ h_{2,1} & h_{2,2} & \cdots & h_{2,N_T} \\ \vdots & \vdots & \ddots & \vdots \\ h_{N_R,1} & h_{N_R,2} & \cdots & h_{N_R,N_T} \end{bmatrix}. \tag{2-1}$$

The component of the matrix **H**, $h_{i,j}$ is the coefficient of the each channel from the *j*th transmit antenna to the *i*th receive antenna. We suppose that the power of the received signal for each receive antennas is equal to the sum of transmit power E_s. Consequently, we acquire the normalization value of the channel matrix **H**, for a deterministic channel condition as follow,

$$\sum_{j=1}^{N_T} \left|h_{i,j}\right|^2 = N_T, \quad i = 1,\ 2,\ \ldots,\ N_R. \tag{2-2}$$

If the channel coefficients are random, the normalization value will apply to the expected value. The received signal at *i*th receive antenna is given by

$$y(t) = \sum_{j=1}^{N_T} h_{i,j}(t) \cdot s_j(t) + n_i(t), \qquad i = 1,2,\ldots N_R, \tag{2-3}$$

where, $s_j(t)$ is the transmit signal at *j*th transmit antenna and $n_i(t)$ is additive white Gaussian noise (AWGN) in the receiver with zero mean and σ^2 variance. In above equation, a transmit signal $s_j(t)$ from each transmit antenna is added to the signal of each receive antenna.

2.1.1 Deterministic channel

To introduce the characteristics of the random channel matrix **H**, first we need to study the deterministic channel model. Coefficient of the deterministic channel model **H** is fixed on H. In other words, the deterministic channel coefficient H is known at the transmitter and receiver.

2.1.2 Flat fading channel

Suppose that the delay spread ($\tau_{\max}$) in the MIMO channel is much smaller than the signal bandwidth (*BW*), i.e., $\tau_{\max} << 1/BW$, the channel is said to be frequency flat fading channel. Frequency flat fading channel has the properties that are known to be exact in non line-of-sight (NLOS) environment with rich scattering and sufficient antenna spacing between transmitter and receiver antennas.

2.1.3 Frequency selective fading channel

Similarly, if the signal bandwidth and MIMO channel delay spread product satisfies $\tau_{\max} >> 0.1/BW$, the MIMO channel is said to be frequency selective. The transfer function of the frequency selective MIMO channel is as follow,

$$\mathbf{H}(f) = \int_0^\infty \mathbf{H}(\tau)\exp(-j2\pi f\tau)d\tau\,. \tag{2-4}$$

2.2 Capacity of each MIMO channel

In this subsection, the capacity of the MIMO channels is introduced. The capacity is defined as the maximum possible transmission rate when the probability of error is almost zero. The capacity of MIMO channel is defined,

$$C = \max_{f(\mathbf{s})} I(\mathbf{s};\mathbf{y})\,, \tag{2-5}$$

where, *f(s)* is the probability distribution function (PDF) of the transmit signal vector **s** and *I*(**s**;**y**) is the mutual information between transmit signal vectors **s** and receive signal vector **y**. The mutual information is given by

$$I(\mathbf{s};\mathbf{y}) = H(\mathbf{y}) - H(\mathbf{y}\,|\,\mathbf{s}), \tag{2-6}$$

where, $H(\mathbf{y})$ is the entropy of the receive signal vector **y**, and $H(\mathbf{y}\,|\,\mathbf{s})$ is the conditional entropy of the receive signal vector **y**. The conditional entropy $H(\mathbf{y}\,|\,\mathbf{s})$ is identical to $H(\mathbf{n})$ because the transmit signal vector **s** and noise vector **n** are independent. So, equation (2-6) is written as

$$I(\mathbf{s};\mathbf{y}) = H(\mathbf{y}) - H(\mathbf{n}). \tag{2-7}$$

For maximize the mutual information, *I(s;y)*, reduces to maximizing $H(\mathbf{y})$. Consequently, mutual information *I*(**s**;**y**) in equation (2-7) is given by,

$$I(\mathbf{s};\mathbf{y}) = \log_2 \det(\mathbf{I}_{N_R} + \frac{E_S}{N_T N_0}\mathbf{H}\mathbf{R}_{SS}\mathbf{H}^H) bps/Hz, \tag{2-8}$$

where, $\mathbf{I}_{N_R}$ is an $N_R \times N_R$ identity matrix, E_S is the power across the transmitter irrespective of the number of antennas N_T, $\mathbf{R}_{SS}$ is the covariance matrix for transmit signal and the superscript ^{H} stands for conjugate transposition. From equation (2-8), the general capacity of the MIMO channel is

$$C = \max_{\mathbf{R}_{SS},\, tr(\mathbf{R}_{SS}) = N_T} \log_2 \det(\mathbf{I}_{N_R} + \frac{E_S}{N_T N_0}\mathbf{H}\mathbf{R}_{SS}\mathbf{H}^H) bps/Hz. \tag{2-9}$$

2.2.1 Capacity of a deterministic MIMO channel

As we mentioned previous, the deterministic channel coefficient H is known at the transmitter and receiver. However, to acquire channel coefficient at the transmitter is very difficult in practical MIMO systems. In the case that the MIMO system do not knows the channel coefficient at the transmitter, generally called an open-loop system, it is a good assumption that the transmitted signals from each transmit antenna has equal power. This condition results in the covariance matrix is identical to the identity matrix, $\mathbf{R}_{SS} = I_{N_T}$. So, from equation (2-8), equal powered mutual information is given by,

$$I(\mathbf{s};\mathbf{y})_{eq} = \log_2 \det(\mathbf{I}_{N_R} + \frac{E_S}{N_T N_0}\mathbf{H}\mathbf{H}^H) bps/Hz, \tag{2-10}$$

where the subscript "eq" stands for "equal power".
Mutual information in equation (2-10) can be calculated by positive eigenvalues of the channel matrix $\mathbf{H}\mathbf{H}^H$. If r is the rank of the matrix **H** and $\lambda_i, i = 1,2,\ldots r$ are the non-zero eigenvalues of the matrix $\mathbf{H}\mathbf{H}^H$, the mutual information in equation (2-10) is re-written as

$$I(\mathbf{s};\mathbf{y})_{eq} = \sum_{i=1}^{r} \log_2(1 + \frac{E_S}{N_T N_0}\lambda_i)\ bps/Hz. \tag{2-11}$$

2.2.2 Capacity of frequency selective fading MIMO channel

In this subsection, we discuss the capacity of MIMO channel in frequency selective fading condition. The capacity of frequency selective fading channel can be obtained by dividing the whole bandwidth into N sub-channel. This results in each sub-channel having BW/N bandwidth. If N is not sufficient large, each sub-channel is undergone frequency selective fading. So, we can derive the capacity of ith sub-channel of frequency selective fading channel is given by

$$I(\mathbf{s};\mathbf{y})_{i,fs} = \log_2 \det(\mathbf{I}_{N_R} + \frac{E_{S,i}}{N_T N_0}\mathbf{H}_i \mathbf{H}_i^H) bps / Hz, \quad (2\text{-}12)$$

where, subscript 'fs' stands for 'frequency selective', $E_{S,i}$ is the energy allocated to the ith sub-channel and $\mathbf{H}_i$ is the $N_R \times N_T$ sub-channel matrix.
And the ergodic capacity of the frequency selective fading MIMO channel is given by [*H. Jafarkhani*(p.38)] as follow,

$$C_{fs} = \varepsilon\left[I(\mathbf{s};\mathbf{y})_{i,fs}\right]. \quad (2\text{-}13)$$

2.3 Transmit signal structure for space time block coding

In this subsection, the basics of the Alamouti STBC with two antennas at the transmitter is briefly introduced. A block diagram of the Alamouti's space time block encoder is shown in Fig. 2.1. The information sources are modulated with an M-ary modulation scheme. Then, the encoder takes a group of two modulated symbols. The each group consist of the two modulated symbol s_1 and s_2 in each encoding operation and then it sends to the transmit antennas according to the block code matrix,

$$S = \begin{bmatrix} s_1 & -s_2^* \\ s_2 & s_1^* \end{bmatrix}. \quad (2\text{-}14)$$

In above equation (2-14), the first column stands for the first transmission symbol period and the second column stands for the second transmission symbol period. Similarly, the first row corresponds to the symbols which are transmitted from the first antenna and the second row corresponds to the symbols which are transmitted from the second antenna. In detail, the first antenna transmits s_1 and the second antenna transmits s_2 during the first symbol period at the same time. Similarly, for the second period, first antenna transmits $-s_2^*$ and simultaneously, second antenna transmits s_1^*. Note that superscript '*' stands for the complex conjugate of the symbol. By using the Alamouti's space time coding, we can transmit symbol both in space and time. This is "space time block coding".
Symbol groups of the each transmit antenna are given are

$$\begin{aligned} \mathbf{S}_1 &= [s_1, \ -s_2^*] \\ \mathbf{S}_2 &= [s_2, \ s_1^*] \end{aligned}, \quad (2\text{-}15)$$

where, $\mathbf{S}_1$ is the first symbol group from the first antenna and $\mathbf{S}_2$ is the second symbol group from the second antenna.
In equation (2-15), two group symbols are orthogonal each other. Here, orthogonal means

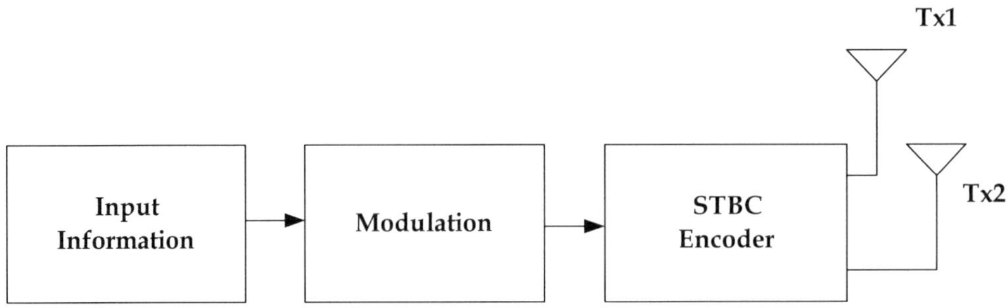

Fig. 2.1. A block diagram of the STBC system

that the inner product of $\mathbf{S}_1$ and $\mathbf{S}_2$ is zero. This orthogonal relationship is given by,

$$\mathbf{S}_1 \cdot \mathbf{S}_2 = s_1 s_2^* - s_2^* s_1 = 0 . \quad (2\text{-}16)$$

2.4 Receiver structure for space time block coding

If we suppose that the system has one antenna at receiver and two antennas at transmit antenna, the receiver structure is illustrated as Fig. 2.2.

The channel coefficient from transmit antenna 1 and 2 are defined as $h_1(t)$ and $h_2(t)$. As these channel coefficients are generally constant across two consecutive symbol periods, $h_1(t)$ and $h_2(t)$ are given by,

$$\begin{aligned} h_1(t) &= h_1(t+T) = |h_1| e^{j\theta_1} \\ h_2(t) &= h_2(t+T) = |h_2| e^{j\theta_2} , \end{aligned} \quad (2\text{-}17)$$

where $|h_i|$ and $|\theta_i|$ are the amplitude gain and phase shift for the path from each transmit antenna to the receive antenna.

At the receiver, the received signals can be expressed as,

$$\begin{aligned} r_1 &= h_1 s_1 + h_2 s_2 + n_1 \\ r_2 &= -h_1 s_2^* + h_2 s_1^* + n_2 , \end{aligned} \quad (2\text{-}18)$$

where, n_1 and n_2 are independent complex variables with zero mean and unit variance, representing additive white Gaussian noise (AWGN) samples.

If the channel coefficients h_1 and h_2 can be recovered perfectly at the receiver, the received signal can be combined as follows,

$$\begin{aligned} \tilde{s}_1 &= h_1^* r_1 + h_2 r_2^* = (\alpha_1^2 + \alpha_2^2) s_1 + h_1^* n_1 + h_2 n_2^* \\ \tilde{s}_2 &= h_2^* r_1^* - h_1 r_2^* = (\alpha_1^2 + \alpha_2^2) s_2 - h_1 n_2^* + h_2^* n_1 , \end{aligned} \quad (2\text{-}19)$$

and these estimated signals are sent to the maximum likelihood detector, which minimizes the following decision metric

$$\left| r_1 - h_1 s_1 - h_2 s_2 \right|^2 + \left| r_2 + h_1 s_2^* - h_2 s_1^* \right|^2 . \quad (2\text{-}20)$$

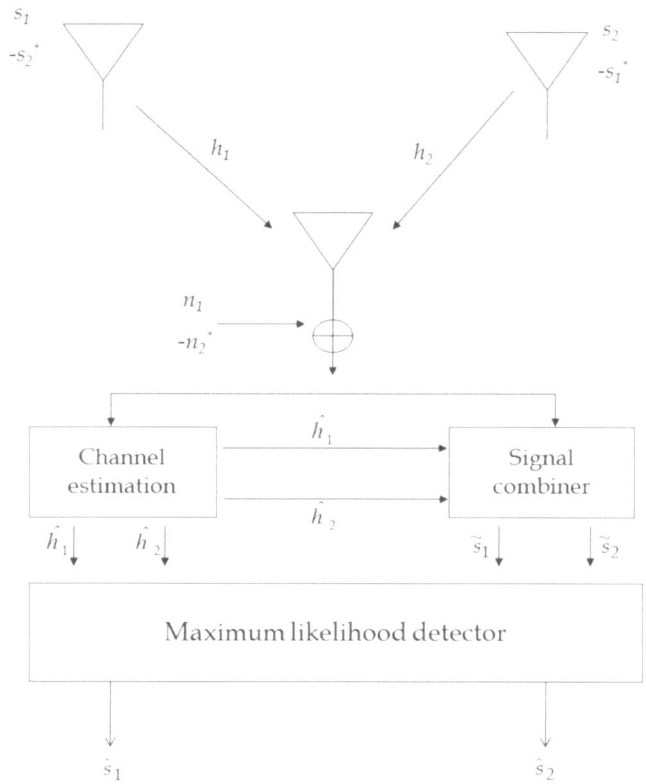

Fig. 2.2. Receiver structure for space time block coding

To expand and delete terms that are orthogonal of the code words, the equation (2-20) is reduced by [*H. Jafarkhani* (p.57)] to,

$$\left|r_1h_1^* + r_2^*h_2 - s_1\right|^2 + (\alpha_1^2 + \alpha_2^2 - 1)|s_1|^2, \tag{2-21}$$

And,

$$\left|r_1h_2^* - r_2^*h_1 - s_2\right|^2 + (\alpha_1^2 + \alpha_2^2 - 1)|s_2|^2. \tag{2-22}$$

Finally, for PSK signal, maximum likelihood detector calculate signal as follow,

$$d^2(\hat{s}_j, s_i) \le d^2(\hat{s}_j, s_k) \qquad \forall i \ne k, \tag{2-23}$$

where, $d^2(x,y) = (x-y)(x^* - y^*) = |x-y|^2$.

3. Technology challenges and issues for MIMO-OFDM system

3.1 Data throughput

3.1.1 Adaptive modulation and coding

Adaptive modulation and coding (AMC) is a technical term used in wireless communications to achieve maximum data throughput. AMC denotes the matching of

coding, modulation and other parameters to the conditions on the channel, as the path loss, the interference, the sensitivity of the receiver and available transmitter power margin.
The MIMO-OFDM system typically consists of convolutional encoder, modulation, inverse fast Fourier transform (IFFT), injection of guard interval (GI) and pre-coder. And the multi-user MIMO OFDM system with AMC is depicted in Fig. 3.1.

Fig. 3.1. Multi-user MIMO OFDM with AMC

The pre-coded signals are summed at each antenna of a base station. The pre-coding matrix is computed by using channel matrix which is estimated from the feedback from each user and base station.

As an example, the scheme here uses AMC that has 6 modulation and coding scheme (MCS) levels. The coding rate of convolutional encoder and the modulation order are changed per MCS level. MCS level is usually decided by SNR which is estimated and computed at the channel estimator of each user.

In Table 3.1, the coding rate and the modulation order are tabled according to SNR in the multi-user and the single-user system. The AMC of the scheme uses BPSK, QPSK, 16QAM modulation and 2/3, 1/2 coding rate at convolution encoder. The SNR range is defined as the SNR range that the error performance of each user is 10^{-4}.

AMC		SNR[dB] of Single-user (IEEE 802.11n)	SNR[dB] of Multi-user (IEEE 802.11n)
Modulation	Coding rate		
BPSK	1/2	0<SNR≤2.5	0<SNR≤2.5
	3/4	2.5<SNR≤4	2.5<SNR≤4
QPSK	1/2	4<SNR≤6.5	4<SNR≤7
	3/4	6.5<SNR≤19.5	7<SNR≤19.5
16QAM	1/2	19.5<SNR≤37	19.5<SNR≤38
	3/4	37<SNR	38<SNR

Table 3.1. AMC selection according to SNR

The process at the user's side is processed in reverse order of the side of the base station.

3.1.2 CP reduction algorithm

In wireless mobile communication systems, there are Doppler shift and delay spread that introduce significant problem to system performance. Doppler shift introduce the channel fading effect with frequency translation caused by movement of mobile station. Doppler shift will be positive or negative depending on whether the mobile receiver is moving toward or away from the base station. Delay spreads are resulted in multiple versions of the transmitted signals that arrive at the receiving antenna, it causes to displace with respect to one another in time and spatial orientation. The random phase and amplitudes of the different multipath components cause fluctuation in signal strength, thereby inducing small-scale fading, signal distortion, or both. Multipath propagation often lengthens the time required for the baseband portion of the signal to reach the receiver, which can cause signal smearing, which is known as inter-symbol interference (ISI).

To prevent ISI effects, first, OFDM divides the high rate data stream into a number of parallel sub-streams. Next, they are modulated onto different orthogonal sub-carriers, thus it has lower symbol rate, and then a cyclic prefix (CP) is added to the head of each symbol to try to eliminate the effect ofISI.

Although CP insertion highly improves the performance of OFDM systems, fixed CP length introduces overhead to overall system. For example, in 802.11a wireless local area network (WLAN) system where CP length is fixed by proportion 1/5 of data block size, the time and energy for CP are wasted.

To reduce the time and energy wasted, adaptive CPs length using correlation value of receive signals can be used. First, we do not consider the received signals whose power level of received signal is lower than noise level, and then, search for correlation value between the first arrived signal and the last delayed signal. Finally, CP lengths are controlled by correlation value from the feedback information of receiver. To control the CP length, we assume that channel varies very slowly. So next symbol length applying adaptive CP control is added to some bit for minimization ISI. However, if every symbol's CP length is changed, next symbol's CP length is very short. For this reason, in deep fading channel condition, BER is increased.

Fig. 3.2 shows the OFDM system with adaptive CP length. Data block is fed to serial-to-parallel (S/P) block and is modulated by sub-carriers. The modulated data block is passed by IFFT as follow equation.

$$x_n = \frac{1}{\sqrt{N}} \sum_{i=0}^{N-1} X_i \exp\left\{\frac{2\pi ik}{N}\right\}, \quad 0 \le i \le N, \tag{3-1}$$

Where, N represents the number of FFT points. CP, which is a proportion of data block size, is added to ahead of the data as shown in equation (3-2).

$$x_n^g = x(n)_N, \quad n = -G, \cdots, 0, 1, \cdots, N-1. \tag{3-2}$$

where G represents length of CP. So, equation (3-3) represents signals with CP inserted. The signals that passed by channel can be represented as follow equation.

$$r_n(t) = x_n^g(t) * h_n(t) + n(t), \tag{3-3}$$

where, '*', n(t) and $h_n(t)$ are represent convolution sum, AWGN, and impulse response of the Rayleigh fading channel, respectively. Rayleigh fading channel has PDF as follow.

$$p(r) = \begin{cases} \frac{r}{\sigma^2} \exp\left(\frac{-r^2}{2\sigma^2}\right) & 0 \le r \le \infty \,. \\ 0 & r < 0 \end{cases} \tag{3-4}$$

where, σ^2 is the time-average power of the received signal.

Transmitted signals are received with reflection, refraction and diffraction. First, we do not consider the received signals whose power level of received signal is lower than noise level, and then, search for correlation value between the first arrived signal and the last delayed signal. Finally, CP lengths are controlled by correlation value from the feedback information of receiver in CP controller of Fig. 3.3.

As shown above Figures, CP length is controlled by correlation value and transmited / received signal are re-calculated as follow.

$$\tilde{x}_n^g = x(n)_N, n = -\tilde{G}, \cdots 0, \cdots, N-1, \tag{3-5}$$

$$r_n(t) = \tilde{x}_n^g(t) * h_n(t) + n(t). \tag{3-6}$$

We obtain the simulation results about data rate and power loss as to mobile speed. Fig. 3.4 shows the gain of data rate when mobile speed is 20km/h. Red line is the conventional OFDM system with fixed CPs length and blue line is the OFDM system with adaptive CPs length.

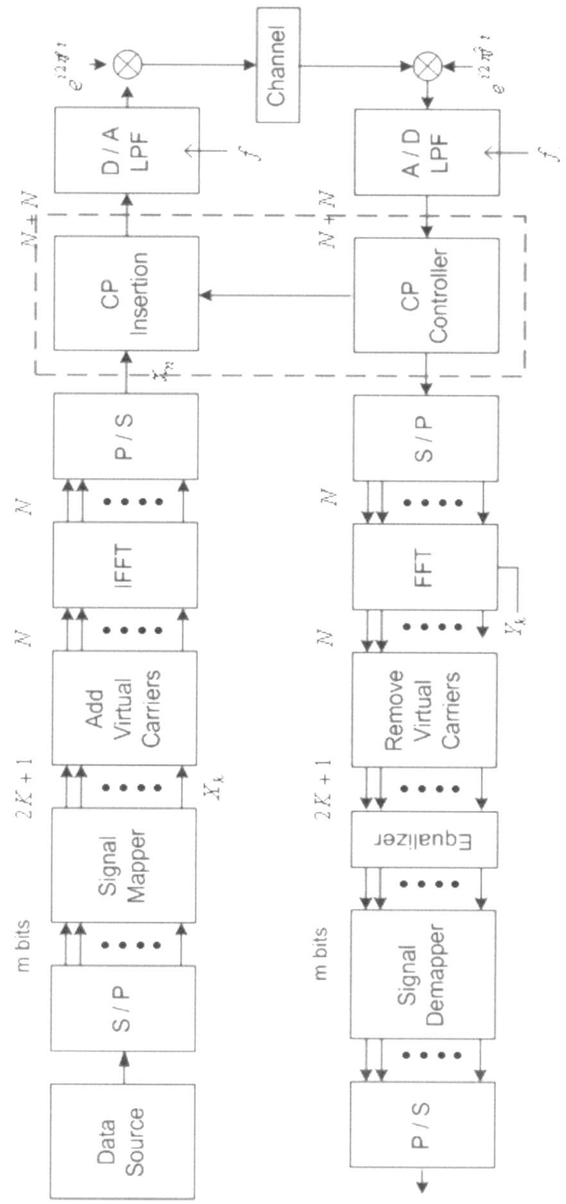

Fig. 3.2. OFDM system with adaptive CP length

In the case of using fixed CPs, there is no gain of data rate. However, the OFDM system using adaptive CP length is able to obtain the gain in data rate about 10Mbps with transmission of 1000 frames.

3.2 Antenna issues

Antenna element numbers and inter-element spacing are key parameters in MIMO system, and especially the latter is really important for the high spectral efficiencies of MIMO to be realized.

Base stations with large numbers of antennas pose environmental concerns. Hence, the antenna element numbers are limited to a modest number, with an inter-element spacing of around 10 λ .

The large spacing is because base stations are usually mounted on elevated positions where the presence of local scatterers to decorrelate the fading cannot be always guaranteed. As an example in four antenna system, four antennas can fit into a linear space of 1.5 m at 10 λ spacing at 2 GHz using dual polarized antennas. For the terminal, (1/2) λ spacing is usually

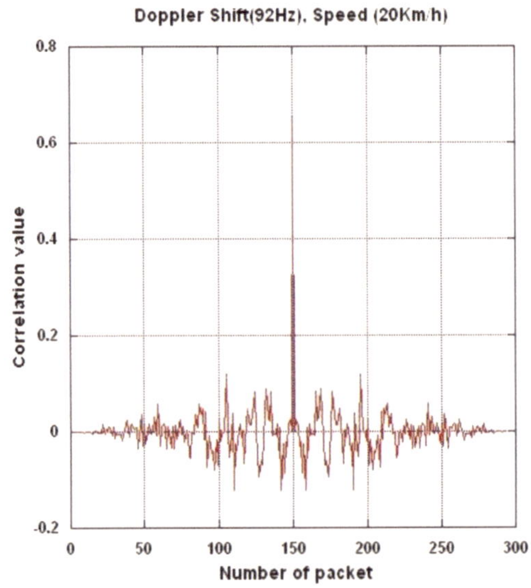

Fig. 3.3. Correlation value of received signals (20km/h)

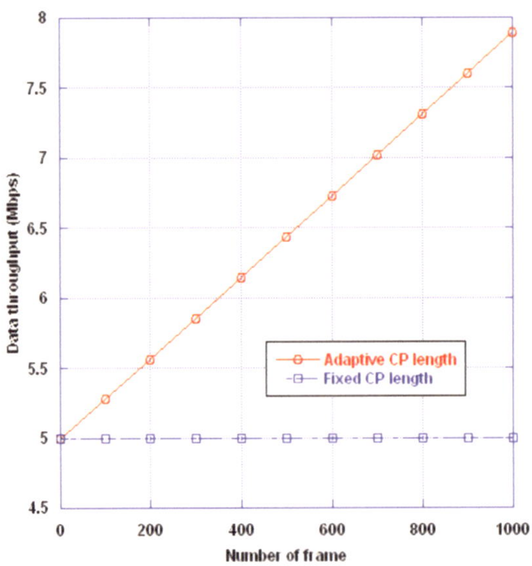

Fig. 3.4. Data rate of proposed scheme (20km/h)

sufficient to ensure a fair amount of uncorrelated fading because the terminal is present amongst local scatterers and quite often there is no direct path. The maximum number of antennas on the terminal is envisaged to be four (or more), though a lower number, say two, is an implementation option. Four dual polarized patch antennas can fit in a linear space of 7.5 cm. These antennas can easily be embedded in casings of lap tops. However, for handsets, even the fitting of two elements may be problematic. This is because, the present trend in handset design is to imbed the antennas inside the case to improve look and appeal. This makes spacing requirements even more critical.

3.3 Precoding schemes for multi-user MIMO system

Precoding scheme linearizes each layer of MIMO and makes beamforming possible. Default precoder can be unitary precoder based on Fourier matrix, and system can utilize specific precoder based on precoder codebook transimitted from mobile station. There are two types of precoder codebook, knockdown precoder and readymade precoder.

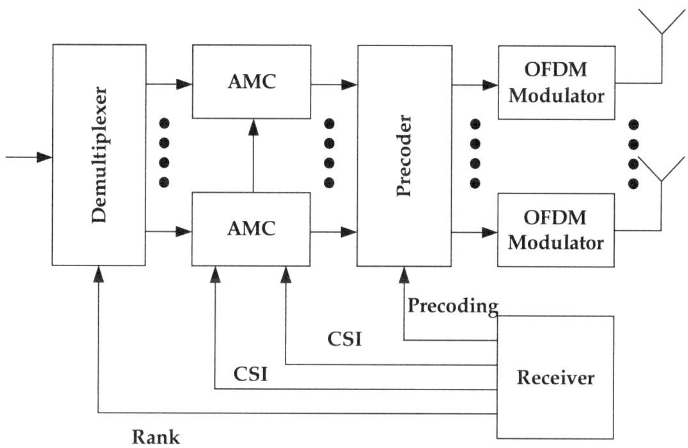

Fig. 3.5. MIMO-OFDM system with a precoder

Knockdown precoder uses the predefined matrix of prime numbers for the formulation of precoder. Then mobile device returns the information about suitable index and column of matrix. And the base station uses the information to select a precoder. This is typically referred to as codebook-based beamforming.

Readymade precoder utilizes the *M* predefined matrices for the precoder. The mobile device feeds the information about the index of the proper matrix back to the base station. Then the base station makes a use of the matrix.

3.4 System complexity

The implementation complexity of the MIMO system represents a substantial increase over existing devices. There are two primary areas of increased complexity associated with the MIMO system: RF and baseband processing. An assessment of FPGA implementation shows that a 2×2 implementation is roughly three times the baseband complexity of current devices. A 4×4 implementation is about eight times the baseband complexity of current devices. Given the continuous increase in transistor density, we anticipate that the baseband processing is not a significant cost driver for next-generation technology.

While additional RF receive and transmit chains are required to support MIMO, some parts of the chains, such as the local oscillator and clock generation circuitry, can be shared. In addition, the transmit power requirement per power amplifier decreases directly in proportion to the number of antennas employed.
Improved support for sleep and idle modes in the MAC will permit highly efficient power utilization for battery-powered devices, achieving charge cycles equivalent to or better than those cell phones achieve today.

4. Acknowledgement

This work was, in part, supported by Basic Science Research Program through the National Research Foundation of Korea(NRF) funded by the Ministry of Education, Science and Technology(MEST)"(No. 2010-0022629) and, in part, supported by Kwangwoon university.

5. References

A. Goldsmith; S. A. Jafar; N. Jindal, & S. Vishwanath, (2003). Capacity limits of MIMO channels, *IEEE J. Select. Areas Commun.*, vol. 21, no. 5, pp. 684-702.

C. Windpassinger; R. F. H. Fischer; T. Vencel & J. B. Huber, (2004). Precoding in multi-antenna and multi-user communications, *IEEE Trans. Wireless Commun.*, vol. 3, no. 4, pp. 1305-1316.

D. Tse & P. Viswanath, (2005). *Fundamentals of Wireless Communication*, 0521845270, Cambridge University Press.

G. Bauch & J. Shamim Malik, (2004). Parameter optimization, interleaving and multiple access in OFDM with cyclic delay diversity, *IEEE Trans. Veh. Technol.*, vol. 1, pp. 505 - 509.

H. Jafarkhani, (2005). *Space-Time Coding - Theory and Practice*, 100521842913, Cambridge University Press.

J. G. Proakis, (2001). *Digital Communications (4th ed.)*, 0072321113, McGraw-Hill, New York.

J. Y. Kim, (2008). *MIMO-OFDM System for High-Speed Wireless Communication Component*, 9788956674599, Gybo Publisher, Seoul, Korea.

L. Hanzo; M. Munster; B. J. Choi, & T. Keller, (2003). *OFDM and MC-CDMA for Broadband Multi-User Communications, WLANs and Broadcasting*, 0470858796, John Wiley & Sons.

M. Jankiraman, (2004). *Space-Time Codes and MIMO Systems*, 1580538657, Artech House Publishers.

Q. H. Spencer; C. B. Peel; A. L. Swindlehurst & M. Haardt, (2004). An introduction to the multi-user MIMO downlink, *IEEE Commun. Mag.*, vol. 42, no. 10, pp. 60-67.

Q.H. Spencer, et al., (2000). Modeling the statistical time and angle of arrival characteristics of an indoor environment, *IEEE J. Select. Areas Commun.*, vol. 18, no. 3, pp. 347-360.

Siavash M Alamouti, (1998). A simple transmit diversity technique for wireless communications, *IEEE J. Select. Areas Commun.*, vol. 16, no. 8, pp. 1451-1458.

12

Time Reversal Technique for Ultra Wide-band and MIMO Communication Systems

Ijaz Naqvi[1] and Ghaïs El Zein[2]
[1]LUMS School of Science and Engineering (SSE) Sector U, D.H.A. Lahore Cantt
[2]European University of Brittany (UEB)
INSA, IETR, UMR 6164, F-35708, 20 avenue des Buttes de Coesmes, 35708 Rennes
[1]Pakistan
[2]France

1. Introduction

Ultra wide band (UWB) technology gained a renewed interest after February 2002, when the Federal Communications Commission (FCC) approved the First Report and Order (R&O) for commercial use of UWB technology under strict power emission limits for various devices. The permission to transmit signals in a wide unlicensed band, opened the doors for the coexistence of UWB technology along with other narrow band and spread spectrum technologies. In UWB communication, extremely narrow RF pulses are employed to communicate between transmitters and receivers. Because of its extremely wide bandwidth, UWB signals result in a large number of resolvable multi-paths and thus reduce the interference caused by the super position of unresolved multi-paths. However, it also results in a complex receiver system. To collect the received signal energy, several kinds of receivers can be applied such as transmit-reference, Rake or decision feedback autocorrelation receiver. The later two techniques are quite complex while the former decreases the data rate of the system. One way to overcome these drawbacks is to make use of a technique that shifts the design complexity from the receiver to the transmitter.

Time Reversal (TR) has been proposed as a technique to shift the design complexity from the receiver to the transmitter. Classically, TR has been applied to acoustics Fink (1992); Fink & et. al. (2000) and underwater systems Edelmann et al. (2002), but recently, it has been widely studied for broadband and UWB communication systems Khaleghi et al. (2007)- Oestges et al. (2004). The received signal in a TR system is considerably focused in spatial and temporal domains and can be received using simple energy threshold detectors. The temporal and spatial focusing of the TR scheme improves with the bandwidth of the signal, therefore, systems with ultra wide bandwidth are inherently suitable for the TR scheme. One of the very first experimental study for TR with wideband electromagnetic waves is carried out in Lerosey et al. (2006). In a TR UWB communication systems, a time-reversed channel impulse response (CIR) is employed as a transmitter pre-filter. The TR technique comprises of two steps. In the first step, the CIR is estimated at the transmitter end. In the second step, the complex conjugated and time-reversed CIR is transmitted in the same channel. The TR wave then propagates in an invariant channel following the same paths in the reverse order. Finally at the receiver, all the paths add up coherently in the delay and spatial domains. Experimental demonstration of TR UWB has been performed in Khaleghi et al. (2007); Naqvi & El Zein (2008). The performance of MISO TR systems has been analyzed in Kyritsi, Papanicolaou, Eggers & Oprea (2004); Qiu et al. (2006). TR performance in a multi-user scenario is studied in a number of articles Naqvi et al. (2007); Nguyen et al. (2006). The performance of TR UWB for different bandwidths is analyzed in Khaleghi & El Zein (2007). For dense multi-path propagation channels, strong temporal compression and high spatial focusing can be achieved with a focusing gain of about 8 dB Khaleghi et al. (2007). For communication purposes, this gain improves the transmission range. Inter symbol interference (ISI) effects are mitigated by temporal compression and multi-user interference is reduced due to spatial focusing. The received signal in a TR system is considerably focused in spatial and temporal domains and can be detected (or demodulated) using simple energy threshold detectors.

For the TR scheme, multiple-input single-output (MISO) TR has been used in the literature to exploit the diversity gain offered by the MISO configuration. In Kyritsi, Eggers & Oprea (2004); Kyritsi, Papanicolaou, Eggers & Oprea (2004), using the data from a fixed wireless 8×1 MISO measurement, a delay compression by a factor of 3 was shown to be possible. In Qiu et al. (2006), using the experimental results, temporal focusing and an increase in collected energy with the number of antennas in MISO-TR systems is verified.

In this chapter, we present results of TR validation with multiple antenna configurations using time domain instruments followed by the parametric analysis of the TR scheme. Different TR properties such as normalized peak power (NPP), focusing gain (FG), signal to side-lobe ratio (SSR), increased average power (IAP) and RMS delay spread are compared for different muli-antenna configurations. In the second part of the chapter, a modified transmission scheme for a multi user time-reversal system is proposed. With the help of mathematical derivations, it is shown that the interference in the modified TR scheme is reduced compared to simple TR scheme. Limitations of the proposed scheme are studied and an expression for maximum number of simultaneous users is proposed.

2. Introduction of Time Reversal

Time reversal (TR) is a transmission scheme in which time-reversed channel impulse response (CIR) is used as a transmitter pre-filter. In a first step, the CIR is estimated between a transmitter and a receiver. Then the CIR is flipped in time and emitted by the transmitter. The time-reversed wave back propagates in the channel following the same paths as the CIR's ones but in the reverse order. Finally at the receiver, all the paths add up coherently in the time and spatial domains. For dense multipath propagation channels, strong temporal compression and high spatial focusing can be achieved. High temporal compression reduces inter symbol interference (ISI) whereas spatial focusing reduces multi-user interference and ensures communication security. The noiseless received signal ($y_j(t)$) at the intended receiver (j) can be mathematically represented as:

$$y_j(t) = s(t) \star h_{ij}(-t) \star h_{ij}(t) = s(t) \star R_{ij}^{auto}(t) \tag{1}$$

where $h_{ij}(t)$ is the CIR from the transmitting point (i) to an intended receiver (j), $s(t)$ is the transmitted signal, $\star$ denotes convolution product and $R_{ij}^{auto}(t)$ is the autocorrelation of the

CIR, $h_{ij}(t)$. The noiseless received signal at any non intended receiver (k) is written as:

$$\begin{aligned} y_k(t) &= s(t) \star h_{ij}(-t) \star h_{ik}(t) \\ &= s(t) \star R_{ikj}^{cross}(t) \end{aligned} \tag{2}$$

where $h_{ik}(t)$ is the CIR from the transmitting point (i) to an unintended receiver (k) and $R_{ikj}^{cross}(t)$ is the cross-correlation of the CIR $h_{ik}(t)$ and $h_{ij}(t)$. If the channels are uncorrelated, then the signal transmitted for one receiver will act as a noise for a receiver at any other location. Thus, a secure communication is achieved with low probability of detection and low probability of interception.

In the practical implementation of the TR systems, the pre-coding filter is truncated in time to reduce the filter length and thus the system complexity. The truncated response is represented as $h'(-t)$. For data communication purpose, the transmitted symbols are modulated by a binary pulse amplitude modulation (BPAM) scheme. The kth symbol, d_k, of the symbol sequence is equal to 1 or -1 for the data bits 1 or 0 respectively. Therefore, the received signal at the intended receiver is written as:

$$\begin{aligned} y(t) &= \underbrace{A\sum_k d_k h'(-t-kT_s)}_{\text{Transmitted RF signal}} \star \underbrace{h(t)}_{\text{CIR}} + n(t) \\ &\approx A\sum_k d_k R'_{hh}(t-kT_s) + n(t) \end{aligned} \tag{3}$$

where A is a normalization factor, T_s is the inter-symbol interval, $n(t)$ is the noise and $R'_{hh}(t)$ is the correlation between the truncated CIR ($h'(t)$) and the original CIR ($h(t)$). For the sake of simplicity we have supposed that the T_s is equal to the length of the measured time-reversed CIR ($h'(-t)$). As the amplitude of the peak of the received signal is proportional to the energy of the transmitted signal ($\int h'^2 dt$), the truncation process decreases the peak of the received signal. Due to BPAM, the polarity of the received signal peaks depends on the transmitted data bit and is used for the detection of the data bits.

3. Time-Reversal with multi-antenna configurations

The temporal compression and spatial focusing properties of the TR scheme makes it an attractive transmission scheme for MIMO systems. One of the main differences between a classical MIMO system and a MIMO-TR system is that in the classic system, the receiving antennas receive multiple superposed signals while in the TR system, each antenna receives only one dominant signal. The spatial focusing property of the TR means that the antennas which are separated in space will have uncorrelated channel impulse responses. Thus, the interference caused by the transmitted signals for unintended receiving antennas is suppressed. At the same time, the time dispersive characteristics of the channel are mitigated by the temporal compression inherent to the TR scheme. Therefore, simultaneous communication with all receiving antennas can be performed using simple detectors at the receiver Nguyen et al. (2006). The received signal with MIMO-TR for N_t transmitting antennas and N_r receiving antennas is given by the expression:

$$y_j(t) = \underbrace{s_j(t) \star \sum_{i=1}^{N_t} R_{ij}^{auto}(t)}_{Signal(j)} + \underbrace{\sum_{i=1}^{N_t} \sum_{k=1;k\neq j}^{N_r} s_k(t) \star R_{ikj}^{cross}(t)}_{Interference(j)} + \underbrace{n_j(t)}_{Noise(j)} \quad (4)$$

where $s_j(t)$ and $s_k(t)$ are the transmitted signals intended for the j_{th} and the k_{th} receiving antenna respectively and $n_j(t)$ is the added noise. There are two types of MIMO communications; one is the multiuser scenario and second is the single user MIMO scenario. In the first case, multiple transmitting antennas communicate with multiple receiving antennas well separated in space. In multi user TR communication, the interference part in (4) may be suppressed because of the large distances between the receiving antennas.

In a single user MIMO scenario, it might be possible to simultaneously transmit signals over several independent channels. (4) is valid in this case as well. Note that the number of users then becomes the number of the receiving antennas. Since the interference power increases with the number of receiving antennas, one cannot send more information by simply adding more receiving antennas. However, with reasonably smaller number of receiving antennas than the number of transmitting antennas and a rich multi-path environment, the desired signal's magnitude might become larger than that of the interference Nguyen et al. (2005). In this case, the application of TR in wireless MIMO could be possible.

MISO-TR has been investigated in a number of papers to benefit from the antenna diversity of the configuration. In Kyritsi, Eggers & Oprea (2004); Kyritsi, Papanicolaou, Eggers & Oprea (2004), using the data from a fixed wireless 8×1 MISO measurement, a delay compression by a factor of 3 was shown to be possible. In Qiu et al. (2006), using the experimental results, temporal focusing and an increase in collected energy with the number of antennas in MISO-TR systems is verified. Also, the reciprocity of realistic channels is demonstrated with the help of MISO-TR. MISO-TR system is investigated for UWB communication over ISI channels in Mo et al. (2007). TR is studied for a multi user scenario in Naqvi et al. (2007); Nguyen et al. (2005; 2006).

The use of multiple element antenna (MEA) systems in wireless communications has recently become a well-known technique to increase the transmission reliability and channel capacity Nguyen et al. (2005). Antenna and diversity gain can be achieved using available combining methods (selection, equal gain, maximum ratio combining). However, for wide-band MEA systems where signals are mixed both in time and space, a combination of advanced signal processing algorithms is required to overcome the effects of multi-path fading and ISI. Therefore, the receiver is expected to have a rather high complexity. Since the setup of MEA systems has some similarity to TR, it becomes an interesting question whether TR can be applied in MEA wireless systems. If this is the case, the advantages will be three fold: i) reducing ISI without the use of an equalizer ii) focusing the signal on the point of interest thereby reducing the interference and iii) applying a rather simple receiver structure.

In this chapter, validation of TR scheme is carried out with different multi-antenna configurations in the reverberation chamber (RC) and the indoor environment. A single user approach is applied for all configurations. Different multi-antenna configurations include SISO, SIMO (1×2), MISO (2×1) and MIMO (2×2). Time reversal (TR) measurements are conducted for ultra wide-band (UWB) signals in a RC for these multi-antenna configurations. A comparison is made among the four configurations. Channel measurement is done by using an arbitrary waveform generator (AWG) at the transmitter and a high speed digital

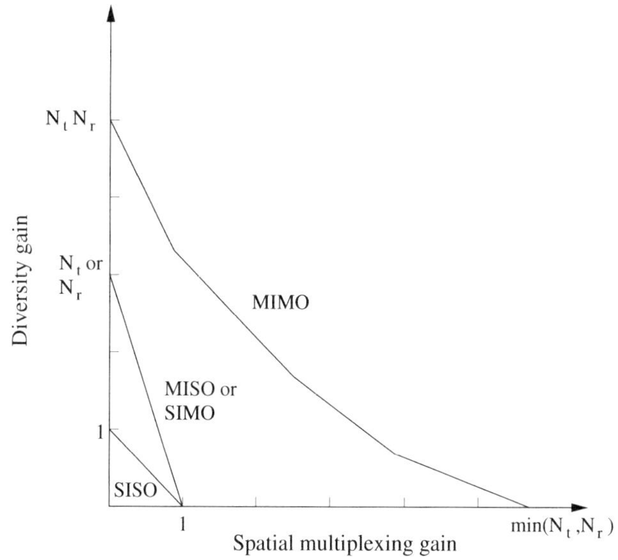

Fig. 1. Multiplexing and diversity gains for different multi antenna configurations

storage oscilloscope (DSO) at the receiver. For all these configurations, the received signals are time-reversed and re-transmitted from the transmitting antenna. TR performance is analyzed and compared for all the configurations by considering different TR characteristics i.e. normalized peak power (NPP), focusing gain (FG), signal to side-lobe ratio (SSR), increased average power (IAP) and RMS delay spread.

There are two types of gains associated with the configurations having more than one antenna either at the transmitting end or at the receiving end or both. One gain is the diversity gain achieved through the antenna diversity. The upper bound for the diversity gain is the product, $N_t N_r$, where N_t and N_r are the number of transmitting and receiving antennas respectively. The upper bound for the multiplexing gain is $min(N_t, N_r)$ Guguen & El Zein (2004). FIG. 1 further elaborates the limits of spatial multiplexing gain and the diversity gain for different multi antenna configurations.

In a TR system, same bounds for the multiplexing gain and diversity gain apply. We have compared different TR properties for different cases of MIMO configurations. The diversity gain is taken into account and the received signal in the case of SIMO and MIMO configurations is combined (or added) whereas transmitted signal is combined for MISO configuration. The results for the MIMO TR validation are published in Naqvi & El Zein (2009; 2010).

3.1 MIMO-TR in a Reverberation Chamber

A comparison of TR with different multi antenna configurations is first made in the RC. These experiments show performance of the TR scheme in an ideal static environment. Multi-antenna TR in the RC makes full use of the multi-path diversity inherent to the environment. The performance evaluation in an ideal environment only gives a general trend of the TR performance, therefore in order to validate our results, experiments are also conducted realistic indoor environment.

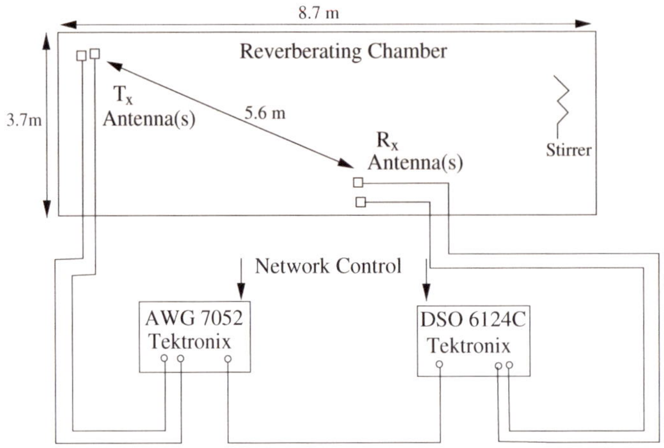

Fig. 2. Experimental setup for different multi-antenna configurations in the reverberation chamber

Fig. 3. The interior of the reverberation chamber with two conical monopole antennas

3.1.1 Experimental setup

An experimental setup is established in the RC for the validation of the TR in multi-antenna configurations. Measurement setup is illustrated in FIG. 2. A set of four conical mono-pole antennas (CMA) are used at the transmitter and receiver with both co-polar and cross-polar antenna orientations and different multi-antenna configurations. FIG. 3 shows two CMAs placed inside the RC. The height of the transmitter and the receiver is 1 m from the ground. The distance between the transmitter and receiver is 5.6 m. The channel sounding pulse with a rise time of 200 ps (see FIG. 4) and the time-reversed measured channel response (MCR) are generated through the AWG. The received signal is measured by a DSO. The DSO captures the MCR of the channel as well as the time-reversed response (TRR). The DSO is operated in average mode so that 256 samples are taken and averaged together to reduce the impact of noise.

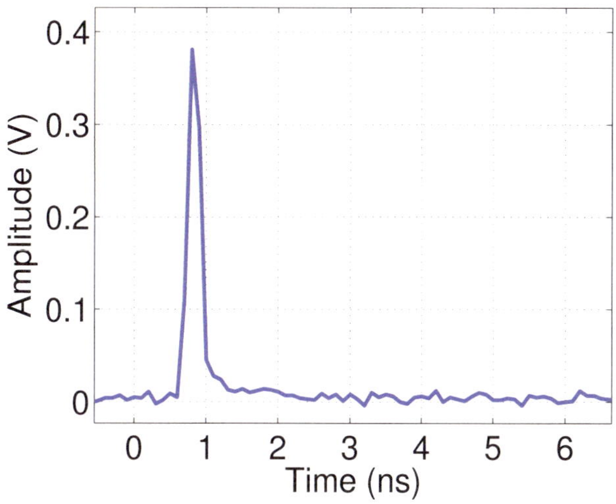

Fig. 4. Channel sounding pulse

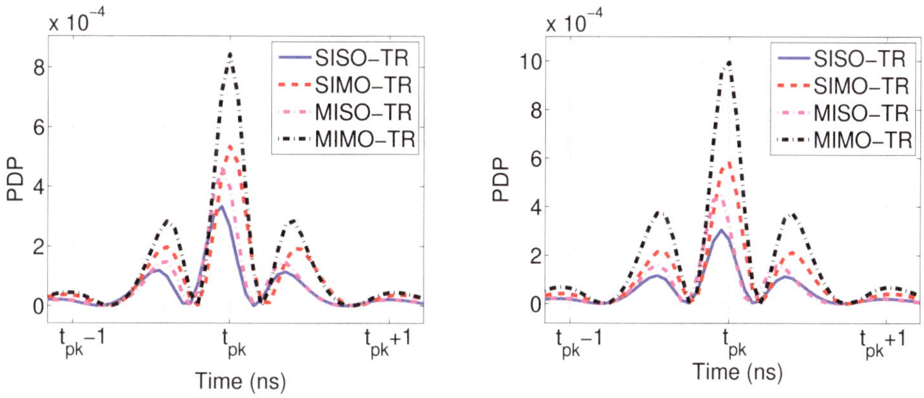

(a) Co-polar antenna orientation

(b) Cross-polar antenna orientation

Fig. 5. PDP of the received TR signal with SISO, SIMO and MIMO configurations

3.1.2 Experimental results

FIG. 5 shows power delay profile (PDP) of the received TR signal in RC for SISO, SIMO, MISO and MIMO configurations for a fixed transmitted power with both co-polar and cross-polar antenna orientations. It is evident that MIMO, MISO and SIMO TR have a better TR peak performance compared to SISO-TR. The comparison for all TR characteristics for these configurations is summarized in Table 1. The peak power of the received signal is normalized to the SISO-TR received peak power. The normalized peak power (NPP) improves with SIMO, MISO and MIMO configurations. MIMO-TR outperforms SISO, SIMO and MISO TR for the same transmitted power. For instance, NPP MIMO-TR is 4.02 dB and 5.16 dB and more than the obtained values with SISO-TR for co-polar and cross-polar antenna orientations respectively.

TR Property	Co-polar antenna orientation				Cross-polar antenna orientation			
	SISO	SIMO	MISO	MIMO	SISO	SIMO	MISO	MIMO
$\sigma_\tau^{MCR}(\mu s)$	2.21	2.11	2.19	2.08	2.21	2.11	2.17	2.21
NPP (dB)	0	2.01	1.37	4.02	0	2.79	1.667	5.16
FG (dB)	26.05	24.62	27.32	27.41	28.02	27.47	30.46	30.67
SSR (dB)	4.51	4.29	4.93	4.68	4.22	4.32	4.43	4.24
IAP (dB)	3.59	4.09	5.02	5.94	3.40	4.50	5.20	5.89
$\sigma_\tau^{TR}(n s)$	0.54	0.57	0.50	0.50	0.52	0.54	0.48	0.55

Table 1. Time-reversal characteristics in the reverberation chamber with different polarizations and multi-antenna configurations

As for the other TR properties, the performance of all the configurations remains almost the same. The configurations which have multiple antennas at the transmitter (MISO and MIMO) have a better FG and IAP than the configurations having one antenna at the transmitter (SISO and SIMO). The SSR remains almost constant for all configurations. The RMS delay spread also remains constant for all configurations. As SSR and RMS delay spread affect the ISI, therefore, all the configurations have a similar signal to interference (SIR) performance. However, the bit rate of the system can be increased taking advantage from the multiplexing gain of multi-antenna configurations.

3.2 SISO and SIMO-TR in the indoor Environment

Experiments are carried out in the indoor environment for SISO and SIMO configurations for a cross-polar antenna orientation for both LOS and NLOS environments. The experimental setup is very similar to the experimental setup in the reverberation chamber except that the environment is different and a power amplifier is used for the measurement of channel response (see Fig. 6).

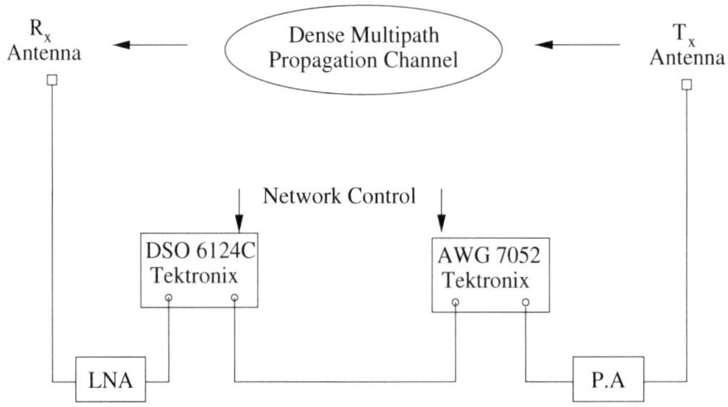

Fig. 6. Experimental setup

3.2.1 Experimental results

Fig. 7 shows for both LOS and NLOS configurations, the power delay profile (PDP) of the received TR signal in an indoor environment with SISO and SIMO configurations for a fixed transmitted power. It is obvious that SIMO TR has a better TR peak performance compared to SISO-TR. TABLE 2 compares different TR properties with SISO-TR and SIMO-TR in the indoor

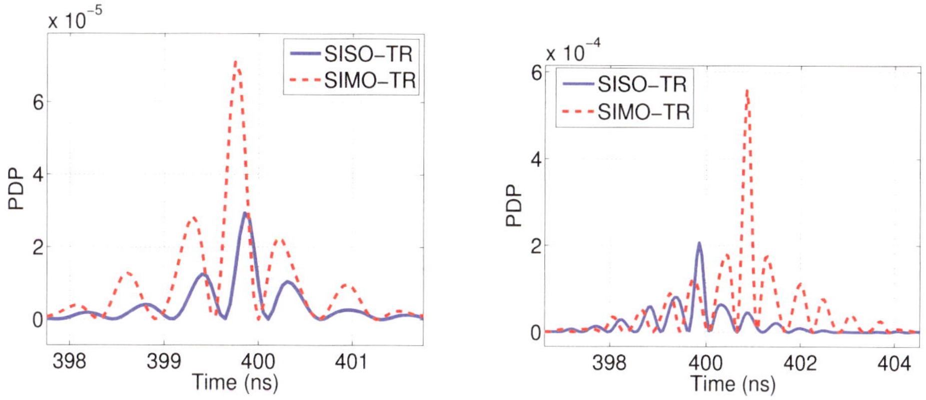

(a) LOS configuration (b) NLOS configuration

Fig. 7. PDP of the received TR signal with SISO and SIMO configurations in an indoor environment

TR Property	LOS		NLOS	
	SISO-TR	SIMO-TR	SISO-TR	SIMO-TR
NPP (dB)	0	4.30	0	3.81
FG (dB)	10.17	9.65	12.67	13.16
SSR (dB)	4.05	4.90	3.7	3.98
IAP (dB)	5.79	5.16	4.14	4.98
$\sigma_\tau^{TR}(ns)$	11.7	14.46	13.29	13.16
$\sigma_\tau^{MCR}(ns)$	18.35	16.07	23.21	22.17

Table 2. Time Reversal characteristics in the indoor environment with different SISO and SIMO configurations

environment. The NPP with SIMO-TR is 4.30 dB and 3.81 dB greater than the obtained values with SISO-TR in LOS and NLOS environments respectively. All other TR properties are very similar for SISO and SIMO-TR. NLOS environment has larger values for RMS delay spread of the MCR (σ_τ^{MCR}) but the RMS delay spread for the TR signal (σ_τ^{TR}) is in the same range for both LOS and NLOS environments.

4. Multi-user TR communications

In this part of the chapter, time-reversal (TR) communication is investigated by modifying the transmission prefilter. Mathematical expressions for received signal and the interference in the modified transmission scheme are derived. It is shown that the modified transmission approach reduces multi-user interference which eventually translates into a better bit error rate (BER) performance than simple TR multiuser scheme. Channel impulse responses (CIR) of a typical indoor channel are measured. In a multi-user scenario, both TR and the modified TR schemes are studied using the measured CIRs. It is shown that the proposed modified TR scheme outperforms the original TR scheme.

4.1 Description of the proposed transmission approach

In a multi user TR system, multiple signals for different users are transmitted simultaneously. The measured and truncated CIR from the transmitter to the user i can be written as:

$$h_i'(-t) = \sum_{m=0}^{L-1} a_m \delta(t - m\,\tau_s) \tag{5}$$

where L is number of time-reversal filter taps which corresponds to $T_{sig} = L\,\tau_s$ in time(seconds), a_m is the associated amplitude and $m\,\tau_s$ is the associated delay of the multi-path components. τ_s is the time between two consecutive samples and depends on the sampling rate of the time-reversal filter. For instance, if the measured CIR is sampled with a sampling rate of $5\,GS/s$, the delay of $\tau_s = 0.2\,ns$ is obtained. Therefore the number of taps (L) in filter having a length of $50\,ns$ is $L = 250$ samples or taps. The transmitted signal for multi user TR can be written as:

$$T_x(t) = \sum_k \sum_{i=0}^{N_u-1} \frac{1}{\sqrt{N_u}} d_{ik} A_i h_i'(-t - kT_s) \tag{6}$$

where d_{ik} is the k_{th} information bit of the i_{th} user, N_u is the total number of simultaneous users, T_s is the inter symbol interval and A_i is the normalization factor which can be written as:

$$A_i = \frac{1}{\sqrt{\left\|h_i'(-t - kT_s)\right\|^2}} \tag{7}$$

where $\|.\|$ is the Frobenius norm operation. The term $\frac{1}{N_u}$ insures that the signals for all the users are transmitted with a constant power. This is in contrast to Nguyen et al. (2006), where this normalization has not been carried out resulting in an unfair comparison of the performance with different number of users. Neglecting the noise, the received signal for the j_{th} user and the k_{th} symbol can be written as:

$$R_{x_{kj}}(t) = \underbrace{\frac{1}{\sqrt{N_u}} d_{jk}\, h_j(t) \star h_j'(-t + jT_u - kT_s)}_{Signal} + \underbrace{\frac{1}{\sqrt{N_u}} \sum_{i=0, i\neq j}^{N_u-1} d_{ik}\, h_j(t) \star h_i'(-t + iT_u - kT_s)}_{Interference} \tag{8}$$

The responses of the modified filter are produced by shifting $h'(-t)$ to either left or right and then forcing the shifted part to zero so that the shifted signal can be packed in the same signal duration. Fig. 8 shows the pattern of the left or right shift for $l = 1, 2$ taps. As shown for the left shift of 1 tap, the last three taps are shifted to left by one tap and the slot for last tap is filled with zero. For the right shift of 1 tap, first three taps are shifted to right and then the slot for the first tap is filled with zero. With the process of filling the shifted taps with zeros, we get rid of the unwanted signal, which causes interference to the adjacent symbols (called *Image* in Naqvi et al. (2009)). As the taps which result in an undesired signal are forced to

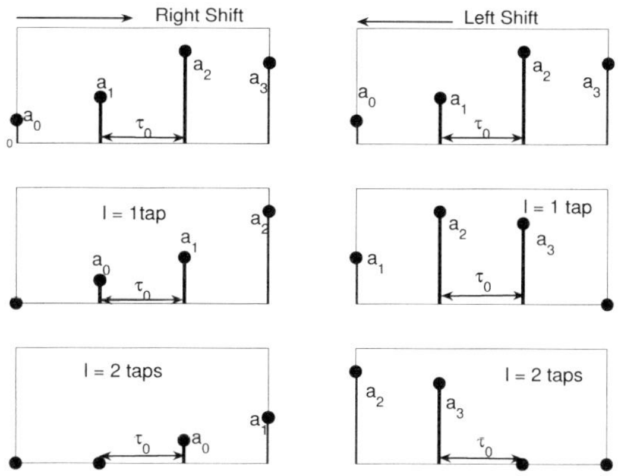

Fig. 8. Pattern for the left and right shift

zero, the received peak signal increases for an equal transmitted power. If $h'(-t)$ is shifted left by $T_u = l\,\tau_s$, the expression is given by:

$$\begin{aligned} left\,shift(h'(-t), T_u) &= \hat{h}(-t + T_u) \\ &= [\sum_{i=0}^{L-l-1} a_{i+l}\delta(t - i\,\tau_s)\,zeros(1,l)] \end{aligned} \tag{9}$$

where $zeros(1,l)$ is a vector containing l number of zeros, l is the number of taps required to carry out a shift of T_u seconds. Note that $\hat{h}(-t + T_u)$ has $L - l$ non zero taps. The transmitted signal with the modified transmission scheme can be thus written as:

$$T_x(t) = \sum_k \sum_{i=0}^{N_u - 1} \frac{1}{\sqrt{N_u}} d_{ik}\, A_i \hat{h}_i(-t + iT_u - kT_s) \tag{10}$$

where $A_i = \frac{1}{\sqrt{\|\hat{h}(-t+iT_u-kT_s)\|^2}}$ and the term $\frac{1}{\sqrt{N_u}}$ insures that the power transmitted for different number of users is constant. The received signal for the k_{th} symbol of the j_{th} user can be written as:

$$\begin{aligned} R_{x_{kj}}(t) = &\underbrace{\frac{1}{\sqrt{N_u}} d_{jk} h_j(t) \star \hat{h}_j(-t + jT_u - kT_s)}_{Signal} \\ &+ \underbrace{\frac{1}{\sqrt{N_u}} \sum_{i=0, i\neq j}^{N_u - 1} d_{ik} h_j(t) \star \hat{h}_i(-t + iT_u - kT_s)}_{Interference} \end{aligned} \tag{11}$$

4.2 Interference analysis of the proposed scheme

To analyze the worst case performance, it is assumed that the transmitter communicates with all users at the same time. Therefore, TR received signal in a multi user scenario consists of a sum of one autocorrelation function and $N_u - 1$ cross correlation functions. The $N_u - 1$ cross correlation functions cause multi user interference. The received signal peak is the sum of the square of the coefficients of CIR (from the properties of the auto-correlation function). The interference term at the time of the peak (t_{peak}) for the j_{th} user in a simple TR scheme can be written as:

$$I_{j_{simple\,TR}}(t_{peak}) = \sum_{i=1, i\neq j}^{N_u} \sum_{m=0}^{L-1} b_{mi} \times a_{mj} \tag{12}$$

where b_{mi} are the coefficients of the time-reversed CIR $h'_i(-t + i\,T_u - k\,T_s)$ (from (8)) specific to the user i, a_{mj} are the coefficients of $h_j(t)$. As (12) uses simple TR transmission scheme, the high powered taps of $h'_i(-t)$ and $h'_j(-t)$ are approximately in the same time interval. Therefore, taps in the propagating channel containing more energy are multiplied by the taps of the transmitted signal with more energy resulting in a relatively higher interference.

To calculate the interference of the modified transmission scheme, we assume that the transmitted signal for the intended receiver is not shifted. Then by using (11) and (12), interference at the peak of the intended signal is then written as:

$$I_{j_{mod.TR}}(t_{peak}) = \sum_{i=0, i\neq j}^{N_u-1} \sum_{m=0}^{L-l-1} b_{(m+l)\,i} \times a_{mj} \tag{13}$$

where b_{mi} and a_{mj} are the same coefficients used in (12). Here the interference is the product of $L - l$ coefficients (as l taps are forced to zero). Furthermore, (13) suggests that in case of modified TR scheme, the taps in the propagating channel containing more energy are multiplied by the taps of the transmitted signal with less energy and vice versa. Therefore, interference is reduced with the new proposed transmission scheme. This reduced interference helps to improve the bit error rate (BER) performance of the system.

4.3 Effects of shift on received signal peak

In a TR communication system, as the received signal is the auto correlation function of the CIR, the received signal peak is the sum of the square of the coefficients of CIR. Neglecting the interference and the noise, the received signal peak with the modified TR scheme for the k_{th} symbol of the j_{th} user is written as:

$$Rx_{modTR}(t_{peak_{jk}}) = d_{jk}\,A_j\Big(\sum_{m=0}^{L-l_j-1} a_m^2\Big) \tag{14}$$

where a_i are the coefficients of taps of $\hat{h}(-t + j\,T_b - kT_s)$ and l_j ($j\,\frac{T_b}{T_s}$) are the number of taps required for a shift of $j\,T_b$. The received signal peak depends on the energy contents of $(L - l_j)$ filter coefficients. Thus, the amplitude of the received peak decreases by the sum of the square coefficients in the shifted part of the transmitted signal. Therefore with the new modulation scheme, the received signal peak reduces in proportion to the energy of the shifted part of the transmitted signal.

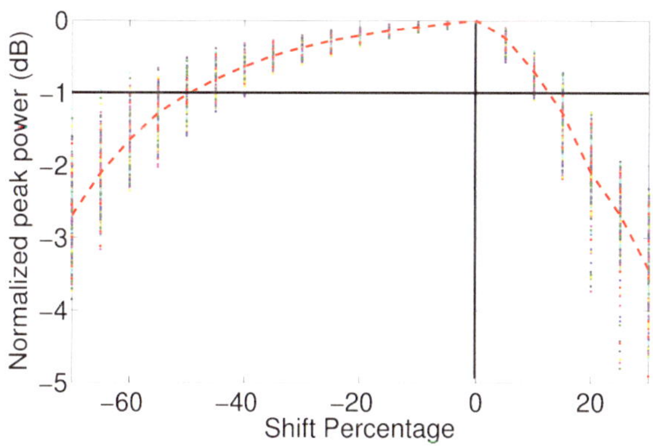

Fig. 9. Received signal peak power with left and right shifts normalized to the peak with no shift

Fig. 9 shows the peak power of the received signal peak for the shifted signals normalized to the received peak with no shift. The shift percentage corresponds to the percentage of the total length of the transmitted signal. A set of 243 measured CIRs are used for the simulation. Experimental setup and the measurement procedure are explained in Section 4.4. The loss of the received peak power for transmitted signals corresponding to individual CIRs is represented by the dots and the dashed line is the mean of power loss. To calculate the maximum number of simultaneous users that a system can support, we must take the decision in accordance to the threshold (say 3 dB) which can vary for different applications. For a 3 dB threshold, our system can support a shift percentage of $0.70L$ taps for left shift and $0.25L$ taps for right shift (see Fig. 9). Thus, the number of users with the proposed scheme can be written as:

$$N_u^{mod.TR} = \lfloor \frac{0.95 \times L}{\delta} \rfloor = \lfloor \frac{0.95 \times T_{sig}}{\Delta TR} \rfloor \tag{15}$$

where $\lfloor . \rfloor$ denotes the floor operator, L is the total number of taps in the transmitted signal, δ is the shift percentage between two simultaneous users, T_{sig} is the channel length in s and ΔTR is shift separation between two users in s. For the same threshold, the previously proposed scheme in Nguyen et al. (2006) can only support a shift of $0.75L$ which is contrary to their claim of 100% shift (as power loss with circular shift operation was not considered by the authors). The power loss for left shift is lesser than the power loss for the right shift as the energy contained in the shifted parts of the right shift is greater than the energy contained in the shifted parts of the left shift. Although a combination of right and left shifts can be used for the communication, for the sake of simplicity we have only used a left shift. In the rest of the paper unless otherwise mentioned, a shift is meant to be a left shift.

The power spectral density (PSD) of the transmitted signal of a TR communication system takes into account the effects of the antennas and the propagation channel including the path loss. In contrast to the pulse signal, the spectrum of a TR signal has a descending shape with increasing the frequency because the higher frequency components experience a greater path loss as compared to the lower frequency components in the spectrum. Fig. 10 shows the PSD plots of the transmitted signal with simple TR and modified TR schemes where a left shift of $0.20N$ taps is carried out for both modified TR scheme. The plots of both schemes have a descending shape. Maximum spectral power is experienced at the same frequency. Therefore,

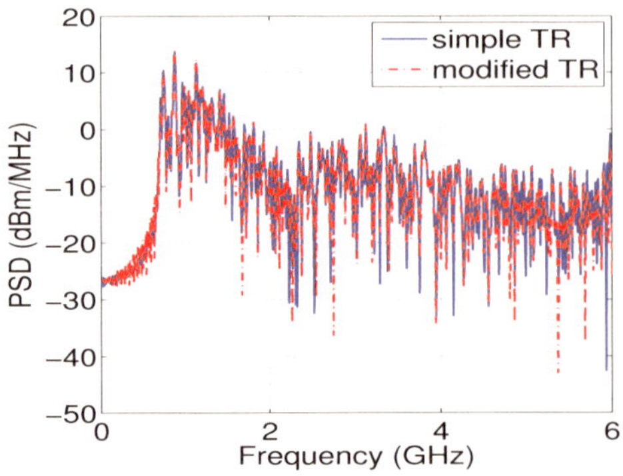

Fig. 10. PSD of transmitted signal with simple TR and modified TR schemes

both the signals must be attenuated with the same factor in order to respect the UWB spectral mask proposed by FCC. Frequency selectivity of the transmitted signals is similar for the two schemes. In short, the both schemes have resembling spectral properties.

4.4 Experimental setup and simulation results

Experiments are performed in a typical indoor environment. The environment is an office space of $14\,m \times 8\,m$ in the IETR[1] laboratory. The frequency response of the channel in the frequency range of 0.7-6 GHz is measured using vector network analyzer (VNA) with a frequency resolution of 3.3 MHz and two wide band conical mono-pole antennas (CMA) in non line of sight (NLOS) configuration. The height of the transmitter antenna and the receiver antenna is 1.5 m from the floor. The receiver antenna is moved over a rectangular surface ($65\,cm \times 40\,cm$) with a precise positioner system. The frequency responses between the transmitting antenna and receiving virtual array are measured. The time domain CIRs are computed using the inverse fast Fourier transform (IFFT) of the measured frequency responses.

4.5 BER performance

In the proposed transmission scheme, one user is separated with the other by a shift of a fixed number of taps. This separation is named as δ, which is a percentage of total number of taps in the transmitted signal. Signal for User 1 is transmitted without any shift. As discussed in Section 4.2, that interference between users is greatly reduced with the proposed modulation scheme. To study the impact of the reduced interference, we evaluate the BER performance with the proposed scheme using left shift for 5, 10 and 15 simultaneous user for $\delta = 0.05\,L$. From the measured CIRs, we generate almost $35 \times (35 - N_u - 1)$ combinations for simulating different number of simultaneous users (N_u). For every combination of simultaneous users, 10000 symbols are transmitted which makes it sufficient for statistical analysis. The measured CIR is truncated for 90% energy contained in the CIR. Thus, the transmitted symbol has a length of 55 ns and a per user bit rate of 18 $Mbps$. Perfect synchronization and no ISI effects are assumed. Signal to noise ratio (SNR) is varied by varying the noise variance, as:

$$SNR = P_j / \sigma^2_{noise} \tag{16}$$

[1] Institute of Electronics and Telecommunications of Rennes

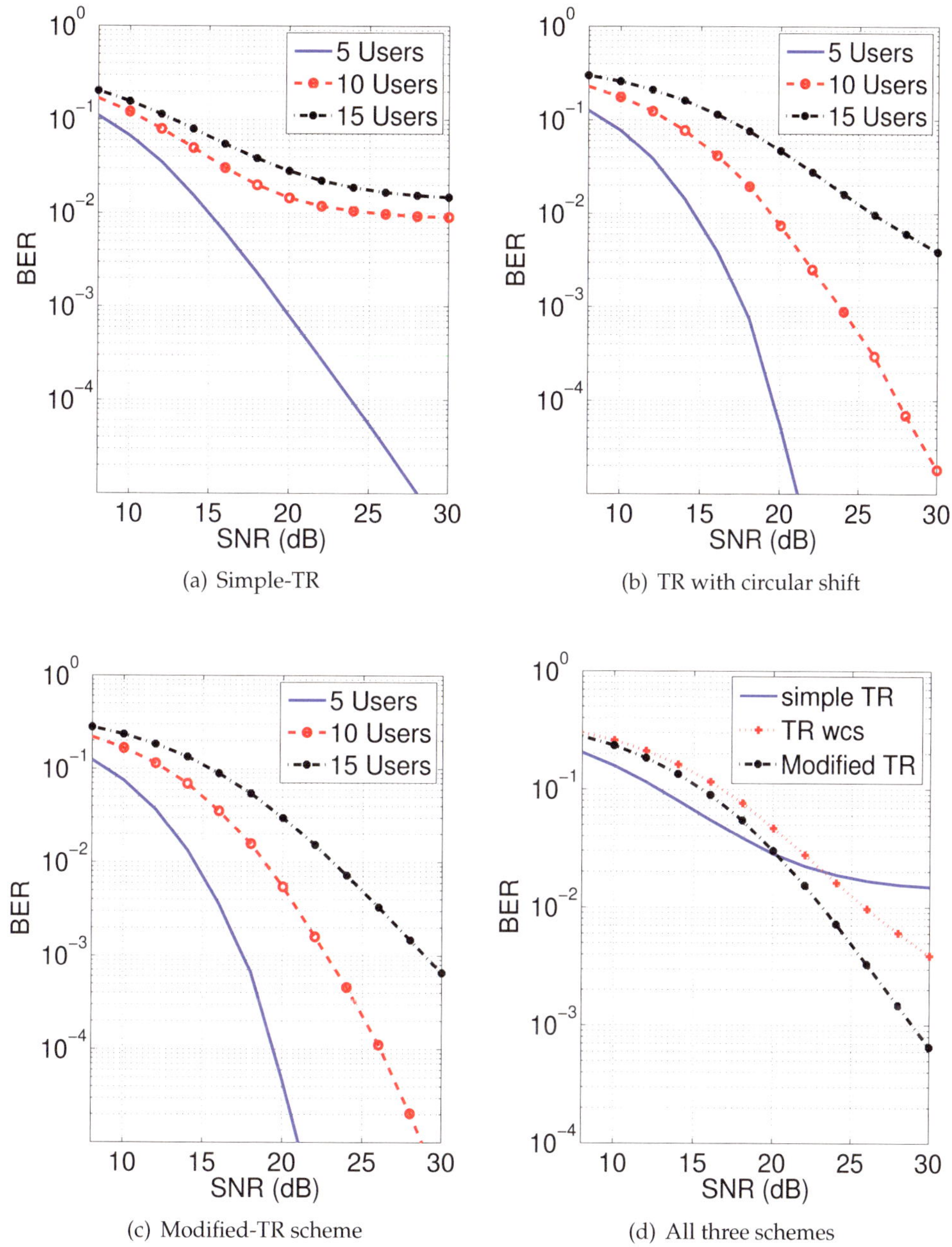

Fig. 11. BER performance with 5, 10, and 20 simultaneous users with a) simple TR, b) TR with circular shift, c) modified TR scheme, d) 15 simultaneous users with all three schemes for $\delta = 0.05\,L$ taps

where P_j is the power of the received signal at its peak and σ^2_{noise} is the noise variance. Bipolar pulse amplitude modulation (BPAM) is used for these simulations. The received signal $y_j(t)$ is sampled at its peak and is detected based on ideal threshold detection, given as:

$$\text{Detected bit} = \begin{cases} 1 & \text{if } y_j(t_{peak}) \geq 0 \\ 0 & \text{if } y_j(t_{peak}) < 0 \end{cases} \quad (17)$$

Fig. 11a-c shows the BER performance of the simple TR, TR with circular shift operation and the modified TR scheme for 5, 10 and 15 simultaneous users. The modified TR scheme outperforms the other two schemes specially for higher number of simultaneous users (10, 15). For instance for 10 simultaneous users, the modified TR scheme results in a 1.4 dB better performance than the TR with circular shift for a BER of 10^{-4}. The simple TR scheme has already reached a plateau. To perform an analysis in the presence of extreme multi user interference, BER performance is studied for 15 simultaneous users. Fig. 11d compares the performance of the three schemes for 15 simultaneous users. The modified TR scheme gives significantly better performance than the other two schemes. The improvement is in the order of 4.5 dB or more.

If a system has a large number of users, the users experiencing higher shift percentages will give poorer performance than the users experiencing lower shift percentages. To have a consistent system, we propose to rotate the shift percentages for different users so that no user is subjected to permanent high shift percentage.

5. Conclusion

In this chapter, TR validation with multiple antenna configuration, followed by the parametric analysis of the TR scheme, is performed by using time domain instruments (AWG and DSO). Different TR properties such as normalized peak power (NPP), focusing gain (FG), signal to side-lobe ratio (SSR), increased average power (IAP) and RMS delay spread are compared for different muli-antenna configurations. It has been found that with multi-antenna configurations, a significantly better TR peak performance is achieved with all other properties remain comparable to the SISO-TR scheme.

In the second part of the chapter, a modified transmission scheme for a multi user time-reversal system is proposed. With the help of mathematical derivations, it is shown that the interference in the modified TR scheme is reduced compared to simple TR scheme. Limitations of the proposed scheme are studied and an expression for maximum number of simultaneous users is proposed. It is shown that the modified TR scheme outperforms simple TR and TR with circular shift scheme specially at higher number of simultaneous users. For instance for 15 simultaneous users, the modified TR scheme improves the performance in the order of 4.5 dB or more for a constant BER.

All these results suggest that the TR UWB, combined with MIMO techniques, is a promising and attractive transmission approach for future wireless local and personal area networks (WLAN & WPAN).

6. Acknowledgment

This work was partially supported by ANR Project MIRTEC and French Ministry of Research.This work is a part of ANR MIRTEC and IGCYC projects, financially supported by French Ministry of Research and UEB.

7. References

Akogun, A. E., Qiu, R. C. & Guo, N. (2005). Demonstrating time reversal in ultra-wideband communications using time domain measurements, *International Instrumentation Symposium*.

Edelmann, G., Akal, T., Hodgkiss, W., Kim, S., Kuperman, W. & Song, H. C. (2002). An initial demonstration of underwater acoustic communication using time reversal, *IEEE Journal of Oceanic Engineering* 27(3): 602–609.

Fink, M. (1992). Time reversal of ultrasonic fields-part i: Basic principles, *IEEE Transactions on Ultrasonics, Ferroelectrics and Frequency Control* 39(5): 555–566.

Fink, M. & et. al. (2000). Time-reversed acoustics, *Rep. Progr. Phys* 63: 1988–1955.

Guguen, P. & El Zein, G. (2004). *Les techniques multi-antennes pour les réseaux sans fil*, Hermes Science Publishers.

Khaleghi, A. & El Zein, G. (2007). Signal frequency and bandwidth effects on the performance of UWB time-reversal technique, *Antennas and Propagation Conference, 2007. LAPC 2007, Loughborough*, pp. 97–100.

Khaleghi, A., El Zein, G. & Naqvi, I. (2007). Demonstration of time-reversal in indoor ultra-wideband communication: Time domain measurement, *International Symposium on Wireless Communication Systems, ISWCS 2007*, pp. 465–468.

Kyritsi, P., Eggers, P. & Oprea, A. (2004). MISO time reversal and time compression, *Proc. URSI International Symposium on Electromagnetic Theory*.

Kyritsi, P., Papanicolaou, G., Eggers, P. & Oprea, A. (2004). MISO time reversal and delay-spread compression for FWA channels at 5 ghz, *IEEE Antennas and Wireless Propagation Letters* 3: 96–99.

Lerosey, G., De Rosny, J., Tourin, A., Derode, A. & Fink, M. (2006). Time reversal of wideband microwaves, *Appl. Phys. Lett.* 15: 154101.

Mo, S. S., Guo, N., Zhang, J. Q. & Qiu, R. C. (2007). UWB MISO time reversal with energy detector receiver over ISI channels, *IEEE Consumer Communications and Networking Conference, CCNC2007*, pp. 629–633.

Naqvi, I. & El Zein, G. (2008). Time domain measurements for a time reversal SIMO system in reverberation chamber and in an indoor environment, *Digest of Papers, IEEE International Conference on Ultra-Wideband, ICUWB 2008*, Vol. 2, pp. 211–214.

Naqvi, I. H. & El Zein, G. (2009). Time reversal UWB system: SISO, SIMO, MISO and MIMO comparison with time domain experiments, *Journées Scientifiques CNFRS-URSI "Propagation et Télédétection"*.

Naqvi, I. H. & El Zein, G. (2010). Retournement temporel en ULB: étude comparative par mesures pour des configurations multi-antennes, *Revue de l'Electricité et de l'Electronique (REE). Dossier: Propagation et Télédétection* (2): 66–72.

Naqvi, I., Khaleghi, A. & El Zein, G. (2007). Performance enhancement of multiuser time reversal UWB communication system, *International Symposium on Wireless Communication Systems, ISWCS 2007*, pp. 567–571.

Naqvi, I., Khaleghi, A. & El Zein, G. (2009). Multiuser time reversal uwb communication system: A modified transmission approach, *IEEE International Symposium On Personal, Indoor and Mobile Radio Communications (PIMRC '09)*.

Nguyen, H., Andersen, J. & Pedersen, G. (2005). The potential use of time reversal techniques in multiple element antenna systems, *IEEE Communications Letters* 9(1): 40–42.

Nguyen, H. T., Kovacs, I. & Eggers, P. (2006). A time reversal transmission approach for multiuser UWB communications, *IEEE Transactions on Antennas and Propagation* 54(11): 3216–3224.

Oestges, C., Hansen, J., Emami, S. M., Kim, A. D., Papanicolaou, G. & Paulraj, A. J. (2004). Time reversal techniques for broadband wireless communication systems, *European Microwave Conference (Workshop)*.

Qiu, R., Zhou, C., Guo, N. & Zhang, J. (2006). Time reversal with MISO for ultrawideband communications: Experimental results, *IEEE Antennas and Wireless Propagation Letters* 5(1): 269–273.

Part 5

Vehicular Systems

13

Connectivity Prediction in Mobile Vehicular Environments Backed By Digital Maps

Robert Nagel and Stefan Morscher
Institute of Communication Networks, Technische Universität München
Germany

1. Introduction

As mobile ad-hoc networks gain momentum and are actively being deployed, providing users and customers with ubiquitous connectivity and novel applications, some challenges implied especially by the mobility of users have not yet been solved. Generally, it can be stated that modern applications impose higher requirements on the underlying communication solutions: more bandwidth, less packet loss, less delay and more reliability of services in terms of availability. These performance metrics are commonly termed *Quality of Service (QoS)*. Due to the variability of node locations in mobile networks, the experienced QoS is highly time-variant. We have discussed in Nagel (2010a) that the level of attained QoS ultimately results from a proper combination of connectivity, i.e., the communication relations in a network, the chosen (and usually invariant) medium access (MAC) protocol and the traffic that is injected into the network at the nodes. If a certain level QoS is desired in a mobile wireless network, at least one of these three properties has to be actively controlled.

We have demonstrated that through controlling the amount of traffic that is injected by the nodes, effective distributed mechanisms can be employed that are, given minimal information about nodes' connectivity, able to provide (and even guarantee) a certain level of QoS. These mechanisms, however, are based on the current connectivity of the network and are effective only at present time. Should an application require a certain amount of QoS over a larger period of time, additional provisions become necessary. Although it is possible to control connectivity in certain boundaries (for instance through power control or adaptive antennas) and at a certain cost, the fundamental physical causes of connectivity themselves (location, mobility, and wireless channel state) cannot be influenced by the application as they are dictated by the user's behavior and the environment. It is, however, possible to anticipate a network's future connectivity – at least for a certain time horizon – and to compute the resulting future QoS. Upon this information, applications, services, and routing protocols could be parameterized accordingly: as an example, if the future QoS of a connection using a certain route is predicted to fall below a necessary level due to a link break, the expected remaining time until the link actually breaks could be used to proactively find and set up a backup route that uses other, potentially more stable links. Also, if a connection was to be set up for a limited time, it may be very helpful to assess if the required QoS can actually be provided by the network for the desired duration before the connection is actually established.

While other work mainly uses mobility prediction in cellular scenarios to estimate hand-over times, or to support ad-hoc routing in random-mobility ad hoc scenarios, this chapter focuses on connectivity prediction in the special case of vehicular networks. Networked vehicular nodes can be assumed to adhere to certain rules that constitute drivers' basic behavior: they move along roads and try to avoid collisions with obstacles, such as buildings and other cars. Founded on the vehicular scenario constraint, we present an algorithm that predicts the location of vehicles based on their current state (position and velocity) and information from digital street maps obtained through the Open Street Map (OSM) project. A filter-based, self-adaptive velocity prediction algorithm is used to model the user-inflicted velocity changes. Using their current positions and the predicted velocities, possible future positions of cars on the street grid and their respective probabilities can be determined. Although the main focus of this chapter is on mobility prediction, we discuss an effective channel parameter estimation technique and propose to predict the network's future connectivity using an adaptive channel model.

It should be noted that the proposed position prediction mechanism does not completely exhaust all opportunities provided by the vehicular scenario. For instance, we assume that vehicles have no information about other vehicles' missions, i.e., the planned route through the road grid. Furthermore, we make no assumptions about other vehicles' capabilities (in terms of maximum acceleration and deceleration, yaw rate, etc.). Also, we do not consider environmental properties, such as weather, street and traffic conditions, etc. We will, however, point out and discuss the potential spots where these additional informations could be exploited to further augment the proposed algorithm.

In the following Section, we present an overview of current work. Subsequently, in Section 3 we formulate the problem mathematically and in Section 4, we describe our algorithm that predicts the future positions of vehicles according to their actual state and a complemental digital road map. In Section 5, we will discuss why the channel model presented in Equation 1 is not sufficient under all conditions and present methods that can adapt to the environment. In Section 6, we discuss some simulation results. Section 7 summarizes this chapter and gives an outlook on further work.

2. Related work

One possible way of predicting a network's future connectivity is to use a model that reflects the individual mobility properties of a node. Given the knowledge of the initial position velocity of a node, a future position could be projected by multiplying the velocity vector with the desired time interval. Obviously, this approach does not account for changes in the length and/or direction of the velocity vector. Several more sophisticated approaches have been suggested and today, mobility prediction has become a common research topic in wireless networks.

Due to the distinct characteristics of vehicular ad-hoc networks, especially the high speeds and restricted degree of freedom in the movement of vehicles, most of the work on prediction for ad hoc networks is too general and thus inappropriate for vehicular networks. Nevertheless, some approaches are discussed here because they give an overview of mobility prediction in general. Material specific to mobility prediction in vehicular networks is very rare and the topic is often neglected in works on vehicular ad hoc networks.

Kaaniche & Kamoun (2010) presents an approach for mobility prediction using neural networks. Although it is not specifically designed for vehicular networks it should perform better than other general approaches as it is independent of the underlying mobility model. A trajectory is calculated for multiple steps in the future using several past positions in quite a similar manner as the adapting FIR filter for velocity prediction presented in this work.

However, the approach does not use any map material and hence the predicted positions may lie far off the road and may thus be unrealistic. The approach using neural networks could be used for velocity prediction in the constellation presented in this works to substitute the FIR filter, however it is expected to perform in a very similar manner and the FIR filter seems less complex to implement.

A similar approach for mobility prediction using spatial contextual maps and Dempster-Shafer's theory for decision making is formulated in Samaan & Karmouch (2005). A framework is presented that allows prediction of the users mobility trajectory based on various bits of contextual information from e.g. user profile and map data. The approach is motivated by the fact that contextual information is becoming more common for adapting services towards the users needs and it uses the additional information in order to predict the users mobility. The concept seems feasible for e.g. cell phone users traveling on foot but does not seem appropriate for vehicular networks as the only contextual information possibly available and relevant to the future mobility is the chosen route to the destination. A complex theory to combine evidence into a prediction is not necessary in this case.

Huang et al. (2008) suggests a prediction algorithm based on fuzzy logic that aims at the prediction of a possible link break or a congested link which then triggers the construction of an alternate route. Similar to our algorithm, the prediction of a link break is based on the prediction of the future vehicle speed, the basis on which the predicted distance to the vehicle can be determined. This requires the generation of a fuzzy rule base that is then dynamically trained using Particle Swarm optimization (which in our approach is done using the adaptive filter for speed prediction). The authors use similar ideas in terms of the speed prediction but implements a fundamentally different concept. Furthermore, it is focussed on route break prediction and hence the performance of the isolated velocity prediction compared to our algorithm cannot be easily evaluated.

In Boukerche et al. (2009), the authors present some general thoughts on mobility prediction in vehicular networks and propose a simple prediction algorithm based on movement vectors in order to reduce the frequency of location beacons without introducing a higher mean error in respect to the positions used for routing packets. In Rezende et al. (2009), the same authors introduce the Network Neighbor Prediction protocol (NNP) that uses the results from their prior works to predict new routes that are going to be available in the near future and to calculate the lifetime of those routes that are currently in use. These works show in their simulation results that mobility prediction is a useful and necessary aspect in vehicular networks and should be researched in greater detail than it currently is.

Another approach, although developed in the context of a different problem, is described by Althoff et al. (2010). The authors compute the set of points that could be reached by vehicles within the prediction times, given the capabilities (minimum and maximum acceleration, yaw rate, etc). of the considered vehicles. The approach is computationally complex and requires a lot of contextual information.

Using the predicted position it should also be possible to predict the future connectivity to a certain extent using an appropriate channel model. In the context of vehicle-to-vehicle (V2V) communications, there is not yet a widely accepted channel model Paier et al. (2009). A common approach for characterizing a channel is to work out a theoretical channel model and then validate it against some appropriate measurements. Channel models are usually classified into stochastic and deterministic channel models, where deterministic channel models use ray tracing and similar techniques based on topological information about the environment in order to solve the the multi-path components (MPC) and derive a precise

channel characterization for a specific realization. Stochastic channel models, on the contrary, try to depict the statistics of the propagation channel in a more general sense that is not so much focussed on a particular situation. An intermittent approach is taken by geometry based channel models (as presented in Cheng et al. (2009)) that do use ray tracing; however, instead of using realistic modeling the calculations are based upon randomly placed objects.
In order to characterize a channel a number of parameters are used:

- The path loss exponent (PLE) α characterizes the average attenuation of the received signal.
- Large scale fading on the one hand refers to slow variations of received power due to shadowing by obstructing objects.
- Small scale fading on the other hand is caused by interference of different MPCs that result in fast fluctuations of the received power. Because these fluctuations are very hard to describe deterministically, they are usually described by means of statistics - most commonly by a Rayleigh distribution.
- In order to determine how much power is carried by the respective MPCs a power delay profile (PDP) is used. The spreading of the received pulse in the time division - often referred to as the channels delay dispersion - is best described in a statistical way by the root mean squared delay spread.
- Because MPCs travel on different paths they experience different Doppler shifts. The root mean square Doppler spread describes the resulting spectrum widening of the received pulse and thus the frequency dispersion.

A large amount of research has been dedicated to the wireless channel in cellular networks. However, looking at the specifics of a vehicular channel, especially in the V2V case it soon becomes clear that its characteristics differ significantly from those of a cellular channel. On the one hand, antennas of both sender and receiver are mounted close to the ground in V2V communications, where with cellular systems usually one of them is mounted high above. This tremendously influences the propagation path of the signals and thus the channel characteristics in terms of diffraction and reflection. On the other hand, communications between vehicles commonly use the 5.9 GHz band which behaves significantly different than the 700-2100 MHz signals used in cellular systems in terms of attenuation and diffraction. Most importantly though, sender and receiver are moving at relatively high speeds in V2V scenarios, which invalidates the assumption of stationarity of the channel characteristics that is commonplace in channel models of cellular systems. That refers not only to a changing impulse response but also to a change of its statistical properties (fading distribution, PDP and Doppler spectrum) Molisch et al. (2009). According to Maurer et al. (2004), Doppler shift and Doppler spread characterize the time-variant behavior of the V2V channel mostly due to movement of the communicating vehicles and the adjacent vehicles.
This section highlights and discusses some of the works into vehicular channel modeling in the context of connectivity prediction - a topic that has not yet received much attention in literature. In Matolak et al. (2006), the authors describe a statistical V2V channel model that is restricted to small scale fading. It uses a tapped delay line model, each tap representing a multi path components received with a certain delay. Each tap has an on/off switching process modeled by a first order Markov chain allowing for persistence parameterization. In general, taps with longer delays have less probability of being on due to their lower energy. Tap amplitudes are modeled using the Weibull distribution where different parameters are proposed for different taps, based on some measurements. The authors differentiate between

different scenarios, in some of which the Weibull parameters are "worse than Rayleigh" ($\beta < 2$), a phenomenon that is often called severe fading.

Maurer et al. present a geometry based IVC channel model in Maurer et al. (2004). They first try to model the dynamic road traffic and the environment adjacent to the road and then try to evaluate multi-path wave propagation through means of ray tracing. The road traffic model is based on the so called Wiedemann model and uses results from the authors previous works. As it seems very difficult to obtain real data with the necessary level of detail and the coverage, a stochastic model is utilized in order to place objects in the surroundings of the road. Different morphographic classes are defined for urban, suburban and highway scenarios that are assigned specific probabilities for different types of objects (trees, buildings, cars, bridges, traffic signs, etc.). Multi-path components are represented by rays, each of which can experience several propagation phenomena like diffraction or reflection. By calculating consecutive snapshots, a time-series of channel impulse responses can be obtained that classifies the channel for the current surrounding. The authors present measurements that validate the channel model with a standard deviation of less than 3 dB in both line-of-sight (LOS) and non-line-of-sight (NLOS) scenarios.

Paier et al. (2009) presents some measurements of V2V propagation in suburban driving conditions using GPS receivers. The authors on the one hand derive both a single slope and a dual slope path loss model from their results where the better dual slope model achieves deviations between 2.6 and 5.6 dB compared to the measured path loss. However, they find that received power is significantly less if no LOS propagation is possible. Fading on the other hand is modeled using a Nakagami distribution with variable parameters as already proposed in other works. While the distribution is Rician $\beta > 2$ as long as a LOS component is present, it turns out that fading can be "worse than Rayleigh" $\beta < 2$ once the LOS connection is lost intermittently at large distances between transmitter and receiver. Furthermore, the authors propose that the Doppler spread is dependent on the effective speed and the distance between transmitter and receiver. The dependance on distance is explained by the increasing number of scatterers at larger distances. Using this dependence, the authors present the speed-separation diagram that can help predict the expected Doppler spread and thus small scale fading characteristics at a certain distance.

In Molisch et al. (2009), the authors provide a survey on V2V channel models and measurements based on a variety of previous works on the subjects, some of which have already been discussed here. We recommend this paper as an introductory reading on the subject as it introduces important factors for channel characterization and includes a table that summarizes important parameters gathered from multiple measurement campaigns. Important aspects like environment characterization and antenna placements are also discussed that we omit here. One important result from the evaluated measurements is that at least path loss coefficients in V2V communication channels are rather similar to well-known cellular systems as long as a LOS connection is given. In terms of small-scale fading and Doppler spread, the results go alongside those presented in Paier et al. (2009). The authors finally conclude that the amount of comparable measurements carried out on V2V channels is too insignificant in order to allow the formulation of a channel model that resembles the real-world V2V channel and important aspects such as antenna placement and shadowing by adjacent vehicles have not yet been sufficiently explored.

Following this conclusion, an adequate prediction of channel quality seems challenging. Analogous to position prediction, an estimation of channel quality can be seen as a trade-off between computational complexity and prediction accuracy. An approach involving ray-tracing similar to the one presented in Matolak et al. (2006) on the one hand produces rather adequate results if provided with the necessary extent of details concerning the surrounding environment (including moving and parked vehicles), building geometries, plants and road signs. However, it seems unrealistic and infeasible to supply an on-board connectivity prediction engine with this amount of knowledge. Measurements suggest a dual-slope model for the path loss exponent as a very simple approach. Small-scale fading is usually modeled using statistical models with strong dependency upon separation distance which limits the possibilities of a prediction to a qualitative worst case approximation. Paier et al. (2009) also identifies significant differences between LOS and NLOS cases in both path loss and fading statistics.

A sophisticated approach to predict the path loss exponent using a particle filter has been proposed in Rodas & Cascon (2010), based on a log-normal fading channel model in wireless sensor networks. Particles are initialized in a random state with their respective weights being iteratively updated to provide an estimation of the path loss exponent. Weak particles with low weights are periodically replaced to avoid degeneration. The filter is parameterized with the type of the fading distribution and its variance. The authors, too, show that the PLE changes significantly as soon as the LOS is lost.

3. Problem statement

In Nagel (2010b), we have outlined how QoS provisioning based on a network's connectivity can be attained. The basis for the computation is the connectivity matrix $\underset{\sim}{\mathbf{C}}$ that describes the communication relations between n networked nodes. Let $\chi(\underline{\mathbf{x}}_i, \underline{\mathbf{x}}_j)$ denote the channel function, taking as parameters the physical positions $\underline{\mathbf{x}}$ of two vehicles in the environment. A very basic channel function could then read:

$$\chi(\underline{\mathbf{x}}_i, \underline{\mathbf{x}}_j) = \begin{cases} 1 & \text{if } \left\| \underline{\mathbf{x}}_i - \underline{\mathbf{x}}_j \right\| \leq r \\ 0 & \text{otherwise} \end{cases} \tag{1}$$

This means that two vehicles i and j are connected if they are located closer than the radio range r; if they are located further apart, they are not connected. The connectivity matrix $\underset{\sim}{\mathbf{C}}$ is then defined as:

$$\underset{\sim}{\mathbf{C}} = (c_{ij}),\ c_{ij} = \chi(\underline{\mathbf{x}}_i, \underline{\mathbf{x}}_j) \tag{2}$$

Every node i is allowed to inject *(source)* traffic amounting to s_i into the network. Multiplying the source vector $\underline{\mathbf{s}}$ with the connectivity matrix results in the load vector $\underline{\mathbf{l}}$:

$$\underline{\mathbf{l}} = \underset{\sim}{\mathbf{C}}\,(\underline{\mathbf{1}} + \underline{\mathbf{s}}) \tag{3}$$

We have shown that the QoS criterion is fulfilled if the injected traffic is dimensioned so that each entry in the load vector l_i does not exceed a certain pre-defined threshold. For more detail, especially on the distributed algorithm, the reader be referred to the original paper. The problem with this approach, however, is that $\underline{\mathbf{s}}|_{t_0}$ is only valid for the current connectivity matrix $\underset{\sim}{\mathbf{C}}|_{t_0}$. As it is desirable to fulfill the QoS criterion over a certain time Δt, we first need to predict the future physical positions of the vehicles, estimate the channel function and then deduce the prospective future connectivity matrix:

$$\underset{\sim}{\mathbf{C}}|_{t_0+\Delta t} = \Bigg(\underbrace{\chi|_{t_0+\Delta t}}_{\substack{\text{Channel}\\ \text{Estimation}}} \underbrace{\left(\underline{\mathbf{x}}_i|_{t_0+\Delta t}, \underline{\mathbf{x}}_j|_{t_0+\Delta t}\right)}_{\substack{\text{Mobility}\\ \text{Prediction}}} \Bigg) \tag{4}$$

After that, the future source vector can be computed (Equation 3) and a decision can be made whether the current demand can be satisfied under the future network conditions and consequently, adequate measures can be taken.

4. Mobility prediction

Generally, the spatial behavior of a vehicle is defined by two factors: On the one hand, speed and direction are controlled by the driver who adapts to the environment and the current situation. On the other hand, movement of a car is restricted to roads so the surrounding road topology is the major limiting factor. This is the key criterion that simplifies location prediction for vehicles compared to regular mobile users. Cars are usually not allowed to travel anywhere, they are bound to a relatively small portion of the world, the lanes. Combined with a small memory of past positions, the current velocity and direction of movement can be calculated. This further limits the amount of available future positions, as cars are usually not expected to u turn spontaneously and velocity changes are bounded by the maximum deceleration and the maximum acceleration.

4.1 Concept

The prerequisite for the prediction is knowledge about a vehicle's current position, direction of movement and the surrounding road topology. The latter is provided by digital street maps (available, for instance, through the OpenStreetMap Project). All of these factors are very stable in terms of prediction. The destination or rather the mission of the car is assumed to be unknown to the algorithm, so at a crossroads basically all directions seem equally probable. The velocity of a car, however, is far less stable and predictable as it is directly controlled by the user and indirectly influenced by environmental factors such as traffic density, road signs and the weather. Especially abrupt speed changes are almost impossible to predict as they are often unexpected, even to the driver himself. The algorithm is sketched in Figure 1.

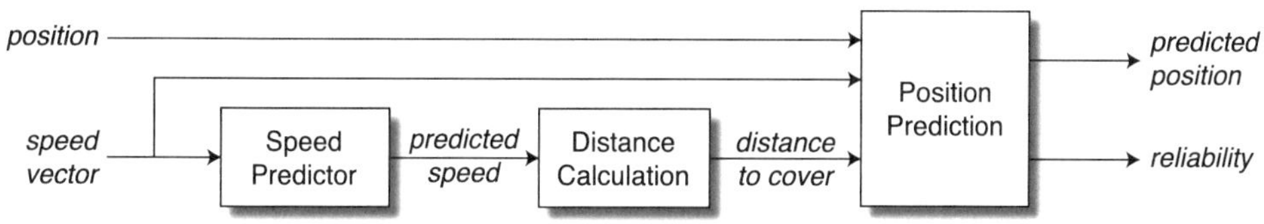

Fig. 1. Algorithm Outline

For speed prediction, we use a filter based approach that employs concepts of adaptive filters initially developed to adapt to varying channel conditions in wireless communications. Like the channel characteristics change depending on the environment, the speed change behavior of a car or rather its driver adapts to various environmental factors. This includes urban scenarios with steep velocity slopes and rural roads with fairly constant speeds. The character of the driver and the performance of the car also influence the prediction to a certain extent and are automatically taken into account by the adaptive filter. A self adapting finite impulse response (FIR) filter approach based on a least mean squares (LMS) algorithm with relatively low depth seems ideal to adapt to both the personal behavior of a driver and the current situation. Using past and current velocities, an ideal weight vector for the past situation is calculated. Due to the low depth of the filter, the weight vector is rather unstable and consequently, it is combined with both the mean weight vector over the last iterations and a "boost" vector to improve reactivity at steep slopes. The resulting weight vector is then used

to predict the future velocity, which is in turn used to calculate the distance covered in the desired interval.
The distance to cover, together with the current position and direction of movement, forms the input for the position predictor that outputs the predicted future location of the vehicle. In some cases, multiple positions are possible, for instance due to a crossroads between the current and the future position. In that case, the position that seems most probable to the algorithm is used as an output; however, internally a list of all possible locations is generated. In many situations, predominantly with cars traveling in sparsely populated areas or on highways, the prediction is rather reliable. In urban areas prediction reliability is reduced by intersections where a sudden change of direction can occur and a certain amount of past predictions may be invalidated. To make applications aware of such differences, an additional output variable was added to resemble the estimated reliability of the output.

4.2 Input data

The algorithm requires a number of input data:

Position data: Obviously, the algorithm requires knowledge about the actual position of a vehicle and a timestamp. The position data used in the performance analysis has been downloaded from the "GPS Tracks" section of the OpenStreetMap online portal. Selected tracks were chosen that were provided by users around the globe and thus constitute a rather broad basis of real life data. Additionally, own traces have been used. The temporal resolution of the recorded tracks was or has been resampled to one second. A statement about the spatial resolution is not generally possible as different positioning hardware from various vendors has been used for the sample data. However, we shall assume a positioning accuracy of a few meters.

Map data: Also, the algorithm needs to be provided with map data of the area surrounding the actual position. This data, too, is provided by and downloaded from the open source OpenStreetMap project. It basically consists of an array of so-called nodes that are uniquely identified and reference a GPS position by latitude and longitude. A street is constructed by a list of subsequent nodes, forming a polyline that represents the shape of the street. Actual contiguous roads may be split apart, for instance if the name of a street changes or if two streets merge, on intersections etc.

Number of steps to predict: The major parameter influencing the algorithm. It is common in most parts of the algorithm and hence introduced in the high level diagram. Many parts of the algorithm also refer to it as n. Depending on the input data, the usual assumption is that one timestep equals one second. Most of the evaluations were done using a medium interval of prediction of 8 seconds - however results using different values are discussed in section 6.4.

4.3 Speed predictor

A car typically moves in different classes of environments: urban, suburban, peripheral and highway. Each of those has different characteristics concerning the speed change of a car. On a highway speed changes are rare but usually with rather steep slopes whereas in urban areas, the speed is hardly ever constant for more than a few seconds. This allows for two different approaches in implementing a speed prediction algorithm. On the one hand, specialized algorithms could be engineered for all of the above scenarios and another algorithm that determines the algorithm that is most appropriate in an actual situation. In typical situations one would expect such an approach to give very accurate results, but clearly there are many

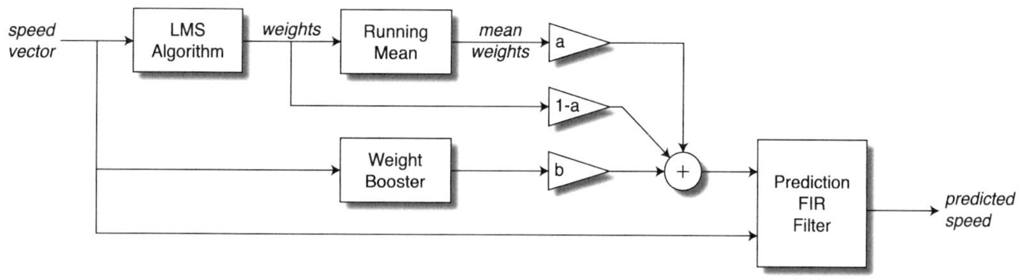

Fig. 2. Speed Predictor Structure

situations where none of the implementations will be adequate. Furthermore, this approach involves increased efforts in development because multiple algorithms need to be designed and there is a high number of factors influencing the situation that are hard to quantize.
On the other hand, it seems more appropriate to design an algorithm that automatically adapts to changing situations and as such can also adapt to factors like driver attitude and others mentioned above. This introduces some delay caused by the responsiveness of the adaption algorithm, but works also in an environment that cannot be properly classified into one of the above scenarios. In some situations, especially with quickly varying conditions, this may result in weaker performance than the approach discussed above, but the overall performance is expected to be better with less development efforts. A solution for this approach is discussed in the next sections.

4.3.1 Structure

The signal flow graph of the speed prediction is shown in Figure 2. The input variables are the current speed of the car and the number of steps n to predict. The only output is the predicted speed for the given time frame.

Prediction FIR Filter: The actual prediction is done in an FIR filter on the right hand side of the signal flow plan. It uses the current speed and a weight vector to predict the velocity from the last speed values. The length of the weight vector is given by the depth of the FIR filter in the evaluations performed here a depth of 12 was used.

LMS algorithm: The most important building block. It is the adaptive part of the algorithm and calculates an ideal weight vector from its two input values the current velocity forms the desired signal, a delayed version forms the input for the algorithm. The weight vector is adapted with a fixed step size in the direction of steepest descent in order to achieve the minimum square error and, at the same time, limit the dynamics of the weight vector.The weight vector is recalculated each time step, for more details see Benvenuto & Cherubini (2002); Guillemin et al. (1971).

Mean Weight: Because the weight vector generated by the *LMS algorithm* is very reactive to acceleration and deceleration processes, it is averaged by a running mean block that calculates the mean weight vector over the length of the situation. Both the mean and the LMS weight vector are combined into a slowed weight vector by multiplication with the parameter a or $1 - a$ respectively.

Weight Booster: The LMS algorithm adapts to new situations with a delay that is roughly its depth l plus the length of the prediction interval n, which equals the number of memory elements involved in the adaption. A change in velocity needs to pass through most of the memory elements before its effect becomes visible in the weight vector. For instance, for

parameter	example value	description
n	8	number of steps to predict
l	12	depth of FIR filters and dimension of weights vector
a	0.275	influence of the mean weights vector
b	2	influence of weight booster
c	0.2	boost limit
d	1	boost gain

Table 1. Speed Prediction Parameters with example values used during development

a car traveling in a city, the weight vector produces rather stable results while the car is traveling at a constant speed but it will react slowly to sharp braking or fast acceleration. The algorithm is designed to fix this problem by manipulating the weight vector in order to emphasize the most recent speed history elements to react more quickly to a spontaneous change in behavior: a length l base vector is multiplied with a scalar calculated from the slope of the velocity curve and is bounded above by the boost limit c. In order for the impact of the booster to remain present for a longer period, the generated "impulse" is broadened using a unity-weight FIR filter.

4.3.2 Parameters

The performance and precision of the speed predictor depends on some fundamental parameters that are summarized in Table 1. The given values are the result of some evaluations during the design phase based on few exemplary scenarios and should give a rough idea to start an implementation. However for a proper implementation a more thorough, numerical optimization is recommended but out of scope of this essay.
It is important to note that all of the below parameters influence the prediction in a way that usually makes adoptions to all parameters necessary if one parameter is changed. In many cases more than one possibility exists that can lead to a desired result for one scenario, but looking at multiple scenarios usually only one if any of the possibilities lead to an overall improvement of performance.

Number of steps to predict (n): This key parameter determines the number of steps to be predicted — $n = 8$ means the algorithm predicts the speed in 8 time steps. Obviously a higher value increases the prediction error, whereas lower values gives more precise predictions. The setting of this parameter is very important because its influence on the other parameters is tremendous, for instance a high value for n will on the one hand require a higher a and on the other hand require more influence of the weight booster, b. Also, this parameter is common with all components of the algorithm, so its influence has to be regarded globally. Different settings and their impact, especially on position prediction, are discussed in section 6.4.

Depth of FIR filters (l): The FIR filters' depth used in the speed predictor is a common value because all blocks share the weight vector. Also the parameter l is, unlike all other parameters mentioned here, a design time parameter that cannot be changed easily as it is hard-coded into the FIR filters and the constants. Nevertheless, its influence on the prediction should be discussed here.
For the fact that the depth of a filter resembles its amount of memory elements, higher values for l give more stable and less reactive prediction results. Changes in the situation need more time to propagate through the memory elements, hence it takes a longer time

to adapt to changes. Smaller values for l improve reaction time but also result in less stable and more fluctuating predictions that often overshoot at slight changes.

Influence of the Mean Weights Vector (a): The weight vector in the standard case (disregarding the weight booster) is combined from the current weight vector produced by the LMS algorithm and its running average. Setting a to the maximal appropriate value $a = 1$ produces a very stable weight vector but also removes the direct influence of the LMS algorithm to the weight vector and thus the reactivity. This is caused by the fact that in this model, the mean weight vector is never reset and thus provides an "all time average".

Influence of the Weight Booster (b): This parameter determines the overall influence of the weight booster. Higher values tend to produce overshoots as a trade-off to slow response to a change in situation if lower values are used. Generally all three values influencing the weight booster should be tuned according to the length of the prediction n. With high n, b should be increased because a faster reaction is necessary due to the latency of the LMS algorithm.

Boost Limit (c): The "boost" vector, or more precisely its scalar values, are influenced by the slope of the velocity curve. The "boost limit" defines an upper bound to those scalar values.

Boost Gain (d): This parameter multiplies the influence of the slope difference before the broadening and limiting of the pulse. Thus a higher value generates very quick increase once a steep slope is detected - in other words, it pushes the boost weight vector more quickly to the limit. Lower values produce a smoother response to steep velocity slopes.

4.4 Distance calculation

The speed predictor predicts the vehicle speed some time steps ahead. The position predictor in turn requires as an input the distance to cover in the next time steps to calculate the future position. The most precise approach is to predict a velocity value for each time step in the prediction period and sum up the difference. Because this requires a set of n speed predictors which increases the computational efforts by n, a simpler approach is chosen in this implementation. Our algorithm uses the current speed and the predicted speed and calculates a linear approximation between the two. The distance to cover s is then the area under the speed curve for a duration of t (n time steps):

$$s = t \cdot \left[v_{current} + 0.5 \cdot \left(v_{pred} - v_{current}\right)\right]$$

4.5 Position predictor

The position predictor uses the current position and direction of movement, digital map data as well as the predicted distance to cover as inputs and outputs a predicted position and its reliability. It is invoked once per time step and tries to first find the current road segment of the vehicle, then determines a number of possible prediction paths and finally chooses the most probable path and returns its end point.

4.5.1 Determine current road segment

All known nearby road segments (taken from the digital map) are evaluated for the distance of the current position to the closest point on the respective road segment. Three criteria must be met in order for a road segment to be chosen:

1. The distance to the closest point is smaller than a threshold.
2. The absolute value of the difference between the direction of movement and the road segment's direction is not larger than $\pi/2$ because vehicles usually do not move perpendicular to streets.
3. It is the closest road segment satisfying both criteria 1 and 2.

In case no road segment is found that fulfills all of the above criteria, the algorithm returns the current position as prediction result with an estimated accuracy of 0%. Possible causes range from wrong GPS positions during the initialization phase of the GPS device and inexact map material to driving or parking on streets or private property that is not (yet) included in the map material.

4.5.2 Determine possible paths

First, the remaining distance from the current position to the respective end point of the road segment s_r is calculated. If the road segment's end point is further away than the distance to cover ($s_r \geq s$), the predicted position will be located between the current position and the road segment's end point. Therefore, the predicted position is determined along the road segment's polyline towards the end point, covering the given distance s.
In the case that the remaining distance s_r is smaller than the distance to cover ($s_r < s$), the predicted position is moved to the road segment's end point and that distance is subtracted from the remaining distance. Subsequently, the next road segment of the prediction path is determined. If the mission of the vehicle is known in advance, the next road segment is chosen according to that mission. Otherwise, in order to find the next road segment, the number of possibilities is determined from the digital map: at a junction, all connected street segments are considered possible candidates. The current road segment, however, is not considered as an alternative — in other words, the vehicle is not expected to u-turn. Three cases exist:

(a) No candidates exist, so the current road segment ends in a node that has no other road segments referenced. In this case the relative probability of the current path is decreased in the relation to the amount of distance already covered.

(b) One candidate means there is no choice and the vehicle is moving along a road without an intersection at the current node. Determining the next road segment and updating the path accordingly is trivial.

(c) Multiple candidates are available, so the predicted path hits some kind of intersection. Hence the process of determining the next road segment becomes a bit more complex: Initially, all candidates must be assumed to be equally probable.

The procedure is repeated recursively until all distance s is covered and all possible paths of length s have been determined (effectively yielding a tree of possible road segments, with leaves at all possible future locations).

4.5.3 Pick best path

It may be desirable for an application that the prediction comprises all possible future realizations. However, if the prediction routine should return the future position along only one predicted path, the best of the alternative paths found must be chosen. If the mission of an observed vehicle is unknown to the algorithm, it must more or less issue a guess as to what option the driver of a car will go for. The range of alternatives is narrowed down in three steps:

(a) Estimated probability: In the current implementation of the algorithm, this first step will only remove the paths that end in a *dead end* and hence have a reduced relative probability. All other paths are considered equally probable and hence cannot be classified by their probability. For instance, the car hits an intersection with three alternatives, one of which being a dead end street. The dead end would be removed from the candidates, whilst the other two possibilities are equally probable.

(b) Way Changes: The number of street changes is the primary decision criterion for the algorithm. It is assumed that in case multiple paths exist, the driver stays on the current street. Hence the path with the least number of street changes is favored for the prediction. It is furthermore assumed that if it is necessary to change the road at some stage in all paths, the driver still stays on the current road as long as possible.

(c) Direction Difference: Should the way change criteria be unable to choose one candidate, the total difference of direction along the path is considered. Assuming the driver to be lazy, the path encountering the least change in direction is chosen to be the best path.

Clearly, criteria (b) and (c) do not increase the probability of a certain path. These are merely decision criteria in order to choose one path from multiple options. Choosing a random path statistically produces the same error, but has a severe disadvantage in terms of continuity: as the algorithm is executed each time step, it should return consistent values from one step to the next; when using a random selection, it is most likely that the algorithm will return a completely different position each time it is invoked. From a statistical point of view, this does not change much but for another program or algorithm that is based on the results of the prediction it may very well change things depending on the application. For the very same reason, it is very important for the algorithm to return the estimated probability of a given prediction because another program can then classify the prediction accordingly.

5. Channel prediction

It is clear from Equation 4 that the network's future connectivity does not only depend on the future vehicles' positions. An adequate channel model has to be chosen and constantly updated to reflect the changing radio environment. In Equation 1, we have shown an exemplary simple channel function, the *disc model*. We shall call two nodes i and j connected if the path loss $\beta(d)$, a function of the distance between the two nodes, does not exceed a certain threshold β_t:

$$\beta_t \overset{!}{>} \beta(d) = 20\log_{10}\frac{4\pi d_0}{\lambda} + 10\alpha\log_{10}\frac{d}{d_0} \tag{5}$$

The path loss consists of two components: a constant addend that reflects the loss related to the wavelength of the signal and a distance-dependent term that represents the propagation of the radio wave through space and the resulting diminishment of power due to the growth of the wave sphere's surface. Due to various propagation effects, the path loss exponent (PLE) α is variable, to reflect various environments' radio properties (and usually ranges between 2 and 3). To account for reflections, scattering and shadowing, an additional stochastic variable β_s is introduced that is log-normally distributed with zero mean and variance σ^2:

$$\underbrace{\beta(d)}_{\text{measured}} = C + \underbrace{10\alpha}_{\text{unknown}}\log_{10}\underbrace{\frac{d}{d_0}}_{\text{known}} + \underbrace{\beta_s}_{\text{unknown}} \tag{6}$$

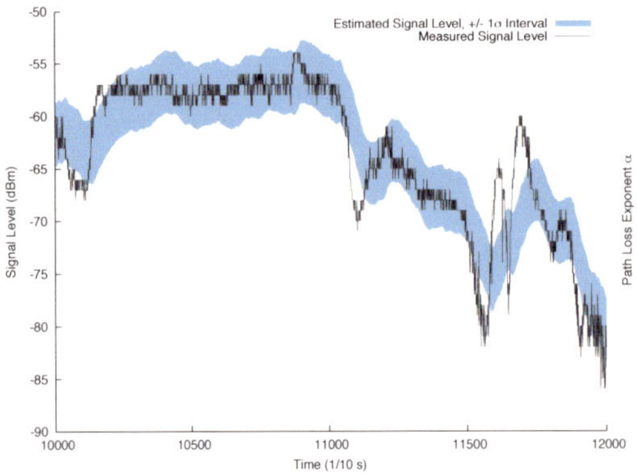

(a)

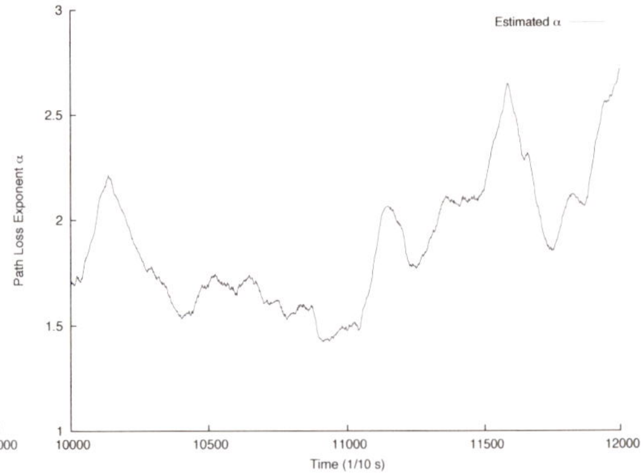

(b)

Fig. 3. Parameter estimation using particle filter: measured and estimated signal level, estimated PLE

Through constant exchange of position messages, two nodes can determine their distance d and at the same time measure the path loss $\beta(d)$ between them (terms marked as "known"). Assuming that β_s is log-normally distributed and knowing the order of magnitude of the variance, we suggest to use a particle filter for online estimation of the PLE α and subsequent prediction, analogous to the work presented in Rodas & Cascon (2010). To study the vehicular channel, we have recorded and evaluated several hours of measurements. Figure 3(a) shows the measured path loss (solid line) and the path loss computed using the estimated PLE plus β_s's 68% (one standard deviation) confidence interval (filled curve). The standard deviation of the measured signal level was estimated around 3 dB, the system constant C was -42 dB and the duration of the displayed dataset is 20 seconds. The estimated PLE is shown in Figure 3(b). For connectivity prediction, we propose to employ the same concepts as used for position prediction to at least estimate the trend of the PLE. Furthermore, as we have discussed in the section on related work, it is very important to distinguish between LOS and NLOS conditions. In Nagel & Eichler (2008), we have introduced a method for V2V channel simulation in environments that include objects that possibly obstruct a direct LOS path and have discussed how a dual-slope channel model can be implemented to account for these objects. Consequently, we propose to complement the path loss formula in Equation 6 accordingly and incorporate the information on buildings and other obstacles from the digital map material (that is already used in the position prediction) to determine if the path between the predicted future vehicle positions is LOS or not. The propagation breakpoint derived from the map should then be accounted for in the PLE estimation. In simulations, we have realized quite accurate channel parameter estimations using a particle filter that accounts for LOS and NLOS conditions, based on information about surrounding radio obstacles.

It is, however, clear that the effects of large-scale fading have a large impact on the future connectivity but are hard to account for. Due to positioning errors, it is virtually impossible to predict small-scale fading effects. When evaluating the connectivity matrix computed from the predicted positions and the predicted channel, additional information about the reliability of the prediction should be provided and accounted for.

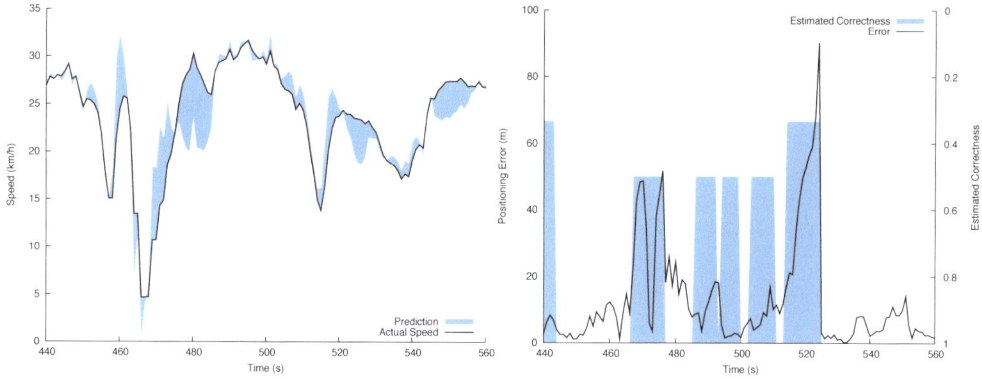

(a) Velocity prediction (b) Prediction error

Fig. 4. City Scenario

6. Results

Three representative scenarios were chosen for the performance evaluation of the developed algorithm. These scenarios are based on GPS tracks downloaded from the OSM portal that were selected to provide maximum diversity in the results presented below: the chosen tracks were recorded in a city as well as in suburban and highway surroundings. We have evaluated the three scenarios concerning the accuracy of both the speed prediction and the resulting predicted position under the three different environmental settings.

6.1 City scenario

The first data set represents a typical city scenario. It has been recorded in the german city of Herne in the Ruhr area, with speeds of up to 50 kilometers per hour and a total length of about 20 minutes.

Figure 4(a) shows a section of the actual vehicle speed (solid line), the area of the filled curve reflects the velocity prediction error where the upper or lower edge of the area marks the predicted speed. For easy comparison, the predicted values are shifted by 8 seconds, so that the real value and the value that has been predicted for that instant are matched in time. The results show that especially at steep slopes, the algorithm overshoots significantly and predicts too low or too high velocity values. This could be tuned using the parameters of the speed prediction in order to achieve better performance in the particular scenario, but the impact on other scenarios is hard to estimate and thus requires significant research efforts.

Figure 8(a) shows the distribution function of the position prediction error in meters (upper blue line). The mean error is 13.4 meters, the median amounts to 7.5 meters. Figure 4(b) shows a section of the prediction error over time; the filled curve represents the estimated probability (correctness) of the prediction. Note that the second Y axis has been reversed for better readability.

As explained in section 4.5, the estimated probability generally equals 1 if the position predictor identifies only one possible path for the vehicle, based on the map data. In the presented case that the mission or route of the car are unknown to the algorithm, the choice of the path used for prediction is arbitrary once it encounters p multiple possible paths. Hence the estimated probability drops to $1/p$. This, in turn, means that if a large error occurs while the estimated probability is 1, an error in the position predictor or the map material should

be assumed, while high prediction errors with low estimated probability are most likely to be produced by the fact that the mission of the car is unclear.
Should the position predictor be either unable to find the current segment or to find any path to continue, the estimated prediction probability drops to zero. This is the case at the beginning of the city scenario and is the result of pulling out of a private parking area in a sort of backyard. As there is no map material covering that area, the position predictor cannot give useful predictions based on the fact that it is unclear on which road the vehicle is driving. In such situations, the position predictor simply returns the current position.

(a) Intersection (time step 500) (b) T-Intersection (time step 200)

Fig. 5. Scenario 1 - Prediction Behaviour at Crossroads

To get an idea of the nature of an error, it is helpful to visualize the real and the predicted path as shown in Figure 5. The actual path is shown as a black solid line while the predicted path is shown as a dashed orange line.
Around time step 520, Figure 5(a) shows a typical situation in which the prediction algorithm encounters a crossroads. For the reasons explained in Section 4.5, the algorithm always prefers to choose the path that continues on the current road. This can be seen in the Figure where the predicted green dots continue straight on, while the real, blue trace turns onto the intersecting road. Once the car is on the new road, the prediction adapts to the new situation and continues its prediction along the new road. This can also be seen in Figure 4(b), where the error peaks due to the large discrepancy between the real and the predicted position. At the same time, the estimated probability drops to 0.33, due to the fact that the algorithm recognizes three alternative paths at the intersection. Figure 5(b) shows a similar example around time step 200 as the car moves towards a T-crossing. The algorithm chooses the path with the lowest total change in angle, which in this case is the wrong choice. This, again, results in a drop of the estimated probability and a peaking error.
As can be seen from the examples above, the high error in urban scenarios is widely based on the fact that usually many intersections lie along the path and high prediction errors are introduced if the algorithm chooses the wrong path. We have argued that this fact can be significantly improved if the cars mission is known to the position predictor and, consequently, the correct path can be used for the prediction.

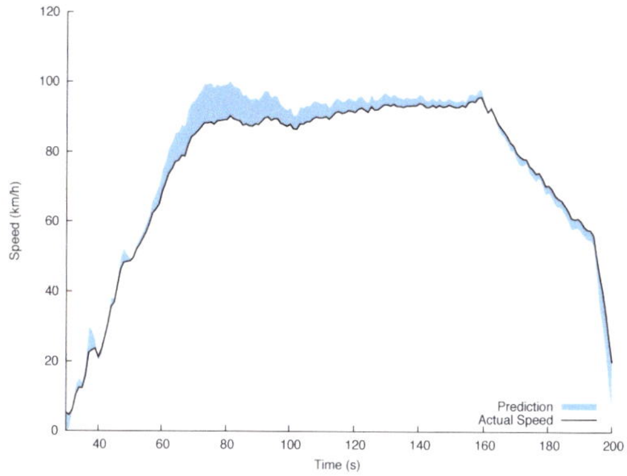

(a) Velocity prediction

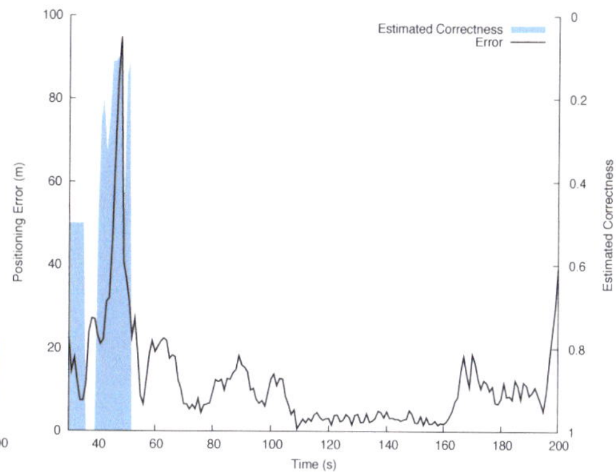

(b) Prediction error

Fig. 6. Suburban Scenario

This also implies that the mean prediction error is not a very good metric in order to assess the precision of the prediction. The algorithm may predict the cars position with an error of less that five meters in cases where there are no intersections, but at each intersection an error of up to 50 meters is possible that will greatly influence the mean error. A more suitable metric to identify the amount of such situations in the scenario is the discrepancy between the mean error and the weighted mean error that includes the estimated probability. The weighted mean error is simply the mean over the prediction error, multiplied with the estimated probability. Because the estimated probability drops at intersections, a prediction error in this situation is weighted less than an error occurring along a straight, intersection-free road. The weighted mean error in this situation amounts to about 7.4 meters, which is significantly less than the mean error of 13.4 meters and therefore shows that the prediction quality could be greatly improved with knowledge of the cars future route.

6.2 Suburban scenario

The second scenario covers the suburban area of Wiener Neustadt in Austria. The driver first hits the B17 road and afterwards enters the suburban area where the car is parked at a shopping center.

The section of the velocity graph in Figure 6(a) shows a short drive to the highway like state road. The speed prediction is rather stable whilst traveling at constant speeds between second 50 and second 200. This is accompanied by a rather small prediction error as shown in Figure 6(b). A peak in the prediction error at second 40 occurs due to a wrong choice of the next segment - again based on the fact that the cars mission is unknown. The fact that the algorithm had the choice of multiple directions is visualized by a significant drop of the estimated correctness curve.

Due to a very sharp deceleration around second 200, Figure 6(b) shows another peak without a drop in probability for the fact that no other possible directions are identified. The reason for the braking is unclear, an explanation cannot be found in the map material nor the satellite image of the area. Figure 6(b) also shows a few more peaks based on decisions for the wrong directions and braking actions.

The distribution function shown in Figure 8(b) (upper blue line) is slightly flatter than the one from scenario 1. The median error (about 10 meters) is slightly higher than in the city,

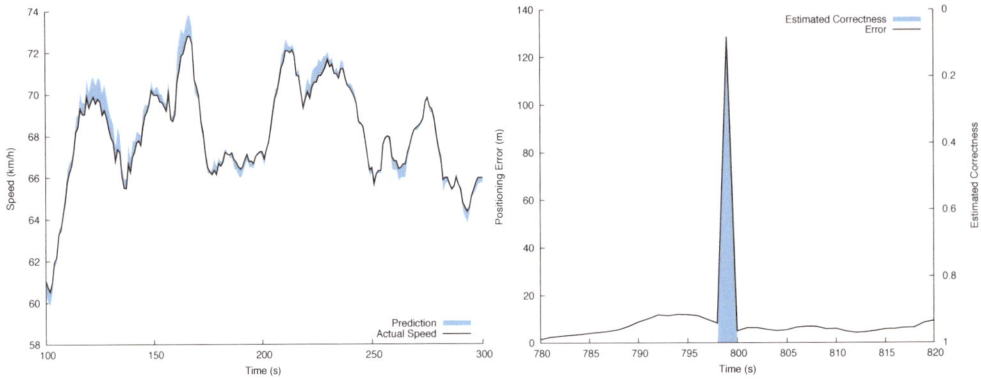

(a) Velocity prediction (b) Prediction error

Fig. 7. Highway Scenario

probably caused by the fact that either map material or the GPS device used to record the track are less precise than in the city scenario. The 90% percentile is significantly smaller (22 meters compared to 34 meters), which supports the before assumption and leads to the conclusion that the overall position prediction is better in the suburban scenario. The mean error of 13.5 meters, however, is almost identical to the city scenario.

6.3 Highway scenario

The third scenario covers a ride on a highway near the English town of Cambridge during rush hour traffic, which explains the unsteady velocity curve shown in Figure 7(a). Again, a representative section has been chosen for presentation.

The prediction error plotted in Figure 7(b) shows constantly low prediction errors. From the distribution function shown in Figure 8(c) (upper blue line) reveals a very steep slope, which means excellent performance of the algorithm as more than 95% of all errors are below 10 meters. The mean error amounts to only 4.6 meters and the median is 3.8 meters.

One notable peak of the error, accompanied by a drop in the estimated probability occurs around time step 800 (see Figure 7(b)). At the instant when the car is crossing a highway bridge the algorithm wrongly chooses the current road segment to be part of the road below the bridge that shares a node with the highway. Consequently, the algorithm chooses the wrong road segment to continue prediction. This error is caused by an unfortunate combination of a small measuring error of the GPS device and an imprecision of the map material, where the highway shares a node with the intersecting road (although they are on different levels).

Another error source stems from the fact that in the used map material, a road is represented by a polyline, and all vehicles are assumed to be positioned on this line. In reality, highways consists of a number of parallel lanes that have a certain lateral displacement. Although a suitable representation of road lanes has been suggested, the data available today does not yet represent different lanes. We expect, however, that the error would be decreased if this information could be accounted for in the prediction.

6.4 Influence of prediction length

The results that we have discussed above were obtained through prediction with period lengths of eight seconds. This sections evaluates the same scenarios with longer prediction lengths of 16 and 32 seconds. The resulting position error distribution functions are shown in Figure 8.

The steepness of the distribution functions decrease as the prediction length increases, due to less prediction accuracy across a longer period of time, i.e., the tendency to produce greater errors. The maximum error also increases dramatically, because in case that a wrong path is chosen, the prediction continues along the wrong path for a much longer time before it is corrected as the car turns the other way. The mean error is also shifted towards higher values with increasing prediction intervals.

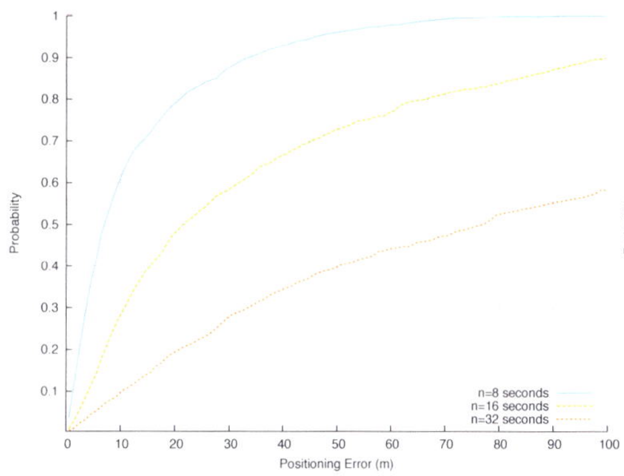

(a) Scenario 1 - City

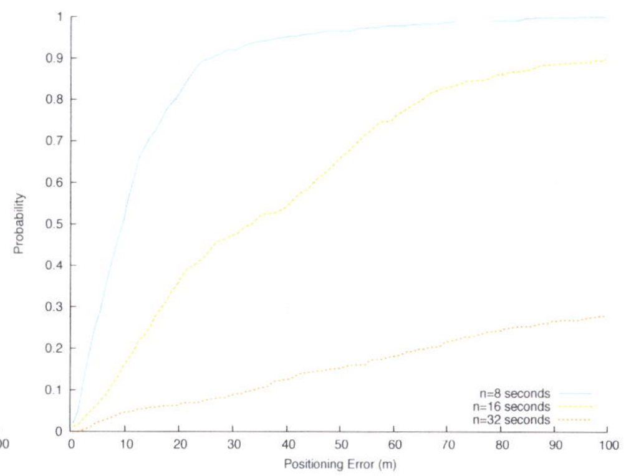

(b) Scenario 2 - Suburban

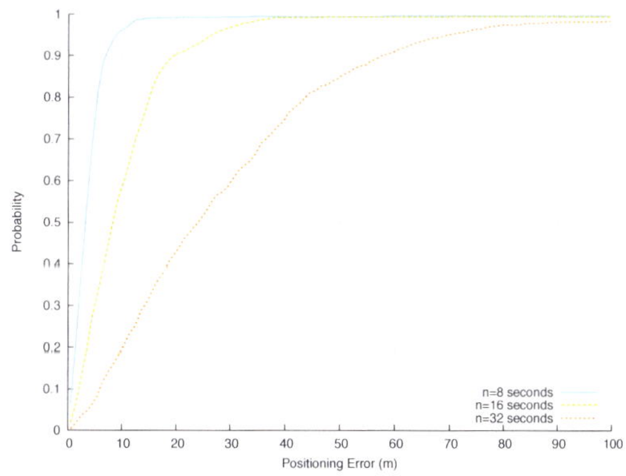

(c) Scenario 3 - Highway

Fig. 8. Prediction Error Histogram - Different Prediction Lengths

In the city and suburban scenarios, the prediction is already significantly less reliable with $n = 16$ time steps (i.e., seconds) as a prediction interval. It is rendered basically useless with a prediction interval of $n = 32$ and the majority of errors are out of scale of the histogram. The highway scenario, however, behaves much more stable as the prediction interval is increased and still returns useful results using a prediction horizon of 32 seconds. To a large extent, this is based on the relatively stable velocities and absent alternative paths along the way.

6.5 Path loss estimation error

To determine the future connectivity of a network, a node has to predict the positions of all relevant vehicles (usually the one- or two-hop radio neighborhood) and determine the resulting path loss to decide whether it will be connected to this vehicle or not. The first error source of the path loss estimation is, of course, the error induced by inaccurate position prediction. Fortunately, this error term strongly depends on the distance d between the two involved vehicles. Let us assume that the estimating vehicle has perfect ego positioning and position prediction and let Δd denote the maximum positioning error. The resulting absolute estimation error range is then:

$$\begin{aligned} \Delta\beta(d, \Delta d) &= \beta(d + \Delta d) - \beta(d - \Delta d) \\ &= 10\alpha \log_{10}\left(\frac{d + \Delta d}{d - \Delta d}\right) \end{aligned} \quad (7)$$

The second influence on path loss estimation is the accuracy of the predicted path loss exponent. Let $\Delta\alpha$ denote the PLE's maximum estimation error. The resulting absolute path loss estimation error is:

$$\begin{aligned} \Delta\beta(d, \Delta\alpha) &= \beta(d, \alpha + \Delta\alpha) - \beta(d, \alpha - \Delta\alpha) \\ &= 20\Delta\alpha \log_{10}\left(\frac{d}{d_0}\right) \end{aligned} \quad (8)$$

Clearly, there exists a strong negative correlation between the path loss estimation error and the distance to the tracked vehicle, d. With increasing d, the implications of prediction errors become less important with respect to the path loss. The situation is contrary regarding the PLE estimation: because the relation is linear, a large path loss estimation error results if the distance d to the tracked vehicle increases. The problem is that Δd and $\Delta\alpha$ are not known at runtime; therefore, we suggest to keep the prediction results and constantly compare them against the predictions to obtain a statistic of the errors. This information should consequently be used to determine a prediction's reliability.

7. Conclusions and outlook

In this chapter, we have presented an algorithm for the self-adaptive prediction of mobile nodes' future positions. The algorithm is targeted at vehicular applications with nodes that move along the road grid, of which a digital map is available at runtime. We have introduced the necessary building blocks along with their parameterization, discussed some performance studies and pointed out individual strengths and shortcomings. Three exemplary scenarios have been studied: city, suburban, and highway. Given a prediction interval of eight seconds, the algorithm performed well in all of the scenarios, resulting in a mean prediction error of only about 14 meters. On a highway, the mean error is less than 5 meters. As the prediction interval increases, the performance of the algorithm degrades significantly in the city and suburban scenario. On a highway, however, the mean error is around 30 meters for an interval of 32 seconds which may still be acceptable, depending on the application.
We have already argued in the discussion that the position prediction accuracy in the city and suburban scenario is mainly degraded due to an incorrect path selection as the considered vehicle approaches an intersection. In our studies, the future path has been selected randomly from the set of possible paths. The necessary assumptions have been

explained in Section 4.5.2. If the information is available, we strongly propose to consider vehicles' missions for path prediction. Considering the city scenario, if only those prediction errors are evaluated for which the path selection is correct (i.e., the predictor estimates the correctness as 1), the mean error can be decreased to about 8 meters, the median to about 5 meters. Taking the mission into account, these extremely low errors seem feasible.

The computation of the distance to cover is currently calculated using the area under a linear graph between the current velocity and the predicted velocity, thus assuming a linear acceleration. Some thoughts should be given to a substitution of this simple approximation with a more sophisticated implementation. One idea that is rather complex in terms of computational efforts is to use n velocity predictors to predict a velocity for each time instant and thus removing the interpolation. Another approach could be to model the acceleration and deceleration behavior of a typical driver. If the vehicle is autonomous, reproducing the design of the longitudinal controller could increase the prediction performance.

Velocity prediction, too, offers some optimizations opportunities. The key measure necessary here is a numerical optimization of the parameters a, b and c mentioned in Table 1 over a large number of scenarios of adequate length. Appropriate parameter sets could be computed beforehand (and even optimized online) and information about the current driving situation could be used to select the most suitable set. This selection, in turn, could be used to provide other applications with valuable information about the current environment. It is expected that an adoption of these parameters will lead to a somewhat significant improvement of the speed prediction. An urban scenario requires much quicker reactions to speed changes and thus needs more contributions and stronger influence of the weight booster than a highway scenario. The highway scenario, in turn, profits from a more stable prediction based to a large extent on the mean weight vector and requires virtually no influence of the weight booster.

Longer-term prediction of the wireless channel still imposes the largest problem when it comes to evaluate the future connectivity from predicted positions. Further work is necessary to evaluate the dynamics of the radio channel and design an appropriate predictor. We propose to include further information about the environment (see above) in order to distinguish between different surroundings and consequently adjust the appropriate channel parameters (such as the variance of the large-scale fading). An interesting idea in this context is to share and aggregate knowledge of the communication channel obtained from measurements between nearby vehicles. Another situation that requires attention is the channel prediction for vehicles that are actually outside of a node's communication range and channel parameter estimation is obviously not possible. In this case, the channel has to be estimated from measurements conducted with and from nearby vehicles.

8. References

Althoff, M., Stursberg, O. & Buss, M. (2010). Computing reachable sets of hybrid systems using a combination of zonotopes and polytopes, *Nonlinear Analysis: Hybrid Systems* 4(2): 233 – 249.

Benvenuto, N. & Cherubini, G. (2002). *Algorithms for Communications Systems and Their Applications*, Wiley, New York.

Boukerche, A., Rezende, C. & Pazzi, R. (2009). Improving neighbor localization in vehicular ad hoc networks to avoid overhead from periodic messages, pp. 1 –6.

Cheng, L., Bai, F. & Stancil, D. (2009). A new geometrical channel model for vehicle-to-vehicle communications, pp. 1 –4.

Guillemin, E. A., Kalman, R. E., DeClaris, N. & Andersen, J. (1971). *Aspects of network and system theory*, Holt Rinehart and Winston, New York.

Huang, C.-J., Chuang, Y.-T., Yang, D.-X., Chen, I.-F., Chen, Y.-J. & Hu, K.-W. (2008). A mobility-aware link enhancement mechanism for vehicular ad hoc networks, *EURASIP J. Wirel. Commun. Netw.* 2008: 1–10.

Kaaniche, H. & Kamoun, F. (2010). Mobility prediction in wireless ad hoc networks using neural networks, *Journal of Telecommunications* 2(1).

Matolak, D. W., Sen, I. & Xiong, W. (2006). Channel modeling for v2v communications, *Mobile and Ubiquitous Systems - Workshops, 2006. 3rd Annual International Conference on*, pp. 1 –7.

Maurer, J., Fugen, T., Schafer, T. & Wiesbeck, W. (2004). A new inter-vehicle communications (ivc) channel model, Vol. 1, pp. 9 – 13 Vol. 1.

Molisch, A., Tufvesson, F., Karedal, J. & Mecklenbräuker, C. (2009). A survey on vehicle-to-vehicle propagation channels, *Wireless Communications, IEEE* 16(6): 12 –22.

Nagel, R. (2010a). Altruistic traffic limits computation in wireless broadcast networks, *Proceedings of the Third Internation Conference on Advances in Mesh Networks*.

Nagel, R. (2010b). The effect of vehicular distance distributions and mobility on vanet communications, *Proceedings of the IEEE Intelligent Vehicles Symposium*.

Nagel, R. & Eichler, S. (2008). Efficient and realistic mobility and channel modeling for vanet scenarios using omnet++ and inet-framework, *Simutools '08: Proc. of the 1st international conference on Simulation tools and techniques for communications, networks and systems & workshops*, ICST, pp. 1–8.

Paier, A., Karedal, J., Czink, N., Dumard, C., Zemen, T., Tufvesson, F., Molisch, A. F. & Mecklenbräuker, C. F. (2009). Characterization of vehicle-to-vehicle radio channels from measurements at 5.2 ghz, *Wirel. Pers. Commun.* 50(1): 19–32.

Rezende, C. G., Pazzi, R. W. & Boukerche, A. (2009). An efficient neighborhood prediction protocol to estimate link availability in vanets, *MobiWAC '09: Proceedings of the 7th ACM international symposium on Mobility management and wireless access*, ACM, New York, NY, USA, pp. 83–90.

Rodas, J. & Cascon, C. J. E. (2010). Dynamic path-loss estimation using a particle filter, *International Journal of Computer Science Issues* 7(3).

Samaan, N. & Karmouch, A. (2005). A mobility prediction architecture based on contextual knowledge and spatial conceptual maps, *Mobile Computing, IEEE Transactions on* 4(6): 537 – 551.

14

Indoors Localization Using Mobile Communications Radio Signal Strength

Luis Peneda, Abílio Azenha and Adriano Carvalho
Institute for Systems and Robotics, Faculty of Engineering, University of Porto, Rua Dr. Roberto Frias s/n, 4200 - 465 Porto Portugal

1. Introduction

Radio frequency (RF) indoors localization is adopted by automated guided vehicles (AGVs) positioning due to availability of communications framework sub-system (*e.g.* ZigBee wireless network) in the entire working system. AGV (*i.e.* a type of wheeled mobile robot) communications sub-system can therefore support RF localization hardware without additional cost. Mobile communications for indoors environments have many applications and are generally implemented with a personal digital assistant (PDA) for people to exchange information efficiently. In this perspective, examples of applications of RF indoors localization are resources (*e.g.* products at an automatic warehouse) or people (*e.g.* doctors in a hospital). The main problem to overcome corresponds to radio signal strength which is difficult to relate to distance to transmitter in indoors environments due to obstacles and objects that cause multi-path, interferences, noise, etc. (Azenha *et al.*, 2010). As radio signal strength is measured with noise, this fact leads to fluctuations on its values which then require filtering (*e.g.* low-pass filtering, Kalman filtering).

At the present, research is being made in order to develop low-cost navigation hardware such as inertial navigation systems (INSs). INSs are composed of inertial sensors such as accelerometers and gyroscopes (Fu & Retscher, 2009). Namely, low-cost gyroscopes with a drift below 1 degree/hour have been described. Position is computed according to double time integration of acceleration and orientation is computed according to time integration of angle rate provided by a gyroscope. Therefore, in indoors environments, INS can become an aiding scheme to the dead-reckoning algorithm (Borenstein *et al.*, 1996; Azenha & Carvalho, 2008b) in the near future. Dead-reckoning is the most adopted scheme for indoors localization, because other systems such as global positioning system (GPS) do not work indoors. Dead-reckoning can use accelerometers and gyroscopes for INS navigation or rotary encoders and gyroscopes or magnetic compasses for wheeled AGVs indoors navigation. RF localization schemes are also being developed for indoors localization purposes, because they increase system efficiency in terms of its lower cost and they can have sufficient accuracy characteristics.

RF indoors localization methods are therefore means of attenuating AGV dead-reckoning navigation errors (Azenha & Carvalho, 2007b; Azenha & Carvalho, 2008a; Azenha *et al.*, 2008; Park *et al.*, 2009). Dead-reckoning (from sailing: deduced reckoning) navigation method makes use of odometry and heading measurement signals. Dead-reckoning is prone to systematic, non-systematic and numerical drift errors which, in general, increase with traveled distance. Dead-reckoning algorithm performs well in indoors quasi-structured environments for a given period of time or for a given traveled distance, which one is more critical and that depends on current AGV trajectory. So, there is a need of attenuating dead-reckoning errors which, as a result, correspond to localization errors. AGV indoors localization can then resort to RF multilateration, trilateration, triangulation or fingerprinting techniques.

In this chapter, state-of-art of RF indoors trilateration technique for AGV indoors navigation is presented. It is described work-in-progress on AGV, or other objects or people, localization in indoors quasi-structured environments (Borenstein *et al.*, 1996; Azenha & Carvalho, 2006; Azenha & Carvalho, 2007a; Zhou & Roumeliotis, 2008; Azenha & Carvalho, 2008b; Roh *et al.*, 2008). In the work of Bekkali *et al.* (2007), an adaptive Kalman filter is adopted to work with Gaussian noise in location estimate for multilateration method with radio frequency identification (RFID) hardware. In this research direction, Fu & Retscher (2009) present a work about RF indoors localization with trilateration which shows some signal power propagation models which are developed to be applied in localization in indoors environments.

RF trilateration method is adopted in this chapter due to the promising characteristics of wireless communications networks, as written above. In this scheme, the distribution of fixed nodes is very important for the trilateration algorithm to be successful. Distribution of fixed nodes is dependent on the building lay-out (*e.g.* machines, buffers, people walking paths) and building dimensions. In this line of thought, the fixed nodes distribution has to be a compromise between number of nodes and localization of them. Using trilateration method, at least three fixed nodes should be in range of a mobile node for trilateration to be possible to be performed. This system is intended to be a modular system in terms of easy setup and of specific applications independence. Nevertheless, some limitations in these properties are addressed in sections three and four. In fact, node concentration properties are very important to be taken into account and they are dependent on other objects lay-out. Another consideration corresponds to system cost. In fact, the low system cost corresponds to the low-cost in devices and in their maintenance.

Results show that a localization accuracy of down to three meters is possible depending on the lay-out of environment (*i.e.* objects and persons moving or placed in the environment and building construction materials). This result shows that some applications of localization in indoors quasi-structured environments, such as automated warehouses, can benefit from this system because those applications may accept these accuracy limitations. This chapter is organized as follows. Next section presents the background of RF indoors localization methods. Following that section, RF indoors trilateration method state-of-art is shown. Next, application of this method is discussed and then the conclusions end this chapter.

2. Background

Four two dimensional (2D) localization methods are considered: multilateration, trilateration, triangulation and fingerprinting. GPS and other similar systems are not considered because they do not work and therefore they do not perform well in indoors environments (Ni *et al.* 2004; Sugano *et al.* 2006; Tadakamadla, 2006).

Multilateration method is based in TDOA (Time Difference of Arrival) (Patwari *et al.*, 2005). It needs at least three nodes to estimate an unknown position. With the measurement of the time difference between two nodes in a single communication, estimating the radius distance between them is possible. The interception of the radius distance measurement gives the estimated position.

Trilateration method (Shareef *et al.*, 2008; Peneda *et al.*, 2009, Azenha *et al.*, 2010) requires at least three fixed nodes with omnidirectional antennas. Receiver Signal Strength Indication (RSSI) of the communications between the fixed node and the unknown node is used to compute the distance between them. As it does not know the direction, this distance is the radius of the circumference with the fixed node in the center. The interception of the circumferences gives the estimated position of the unknown location node. However, due to the presence of reflection, multi-path, etc. phenomena, trilateration method becomes a challenger task for engineers. In fact, these phenomena make RSSI, an indication of RF signal strength for trilateration method, to have a difficult behavior to adopt by localization systems. For example, a stronger RSSI may not be corresponding to a closer communication node.

Triangulation technique uses the geometry of triangles to compute object location (Hightower & Borriello, 2001). It requires at least two reference nodes and this technique uses the AOA (Angle of Arrival) to estimate the communication angle between the reference and the direction of unknown node. It uses the properties of directional antennas to find a maximum of RSSI signal in order to obtain the direction of object location.

Fingerprinting technique (Tadakamadla, 2006) requires measurement of RSSI at several locations to build a database of location fingerprints. In order to calculate a position, some measurements of RSSI of fixed nodes are obtained and then it is queried to the database and tried to find the same conditions. Fingerprinting method is not appropriated when the lay-out of environment changes very often, because all the calculations and RSSI measurements must be done again.

Multilateration method has the crucial problem that an accurate time synchronization of the received signals is needed. Triangulation method has the disadvantage of using directional antennas to compute a position. Fingerprinting technique requires large time consuming to perform an exhaustive data collection for a wide area network (Kaemarungsi, 2005).

The method that is discussed in this chapter is the trilateration one. This method is efficiently implemented in a wireless communication framework and it only requires that the hardware can measure RSSI with some accuracy. It is modular and, in general, it does not require too much processing to estimate a position. With its modularity properties, trilateration is superior to triangulation and fingerprinting because it is easier to build localization system into existing communications hardware. So, the communications sub-system can therefore support RF localization hardware without additional cost. Then, a low-cost solution can be obtained. Localization accuracy requirements are dependent on the application. In indoors industrial environments, some meters down to some centimeters is the accuracy range which can be found. For example, in an automatic warehouse, some products are required to be located with an accuracy of some meters or, on the other hand, in a control application, AGVs may require a localization accuracy of some centimeters.

3. Indoors localization using RF trilateration

In the following, RF trilateration localization algorithm is shown. Consider n fixed points or beacons with Cartesian coordinates (x_{1i}, x_{2i}) with $RSSI_i$ (dBm), $i = 1,\ldots,n$. $RSSI_i$ (Alavi *et al.*, 2009) is measured for mobile node communication link i ($i = 1,\ldots,n$). In Figure 1 trilateration approach is depicted for three beacons example. Each RF transceiver sends and receives its signals through an omnidirectional antenna. So, signal propagation is independent from direction. Then, distance d_i between mobile node and fixed point i (beacon) can be calculated according to equations (1a-d). Equation (1a) stems from corresponding isotropic RF propagation signal attenuation due to its spatial power distribution (Goldsmith, 2005). This is a linear logarithm model of RSSI as function of distance d_i. It is an approximation of free space RSSI attenuation model which takes into consideration non-ideal medium characteristics by the introduction of n_{Ai} parameter. Equations (1c-d) are a rewrite of equation (1a). Equations (1e-g) show sensitivity of distances d_i to RF experimental parameters.

$$\mathrm{RSSI}_i = A - 10 n_{Ai} \log_{10}(d_i), i = 1,\dots,n \tag{1a}$$

$$d_i = \sqrt{(x_1 - x_{1i})^2 + (x_2 - x_{2i})^2}, i = 1,\dots,n \tag{1b}$$

$$n_{Ai} = -\frac{\mathrm{RSSI}_i - A}{10 \log_{10}(d_i)}, i = 1,\dots,n \tag{1c}$$

$$d_i = 10^{-\frac{\mathrm{RSSI}_i - A}{10 n_{Ai}}}, i = 1,\dots,n \tag{1d}$$

$$\frac{\partial d_i}{\partial \mathrm{RSSI}_i} = -d_i \frac{\log_e 10}{10 n_{Ai}}, i = 1,\dots,n \tag{1e}$$

$$\frac{\partial d_i}{\partial A} = -\frac{\partial d_i}{\partial \mathrm{RSSI}_i}, i = 1,\dots,n \tag{1f}$$

$$\frac{\partial d_i}{\partial n_{Ai}} = \frac{\partial d_i}{\partial \mathrm{RSSI}_i} \frac{A - \mathrm{RSSI}_i}{n_{Ai}}, i = 1,\dots,n \tag{1g}$$

Parameters A (dBm) and n_{Ai} are obtained by experimentation and are variables depending on radio propagation environment properties. A (dBm) is RSSI measurement value at distance $d_i = 1$ m and n_{Ai} is attenuation constant which is dependent on medium propagation characteristics. In general, parameter n_{Ai} uncertainty has more influence on d_i calculation error than parameters RSSI_i and A uncertainty.

Knowledge of distances d_i ($i = 1,\dots,n$) makes possible the calculation of mobile node location (x_1, x_2) through intersection of the circumferences i with centre at point (x_{1i}, x_{2i}) and with radius d_i ($i = 1,\dots,n$) (Azenha & Carvalho, 2008a). For three beacons case study, if the Cartesian coordinate system is chosen with $x_{11} = 0$ m, $x_{12} = 0$ m, $x_{22} = 0$ m, then a simple closed-form system solution (x_1, x_2) can be obtained. On the other hand, as in practical studies beacons are chosen to be different for distinct location calculations and more than three beacons are usually present in the environment, some more general solution algorithms are adopted as for example numerical algorithms.

In indoors environments, due to some observed phenomena (*e.g.* interferences, changing objects, multi-path) in RF signals propagation, RSSI_i must be carefully acquired (Azenha *et al.*, 2008) to minimize error in distances d_i ($i = 1,\dots,n$) calculation. In the following sub-sections, RSSI measurement considerations and fixed node distribution are described.

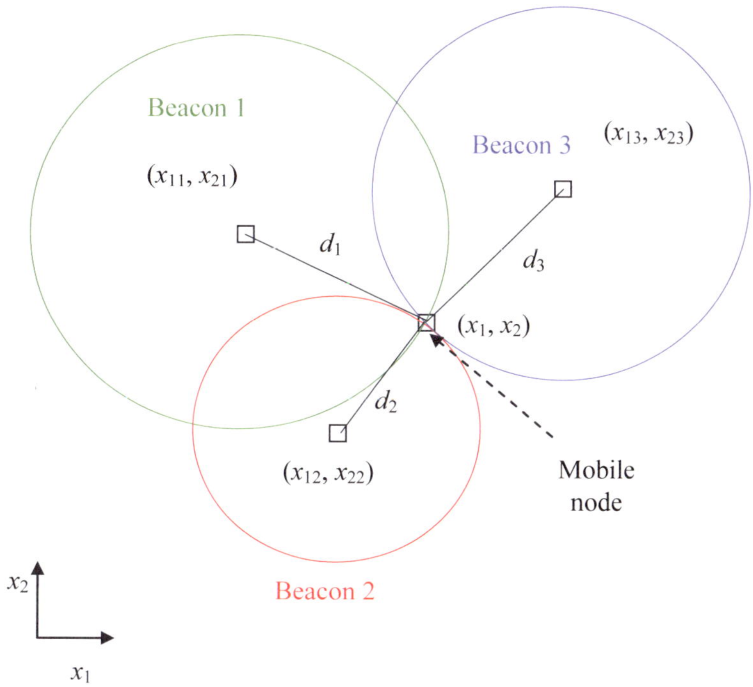

Fig. 1. Trilateration approach example for three beacons

3.1 Most frequent errors in indoors wireless communications

In what concerns RSSI measurement procedure, two types of errors are considered: systematic errors and random errors (Peneda *et al.*, 2009). For the first type the errors can be compensated or their effect minimized in acquisition process. The random errors are the ones that cannot be sufficiently modeled.

3.1.1 Systematic errors

Systematic errors are the ones that are possible to directly compensate (Peneda *et al.*, 2009). In trilateration method, the omnidirectional antennas properties are crucial. So any kind of errors that they introduce in the system make the results become worse. The omnidirectional antennas are not isotropic antennas, so for some directions the transmission power is different. One of these particular cases is when the transmission nodes have different heights. The power of transmission changes with the direction. In fixed nodes and target nodes, it is necessary to be careful with the position of each antenna because, the radiation pattern is not ideal.

So, to compensate these errors, ensuring that the nodes have the same height and the antennas position is the same is needed. With this configuration, some integrity in the results can be guaranteed. The solution could be achieved using antennas with a better radiation pattern, but this can make the localization system more expensive.

In this localization method, the distribution of fixed nodes is very important to the final result. As much more nodes localization system has the final result accuracy is better. Also, the distribution can not have an exceeding number of nodes, because this increases costs. Distribution has to take into consideration the metallic objects placed in industrial environment (Tadakamadla, 2006). These objects induce a signal reflections problem and in a RSSI measurement this reflected signal can add to the received and measured signal without system knowledge.

If target node is in the middle of two metallic objects this could be a serious problem, because target node can communicate but signal reflections make target node estimate other position than the correct position. To improve a good distribution some distance from nodes to this metallic objects are sufficient to decrease the signal reflection errors.

The weather conditions, like temperature, relative humidity and pressure, in indoors environment, could influence the final result in the localization system. Equation (1a) shows that the RSSI measurement has a relationship with the RF propagation parameters A (dBm) and n_{Ai} ($i = 1,\ldots,n$). These parameters change with these weather conditions and have different values as the signal attenuation in the atmosphere is not the same for all conditions. So, if RF propagation parameters are different, RSSI measurement changes for the same position. To prevent this error, target node has to know the accurate RF propagation parameters. The implemented framework, in this study, has a function that estimates the signal propagation parameters without the measurement of temperature, relative humidity and pressure. This function implements a mathematical process to estimate the RF propagation parameters but this process also depends on the RSSI measurements. So the measurement of temperature, relative humidity and pressure with this process could help to find better accurate RF propagation parameters. In addition, weather conditions also influence electronic components such as integrated circuits and batteries. Experimental results show, meanwhile, that if temperature and humidity do not change more than 10 % then RSSI measurements are not changed by these conditions. In fact, in indoors industrial environments, temperature and humidity usually do not change significantly in one day. This is confirmed by experimentation as humidity does not change in the same location and temperature also remains constant in one day in the same location. Because in indoors industrial environments, temperature and humidity are nearly constant in one day, RF propagation parameters A (dBm) and n_{Ai} ($i = 1,\ldots,n$) need only to be adapted periodically (*i.e.* to perform system calibration). On the other hand, calibration can be made in an automatic way by the localization framework.

3.1.2 Random errors

Random errors are also possible to compensate, but a better result is not guaranteed (Peneda *et al.*, 2009). Signal reflection causes a random error because it is impossible to detect if a RF signal is reflected or not. Decreasing the signal reflection effect is possible as suggested previously. In addiction, signal diffraction and scattering are also found as random errors (Tadakamadla, 2006).

Transmission power and transmission frequency could induce some errors to the system. If power transmission is not controlled, all localization system fails because, to the same distance and the same RF propagation parameters, RSSI measurement becomes different. Also, due to electronics tolerance, some frequency deviations may appear which introduce errors.

RSSI measurement may not have enough resolution because it does not make a strong contribution to localization error. RSSI measurement of 1 dBm resolution is sufficient to not introduce conversion errors, because these errors do not have an influence to the localization accuracy. Other errors such as multi-path and interferences are the dominant contributions to localization errors.

3.2 Fixed nodes distribution

In this sub-section, fixed nodes distribution considerations are described, because this subject is very important to have good system performance. The distribution of fixed nodes is very important for the trilateration algorithm to be successful. Distribution of fixed nodes is dependent on the building lay-out (*e.g.* product buffers, machines, people walking paths) and building dimensions. In this line of thought, the fixed nodes distribution has to be a compromise between number of nodes and localization of them. Using trilateration method, at least three fixed nodes should be in range of a mobile node for trilateration to be possible to be performed. In practice, due to limitations in battery of fixes nodes or to obstacles in the middle of communicating nodes, at least four fixed nodes are adopted for this purpose. Four nodes at the worst case are adopted in order to face system difficulties such as node low battery voltage (*i.e.* needing to be replaced) or obstacles in range of the communication link which deteriorates RSSI measurement.

Also, at locations where product buffers are located, fixed node concentration is intended to be higher. Product buffers which have dimensions dependent on the requirements of storage space are also evaluated in terms of node concentration. Node distribution has to be rationalized in terms of cost with factors such as of battery replacement, software updates of reconfigurations, nodes replacement, etc. On the other hand, a zone that is better to make calibration of RF propagation parameters can be identified to be adopted by this system. There is a need of identifying several calibration zones and if a product buffer is very large then several calibration zones inside it can be chosen. Each calibration zone is chosen in order to identify typical RF propagation parameters A (dBm) and n_{Ai} ($i = 1,\ldots,n$). This procedure is applied in warehouses where this system is deployed.

This system is intended to be a modular system in terms of easy setup and of specific applications independence. As much more nodes localization system has the final result accuracy is better. Also, distribution can not have an exceeding number of nodes, because this fact increases costs. Maintenance of system nodes also increases cost, so the higher the number of nodes the higher the system cost. Nodes distribution can be adapted to lay-out of environment in order to take advantage of more important zones where more mobile nodes are located (accuracy can be improved with more placed beacons). Distribution also has to take into consideration the metallic objects placed in industrial environment. Because of these limitations, the modularity of the systems becomes reduced and so these are some limitations of the localization system. As a communications framework can be adopted by this localization system, it may be necessary to add more fixed nodes to existing network in order to make possible locating mobile nodes. This is a constraint to the modular and low-cost localization system properties.

4. Error mitigation and experimental results

RSSI measurement accuracy is critical to get acknowledge on position in a localization system. A bad RSSI acquisition value makes localization system to have poor estimation. This makes the entire system to fail and there is no way to detect it. In order to improve localization system results, some compensation filters are applied in RSSI measurement process. Power consumption in ZigBee networks is low. Nevertheless, for reducing power consumption, the nodes should only communicate when necessary, transmitting power should be low but significant and therefore the system is able to perform well without the need of replacing batteries too many times.

This section presents some experimental results on RSSI measurements and on different height of beacons and of mobile node considerations which have to be taken into account.

4.1 Filters

Some measurement filters can be adopted to improve RSSI acquisition quality, namely that in equation (2) and others which save and compare past RSSI acquisitions and outputs most repeated RSSI value.

$$\mathrm{RSSI}_i(k)_{acquired} = 0.75 \cdot \mathrm{RSSI}_i(k)_{measured} + 0.25 \cdot \mathrm{RSSI}_i(k-1)_{acquired},\ i = 1,\ldots,n \tag{2}$$

In equation (2), variable $\mathrm{RSSI}_{acquired}$ is post-processed RSSI value and $\mathrm{RSSI}_{measured}$ is RSSI value in raw input just after measurement. Parameter k is acquisition value order index.

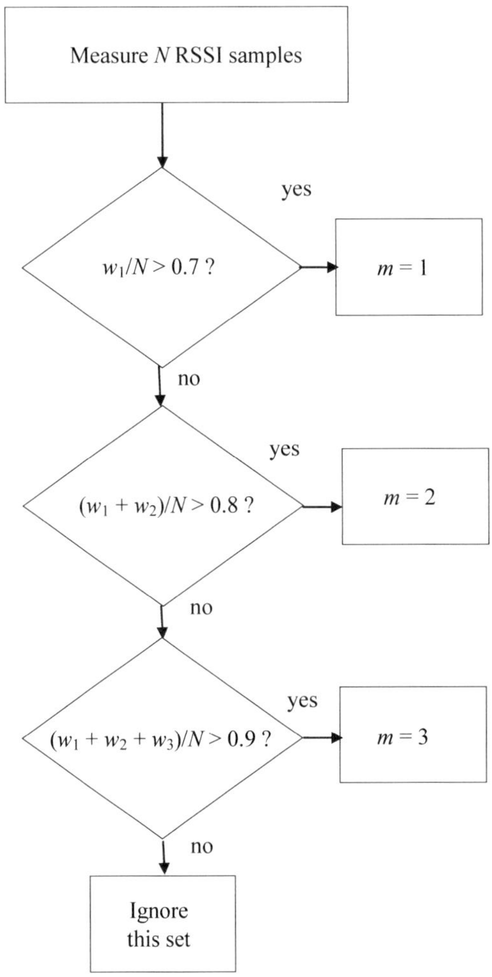

Fig. 2. Weighted-mean filter (3) algorithm

Weighted-mean filter (3) provides an average of the most repeated RSSI in set values. In set values there are some different RSSI values but only the most repeated values (one, two or three different values) are considered. If there are more than three most repeated different values, the set values have too much variations and it is better not to work with this set.

$$\mathrm{RSSI} = \frac{w_1 \mathrm{RSSI}_{w1} + w_2 \mathrm{RSSI}_{w2} + \ldots + w_m \mathrm{RSSI}_{wm}}{w_1 + w_2 + \ldots + w_m} \quad m \leq 3 \tag{3}$$

In equation (3) w_i $(i = 1,\ldots,m)$ is the number of repetitions of a RSSI value, and RSSI_{wi} $(i = 1,\ldots,m)$ is RSSI sample value repeated with number of repetitions w_i $(i = 1,\ldots,m)$. Figure 2 depicts filter (3) algorithm.

From knowledge of signal propagation conditions it is reasonable to estimate a signal level threshold which allows distinguishing 'good' measurements from 'bad' measurements. So, if w_1 is larger than 70 % of the measurements then $\mathrm{RSSI} = \mathrm{RSSI}_{w1}$ is considered, else if $w_1 + w_2$ is larger than 80 % of them then $m = 2$ is considered.

These two types of filters have some differences between them. The first filter (2) is applied for every RSSI measurement in the sample. So it is difficult to get which RSSI measurement is good. The set of measurements in a sample, from which measurements are more constant, is considered as the good RSSI value. The second filter (3) is applied only after the sample set of RSSI measurements is completed and it ignores the measurements that have a low repeatability, which are considered as errors.

Filter (3) assumes that if w_1 is larger than 70 % of the measurements then $\mathrm{RSSI} = \mathrm{RSSI}_{w1}$ is considered. RSSI is measured with a resolution of 1 dBm. So, for example, if w_1 is 70 % and w_2 is 30 % and $\mathrm{RSSI}_{w1} = -40$ dBm and $\mathrm{RSSI}_{w2} = -39$ dBm, then filter (3) outputs $\mathrm{RSSI} = -40$ dBm. This fact is supported by the reason that having another scheme of calculating RSSI with for example an arithmetic mean leads to an output that is not appropriate for dealing with practical RSSI measurement accuracy. With another example, if w_1 is 70 % and w_2 is 30 %and $\mathrm{RSSI}_{w1} = -40$ dBm and $\mathrm{RSSI}_{w2} = -35$ dBm, then filter (3) outputs $\mathrm{RSSI} = -40$ dBm. This fact is supported by the reason that probably this result is the correct RSSI measurement. These assumptions are based on the fact that a resolution of 1 dBm is sufficient to be considered for the RSSI measurements. In fact, increasing this resolution does not increase system performance due to the noise added to those measurements and to the random errors. These errors are not possible to compensate in order to make worthwhile increasing resolution. Then, these errors, which are not possible to compensate, do not influence system accuracy, because a resolution of 1 dBm for RSSI measurement is sufficient.

Another task to be performed corresponds to RF output power. For example in ZigBee networks, the nodes should be requested to send a signal only when strictly necessary, being transmitting power low but strong enough to be effective. Using these recommendations, batteries can be used in an acceptable lifetime cycle for all communication nodes.

4.2 RSSI measurements

In Figure 3, working environment lay-out for experimental setup is depicted. There are four beacons (P2, P3, P4, P5) and a mobile node with unknown location. Lay-out corresponds to an indoors quasi-structured environment where temperature is about 23 °C and relative humidity is about 49 %. RSSI measurements for distinct time instants are shown in Figure 4 ($A = -41$ dBm). Each RSSI value is shown in Figure 4 after applying filter (3).

There are fluctuations in RSSI values during the time interval of measurements due to interferences in RF signal propagation. For the first two hours the fluctuations are larger and then, due to the removal of a computer located near the mobile node, the interferences decreased. So, due to the presence of metallic objects near the nodes, some large RSSI measurement errors may arise. An active component, like a computer or industrial machines, has a contribution to RSSI fluctuations stronger than a passive metallic object. Having RSSI measurement errors, RF localization methods have then corresponding errors. This is the most important problem to handle in this type of localization method.

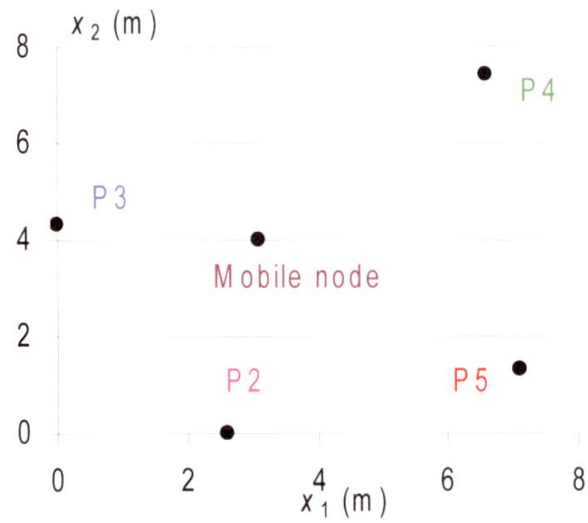

Fig. 3. Tested environment lay-out

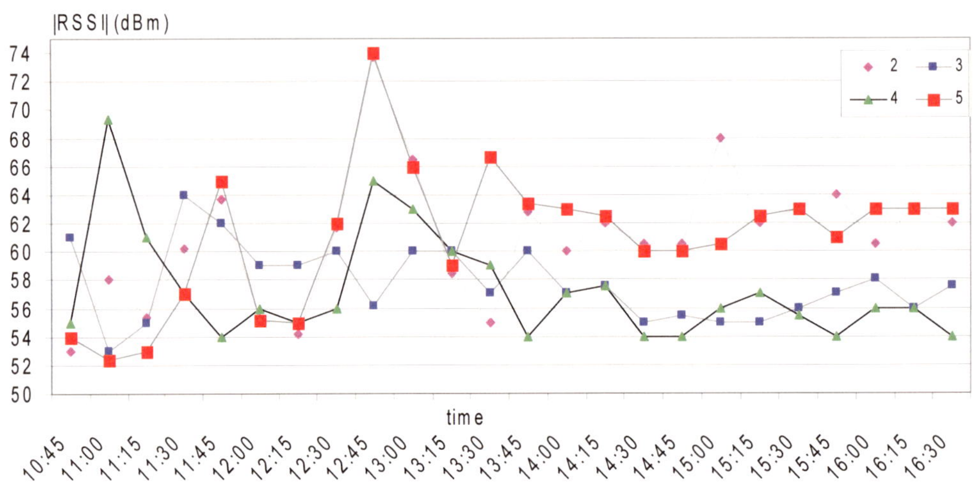

Fig. 4. RSSI measurements during nearly six hours with the same environment lay-out

Even in a good distribution for an industrial environment, some persons and objects could be moving (*e.g.* cars, automated guided vehicles, products) and this causes a poor acquisition. In fixed nodes distribution it is important that the localization system works well in these cases.

In this experiment four fixed nodes are used and the results corresponding to some of them are poor. In order to improve the final result, the network should provide all possible locations with more fixed nodes around them.

In the trilateration method, omnidirectional antennas properties are crucial. So any kind of errors that they introduce in the system make the results become worse. The radiation pattern is not completely a symmetrical one, so transmitted power is slightly different according to the transmitted direction. One of these particular cases is when the transmission nodes have different heights. The power of transmitted signals changes with the direction. In fixed nodes and target nodes, it is necessary to be careful with the position of each antenna because, as mentioned before, the radiation pattern is not ideal. So, indoors localization methods based on this approach requires calibration for different directions.

4.3 Different height of nodes

As written above and keeping the antennas orientation 'stable' in the time, trilateration algorithm is developed to apply to same height of both beacons and AGV. Otherwise, some corrections to RSSI values must be made to take advantage of trilateration algorithm. For example, consider Figure 5a where a beacon i is located at height h_i relatively to AGV. A special case occurs when h_i is smaller than 10 % of d_i. Then, this correction can be ignored because the approximation error is not significant (Figure 5b). In this case RSSI ≈ RSSI' can be assumed. This corresponds to the area between the line $h_i = 0.1\ d_i$ and $h_i = 0$ meters (grey area in Figure 5b). In these working points the correction can be ignored due to the small error of approximation.

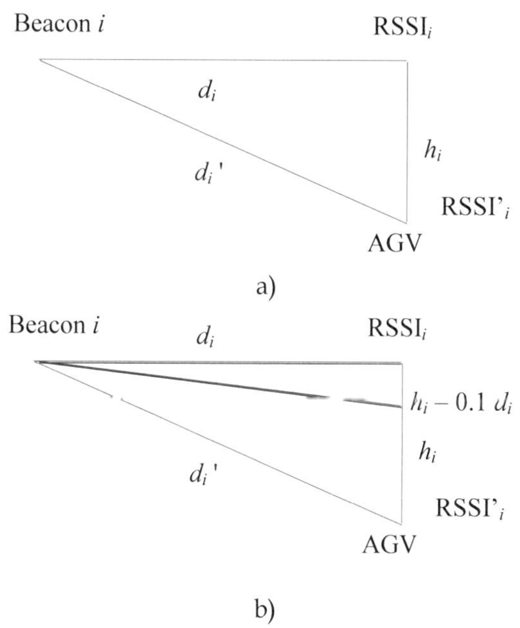

Fig. 5. Different height positions correction

Considering Figure 5a, the following equations (4a-e) are derived:

$$d_i = \sqrt{d_i'^2 - h_i^2} \tag{4a}$$

$$\text{RSSI}_i = A - 10 n_{Ai} \log_{10}(d_i) \tag{4b}$$

$$\mathrm{RSSI}'_i \approx A - 10 n_{Ai} \log_{10}(d'_i) \tag{4c}$$

$$\mathrm{RSSI}_i - \mathrm{RSSI}'_i \approx -10 n_{Ai} \log_{10}(d_i) + 10 n_{Ai} \log_{10}(d'_i) \tag{4d}$$

$$\mathrm{RSSI}_i \approx \mathrm{RSSI}'_i - 10 n_{Ai} \log_{10}\left(\frac{d_i}{d'_i}\right) \tag{4e}$$

where equations (4a-e) are the corrections to apply to RSSI values in order to make possible the adoption of trilateration algorithm without modifications. Some issues are also raised now because distances from AGV to beacons are unknown. So, some type of distance estimation should be made or, by other means, a look-up table relating RSSI values can be made off-line. Using a look-up table eliminates the need of estimating distances but introduces interpolating errors which for high distances can become unpractical. In some cases, a look-up table can be used for correcting RSSI values obtained in range of obstacles with known location in order to overcome limitations of RSSI measurement in indoors quasi-structured environments.

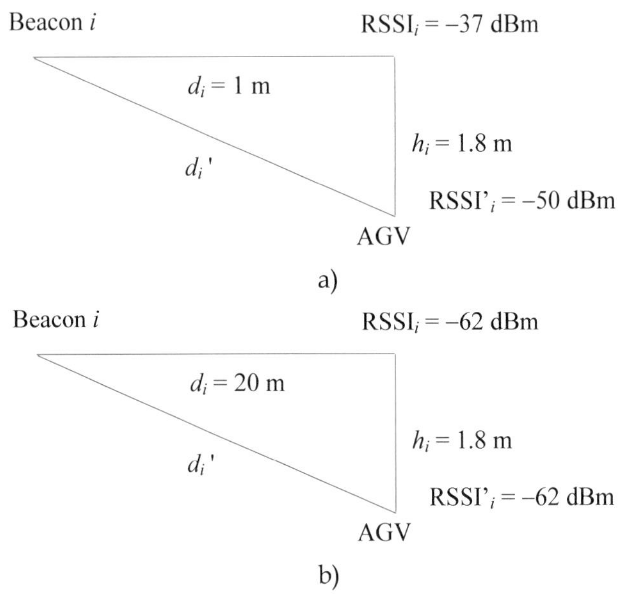

Fig. 6. Different height positions experimental results

Considering Figure 6, an example of RSSI measurements is shown. Figure 6a confirms the need of taking into account the different height for the beacon and for the mobile node antennas. So, this result confirms equation (4e) for $n_{Ai} = 3.25$. Figure 6b, on the other hand, confirms the negligible error occurred when the height difference of antennas can be neglected as h_i is smaller than 10 % of d_i.

So, to compensate these errors, ensuring that the nodes have the same height and the antennas position is the same is a good practice. With this configuration some integrity in the results can be guaranteed. The solution could be achieved using antennas with a better radiation pattern, but this can make the localization system more expensive. Nevertheless, some constraints on space limitations can lead to the different heights of nodes occurrence.

5. Trilateration experiments

Some localization results using commercial chip CC2431 from Chipcon (Texas Instruments) are shown in this section. This chip accepts location of fixed nodes and their corresponding $RSSI_i$ ($i = 1,\ldots,n$) and it accepts a single RF propagation parameters set (*e.g.* $A = -40.0$ dBm, $n_{Ai} = 2.50$). Then, after computing mobile node location estimate, this output result can be analyzed in order to obtain the chip localization performance.
Locations of beacons and of mobile node are depicted in Figure 7. Beacon i is located at position P_i ($i = 1,\ldots,4$). $RSSI_1 = -51$ dBm, $RSSI_2 = -52$ dBm, $RSSI_3 = -43$ dBm and $RSSI_4 = -60$ dBm are measured within communications sub-system. Filter (3) is applied in order to obtain these RSSI results. In this experiment, RSSI values after filtering are nearly constant in time, in contrast to that results encountered in Figure 4. This fact leads to a better performance of localization system.
Trilateration is made using localization engine of commercial ZigBee network chip CC2431 with several RF propagation parameters combinations: i) $A = -40.0$ dBm, $n_{Ai} = 2.50$; ii) $A = -36.5$ dBm, $n_{Ai} = 3.00$; iii) $A = -36.5$ dBm, $n_{Ai} = 2.75$; iv) $A = -37.5$ dBm, $n_{Ai} = 3.00$. This chip considers A and n_{Ai} communication link i parameters ($i = 1,\ldots,n$) equal respectively to all links i. So, this is a constraint for this localization engine, because parameters A and n_{Ai} are the same for every link i ($i = 1,\ldots,n$).
Nodes transmitting power is programmable within this ZigBee network and it must be set according to a compromise between battery lifetime and effective communications power for at least a twenty meters span workspace. In free space, ZigBee protocol can meet requirements of some 64 meters for workspace span.

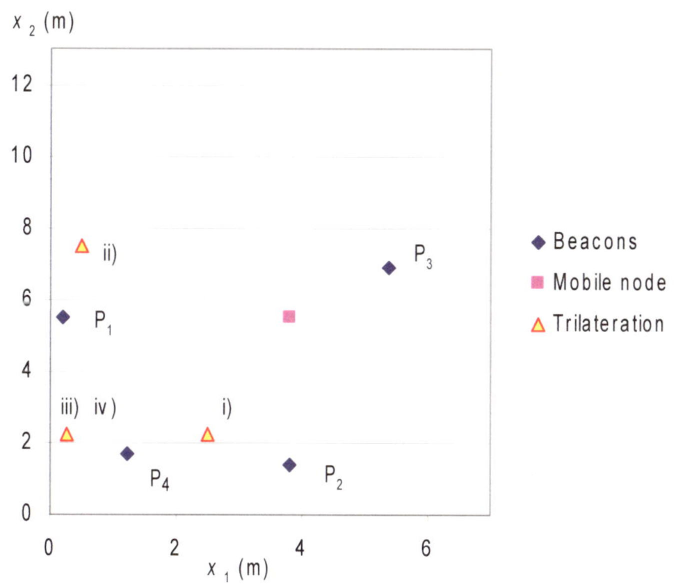

Fig. 7. Trilateration example using ZigBee commercial hardware

As it can be concluded by analyzing Figure 7, parameters A and n_{Ai} strongly influence trilateration localization error. So, in order to obtain better localization results, these parameters should be carefully estimated. Parameters A and n_{Ai} estimation is therefore a crucial factor in order to get a good localization performance using this commercial chip. In this experiment, parameters A and n_{Ai} variations are small but, as it can be concluded, they influence greatly the localization accuracy. This workspace dimensions are reduced in terms of maximum workspace dimensions. In fact, workspace dimensions are only limited by the total number of network nodes accepted by the system specifications (which are related to maximum radiation allowed by ZigBee protocol and transmitting power). Therefore, maximum transmitting power is limited by ZigBee protocol and so, in this way, workspace dimensions are limited.

6. Future research directions

Future research work is planned to develop computation of distances from receiver to transmitter using RSSI for trilateration schemes and are intended to be compared in terms of interpolation algorithms. Filters that process RSSI raw measurements are a key research direction in order to improve distances evaluation. Using available commercial chips to carry out trilateration schemes using RSSI measurements is also a future research direction. New commercial chips are now a main experimental material under test. New chips may have more stable transmission power signals and better frequency stabilization. Studying and comparing AGV localization performance of triangulation and trilateration is also intended to be exploited. Experimental work with artificial neural networks for localization improvement is also in progress.

According to experimental results, systematic errors resulted from increasing received signal power when reflections happen. Then, it points out to optimize the physical configuration of the mobile network through elimination of reflection paths between the nodes. For instance, the current communicating node (*i.e.* current beacon to perform trilateration) must be installed closed to the ceiling of the space where the measurements are performed.

7. Conclusion

In this chapter, a trilateration scheme based on RSSI measurements for indoors localization in quasi-structured environments is presented. Procedure for trilateration has some characteristics which are summarized below:

- Localization error in general increases with increasing distance d_i ($i = 1,\ldots,n$);
- $RSSI_i$ ($i = 1,\ldots,n$) values need to be accurately acquired to minimize localization error.

In current chapter, research is done in an indoors quasi-structured environment. Results show that a localization accuracy of down to three meters is possible depending on the lay-out of environment (*i.e.* objects and persons moving or placed in the environment and building construction materials). If post-processing filters are developed then an increase of accuracy is expected to be obtained. The main radio propagation link i parameter with influence on the localization accuracy is n_{Ai} ($i = 1,\ldots,n$). For long distances d_i ($i = 1,\ldots,n$), corresponding RSSI is lower, so localization error increases accordingly. Errors affecting attenuation parameters evaluation correspond to localization errors and minimizing them is therefore a current research direction.

An experiment on RSSI measurement with application of filtering is shown to minimize interference effects. In this localization method, the distribution of fixed nodes is very important to the final result. As much more nodes localization system has the final result accuracy is better. Also, distribution can not have an exceeding number of nodes, because this fact increases costs. Nodes distribution can be adapted to lay-out of environment in order to take advantage of more important zones where more mobile nodes are located (accuracy can be improved with more placed beacons). Distribution also has to take into consideration the metallic objects placed in industrial environment. Because of these limitations, the modularity of the systems becomes reduced and so these are some limitations of the localization system. These objects could induce a signal reflections problem and, in a RSSI measurement, this signal reflection effect changes the power of the received and measured signal being difficult to process it. Some issues on systematic and random errors found in this RF trilateration scheme are therefore presented such as antennas imperfections, different heights of fixed nodes antennas and mobile nodes antennas, interferences and other problems required to have their effects minimized.

This approach has properties which are dependent on the application of localization, because lay-out influences beacons distribution. Nevertheless, this system can be considered a modular system because, having taken some care in choosing distribution of nodes, this system is easy to setup and it can be deployed in a systematical way.

Weather conditions in indoors quasi-structured environments are not a question to be taken into consideration, because they do not change in a day according to experimental results. So, calibration (*i.e.* of RF propagation parameters) is made periodically in order to take weather changes into account. Also, automatic calibration (*e.g.* daily) can be programmed.

This chapter ends with a trilateration experiment (section five) using ZigBee commercial hardware and some insights on RF propagation parameters influence are presented. In fact, these parameters are very important to be estimated accurately in order to reduce localization error.

8. Acknowledgements

This chapter was developed under the grant SFRH/BPD/21033/2004 from Fundação para a Ciência e a Tecnologia (Portugal) and Fundo Social Europeu - QREN (European Union).

9. References

Alavi, S. M. M., Walsh, M. J. & Hayes, M. J. (2009). Robust distributed active power control technique for IEEE802.15.4 wireless sensor networks — A quantitative feedback theory approach. *IFAC Control Engineering Practice*, Vol. 17, No. 7, 805–814.

Azenha, A. & Carvalho, A. (2006). Indoor localization systematical errors analysis for AGVs. *Proceedings of 13th Saint Petersburg International Conference on Integrated Navigation Systems*, pp. 199-204, Saint Petersburg, Russian Federation.

Azenha, A. & Carvalho, A. (2007a). AGV control in the presence of localization systematical errors. *Proceedings of 14th Saint Petersburg International Conference on Integrated Navigation Systems*, pp. 225-229, Saint Petersburg, Russian Federation.

Azenha, A. & Carvalho, A. (2007b). Radio frequency localization for AGV positioning. *Proceedings of 14th Saint Petersburg International Conference on Integrated Navigation Systems*, pp. 301-302, Saint Petersburg, Russian Federation.

Azenha, A. & Carvalho, A. (2008a). Integration of communications sub-system into localization and control of AGVs. *Proceedings of the 15th Saint Petersburg International Conference on Integrated Navigation Systems*, pp. 294-301, Saint Petersburg, Russian Federation.

Azenha, A. & Carvalho, A. (2008b). Dynamic analysis of AGV control under dead-reckoning algorithm. *Robotica*, Vol. 26, No. 5, 635-641.

Azenha, A., Peneda, L. & Carvalho, A. (2008). Radio frequency propagation parameters analysis for AGV localization using trilateration. *Proceedings of 2008 IEEE Multi-conference on Systems and Control*, San Antonio, Texas, USA.

Azenha, A., Peneda, L. & Carvalho, A. (2010). Accuracy improvement of indoors localization with radio signal strength measurements. *Proceedings of the 17th Saint Petersburg International Conference on Integrated Navigation Systems*, pp. 349-355, Saint Petersburg, Russian Federation.

Bekkali, A., Sanson, H. & Matsumoto, M. (2007). RFID indoor positioning based on probabilistic RFID map and Kalman filtering. *Proceedings of 3rd IEEE International Conference on Wireless and Mobile Computing, Networking and Communications (WiMob 2007)*. Crowne Plaza Hotel, White Plains, New York, USA.

Borenstein, J., Everett, H. R. & Feng, L. (1996). *Navigating Mobile Robots: Systems and Techniques*. MA, USA: A K Peters Wellesley.

Fu, Q. & Retscher, G. (2009). Active RFID trilateration and location fingerprinting based on RSSI for pedestrian navigation. *The Journal of Navigation*, Vol. 62, No. 2, 323-340.

Goldsmith, A. (2005). *Wireless Communications*. New York: Cambridge University Press.

Hightower, J. & Borriello, G. (2001). *Location Sensing Techniques*. Technical report, University of Washington, Seattle, Washington, USA.

Kaemarungsi, K. (2005). *Design of Indoor Positioning Systems Based on Location Fingerprinting Technique*. University of Pittsburgh, Pennsylvania, USA.

Ni, L. M., Liu, Y., Lau, Y. C. & Patil, A. P. (2004). LANDMARC: Indoor location sensing using active RFID. *Wireless Networks*, Vol. 10, 701–710.

Park, B. S., Yoo, S. J., Park, J. B. & Choi, Y. H. (2009). Adaptive neural sliding mode control of nonholonomic wheeled mobile robots with model uncertainty. *IEEE Transactions on Control Systems Technology*, Vol. 17, No. 1, 207-214.

Patwari, N., Ash, J. N., Kyperountas, S., Hero III, A. O., Moses, R. L. & Correal, N. S. (2005). Locating the nodes - cooperative localization in wireless sensor networks. *IEEE Signal Processing Magazine*, July, 54–69.

Peneda, L., Azenha, A. & Carvalho, A. (2009). Trilateration for indoors positioning within the framework of wireless communications. *Proceedings of IEEE Industrial Electronics Conference 2009*, pp. 2752-2757, Porto, Portugal.

Roh, H., Han, J., Lee, J., Lee, K., Lee, S. & Seo, D. (2008) Development of a new localization method for mobile robots. *Proceedings of 2008 IEEE Multi-conference on Systems and Control*, pp. 383-388, San Antonio, Texas, USA.

Shareef, A., Zhu, Y. & Musavi, M. (2008) Localization using neural networks in wireless sensor networks. *Proceedings of. ACM Mobile'08*. Innsbruck, Austria.

Sugano, M., Kawazoe, T., Ohta, Y. & Murata, M. (2006). Indoor localization system using RSSI measurement of wireless sensor network based on Zigbee standard. *Proceedings of IASTED Wireless Sensor Networks (WSN'06)*. Banff, Alberta, Canada.

Tadakamadla, S. (2006). *Indoor Local Positioning System For ZigBee, Based On RSSI*. M.Sc. Thesis, Mid Sweden University, The Department of Information Technology and Media (ITM).

Zhou, X. S. & Roumeliotis, S. I. (2008). Robot-to-robot relative pose estimation from range measurements. *IEEE Transactions on Robotics*, Vol. 24, No. 6, 1379-1393.

15

Intermittent Connectivity Wireless Communication Networks

Genaro Hernández-Valdez[1] and Felipe A. Cruz-Pérez[2]
[1]*Electronics Department, UAM-A,*
[2]*Electrical Engineering Department,*
CINVESTAV-IPN
Mexico

1. Introduction

Modern computer communication has been developed for providing continuous end-to-end connectivity. There are, however, communications services that are tolerant to both disruptions and transmission delay and, do not require (or cannot be given) continuous connectivity. This chapter focuses on communication over infrastructural wireless communication networks with intermittent connectivity (WCN-IC). Intermittent connectivity is due to either planned or unexpected link disruptions that may results in long delays for the communicating parties. The key assumption for WCN-IC networks is that the coverage is sparse; consequently, as long as the mobile user is in the coverage area of an information node (infocell) the user may download information to the mobile terminal storage for later usage. The communication services that may use such intermittent and high delay connections are characterized by a low degree of interactivity (i.e., broadcasting, messaging, data collection, background file downloading such as a video file, a piece of music, a weather report, etc., and background download of e-mails). In specific, two network paradigms for WCN-IC are studied in this chapter; say the *spatial intermittent connectivity* (SIC) and the *spatial and temporal intermittent connectivity* (STIC) paradigms.

SIC and STIC network models are intended to operate in high traffic-density (sit-through or walk-through) and/or high mobility (drive-through) scenarios such as city centres, business districts, airports, campuses, tourist zones, and highways (Hernández-Valdez & Cruz-Pérez, 2008). Infostations (Ahmed & Miguel-Calvo, 2009; Chowdhury et al., 2010; Chowdhury et al., 2006; Frenkiel et al., 2000; Small & Haas, 2007; Small & Haas, 2003), hotspots (Doufexi et al., 2003; Goodman et al., 1997; Frenkiel & Imielinski, 1996), drive-through internet and wireless local networks-based architectures (Ott & Kutscher, 2005; Ott & Kutscher, a, 2004; Ott & Kutscher, b, 2004; Zhou et al., 2003), roadside infrastructures (Sichitiu & Kihl, 2008; Tan et al., 2009; Wu and Fijumoto, 2009), cell-hoping systems (Hassan & Jha, 2004; Hassan & Jha, 2003; Hassan & Jha, 2001), and relay stations (Pabst et al., 2004; Yanikomeroglu, 2004) are examples of SIC networks, while the Intermitstations system proposed in (Hernández-Valdez et al., a 2003; Hernández-Valdez et al., b 2003) is an example of a STIC network. Even though the naming varies in terms of functionalities they share the main characteristic of WCN-IC networks: the overall spatial coverage of these networks is sparse.

1.1 Capacity-delay trade-off in wireless networks with intermittent connectivity

In general, wireless communication networks are characterized by their capacity-delay trade-off (Small & Haas, 2003). In traditional cellular systems, for instance, within the limitations of wireless radio link reliability, constant connectivity is provided and the worst case signal to noise ratio (SIR) dictates the data rate that can be used. Thus, although both the delay and probability of disruption are small, the capacity is limited as well. Instead, wireless communication networks with spatial intermittent connectivity provide reduced coverage keeping the distance between information nodes (base stations or access points) unchanged (Hernández-Valdez & Cruz-Pérez, 2008). This allows the worst case SIR to be improved and, as a consequence, higher data rates provisioning (Iacono & Rose, 2000). However, due to both, the lack of continuous spatial coverage and users' mobility, these high data rates comes at the expense of providing spatial intermittent connectivity only. In mobile ad hoc networks, the transmission range is significantly smaller than in cellular networks and, as a result, the reuse of radio channels can significantly improve the overall network capacity. Nevertheless, continuous temporal connectivity cannot be guaranteed; nodes can separate from the network leading to network partition.

Clearly, the choice of technology depends on the traffic types that the network is intended to support. In IMT-2000, supported traffic types are divided into four different quality of service (QoS) classes (Recommendation, 2000). These traffic classes are: conversational, streaming, interactive, and background. The main distinguishing factor among these traffic classes is their ability to tolerate delay. Under this framework, a cellular system could be more suitable to support conversational and streaming applications such as real-time constant bit rate voice traffic, videoconferencing, etc. On the other hand, SIC networks could be used mainly for applications that can tolerate significant delay; that is, SIC networks can easily and efficiently support background applications. The main difference between interactive and background classes is that the former is mainly used by interactive applications (i.e., gaming, interactive e-commerce, interactive Web browsing, database read types of traffic, telemetry traffic, etc.); while the later is meant for best effort services (i.e., background download of e-mails or background file downloading) (Recommendation, 2000).

On the other hand, STIC networks have been conceived to improve system performance in terms of both delay and delivery probability (disruption connectivity) relative to SIC networks. The STIC paradigm consists of one or more spatially non-overlapping and coordinated sets of information nodes operating in a temporal intermittent and sequential fashion. This temporal sequential operation mode allows STIC systems to spatially distribute the total system capacity. STIC networks can easily and efficiently support background, interactive, and in some special cases, conversational applications.

To clearly and directly quantify performance improvement of STIC over SIC wireless communication networks, a simple but illustrative one-dimensional (drive-through) scenario is considered. Then, general mathematical expressions for the probability distribution function (pdf) of the connectivity delay[1] in terms of the information node radius, distance between adjacent coverage zones, *temporal reuse factor*, *temporal intermittence factor*, minimum necessary time to establish connectivity, and parameters of the user's

[1] Connectivity delay is the time elapsed from the session attempt to the moment at which the mobile node first come within transmission range of an information node.

velocity probability distribution function, are derived and numerically evaluated. The connectivity delay improvement in STIC networks is achieved at the expense of a slight system capacity (per area unit) loss. Nevertheless, as discussed in Section 4.4, this capacity loss of STIC relative to SIC networks could be negligible and/or acceptable because of the spatial random nature of information generation/request by mobile terminals and the greater disruption periods in SIC networks; and, more importantly, the broader gamma of traffic classes that could be supported in STIC networks.

2. Wireless communication networks with spatial intermittent connectivity

Cellular systems are deployed to provide anywhere/anytime services. This is translated into ubiquitous connectivity requirements, which in turn requires significant and expensive infrastructure. To keep good quality of service, ubiquitous connectivity requires that transmitted power should be increased as the distance from the information node (base station/access point) increases. While this is an appropriate design for conversational, and in general, real-time services, it has been shown that this is not the case for data services (Yates & Mandayam, 2000; Yuen et al., 2003, Iacono & Rose, a 2000; Iacono & Rose, a 2000). It is well known that the optimal use of a set of channels is achieved by water-falling solutions, in which more power is transmitted on the better channels (Yates & Mandayam, 2000). These arguments imply that more power should be transmitted the closer the mobile node is to the information node. This was the driving force in developing the here generically referred to as wireless communication networks with *spatial intermittent connectivity* (SIC). An example of a SIC architecture is the Infostations system which was originally proposed at Wireless Information Networks Laboratory (WINLAB) (Frenkiel & Imielinski, 1996) and has been classified as a promising 4th generation (4G) wireless data system concept. The issue of cost-per-bit was the driving force that motivated the development of the Infostations model at WINLAB (Frenkiel, 2002). Researchers at WINLAB realized that "free bits" are as a matter of course provided by the Internet. Additionally, Infostations systems and, in general, WCN-IC networks are intended, but not limited, to use unlicensed bands. In these bands, the cost of wireless data transfers need not be greater than that of wire-line LAN technology and, as a consequence, SIC wireless communication networks are expected to provide the free bits that wireless data services require (Frenkiel et al., 2000).

In SIC networks, small and separated zones of high bit rate connectivity provide low cost and low power access to information services in a mobile environment. The use of small disjoint geographical connectivity areas in SIC networks is translated into a significant increase in cell (or per information node) capacity compared to cellular systems. The reason is twofold: reduced coverage allows smaller frequency reuse cluster size and higher-level modulations and/or more spectrally efficient channel coding schemes. The first effect leaves more bandwidth available per information node, whereas the second improves the efficiency per unit of bandwidth (Yates & Mandayam, 2000). As a result, the vast array of contiguous cells which is needed in conversational systems to provide continuous connectivity (ubiquitous coverage) is reduced to a relatively small number, with a considerable reduction in infrastructure.

Furthermore, efficient utilization of the limited battery power of the mobile nodes is an added incentive to employ SIC networks. Nevertheless, because of users' mobility, the high data rates in SIC networks come at the expense of providing spatial intermittent connectivity only. At this point, it is important to mention that SIC networks can be also defined as manywhere/anytime architectures because they provide, from the spatial point of view, intermittent connectivity (*manywhere*) and within the coverage of an information node connection can be provided in a continuous fashion (*anytime*). On the other hand, cellular networks are defined as anywhere/anytime architectures because they provide, from the spatial point of view, continuous connectivity (*anywhere*) and, within the coverage of a base station, the connectivity can be provided in a continuous fashion (*anytime*). To avoid confusion, it is important to remark that the anywhere, manywhere, anytime, and manytime adjectives used in this chapter are given from the network (not the user) point of view.

On the other hand, the main drawbacks of SIC networks are the significant connectivity delays and service disruption that mobile nodes may experience. Thus, SIC networks are mainly suitable and efficient for applications that need to transfer huge information data files and tolerate significant delays. Fig. 1.a illustrates the SIC paradigm and compares it against the cellular model (Fig. 1.b). In Fig. 1 both infocells coverage area and cells coverage area are represented by continues-line hexagons.

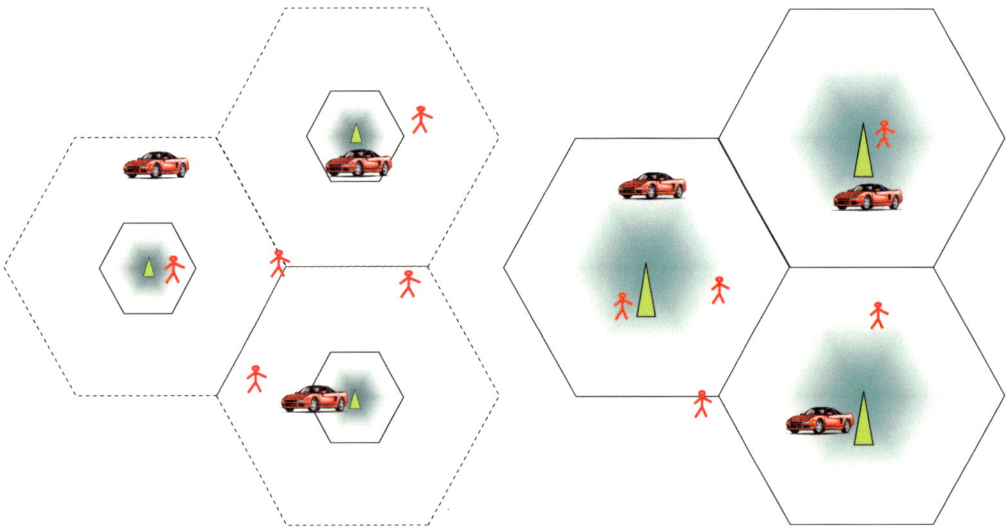

(a) (b)

Fig. 1. Wireless communication networks: (a) SIC and (b) Cellular paradigms

SIC networks are definitively not suitable for delay sensitive applications and, as stated before, their main drawbacks are connectivity delay and probability of disruption that mobile nodes can suffer. Moreover, no matter how creative and successful the placement of the information nodes is, there remains the possibility that a particular user will not access an information node within an acceptable time period. In order to overcome this problem, the authors of (Yuen et al., 2003) extended the Infostation concept by allowing mobile nodes to act as mobile Infostations and exchange files to other nodes in their proximity. In this way, the delay and the probability of delivery can be significantly reduced. However, spreading the information to other nodes consumes network capacity and entails routing problems. Thus, again, a capacity-delay trade-off has to be faced. To overcome these drawbacks, wireless communication networks with *spatial and temporal intermittent connectivity* (STIC networks) were proposed in the literature (Hernández-Valdez & Cruz-Pérez, 2008). STIC networks are studied in the next section.

3. Wireless communication networks with spatial and temporal intermittent connectivity

In this section, the *spatial and temporal intermittent connectivity* (STIC) network paradigm is explained. The STIC paradigm consists of one or more spatially non-overlapping but coordinated sets of information nodes (i.e., access points) operating in an intermittent and sequential fashion. Each set of information nodes works periodically during a fixed time period. In other words, the transceivers of each set of information nodes are sequentially switched from *active* to *sleep* cycles[2]. The time interval a set of information nodes is in the *active* cycle is denoted as t_{on}, and the time interval a set of information nodes is in the *sleep* cycle is denoted as t_{off}. This temporally-intermittent and sequentially-coordinated operation mode allows STIC networks (relative to SIC networks) to spatially distribute the total system capacity. In this way, STIC networks can significantly reduce both connectivity delay and probability of disruption relative to SIC networks at expense of increased system complexity[3] and slight reduction of capacity per information node. Clearly, this capacity loss is due to both the spatial distribution of mobile nodes and the spatial distribution of the total system capacity by temporal intermittent connectivity (Section 4.4 of this chapter presents a comprehensive discussion on system capacity loss of STIC networks relative to SIC networks). Additionally, this capacity loss is a function of both the spatial reuse factor and the *temporal reuse factor* (defined as the inverse of the fraction of time a given set of information nodes is in the *active* cycle). For instance, Fig. 2. illustrates the architecture of a hexagonal shaped STIC network composed of two different sets of information nodes (one of them represented by the light grey infocells and the other by the diffusive blue ones). These two different sets of information nodes operate in a coordinated sequential form, that is, while the light grey information nodes are in the *active* cycle, the diffusive blue ones are in the *sleep* cycle, and vice versa. Notice that t_{on}, t_{off}, *temporal reuse factor*, *temporal intermittence factor* (defined as the ratio between t_{on} and t_{off}), cell size of information nodes, and distance between adjacent coverage zones, for each set of information nodes in STIC networks are design parameters and could be chosen according to the nature of traffic classes (i.e., required QoS in terms of delay), spatial distribution of mobile nodes, interference conditions, etc.

To clearly appreciate the real difference between SIC and STIC networks the following example is given. Let us consider the SIC and STIC networks represented, respectively, by figure 1.a and figure 2. Suppose that cell sizes of STIC and SIC networks are equals, that is the radius of infocells shown in Fig 1.a and 2 are equal. Suppose, also, that propagation characteristics and interference conditions are similar in both systems. Then, in the SIC

[2] Observe that this sequential and intermittent operation mode can be implemented at the data-link layer using well-developed and efficient MAC protocols. Choosing the more suitable MAC protocol or proposing new ones for STIC networks is out of the scope of this work and, it is left as material of future research.

[3] Contrary to SIC networks, a large number of information nodes and synchronization between sets of information nodes are required in STIC networks. Moreover, in STIC networks some kind of handover technique could be required (in order to provide, for example, real time services).

network, the total system capacity (say C_T) is provided only within the coverage area of each information node. On the other hand, in the STIC network, C_T is shared (in a sequential and temporally intermittent fashion) by each pair of two information nodes (referring to Fig. 2, one of them from the light grey set of information nodes and the other from the diffusive blue one). Here, it is important to mention that in SIC networks it is assumed that high-speed information islands may be provided by different administrations (Yates & Mandayam, 2000; Yuen et al., 2003, Iacono & Rose, a 2000; Iacono & Rose, a 2000). Also, of importance, it is assumed that no synchronization between information nodes is required in SIC networks. On the other hand, in STIC networks, coordinated sets of high-speed information nodes could be provided by a larger telecommunication provider or by different small administrations working cooperatively. In any case, synchronization between sets of information nodes in STIC networks is required. This synchronization task could be based, for example, on the global position system (GPS).

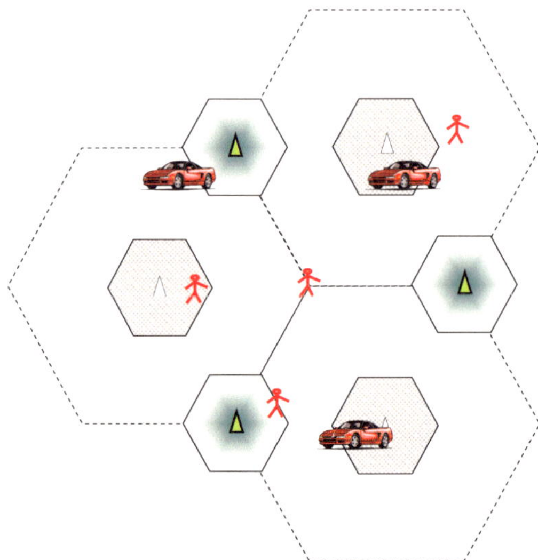

Fig. 2. Wireless communication network with spatial and temporal intermittent connectivity

3.1 Configuration modes in STIC networks

Now let us move to the STIC network configuration. In general, STIC networks have two possible configurations. One of them is the so called *manywhere/manytime* (STIC-M/M) approach and the other one is the so called *anywhere/manytime* (STIC-A/M) approach. For an easy explanation, let us consider the one-dimensional scenarios shown in Fig. 3. Fig. 3 compares the cellular, SIC and STIC paradigms. In Fig. 3.a, r_c represents cell size for the cellular network; in Fig. 1.b, r_s and l represent, respectively, the coverage size of information nodes and distance between adjacent information nodes for the SIC network; in Fig. 1.c, r_m and l_m represent, respectively, the coverage size of information nodes and distance between adjacent information nodes for a STIC-M/M network.The STIC-M/M and STIC-A/M approaches are represented, respectively, by Figs. 3.c and 3.d. The former provides, from the spatial point of view, intermittent connectivity (*manywhere*) and within the coverage of an information node the *information service* (connection) is provided in a sequential and temporally intermittent fashion (*manytime*). The later provides, from the spatial point of view, continuous connectivity (*anywhere*) and within the coverage of an information node the *information service* (connection) is provided in a sequential and temporally intermittent fashion (*manytime*).

The STIC-M/M network paradigm is characterized by discontinuous coverage service but with lower connectivity delay and probability of service disruption relative to the SIC network paradigm. On the other hand, the STIC-A/M paradigm, similar to cellular networks, provides continuous connectivity but in a temporal intermittent and sequential fashion. It is important to note that, for practical purposes, some degree of overlapping between adjacent information nodes of STIC-A/M networks will be necessary to support handover. In fact, assuming there exist IP address change at each information node (all IP networks), a smooth handover technique could be implemented. Also, of importance is to note that, with an appropriated design, the STIC-A/M network model opens the possibility to support more delay sensitive applications services than those supported by SIC networks. Thus, the STIC network paradigm gives network designers more control and flexibility over both the degree of delay and disruption tolerance that WCN-IC systems can achieve. Due to this flexibility, STIC networks are intended to provide wireless communication services in a variety of different environments, including highways, hot spots in urban zones, airports, etc. The type of configuration used depends on market and operator needs. STIC networks could be used to cover hotspot areas where intensive high data rate transfers are requested, such as tourist and business zones. We would like to emphasize, however, that STIC and cellular networks are meant to be complementary rather than competitive technologies that altogether provide a complete set of mobile communication services. Also, SIC networks such as WLAN-based architectures, Infostations, and Ad-hoc Networks (Grossglauser & Tse, 2001; Perkins, 2001; Wu & Fujimoto, 2009) will play an important role to this end.

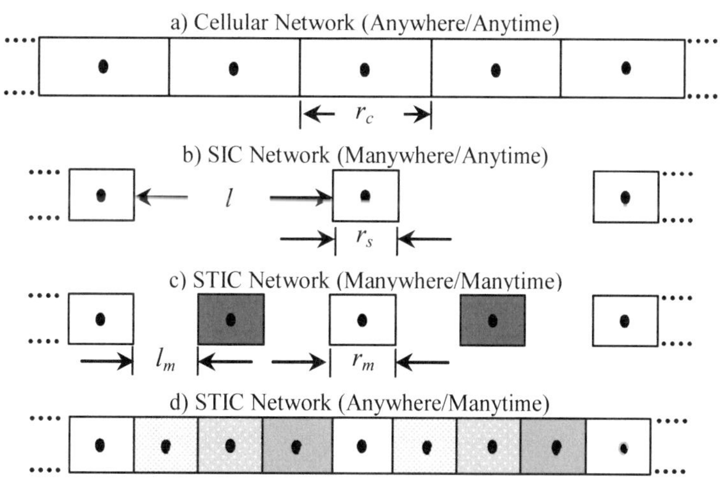

Fig. 3. Cellular, SIC, and STIC one-dimensional network scenarios

4. Connectivity delay analysis

In this section, the time elapsed from the session attempt to the moment at which the mobile node first come within transmission range of an information node in both SIC and STIC one-dimensional networks is mathematically analysed using the system model presented in Section 4.1. We refer to this time as the connectivity delay. The analysed one-dimensional SIC and STIC models (represented, respectively, by an Infostations and Intermitstations systems) are shown in Fig. 3.b and 3.d, respectively. Sub-sections 4.2 and 4.3 are devoted to the connectivity delay analysis for SIC and STIC networks, respectively. In both cases, the following methodology is used to study the connectivity delay. First, using the total probability theorem and transformations of random variables, general mathematical expressions for the cumulative distribution function (cdf), probability density function (pdf), and the moment generating function (mgf) of the connectivity delay are derived. Then, using the mgf, mathematical expressions for the mean and standard deviation of the connectivity delay are obtained. In the analysis, the minimum necessary time to establish connectivity, say Δt, is taken into account. Finally, in sub-section 4.4 a comprehensive discussion on the system capacity loss of STIC networks relative to SIC networks is offered.

4.1 System model

A one-dimensional drive-through scenario is considered where the SIC system is composed of discontinuous cells (small coverage areas or information islands) of length r_s and equally spaced by a distance l, see Fig. 3.b. On the other hand, the STIC model is composed of one (or more) non-overlapping but coordinated sets of information nodes operating sequentially, see Figs. 3.c and 3.d. Free-flowing highway traffic is considered where the velocity, **V**, of mobile nodes is assumed to be a random variable (RV) with arbitrary probability distribution with maximum speed d, and minimum speed c, and it is assumed to remain constant at least from the duration of the session (El-Dolil et al., 1989). For numerical evaluations, two particular cases for the pdf of **V** were considered: truncated normal (TN) and uniform (UN). The pdf of **V** is given by

$$f_V(v) = \begin{cases} k\dfrac{1}{\sqrt{2\pi}\sigma}e^{-\frac{(v-\mu)^2}{2\sigma^2}} & ;\text{for } c < v \le d \\ 0 & ;\text{otherwise} \end{cases} \tag{1}$$

if **V** is truncated normally distributed, or by

$$f_V(v) = \begin{cases} \dfrac{1}{(d-c)} & ;\text{for } c < v \le d \\ 0 & ;\text{otherwise} \end{cases} \tag{2}$$

if **V** is uniformly distributed. Where $k = \Phi[(d+\mu)/\sigma] - \Phi[(d-\mu)/\sigma]$, μ and σ are, respectively, the mean and standard deviation of a Gaussian random variable and

$$\Phi(x) = \frac{1}{\sqrt{2\pi}}\int_{-\infty}^{x} e^{-\frac{\xi^2}{2}} d\xi . \tag{3}$$

It can be readily shown that μ and σ are related with the mean (μ_t) and variance (σ_t^2) of the truncated normal random variable **V** as follows

$$\mu_t = \mu + \frac{k\sigma}{\sqrt{2\pi}}\left(e^{-\frac{(c-\mu)^2}{2\sigma^2}} - e^{-\frac{(d-\mu)^2}{2\sigma^2}} \right) \tag{4a}$$

$$\sigma_t^2 = \sigma^2 + \frac{k\sigma}{\sqrt{2\pi}}\left[\left(c-\mu+\frac{k\sigma}{\sqrt{2\pi}} \right) e^{-\frac{(c-\mu)^2}{2\sigma^2}} - \left(d-\mu+\frac{k\sigma}{\sqrt{2\pi}} \right) e^{-\frac{(d-\mu)^2}{2\sigma^2}} \right] \tag{4b}$$

4.2 Connectivity delay analysis in the SIC network

In this section analytical expressions for the pdf, cdf, and mgf of the connectivity delay in a one-dimensional SIC network are obtained. Let the random variable (RV) $\mathbf{T}_i$ be the connectivity delay and let us define the random variables (RVs) $\mathbf{X}_1$ and $\mathbf{X}_2$ as follows. Assume that the session is originated outside (inside) the *information node coverage area* (infocell), the random variable $\mathbf{X}_1$ ($\mathbf{X}_2$) represents the distance; from the session attempt, between the *mobile node* (MN) and the nearest *information node* (IN) boundary in the direction of user's movement, see Fig. 4. It is reasonable to assume that the RVs $\mathbf{X}_1$ and $\mathbf{X}_2$ are uniform in the intervals $(0, l)$ and $(0, r_s)$, respectively. Then, given the following events:

A={The session attempt occurs when the MN is outside the infocell},

A^c={The session attempt occurs when the MN is inside the infocell},

B={The MN successfully access the system via the current IN | A^c},

B^c={The MN does not access the system via the current IN | A^c}, the cdf of $\mathbf{T}_i$ can be expressed as:

$$F_{\mathbf{T}_i}(\tau) = P(\mathbf{T}_i \le \tau) = P(\mathbf{T}_i \le \tau | A)P(A) + P(\mathbf{T}_i \le \tau | A^c)P(A^c) \tag{5}$$

where

$$P(A) = P_{out} = \frac{l}{r_s + l},$$

$$P(A^c) = P_{in} = \frac{r_s}{r_s + l},$$

$$P(\mathbf{T}_i \le \tau | A) = P\left(\frac{\mathbf{X}_1}{\mathbf{V}} \le \tau \right),$$

$$\begin{aligned} P(\mathbf{T}_i \le \tau | A^c) &= P(\mathbf{T}_i \le \tau | B)P(B) + P(\mathbf{T}_i \le \tau | B^c)P(B^c) \\ &= P\left(\frac{\mathbf{X}_2}{\mathbf{V}} > \Delta t \right) u(\tau) + P\left(\frac{\mathbf{X}_2 + l}{\mathbf{V}} \le \tau \,\middle|\, \frac{\mathbf{X}_2}{\mathbf{V}} \le \Delta t \right) P\left(\frac{\mathbf{X}_2}{\mathbf{V}} \le \Delta t \right) \\ &= P\left(\frac{\mathbf{X}_2}{\mathbf{V}} > \Delta t \right) u(\tau) + P\left(\frac{\mathbf{X}_2}{\mathbf{V}} \le \Delta t, \frac{\mathbf{X}_2 + l}{\mathbf{V}} \le \tau \right), \end{aligned}$$

where u(τ) is the unit step function. The first (second) term on the right hand of (5) does represent the case when the session attempt is originated outside (inside) the infocell.

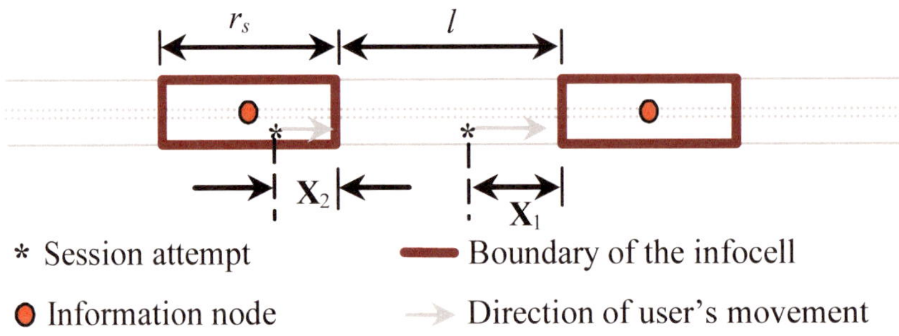

Fig. 4. One-dimensional SIC scenario

Given the following transformations: $\mathbf{Z}_1=\mathbf{X}_1/\mathbf{V}$, $\mathbf{Z}_2=\mathbf{X}_2/\mathbf{V}$, $\mathbf{Z}_3=(\mathbf{X}_2+l)/\mathbf{V}$, it is necessary to find the cdf of $\mathbf{Z}_1$, $\mathbf{Z}_2$, and the joint cdf of $\mathbf{Z}_2$ and $\mathbf{Z}_3$. To this end, let us define the RV $\mathbf{Z}$ as follows: $\mathbf{Z}=\mathbf{X}/\mathbf{V}$, where $\mathbf{X}$ is a uniform RV in the interval (a, b), and $\mathbf{V}$ is a RV with general probability distribution whose possible outcomes are limited in the interval (c, d). Assuming that $\mathbf{X}$ and $\mathbf{V}$ are statistically independent, the cdf of $\mathbf{Z}$ can be written as follows

$$F_Z(z)=\begin{cases} 0 & ;\text{ for } z<a/d \\ G_1(z)=\int_{a/z}^{d}\int_{a}^{zv} f_V(v)f_X(x)dxdv & ;\text{ for } a/d\le z\le a/c \\ G_2(z)=\int_{c}^{d}\int_{a}^{zv} f_V(v)f_X(x)dxdv & ;\text{ for } a/c<z\le b/d \\ G_3(z)=1-\int_{c}^{b/z}\int_{zv}^{b} f_V(v)f_X(x)dxdv & ;\text{ for } b/d<z\le b/c \\ 1 & ;\text{ for } z>b/c \end{cases} \tag{6a}$$

if $a/c\le b/d$, and as

$$F_Z(z)=\begin{cases} 0 & ;\text{ for } z<a/d \\ G_1(z)=\int_{a/z}^{d}\int_{a}^{zv} f_V(v)f_X(x)dxdv & ;\text{ for } a/d\le z\le b/d \\ G_4(z)=\int_{a}^{b}\int_{x/z}^{d} f_V(v)f_X(x)dvdx & ;\text{ for } b/d<z\le a/c \\ G_3(z)=1-\int_{c}^{b/z}\int_{zv}^{b} f_V(v)f_X(x)dxdv & ;\text{ for } a/c<z\le b/c \\ 1 & ;\text{ for } z>b/c. \end{cases} \tag{6b}$$

if $a/c>b/d$, where $f_X(x)$ is the pdf of $\mathbf{X}$.

For $\Delta t<r_s/d$, and Δt given as a parameter, the joint cdf of $\mathbf{Z}_2$ and $\mathbf{Z}_3$ is given by

$$F_{Z_2,Z_3}(\tau)=\begin{cases}0 & ;\text{for } \tau<l/d\\ G_5(\tau)=\int_0^{d\tau-l}\int_{\frac{x+l}{\tau}}^{d} f_V(v)f_X(x)dvdx & ;\text{for } l/d\le\tau\le\Delta t+l/d\\ G_6(\tau)=\int_{l/\tau}^{\frac{l}{\tau-\Delta t}}\int_0^{\tau v-l} f_V(v)f_X(x)dxdv+ & \\ \quad+\int_{\frac{l}{\tau-\Delta t}}^{d}\int_0^{\Delta t v} f_V(v)f_X(x)dxdv & ;\text{for } \Delta t+l/d<\tau\le l/c\\ G_7(\tau)=\int_c^{\frac{l}{\tau-\Delta t}}\int_0^{\tau v-l} f_V(v)f_X(x)dxdv+ & \\ \quad+\int_{\frac{l}{\tau-\Delta t}}^{d}\int_0^{\Delta t v} f_V(v)f_X(x)dxdv & ;\text{for } l/c\le\tau\le\Delta t+l/c\\ G_8(\tau)=\int_c^{d}\int_0^{\Delta t v} f_V(v)f_X(x)dxdv & ;\text{for } \Delta t+l/d<\tau\le\infty\end{cases}\tag{7a}$$

if $\Delta t \le l/c - l/d$, and as

$$F_{Z_2,Z_3}(\tau)=\begin{cases}0 & ;\text{for } \tau<l/d\\ G_5(\tau)=\int_0^{d\tau-l}\int_{\frac{x+l}{\tau}}^{d} f_V(v)f_X(x)dvdx & ;\text{for } l/d\le\tau\le l/c\\ G_9(\tau)=\int_c^{d}\int_0^{\tau v-l} f_V(v)f_X(x)dxdv & ;\text{for } l/c<\tau\le\Delta t+l/d\\ G_7(\tau)=\int_c^{\frac{l}{\tau-\Delta t}}\int_0^{\tau v-l} f_V(v)f_X(x)dxdv+ & \\ \quad+\int_{\frac{l}{\tau-\Delta t}}^{d}\int_0^{\Delta t v} f_V(v)f_X(x)dxdv & ;\text{for } l/d\le\tau-\Delta t\le l/c\\ G_8(\tau)=\int_c^{d}\int_0^{\Delta t v} f_V(v)f_X(x)dxdv & ;\text{for } \Delta t+l/c<\tau\le\infty\end{cases}\tag{7b}$$

if $\Delta t > l/c - l/d$, where $f_X(x)$ is the pdf of **X** with a=0, and b=r_s.

Using (6) it is straightforward to obtain the cdf, pdf, and mgf, of the RVs $\mathbf{Z}_1$ and $\mathbf{Z}_2$. This task is left to the reader as an exercise. In the following analysis, $F_{Z_n}(\tau)$, $f_{Z_n}(\tau)$, and $\varphi_{Z_n}(\tau)$, represent, respectively, the cdf, pdf, and mgf, of the RV $\mathbf{Z}_n$ (n = 1, 2). In this way, the cdf of the connectivity delay for the SIC network can be written as

$$F_{T_i}(\tau)=P_{out}F_{Z_1}(\tau)+P_{in}F_{Z_2,Z_3}(\tau)+P_{in}\langle 1-F_{Z_2}(\Delta t)\rangle u(\tau).\tag{8}$$

Thus, the pdf of $\mathbf{T}_i$ is found by differentiating (8). Thus

$$f_{T_i}(w)=P_{out}f_{Z_1}(\tau)+P_{in}f_{Z_2,Z_3}(\tau)+P_{in}\langle 1-F_{Z_2}(\Delta t)\rangle \delta(\tau),\tag{9}$$

where

$$f_{Z_2,Z_3}(\tau)=\frac{\partial F_{Z_2,Z_3}(\tau)}{\partial \tau}.\tag{10}$$

The moment generating function of $\mathbf{T}_i$ is given by the Laplace-Stieltjes Transform of $f_{\mathrm{T}_i}(\tau)$, evaluated for $-s$:

$$\phi_{\mathrm{T}_i}(s)=\int_0^{\infty} f_{\mathrm{T}_i}(\tau)e^{s\tau}d\tau = P_{out}e^{s\Delta t}\phi_{Z_1}(s)+P_{in}\int_0^{\infty} f_{Z_2,Z_3}(\tau)e^{s\tau}d\tau + P_{in}\left\langle 1-F_{Z_2}(\Delta t)\right\rangle. \quad (11)$$

Then, the derivatives of $\phi_{\mathrm{T}_i}(s)$ at s=0 equal the moments of $\mathbf{T}_i$. Thus, the mean and variance of $\mathbf{T}_i$ can be expressed as follows

$$\begin{aligned}
E\{\mathbf{T}_i\} &= \frac{d\phi_{\mathrm{T}_i}(s)}{ds}\Big|_{s=0} = P_{out}\left[E\{\mathbf{Z}_1\}+\Delta t\right]+P_{in}\int_0^{\infty}\tau f_{Z_2,Z_3}(\tau)d\tau \\
E\{\mathbf{T}_i^2\} &= \frac{d^2\phi_{\mathrm{T}_i}(s)}{d^2 s}\Big|_{s=0} = P_{out}\left[E\{\mathbf{Z}_1^2\}+2\Delta t E\{\mathbf{Z}_1\}+(\Delta t)^2\right]+P_{in}\int_0^{\infty}\tau^2 f_{Z_2,Z_3}(\tau)d\tau \\
Var\{\mathbf{T}_i\} &= E\{\mathbf{T}_i^2\}-E^2\{\mathbf{T}_i\}
\end{aligned} \quad (12)$$

where $E\{\bullet\}$ and $Var\{\bullet\}$ represent, respectively, the expected value and variance operators.

4.3 Connectivity delay analysis in the STIC network

In this section an analytical expression for the cdf of the connectivity delay; $\mathbf{T}_l$, in the Anywhere/Manytime STIC network architecture (STIC-AM) is obtained. The STIC-AM model analysed in this section consist of two spatially non-overlaping but coordinated sets of information nodes operating in a temporal sequential form. In this section, it is considered that the radius of each information node is r_m and that t_{on}=t_{off}, that is, the temporal intermittence factor equals 1/2, and the temporal reuse factor equals 2.

A session attempt can arrive when the current information node (MN within the area of nominal coverage of a given information node) is *on* or when it is *off*. Obviously, when the current information node is *on* (*off*), the adjacent ones are *off* (*on*). Let the random variable $\mathbf{T}_o$ be the time interval from the moment when the session attempt arrives to the time when the current information node switches from the *on* (*off*) state to the *off* (*on*) state. Also, we define the RV $\mathbf{X}$ as the distance (from the session attempt) between the mobile node and the current information node boundary in the direction of user's movement. It is reasonable to assume that $\mathbf{X}$ and $\mathbf{T}_o$ are uniform RVs in the intervals (0, r_m) and (0, t_{on}), respectively.

Given the following events:

C={The session attempt occurs when the current IN is *off*},

D={The MN moves out of the current IN coverage area before it switches to the *on* state | C},

E={When the MN moves into a New IN and it is *on*, the MN does not get access before the IN switches to the *off* state | D},

F={The MN does not get access in the current infocell | D^C}

G={The current IN switches to the *off* state after the MN moves out of its coverage area | C^C},

H={The MN does not get access in the current infocell | G}

I={The MN gets access before the current IN switches to the *off* state | G^C},

J={The current IN switches again to the *on* state before the MN moves out of its coverage area | I^C},

K={The MN does not get access at the current IN coverage area | J},

L={When the MN moves into the IN, it gets access before the IN switches to the *off* state | J^c}, and their respective complements, the cdf of the connectivity delay $\mathbf{T}_I$ can be expressed as follows

$$F_{\mathrm{T}_I}(\tau) = P(\mathbf{T}_I \le \tau) = P(\mathbf{T}_I \le \tau | C)\cdot P(C) + P(\mathbf{T}_I \le \tau | C^c)\cdot P(C^c) \tag{13}$$

where

$$P(C) = P_{off} = \frac{t_{off}}{t_{on}+t_{off}},$$

$$P(C^c) = P_{on} = \frac{t_{on}}{t_{on}+t_{off}},$$

$$\begin{aligned} P(\mathbf{T}_I \le \tau | C) = \; & P(D)\left[P(\mathbf{T}_I \le \tau | E)\cdot P(E) + P(\mathbf{T}_I \le \tau | E^c)\cdot P(E^c)\right] + \\ & P(D^c)\left[P(\mathbf{T}_I \le \tau | F)\cdot P(F) + P(\mathbf{T}_I \le \tau | F^c)\cdot P(F^c)\right] \end{aligned}$$

$$\begin{aligned} P(\mathbf{T}_I \le \tau | C^c) = \; & P(G)\left[P(\mathbf{T}_I \le \tau | H)\cdot P(H) + P(\mathbf{T}_I \le \tau | H^c)\cdot P(H^c)\right] + \\ & P(G^c)\left[P(\mathbf{T}_I \le \tau | I)\cdot P(I) + \right. \\ & P(I^c)\left\{P(J)\left\langle P(\mathbf{T}_I \le \tau | K)\cdot P(K) + P(\mathbf{T}_I \le \tau | K^c)\cdot P(K^c)\right\rangle + \right. \\ & \left.\left. P(J^c)\left\langle P(\mathbf{T}_I \le \tau | L)\cdot P(L) + P(\mathbf{T}_I \le \tau | L^c)\cdot P(L^c)\right\rangle\right\}\right] \end{aligned}$$

Using the involved random variables, equation (13) can be written as follows

$$\begin{aligned} F_{\mathrm{T}_I}(\tau) = \; & P_{off}\left\{F_{\mathrm{U}}(0)\left\langle F_{\mathrm{T}_1}(\tau)\left[1-F_{\mathrm{U}}(-\Delta t)\right] + F_{\mathrm{Z}}(\tau)F_{\mathrm{U}}(-\Delta t)\right\rangle + \right. \\ & \left. \left[1-F_{\mathrm{U}}(0)\right]\left\langle F_{\mathrm{T}_1}(\tau)F_{\mathrm{U}}(\Delta t) + F_{\mathrm{T}_o}(\tau)\left[1-F_{\mathrm{U}}(\Delta t)\right]\right\rangle\right\} + \\ & P_{on}\left\{F_{\mathrm{U}}(0)\left\langle F_{\mathrm{T}_o}(\tau)F_{\mathrm{Z}}(\Delta t) + \left[1-F_{\mathrm{Z}}(\Delta t)\right]\right\rangle + \left[1-F_{\mathrm{U}}(0)\right]\left\langle\left[1-F_{\mathrm{T}_o}(\Delta t)\right] + \right.\right. \\ & F_{\mathrm{T}_o}(\Delta t)\left(\left[1-F_{\mathrm{U}}(t_{on})\right]\left[F_{\mathrm{T}_1}(\tau)\left[1-F_{\mathrm{U}}(t_{on}+\Delta t)\right] + F_{\mathrm{T}_2}(\tau)F_{\mathrm{U}}(t_{on}+\Delta t)\right] + \right. \\ & \left.\left.\left. F_{\mathrm{U}}(t_{on})\left[F_{\mathrm{Z}}(\tau)F_{\mathrm{U}}(t_{on}-\Delta t) + \left[1-F_{\mathrm{U}}(t_{on}-\Delta t)\right]F_{\mathrm{T}_2}(\tau)\right]\right)\right\rangle\right\} \end{aligned} \tag{14}$$

where, $F_{\mathrm{T}o}(\tau)$, $F_{\mathrm{T}1}(\tau)$, $F_{\mathrm{T}2}(\tau)$, $F_{\mathrm{Z}}(\tau)$, and $F_{\mathrm{U}}(\tau)$, are the cdf of the following random variables: $\mathbf{T}_o$, $\mathbf{T}_1$ (=$\mathbf{T}_o$+t_{on}), $\mathbf{T}_2$ (=$\mathbf{T}_o$+2t_{on}), **Z** (=**X**/**V**), and **U** (=**Z**-$\mathbf{T}_o$), respectively. Note that, $\mathbf{T}_1$ and $\mathbf{T}_2$ are uniform RV in the intervals (t_{on}, 2t_{on}) and (2t_{on}, 3t_{on}), respectively (Papoulis & Pillai, 2002). The cdf of **Z** is given by equation (2) with a=0, b=r_m, c=v_{min}, and d=v_{max}. Using the methodology described in (Papoulis & Pillai, 2002, page 185) and assuming that **Z** and $\mathbf{T}_o$ are independent, it is straightforward to obtain the cdf, pdf, and mgf of **U**. This task is left to the reader as an exercise.

Finally, as in the case of SIC networks (sub-section 4.2), using de cdf of $\mathbf{T}_I$ given by equation (14), mathematical expressions for the mean value, standard deviation, pdf, and mgf, of this random variable can be obtained.

4.4 Comments on the system capacity loss of STIC networks relative to SIC networks

In STIC networks, information nodes (access points) are available (or active) only for a fraction of time. Hence, their system capacity per spatial area unit[4] (in bps/m^2) of STIC networks is smaller relative to SIC networks. This capacity loss depends mainly on the temporal reuse factor and it is discussed next.

In order to carry out a fair comparison among the performance of STIC and SIC networks, let us assumed that a STIC network is designed in such a way that the amount of interference experienced (determined by the access points separation and channel gain) is the same as that of a reference SIC network[5]. Under these conditions, the capacity in bps (i.e., throughput) of each access point in SIC and STIC networks is the same. However, system capacity per spatial area unit in the STIC network is less than that in the SIC network because of the intermittent operation of its access points. That is, in STIC networks connectivity is available only a fraction of time that depends on the temporal reuse factor. This capacity loss per spatial area unit is the price to pay for the connectivity delay improvement in STIC networks. Nevertheless, depending on the system and design parameters (i.e., infocell length, separation between adjacent infocells, number of sets of information nodes, temporal reuse factor, temporal intermittence factor, etc.), and on the network architecture (i.e., manywhere/manytime or anywhere/manytime STIC configurations), this capacity loss can be acceptable and/or negligible. This asseveration is reinforced by the following facts.

Commonly in mobile wireless communications networks, it is either worthless or inefficient to have system capacity concentrated in only a fraction of the total area where terminals/users freely roam (here referred to as system area). In particular, in SIC networks, if mobile nodes (terminals) in the spatial region where the system capacity is concentrated (or, equivalently, where terminals have connectivity) have not more information to transmit/receive, then the system capacity is wasted and cannot be used to attend terminals in other regions (because of the spatial intermittent connectivity). The probability of occurrence of this event is not negligible due to the fact that terminals always have the necessity to transmit/receive only a limited amount of information (finite number of bits) and that the transmitted/received information is not instantaneously processed (then, the time period between packets generation/request is always greater than zero). Additionally in SIC networks, due to the inherent and fundamental mobility freedom of users' characteristic in mobile wireless communications networks, in general, and because of the random nature of the time instants when users generate (request) information; it is not unlikely that terminals require to transmit (receive) information in zones where there is not connectivity (Cavalcanti et al., 2002; Chowdhury et al., 2010)). Then, because of the

---

[4] System capacity per unit area refers to capacity in bps/m^2 considering the total area where terminals/users freely roam.

[5] In a homogeneous environment, this can be achieved by keeping the access points separation equal in SIC and STIC networks, as explained in (Hernández-Valdez & Cruz-Pérez, 2008). Please note that intertmittstations architecture proposed in (Hernández-Valdez & Cruz-Pérez, 2008) to achieve continuous connectivity is a particular case of a STIC network.

inhomogeneous spatial capacity distribution in SIC networks, it is possible that some spatial areas have more capacity than the necessary and other zones do not have capacity at all.
The quantitative comparison of SIC and STIC networks in terms of its capacity is a subject of further future research. Nevertheless, as explained above, it is expected that the system capacity loss of STIC networks relative to SIC networks be significantly smaller to the fraction of time that the access points are active (i.e., inverse to the temporal reuse factor). This is particularly true for uniform spatially distributed traffic demand systems with non-interactive service classes[6]. For mobile wireless communications with interactive services, the capacity loss of STIC networks relative to SIC networks could be reduced with the use of *adaptive temporal reuse factor*. Basically, in scenarios with non-uniform spatial distribution traffic, in general, access points in regions where there is larger capacity demand could be adaptively activated a larger fraction of time (*adaptive temporal reuse factor*). The impact of both the non uniformity in the spatial traffic distribution caused by the correlation of traffic demand with users' position, and the use of *adaptive temporal reuse factor* in intermittent connectivity networks needs to be evaluated and it is also a topic of further future research.
More importantly, because of its smaller connectivity delay, a fundamental advantage of STIC networks relative to SIC networks is their capability to support more delay constrained services. Then, the price to pay in terms of capacity loss could be acceptable and/or insignificant.

5. Performance evaluation

The goal of the numerical evaluations presented in this section is to compare in terms of connectivity delay drive-through SIC and STIC networks. For the numerical evaluations, typical values for the users' velocity pdf are used (El-Dolil et al., 1989). In the following figures, the labels UN and TN stand for uniform distribution and truncated normal distribution of the pdf of users' velocity, respectively. As stated before, SIC networks are based on ultra-high speed radios transmitting to very small and discontinuous zones of coverage through which the users pass by a few seconds and, in general, the distance between zones of coverage is much greater than the information node radius (Cavalcanti et al., 2002; Frenkiel et al., 2000).
Figs. 3.a and 3.b show, respectively, the cdf of $\mathbf{T}_i$ and $\mathbf{T}_l$ with c=11.11 m/s, d=44.44 m/s, μ_t=27.77 m/s, and σ_t=5.55 m/s. In Fig. 5.a Δt=0.05 s, with $r_s=l$ as a parameter. In Fig. 5.b $\Delta t=0.1t_{on}$ s, r_m=250m, with t_{on} as a parameter. Figs. 6.a and 6.b show, respectively, the pdf of $\mathbf{T}_i$ and $\mathbf{T}_l$ with c=11.11 m/s, d=44.44 m/s, Δt=0.05 s, l=600 m, and r_s=250 m, with the mean and standard deviation of the pdf of the velocity of mobile nodes as parameters. The delta function given by the last term on the right of (9) is not plotted in any curve of Fig. 6 and, the value of this term is equal $0.497\delta(\tau)$ and $0.451\delta(\tau)$ for all the plots of Figs. 6.a and 6.b, respectively. The coefficient of the delta function does represent the proportion of session

[6] In the interactive class of services (the interactive class supports services typically supported by today's best effort IP networks, including file transfer, web browsing, or telnet applications), the reception of information can trigger the generation/request of new or additional information to be transmitted/received. Due to the fact that the transmission and reception in SIC networks can only occur in spatial regions where there is connectivity, traffic demand in SIC networks with interactive services is correlated with users' position. Then, it is expected that the spatial traffic distribution in a homogeneous SIC network with interactive services be non uniform.

attempts with connectivity delay equals 0 seconds. The following important observations can be extracted from Figs. 5 and 6. The connectivity delay in SIC networks depends strongly on the distance between zones of coverage (l), the type of pdf velocity (uniform or truncated normal), and the parameters of the pdf velocity (mean, variance, maximum speed d, and minimum speed c). On the other hand, the information node radius has a minor effect on connectivity delay. On the contrary, in STIC networks the connectivity delay is not sensitive to the pdf of mobile nodes' velocity.

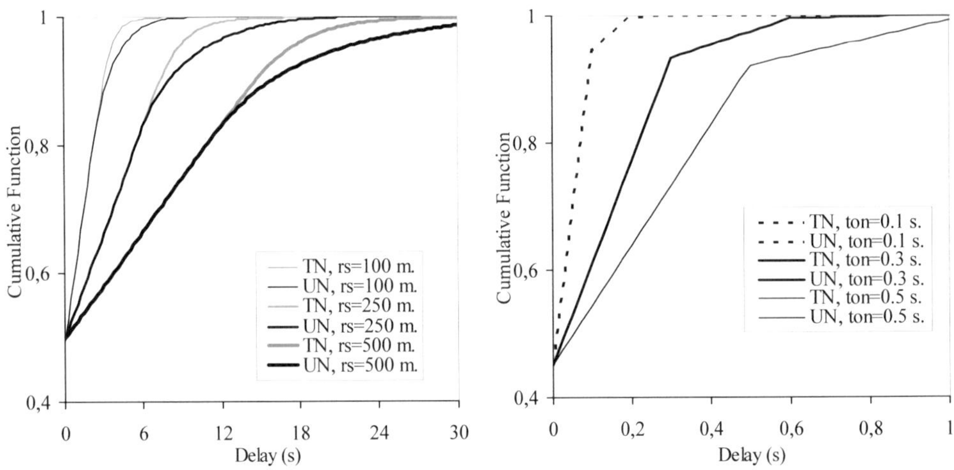

Fig. 5. cdf of the connectivity delay for a one-dimensional (a) SIC network with Δt=0.05 s, and r_s=l as a parameter, (b) STIC network with l_m=0 m, Δt=0.1t_{on}, r_m=250 m, and t_{on} as a parameter

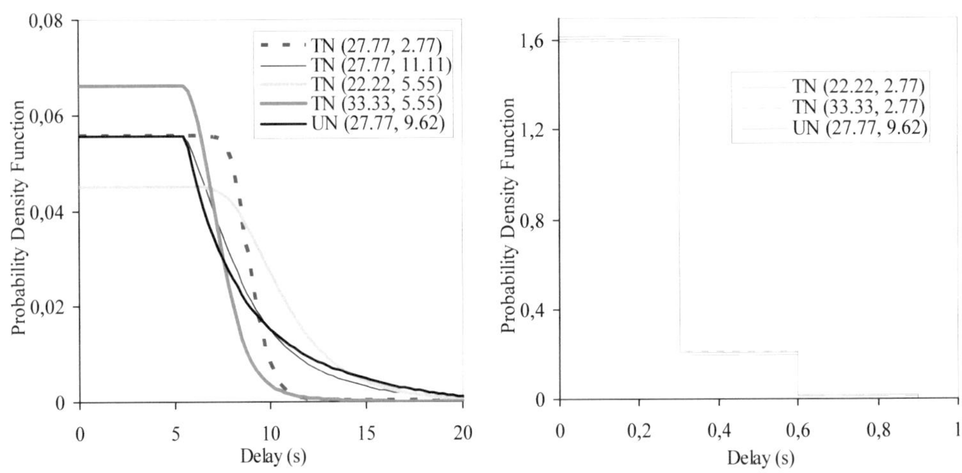

Fig. 6. pdf of the connectivity delay for a one-dimensional (a) SIC network with, r_s=l =250 m, (b) STIC network with l_m=0 m, t_{on}=0.3 s, r_m=250 m, and the mean and standard deviation of pdf velocity as parameters. In both systems Δt=0.05 s

Table 1 shows the mean (μ_{Ti}) and the standard deviation (σ_{Ti}) of the connectivity delay for the SIC network with Δt=0.05 s and v_{min}, v_{max}, r_s, and l, as parameters. On the other hand, Table 2 shows the mean (μ_{TI}) and the standard deviation (σ_{TI}) of the connectivity delay for the STIC network with v_{min}=60 km/h, v_{max}=140 km/h, and r_m=250 m, with Δt and t_{on} as parameters.

(v_{min}, v_{max}) (km/h)	r_s=l=100 m		r_s=l=250 m		r_s=l=500 m	
	μ_{Ti}	σ_{Ti}	μ_{Ti}	σ_{Ti}	μ_{Ti}	σ_{Ti}
(80, 180)	0.77	1	1.9	2.5	3.7	4.9
(80, 120)	0.95	1.2	2.3	3	4.6	6
(40, 120)	1.3	1.7	3.1	4.3	6.2	8.6
(40, 180)	1	1.5	2.5	3.6	4.9	7.2

Table 1. Mean value and standard deviation of Connectivity Delay in the SIC Network. All the values are given in seconds (s)

Δt	t_{on}=1 ms		t_{on}=10 ms		t_{on}=100 ms	
	μ_{TI}	σ_{TI}	μ_{TI}	σ_{TI}	μ_{TI}	σ_{TI}
0.01t_{on}	0.26	0.41	2.6	4.1	26	42
0.1t_{on}	0.33	0.51	3.3	5.1	33	52
0.3t_{on}	0.5	0.65	4.8	6.5	49	67

Table 2. Mean value and standard deviation of Connectivity Delay in the STIC Network. All the values are given in milliseconds (ms)

From Table 2, it is observed that the mean and standard deviation of the STIC connectivity delay are as small as t_{off} is and their values increase as Δt increases. Notice that in STIC networks t_{on} is a design parameter. On the other hand, Table I shows that, in SIC networks, μ_{Ti} and σ_{Ti} are very sensitive to both the distance between zones of coverage and the parameters of the pdf velocity. Finally, from Tables I and II, it is evident that the values of the mean and standard deviation of the connectivity delay in STIC networks are to a great extent smaller than those presented in SIC networks. Then, STIC networks support more restrictive delay sensitive applications than those supported by SIC networks. More importantly, STIC networks offer network designers control and flexibility over the degree of delay and disruption tolerance that intermittent connectivity systems can achieve. Due to this flexibility, STIC networks are intended to provide wireless communication services in a variety of different environments, including highways, hot spots in urban zones, airports, city centres, business districts, tourist zones, etc.

6. Conclusion

This Chapter focused on the delay coverage study in wireless communication networks with intermittent connectivity. Special emphasis was made in spatial and spatial/temporal intermittent connectivity paradigms. We stated that the tremendous growth in demand for wireless mobile multimedia services claims for the development of new techniques and/or network architectures to support the delay requirement of the real-time and/or conversational/streaming part of these applications. With this in mind, the *spatial and temporal intermittent connectivity* (STIC) paradigm was proposed in the literature. STIC networks were conceived to improve system performance in terms of both delay and service disruption probability relative to and without sacrificing the main advantages of spatial intermittent connectivity (SIC) networks (i.e., low cost and low power access to high data rate information services). This is achieved at the expense of a negligible and/or acceptable system capacity per area unit reduction. This capacity reduction of STIC relative to SIC networks depends mainly on the spatial distribution of mobile nodes, spatial reuse factor, *temporal reuse factor*, and *temporal intermittence factor*. The STIC paradigm consists of one or more non-overlapping and coordinated sets of information nodes operating in a temporal intermittent and sequential fashion. This temporal sequential operation mode allows STIC systems to spatially distribute the total system capacity. Then, the STIC network model gives network designers more control and flexibility over both the degree of delay and disruption tolerance that intermittent connectivity systems claim. By allowing the designers to choose the most important parameters to constrain, the model effectively improves both delay and disruption probability at the expense of slight system capacity per unit area reduction. Although, our results are extracted for particular scenarios, with a certain set of parameters values, the contribution clearly and directly quantify the connectivity delay improvement of STIC networks relative to SIC networks. Further research in this topic includes exploring the impact of both the non uniformity in the spatial traffic distribution caused by the correlation of traffic demand with mobile users' position, and the use of *adaptive temporal reuse factor* in STIC networks.

7. References

Ahmed B. T. & Miguel-Calvo R. (2009), Infostation for highway cigar shape cells, *Computer Communications*, no. 32, pp. 730-735, 2009.

Chowdhury H. , Lehtomäki J. , Mäkelä J.-P. , & Sastri Kota (2010), Data downloading on the sparse coverage-based wireless networks, *Journal of Electrical and Computer Enginneering*, vol. 2010, Article ID 843272, 7 pages, 2010. doi:10.1155/2010/843272.

Chowdhury H., Makela J.-P., and Pahlavan K. (2006), On the random crossing of an infostation coverage, in *Proceedings of the IEEE Vehicular Technology Conference*, vol. 1, pp. 1–5, Sept. 2006.

Cavalcanti D., Sadok D., & Kelner J. (2002), Capacity study of one-dimensional mobile infostations network, available on-line.

Doufexi A., Tameh E., Nix A., Armour S., & Molina A. (2003), Hotspot Wireless LANs to Enhance the Performance of 3G and Beyond Cellular Networks, *IEEE Commun. Mag.*, vol. 41, no. 7, pp. 58-65, July 2003.

El-Dolil S. A., Wong W. C., & Steel R. (1989), Teletraffic Performance of Highway Microcells with Overlay Macrocell, *IEEE JSAC*, vol. 7, no.1, pp. 71-78, January 1989.

Frenkiel R. H. (2002), 3G and the Cost of Bits, *Business Briefing, Wireless Technology 2002*, World Markets Research Center, Ltd., London 2002.

Frenkiel R. H., Badrinath B. R., Borràs J., & Yates R. D. (2000), The Infostations Challenge: Balancing Cost and Ubiquity in Delivering Wireless Data, *IEEE Per. Commun.*, vol. 7, no. 2, pp. 66-71, April 2000.

Frenkiel R. H., & Imielinski T. (1996), Infostations: The Joy of 'Many-time, Many-where' Communications, *WINLAB Technical Report* (WINLAB-TR-119), Rutgers University, April 1996.

Goodman D. J., Borràs J., Mandayam N. B. & Yates R. D. (1997), INFOSTATIONS: A New System Model for Data and Messaging Services, 47th *IEEE VTC'97*, pp. 969-973, May 1997.

Grossglauser M. & Tse D. (2001), Mobility Increases the Capacity of Ad Hoc Wireless Networks, *Proc. INFOCOM*, pp.477-486, 2001.

Hassan J. & Jha S. (2004), Design and Analysis of Location Management Schemes for a New Light-Weight Wireless Network, *Computer Communications*, vol. 27, no. 8, pp. 743-750, May 2004.

Hassan J. & Jha S. (2003), Cell hopping: A Lightweight Architecture for Wireless Communications, *IEEE Wireless Communications*, vol. 10, no. 5, pp. 16-21, Oct. 2003.

Hassan J. & Jha S. (2001), Cell hopping: A New Model for Wireless Communications, in *Proc. IEEE International Conference on Telecommunications* (ICT'2001), Bucharest, Romania, June 2001.

Hernández-Valdez G. & Cruz-Pérez F. A. (2008), "Spatial and Temporal Intermittent Connectivity for Delay Improvement in Wireless Communication Networks", *in Proc. the 19th IEEE International Symposium on Personal, Indoor and Mobile Radio Communications* (PIMRC'2008), Cannes, Francia, Septiembre 15-18, 2008

Hernández-Valdez G., Cruz-Pérez F. A., & Lara-Rodríguez D. (2003), INTERMITSTATIONS: The Anywhere/Manytime and Manywhere/Manytime Wireless Communication Approaches, *in Proc. 58th IEEE Vehicular Technology Conference* (*VTC'2003-Fall*), Orlando, Florida, USA, vol. 3, pp. 1848-1852, October 6-9, 2003.

Hernández-Valdez G., Cruz-Pérez F. A., & Lara-Rodríguez D. (2003), A New Wireless Network Approach for High Speed Communication, *in Proc. the 14th IEEE International Symposium on Personal, Indoor and Mobile Radio Communications* (*PIMRC'2003*), Beijing, China, vol. 3, pp. 2363-2367, September 7-10, 2003.

Hong D. & Rappaport S. S. (1986), Traffic Model and Performance Analysis for Cellular Mobile Radio Telephone Systems with Prioritized and Non-prioritized Handoff Procedures, *IEEE Trans. Veh. Technol.*, vol. 35, no. 3, pp. 77-92, Aug. 1986.

Honkasalo H., Pehkonen K., Niemi M.T., & Leino A.T. (2002), WCDMA and WLAN for 3G and Beyond, *IEEE Wíreless Commun.*, vol. 9, no. 2, pp. 14-18, Apr. 2002.

Hu H., Yanikomeroglu H., Falconer D. D., & Periyalwar S. (2004), Range Extensión without Capacity Penalty in Cellular Networks with Digital Fixed Relays, in *Proc. IEEE GLOBECOM'2004*, Dallas, TX, Nov.-Dec. 2004, pp. 3053-3057, 2004.

Iacono A. L. & Rose C., a (2000), Mine, Mine, Mine: Information Theory, Infostation Networks, and Resource Sharing, *IEEE Wireless Communications and Networking Conference, WCNC'2000*, pp. 1541-1546, 2000.

Iacono A. L. & Rose C., b (2000), Bounds on File Delivery Delay in an Infostations System, 51st *IEEE VTC 2000 Spring*, vol. 3, pp. 2295-2299, 2000.

Ott J. & Kutscher D. (2005), A disconnection-tolerant transport for drive-thru internet environments, in *Proceedings of IEEE INFOCOM*, pp. 1849-1862, 2005.

Ott J. & Kutscher D., a (2004), The drive-thru architecture: WLAN-Based Internet Access on the Road, in *Proc. IEEE VTC'04-Spring*, Milan, Italy, vol. 5, May 2004, pp. 2615-2622.

Ott J. & Kutscher D., b (2004), Drive-Thru Internet: IEEE 802.11b for 'Automobile' Users, in *Proc. IEEE INFOCOM'*04, Hong Kong, China, Mar. 2004.

Pabst R., Walke B. H., Schultz D. C., Herhold P., Yanikomeroglu H., Mukherjee S., Viswanathan H., Lott M., Zirwas W., Dohler M., Aghvami H., Falconer D. D., & Fettweis G. P. (2004), Relay-Based Deployment Concepts for Wireless and Mobile Broadband Radio, *IEEE Commun. Mag.*, vol. 42, no. 9, pp. 80-89, Sept. 2004.

Papoulis A. & Pillai S. U. (2002), *Probability, Random Variables, and Stochastic Processes*, 4th ed., McGraw-Hill, 2002.

Perkins C. (2001), *Ad Hoc Networking*, first ed., Addison-Wesley, 2001.

Recommendation ITU-R M.1079-1 (2000), Performance and Quality of Service Requirements for International Mobile Telecommunications-2000 (IMT-2000), 1994-2000.

Sichitiu M. L. & Kihl M. (2008), Inter-vehicle communication systems: a survey, *IEEE Communications Surveys and Tutorials*, vol. 10, no. 2, pp. 88–105, 2008.

Small T., & Haas Z. J. (2007), Quality of Service and Capacity in Constrained Intermittent-Connectivity Networks, *IEEE Trans. on Mobile Computing*, vol. 6, no. 7, pp. 803-814, July 2007.

Small T., & Haas Z. J. (2003), The Shared Wireless Infostation Model - A New Ad Hoc Networking Paradigm (or where there is a whale, there is a way), *Proc. MobiHoc*, pp. 233-244, 2003.

Tan W. L., Lau W. C., & Yue O. (2009), Modeling resource sharing for a road-side access point supporting drive-thru internet, *Proceedings of the sixth ACM international workshop on VehiculAr InterNETworking* (VANET 2009), ISBN:978-1-60558-737-0, pp. 33-42, 2009.

Wu H. & Fujimoto R. H. (2009), Spatial propagation of information in vehicular networks, *IEEE Transaction on Vehicular Technology*, vol. 58, no. 1, pp. 420-431, January 2009.

Yanikomeroglu H. (2004), Cellular Multihop Communications: Infrastructure-Based Relay Network Architecture for 4G Wireless Systems, in *Proc. 22nd Queen's Biennial Symp. Commun.* (QBSC'04), 2004, pp. 76-78.

Yates R. D., & Mandayam N. B. (2000), Challenges in Low Cost Wireless Data Transmission, *IEEE Signal Processing Mag.*, vol. 17, no. 3, pp. 93-102, May 2000.

Yuen W. H., Yates R. D., & Mau S-C. (2003), Exploiting Data Diversity and Multiuser Diversity in Noncooperative Mobile Infostation Networks, *IEEE INFOCOM* 2003, vol. 3, pp. 2218-2228, 2003.

Zhou S., Zhao M., Xu X., Wang J., & Yao Y. (2003), Distributed Wireless Communications System: A New Architecture for Future Public Wireless Access, *IEEE Commun. Mag.*, vol. 41, no. 3, pp. 108-113, Mar. 2003.

Part 6

Optical Communications

16

Trends of the Optical Wireless Communications

Juan-de-Dios Sánchez- López[1], Arturo Arvizu M[2],
Francisco J. Mendieta[2] and Iván Nieto Hipólito[1]
[1]*Autonomus University of Baja California,*
[2]*Cicese Research Center*
México

1. Introduction

The Optical Wireless Communications (OWC) is a type of communications system that uses the atmosphere as a communications channel. The OWC systems are attractive to provide broadband services due to their inherent wide bandwidth, easy deployment and no license requirement. The idea to employ the atmosphere as transmission media arises from the invention of the laser. However, the early experiments on this field did not have any baggage of technological development (like the present systems) derived from the fiber optical communications systems, because like this, the interest on them decreased (Willebrand, 2002). At the beginning of the last century, the OWC systems have attracted some interest due to the advantages mentioned above. However, the interaction of the electromagnetic waves with the atmosphere at optical frequencies is stronger than that corresponding at microwave. (Wheelon, 2002)

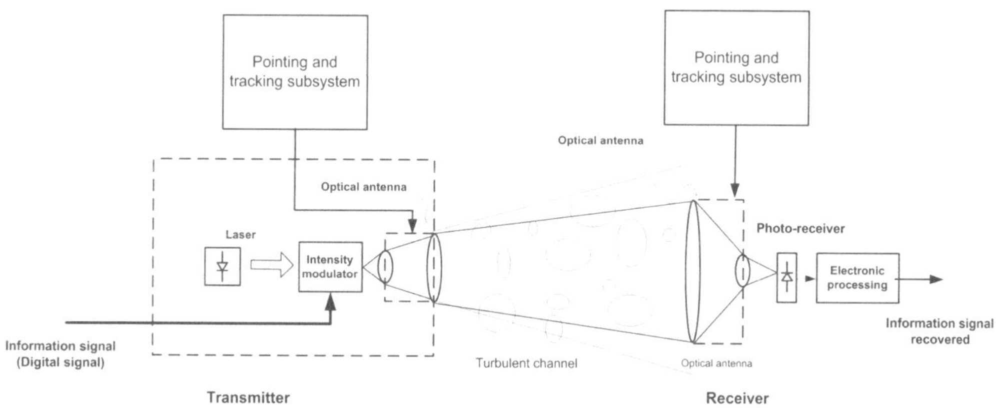

Fig. 1. Model of a typical atmospheric optical communications link

The intensity of a laser beam propagating through the atmosphere is reduced due to phenomena such as scattering and molecular absorption, among other (Willebrand, 2002). The changes in the refractive index of the atmosphere due to optical turbulence affect the quality of laser beam through distortion of its phase front and random modulation of its optical power (Zsu, 2002). Also the presence of fog may completely prevent the passage of the optical beam that leads to a no operational communications link (Kedar, 2003).

The figure 1 shows the block diagram of an OWC communications system (also called Free Space optic communications system or FSO) (Zsu, 2002). The information signal (analog or digital) is applied to the optical transmitter to be sent through the atmosphere using an optical antenna. At the receiver end the optical beam is concentrated, using an optical antenna, to the photo-detector sensitive area, which output is electrically processed in order to receiver the information signal.

2. Important access technologies (first and last mile)

In the past decades, the bandwidth of a single link in the backbone of the networks has been increased by almost 1000 times, thanks to the use of wavelength division multiplexing (WDM) [Franz, 2000]. The existing fiber optic systems can provide capabilities of several gigabits per second to the end user. However, only 10% of the businesses or offices, have direct access to fiber optics, so most users who connect to it by other transmission technologies which use copper cables or radio signals, which reduces the throughput of these users. This is a bottleneck to the last mile (Zsu, 2002).
While there are communication systems based on broadband DSL technology or cable modems, the bandwidth of these technologies is limited when compared against the optical fiber-based systems (Willebrand, 2002). In the other hand, the RF systems using carrier frequencies below the millimeter waves can not deliver data at rates specified by IEEE 802.3z Gbit Ethernet. Rates of the 1 Gbps and higher can only be delivered by laser or millimeter-wave beams. However, the millimeter wave technology is much less mature than the technology of lasers (Willebrand, 2002), which leaves the optical communications systems as the best candidates for this niche market. Therefore, the access to broadband networks based on optical communications may be accomplished through passive optical networks (or PON's, which are based on the use of fiber optics) or via optical wireless communication systems (Qingchong, 2005).
The optical wireless communications industry has experienced a healthy growth in the past decade despite the ups and downs of the global economy. This is due to the three main advantages over other competing technologies. First, the wireless optical communications cost is on average about 10% of the cost of an optical fiber system (Willebrand, 2002). It also requires only a few hours or weeks to install, similar time to establish a radio link (RF), while installing the fiber optics can take several months. Second, OWC systems have a greater range than systems based on millimeter waves. OWC systems can cover distances greater than a kilometer, in contrast with millimeter-wave systems that require repeaters for the same distance. In addition, millimeter wave systems are affected by rain, but the OWC systems are affected y fog, which makes complementary these transmission technologies (Qingchong, 2005). Finally, this type of technology as opposed to radio links, does not require licensing in addition to not cause interference.

2.1 Applications of the OWC systems

Optical wireless communications systems have different applications areas:

a. Satellite networks
   The optical wireless communications systems may be used for in satellite communication networks, satellite-to-satellite, satellite-to-earth (Hemmati et al, 2004).
b. Aircraft
   In applications satellite to aircraft or the opposite (Lambert et al, 1995).

c. Deep Space
   In the deep space may be used for communications between spacecraft - to - earth or spacecraft to satellite. (Hemmati et al, 2004).
d. Terrestrial (or atmospheric) communications
   In terrestrial links are used to support fiber optic, optical wireless networks "wireles optical networks (WON)" last mile link, emergency situations temporary links among others (Zsuand & Kahn, 2002).

Each application has different requirements but this book chapter deals primarily with terrestrial systems.

2.2 Basic scheme of OWC systems communications

Optical communications receivers can be classified into two basic types. (Gagliardi & Karp, 1995): non-coherent receivers and coherent receivers. Noncoherent detect the intensity of the signal (and therefore its power). This kind of receivers is the most basic and are used when the information transmitted is sent by the variations in received field strength. On the other hand are coherent receivers, in which the received optical field is mixed with the field generated by a local optical oscillator (laser) through a beam combiner or coupler, and the resulting signal is photo-detected.

2.2.1 Noncoherent optical communications systems

The commercially deployed OWC systems use the intensity modulation (IM) that is converted into an electrical current in the receiver by a photodetector (usually are a PIN diode or an avalanche photo diode (APD)) which is known as direct detection (DD).
This modulation scheme is widely used in optical fiber communications systems due to its simplicity.
In IM-DD systems, the electric field of light received, E_s is directly converted into electricity through a photoreceiver, as explained above. The photocurrent is proportional to the square of E_s and therefore the received optical power P_r, i.e.:

$$i(t) = \frac{e\eta}{h\nu} E_s^2(t) \tag{1}$$

where e is the electronic charge, η is the quantum efficiency, h is Planck's constant, υ is the optical frequency. The block diagram of the system is shown in Figure 2.

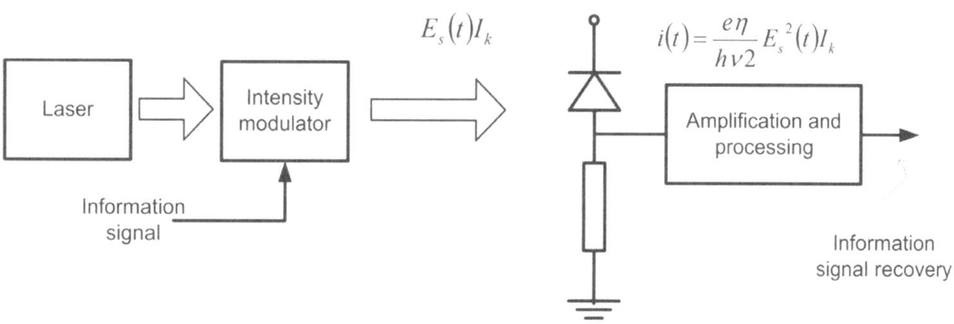

Fig. 2. Block diagram using an optical communication system of intensity modulation and direct detection (noncoherent)

The optical direct detection can be considered as a simple process of gathering energy that only requires a photodetector placed in the focal plane of a lens followed by electronic circuits for conditioning the electrical signal derived from the received optical field (Franz & Jain, 2000).

2.2.2 Coherent optical communications systems

In analog communications in the radio domain [Proakis, 2000, Sklar, 1996], the coherent term is used for systems that recover the carrier phase. In coherent optical communications systems, the term "coherent" is defined in a different way: an optical communication system is called coherent when doing the mixing of optical signals (received signal and the signal generated locally) without necessarily phase optical carrier recovered [Kazovsky, 1996]. Even if it does not use the demodulator carrier recovery but envelope detection, the system is called coherent optical communication system due to the mixing operation of the optical signals. In turn, the coherent receivers can be classified into two types: asynchronous and synchronous. They are called synchronous when the tracking and recovering of the carrier phase is performed and asynchronous when is not performed the above mentioned process. The asynchronous receivers typically use envelope detection (Kazovsky, 1996), (Franz & Jain, 2000) Figure 3 shows the basic structure of a communications system with digital phase modulation and coherent detection. The output current of the photodetectors array is:

$$i(t) = \Re\frac{E_S^2(t)}{2} + \Re\frac{E_{LO}^2(t)}{2} + \Re\sqrt{E_S(t)E_{LO}}\cos\{[\omega_{LO} - \omega_s]t + \phi_{LO} - \phi_S\} \quad (2)$$

where $\Re = en/hv$ is the responsivity, E_{LO} is the electric field generated by the laser that operates as a local oscillator, ω_{LO} is the frequency of the local oscillator and ω_s is the carrier frequency of the optical received signal ϕ_{LO} is the phase of the carrier signal received, and ϕ_S is the carrier phase of the received optical signal. The coherent mixing process requires that the local beam to be aligned with the beam received in order to get efficient mixing. This can be implemented in two different ways; if the frequency of signal and local oscillator are different and uncorrelated the process is referred to as heterodyne detection (Fig. 4) (Osche, 2002); if the frequencies of the signal and local oscillator are the same and are correlated, is

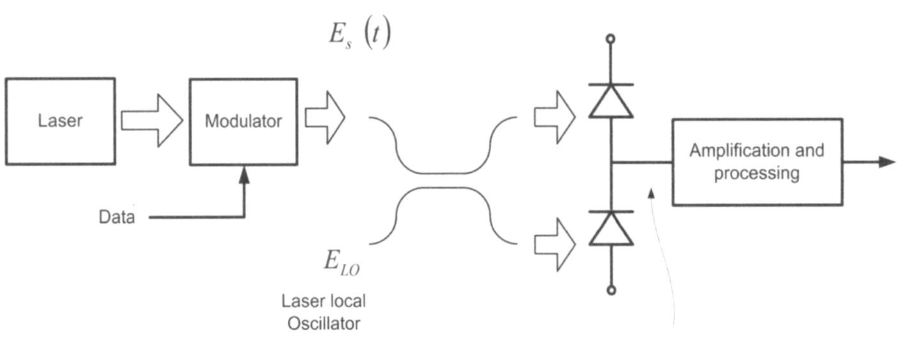

$$i(t) = \Re\frac{E_S^2(t)}{2} + \Re\frac{E_{LO}^2}{2} + \Re\sqrt{E_S(t)E_{LO}}\cos\{[\omega_{LO} - \omega_s]t + \phi_{LO} - \phi_s\}$$

Fig. 3. Optical Communication System with coherent detection

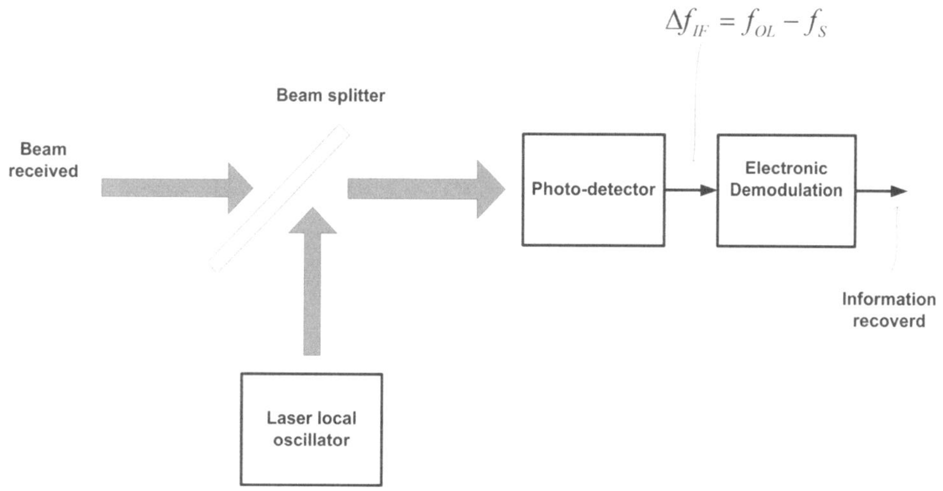

Fig. 4. Optical heterodyne receiver

called homodyne detection (Fig. 5) (Osche, 2002).Due to the process of mixing, coherent receivers are theoretically more sensitive than direct detection receivers (Kazovsky, 1996).
In terms of sensitivity, the coherent communications systems with phase modulation, theoretically have the best performance of all (e.g. BPSK is about 20 dB better than OOK). Sensitivity is the number of photons per bit required to get a given probability of error (Kazovsky 1996).

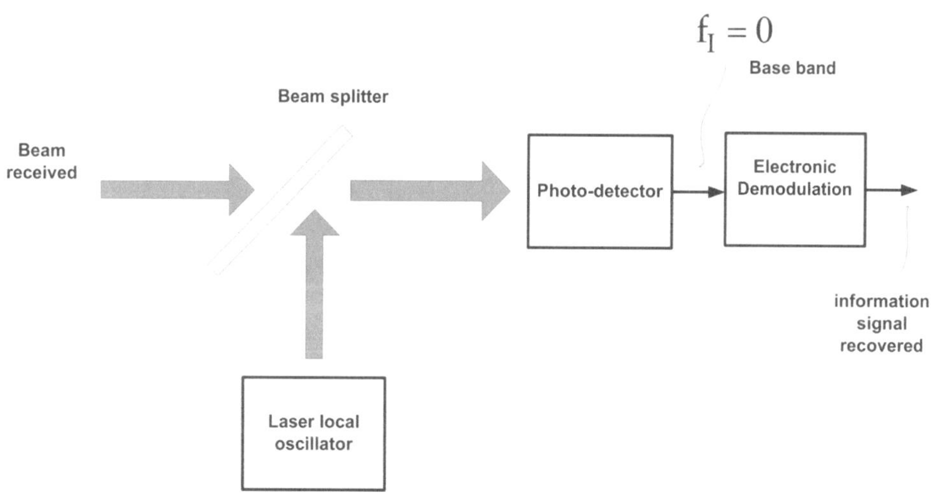

Fig. 5. Optical homodyne receiver

2.2.3 Advantages of optical communications systems with coherent detection

As mentioned previously the coherent optical communications systems have better performance than incoherent optical communications systems and may be used the phase, amplitude and frequency and state of polarization (SOP) of the optical signal allowing various digital modulation formats of both amplitude, phase and SOP combination. However, the coherent detection systems are expensive and complex (Kazovsky, 1996),

(Ryu, 1995) and require control mechanisms or subsystems of the state of polarization of the received signal with the optical signal generated by local oscillator (laser). Moreover, homodyne optical communications systems require coherent phase recovery of the optical carrier, and usually this is done through optical Phase Lock Loop (OPLL), Costas loop or other sinchronization technique, which increases the complexity of these systems.

3. Optical and optoelectrónic components

Devices such as the laser diodes, high-speed photo-receivers, optical amplifiers, optical modulators among others are derived of about thirty years of investigation and development of the fiber optics telecommunications systems. These technological advances has made possible the present OWC systems. Additionally, OWC systems have been benefited by the advances in the telescopes generated by the astronomy.

3.1 Optical sources for transmitters

In modern optical wireless communications, there are a variety of light sources for use in the transmitter. One of the most used is the semiconductor laser which is also widely used in fiber optic systems. For indoor environment applications, where the safety is imperative, the Light Emitter Diode (LED) is prefered due to its limited optical power. Light emitting diodes are semiconductor structures that emit light. Because of its relatively low power emission, the LED's are typically used in applications over short distances and for low bit rate (up to 155Mbps). Depending on the material that they are constructed, the LED's can operate in different wavelength intervals. When compared to the narrow spectral width of a laser source, LEDs have a much larger spectral width (Full Width at Half Maximun or FWHM). In Table 1 are shown the semiconductor materials and its emission wavelength used in the LED's (Franz et al, 2000).

Material	Wavelength Range (nm)
AlGaAs	800 - 900
InGaAs	1000 - 1300
InGaAsP	900 - 1700

Table 1. Material, wavelength and energy band gap for typical LED

3.1.1 Laser

The laser is an oscillator to optical frequencies which is composed by an optical resonant cavity and a gain mechanism to compensate the optical losses. Semiconductor lasers are of interest for the OWC industry, because of their relatively small size, high power and cost efficiency. Many of these lasers are used in optical fiber systems, there is no problem of availability. Table 2 summarize the materials commonly used in semiconductor lasers (Agrawal, 2005)

Material	Wavelength Range (nm)
GaAlAs	620 - 895
GaAs	904
InGaAsP	1100 - 1650 1550

Table 2. Materials used in semiconductor laser with wavelengths that are relevant for FSO

3.2 Photodetectors

At the receiver, the optical signals must be converted to the electrical domain for further processing, this conversion is made by the photo detectors. There are two main types of photodetectors, PIN diode (Positive-Intrinsic-Negative) and avalanche photodiode" avalanche photodiode (APD) (Franz et al, 2000). The main parameters that characterize the photodetectors in communications are: spectral response, photosensitivity, quantum efficiency, dark current, noise equivalent power, response time and bandwidth (Franz et al, 2000). The photodetection is achieved by the response of a photosensitive material to the incident light to produce free electrons. These electrons can be directed to form an electric current when applied an external potential.

3.2.1 Pin photodiode

This type of photodiodes have an advantage in response time and operate with reverse bias. This type of diode has an intrinsic region between the PN materials, this union is known as homojunction. PIN diodes are widely used in telecommunications because of their fast response. Its responsivity, i.e. the ability to convert optical power to electrical current is function of the material and is different for each wavelength. This is defined as:

$$\Re = \frac{\eta e}{h\nu} \quad [A/W] \tag{3}$$

Where η is the quantum efficiency, e is the electron charge (1.6×10^{-19} C), h is Planck's constant (6.62×10^{-34} J) and ν is the frequency corresponding to the photon wavelength.
InGaAs PIN diodes show good response to wavelengths corresponding to the low attenuation window of optical fiber close to 1500nm. The atmosphere also has low attenuation into regions close to this wavelength.

3.2.2 Avalanche photodiode

This type of device is ideal for detecting extremely low light level. This effect is reflected in the gain M:

$$M = \frac{I_G}{I_p} \tag{4}$$

I_G is the value of the amplified output current due to avalanche effect and I_p is the current without amplification. The avalanche photo diode has a higher output current than PIN diode for a given value of optical input power, but the noise also increases by the same factor and additionally has a slower response than the PIN diode (see table 3).

Material and Structure	Wavelength (nm)	Responsivity (A/W)	Gain	Rise time
PIN. Silicon	300 - 1100	0.5	1	0.1-5 ns
PIN InGaAs	1000 - 1700	0.9	1	0.01-5 ns
APD Germanium	800 - 1300	0.6	10	0.3-1 ns
APD InGaAs	1000 - 1700	0.75	10	0.3 ns

Table 3. Characteristics of photo detectors used in OWC systems

Table 3 shows some of the materials and their physical properties used to manufacture of photo-detectors (Franz et al, 2000).

3.3 Optical amplifiers

Basically there are two types of optical amplifiers that can be used in wireless optical communication systems: semiconductor optical amplifier (SOA) and amplifier Erbium doped fiber (EDFA). Semiconductor optical amplifiers (SOA) have a structure similar to a semiconductor laser, but without the resonant cavity. The SOA can be designed for specific frequencies. Erbium-doped fiber amplifiers are widely used in fiber optics communications systems operating at wavelenghts close to 1550 nm. Because they are built with optical fiber, provides easy connection to other sections of optical fiber, they are not sensitive to the polarization of the optical signal, and they are relatively stable under environment changes with a requirement of higher saturation power that the SOA.

3.4 Optical antennas

The optical antenna or telescope is one of the main components of optical wireless communication systems. In some systems may have a telescope to the transmitter and one for the receiver, but can be used one to perform both functions. The transmitted laser beam characteristics depend on the parameters and quality of the optics of the telescope. The various types of existing telescopes can be used for optical communications applications in free space. The optical gain of the antennas depends on the wavelength used and its diameter (see equations 5, 40 and 41). The Incoherent optical wireless communication systems typically expands the beam so that any change in alignment between the transmitter and receiver do not cause the beam passes out of the receiver aperture. The beam footprint on the receiver can be determined approximately by:

$$D_f \approx \theta L \tag{5}$$

D_f is the footprint diameter on the receiver plane in meters, θ is the divergence angle in radians and L is the separation distance between transmitter and receiver (meters). The above approximation is valid considering that the angle of divergence is the order of milliradians and the distances of the links are typically over 500 meters.

4. Factors affecting the terrestrial optical wireless communications systems

Several problems arise in optical wireless communications because of the wavelengths used in this type of system (Osche, 2002). The main processes affecting the propagation in the atmosphere of the optical signals are absorption, dispersion and refractive index variations (Collet, 1970), (Goodman, 1985) (Andrews, 2005), (Wheelon, 2003). The latter is known as atmospheric turbulence. The absorption due to water vapor in addition with scattering caused by small particles or droplets or water (fog) reduce the optical power of the information signal impinging on the receiver (Willebrand, 2002). Because of the above mentioned previously, this type of communications system is suscpetible to the weather conditions prevailing in its operating enviroment. Figure 6 shows the disturbances affecting the optical signal propagation through the atmosphere.

4.1 Fog

Fog is the weather phenomenon that has the more destructive effect over OWC systems due to the size of the drops similar to the optical wavelengths used for communications links (Hemmati et al, 2004.). Dispersion is the dominant loss mechanism for the fog (Hemmati et al, 2004.). Taking into account to the effect over the visibility parameter the fog is classified as low (1-5 km), moderate (0.2-1 km) and dense (0.034 - 0.2 km). The attenuation due to visibility can be calculated using the following equation (Kim et al, 2000):

$$P_v = \exp\left[\frac{-3.9}{V}\left(\frac{\lambda}{0.55}\right)^m L\right] \tag{6}$$

Where V is the visibility [km], L is the propagation range and m is the size distribution for the water drops that form the fog.

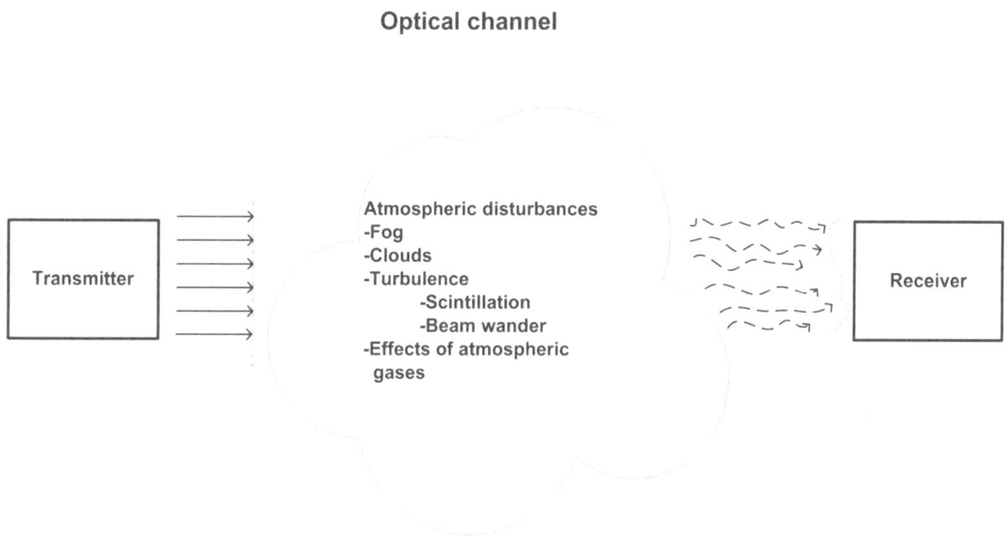

Fig. 6. Optical link over a terrestrial atmospheric channel

4.2 Rain

Other weather phenomena affecting the propagation of an optical signal is the rain, however its impact is in general negligible compared with the fog due to the radius of the drops (200µm - 2000µm) which is significantly larger than the wavelength of the light source OWC systems [Willebrand 2002].

4.3 Effects due to atmospheric gases. Dispersion and absorption

The dispersion is the re-routing or redistribution of light which significantly reduces the intensity arriving into the receiver (Willebrand, 2002). The absorption coefficient is a function of the absorption of each of the the particles, and the particle density. There absorbent which can be divided into two general classes: molecular absorbent (gas) []; absorbing aerosol (dust, smoke, water droplets).

4.4 Atmospheric windows

The FSO atmospheric windows commonly used are found in the infrared range.

The windows are in 0.72µm and 1.5µm, and other regions of the absorption spectrum. The region of 0.7µm to 2.0µm is dominated by the absorption of water vapor and the region of 2.0µm to 4.0µm is dominated by the combination of water and carbon dioxide.

4.5 Aberrations losses

These losses are due to the aberrations of the optical elements and can be expressed as:

$$L_{ab} = e^{-(k\sigma_a)^2} \tag{7}$$

$k=2\pi/\lambda$
σ_a=rms aberrations error

4.6 Atmospheric attenuation

Describes the attenuation of the light traveling through the atmosphere due to absorption and dispersion. In general the transmission in the atmosphere is a function of link distance L, and is expressed in Beer's law as [Lambert et al, 1995]

$$L_{atm} = 10 \log \tau \left[\frac{dB}{Km}\right] \tag{8}$$

with

$$\frac{I_d}{I_{Tx}} = \tau = \exp(-\gamma L) \tag{9}$$

I_d/I_{Tx} is the relationship between the intensity detected and the transmitted output intensity and γ is the attenuation coefficient. The attenuation coefficient is the addition of four parameters; the dispersion coefficients of molecules and aerosols, α and absorption coefficient, β of molecules and aerosols, each depending on the wavelength and is given by (Lambert et al 1995).

$$\gamma = \alpha_{molecule} + \alpha_{aerosol} + \beta_{molecule} + \beta_{aerosol} \tag{10}$$

4.7 Atmospheric turbulence

Inhomogeneities in temperature and pressure variations of the atmosphere cause variations in the refractive index, which distort the optical signals that travel through the atmosphere. This effect is known as atmospheric turbulence.The performance of atmospheric optical communications systems will be affected because the atmosphere is a dynamic and imperfect media. Atmospheric turbulence effects include fluctuations in the amplitude and phase of the optical signal (Tatarski, 1970), (Wheelon, 2003). The turbulence-induced fading in optical wireless communication links is similar to fading due to multipaths experienced by radiofrequency communication links (Zsu, 2002). The refractive index variations can cause fluctuations in the intensity and phase of the received signal increasing the link error probability.

As mentioned briefly above, the heating of air masses near the earth's surface, which are mixed due to convection and wind generates atmospheric turbulence. These air masses have different temperatures and pressure values which in turn leads to different refractive index values, affecting the light traveling through them. The atmospheric turbulence has important effects on a light beam especially when the link distance is greater than 1 km (Zsu, 1986). Variations in temperature and pressure in turn cause variations in the refractive index along the link path (Tatarski, 1971) and such variations can cause fluctuations in the amplitude and phase of the received signal (known as flicker or scintillation) (Gagliardi, 1988). Kolmogorov describe the turbulence by eddies, where the larger eddies are split into smaller eddies without loss of energy, dissipated due to viscosity (Wheelon, 2003, Andrews, 2005), as shown in Figure 7. The size of the eddies ranges from a few meters to a few millimeters, denoted as outer scale L_0, and inner scale, l_0, respectively as shown in Figure 7 and eddies or inhomogeneities with dimensions that are between these two limits are the range or inertial subrange (Tatarski, 1971).

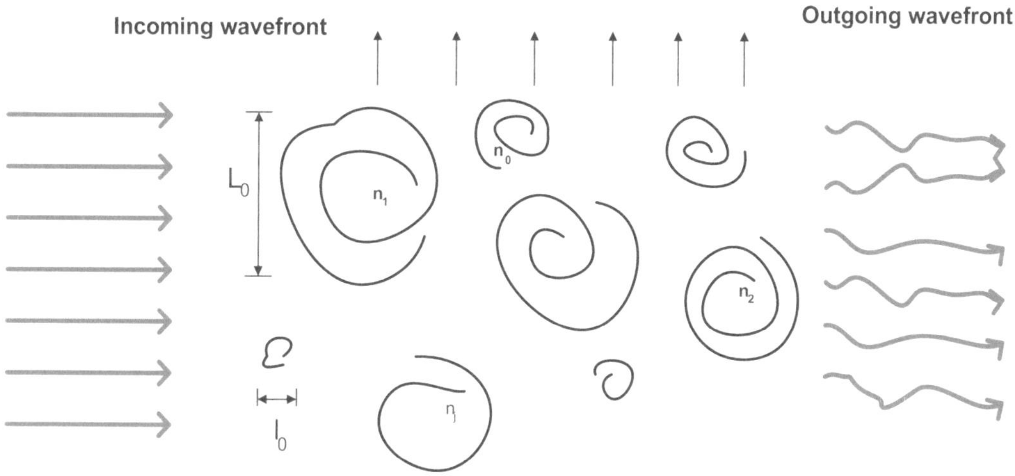

Fig. 7. Turbulence model based on eddies according to the Kolmogorov theory

A measure of the strength of turbulence is the constant of the structure function of the refractive index of air, C_n^2, which is related to temperature and atmospheric pressure by (Andrews, 2005):

$$C_n^2 = \left(79 \times 10^{-6} \frac{P}{T}\right)^2 C_T^2 \tag{11}$$

Where P is the atmospheric pressure in millibars, T is the temperature in Kelvin degrees and C_T^2 is the constant of the structure function. In short intervals, at a fixed propagation distance and a constant height above the ground can be assumed that C_n^2 is almost constant, (Goodman, 1985). Values of C_n^2 of 10-17 $m^{-2/3}$ or less are considered weak turbulence and values up to 10-13$m^{-2/3}$ or more as strong turbulence (Goodman, 1985). We can also consider that in short time intervals, for paths at a fixed height, C_n^2 is constant (the above for horizontal paths). C_n^2 varies with height (Goodman, 1985).
Another measure of the turbulence is the Rytov variance, which relates the structure constant of refractive index with the beam path through the following equation:

$$\sigma_R^2 = 1.23 C_n^2 k^{7/6} L^{11/6} \tag{12}$$

where λ is the wavelength, L is the distance from the beam path and $k=2\pi/\lambda$.
An optical light beam is affected by turbulence in different ways: variations in both intensity and amplitude, phase changes (phase front), polarization fluctuations and changes on the angle of arrival.

4.8 Intensity and amplitude fluctuations

The atmospheric turbulence affects the amplitude and phase of the optical signal that propagates through the medium in two points separated by a distance r, and can be described by the following equation according to the Rytov method for solving Maxwell's equations (Goodman, 1985):

$$U(\vec{r}) = U_0(\vec{r})\exp(\psi(\vec{r})) \tag{13}$$

where $U_0(r)$ is the undisturbed field. The complex phase perturbation can be written (Andrews, 2005):

$$\psi_1(\vec{r}) = \chi + iS_1 \tag{14}$$

or

$$\psi_1(\vec{r}) = \ln\left(\frac{A}{A_0}\right) + i(S - S_0) \tag{15}$$

where χ is the logarithm of the amplitude A and S is the phase of the field *U*(*r*) and A_0 and S_0 are the amplitude and phase without disturbing respectively. This analysis is done based on the Rytov approximation and shows that the irradiance (or intensity) fluctuations follow a lognormal distribution due to that the logarithm of the amplitude and the irradiance are related by (Goodman, 1985):

$$\chi = \frac{\left[\ln\left(\frac{I}{A^2}\right)\right]}{2} \tag{16}$$

According to the Rytov approximation, the variance of the logarithm of the amplitude $\langle\chi^2\rangle$ for a plane wave is (Goodman 1985):

$$\left\langle \chi^2 \right\rangle = \sigma_\chi^2 = 0.307 C_n^2 L^{11/6} k^{7/6} \tag{17}$$

It has been shown that the above equation (13) is a good approximation for values of $\sigma^2_\chi<1$ (Wheelon, 2003]. The variance of the logarithm of the intensity is related to the variance of the logarithm of the amplitude of (Wheelon, 2002).

$$\sigma_{\ln I}^2 = \left\langle \left|\ln I - \langle \ln I \rangle\right|^2 \right\rangle = 4\sigma_\chi^2 \tag{18}$$

and

$$\sigma_{\ln I}^2 = 1.23 C_n^2 L^{11/6} k^{7/6} = \sigma_R^2 \tag{19}$$

Where σ_R^2 is known as the Rytov variance. The Rytov variance for an infinite plane wave gives information about the strength of the fluctuations in the irradiance and hence gives us an idea of the strength of the atmospheric turbulence. Table II shows the relationship between values of Rytov variance and the strength of fluctuations (Wasiczko, 2004).

Strength levels of turbulence	Rytov variance
Weak	$\sigma_R^2 < 0.3$
Medium	$\sigma_R^2 \sim 1$
Strong	$\sigma_R^2 \gg 1$

Table 4. Typical values of turbulence for turbulence levels from weak to strong

Probability distribution function	Theory	Features	Application
Rician [Wheelon, 2001]	Born approximation	Little agreement with experimental data	Extremely weak turbulence regime
Lognormal [Tatarski, 1970]	Rytov approximation	Matching moments with experimental data	Weak turbulence regime
Negative Exponential [Andrews, 2005]	Heuristics	Easy to handle analytically	Saturation regime
I-K [Andrews, 2005]	Modulation effects of large scales to small scales	Difficult to relate PDF* parameters with the turbulence ones	Strong Turbulence
Lognormal - Rician [Andrews, 2005]	Modulation effects of large scales to small scales	Difficult to relate PDF* parameters with the turbulence ones	Strong Turbulence
Gamma-Gamma [Andrews, 2005]	Modulation effects of large scales to small scales	Its parameters are directly related to the turbulence.	Weak to strong turbulence

Table 5. Models for irradiance distributions (*PDF: Probability destribution function)

Another parameter used to compare the magnitude of the fluctuations of the irradiance is the transverse coherence length of an electromagnetic wave at optical frequencies (Wheelon, 2001). The coherence length for a plane wave is obtained from (Wheelon, 2003).

$$\rho_0 = \left(1.46k^2LC_n^2\right)^{-3/5} \tag{20}$$

For a spherical wave coherence length is given by (Wheelon, 2003)

$$\rho_0 = \left(0.546k^2LC_n^2\right)^{-3/5} \tag{21}$$

The coherence radius ρ_0 defined by Fried (Andrews, 2005) is:

$$r_0 = 2.099\rho_0 \tag{22}$$

The meaning of ρ_0, can be interpreted as follows: the phase in the wave front does not experience fluctuations in the sense of mean square root of greater than one radian at a distance ρ_0 wavefront at the receiver (Wheelon, 2003). The following table summarizes and compares differents models for irradiance distribution that have been proposed by several authors (Andrews, 2005), (Zsu, 2002).

4.9 Phase variations

The phase fluctuations not are usually take into account in incoherent optical wireless communication systems. However, in coherent optical wireless communication systems they should be considered. The phase fluctuations are caused by large eddies including those of outer scale (Goodman, 1985). It follows that the analysis of phase fluctuations are based on geometrical optics. Diffraction effects due to small-scale inhomogeneities have little effect on the result obtained based on geometrical optics (Wheelon, 2001). The complex phase disturbance [equation (40)], the phase *S*(*r*,*L*) can be expressed (Tatarski, 1971) as:

$$S(\vec{r},L)=\frac{1}{2i}\left[\psi(\vec{r},L)-\psi^{*}(\vec{r},L)\right] \tag{23}$$

considering that the turbulence in the atmosphere is homogeneous and isotropic, the phase variance (Andrews, 2005) is :

$$\sigma_S^2 \cong 4\pi^2k^2L\int_0^\infty \kappa\Phi_n(\kappa)d\kappa \tag{24}$$

the phase covariance function or the spatial covariance function for plane wave can be expressed as:

$$B_{S,pl}(\rho,L)=0.78C_n^2k^2\left(\frac{\rho}{\kappa_0}\right)^{-5/6}K_{5/6}(\kappa_0\rho) \tag{25}$$

where K is the modified Bessel function of second class. The temporal covariance function can be obtained from the spatial function using the frozen turbulence hypothesis of Taylor (Zhu and Kahn, 2002) replacing $\rho=V\perp$ where $V\perp$ is the average wind speed transverse to the propagation path. Therefore, the spatial covariance function is (Wheelon, 2003].

$$B_{S,pl}(\tau,L)=0.78C_n^2k^2\kappa_0^{-5/3}(\kappa_0V_\perp\tau)^{5/6}K_{5/6}(\kappa_0V_\perp\tau) \tag{26}$$

The power spectrum of phase variations was first published in the work of (Clifford, 1970) and can be obtained using the Wiener Khintchine theorem (Tatarski, 1970) as shown below. Applying the Fourier transform of the function of temporal phase covariance, we obtain the temporal spectrum of phase variations [Tatarski, 1970].

$$\begin{aligned}S_{S,pl}(\omega)&=4\int_0^\infty B_{S,pl}(\tau,L)\cos(\omega\tau)d\tau\\&=3.13C_n^2k^2L\kappa_0^{-5/3}\int_0^\infty(\kappa_0V_\perp\tau)^{5/6}K_{5/6}(\kappa_0V_\perp\tau)\cos(\omega\tau)d\tau\end{aligned} \tag{27}$$

Evaluating the integral gives [Wheelon, 2003] we obtain the aproximated expression

$$S_{S,pl}(\omega)=\frac{5.82C_n^2LV_\perp^{5/3}}{\left(\omega^2+\kappa_0^2V_\perp^2\right)^{4/3}} \tag{28}$$

4.10 Polarization fluctuations

The electromagnetic field is characterized by an electric field and a magnetic field which are vector quantities. The direction taken by the electric field vector at each point along the path is defined by the polarization of the field (Fowles, 1968). There have been several studies to estimate the magnitude of the change of polarization in an optical frequency electromagnetic signal as it travels through the turbulent atmosphere (Collet, 1972) (Strohbehn, & Clifford, S. 1967). These studies conclude that the change in the state of polarization of a beam traveling in a line of sight path in the turbulent atmosphere is negligible. Depolarization is usually measured as the ratio between the average intensity of the orthogonal field component and the incident plane wave (Wheelon, 2003). Under certain considerations depolarization can be obtained through:

$$\delta \text{Pol} = 0.070 C_n^2 \left(\kappa_0\right)^{7/3} k^{-2} \tag{29}$$

Various expressions have been obtained to determine the depolarization of an electromagnetic field at optical frequencies, considering quasi-monochromatic light sources and the results are similar. For example for L = 1500m, λ= 1550 nm and $C_n^2 = 1 \times 10^{-13}$ the depolarized component is 2.1×10^{-18} smaller in terms of the polarized component (Wheelon, 2001).

4.11 Arrival angle fluctuations

Fluctuations on the angle of arrival is another effect of atmospheric turbulence and seriously affects the performance of the communications system (Andrews, 2005). The movement of the centroid of the spot intensity on the receiver due to local inhomogeneities in the transmitter are responsible for this phenomenon. In the case of of non-coherent optical wireless communications wireless systems, this effect can be decreased by expanding the transmitted beam, so you always get intensity above the detection threshold to the receiver at the expense of the decrease in the average intensity (Wheelon, 2003). A more sophisticated technique is the use of pointing and tracking mechanisms of the centroid of the optical signal which makes adjustments on both the receiver and transmitter to ensure the highest possible alignment between them (Hemmati, 2006). Another way of reducing the effects of the variations on the angle of arrival is the use of adaptive optics, which correct these variations provided that the receiver aperture is large enough (Wheelon, 2001), (Andrews, 2005). The variance of the perturbations of the angle of arrival are obtained from the following equation (Wheelon, 2003).

$$\left\langle \delta\theta^2 \right\rangle = 2\pi R \int_0^\infty d\kappa \kappa^2 \Phi(\kappa) \tag{30}$$

4.12 Statistical models of wireless optical channel

As mentioned above, various probability distribution functions have been proposed to describe the statistical behavior of atmospheric optical communications channel. It was found that the amplitude distribution (or intensity) and phase is dependent on the theory of propagation of optical beams used. The phase distribution is obtained from geometrical optics and found that is suitable for the various regimes of turbulence (Andrews, 2005). Under the condition that the beam path is much larger than the size of the outer scale, based on the application of central limit theorem phase fluctuations of the optical signal is Gaussian and several experiments have supported the outcome (Clifford, 1970).

4.13 System design

This section will show the basics for the design of a OWC link. The power budget of an optical link must consider different impairments that affect the system performance such as : a) finite transmission power, b) optical gains and losses, c) Receiver sensitivity, d) propagation losses, e) electronics noise, f) phase noise of optical sources g) imperfect synchronization for coherent detection optical carrier, among others. First, we determine the fade margin between the transmitted optical power and minimum receiver sensitivity needed to establish a specified BER. It also should be considered the system margin (M_S), to compensate for the degradation of components and temperature factors. It is required to estimate a margin of availability (*M*) or link power budget, which is given by the following equation.

$$M = L_f - L_{tur} - L_{prop} - L_{poin} - L_{atm} - M_s \tag{31}$$

where:

L_f : fade margin

L_{tur} : turbulence losses

L_{prop} : propagation losses

L_{poin} : Pointing losses

L_{atm} : atmospheric losses

M_s : system margin

Parameters to be considered in the design are: wavelength, transmission rate, signal to noise ratio (SNR), link distance, diameter of the optical transmitter and receiver antennas, transmitter power and receiver sensitivity. We describe below the relationship among the parameters mentioned.

4.13.1 Fade margin

It is defined as the amount of the total losses allowed by the system to perform the optical link and is obtained from the equation:

$$L_f = P_{Tx} - P_{sens} \tag{32}$$

4.13.2 Propagation losses

Propagation losses are given by (Santamaria A., Lopez-Hernandez F.J., 1994):

$$L_{prop} = 10\log_{10}\left(\frac{4\pi Z}{\lambda}\right)^2 \tag{33}$$

where Z is the distance between the transmitter and receiver.

4.13.3 Turbulence losses

These losses take into account the effects of the variation of intensity of the laser beam due to atmospheric turbulence (scintillation) and can be estimated through:

$$L_{turb} = 10\log_{10}\left[1 + \left(\frac{\Omega_0}{\Omega_{turb}}\right)^2\right] \tag{34}$$

where

$$\Omega_0 = \frac{2\lambda}{\pi D_{Lens\_Tx}} \qquad (35)$$

With D_{Lens_Tx} is the lens transmitter diameter, and

$$\Omega_{turb} = \frac{\lambda}{\pi \rho_o} \qquad (36)$$

where ρ_b is the coherence radius.

4.13.4 Pointing losses

Pointing losses are due to misalignment between the transmitter and receiver the which causes reduction in the power captured by the receiver (A. Santamaria, FJ Lopez-Hernandez, 1994), are given by (A. Santamaria, FJ Lopez-Hernandez, 1994)

$$L_{pointing} = 4.3229\left(\frac{\phi_e}{\Omega_0}\right)^2 \qquad (37)$$

Where ϕ_e is the boundary angle of diffraction-limited beam of the transmitter and is given by

$$\phi_e \cong \frac{\lambda}{2D_{Lens\_Tx}} \qquad (38)$$

4.13.5 Atmospheric losses

They appears when the particle causing the scattering has the diameter equal to or greater than the wavelength of the radiation signal. These lossess are due to atmospheric gases (Beer's law). The attenuation and scattering coefficients are related with the visibility (Kim et al).

4.13.6 Geometric losses

Geometric path losses for a FSO link depends on the beamwidth of the optical transmitter (θ), the path length (L) and the receiver aperture area (D_r) (Figure 8):

$$L_{geo} = 20\log\left(\frac{\theta L}{D_r}\right) \quad dB \qquad (39)$$

L=transmitter-receiver distance
θ=Beam Divergence
D_r=Receiver diameter

4.13.7 Transmitting and receiving antenna gain

The gain of the transmitting antenna for free space is given by (A. Santamaria, FJ Lopez-Hernandez, 1994)

$$G_{Tx} = 10\log_{10}\left(\frac{2}{\Omega_0}\right)^2 \quad (40)$$

The receiving antenna gain is given by (A. Santamaria, FJ Lopez-Hernandez, 1994)

$$G_{Rx} = 10\log_{10}\left(\frac{4\pi A_r}{\lambda^2}\right) \quad (41)$$

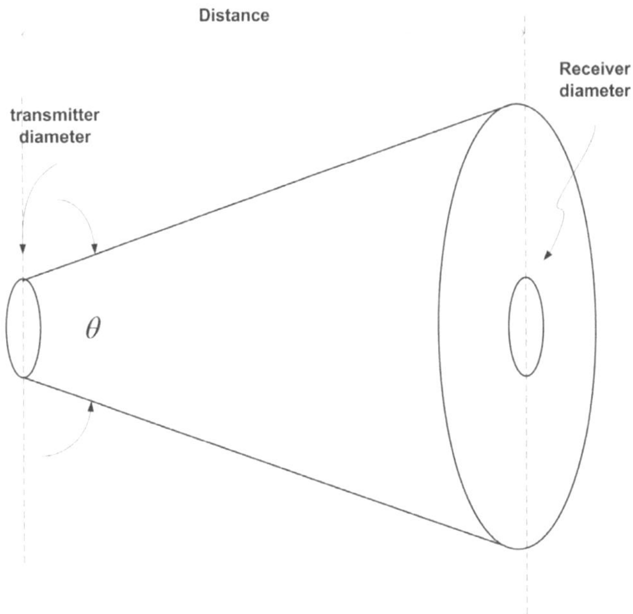

Fig. 8. Geometric losses scheme

5. Mitigating the effects of turbulent optical channel

One of the problems to be resolved in optical communication systems is to reduce the effects of turbulence, i.e. the scintillation and variations of the angle of arrival of the beam. Various techniques are used to reduce these phenomena. Among them we can mention the use of encryption, the use of large aperture receivers, using alignment systems, spatial diversity and amplifiers using erbium-doped fiber (EDFA).

5.1 Using coding to reduce the effects of turbulence in OWC systems

One way to improve the performance of wireless optical communication systems is the use of channel coding techniques. Several studies have been conducted to study the effect of the use of channel coding techniques in conditions of strong turbulence (Tisftsis, 2008) which is the scenario that offers the worst operating conditions. Pulse modulations such as PPM (Pulse Position Modulation) have been analyzed under the effects of weak turbulence (Hemmati, 2006). These results indicate the need for error correction in the receiver (FEC) to make communication possible under these conditions (Ohtsuki, 2003).

5.2 Large aperture receiver

It is known that for incoherent optical communications systems, such as IM-DD systems, the use of larger receiver apertures, increase the optical power collected leading to a reduction in scintillation. This effect is known as aperture averaging. This means that the larger the diameter of the receiving aperture, the power collected is higher, the signal has a better signal to scintillation noise ratio and the photo-current fluctuations are reduced (Fried, 1967).

5.3 Tracking and pointing systems

To reduce the effects of drift in the beam and the transmitter-receiver misalignment, phenomena that reduce the performance of wireless optical communication systems, mechanical systems can be used to correct both transmitter and receiver to compensate for variations tilt and pitch. This is possible because both changes occur at speeds of tenths of seconds (corresponding to frequencies below 100 Hz) (Andrews, 2005).

5.4 Use of spatial diversity to mitigate the effects of turbulence

One way to reduce the effect of signal fading due to turbulence, which is mainly caused by beam wander, is the use of arrangements of receivers (Andrews, 2005).

5.5 Erbium-doped fiber amplifiers (EDFA)

The use of EDFA in the receiver avoids the use of high power transmission. It has been shown that the use of these devices also reduces the scintillation due to increased average received optical power (Franz & Jain, 2000), but these devices could be expensive for certain applications of OWC systems.

6. Methods of modulation and coding

Traditionally, wireless communications systems use optical modulation formats OOK (On-Off Keying), which is also widely used in fiber optic systems and is characterized by its simplicity and robustness. This system consists of intensity modulated optical carrier and digital information is sent with the presence or absences of the optical carrier. Other modulation techniques have been used in optical wireless communication systems, such as pulse position modulation and the use of phase-modulated subcarriers. One of the problems present in the transmission of optical signals is scintillation, which reduces the optical power available at the receiver for periods that can be several milliseconds to values below the detection threshold and thus interruption link. Different alternatives for the solution to this problem have been proposed and analyzed. You can increase the received optical power using erbium-doped fiber amplifier (EDFA). The atmospheric turbulence reduces the received optical power which is caused by the low frequency components of the scintillation and is expressed as the displacement of the centroid of the spot or footprint of the beam in the plane of the receiver (beam wander).

6.1 Incoherent optical communication systems. OOK modulation

Within the methods of direct detection and intensity modulation, one of the most used techniques is the On-Off Keying modulation. For this modulation has been found that the probability of error (Andrews, 2005) is:

$$P_e = \frac{1}{2}\int_0^{\infty} f_I(i)\,\mathrm{erfc}\left(\frac{SNR(i)}{2\sqrt{2}}\right)di \tag{42}$$

where SNR is the signal to noise ratio as a function of intensity and erfc is the complementary error function. $f_I(.)$ is the probability density function of changes in signal strength.

6.2 Use of subcarriers

Basically, the resurgence of practical OWC systems is due to the technological developments of the systems of fiber optic communications. One of the techniques used to improve the performance of OWC systems is the use of sub-carriers. In this method, the laser beam intensity is modulated by an electrical signal derived from a combination of these subcarriers. Figure 9 shows the block diagram for subcarrier intensity modulations systems.

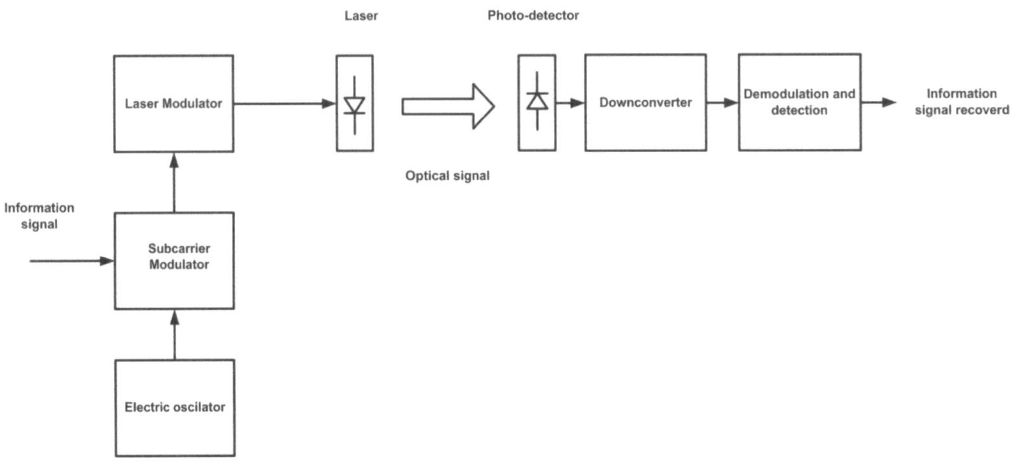

Fig. 9. Subcarrier intensity modulation OWC

6.3 Coherent optical communication systems

As indicated above, the current optical communications systems are based on incoherent modulation techniques which are relatively simple to implement and robust, but its theoretical performance is below the coherent modulation format. This type of system has advantages in relation to sensitivity, frequency selectivity and increased lodging capacity of channels in the bandwidth of the optical carrier. The coherent optical communication systems in atmospheric space applications have interesting characteristics that make them attractive for potential commercial use. For example, the homodyne detection of binary phase modulated signals (BPSK), the quantum limited is obtained with only 9 photons per bit, when in the OOK systems are needed 38 photons per bit. The BER for BPSK modulation is an average over the all possible intensity levels of a given probability density function, $p_I(I)$ without regard phase noise (Sánchez, 2008):

$$BER = \int_0^{\infty} p_I(\xi)\,\mathrm{erfc}\left(\sqrt{SNR(\xi)}\right)d\xi \tag{43}$$

The optical phase synchronization, and control of the state of polarization are the main challenges for the practical implementation of coherent systems using optical fiber as transmission medium (Kazovsky, 2006).
In the case of wireless systems, in clear sky conditions, the state of polarization suffers little variation and these changes are slow (Hodara, 1966) (Wheelon, 2001), but it is required that the state of polarization of the signal optical input matches the local oscillator. Carrier synchonization is neccesary to achieve the demodulation in coherent systems. The phase modulation techniques are usually suppressed carrier. Techniques such as injection locking, optical phase lock loop (OPLL) can not be used directly to lock the local oscillator phase [Kazovsky, 1986]. With the advent of high-speed digital components, the compensation of polarization, as well as other phenomena of the optical channel can be obtained in the electrical domain, opening up new possibilities for the practical implementation of optical communication systems consistent (Sánchez, 2008), (Arvizu, 2010). Figure 10 shows the block diagram of a coherent optical wireless communication system which shows the possible subsystems required to enable proper operation. At the transmitter, the optical phase modulation is performed while at the receiver is used an phase lock loop (PLL) to maintain synchronized the optical carrier signal with the optical local oscillator [Kazovski et al, 1995], and a state of polarization control system (Sánchez 2008), (Arvizu, 2010), as well as a balanced photo-reception stage.
Due to the loss of spatial coherence can not use aperture averaging in coherent optical communications systems and diameter in the aperture receiver must be smaller than the coherence distance r0 (equation 22). For example, with L=1500 m, λ=1.550μm and C_n^2 = 7×10^{-13}, r_0=2.5 cm (Figure 11).
However, the small apertures require the use of less divergence beams so that more optical power is collected by the receiver, which involves the use of pointing and tracking systems more fine and precise, making the system more complex and expensive. Another solution is the use of spatial diversity system. The space diversity coherent systems require that each unit receiving signals are processed individually before combining it and then perform the symbol detection process (Arvizu et al, 2010). That is, it requires that the signals to be synchronized in phase due to the loss of spatial coherence so that the combination of signals is not destructive and attenuates the signal received. This process can be performed optically or electronically (Arvizu et al, 2010). The distance between these coherent diversity receivers must be greater than r_0, so that the signals collected by each unit are uncorrelated.
Other proposed systems is the use of OWC systems with spatial diversity and coherent detection using (linear post detection combiner) (PDLC), which uses "n" receivers and develops individually detection by estimating the symbol for each (hypothesis "1" and "0") then becomes the weighting of the signal with better signal to noise ratio which is selected to obtain the output data (Arvizu et al, 2010).
Coherent optical communications systems offer several advantage in deep space applications, such as high sensivity, which is important because of the small signals existent in this scenery and the absence of atmospheric turbulence. Additionally coherent receivers have an inherent frequencial selectivity, as well as rejection of the background radiation, characteristics important in deep space applications.
Next generations of optical wireless communications could use differents strategies for reduce the turbulence effects. Adaptive optics is a technology utilized for improve the performance of astronomical telescopes by reducing the wavefront distortions and can be

used in OWC systems. However, still is a technology expensive for terrestrial OWC applications.

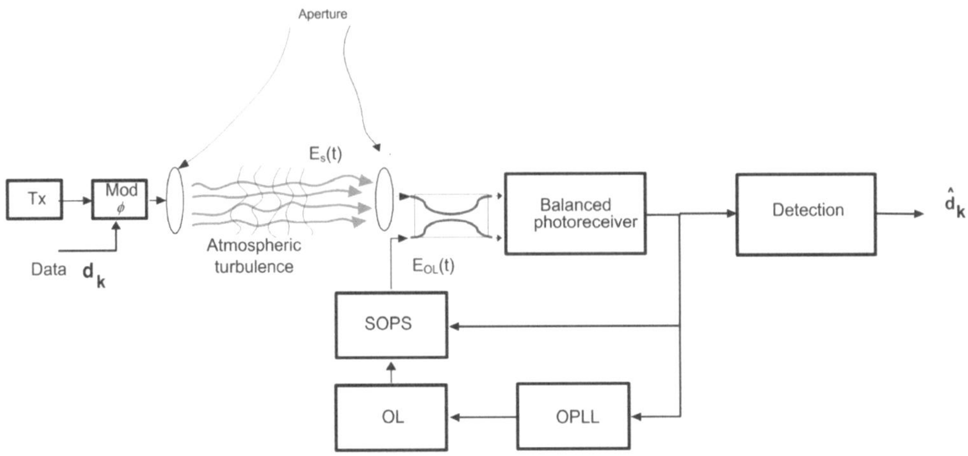

Fig. 10. Block diagram of the Coherent optical wireless communications system. SOPS: State of polarization system; OL: Local Oscillator: OPLL: Optical Phase lock loop

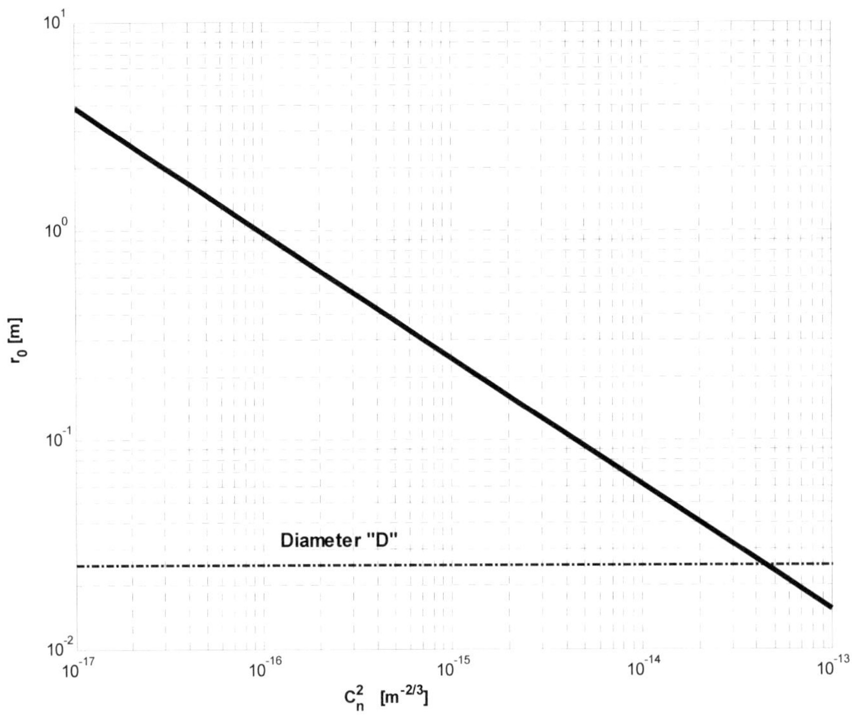

Fig. 11. Coherence diameter as function of the refractive index structure constant

7. Conclusions

In this chapter, the wireless optical communication systems have been discussed from first principles to systems that use different techniques to improve their performance. Different atmospheric channel characteristics have been emphasized and in general have shown the most relevant such as scintillation, the variations of the angle of arrival, the attenuation due to atmospheric gases and the effects of weather conditions. We analyzed the performance of communications systems for detecting incoherent modulations (OOK) and coherent (BPSK).This technology is becoming commonly used in civil applications and in the future be developed to have a scope similar to fiber optic systems in scope and availability.

8. References

Agrawal, P, Govind (2005). *Light Wave Telecommunications Systems* John Wiley and Sons, Inc, ISBN -13 978-0-471-21572-2, New York.

Andrews, L. C. & Phillps, R.L. (2005). *Laser beam propagation through random Media.* SPIE Press, ISBN 0-8194-5948-8 Bellingham, Washington.

Arvizu M. Mondragón, Sánchez L. Juan de Dios, Mendieta J. Francisco Javier, Coherent Optical Wireless Link Employing Phase Estimation with Multiple Beam, Multiple Aperture, for Increased Tolerance to Turbulence, *IEICE Transactions communications,* Vol. E93-B, No. 1, (January 2010), 226-229, ISSN 1745-1345.

Collet, E. & Alferness, R. (1972). Depolarization of a laser beam in a turbulent medium. *Journal of the Optical Society of America.* Vol. 62, No. 4, (529-533), ISSN 0030-3941.

Clifford, S.F. (1970). Phase Variations in Atmospheric Optical Propagation, *Journal of the Optical Society of America.* Vol. 61, No. 10, (529-533), ISSN 0030-3941.

Fowles G. R. 1975. *Introduction to modern optics.* Dover Publications. 2 edition, ISBN 0486659577, New York.

Franz, J. H. & Jain,V.K. (2000). *Optical communications, components and systems.* CRC Press. ISBN 0-8493-0935-2, New Delhi.

Fried. D.L. 1967. Optical heterodyne detection of an atmospherically distorted signal wave front. *Proceedings of IEEE.* Vol. 55, No. 1 (47-67).

Gagliardi, Robert M. and Karp, Sherman (1995). *Optical Communications,* John Wiley and Sons, Inc., Second Edition, ISBN 978-0471542872, New York.

Goodman, J. W. (1985). *Statistical Optics.* Wiley and Sons. ISBN 0471015024, New York.

Hemmati, H. (2006). *Deep Space Optical Communications,* John Wiley and Sons, Inc., ISBN 978-0-04002-7.

Kazovsky, L., Benedetto, S., Willner, A (1996). *Light Wave Telecommunications Systems.* Artech House, Inc. Norwood, ISBN 0-89006-756-2.

Kedar, D. y Arnom, S. (2003). Optical wireless communications through fog in the presence of pointing errors. *Applied Optics.* Vol. 42 No.24, (4946-4954) ISSN 2155-3165.

Kim, I.I, Mc Arthur, B., Korevaar, E. (2000), Comparison of Laser Beam Propagation at 785 nm and 1550 nm, in Fog and Haze for Optical Wireless Communications. *Proceedings of SPIE Optical Wireless Communications* III, Vol. 4214, (26-37)

Lambert, G. Stephen and Casey, L. William. (1995). *Laser Communication in Space.* Artech House, inc., Norwood. ISBN 0-89006-722-8.

Ohtsuki, T. (2003). Performance analysis of atmosferic optical PPM CDMA systems. *Journal of Lightwave Technology.* Vol. 21 No. 2 (406-411), ISSN: 0733-8724.

Osche, G. 2002. *Optical detection theory for laser applications*. John Wiley and Sons, ISBN 0-471-22411-1, New Jersey.

Qingchong L., Chunming Q., Mitchell G., & Stanton S. (2005). Optical wireless communications networks for first-and last-mile broadband access. *Journal of Optical Networking*. Vol. 4 No. 12 (807-828), ISSN 1536-5379.

Santamaria A., López-Hernández F.J. (1994). *Wireless LAN systems*, Artech House, ISBN 9780890066096.

Sánchez L. Juan de Dios, Arvizu M., Arturo, Mendieta J., Francisco (2008). Optical Phase Estimation in an Urban Wireless Communications, *IEICE Transactions communications*, Vol. E91-B, No. 7, (July 2008), 2447-2450, ISSN 1745-1345.

Strohbehn, J.W., y Clifford, S. (1967). Polarization and angle-of-arrival fluctuations for a plane wave propagated through a turbulent medium. *IEEE Transactions on Antennas and Propagation*, Vol. 15, No. 3 (416-421), ISSN 0018-926X.

Tatarski, V.I. (1971). *The effects of turbulence atmosphere on wave propagation*. The National Oceanic and Atmospheric Administration. U.S. Departament of Commerce, ISBN 07065-0680-4, Springfield, VA.

Tisftsis T.A. 2008. Perfomance of heterodyne wireless optical communications systems over gamma atmospheric channels. *Electronics letters*. Vol. 44, No. 5, (373-375), *ISSN*: 0013-5194

Wasiczko, L.M. (2006 *Techniques to mitigate the effects of atmospheric turbulence on free space optical communications link*. Ph.D Thesis. University of Maryland. 135 pp.

Willebrand, H. Ghuman, B.S. (2000). Free-space optics: enabling optical connectivity in today's networks", Sams Publishing, Indiana, ISBN 0-672-32248-x, USA.

Wheelon , A. D. (2001). *Electromagnetic scintillation Vol, I. Geometrical optics*. Cambridge University Press. Cambridge, ISBN 0521-801982

Wheelon, A.D. (2003). *Electromagnetic scintillation Vol, II. Weak Scattering*. Cambridge University Press. Cambridge, ISBN: 0521801990.

Zhu, X., Kahn J. M. (2002) Free Space Optical Communications Through Atmospheric Turbulence Channels, *IEEE Transactions on Communications*, Vol. 50, No. 8, August 2002. ISSN 0090-6778.

17

Visible Light Communication

Chung Ghiu Lee
Chosun University
South Korea

1. Introduction

The visible light communication (VLC) refers to the communication technology which utilizes the visible light source as a signal transmitter, the air as a transmission medium, and the appropriate photodiode as a signal receiving component.
The visible light communication technology has a short history compared with other communication technology, for example, public old telephone service, Ethernet, high-speed optical communication, wireless cellular communication, IrDA, etc.
It is due to that the development and commercialization of light emitting diodes (LEDs) which emits the light in visible wavelength range have been successful for illumination in recent decade. It is said that the illumination LEDs will replace the conventional illumination lightings such as incandescent bulbs and fluorescent lamps since they have the characteristics of long lifetime, mercury free, color mixing, fast switching, etc.
By utilizing the advantage of fast switching characteristic of the LEDs compared with the conventional lightings, i.e., modulating the LED light with the data signal, the LED illumination can be used as a communication source. Since the illumination exists everywhere, it is expected that the LED illumination device will act as a lighting device and a communication transmitter simultaneously everywhere in a near future.
There have been researches on application of visible LEDs. The audio system using visible light LEDs was reported in Hong Kong by G. Pang et al. (Pang, 1999) and the visible light communication with the power line communication was reported in Japan by Komine et al. It can be considered that the active research has been started since 2005. Still the VLC system is not close to commercialization, but in the basic research.
From the above technical backgrounds, the technical issues will be described in system viewpoint with the recent developments and research results. The VLC link configuration is explained in Section 2. The VLC transmitter (Section 3) and the VLC receiver (Section 4) are described. Section 5 is about VLC considerations including LED characteristics and data format considering the illumination perspectives, including the international efforts on standardization for helping commercialization. The chapter will be concluded with Section 6.

2. System description

2.1 Channel configuration

The optical wireless communication (OWC) is a general term for explaining wireless communication with optical technology. Usually, OWC includes infrared (IR) communication for short range (Knutson, 2004) and free-space optics (FSO) communication (FSO website) for longer range.

The visible light communication (VLC) denotes a communication technology which uses visible light as optical carrier for data transmission and illumination. Nowadays, light-emitting diode (LED) at visible wavelengths (380 nm ~ 780 nm) has been actively developed (Schubert, 2003) and can be used as a communication source and, naturally, the silicon photodiode which shows good responsivity at visible wavelength region is used as receiving element. The transmission channel is the air, whether it is indoor or outdoor.

At present, the researches on VLC are focused on indoor applications. The indoor VLC channels are classified adopted from the conventional IR communication (Kahn, 1999) and (Ramirez-Iniguez, 2008), since the link configurations of VLC are similar to IR communication. The different characteristics come from the different operating wavelength and wavelength-dependent devices (visible LED, silicon photodetector, etc), and the fact that the VLC has the dual nature of communication and illumination. The other physical principles related to optics can be applied similarly, including the light transmission and reflections.

The link configurations are classified into four basic types (Ramirez-Iniguez, 2008), according to the existence of obstacles in light path and the directionality of the transmitter to the receiver.

The basic link types include the directed line-of-sight (LOS), the non-directed LOS, the directed non-LOS, and the non-directed non-LOS. The decision that the link is directed or non-directed depends on whether the transmitter has the direction to the receiver. The decision that the link is LOS or non-LOS depends on whether there exist a barrier to block the transmission of light between a transmitter and a receiver.

In a VLC system, the non-directed LOS link is important since the general illumination operates for LOS environment and it is not focused or directed.

From now on, we concentrate on indoor application of VLC and non-directed, line-of-sight (LOS) link, since the indoor application is expected to be developed in a near future.

Fig. 1 shows the simplified geometry for an indoor, non-directed LOS link, with the transmitter on the ceiling and the receiver on the bottom surface.

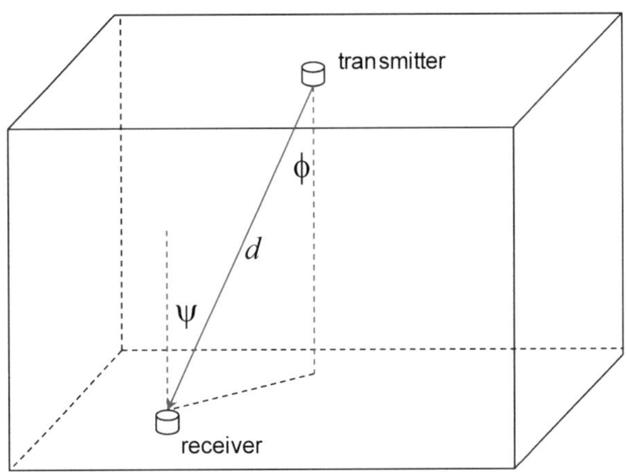

Fig. 1. Geometry for an indoor, non-directed LOS VLC link

Following the analysis for the directed LOS link (Kahn, 1997), the received optical power P at a receiver is expressed as

$$P = P_t \cdot \frac{(m+1)}{2\pi d^2} \cdot \cos^m(\phi) \cdot T_s(\psi) \cdot g(\psi) \cdot \cos(\psi), \qquad 0 \le \psi \le \Psi_C, \tag{1}$$

where P_t is the transmitted power from an LED, ϕ is the angle of irradiance with respect to the axis normal to the transmitter surface, ψ is the angle of incidence with respect to the axis normal to the receiver surface, d is the distance between an LED and a detector's surface. $T_S(\psi)$ is the filter transmission. $g(\psi)$ is the concentrator gain. Ψ_C is the concentrator field of view (FOV), i.e., semiangle at half power. m is the order of Lambertian emission, and is given with the transmitter semiangle (at half power) $\Phi_{1/2}$ as

$$m = -\ln 2 / \ln(\Phi_{1/2}). \tag{2}$$

Here, $m = 1$ in the case of $\Phi_{1/2} = 60°$ (Lambertian transmitter). From the axial symmetry in Fig. 1, we can set as $\phi = \psi$. A concentrator and an optical filter can be used in front of the photodetector. At the time of experiment, it was not optimized for the beam profile from the LED. With $\Psi_C \approx 90^\circ$, $g(\psi) \approx n^2$, where n is the refractive index of the CPC.

2.2 Comparison with IR communication

To have a clear notion about VLC, it is needed to compare it with the infrared communication technology. The differences between VLC and infrared communication are listed in Table 1.

	Visible light communication	Infrared communication
Data rate	>100Mb/s possible (LED dependent)	4 Mb/s (FIR), 16 Mb/s (VFIR)
Status	Research and standardization in IEEE	Standardization (IrDA)
Distance	~meters	~3 meters
Regulation	No	No
Security	Good	Good
Carrier wavelength (frequency)	380~780 nm visible light (multiple wavelengths)	850 nm infrared
Services	Communication, illumination	Communication
Noise source	Sun light, Other illumination	Ambient light
Environmental	Daily usage Eye safe (visible)	Eye safe for low power (invisible)
Applications	Indoor & vehicular communication, Optical ID	Remote control, Point-to-point connection

Table 1. Comparison of short-range wireless communication technologies. (FIR: fast infrared, VFIR: very fast infrared)

The infrared communication is standardized by the IrDA (Infrared Data Association) and the IrDA is still developing advanced application of infrared communication. The data rate for infrared communication (Knutson, 2004) includes 4 Mb/s (FIR), 16 Mb/s (VFIR), and etc. On the other hand, the VLC data rate is dependent on the LED's modulation bandwidth and the standardization on physical layer specifications has not yet been published. Some of researches have reached around 20 Mb/s. Since the resonant-cavity LEDs shows the modulation bandwidth > 100 Mb/s, it is expected that the VLC system with > 100 Mb/s data rate is possible by using the high-speed LEDs and appropriate multiplexing techniques. The transmission distance for VLC is possible up to several meters due to its illumination requirement. Since the infrared communication is used for a remote controller, the maximum distance is ~ 3 meters. The VLC transmitter emits multiple-wavelength light from red to violet and the exact analysis will become more complex than infrared communication. Due to the wavelength of the light source, the noise sources will be different. For infrared communication, noise comes from ambient light containing infrared light. In the case of VLC, the sunlight and other illumination light can be noise sources. Also, the visible light is in our daily lives and we can detect it with human eye. Therefore, the VLC is eye safe. The infrared communication has the long history and many applications have been developed and are listed in (IrDA website). On the other hand, the VLC has shorter history and the small number of applications has been proposed. Nevertheless, the illumination exists everywhere and the VLC using the illumination infrastructure can be used easily.

By utilizing the characteristics of VLC link, it is expected to be candidate infrastructure for indoor/outdoor public ubiquitous communication technology in the near future.

3. VLC transmitter

The technical considerations for VLC transmitter are mentioned. The main components of VLC transmitter are visible LEDs Fig. 2 shows a configuration of a VLC link and an VLC transmitter is shown. The VLC transmitter is different from conventional communication transmitter in viewpoint that it must act as a communication transmitter and an illumination device simultaneously. Therefore, we must consider the following two requirements simultaneously.

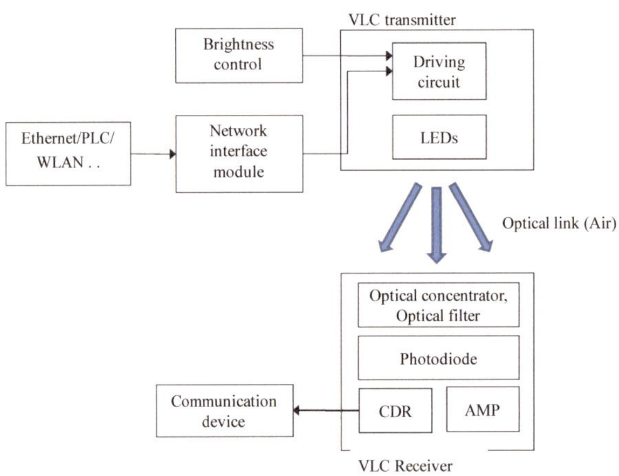

Fig. 2. Configuration of a VLC link. (CDR: clock and data recovery, AMP: amplifier, PLC: power line communication, WLAN: wireless LAN)

Firstly, the VLC transmitter for communication usually uses visible LEDs as a modulation device on optical carrier at visible light. For data modulation on the LEDs, the modulation bandwidth of visible LEDs must be considered. The visible LEDs are usually high-brightness LEDs and the manufacturers do not develop the high-brightness LEDs for communication applications. There were research reports on measured modulation bandwidth of high-brightness LEDs (Lee, 2007). Still, most of visible LEDs for illumination have the modulation bandwidth around tens of megahertz. Although the data rate using visible LEDs would be limited to tens of megahertz, the VLC will find the appropriate low data rate applications, for example, optical ID, simple message delivery, etc.

There was a research on increasing the modulation bandwidth of arrayed white LEDs using multiple-resonant modulation for VLC system (Minh, 2008). The experiment demonstrated the VLC system with 16 LEDs to achieve 25 MHz bandwidth and low error rate data transmission at 40 Mb/s.

Secondly, the VLC transmitter must act as an illumination as well. The illumination requirement is that the illuminance must be 200 - 1000 lx for indoor office illumination according to ISO recommendation (Tanaka, 2003). The high-brightness LEDs operates with the forward current > 100 mA and it is quite large, compared with usual communication devices. Thus, to modulate data on the high-brightness LEDs while maintaining the illumination level makes the VLC transmitter design more complex than the conventional communication transmitter design. Transmitting low rate data transmission with illumination simultaneously was reported in (Choi, 2010), where pulse position modulation (PPM) data was transmitted over pulse width modulation (PWM) dimming control signal.

3.1 LED characteristics

For appropriate VLC transmitter design, the LED characteristics needs to be understood.

The general characteristics of LED are well described in (Schubert, 2003). Here, we focus on the high-brightness LED for visible wavelength range.

There are two types of visible wavlength LEDs. One category is single color LED, for example, red (R), green (G), blue (B) LEDs. The other category is white LED, which uses phosphors for converting the emission wavelength from the original active area. We will discuss the white LEDs later in this section. Typically, red, green, and blue LEDs emits a band of spectrum, depending on the material system. Red LEDs emits the wavelength around 625 nm, green LEDs around 525 nm, and blue LEDs around 470 nm.

The output optical power versus the input current into the LED is one of important parameter. The linear dependence of the output optical power on the input current makes the LED operation easy and is closely related to the data modulation performance. The output optical power depends on the ambient temperature. Depending on the material system, the temperature dependence of the output optical power varies. Generally, the temperature increases, the output optical power decreases.

On the other hand, the white LED draws much attention for the illumination devices. Comparing the LED illumination with the conventional illumination such as fluorescent lamps and incandescent bulbs, the LED illumination has many advantages such as high-efficiency, environment-friendly manufacturing, design flexibility, long lifetime, and better spectrum performance.

Most of white LEDs is comprised of LED chip emitting short wavelength and wavelength converter (for example, phosphor). The short wavelength light from the LED chip is absorbed by the phosphor and then the emitted light from the phosphor experiences wavelength shift to a longer wavelength. As a result, the many wavelength components are observed outside the LED. A white light can be generated from a blue LED with appropriate phosphor. The emission spectrum of a phosphor based LED has the strong original blue specrum and the longer wavelengths shifted by the phosphor.

From the illumination viewpoint, the RGB or white LEDs can be used for VLC. However, we consider the response time of each LED from the communication viewpoint, since the response time is directly related to the maximum data rate to be transmitted by the LED. Basically, the phosphor based white LED has longer rise/fall times due to phosphor absorption/re-emission times. It is noted that each LED can find its appropriate applications for VLC systems.

3.2 Brightness control of LED

For LED illumination, dimming, i.e., brightness control, is needed. Several dimming control methods are widely used (Garcia, 2009) and new methods have been proposed (Doshi, 2010). AM dimming is the way of LED dimming which controls the DC forward current injected into the LED. By changing the DC forward current, the emitted luminous flux is controlled. It is very simple to implement, but it could cause a change of the chromaticity coordinates of the emitted light.

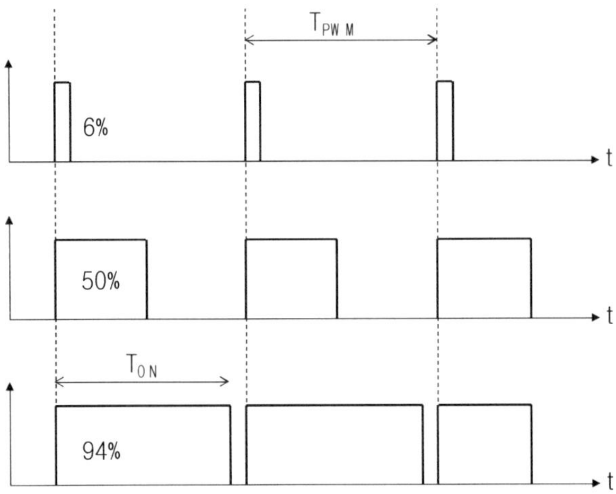

Fig. 3. Waveform of pulse width modulation (PWM) signal for dimming control

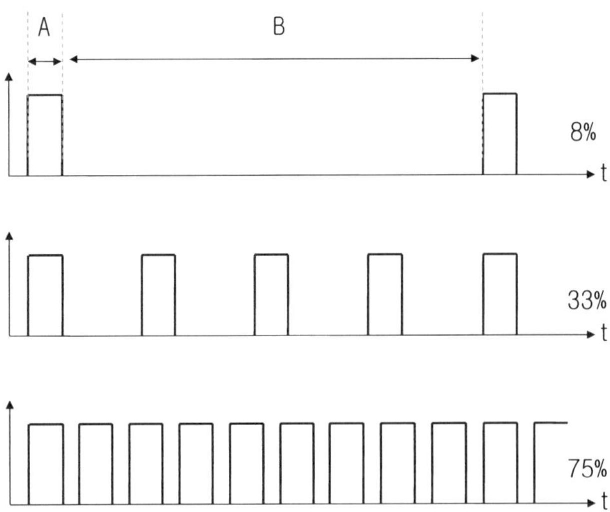

Fig. 4. Waveform of pulse frequency modulation (PFM) signal for dimming control

The pulse width modulation (PWM) method controls the width of the current pulse, thus the average current into the LED, as shown in Fig. 3. While the PWM pulses have a constant amplitude, the pulse width varies according to the dimming level (duty ratio) within the PWM period. Since the PWM pulses have a constant amplitude, the spectrum of the emitted light from the LED is constant.

The pulse frequency modulation (PFM) method controls the frequency of the contant width pulses as shown in Fig. 4, and thereby, the average current into the LED.

The bit angle modulation (BAM, also known as binary code modulation) method is shown in Fig. 5, which is invented by Artistic License Engineering Ltd., uses the binary data pattern encoding the LED dimming level (Artistic License website). Each bit in the BAM pulse train matches to the binary word. For example, in the 8-bit BAM system, the most significant bit (MSB), b7, matches to the pulse with the width of $128=2^7$, the sixth bit, b6, matches to the pulse with the width of $64=2^6$. Similarly, b5 to 2^5 pulse width, b4 to 2^4 pulse width, b3 to 2^3 pulse width, b2 to 2^2 pulse width, b1 to 2 pulse width. The least significant bit (LSB), b0, matches to the pulse width of a unit width. The BAM is simple to implement and reduces the potential to flicker.

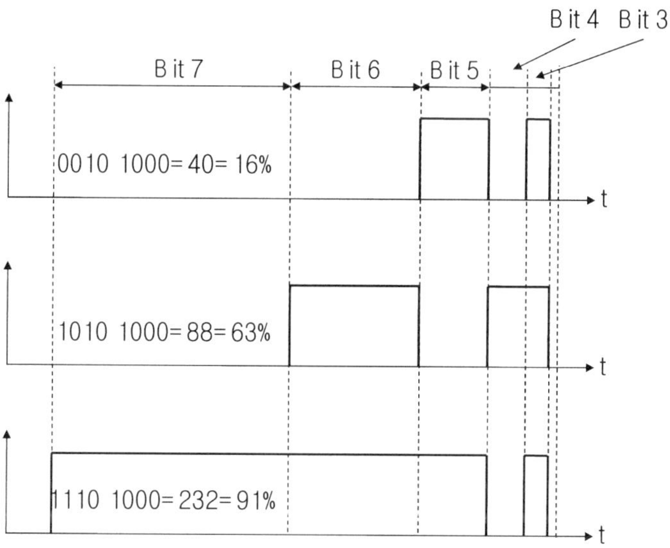

Fig. 5. Waveform of bit angle modulation (BAM) signal for dimming control

The multiphase PWM method is proposed (Doshi, 2010) to reduce the output current transients and electromagnetic interference (EMI) generated by the power circuit, which are associated with visible flicker and audible noise in the power circuit. It is achieved by shifting the individual PWM signals for different LED.

Recently, the signal formats considering the brightness control and data communication simultaneously have been introduced for VLC (Linnartz, 2009) (Choi, 2010) (Bai, 2010). Usually, the brightness of LED light depends on average current into the LED light. The above methods are based on PWM dimming techniques.

3.3 LED driver circuit

Usually, the VLC transmitter employs direct modulation of visible LEDs since the VLC system needs cheap transmitter design. To utilize LEDs as a communication source and as

an illumination simultaneously, it is required to add the digital data signal over the dimming control signal. To modulate the LEDs, the drive current is fed into the LEDs with the appropriate DC bias.
For modulating an LED or LD directly, a transistor is switched for feeding the LED or an FET can be used (Ramirez-Iniguez, 2008). Also, the integrated circuit (IC) based driver chip can be used. We can get application diagrams for such IC based LED driver from the driver chip manufacturer (Maxim website).
Since the drive current contains the DC current for illumination or the dimming current for data signal, a bias Tee can be used for mixing the DC current and digital data for low data rate application.
To design an appropriate driver circuit for VLC system, the following items must be considered:

- Current requirement of LED(s) : modulation depth and bias current
- Rise and fall times of LED(s) and component(s) : related to maximum bit rate
- Illumination compatibility with communication
- Design approach : whether driver IC is used or not
- Power dissipation and thermal design of the transmitter

4. VLC receiver

The VLC receiver is composed of receiving optical elements including optical concentrator and optical filter, photodiode, amplifier, and signal recovery circuit, as shown in Fig. 2. Basically, the VLC system is designed to employ direct detection at the photodiode.
The optical concentrator is used to compensate for high spatial attenuation due to the beam divergence from the LEDs to illuminate large area. By using the appropriate concentrator, the effective collection area can be increased. The methods using compound parabolic concentrator (CPC) and imaging lens for infrared communications are described in (Kahn, 1997) and (Ramirez-Iniguez, 2008). Since the wavelength range is different from the infrared communication, the specific design parameters for the VLC system will be changed from the design for the infrared communication.
The VLC system is vulnerable to the sunlight and other illuminations, and therefore, it is important to employ appropriate optical filter to reject unwanted DC noise components in the recovered data signal.
The photodiodes with good responsivity to visible light are silicon p-type-insulator-n-type photodiode (Si PIN-PD) and silicon avalanche photodiode (Si APD). The silicon material photodiode operates from 400 nm to 1200 nm, which includes the visible wavelength range. There are many photodiodes whose bandwidths are over 200 MHz and is much wider than the VLC LED transmitter.
There are several types of signal amplification circuits. Among them, high impedance amplifier and transimpedance amplifier are briefly described. The high impedance amplification is simple to implement. The series resistor is connected to the anode of the photodiode and the high input-impedance amplifer senses the voltage across the series resistor and amplifies it. The transimpedance amplifier provides current-to-voltage conversion by using shunt feedback resistor around an inverting amplifier
Generally, the noise in the VLC receiver is similar to the usual optical communication receiver, for example, the thermal noise from the load resistor and the photodiode, the shot noise in the photodiode, the excess noise from the amplifier. The main noise components are the sunlight and the other illumination light.

5. VLC considerations

5.1 Multiple wavelengths

The system design and analysis on IR are based on the assumption that the IR source emits a monochromatic light. Most of researches on VLC have been performed also on the same assumption. The optical power [Watt] of monochromatic light at wavelength λ is related to the illuminance $I(0)$ as :

$$P_{rec} = \frac{I(0)\cos^m(\phi)}{683V(\lambda)D_d^2\cos(\psi)}, \tag{3}$$

where $V(\lambda)$ is the eye sensitivity function (Schubert, 2003). Referring to Fig. 1, ϕ is the angle of irradiance with respect to the axis normal to the transmitter surface and ψ is the angle of incidence with respect to the axis normal to the receiver surface. D_d is the distance between an LED and a detector's surface. The constant 683 in the denominator comes from the conversion equation between radiometric [Watt] and photometric unit [lx]:

$$Photometric\ unit[lx] = radiometric\ unit[Watt] \times 683\left(\frac{lm}{W}\right) \times V(\lambda) \tag{4}$$

According to the photometry (Schubert, 2003), at the wavelength of 555 nm (green color), we have the eye sensitivity $V(550)=1$; and at the wavelength of 720 nm (red color), the eye sensitivity is given as $V(720)=0.001$.

However, practically, the illumination LED is a multiple-wavelength source in visible range, for example, 380 nm ~ 780 nm. Therefore, the calculations of the illuminance and received optical power must involve the integration over wavelengths occupied by the light in the eye sensitivity function. The received optical power is given as

$$P_{rec} = \frac{I(0)\cos^m(\phi)}{683D_d^2\cos(\psi)\int_{380}^{780} V(\lambda)P(\lambda)d\lambda} \tag{5}$$

$P(\lambda)$ is the power spectral density (Schubert, 2003).

5.2 Optical interference noise

The noise sources in VLC system include the sunlight, the incandescent light and the fluorescent light. Moreira et al. measured the average background current for a couple of typical optical interferences (Moreira, 1997). The background current was detected with a 0.85 cm^2 silicon PIN photodiode in a differential structure.

Table 1 shows the measured background currents from 60 Watt incandescent bulb at 1 m distance and from eight 36 Watt fluorescent lamps at 2.2 meters distance in a 5 m × 6 m room. From the Table, the background current of the sunlight is the largest one. Also, the background current of the incandescent bulb is larger than that of the fluorescent lamps. If the optical filter is used, the backgound current can be reduced effectively by filtering out appropriate wavelength components. Specifically, the optical filter works effectively for fluorescent lamps due to its optical spectrum.

	without optical filter	with optical filter
Direct sunlight	5100	1000
Indirect sunlight	740	190
Light from an incandescent bulb	84	56
Light from a fluorescent lamp	40	2

Table 2. Background current from the optical interferences (Moreira, 1997)

In (Moreira, 1997), the interference signal from the incandescent bulbs has the Fourier series expression given by

$$i_{incandescent}(t) = \frac{I_B}{A_1}\sum_{i=1}^{\infty} a_i \cos(2\pi \cdot 100it + \phi_i), \quad (6)$$

where a_i and ϕ_i are the relative amplitude and phase of each harmonic of 100 Hz. A_1 is the constant that relates the interference amplitude with I_B. The constants a_i, ϕ_i, and A_1 can be estimated from the measurement data for a specific incandescent bulb.

The reference (Moreira, 1997) provides the mathematical equations for the other interference signals from incandescent bulbs and fluorescent lamps, and the related constants. For a specific photodiode and receiver circuit, the equation needs to be estimated for more exact analysis.

5.3 Recent research

Most of researches on optical wireless communication (OWC) have been performed in the field of infra-red (IR) communication. The modulation formats for optical wireless communication system have been reported such as on-off keying (OOK) (Dickenson, 2004), dual-header pulse interval modulation (DH-PIM) (Aldibbiat, 2005), subcarrier PSK intensity modulation (Lu, 2004), multiple-subcarrier modulation (Ohtsuki, 2003). From the fact that the IR and visible light are light with different wavelength spectra, the modulation formats for IR system can be adopted in VLC considering geometrical environment, mobility and multi-user connectivity.

Recently, the VLC research has been started actively in Japan. Nakagawa laboratory in Keio University has published many research papers on VLC, including the fundamental analysis (Komine, 2004) and the interconnection of VLC with power line communication (Komine, 2003). The Korea Photonics Technology Institute (KOPTI) published a research on measurement results for modulation bandwidth of high-brightness LEDs to prove the feasibility of VLC from the source bandwidth (Lee, 2007). The research group in Oxford University reported the multiple resonant equalization technique for enhancing LED bandwidth for VLC (Minh, 2008).

Recently, Linnartz et al. published the code-time division multiple access - pulse position modulation (CTDMA-PPM) and code-time-division multiple access - pulse width modulation (CTDMA-PWM) for tagging each LED lamp by transmitting PPM and PWM coded data in high-power LED system, respectively (Linnartz, 2010). The scheme is proposed for illumination, transmission of identifiers and lighting control. As stated in Section 3.2, the signal formats for brightness control and data communication simultaneously have been reported (Choi, 2010) (Bai, 2010).

5.4 Standardization activities

In Japan, the visible light communication consortium (VLCC) is organized for collaboration between industrial companies, universities, and research institutes (VLCC website). The VLCC member includes NEC corporation, Panasonic Electric Works, Nippon Signal, Toshiba corporation, Samsung Electronics, NTT DoCoMo, Casio Computer, Nakagawa Laboratories, Sumitomo Mitsui Construction, Sharp corporation, etc. The VLCC concentrates on activating technology exchange, system development, demonstration, and standardization of VLC inside Japan.

In Europe, the working group 5 of the wireless world research forum (WWRF) deals with VLC technology as one of next-generation wireless access technology (WWRF website). The WWRF has published a white paper on killer application of VLC, market forcast, and technology roadmap.

In IEEE, 802.15 in IEEE 802 LMSC (LAN/MAN Standards Committee) has organized the study group on VLC and the group is now the task group 7 (TG7) (TGVLC website).

In South Korea, the telecommunications technology association (TTA) (TTA website) supports standardization of VLC for Korean standard and international standard.

6. Conclusion

In this chapter, the key ideas on visible light communication (VLC) have been reviewed in relationship with optical wireless communication and infrared communication. The channel characteristics for VLC system were mentioned comparing it with infrared communication and the VLC transmitter and receiver are described including the basic characteristics of LED. Also, the considerable topics have been described including LED dimming, optical devices, and the effect of multiple wavelengths. The recent research results and standardization activities are summarized.

7. References

Aldibbiat, N.M. ; Ghassemlooy, Z., McLaughlin, L. (2005) Indoor optical wireless systems employing dual header pulse interval modulation (DH-PIM), *International Journal of Communication Systems*, Vol. 18, No. 3 (2002) (285-306) 1074-5351

Artistic License website ; http://www.artisticlicence.com (Application Note 11)

Bai, B.; Xu, Z.; Fan, Y.; (2010) Joint LED dimming and high capacity visible light communication by overlapping PPM, Presented in *19th Annual Wireless and Optical Communications Conference (WOCC)*, 978-1-4244-7597-1 , Shanghai, May 2010, IEEE

Choi, J.H. ; Cho, E.-B. ;Kang, T.-G. ;Lee, C.G. (2010) Pulse-width modulation based signal format for visible light communications, *Technical Digest of OECC 2010*, pp. 276-277, 978-1-4244-6785-3, Sapporo, (July 2010) IEICE

Dickenson, R.J. ; Ghassemlooy, Z. (2004) Bit error rate performance of 166 Mb/s OOK diffuse indoor IR link employing wavelents and neural networks, *IEE Electronics Letters*, Vol. 40, No. 12, (2004) (753-755) 0013-5194

Doshi, M. ; Zane, R. (2010) Control of Solid-State Lamps Using a Multiphase Pulsewidth Modulation Technique, *IEEE Transactions on Power Electronics*, Vol. 25, No. 7, (July 2010) (1894-1904), 0885-8993

FSO website ; http://www.freespaceoptics.org

Garcia, J. ; Dalla-Costa, M.A. ; Cardesin J. ; Alonso J.M. ;Rico-Secades M. (2009) Dimming of High-Brightness LEDs by Means of Luminous Flux Thermal Estimation, *IEEE Transactions on Power Electronics*, Vol. 24, No. 4, (April 2009) (1107-1114), 0885-8993

Kahn, J.M. ; Barry, J.R. (1997) Wireless Infrared Communications, *Proceedings of the IEEE*, Vol. 85, No. 2, (February 1997) (265-298), 0018-9219

Knutson, C. D.; Brown, J. M. (2004) *IrDA Principles and Protocols*, MCL Press, 0-9753892-0-3, USA

Komine, T. ; Nakagawa, M. (2003) Integrated System of White LED Visible-Light Communicaiton and Power-Line Communication, *IEEE Transactions on Consumer Electroincs*, Vol. 49, No. 1, (2003) (71-79), 0098-3063

Komine, T. ; Nakagawa, M. (2004) Fundamental analysis for visible-light communication system using LED lights, *IEEE Transactions on Consumer Electronics*, Vol. 50, No. 1, (2004) (100-107), 0098-3063

Lee, C.G. ; Park, C.S. ;Kim, J.-H . ;Kim, D.-H. (2007) Experimental verification of optical wireless communication link using high-brightness illumination light-emitting diodes, *Optical Engineering*, Vol. 46, No. 12, (December 2007) (125005), 0091-3286

Linnartz, J.-P. M. G. ; Feri, L. ; Yang, H. ; Colak, S. B. ; Schenk, T. C. W. (2009) Code Division-Based Sensing of Illumination Contributions in Solid-State Lighting Systems, *IEEE Transactions on Signal Processing*, Vol. 57, No. 10, (October 2009) (3984-3998), 1053-587X

Lu, Q. ; Mitchell, G.S. (2004) Performance Analysis for Optical Wireless Communication Systems Using Subcarrier PSK Intensity Modulation through Turbulent Atmospheric Channel, *IEEE Globecom 2004*, pp.1872-1875, 0-7803-8794-5, Dallas, November 2004, IEEE

Maxim website ; http://www.maxim-ic.com

Minh, H.L. ; O'Brien, D.C. ; Faulkner, G.F. ; Zeng, L. ; Lee, K. ; Jung, D. ; Oh, Y. (2008) High-speed visible light communicaitons using multiple-resonant equalization, *IEEE Photonics Technology Letters*, Vol. 20, No. 14, (July 2008) (1243-1245), 1041-1135

Moreira, A.J.C. ; Valadas, R.T. ; de Oliveira Duarte, A.M. (1997) Optical interference produced by artificial light, *Wireless Networks*, Vol. 3, No. 2, (June 1997) (131-140), 1022-0038

Ohtsuki, T. (2003) Multiple-Subcarrier Modulation in Optical Wireless Communicaitons, *IEEE Communications Magazine*, Vol. 41, No. 3, (2003) (74-79), 0163-6804

Pang, G. ; Ho, K.-L. ;Kwan, T. ; Yang, E. (1999) Visible Light Communication for Audio Systems, *IEEE Transactions on Consumer Electronics*, Vol. 45, No. 4, (November 1999) (1112-1118) 0098-3063

Ramirez-Iniguez, R. ; Idrus, S. M. ; Sun, Z. (2008) *Optical Wireless Communications : IR for wireless connectivity*, CRC Press, 978-0-8493-7209-4, USA

Schubert, E. F. (2003). *Light-Emitting Diodes*, Cambridge University Press, 0-521-82330, UK

Tanaka, Y. ; Komine, T. ; Haruyama, S. ; Nakagawa, M. (2003) Indoor Visible Light Data Transmission System Utilizing White LED Lights, *IEICE Transactions on Communications*, Vol. E86-B, No. 8, (August 2003) (2440-2454) 1745-1345

TGVLC website ; http://www.ieee802.org/15/pub/TG7.html

TTA website ; http://www.tta.or.kr/English/index.jsp

VLCC website ; http://www.vlcc.net

WWRF website; http://www.wireless-world-research.org/

Williams, S. (2000) IrDA : Past, Present and Future, *IEEE Personal Communiations*, Vol. 7, No. 1, (February 2000) (11-19), 1070-9916

18

Non-mechanical Compact Optical Transceiver for Optical Wireless Communications

Morio Toyoshima, Hideki Takenaka and Yoshihisa Takayama
National Institute of Information and Communications Technology
Japan

1. Introduction

The advantages of optical communications as compared to radiowave (RF) communications include broader bandwidth, larger capacity, lower power consumption, more compact equipment, higher security against eavesdropping, better protection against interference, and the absence of regulatory restrictions (Hyde & Edelson, 1997). Moreover, the demand for high-data-rate transmission from spaceborne observation platforms is steadily increasing (Toyoshima, 2005a). Free-space optical (FSO) communications systems are expected to play an important role in providing such high-data-rate communications, and optical technologies for satellite networks are expected to revolutionize space system architecture (Chan, 2003). For terrestrial optical wireless communications, a transmitter with a 3 × 3 square array of vertical-cavity surface-emitting lasers (VCSELs) was evaluated in Parand et. al. (2003). Multiple-input multiple-output (MIMO) systems were presented based on optical code-division multiple-access (OCDMA), imaging diversity receivers, and white LEDs (Hamzeh et. al., 2004; Djahani et. al., 1999; Zeng et. al., 2009; Minh et. al., 2009). For long-range free-space laser communications, however, maintaining a line of sight between transceivers is particularly difficult because of the small divergence angle of the laser beams. Minimizing the requirements for the tracking system and ensuring the steady operation of the onboard optical terminal are therefore important for realization of commercial applications. FSO links are also well known for their susceptibility to adverse weather conditions such as cloud and fog, which pose great challenges to link availability. For terrestrial FSO links, RF links can be backed up to ensure continuous availability (Wu et. al., 2007).

Optical terminals for long-distance communications tend to have large mass because optical tracking systems require mechanically movable parts for coarse laser pointing and tracking. Reductions in mass, power, and volume can decrease interference with other missions on satellites. Non-mechanical movable architecture is extremely attractive for robust and lifelong operation of an optical terminal in orbit. The small satellite community still uses 9.6-kbps communication links by employing ham radio communications due to resource constraints in nano-class satellites (Nakaya et al., 2003; Miyashita et al., 2006). Compact terminals can be used in nano-class satellites that have a mass of the order of a few tens of kilograms. There is also a significant advantage concerning frequency-licensing problems faced by satellites, and in this regard optical frequency carriers will be of great use to the small satellite community. Research and development at National Institute of Information and Communications Technology (NICT) on FSO communications indicates that compact communications terminals will have good applicability in the future. NICT has developed a non-mechanical, compact optical terminal equipped with a two-dimensional laser array for space communications, and this paper considered its application toward indoor optical wireless communications.

In section 2, we propose the concept of a compact free-space laser communications terminal via the first implementation of an 8 × 8 VCSEL array. This optical system has no mechanically moving parts. This compact terminal can receive optical communications signals from multiple platforms and transmit multiple optical communications beams to the counter terminals. Such an optical system can therefore serve as a MIMO system. Section 3 presents the system analysis of the optical link budget for indoor optical wireless communications between an optical base station and distributed stations. Background noise is estimated during the daytime and eye safety is discussed with respect to the optical base station and the distributed stations.

2. Conceptual terminal design

2.1 System configuration

Figure 1 shows the configuration of the proposed compact laser communications transceiver. The laser beam from the counter terminal passes through the telescope lens, is reflected from the beam splitter, and is detected by the CCD sensor. The CCD sensor detects the direction of the counter terminal's line of sight, and one of the array lasers is selected according to the direction of the signal received by the CCD. A CCD with a pixel size equal to that of the XGA (1280 × 1024) is used. The centroid of the pixels is calculated in the computer, and the laser beam corresponding to the direction of the centroid is turned on. Figure 2 shows a photograph of the manufactured compact laser communications transceiver and control computer system. With this configuration, multiple inputs from multiple platforms are possible with the parallel laser spot detection processing, and MIMO configuration is also possible (Short et al., 1991).

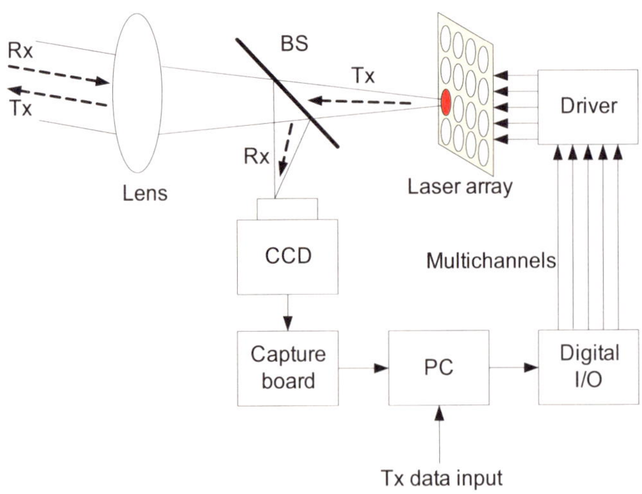

Fig. 1. Configuration of the proposed compact laser communications transceiver

2.2 Optical part of the transceiver

The laser beam is transmitted from the two-dimensional laser array through the beam splitter and telescope lens. The beam is selected by the centroid calculation in the computer. The beam divergence angle of the selected laser beam covers the angular interval between adjacent laser arrays (Cap et al., 2007). Two adjacent laser beams are turned on simultaneously to ensure that the laser transmission is not interrupted and to maintain a constant optical intensity at the counter terminal. Figure 3 shows the beam transmission configuration for a two-dimensional laser array. With this transmission method, the transmitted laser beam is not interrupted during the tracking of the counter terminal. Each laser beam is combined by an interval at the half width at half maximum (HWHM). Therefore, if the two adjacent laser beams are turned on simultaneously the optical intensity can be almost constant at the counter terminal.

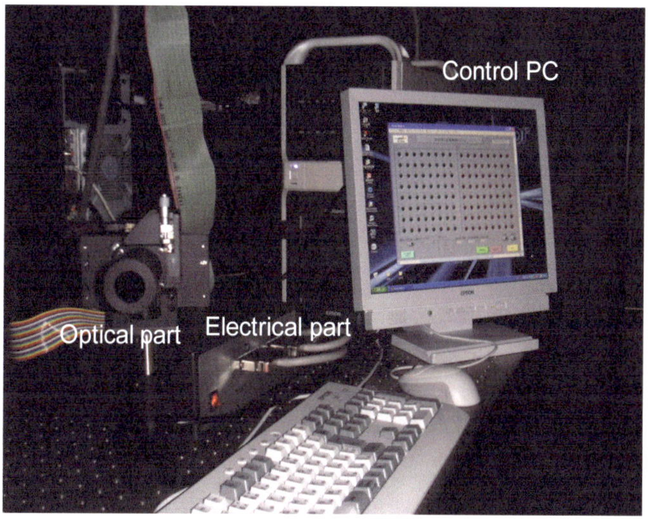

Fig. 2. Manufactured compact laser communications transceiver

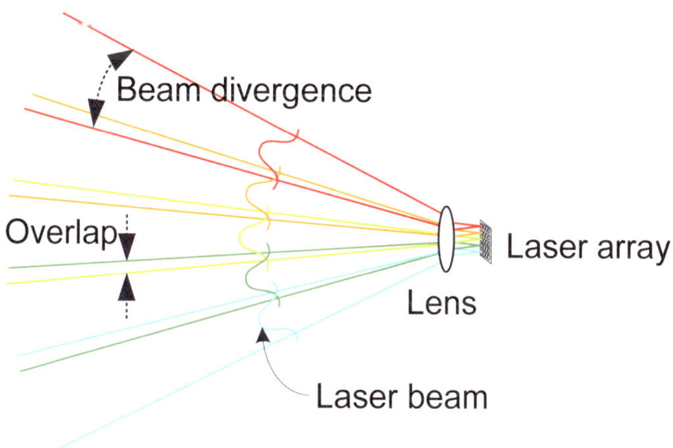

Fig. 3. Laser beam transmission method

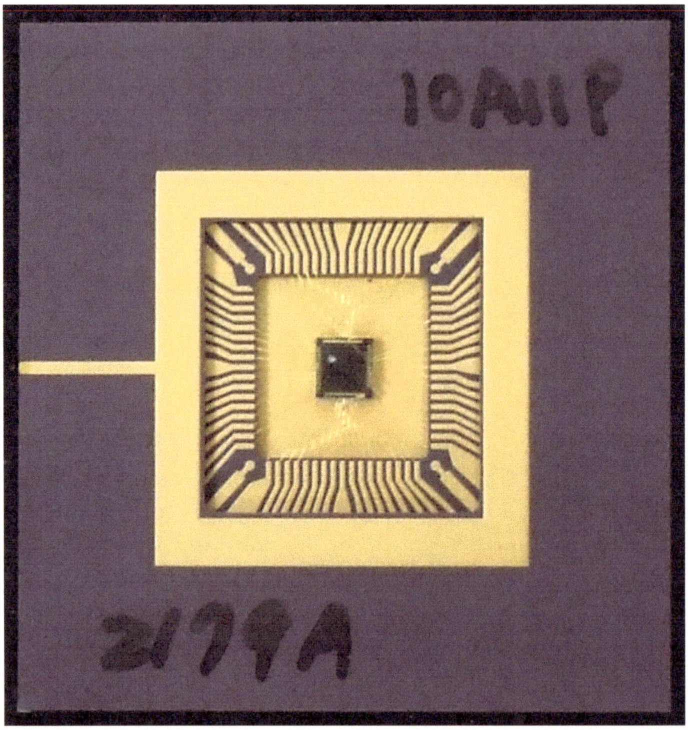

Fig. 4. 8 × 8 VCSEL array

Fig. 5. Optical part of the compact laser communication transceiver

For the transmitter, we use an 8 × 8 VCSEL array, as shown in Figure 4, for the first evaluation model. VCSELs were chosen because they are easy to arrange in an array, there are no mechanical parts, and they are readily available. The maximum output power of one pixel is 4 mW at a wavelength of 850 nm, as shown in Table 1. The laser diode can be modulated at above 2.5 GHz. All the VCSELs could be turned on individually. The beam divergence for this evaluation model was designed to be 2 degrees for one VCSEL.

Fig. 6. Electrical part of the compact laser communication transceiver

Parameter	Value
Array number	64 (8 × 8)
Maximum output power of one pixel	4 mW
Wavelength	850 nm
Beam divergence angle	20-30 degrees
Minimum frequency response	2.5 GHz

Table 1. VCSEL array specifications

Figure 5 shows the optical part of the manufactured compact laser communications transceiver. The small telescope consists of nine lenses. The VSCEL is mounted at the end of the small telescope and the CCD sensor is mounted on the upper side of the telescope, as shown in Fig. 5. The size of the optical part of the telescope (lens mount) is 13.5 × 6 × 11 cm, power consumption is less than 10 W, and mass is 1 kg, as shown in Table 2. Commercial-off-the-shelf (COTS) transceivers usually have a tracking system and a COTS transceiver has power consumption of 20 W and mass of about 8 kg at 1.25 Gbps. Our system, however, has no mechanical tracking system; thus there is the potential of reduced mass, power, and volume in the proposed transceiver.

2.3 Electrical part of the transceiver

Laser beams in the VCSEL array are modulated according to the received laser spot extracted by the control computer system, as shown in Fig. 1. Two 32-channel digital I/O boards are installed and can transmit data at a rate of 25 Mbps. Figure 6 shows a photograph of the electrical part of the manufactured laser driver. The electrical part, as shown in Fig. 6, can drive 64 channels of the VCSELs by the selected signal from the digital I/O boards. The laser diode is driven at an average power of 2 mW by the driver electronics. The electrical part of the compact laser communications transceiver has mass of 3.1 kg, size of 27 × 26 × 10 cm, and power consumption of less than 10 W, as shown in Table 2.

Resource		Value
Optical part	Mass	1 kg
	Size (lens mount)	15 × 12 × 12 cm (13.5 × 6 × 11 cm)
Electrical part	Mass	3.1 kg
	Size	27 × 26 × 10 cm
	Power	< 10 W

Table 2. Compact laser communication transceiver resources

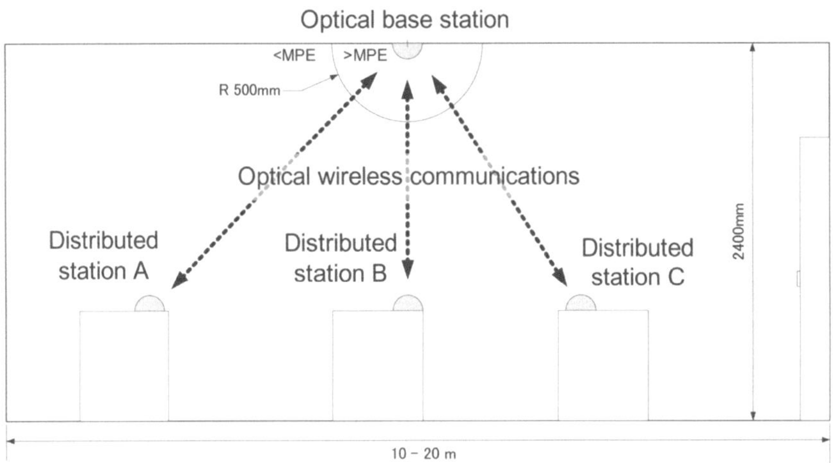

Fig. 7. Optical base station and distributed optical station layout

3. System analysis and experimental results

3.1 Link budget analysis

Table 3 summarizes the results of the link budget analysis for the proposed compact optical transceiver applied to indoor optical wireless communications. The optical link is designed to connect an optical base station on the ceiling with distributed optical terminals in a room, as shown in Fig. 7. The output laser power for a pixel of the VCSEL array is assumed to be 2 mW at 850 nm wavelength. The beam divergence angle is set at 0.33 rad for a single laser pixel for the full width at $1/e^2$ maximum (FWe^{2}M), and the angular coverage of the transmitter is 180° for a 8 × 8 array, which is sufficient to cover the number of distributed optical terminals in the room. The overlap of the beams is set to occur at the HWHM. The

beam pointing error can be considered as zero because the transmitting power can be doubled by turning on the adjacent two VCSELs simultaneously.
If stations A, B, or C simultaneously communicate with the base station, the spatial diversity can be performed by the different VCSEL lasers. If some stations can be within one laser beam, time-division multiple-access (TDMA), CDMA, or frequency-division multiple-access (FDMA) can be used for the communication scheme. By using these techniques, MIMO can be achieved with a single photo detector with the sufficient field of view (FOV) and appropriate optical filter. Figure 8 shows an example image of simultaneous two-target tracking measured by CCD. Figures 9 and 10 show the CCD pixels for simultaneous two-target tracking when one target is fixed and the other is oscillating at 5 and 10 Hz, respectively. These results show successful simultaneous two-target tracking, demonstrating the capability of MIMO for free-space laser communications.

Item	Unit	Value
TX power	mW	2.0
	dBm	3.0
Laser array pixel size	-	8x8
Beam diameter at telescope	μm	3.2
TX beam divergence	rad	0.33
Angular coverage	deg	180.0
TX optics loss	dB	-2.0
Wavelength	m	8.50E-07
Average pointing loss	dB	0.0
TX gain	dB	24.6
Distance	m	10.0
Space loss	dB	-163.4
Atmospheric transmission	dB	0.0
RX antenna diameter	cm	5.0
RX gain	dB	105.3
RX optics loss	dB	-2.0
RX power	dBm	-34.5
Data rate	bps	1.00E+09
Sensitivity (@BER of 10^{-6})	photons/bit	1000
	dBm	-36.3
Average margin for BER	dB	**1.9**
MPE	W/m^2	20.0
Margin for MPE	dB	0.4

Table 3. Link budget analysis between an optical base station on the ceiling and distributed optical terminals in a room

3.2 Background noise and eye safety

If we consider the FOV of about 10 degrees, the background level during the daytime becomes about -44 dBm by using an optical filter with 1 nm optical bandwidth and 5 cm aperture diameter. In this case, the signal-to-noise ratio (SNR) can be about 10 dB for the received level at a BER of 10^{-6}, as shown in Table 3. Due to the background, a detector array with FOV of 10 degrees should be used to achieve a 1 Gbps data rate. Pointing therefore needs to be achieved at the receiver.

The link distance is assumed to be 10 m from the optical base station on the ceiling to the distributed optical stations. If we use on-off-keying (OOK) non-return-to-zero (NRZ) data transmission with a receiving aperture with a 5 cm diameter in the proposed system, the link margin will be 1.9 dB at a data rate of 1 Gbps with BER of 10^{-6}. In order to keep the eyes safe from laser beam radiation, the irradiance from the optical base station should be lower than the maximum permissible exposure (MPE) beyond a distance of 50 cm. On the other hand, the laser beam in the distributed stations close to the users can be never transmitted until when the laser beam from the optical base station is received as the protocol. If the laser beam is received by the distributed optical stations it will not contact the human eyes. Therefore, by this procedure the eye safety can be preserved in the distributed optical stations close to the users.

As shown in Table 3, the proposed non-mechanical method can be applied to terrestrial free-space laser communications. If the proposed terminal can be greatly compacted, mobile users can use the high-data-rate optical link without a mechanical tracking system on the ground, like a digital camera. Setting up the optical transceivers is easy and their installation is uncomplicated. In the future, applicable fields for the optical transceivers will include not only satellite communications but also high-speed cell phone communications, wireless LAN, mobile communications, and building-to-building fixed high data rate communications with no difficulties. The reliability of VCSELs, however, must be examined in the future based on the given environment.

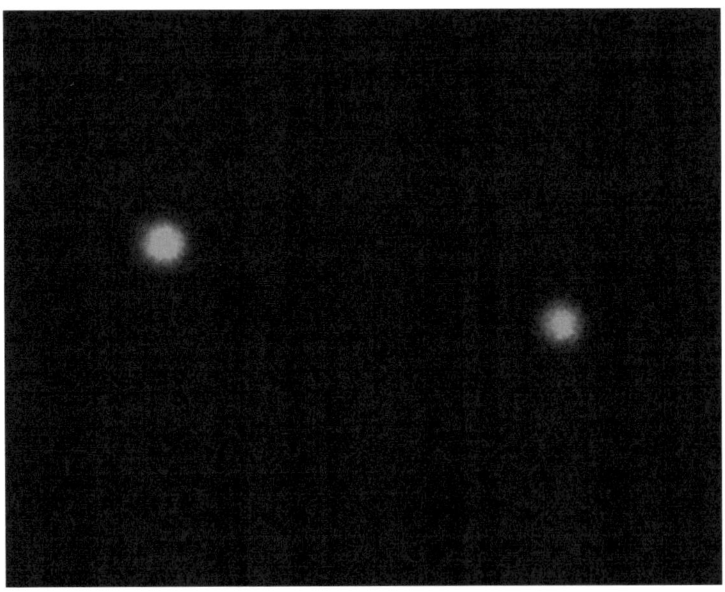

Fig. 8. Example of simultaneous two-target tracking measured by CCD

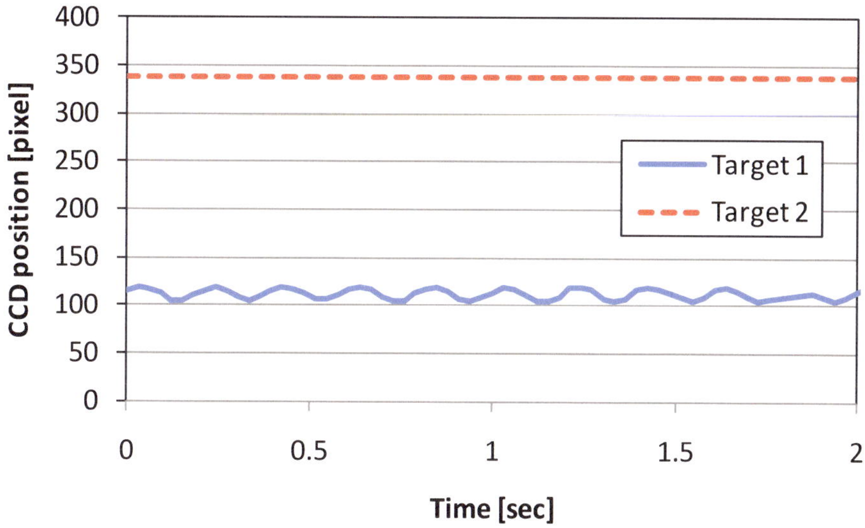

Fig. 9. CCD pixels for simultaneous two-target tracking when one target is fixed and the other is oscillating at 5 Hz

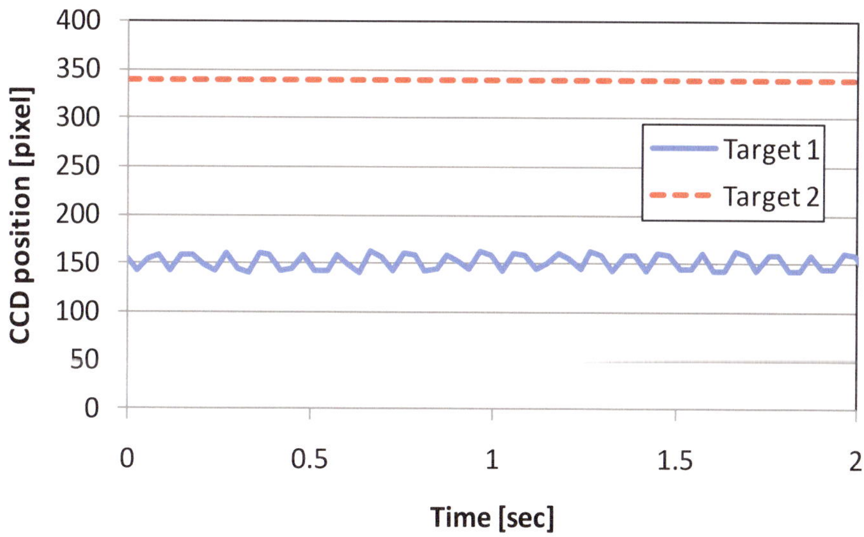

Fig. 10. CCD pixels for simultaneous two-target tracking when one target is fixed and the other is oscillating at 10 Hz

3.3 Future issues

The system proposed in this paper was developed for space communications but applied for indoor networks. Indoor optical wireless systems face stiff competition from future WiFi (802.11n) and 3GPP evolutions (IMT-Advanced), which will have data rates respectively exceeding 300 Mbps and 100 Mbps. The Gbps-class optical indoor wireless system may, however, play an interesting role in high data transmission and supplementing for drawbacks of frequency and bandwidth allocation and interference problems between RF and optical systems. Optical wireless systems should not compete with each other. Standardization efforts will be carried out with respect to the supplementing and also to ensure Gbps-class optical wireless interfaces on future user devices.

4. Conclusion

We have presented a non-mechanical and highly compact optical transceiver. A VCSEL array is used in the transceiver, and the laser pixel turned on depends on the direction of the counter terminal from which the CCD receives a signal. The mass, volume, and power of the proposed system can be reduced because it contains no mechanically movable structures. This study used an 8 × 8 VCSEL, which, to the best of our knowledge, is the first such implementation. The VCSEL number can be increased for improving the number of counter terminals but the MPE must be reduced, which is the tradeoff in the system design, and a novel protocol was proposed for eye safety. A simultaneous two-target tracking test was performed and demonstrated the capability of MIMO for free-space laser communications. As there are no regulatory restrictions on the use of the optical frequency, the proposed compact laser communications transceiver will be useful not only for satellites but also terrestrial optical wireless communications in future applications.

5. References

Arimoto, Y.; Toyoshima, M., Toyoda, M., Takahashi, T., Shikatani, M. & Araki K. (1995). Preliminary result on laser communication experiment using Engineering Test Satellite-VI (ETS-VI), *Proc. SPIE*, Vol. 2381, pp. 151–158

Cap, G. A.; Refai, H. H. & Sluss, Jr., J. J. (2007). Omnidirectional free-space optical (FSO) receivers, *Proc. SPIE*, Vol. 6551-26, pp. 1–8

Chan, V. W. S. (2003). Optical satellite networks, *Journal of Lightwave Technology*, Vol. 21, pp. 2811–2827

Djahani, P. & Kahn, J. M., (1999). Analysis of Infrared Wireless Links Employing Multi-Beam Transmitters and Imaging Diversity Receivers, *Global Telecommunications Conference - Globecorn'99*, 1999.

Hyde, G. & Edelson, B. I. (1997). Laser satellite communications: Current status and directions, *Space Policy*, Vol. 13, pp. 47–54

Hamzeh, B. & Kavehrad, M., (2004). OCDMA-coded free-space optical links for wireless optical-mesh networks, *IEEE Transactions on Communications*, Vol. 52, No. 12, pp. 2165–2174

Jono, T.; Takayama, Y., Kura, N., Ohinata, K., Koyama, Y., Shiratama, K., Sodnik, Z., Demelenne, B. Bird, A. & Arai, K. (2006). OICETS on-orbit laser communication experiments, *Proc. SPIE*, Vol. 6105, pp. 13–23

Kim, I. I.; Riley, B., Wong, N. M., Mitchell, M., Brown, W., Hakakha, H., Adhikari, P. & Korevaar, E. J. (2001). Lessons learned from the STRV-2 satellite-to-ground lasercom experiment, *Proc. SPIE*, Vol. 4272, pp. 1–15

Lightsey, P. A. (1994). Scintillation in ground-to-space and retroreflected laser beams, *Opt. Eng.*, Vol. 33, No. 8, pp. 2535–2543

Minh, H. L., O'Brien, D., Faulkner, G., Zeng, L., Lee, K., Jung, D., Oh, Y., and Won, E. T., (2009). 100-Mb/s NRZ Visible Light Communications Using a Postequalized White LED, *IEEE Photonics Technology Letters*, Vol. 21, No. 15, pp. 1063–1065

Miyashita, N.; Konoue, K., Omagari, K., Imai, K., Yabe, H., Miyamoto, K., Iljic, T., Usuda, T., Fujiwara, K., Masumoto, S., Konda, Y., Sugita, S., Yamanaka T., & Matunaga, S. (2006). Ground operation and flight report of Pico-satellite Cute-1.7 + APD, *International Symposium on Space Technology and Science (25th ISTS)*

Nakaya, K.; Konoue, K., Sawada, H., Ui, K., Okada, H., Miyashita, N., Iai, M., Urabe, T., Yamaguchi, N., Kashiwa, M., Omagari, K., Morita, I. & Matunaga, S. (2003). Tokyo Tech CubeSat: CUTE-I -Design and development of flight model and future plan-, *21st AIAA International Communication Satellite System Conference & Exhibit*, Yokohama, Vol. 2003-2388, April 15–19

Nielsen, T. T.; Oppenhaeuser, G., Laurent, B. & Planche, G. (2002). In-orbit test results of the optical intersatellite link, SILEX. A milestone in satellite communication, *Proceedings of the 53rd International Astronautical Congress*, Vol. IAC-02-M.2.01, pp. 1–11, Houston, October

Parand, F., Faulkner, G. E. & O'Brien, D. C. (2003). Cellular tracked optical wireless demonstration link, *IEE Proc. Optoelectron.*, Vol. 150, No. 5, pp. 490–496

Reyes, M.; Chueca, S., Alonso, A., Viera, T. & Sodnik, Z. (2003). Analysis of the preliminary optical links between ARTEMIS and the Optical Ground Station, *Proc. SPIE*, Vol. 4821, pp. 33–43

Short, R. C.; Cosgrove, M., Clark, D. L. & Oleski, P. (1991) Performance of a demonstration system for simultaneous laser beacon tracking and low data rate optical communications with multiple platforms, *Proc. SPIE*, Vol. 1417, pp. 464–475

Takayama, Y.; Jono, T., Toyoshima, M. Kunimori, H., Giggenbach, D., Perlot, N., Knapek, M., Shiratama, K., Abe, J. & Arai, K. (2007) Tracking and pointing characteristics of OICETS optical terminal in communication demonstrations with ground stations (Invited Paper), *Proc. SPIE*, Vol. 6457A, 6457A-06

Toyoshima, M. (2005a). Trends in satellite communications and the role of optical free-space communications [Invited], *Journal of Optical Networking*, Vol. 4, pp. 300–311

Toyoshima, M.; Yamakawa, S., Yamawaki, T., Arai, K., Reyes, M., Alonso, A., Sodnik, Z. & Demelenne, B. (2005b). Long-term statistics of laser beam propagation in an optical ground-to-geostationary satellite communications link, *IEEE Trans. Antennas and Propagat.*, Vol. 53, No. 2, pp. 842–850

Toyoshima, M.; Kunimori, H., Jono, T., Takayama, Y. & Arai, K. (2006) Measurement of atmospheric turbulence in a ground-to-low earth orbit optical link, *2006 Joint Conference on Satellite Communications (JC-SAT 2006)*, Vol. SAT2006-37, pp. 119–124, Jeju-do, Korea, October 20

Toyoshima, M.; Takahashi, T., Suzuki, K., Kimura, S., Takizawa, K., Kuri, T., Klaus, W., Toyoda, M., Kunimori, H., Jono, T., Takayama, Y. & Arai, K. (2007). Laser beam propagation in ground-to-OICETS laser communication experiments, *Proc. SPIE*, Vol. 6551, 6551-09

Wilson, K. E.; Lesh, J. R., Araki, K. & Arimoto Y. (1998). Overview of the Ground-to-Orbit Lasercom Demonstration, *Space Communications*, Vol. 15, pp. 89–95

Wu, H., & Kavehrad, M., (2007). Availability Evaluation of Ground-to-Air Hybrid FSO/RF Links, *International Journal of Wireless Information Networks*, Vol. 14, No. 1, pp.33–45

Zeng, L., O'Brien, D. C., Minh, H. L., Faulkner, G. E., Lee, K., Jung, D., Oh, Y. & Won, E. T., (2009). High Data Rate Multiple Input Multiple Output (MIMO) Optical Wireless Communications Using White LED Lighting, *IEEE Journal on Selected Areas in Communications*, Vol. 27, No. 9, pp. 1654–1662

Part 7

Communication Protocols and Strategies

Efficient Medium Access Control Protocols for Broadband Wireless Communications

Suvit Nakpeerayuth[1], Lunchakorn Wuttisittikulkij[1], Pisit Vanichchanunt[2], Warakorn Srichavengsup[3], Norrarat Wattanamongkhol[1], Robithoh Annur[1], Muhammad Saadi[4], Kamalas Wannakong[1] and Siwaruk Siwamogsatham[5]
[1]Chulalongkorn University
[2]King Mongkut's University of Technology North Bangkok
[3]Thai-Nichi Institute of Technology
[4]University of Management and Technology
[5]National Electronics and Computer Technology Center
[1,2,3,5]Thailand
[4]Pakistan

1. Introduction

In wireless communication systems, an efficient medium access control (MAC) protocol is usually required so that multiple wireless stations can efficiently share the scarcely-limited wireless channel. In a typical wireless environment, wireless stations are usually geographically distributed over a service area and are not synchronized. As a consequence, wireless stations are typically required to contend for transmission opportunities. In general, if the MAC protocol is not properly designed, channel contention may cause serious transmission collisions and can considerably degrade the system throughput performance.

Over the past several decades, numerous MAC protocols have been developed to smartly utilize the wireless channel, e.g., ALOHA (Abramson, 1970), carrier-sense multiple access (CSMA) (Kleinrock & Tobagi, 1975; Tobagi & Hunt, 1980), and many other variants (Tasaka & Ishibashi, 1984; Karn, 1990; Frigon, et al., 2001; Amitay & Greenstein, 1994). These conventional MAC protocols have been successfully deployed in practice for different applications and environments, including the widely adopted IEEE 802.11 a/b/g/n wireless local area network systems, the emerging IEEE 802.16 (WiMAX) wireless metropolitan area network, the IEEE 802.15.4 (Zigbee) wireless sensor networks, and various famous MAC protocols for satellite communication networks. In addition, the emerging multimedia technologies in recent years have continuously driven the requirements for higher and higher system transmission throughput. In such an environment, the round trip propagation delays between the base station and wireless stations have increasingly become relatively larger and larger compared with a packet transmission time. As a consequence, a fair deal of recent research work has been directed toward the renewed studies of efficient MAC schemes for systems with relatively large propagation delays.

This chapter overviews the existing MAC technologies and summarizes recent research advancements toward the improvements and analysis of various MAC protocols. In particular, a class of efficient modified random channel contention and reservation schemes based on our proposed work (Sivamok, et al, 2001; Srichavengsup, et al, 2005) is presented with a complete discussion of mathematical performance evaluation and numerical results.

2. Pure ALOHA

In 1970, Norman Abramson and his colleagues at the University of Hawaii proposed a new medium access control, known as ALOHA or Pure ALOHA, as part of the ALOHA system, that aimed to interconnect a central computer at the university main campus near Honolulu to remote consoles at colleges and research institutes on several islands using UHF radio communications. Two 100 kHz channels at 407.350 MHz and 413.475 MHz are assigned for transmission in each direction, each operating at a bit rate of 24,000 baud. In the ALOHA system, information is transmitted in the form of packets, and all packets are of fixed length, i.e. 88 bytes (8 bytes for header and 80 bytes for data). Therefore, the packet transmission time is about 29 msec and this time becomes 34 msec when information for receiver synchronization is included.

The basic idea of the Pure ALOHA protocol is simple, but elegant: each station is allowed to send its packet whenever it has a packet ready for transmission. Since a common channel is shared among stations, collision between packets from different stations will result when they are sent at nearly the same time. Fig. 1 shows an example of packet transmissions and possible collisions of four stations contending for the same channel. Those packets that are overlapped in time are collided and destroyed. In this example, only two packet transmissions are successful, and the rest of them need to be retransmitted.

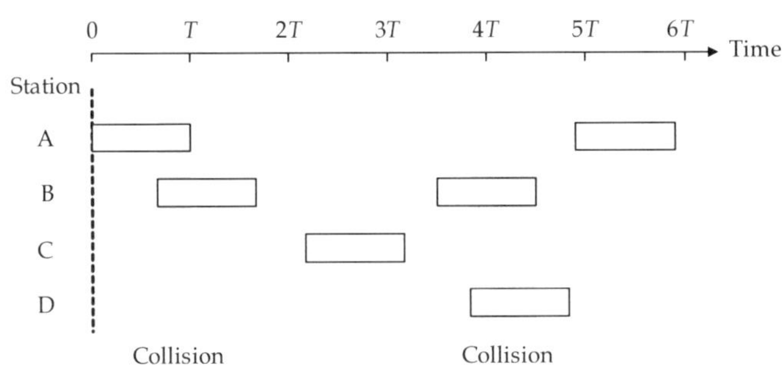

Fig. 1. Packet transmissions in a Pure ALOHA system

After a packet transmission, the sending station waits for an acknowledgement from the receiver to indicate successful transmission of the packet. However, if no acknowledgement is returned within a time-out period, the sending station assumes that the packet is destroyed and starts a retransmission procedure. In principle, the time-out period must be set at least equal to the maximum possible round trip delay between two most widely separated stations to ensure correct functioning of the protocol. Obviously, if the colliding stations try to retransmit their packets immediately, they will collide again. Therefore, each station is required to wait for a random amount of time, called back-off time, before resending the packet. This random back-off mechanism is intended to keep multiple stations from trying to transmit at the same time again which helps reduce probability of collisions. The back-off time is randomly chosen from the range $[0, 2^k - 1]$ multiplied by the maximum propagation delay (or alternatively the packet transmission time), where k is the number of previous unsuccessful transmission attempts. This means that the mean value of back-off time is doubled each time the packet is retransmitted. This retransmission is repeated until either the packet is acknowledged or a predetermined number of retransmissions, typically set as 15 attempts, is exceeded.

To see how well such a simple protocol will perform, a throughput analysis for the Pure ALOHA protocol is carried out with the following basic assumptions. There is an infinite number of stations that are generating new packets according to a Poisson process with an average of S packets per packet transmission time. All packets are of equal length and the packet transmission time is T seconds. Packets that fail to reach the intended receivers due to collisions are retransmitted. Since retransmitted packets are vulnerable to collisions too, they will also require retransmission again if not successful. Let us define G as the average number of packets both new and retransmitted combined per packet transmission time. Obviously, G is always greater than or equal to S. It is further assumed that generations of these combined packets during one packet transmission time also follow Poisson distribution. The ratio of S to G is essentially the probability of a successful packet, that is

$$P_S = \frac{S}{G} \tag{1}$$

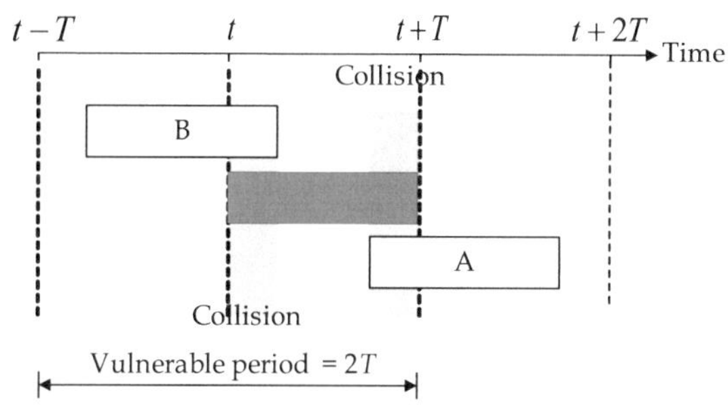

Fig. 2. Vulnerable time for Pure ALOHA

Fig. 2 shows the vulnerable time of a shaded packet, which starts its transmission at time t and finishes at $t+T$. This shaded packet is successfully transmitted, as long as no other packet is transmitted during the interval $t-T$ to $t+T$, so-called vulnerable period. If another packet begins a transmission within the interval $t-T$ to t, such as packet B, the end of this packet will collide with the start of the shaded packet. If another packet begins a transmission within the interval t to $t+T$, such as packet A, the start of this packet will collide with the end of the shaded packet. Based on this observation, it is clear that the shaded packet has a vulnerable period of $2T$, in which if no other packet starts any packet transmission, no collision will occur and the shaded packet will reach the receiver successfully. Therefore, the probability of a successful packet (P_s) in Pure ALOHA is equal to the probability of no generation of packet within $2T$ seconds. Since the probability of k packets are generated within 2 times the packet transmission time according to the Poisson distribution is given by:

$$\Pr[k] = \frac{(2G)^k e^{-2G}}{k!} \tag{2}$$

the probability of no packet generated is

$$\Pr[k=0] = e^{-2G} \tag{3}$$

By combining Equations (1) and (3), we get

$$S = Ge^{-2G} \tag{4}$$

This relation between G which represents the total offered traffic on the channel and S which represents the throughput of the Pure ALOHA system is plotted in Fig. 3. It shows that initially at low traffic load throughput increases with increasing offered traffic up to a maximum of $1/2e = 0.184$ occurring at a value of $G = 0.5$. A further increase of traffic leads to a higher collision probability due to more intense contention, causing a reduction of throughput.

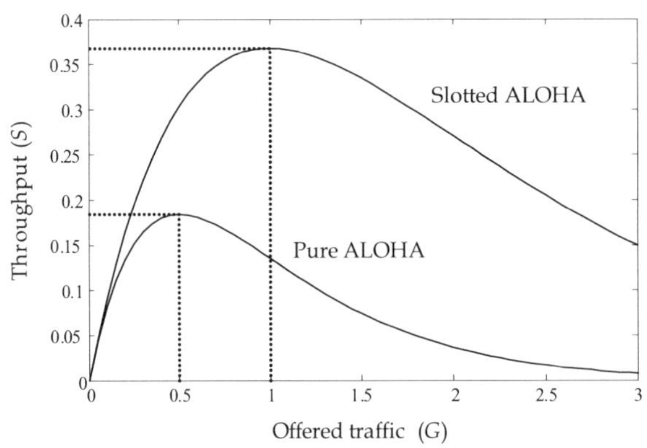

Fig. 3. Throughput versus offered traffic for Pure and Slotted ALOHA

3. Slotted ALOHA

In 1972, Robert introduced a simple modification to Pure ALOHA for improved performance. Time is divided into slots, where each time slot has a fixed size equal to the time required to transmit one packet. Unlike Pure ALOHA, a station is allowed to start a packet transmission only at the beginning of each time slot. If the station has a packet ready to send, it must wait until the beginning of the next time slot. If more than one packet are transmitted in the same slot, they are collided and retransmissions are required. In case of collision, each station involved retransmits its packet in each subsequent slot with probability p until success. Since a packet transmission is confined within the slot boundary, when a collision between packets from different stations occurs, they will overlap completely. This means that the vulnerable period for Slotted ALOHA is reduced by half compared to Pure ALOHA. This modified protocol is commonly known as Slotted ALOHA. Fig. 4 shows an example of packet transmissions and possible collisions in the Slotted ALOHA system. Notice that most packets are generated during a slot interval, and they are kept waiting until the start of the next slot before transmitted. Indeed, the traffic pattern is deliberately selected to be the same as in Fig. 1 for comparison purpose with Pure ALOHA. Slotted ALOHA appears to reduce collision in this example; only two packets are collided compared to four in case of Pure ALOHA.

Since the throughput of Slotted ALOHA can be analyzed in the same way as Pure ALOHA except that the vulnerable period is now equal to the packet transmission time, the probability of no other packet is sent in the same slot is

$$\Pr[k=0]=e^{-G} \tag{5}$$

and thus the relation between throughput and offered traffic for Slotted ALOHA can be obtained as

$$S=Ge^{-G} \tag{6}$$

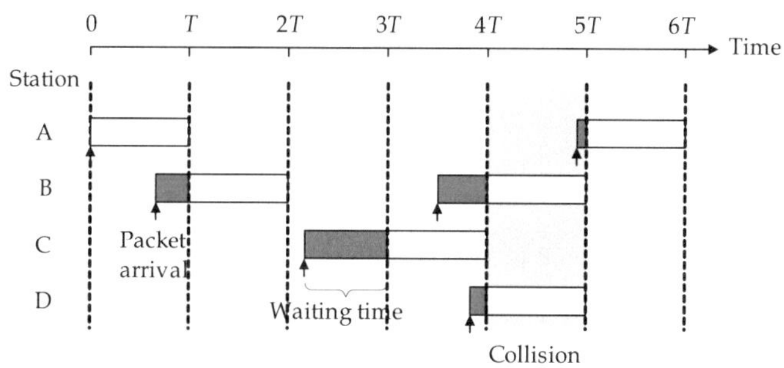

Fig. 4. Packet transmissions in a Slotted ALOHA system

Fig. 3 illustrates the comparison of throughput performance of Pure and Slotted ALOHA. The maximum throughput of Slotted ALOHA is $1/e=0.368$, which occurs at $G=1$; this is doubled of that of Pure ALOHA. As we can see, the efficiency of Pure ALOHA can be improved by the introduced time slot structure. However, time synchronization is required to align stations to the slot structure. One possible solution is to have a central station send a kind of clock signal at a regular interval.

Both Pure and Slotted ALOHA have advantageous features. First, they are highly decentralized and quite simple to implement, especially Pure ALOHA. Second, when there is only one active station, the station can continuously transmit its packets at the maximum channel capacity. These two key features make the ALOHA system particularly useful for large population of stations each with light and burst traffic demand. However, due to their simplicity of operation, ALOHA makes inefficient use of channel capacity and is low in throughput performance.

4. Carrier Sense Multiple Access (CSMA)

Pure ALOHA has a shortcoming in that a station still transmits its packet even if the channel is already occupied by another station. Such collisions can be avoided, if only the sending station senses the channel before using it. This led to the development of an important class of MAC protocols called Carrier Sense Multiple Access (CSMA). A station that wishes to send a packet is required to sense if the channel is busy or idle first. If the channel is sensed busy, the station must wait until the channel becomes idle again before making any transmission. Such a "listen before talk" strategy helps reduce unnecessary packet collisions, thereby increasing channel efficiency. Fig. 5 shows an example of possible packet transmissions in a CSMA system for the same traffic situation as in Fig. 1 of Pure ALOHA. As we can see, each packet waits until the channel becomes idle before transmission and in this particular example, no collisions occur at all; all packets are successfully transmitted.

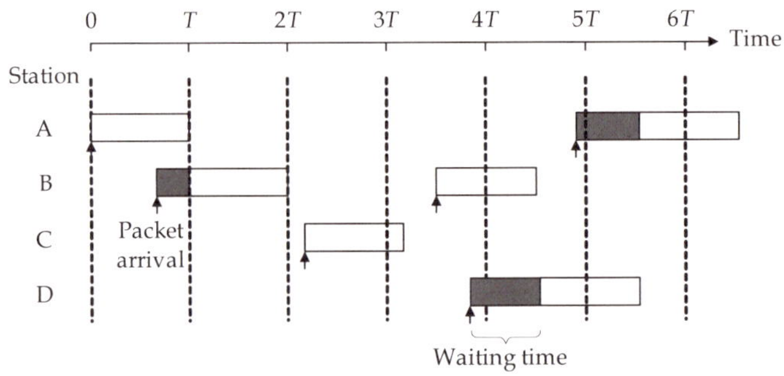

Fig. 5. Packet transmissions in a CSMA system

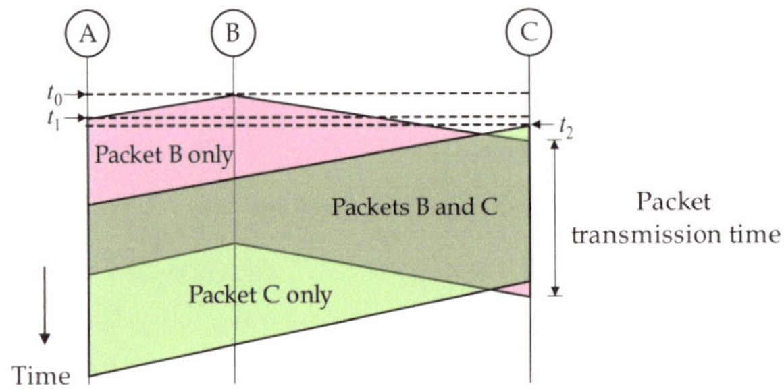

Fig. 6. An example of a collision in CSMA

Even if the channel is sensed by all stations before their transmissions, collisions can nonetheless occur in CSMA due to propagation delay. That is, when a station transmits a packet, it takes time equal to propagation delay before all other stations detect this transmission. During this period, if another station has a packet ready to send and not yet detect that transmitted packet, it will send its own packet and a collision will result. Fig. 6 shows an example of a possible collision of two packets in CSMA. Station B starts a packet transmission at time t_0 . A moment later at time t_1 , station A receives the first bit of the packet and thus refrains from transmission. However, at time t_2 station C has a packet ready to send and does not detect any signal on the channel, so it starts a packet transmission, which of course will collide with the packet from station B. Therefore, the vulnerable period of CSMA is equal to the propagation delay, which is the time required for a signal to traverse from one station to another at the opposite end. This means that the smaller the propagation delay between two most widely separated stations gets, the less the collisions are, and the more the performance improvement can be achieved. Note however that even if the propagation delay is zero, collisions still occur. Consider two or more persistent stations, awaiting the channel to become idle. As soon as the ongoing packet transmission is ended, all persistent stations will transmit their packets immediately, and results in a definite collision.

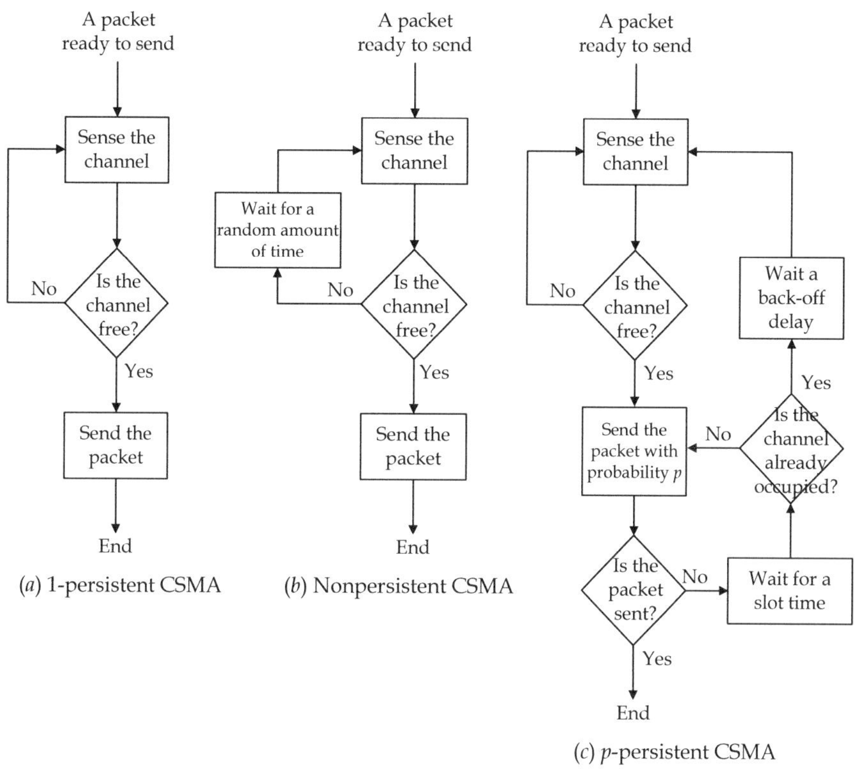

Fig. 7. Flow diagrams for CSMA systems

CSMA has several variations which differ in the strategy used in waiting for the channel to become idle. Three most commonly known strategies, namely 1-persistent CSMA, nonpersistent CSMA and p persistent CSMA, are considered below. Note that Fig. 7 shows flow diagrams for these three persistent strategies.

1-persistent CSMA When a station is ready for a packet transmission, it first senses whether the channel is busy or idle. If the channel is idle, it sends the packet immediately. If the channel is busy, the station keeps on sensing the channel until it becomes idle and then sends the packet immediately. The problem of 1-persistent CSMA is that if two stations have a packet ready to send in the middle of another packet transmission. Both stations will wait until the end of the transmission and start their packet transmissions at the same time, guaranteeing a collision. Thus, 1-persistent CSMA can be perceived as a greedy strategy.

Nonpersistent CSMA When a station wishes to transmit a packet, it first senses the channel to see if it is idle, if so the station sends the packet immediately. If the channel is busy, instead of continuing to listen for the channel to become idle and transmitting immediately, it waits a random amount of time, then tries again. In contrast to 1-persistent CSMA, nonpersistent CSMA is much less greedy. Therefore, in high load situations, there is less chance of collisions occurring. On the other hand, in low load conditions, the channel capacity is left unused despite some ready stations.

***p*-Persistent CSMA** When a station has a packet ready to send, it first senses the channel. If the channel is sensed busy, the station keeps on sensing the channel until it becomes idle and uses the following procedure. Note that this same procedure is applied if the channel is sensed idle right from the start. The station transmits its packet with probability p, and delays one time slot with probability $1-p$, where the duration of a time slot is set equal to or greater than the maximum propagation delay. If the station decides to delay one time slot, it checks whether the skipped slot has been occupied by another station. If it is, the station assumes as if there is a collision and starts its back-off procedure. Otherwise, the station repeats the same procedure as before. That is, it transmits the packet with probability p, and delays one time slot with probability $1-p$, and so on.

Fig. 8 shows an example of packet transmissions in each of the three CSMA systems for the same packet arriving scenario. Station A is the first to have a packet ready to send and then followed by stations B and C. For 1-persistent CSMA as shown in Fig. 8(a), a packet from station A is transmitted immediately as it arrives because the channel is sensed idle. Packets from stations B and C arrive while the channel is busy, hence they wait until the end of packet A transmission and start their transmissions immediately, resulting a collision. Both of them start a back-off procedure, by delaying their next attempt by a random amount of time. In this example, station C selects a shorter back-off time, so it begins a packet transmission before station B. As a result, when station B wishes to retransmit its packet, the channel is already occupied by station C. So station B waits until the end of transmission and then sends its packet. For nonpersistent CSMA as shown in Fig. 8(b), similar to the previous case packet A is successfully transmitted as it arrives first and finds the channel idle. Packets from stations B and C arrive a little while later when the channel is already occupied by station A, they are rescheduled for later transmission. After a random delay, the packet from C is transmitted. During its transmission, the packet from B tries again, but unfortunately finds the channel busy, so it is rescheduled again. After another random delay later, the packet from B is finally transmitted successfully. For *p*-persistent CSMA as shown in Fig. 8(c), unlike the previous two schemes station A that has a packet ready to send first and finds the channel idle does not transmit its packet immediately. Instead it waits until the beginning of the next slot and makes a decision based on the *p*-persistent CSMA's rule. That is, it transmits its packet with probability p, and delays one time slot with probability $1-p$. In this example, station A does not send its packet in the first slot, but it does in the second. When packets from stations B and C arrive, the channel is already used by station A, so they wait until the end of the packet transmission. Then the same *p*-persistent CSMA's rule as before is applied. In this example, packet B decides to send its packet in the third slot. Once station C learns at the end of the third slot that the channel is already taken by other station it assumes as if there is a collision and starts its back-off procedure. After a random back-off time later, station C try to retransmit with the same rule and it sends its packet in the second slot. It should be noted that the packet transmission time is assumed to be a multiple integer number of the propagation delay.

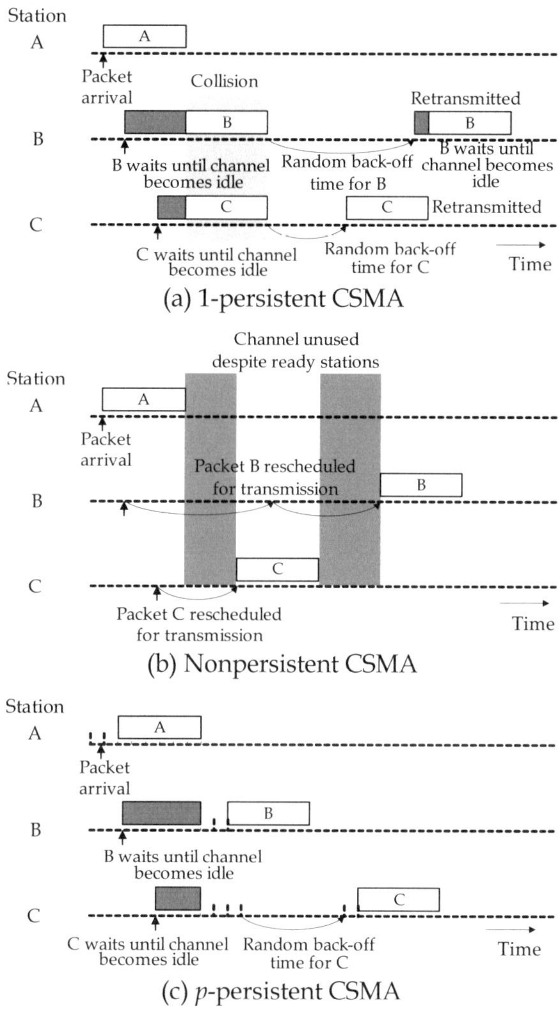

Fig. 8. An example of packet transmissions in different CSMA systems

5. Performance analysis of nonpersistent CSMA

Like other CSMA protocols, the nonpersistent CSMA reduces interferences from collision by listening to the channel before packet transmission. If the channel is busy, the stations reschedule the packet transmission to some random time in the future. To analyze the performance, we assume that the offered traffic rate which is the sum of the new arrival rate and the retransmission rate is constant and follows the Poisson point process. The average retransmission delay is also assumed to be large compared to the transmission time of each packet. From Fig. 9, a packet from station A arrives at time t and is immediately sent out through the channel, because the channel is sensed idle. As it takes another τ seconds for the packet to reach other stations, if there are other stations that have a packet ready to send during t to $t+\tau$, then they send their packets, causing inevitable collisions. So, the nonpersistent CSMA has a vulnerable period of τ. In this example, two other stations B and

C each send a packet a moment later with station C being the last station to send during this vulnerable period. As a result, all these three packets need to be retransmited. The duration that there is one or more packet transmitted is referred to as the transmission period (TP). A transmission period can be a successful transmission period or an unsuccessful transmission period depending on whether there is collision or not. The time duration between two TPs will be referred to as an idle period. A cycle of the transmission along the time axis consists of a busy period B and an idle period I, where the busy period can be a successful or unsuccessful TP. Let us define a useful transmission period U as the time duration that the channel carries useful information without collision in a cycle. From the renewal theory, the average channel utilization can be expressed as

$$S = \frac{\bar{U}}{\bar{B} + \bar{I}} \tag{7}$$

where " $\bar{}$ " stands for the average.

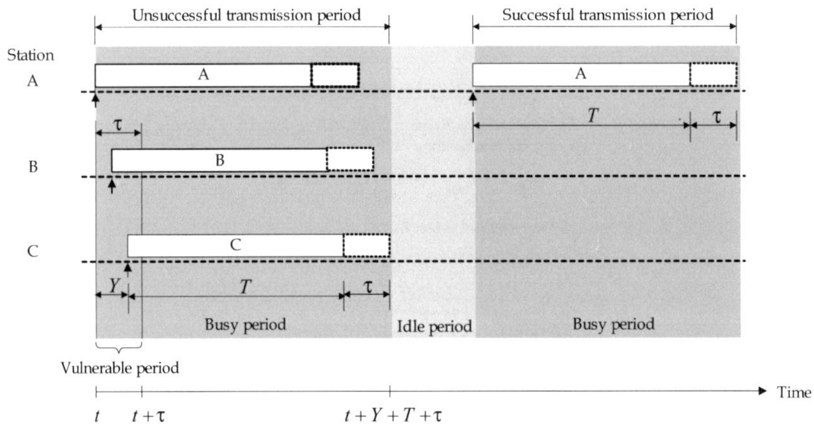

Fig. 9. The busy and idle periods of the nonpersistent CSMA

Let T be the packet time and g be the offered traffic rate (the number of packets per second). A TP is successful if there is no other packet transmitted in the vulnerable period $(t, t+\tau)$ and the useful transmission time is T. This occurs with the probability of $e^{-g\tau}$ and we get

$$\bar{U} = Te^{-g\tau} \tag{8}$$

Let $t + Y$ be the time that the last packet arrives in the vulnerable period (which is the packet from station C in Fig. 9). For an unsuccessful transmission period, the busy period B includes a packet time T, Y, and τ which is the time for the last bit of the packet to leave the channel.

$$B = T + Y + \tau \tag{9}$$

and the cumulative distribution function of Y is

$$\begin{aligned} F_Y(y) &= \Pr\{Y \le y\} = \Pr\{\text{no arrival occurs in an interval } (t+Y, t+\tau)\} \\ &= e^{-g(\tau - y)}, \quad y \le \tau \end{aligned} \tag{10}$$

The average of Y is

$$\bar{Y} = \tau - \frac{1}{g}(1 - e^{-g\tau}) \tag{11}$$

Since the mean of inter-arrival time is $1/g$, and it is assumed to be large compared to T, the average of the idle period is

$$\bar{I} = \frac{1}{g} \tag{12}$$

Substituting $\bar{U}$, $\bar{B}$ and $\bar{I}$ into (7), we obtain

$$\begin{aligned} S &= \frac{Te^{-g\tau}}{T + 2\tau - \frac{1}{g}(1 - e^{-g\tau}) + \frac{1}{g}} \\ &= \frac{gTe^{-g\tau}}{gT(1 + 2\tau / T) + e^{-g\tau}} \\ &= \frac{Ge^{-aG}}{G(1 + 2a) + e^{-aG}} \end{aligned} , \tag{13}$$

where $a = \tau / T$ is the propagation time relative to the packet time and $G = gT$ is the offered traffic rate per packet time.

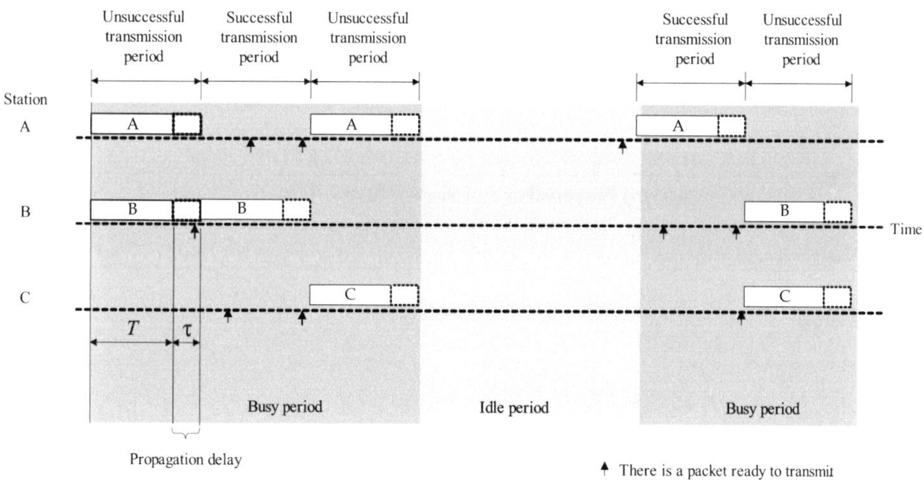

Fig. 10. The busy and idle periods of the slotted nonpersistent CSMA

For slotted nonpersistent CSMA, the time duration of each slot is set to τ and the packet time T is an integer multiple of τ (see Fig. 10 for details). When there is a packet ready to send, each station waits for the beginning of the next slot and senses whether the channel is idle. If so, the packet will be sent otherwise the packet is rescheduled for transmission later on. The probability mass function (PMF) of the idle period is a geometric function of the form

$$\Pr\{I = k\tau\} = (e^{-g\tau})^{k-1}(1 - e^{-g\tau}), \quad k = 1,2,... \tag{14}$$

This gives us

$$\overline{I} = \sum_{k=1}^{\infty} k\tau \Pr\{I = k\tau\} = \frac{\tau}{1 - e^{-g\tau}} \tag{15}$$

In the slotted nonpersistent CSMA, both successful and unsuccessful TPs are $T + \tau$. The busy period B contains k TPs if at least one arrival occurs at the last slot of (k - 1)th TPs, and no arrival occurs at the last slot of the kth TP.

$$\Pr\{B = k(T + \tau)\} = (1 - e^{-g\tau})^{k-1} e^{-g\tau}, \quad k = 1,2,... \tag{16}$$

The average busy period is

$$\overline{B} = \sum_{k=1}^{\infty} k(T + \tau)\Pr\{B = k(T + \tau)\} = \frac{T + \tau}{e^{-g\tau}} \tag{17}$$

The average number of TPs per cycle is $\overline{B} / (T + \tau)$. When the transmission is successful, the useful transmission period is T. The average of the useful transmission period is

$$\overline{U} = T\left(\frac{\overline{B}}{T + \tau}\right)P_{success} \tag{18}$$

where $P_{success}$ is the probability that a TP is successful.

$$\begin{aligned} P_{success} &= \Pr\{\text{Only one arrival in the last slot before a TP} \mid \text{At least one arrival in the last slot before a TP}\} \\ &= \frac{\Pr\{\text{Only one arrival in the last slot before a TP}\}}{\Pr\{\text{At least one arrival in the last slot before a TP}\}} \\ &= \frac{g\tau e^{-g\tau}}{1 - e^{-g\tau}} \end{aligned} \tag{19}$$

Now we obtain

$$\begin{aligned} S = \frac{\overline{U}}{\overline{B} + \overline{I}} &= \frac{T\left(\frac{(T + \tau)/e^{-g\tau}}{T + \tau}\right)\left(\frac{g\tau e^{-g\tau}}{1 - e^{-g\tau}}\right)}{\frac{T + \tau}{e^{-g\tau}} + \frac{\tau}{1 - e^{-g\tau}}} = \frac{gT\tau e^{-g\tau}}{T + \tau - Te^{-g\tau}} = \frac{gT(\tau / T)e^{-g\tau}}{1 + (\tau / T) - e^{-g\tau}} \\ &= \frac{aGe^{-aG}}{1 + a - e^{-aG}} \end{aligned} \tag{20}$$

If a approaches zero, we obtain

$$\lim_{a \to 0} S = \frac{G}{1 + G}. \tag{21}$$

The unity throughput can theoretically be obtained when the offered traffic rate G approaches infinity. The throughputs S versus the offered traffic rate per packet time G of the nonpersistent CSMA and the slotted nonpersistent CSMA are plotted for various values of a in Figs. 11 and 12, respectively.

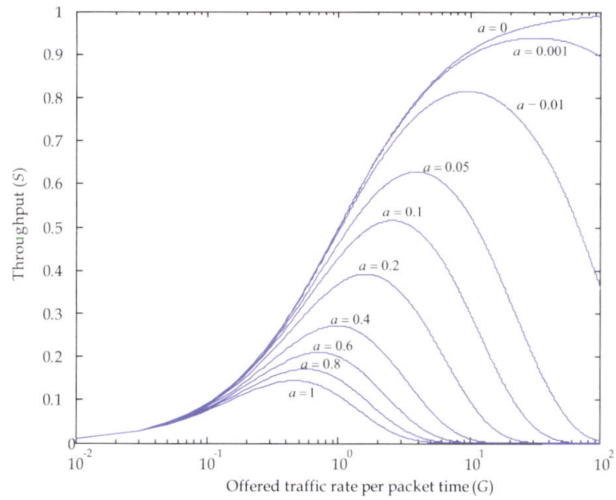

Fig. 11. Throughput versus offered traffic for nonpersistent CSMA

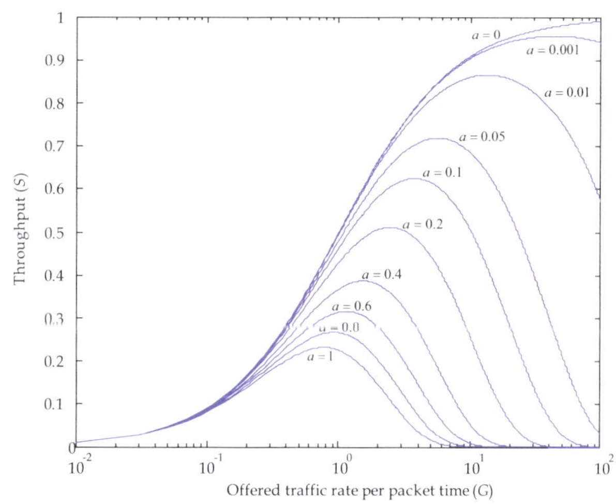

Fig. 12. Throughput versus offered traffic for slotted nonpersistent CSMA

6. Proposed channel reservation algorithms

This section presents a class of MAC protocols that organizes the channel bandwidth into a frame structure consisting of two alternate periods, namely contention period and information transfer period, see Fig. 13. The contention period consists of a fixed number of contention slots, which are used by all users to reserve for channel bandwidth on a contention basis. Users who succeed in the reservation process will be assigned data slots by the base station in the information transfer period for their information transmission. Since the overall system performance very much depends on the efficiency during reservation period, we have proposed a number of efficient channel reservation algorithms to meet the required performance. They include CFP, CAP, COP, COP+SPL, CFP+SPL, UNI, UNI+LA, MT-CFP, MT-CFP+SPL, MT-UNI, MT-UNI+LUA and MT-UNI+LUT. We will explain each algorithm in turn together with their performance analysis.

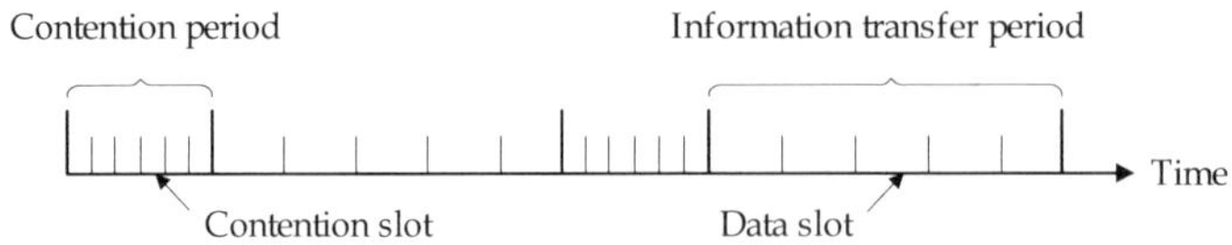

Fig. 13. A frame structure of MAC protocols

6.1 Cascade Fixed Probability (CFP)

In the first algorithm, each user will attempt to make reservation on each contention slot in sequence from the first slot to the last. In each slot, the user will decide whether it will access the present slot with a certain probability (p) and the value of this probability is the same for all users and fixed throughout all contention slots. As a result, this algorithm will be referred to as Cascade Fixed Probability (CFP). It is apparent that the value of probability p is the key parameter to the system performance, hence must be chosen with care. We shall now derive the average number of successful users as a function of the number of active users and the number of available slots.

Let $S[M,N]$ be the average number of successful users for the system with M users and N contention slots and $b[M,i,p]$ be the binomial probability that i out of M users access a particular contention slot with permission probability p, which is expressed as:

$$b[M,i,p] = \binom{M}{i} p^i (1-p)^{M-i}, \text{ where } \binom{M}{i} = \frac{M!}{i!(M-i)!} \tag{22}$$

In each contention slot, only a single user can succeed in reservation, which will occur only when no other users access the slot. A detailed analysis of $S[M,N]$ is formulated in the following recursive formula:

$$\begin{aligned} S[M,N] &= b[M,0,p]S[M,N-1] + b[M,1,p](1+S[M-1,N-1]) + \sum_{i=2}^{M} b[M,i,p]S[M-i,N-1] \\ &= b[M,1,p] + \sum_{i=0}^{M} b[M,i,p]S[M-i,N-1] \end{aligned} \tag{23}$$

where $M \geq 0, N \geq 0$.

The boundary conditions of (23) are $S[a,0] = S[0,b] = 0$ where $a = 0,1,2,....,M$ and $b = 0,1,2,....,N$. We can then find an appropriate permission probability $p_{CFP}[M,N]$ of each frame by differentiating (23) with respect to p, setting it to 0, i.e. $\frac{\partial}{\partial p} S[M,N] = 0$ and determining p that gives the maximum average number of successful users $S_{CFP}[M,N]$.

6.2 Cascade Adaptive Probability (CAP)

In the CFP algorithm, it is seen that an appropriate value of p exists and can be formulated as a function of the number of active users at the start of each frame (M) and the number of slots in each frame (N). It is interesting to further explore this finding to improve the system performance by introducing an idea of adaptive probability. Like the CFP algorithm, all users still use the same value of probability at each slot, but the permission probability may change from one slot to another by considering the current number of remaining users and slots. At the beginning of each contention slot, each user must somehow acquire the present system conditions, i.e. the current number of remaining users and slots. Note that this requirement contradicts with the fundamental system assumption made here. Nevertheless, its analysis provides and interesting new aspect to this study. Once the user knows both parameters the user will choose the value of p based on these values using the formulation derived in the CFP algorithm. Since the permission probability is properly selected in response to the current system scenarios, an improved system performance can be intuitively expected. This algorithm will be known as Cascade Adaptive Probability (CAP). The model for throughput analysis of this algorithm is similar to that of the CFP algorithm, though details may differ.

Let $S_{CAP}[M,N]$ be the average number of successful users of the CAP system with M users and N contention slots and $p_{CFP}[M,N]$ is the optimal permission probability derived from the CFP system with M users and N contention slots. $S_{CAP}[M,N]$ is computed as a recursive formula.

$$\begin{aligned} S_{CAP}[M,N] &= b[M,0,p_{CFP}[M,N]]S_{CAP}[M,N-1] + b[M,1,p_{CFP}[M,N]](1+S_{CAP}[M-1,N-1]) \\ &\quad + \sum_{i=2}^{M} b[M,i,p_{CFP}[M,N]]S_{CAP}[M-i,N-1] \\ &= b[M,1,p_{CFP}[M,N]] + \sum_{i=0}^{M} b[M,i,p_{CFP}[M,N]]S_{CAP}[M-i,N-1] \end{aligned} \tag{24}$$

where $M \geq 0, N \geq 0$.

The boundary conditions of (24) are $S[a,0] = S[0,b] = 0$ where $a = 0,1,2,....,M$ and $b = 0, 1,2,....,N$.

6.3 Cascade Optimal Probability (COP)

The adaptive algorithm described above can indeed enhance the system performance, see the comparative results in the next section. However, there exists a more effective way to adapt the permission probability in accordance with the present system status, which can provide truly optimal results. That is, instead of using $p_{CFP}[M,N]$ in the adapting process, the optimal value of permission probability that maximizes $S_{COP}[M,N]$ is determined for given system parameters, i.e., M users and N slots. This algorithm is referred to as Cascade Optimal Probability (COP) and its mathematical analysis is given by:

$$\begin{aligned} S_{COP}[M,N] &= b[M,0,p_{COP}[M,N]]S_{COP}[M,N-1] + b[M,1,p_{COP}[M,N]](1+S_{COP}[M-1,N-1]) \\ &\quad + \sum_{i=2}^{M} b[M,i,p_{COP}[M,N]]S_{COP}[M-i,N-1] \\ &= b[M,1,p_{COP}[M,N]] + \sum_{i=0}^{M} b[M,i,p_{COP}[M,N]]S_{COP}[M-i,N-1] \end{aligned} \tag{25}$$

The boundary conditions of (25) are the same as in the CFP system, except that in each step of recursion, the appropriate permission probability $p_{COP}[M,N]$ is selected such that it yields the maximum average number of successful users.

6.4 Cascade Optimal Probability + Split (COP+SPL)

This algorithm is further developed from the COP algorithm. The concept of this algorithm is based on the observations that the success rate for the system with small number of users and slots tends to be superior to the system with an increased number of users and slots with the same factors. As a result, it may be useful and effective to split the number of slots into halves and randomly divide users into two groups. Users in one group will make reservation in the first half of contention slots and users in the other group utilize the second half. Each user determines which group it belongs to by simply flipping a coin. If users can be grouped perfectly, i.e. equally split between the two groups, improvement of the overall system performance will result. However, since users are split in a random manner, it is not known what pattern of grouping will appear. In the worst case half of the slots are heavily loaded with all users while the other half are left totally unused. Under this condition, the overall performance will clearly degrade. The uncertainty in various grouping possibilities raises the concern whether such an idea will really offer benefit or it may actually make things even worse. To answer this problem, we shall derive its performance analytically as follows. It is noted that the number of groups can be set to an arbitrary values, not neccessarily limited to two.

Let g be the number of groups and N/g is the number of contention slots in each group which must be an integer number. The average number of successful users of the COP+SPL system can be expressed as follows:

$$S_{COP+SPL}[M,N] = g\sum_{i=0}^{M} b[M,i,\frac{1}{g}]S_{COP}[i,\frac{N}{g}] \tag{26}$$

6.5 Cascade Fixed Probability + Split (CFP+SPL)

This algorithm can be considered as a simplified version of the previously described COP+SPL algorithm. It functions in the same manner as the COP+SPL except for the permission probability used in each group split. The permission probability for this algorithm is set to a fixed value for all the groups, not optimized for individual group separately as in the COP+SPL algorithm. We shall call this technique as the Cascade Fixed Prob + Split (CFP+SPL) algorithm. The average number of successful users of the CFP+SPL algorithm can be expressed as follows:

$$S_{CFP+SPL}[M,N] = g\sum_{i=0}^{M} b[M,i,\frac{1}{g}]S[i,\frac{N}{g}] \tag{27}$$

where $S[i,\frac{N}{g}]$ is the recursive formula as in (23).

The maximum average number of successful users of the CFP+SPL algorithm can be determined in a similar fashion as in the CFP algorithm. The same boundary conditions as in (23) can be applied here.

6.6 Uniform (UNI)

All four previous algorithms have one feature in common: users consider reservation on each contention slot in sequence. This is a common method adopted in most well-known access control algorithms, as it fits well with the conventional system environment where users can repeatedly make reservation attempts on consecutive contention slots. In some systems, the round trip propagation delay between the base station and users is relatively larger than a packet transmission time. In this situation, users will not receive such a chance, i.e. only a single attempt is possible at each frame. Under this system condition, the order of contention slots becomes irrelevant. Users need not consider each slot in sequence. They may simply select one slot for reservation out of the available slots uniformly. Therefore this technique will be called the Uniform (UNI) algorithm. This UNI algorithm poses some interesting properties. First, the system no longer needs to know the number of active users at the start of each frame, making this algorithm more practical. Second, unlike the previous algorithms where early slots tends to experience greater reservation demands than later slots, all contention slots can now be uniformly loaded and thus better utilized. The average number of successful users can be computed as follow:

$$\begin{aligned} S_{UNI}[M,N] &= b[M,0,\frac{1}{N}]S_{UNI}[M,N-1] + b[M,1,\frac{1}{N}](1+S_{UNI}[M-1,N-1]) \\ &\quad + \sum_{i=2}^{M} b[M,i,\frac{1}{N}]S_{UNI}[M-i,N-1] \\ &= b[M,1,\frac{1}{N}] + \sum_{i=0}^{M} b[M,i,\frac{1}{N}]S_{UNI}[M-i,N-1] \end{aligned} \tag{28}$$

where $M \geq 0, N \geq 0$.

The boundary conditions of (28) are $S[a,0] = S[0,b] = 0$ where $a = 0,1,2,....,M$ and $b = 0,$ $1,2,....,N$.

6.7 Uniform with Limited Access (UNI+LA)

One problem associated with the *Uniform* algorithm is that it does not take the number of users into account. Accordingly, its performance can be significantly deteriorated when the number of users is relatively much higher than the number of slots available. This is because all users will definitely place a reservation in one of the slots, collision will most likely be hard to avoid. For example, if only two slots are available for ten active users, it is better for most users not to make request. Otherwise, collisions will inevitably take place in both slots. As all users will access the slots, the maximum number of successful users is one and this occurs with a very small chance, i.e. nine users access one slot and one of them accesses the other slot. Clearly the UNI algorithm is not at all effective in this situation. To eliminate such shortcomings, it is essential to find some means to limit the user attempts in accordance with the number of users and available slots. This is achieved by introducing a probability (p) that limits each user in contending for a slot. That is, each user will not access in the current contention period and wait till the next period with probability of $1-p$, and with probability of p users will follow exactly the same step as the Uniform algorithm. We shall refer to this algorithm as Uniform + Limited Access (UNI+LA). The average number of successful users can be derived as follow:

$$S_{UNI+LA}[M,N]=\sum_{i=0}^{M}b[M,i,p]S_{UNI}[i,N] \quad (29)$$

The boundary conditions of (29) are the same as in the CFP system.

6.8 Multi-Token Cascade Fixed Probability (MT-CFP)

All seven proposed algorithms described earlier have one feature in common, i.e. each user is entitled to make reservation only once in each frame. For the remaining five algorithms, users are no longer limited by such a constraint. It is possible for users to send multiple requests. Nonetheless, as before the outcome of each of their requests do not return immediately. In principle, giving users more chances of making reservations should enable them to achieve greater success. This more flexible mechanism will be referred to as Multi-Token, where the number of tokens defined as T represents the number of accesses allowed per frame. The first Multi-Token algorithm to describe here is MT-CFP (Multi-Token CFP), which is the extension to the CFP algorithm. This MT-CFP is almost the same as the CFP except that each user may repeat reservation attempts as long as the number of attempts remains less than or equal to the predefined number of tokens. In a special case where the number of tokens is set to 1 the MT-CFP becomes the CFP.

Let us first define the following variables which are to be used correspondingly in the mathematical analysis:

T_i = the number of tokens for user i.

B_i = the successful status bit for user i, where "0" means user i has not succeeded yet and "1" means user i has already succeeded.

M = the number of users.

N = the number of reservation slots.

R = the number of remaining users in the system.

In terms of the performance analysis, we can calculate the probability that there are k successful users given the number of tokens T_i, successful status bit B_i and the number of slots N by using the following equation:

$$P_{MT-CFP}[k\,|\,T_1,T_2,...,T_M,B_1,B_2,...,B_M,N]=(1-p)^R\times P_0+p(1-p)^{R-1}\times P_1+\sum_{i=2}^{R}p^i(1-p)^{R-i}\times P_i \quad (30)$$

where

$R=M$ - summation of zero bit of $T_1,T_2,...,T_M$

$$\begin{aligned}
P_0 &= P[k\,|T_1,T_2,T_3,...,T_{M-1},T_M,B_1,B_2,B_3,...,B_{M-1},B_M,N-1]\\
P_1 &= P[k-x\,|T_1-1,T_2,T_3,...,T_{M-1},T_M,B_1+x,B_2,B_3,...,B_{M-1},B_M,N-1]\\
&\quad +P[k-x\,|T_1,T_2-1,T_3,...,T_{M-1},T_M,B_1,B_2+x,B_3,...,B_{M-1},B_M,N-1]\\
&\quad +P[k-x\,|T_1,T_2,T_3-1,...,T_{M-1},T_M,B_1,B_2,B_3+x,...,B_{M-1},B_M,N-1]\\
&\quad \vdots\\
&\quad +P[k-x\,|T_1,T_2,T_3,...,T_{M-1}-1,T_M,B_1,B_2,B_3,...,B_{M-1}+x,B_M,N-1]\\
&\quad +P[k-x\,|T_1,T_2,T_3,...,T_{M-1},T_M-1,B_1,B_2,B_3,...,B_{M-1},B_M+x,N-1]
\end{aligned}$$

$$x = \begin{cases} 0 \text{ if repeated success} \\ 1 \text{ if new success} \end{cases}$$

$$\begin{aligned} P_2 = \; & P[k \,|\, T_1-1, T_2-1, T_3, T_4, \ldots, T_{M-1}, T_M, B_1, B_2, \ldots, B_{M-1}, B_M, N-1] \\ & + P[k \,|\, T_1-1, T_2, T_3-1, T_4, \ldots, T_{M-1}, T_M, B_1, B_2, \ldots, B_{M-1}, B_M, N-1] \\ & + P[k \,|\, T_1-1, T_2, T_3, T_4-1, \ldots, T_{M-1}, T_M, B_1, B_2, \ldots, B_{M-1}, B_M, N-1] \\ & \vdots \\ & + P[k \,|\, T_1, T_2, T_3, \ldots, T_{M-2}-1, T_{M-1}-1, T_M, B_1, B_2, \ldots, B_{M-1}, B_M, N-1] \\ & + P[k \,|\, T_1, T_2, T_3, \ldots, T_{M-2}-1, T_{M-1}, T_M-1, B_1, B_2, \ldots, B_{M-1}, B_M, N-1] \\ & + P[k \,|\, T_1, T_2, T_3, \ldots, T_{M-2}, T_{M-1}-1, T_M-1, B_1, B_2, \ldots, B_{M-1}, B_M, N-1] \\ & \vdots \end{aligned}$$

$$P_R = P[k \,|\, T_1-1, T_2-1, \ldots, T_{M-1}-1, T_M-1, B_1, B_2, \ldots, B_{M-1}, B_M, N-1]$$

The boundary conditions are set according to the following:

$$P_{MT-CFP}[k \,|\, T_1, T_2, \ldots, T_M, B_1, B_2, \ldots, B_M, N] = \begin{cases} 0 & if\ k < 0,\ T_i \geq 0, B_i \geq 0, N \geq 0 \\ 1 & if\ k = 0,\ T_i \geq 0, B_i \geq 0, N = 0 \\ 1 & if\ k = 0, T_i = 0, B_i \geq 0, N \geq 0 \\ 0 & if\ k > N,\ T_i \geq 0, B_i \geq 0 \end{cases}$$

The average number of successful users of the MT-CFP system can be expressed as follows:

$$S_{MT-CFP}[M,N,T] = \sum_{k=0}^{M} k \times P_{MT-CFP}[k \,|\, T_1, T_2, \ldots, T_M, B_1, B_2, \ldots, B_M, N] \tag{31}$$

6.9 Multi-Token Cascade Fixed Probability with Split (MT-CFP+SPL)

This algorithm is further developed from the MT-CFP algorithm by applying Split mechanism to MT-CFP algorithm. We shall call this technique as the Multi-Token Cascade Fixed Prob + Split (MT-CFP+SPL) algorithm. Let g be the number of groups and N/g be the number contention slots in each group which must be an integer number. In this algorithm, each user randomly chooses any group from g groups with equal probability $1/g$. Then each user will attempt to make a reservation in sequence from the first slot to the last slot in that group until there is no remaining token for making a request. The average number of successful users of the MT-CFP+SPL algorithm can be expressed as follows:

$$S_{MT-CFP+SPL}[M,N,T] = g\sum_{i=0}^{m} b[M,i,\frac{1}{g}] S_{MT-CFP}[i,\frac{N}{g},T] \tag{32}$$

The boundary conditions of (32) are the same as in the MT-CFP system.

6.10 Multi-Token Uniform (MT-UNI)

This algorithm is an alteration of UNI by applying the Multi-Token mechanism which allows each user to randomly choose any T slots from N slots for reservation with equal probability. Therefore, we can calculate $P[k|M,N,T]$, the probability that k successful users given the number of users M, the number of slots N and the number of tokens T by using the following equation:

$$P[k|M,N,T]=\frac{C[k|M,N,T]}{\sum_{k=0}^{M}C[k|M,N,T]}. \tag{33}$$

$C[k|M,N,T]$ is now given as the number of cases that k successful users given the number of users M, the number of slots N and the number of tokens T.

$\sum_{k=0}^{M}C[k|M,N,T]$ is now given as the number of all cases that each of M users uses T tokens to reserve T slots from N slots. Then

$$\sum_{k=0}^{M}C[k|M,N,T]=\left[N\cdot(N-1)\cdot(N-2)\cdot\ldots\cdot(N-(T-1))\right]^{M}. \tag{34}$$

The average number of successful users of the MT-UNI system can be expressed as follows:

$$S_{MT-UNI}[M,N,T]=\sum_{k=0}^{M}k\times P[k|M,N,T] \tag{35}$$

6.11 Multi-Token Uniform with Limited User's Access (MT-UNI+LUA)

The MT-UNI algorithm described earlier can become ineffective when there are high traffic. To improve the MT-UNI performance, we introduce Limited Access (LA) mechanism to the MT-UNI algorithm. In this paper, we propose 2 types of LA for MT-UNI. The first one is Limited User's Access (LUA) mechanism. We use LUA to limit the user attempts by introducing a probability (p). Users that find themselves not to access the slots will do nothing whereas other users will follow exactly the same step as the Multi-Token Uniform algorithm. This technique is referred to as Multi-Token Uniform + Limited User's Access (MT-UNI+LUA). The average number of successful users of the MT-UNI+LUA system can be expressed as follows:

$$S_{MT-UNI+LUA}\left[M,N,T\right]=\sum_{i=0}^{M}b\left[M,i,p\right]S_{MT-UNI}\left[i,N,T\right] \tag{36}$$

We can identify the appropriate permission probability $p_{MT-UNI-LUA}[M,N]$ of the MT-UNI+LUA algorithm by differentiating (36) with respect to p, setting it to 0, and finding p that gives maximum average number of successful users $S_{MT-UNI+LUA}\left[M,N,T\right]$.

6.12 Multi-Token Uniform with Limited User's Token (MT-UNI+LUT)

Another type of LA is Limited User's Token (LUT) mechanism. If we choose LUT mechanism for the MT-UNI algorithm, we shall refer to this algorithm as Multi-Access

Uniform + Limited User's Token (MT-UNI+LUT). In this algorithm, each user's token will be decided to use or not by a probability (p). As a result, each user has a limited use of his available number of tokens. The value of p certainly plays an important role to the system performance and we will now illustrate how the optimal value of p can be analytically determined.
The average number of successful users of the MT-UNI+LUT system can be expressed as follows:

$$S_{MT-UNI+LUT}[M,N,T] = \frac{\sum_{k=0}^{M} k \sum_{u=0}^{MT} (p^{u}(1-p)^{MT-u}) C[k,u|M,N,T]}{\sum_{k=0}^{M} \sum_{u=0}^{MT} (p^{u}(1-p)^{MT-u}) C[k,u|M,N,T]} \quad (37)$$

$C[k,u|M,N,T]$ is now given as the number of cases that k successful users use u tokens from all of user's tokens (MT) given the number of users M, the number of slots N and the number of tokens for each user T.
We can identify the appropriate permission probability $p_{MT-UNI+LUT}[M,N,T]$ of the MT-UNI+LUA algorithm by differentiating (37) with respect to p, setting it to 0, and finding p that gives maximum average number of successful users $S_{MT-UNI+LUT}[M,N,T]$.
The relationship among CFP, CAP, COP, COP+SPL, CFP+SPL, UNI, UNI+LA, MT-CFP, MT-CFP+SPL, MT-UNI, MT-UNI+LUA and MT-UNI+LUT protocols can be shown in Fig. 14.

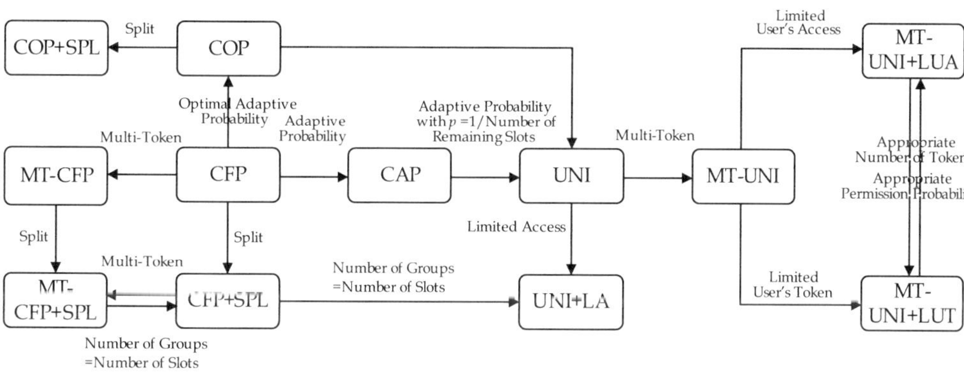

Fig. 14. The relationship among CFP, CAP, COP, COP+SPL, CFP+SPL, UNI, UNI+LA, MT-CFP, MT-CFP+SPL, MT-UNI, MT-UNI+LUA and MT-UNI+LUT protocols

The required information for each algorithm can be illustrated in Table I, it appears that only the CFP, CFP+SPL, MT-CFP, MT-CFP+SPL, UNI, UNI+LA, MT-UNI, MT-UNI+LUT and MT-UNI+LUA algorithms are practically applicable to the system assumption that the base station can obtain the number of active users at the start of each reservation period. Other algorithms CAP, COP and COP+SPL require additional information, i.e. the number of remaining users at each contention slot or the number of users in each split group. Such information is hard to acquire instantly in the system where the round trip propagation delay between the base station and users is relatively larger than a packet transmission time. Therefore, these algorithms will not be practical in this situation.

Table II shows the applied mechanisms of each algorithm, for example, starting with the CAP algorithm, it can be seen that CAP applies Adaptive Probability. The COP and COP+SPL algorithms employ the mechanism namely Optimally Adaptive Probability. The applied mechanisms for other algorithm are fully illustrated in Table II.

Algorithm	Know the number of active users at the start of each reservation period	Know the number of remaining users at each contention slot
CFP	√	
CAP	√	√
COP	√	√
CFP+SPL	√	
COP+SPL	√	√
MT-CFP	√	
MT-CFP+SPL	√	
UNI	√	
UNI+LA	√	
MT-UNI	√	
MT-UNI+LUT	√	
MT-UNI+LUA	√	

Table 1. The Required Information for Each Algorithm

Algorithm	Multi-token	Split	Adaptive Probability	Optimally Adaptive Probability
CFP				
CAP			√	
COP				√
CFP+SPL		√		
COP+SPL		√		√
MT-CFP	√			
MT-CFP+SPL	√	√		
UNI				
UNI+LA				
MT-UNI	√			
MT-UNI+LUT	√			
MT-UNI+LUA	√			

Table 2. The Applied Mechanisms of Each Algorithm

6.13 Numerical results

All results given here are obtained from the mathematical formulations described in the previous sections. We shall first illustrate how the permission probability has an effect on the system performance, which is measured in terms of the average number of successful users. The CFP algorithm is specifically selected for discussion, as it is ideal for this purpose.

By using equation (23), it is possible to obtain a relation between the average number of successful users and the permission probability *p*; this is depicted in Fig. 15. In this figure, the number of slots *N* is fixed at 16 and the total number of users *M* varied from 1 to 16. As we can see, at small values of permission probability the average number of successful users increases with the permission probability. This is simply because under this condition users do not access the contention slots frequently enough; a lot of time these slots are idle. Therefore, an increase in the permission probability will reduce the number of idle slots and thus improving the system throughput. When increasing the permission probability up to a certain value, the number of successful users begins to decline. This performance degradation is due to an increase in the number of collisions caused by too many accessing attempts. A further increment of the permission probability beyond this will only generate more collisions and results in the reduction of the number of successful users.

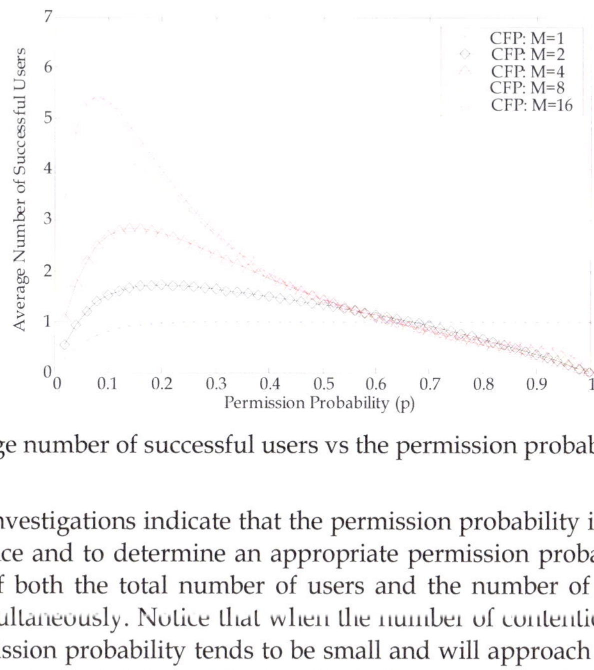

Fig. 15. The average number of successful users vs the permission probability with $N = 16$ for CFP

All of the above investigations indicate that the permission probability is a key factor to the system performance and to determine an appropriate permission probability it is essential to take account of both the total number of users and the number of slots available into consideration simultaneously. Notice that when the number of contention slots is large, the appropriate permission probability tends to be small and will approach zero in the extreme case where the number of slots is infinite. This is because when there are an increased number of contention slots, users gain greater opportunity for access. Therefore, they can access using the lower permission probability to avoid collision. In other words, in the system with a small number of contention slots, the users must attempt to increase their success opportunity by increasing their permission probability.

Fig. 16 illustrates the performance comparison of the CFP, CFP+SPL, MT-CFP and MT-CFP+SPL algorithms. These numerical results are obtained by using the appropriate number of tokens and appropriate permission probability. It is clear that MT-CFP algorithm generally performs better at small number of users. On the other hand, in case of heavy loads the CFP+SPL with 16 groups and MT-CFP+SPL with 16 groups offer relatively superior performance. Moreover, it can be noticed that at the large number of users the performance of MT-CFP algorithm is equal to the performance of CFP algorithm. This is because at the large number of users, the best value of the number of tokens is equal to 1.

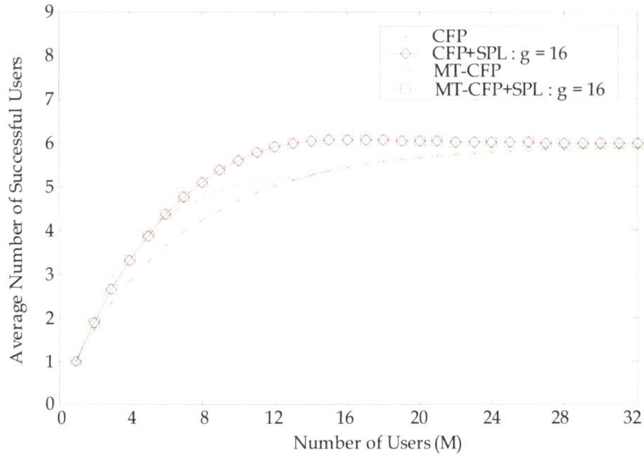

Fig. 16. The average number of successful users vs the number of users (M) with $N = 16$ using the appropriate probability of limitation and appropriate number of tokens for CFP, CFP+SPL, MT-CFP and MT-CFP+SPL

Fig. 17 illustrates the performance comparison of the UNI, UNI+LA, MT-UNI, MT-UNI+LUA and MT-UNI+LUT algorithms. These numerical results are obtained by using the appropriate probability of limitation and the appropriate number of tokens. It can be noticed that under the light load condition, when the number of users is not more than the number of slots divided by 2, the average number of successful users of MT-UNI algorithm is comparatively equal to MT-UNI+LUT and MT-UNI+LUA algorithms and the average number of successful users of UNI algorithm is comparatively equal to UNI+LA algorithm. This is because at the small number of users, the appropriate probability of limitation is equal to 1. In case of heavy load condition, when the number of users is more than the number of slots, the average number of successful users of UNI algorithm is comparatively equal to MT-UNI algorithm and the average number of successful users of UNI+LA algorithm is comparatively equal to MT-UNI+LUT and MT-UNI+LUA algorithms. This is because at the large number of users, the best value of the number of tokens is equal to 1. In this case, limiting the number of user's token is the same meaning as limiting the user's access.

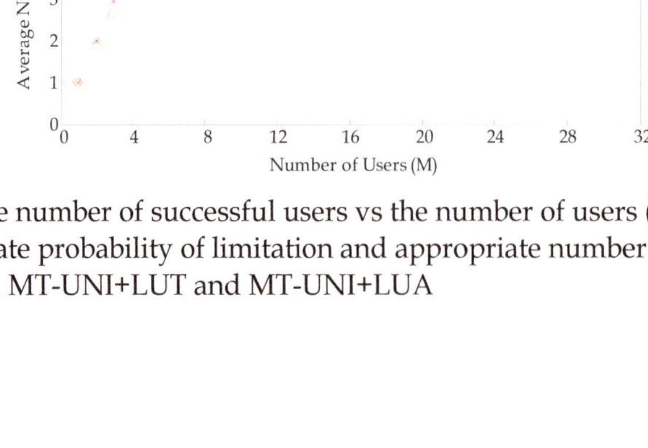

Fig. 17. The average number of successful users vs the number of users (M) with $N = 16$ using the appropriate probability of limitation and appropriate number of tokens for UNI, UNI+LA, MT-UNI, MT-UNI+LUT and MT-UNI+LUA

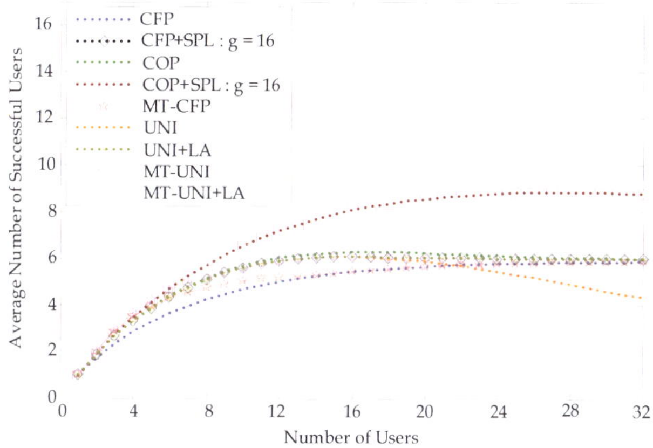

Fig. 18. The number of successful users vs the number of users with $N = 16$

From the above results, it can be noticed that when using the appropriate probability of limitation and appropriate number of tokens the MT-UNI+LUT algorithm is completely identical to the MT-UNI+LUA algorithm under any load condition. Thus, we shall call MT-UNI+LUT and MT-UNI+LUA algorithms as the Multi-Token Uniform + Limited Access (MT-UNI+LA) algorithm for the following discussion.

The performance comparison of all algorithms is depicted in Fig. 18. It is clear that the MT-CFP, MT-UNI and MT-UNI+LA algorithms are effective at systems with light to medium loads. In case of heavy load condition, the COP+SPL algorithm offers relatively superior performance.

7. Conclusions

In this chapter, several well known MAC protocols for the wireless networks are overviewed such as ALOHA, slotted ALOHA, CSMA including 1-pesistent, non-persistent, and p-persistent. Performance analyses for some of these MAC protocols are given in details. Due to the nature of randomness in ALOHA systems, packets can easily collide. In order to minimize collisions, carrier sensing technique, i.e. stations monitor the channel status before transmission, can be applied to improve the throughput performance. In addition, a class of MAC protocols that organizes the channel bandwidth into a frame structure consisting of two alternate periods, namely contention period and information transfer period, are presented. For contention period, we have proposed a number of efficient channel reservation algorithms, namely CFP, CAP, COP, COP+SPL, CFP+SPL, UNI, UNI+LA, MT-CFP, MT-CFP+SPL, MT-UNI, MT-UNI+LUA and MT-UNI+LUT, which are designed for systems where the round trip propagation delays between the base station and wireless stations is relatively larger than the packet transmission time. Mathematical analyses of these algorithms are described and some numerical results are given to compare their performance.

Due to many newly emerging wireless applications, such as entertainment applications, interactive games, medical applications and high speed data transmission, the global demand for multimedia services such as data, speech, audio, video, and image are growing at rapid pace. Future MAC protocols are therefore required not only to handle high speed transmission, but also support various different Quality of Services (QoS). In addition, misbehaviors at the MAC layer, such as DoS attack, have become another concern, as it can potentially cause serious damages to the entire networks. Much ongoing research work in the literature has also been active toward these emerging directions.

8. References

Abramson, N. (1970). The ALOHA System - Another Alternative for Computer Communications. *AFIP Conf. Proc Fall Joint Computing Conf.*, pp. 281–285, 1970.

Amitay, N. & Greenstein, L. J. (1994) Resource Auction Multiple Access (RAMA) in the Cellular Environment. *IEEE Trans. Veh. Technol.*, Vol. 43, No. 4, (January 1994) pp. 1101–1111.

Frigon, J. F.; Leung V.C.M. & Chan, H.C.B. (2001) Dynamic Reservation TDMA Protocol for Wireless ATM networks. *IEEE J. Select. Areas Commun.*, Vol. 19, No. 2, (February 2001) pp. 370–383.

Karn, P. (1990) MACA: a new channel access method for packet radio. *Proceedings of the ARRL/CRRL Amateur Radio 9th Computer Networking Conference*, pp. 134-140, September 1990, Ontario, Canada.

Kleinrock, L. & Tobagi, F. A. (1975). Packet switching in radio channels: part I-carrier sense multiple-access modes and their throughput-delay characteristics. *IEEE Trans. on Commun.*, Vol. COM-23, No. 12, (December 1975) pp. 1400–1416.

Sivamok, N.; Wuttisttikulkij, L. & Charoenpanitkit, A. (2001). New channel reservation techniques for media access control protocol in high bit-rate wireless communication systems. *IEEE Proc. of Globecom*, vol.6, pp. 3558–3562, 2001.

Srichavengsup, W.; Sivamok, N.; Suriya, A. & Wuttisttikulkij, L. (2005). A design and performance evaluation of a class of channel reservation techniques for medium access control protocols in high bit-rate wireless communications. *IEICE Transactions on Fundamentals of Electronics, Communications and Computer Sciences*, Vol. E88-A, No.7, (July 2005) pp. 1824–1835.

Tasaka, S. & Ishibashi, Y. (1984) A Reservation Protocol for Satellite Packet Communication – A Performance Analysis and Stability Considerations. *IEEE Trans. Wireless Commun.*, Vol. COM-32, No. 8, (Aug. 1984) pp. 920–927.

Tobagi, F. A. & Hunt, V.B. (1980) Performance analysis of carrier sense multiple access with collision detection. *Comput. Netw.*, Vol. 4, (October/November 1980) pp.245–259.

Yang, Y. & Yum, T-S. P., Delay distributions of slotted ALOHA and CSMA. *IEEE Trans. on Commun.*, Vol. 51, No. 11, (November 2003) pp. 1846–1858.

20

Wireless Communication-based Safety Alarm Equipment for Trackside Worker

Jong-Gyu Hwang and Hyun-Jeong Jo
Korea Railroad Research institute
Korea

1. Introduction

According to results of the analysis on present condition of railway accidents in Korea, about 50% of them are recorded as railway casualties based on the number of incidence in railway accident, and if converted into the equivalent fatality index(1 fatality = 10 seriously injured persons = 200 slightly injured persons), the equivalent fatality index caused by casualties occupies 94% of the equivalent fatality index for total railway accidents[1]. These railway casualties are consisted of the casualties by railway transportation and the casualties by railway safety. Casualties by railway transportation refer to the accidents where casualties occur to the passengers, crews, workers, etc. by railway vehicles, and the casualties by railway safety mean the accidents where casualties occur to the passengers, crews, workers, etc. by railway facilities without any direct rear-end collision or contact with railway vehicles. That is, accidents such as the falling down or misstep at platform, electric shock, getting jammed to vehicle doors, etc. correspond to casualties by railway safety. Many measures are being studied to prevent and reduce casualties by railway transportation in such a way that casualties by railway transportation are analyzed to have occupied about 87% among casualties which occupy more than 90% of the equivalent fatality index for total railway accidents, etc.[2-7]. As explained previously, in case of the public casualties by railway transportation which occupy most of the railway accidents, since screen doors were installed or are under progress at almost all of the station buildings for metropolitan transit, they play epoch-making roles in the reduction of casualties. However, studies on safety equipment to protect trackside workers who are employees as target persons of casualties have seldom accomplished yet.

When doing maintenance works for the track or signaling equipment at the trackside of railway, the method which delivers information on approaching of train to maintenance workers through alarm devices such as the flag or indication light, etc., if they recognize the approach of train, is being used by locating persons in charge of safety alarm in addition to the maintenance workers at fixed distances in the front and rear of the workplace. Workers maintaining at the trackside may collide with the train since they cannot recognize the approach of train although it approaches to the vicinity of maintenance workplace because of the sensory block phenomenon occurred due to their long hours of continued monotonous maintenance work. And in case of the metropolitan transit section, when doing the maintenance work at night for track facilities, clash or rear-end collision accidents between many maintenance trainses called motor-cars can be occurred since there are cases where the signal systems for safe operation of motor-car such as track circuit etc. are blocked or not operated normally. Since the motor-car driver is not able to accurately locate the points where maintenance works and other motor-cars are done, accidents can occur at any times. In other words, workers are exposed to the accident risks when they are performing maintenance works at tracks, because they are sometimes unable to recognize the approaching motor-cars[8].

To reduce these casualty accidents of maintenance workers working at the trackside of and the clash or rear-end collision accidents between motor-cars, we developed safety alarm equipment preventing the accidents by transmitting specific RF-based communicaiton signals from the motor-car periodically and by making the terminal equipment being carried by workers at the trackside provide various alarm signals such as vibration, sound, LED, etc. to workers through receiving wireless signals from terminal equipment of approaching motor-car. Further, the safety equipment held by the maintenance personnel sends signals telling the location of personnel to motor-cars, allowing motor-car driver to know exactly where maintenance personnel work. Such interactive wireless communication links may contribute to reduction of motor-car accidents[9-11]. In addition, if more than two motor-cars are operated, we made it possible to alarm that another motor-car is approaching through bidirectional wireless communications even between the on-board equipment of motor-cars[12][13].

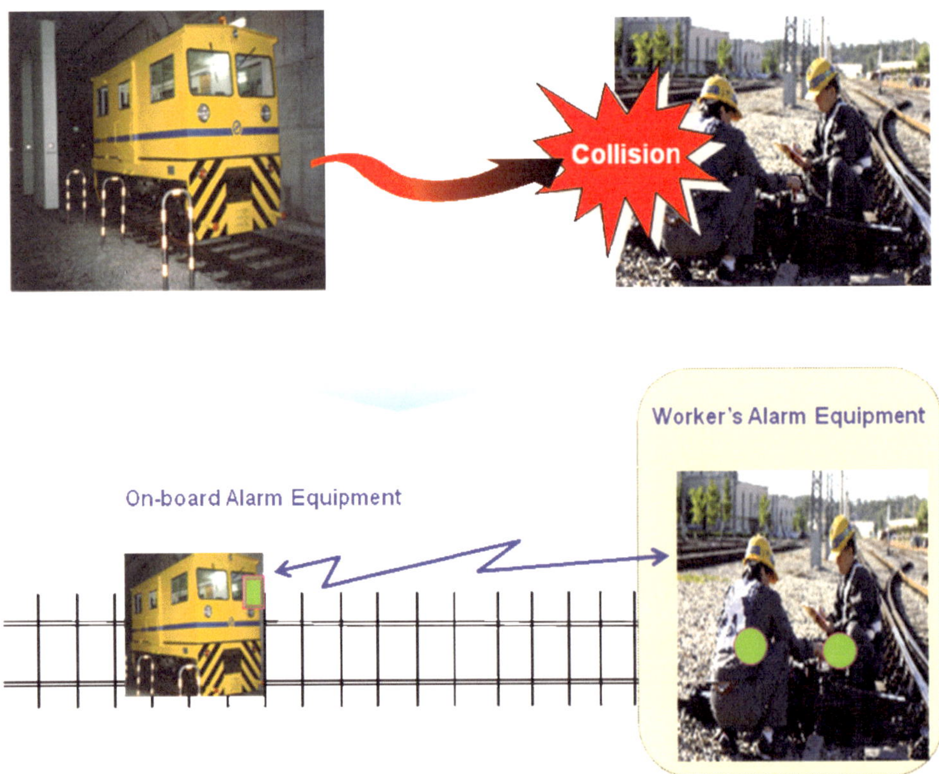

Fig. 1. Configuration of proposed safety equipment

Figure 1 is the one showing an configuration of safety alarm equipment to secure the safety through bidirectional detection between the motor-car and trackside worker proposed in this thesis, and it is the safety equipment making workers evacuate by providing various forms of alarm sounds through recognition of the approaching motor-car by worker's safety equipment if the motor-car approaches within the some distance of front, and on the contrary, inducing to drive carefully by making it possible to check even in the motor-car also if there is any worker existed in the front or not. This is to induce careful driving by providing a motor-car driver with the information also so that the driver can check if there is any work conducted by worker within the fixed distance of front or not, and the alarm signal at the on-board equipment was made to be expressed by LED and alarm sound.

2. Wireless communication-based safety equipment

2.1 Structure of safety equipment using the wireless communication

We designed the safety equipment transmitting alarm signals bidirectionally by using the wireless communication to reduce casualties of trackside workers. Designed safety equipment is consisted of the on-board equipment and the portable device for worker, and it is the safety equipment to reduce casualties by enabling careful driving and evacuation to the safe area by making information on approaching motor-car in the front or information on workers output in the form of various alarm signals respectively. Basic mechanism of the designed safety equipment is made of the structure which makes the signal in a specific frequency band transmitted periodically from the motor-car, and delivers alarm signals in the form of buzzer, LED and vibration, etc. by receiving periodic signals coming from the motor-car to the safety equipment carried by the trackside worker working within a fixed distance in the front. If any worker recognizes alarm signals to alert an approaching motor-car from the safety equipment carried by the worker, the worker will evacuate to the safe area and the alarm sounds can be cutoff. On the contrary, it was developed to make bidirectional communications possible so that whether there is any worker existed in the front or not can be checked from the on-board also[14][15].

Figure 2 is the one showing the configuration of on-board terminal of safe alarm equipment, and it is consisted of RF module to send and receive RF signals periodically, MCU module handling the occurrence of periodic RF signal and operation mechanism of alarm signal, LED module for the output of alarm signal by the light, LCD module to display the information, AMP and speaker parts for the output of alarm signal by the sound, and the power supply module for the input of power supply from a motor-car. Power supply module was made to be input from 5V to 40V so that the power supply of various motor-cars can be input. The frequency band of wireless signal used in this prototype was 424 MHz which is the ISM band. The alarm signal by LED was made to be displayed in different color respectively in accordance with that whether there is any worker existed in the front or another motor-car existed in the front. The alarm sound was made to be adjusted by the motor-car driver, and the LCD panel was made so that the unique number of approached worker's terminal or terminal of another motor-car can be displayed. If wireless signals are being fed back by various terminals within an approaching section, the ID number of terminal was made to be expressed successively in the order of wireless signal feedback. The output of wireless signal of the motor-car terminal of motor-car and that for worker is in the ISM band, and it was adjusted within 10 mW so that the radio wave range can be about 250~300m to suit for the metropolitan rapid transit.

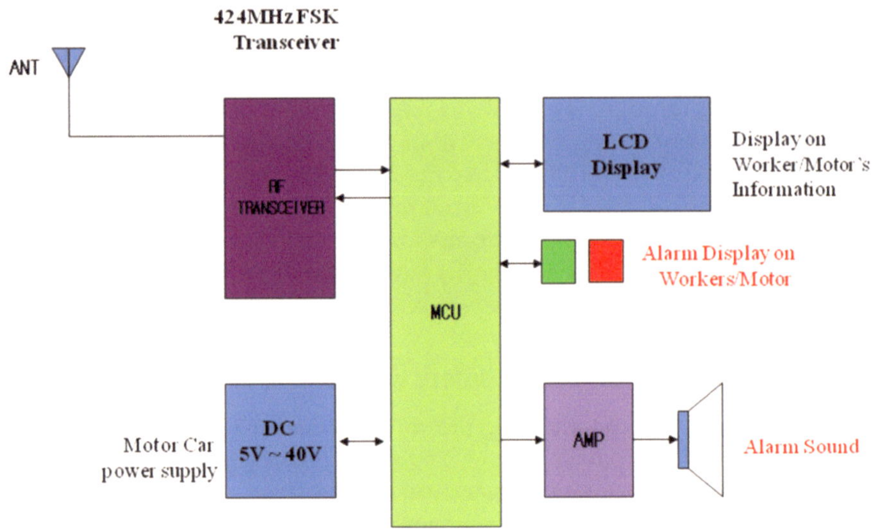

Fig. 2. Configuration of the on-board terminal

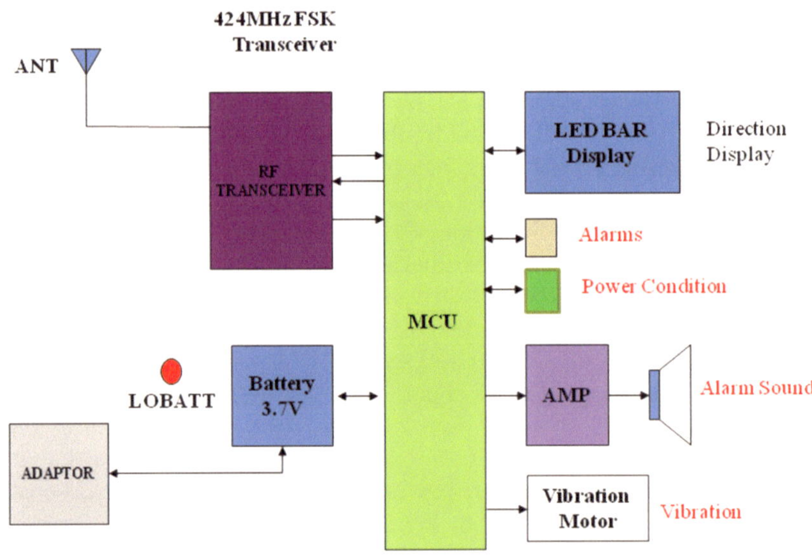

Fig. 3. Configuration of the worker terminal

Figure 3 is the one showing the configuration of terminal for worker and, although its basic configuration is the same as that for on-board terminal in Fig. 2, there is a difference in output part and power supply part of alarm signal. Different from that for on-board terminal, the alarm signal of terminal for worker enhanced its transmission function of alarm signal to the worker through adding an alarm signal by vibration in addition to the alarm signal by LED and sound. Therefore, the vibration motor part was added to the terminal for worker, and the LED alarm was consisted of two kinds of LED displaying the approaching direction of motor-car and the general high brightness LED. In case of the power supply part, although on-board terminal uses power supply inside of the motor-car directly, in case of that for worker, it was made to use batteries after charging them from outside since it is portable, and if the battery charging time is less than three hours, we made the alarm light of 'LOBATT' LED operated. In addition, we made its structure possible to be attached to the worker's waist or put around neck so that it is convenient for the worker to carry with. Table 1 is the one organizing main specifications of the terminal for worker and that for on-board explained previously.

On-board terminal	Frequency	424Mhz
	Output	Within 10mW
	Strength of receipt	-110dbm
	Antenna	External antenna (150mm)
	Input voltage	12V~40V
	Battery	Power supply for motor-car
	Size	190mmx130mmx50mm
	Modulation	F(G)1D/F(G)2D
	Frequency Deviation	±5 kHz
	Bandwidth	8.5 kHz
	Tx Deviation	5 kHz
	S/N Ration	50 dBm
Terminal for worker	Frequency	424Mhz
	Output	Within 10mW
	Strength of receipt	-110dbm
	Antenna	External antenna (50mm)
	Input voltage	3.3~4.2V
	Battery	Storage battery (rechargeable)
	Size	50mmx90mmx25mm
	Modulation	F(G)1D/F(G)2D
	Frequency Deviation	±5 kHz
	Bandwidth	8.5 kHz
	Tx Deviation	5 kHz
	S/N Ration	50 dBm

Table 1. Main Specification of Developed Equipment

2.2 Structure of the transmission frame between on-board and worker terminals

As explained in the previous section, the safety equipment to protect trackside workers is consisted of the on-board equipment to be installed at the motor-car for maintenance work and the worker terminal to be carried by the worker, and the safety mechanism is operated through wireless communicaiton between these two terminals. That is, if the first motor-car in advance approaches the trackside worker, portable worker terminal receive the signal from onboard equipments and indicate warning. If the worker recognizes a warning signal from his alarm terminal, it cut off the alert sounds through "stop key" activity. And then, in case the other motor-car approaches the worker in a row, it must show alert sound notifying the access of the second motor-car regardless of the "stop key" activity which is resulted from the recognition of the access of the first motor-car. For this reason, the transmitted frame architecture is designed such as Fig. 4 (a) to transmit the ID information of the motor-car to trackside worker terminal together with the warning indication. It can assign ID of the 64 motor-cars like transmitted frame in the figure. In case it needs to assign more than 64 motor-car's ID, it is possible if it sets up the transmission frame to 2 bits. We also added the information of the proceed direction of the motor-car as we verified in this frame. Because there are only two directions, which are upward and downward, we send this information with transmission frame and display the worker to show which direction the motor-car is approaching in classifying the LED color and displaying them. Figure 4(b) shows the structure of the transmitted frame which sends from portable equipments for workers to onboard terminal. It is not assigned the ID number because it is unnecessary to classify the rail workers in onboard unlike (a).

As explained previously, the safety equipment for on-board and for worker has several operation switches such as the power supply switch, mode conversion switch, etc. In case of the power supply switch, if this is the case of safety equipment for motor-car, the power supply switch for motor-car was not added separately so that it could not transmit wireless signals to the front periodically and continuously and the driver could not turn off the output signal arbitrary when the power supply of motor-car was input. Checkup button is the button added to enable buzzer sounds cut off if the worker recognizes the approach of motor-car. When making this button operated, it was designed so that the buzzer sound could be operated again if any new wireless signal was received from another approaching motor-car, although the buzzer sound was not expressed if any wireless signal from currently approaching motor-car was received.

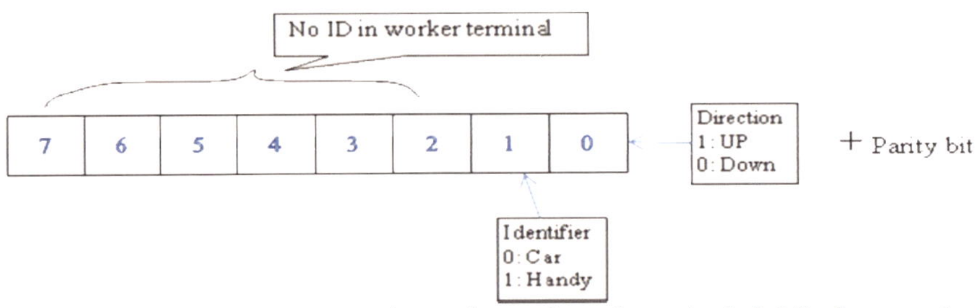

(a) Structure of the transmission frame for on-board terminal ➔ Worker terminale

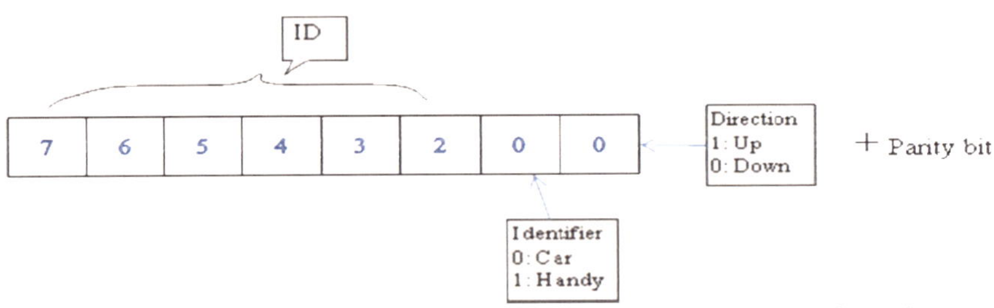

(b) Structure of the transmission frame for worker terminal ➔ On-board terminal

Fig. 4. Transmitted frame between worker and on-board terminal

2.3 Operation mechanism of the alarm signal

Since the motor-car terminal or worker one have the same wireless aignal transmission distance respectively, the alarm of the motor-car and worker terminals will be expressed if the motor-car approaches within the wave transmission distance on the basis of worker. Then, if the worker recognizes this alarm, he/she will push an alarm stop button and the expression of alarm signal at the terminals for worker and motor-car will be stopped accordingly.

Figure 5 is the figure explaining this basic alarm operation mechanism. That is, if the motor-car #01 enters within the wave transmission area of worker terminal, the worker terminal will receive RF signals coming from the motor-car #01 terminal and make alarm signal occurred. And right away, it makes drive carefully by making the alarm informing that there is a worker in the front occurred at the terminal of motor-car #01 by feeding back to the terminal of motor-car #01. The trackside worker will evacuate if he/she acknowledges an alarm signal of worker's terminal, and afterwards since continued alarm signal is not required to be occurred, the alarm signal at the terminal for worker and for motor-car is made to be stopped by handling the checkup button in the terminal for worker. At this time also, although the terminal of motor-car #01 transmits RF signal periodically and the terminal for worker also receives the signal of motor-car #01 periodically, it was made that the alarm signal was not output if an alarm checkup button was pushed. Since then, if the motor-car #02 approaches within the wave transmission area as shown in the figure, it is implemented as a mechanism where the worker's terminal makes alarm signal occurred again like Fig. 5 and at the same time makes alarm signal occurred at the motor-car #02 by feeding it back to the on-board terminal.

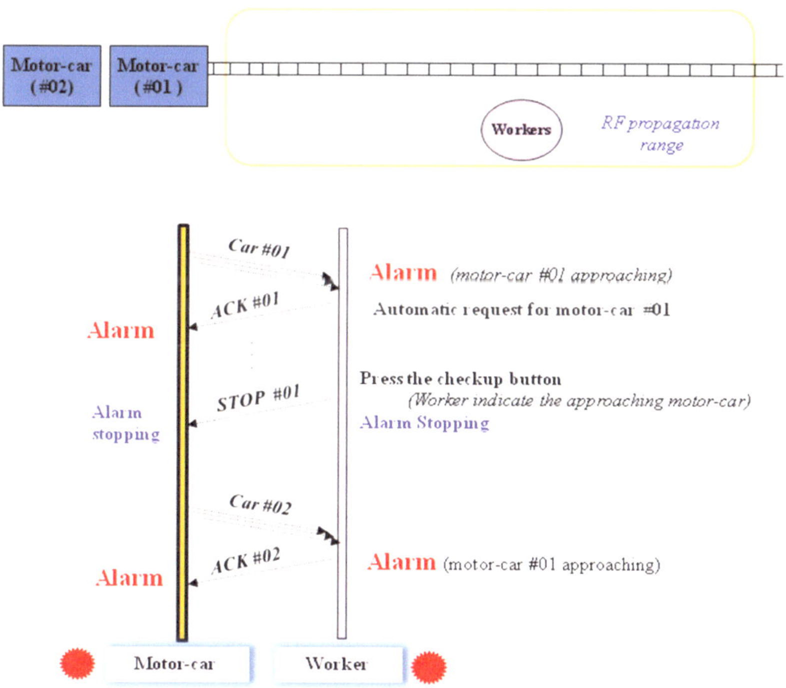

Fig. 5. Basic alarm operation mechanism

In addition to the basic alarm operation mechanism like Fig. 5, certain situation where one motor-car entered within the wave transmission area and then entered again after having left it can be occurred. Since this is the operation of motor-car to be used for works for the trackside maintenance not as a generally operated motor-car, it is possible to repeat frequent forward and backward driving in a narrow area. This case is the one like Fig. 6, and at this time, the terminal for worker will be stopped if it does not receive any RF signal, and the alarm signal of on-board terminal will be stopped also if it does not receive any feedback signal from the terminal for worker. Since then, when the motor-car #01 newly enters within the wave transmission area, it was made to express alarm signals in the same mechanism as that expressed at the time of first entrance. Unlike the basic mechanism like Fig. 5, this is the mechanism making alarm signals operated from the beginning newly if any RF signal is received again after being disconnected although the signal of on-board terminal with same ID is received.

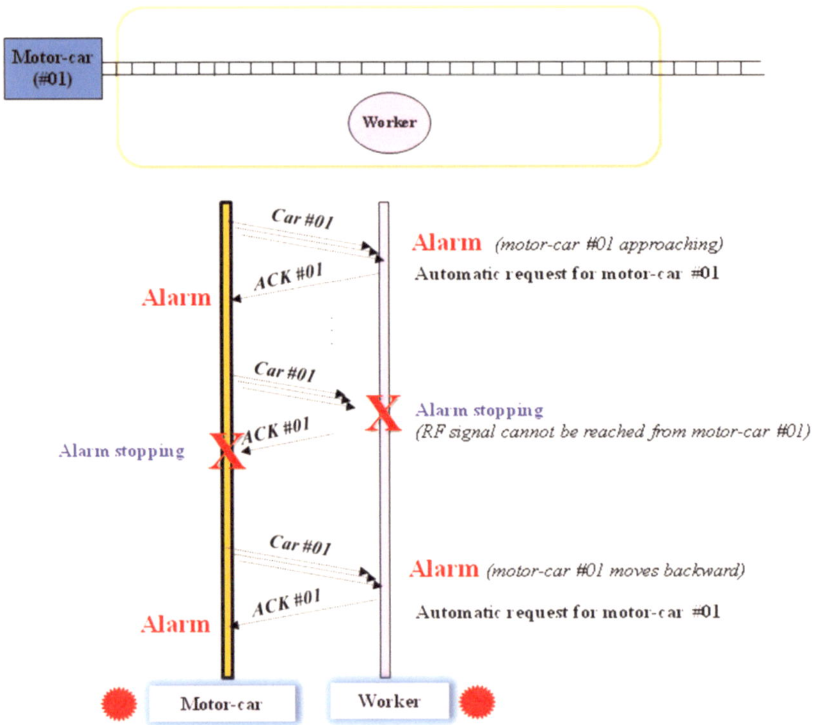

Fig. 6. Alarm mechanism when the motor-car moves backward after leaving its propagation area

Although Fig. 6 is the case where the motor-car enters again after going out of the wave transmission area, there is a case where the motor-car, which is the trackside maintenance motor-car, is operated forward and backward to work within the short area due to its characteristics. This situation is the case where the corresponding motor-car approaches to the worker again by moving backward again within the wave transmission area after the check button is pushed by the worker to stop the alarm after that worker recognizes the approaching motor-car first. That is, in this situation, if the worker terminal does not output the alarm signal again, the clash and rear-end collision accident with motor-car can be occurred again. Thus, the alarm operation mechanism is necessary to solve this problem. Figuer 7 is the one explaining a mechanism to cope with this situation, and the situation mentioned previously was solved by making the alarm signal occurred again if the signal was received from the same motor-car ID after passing a setting time following that the check button was pushed by the worker. The setting time of worker terminal can be varied in accordance with the characteristics of motor-car operation of the railway operation agency, and in the prototype for this study, it was set to 2 minutes by reflecting opinions of motor-car driver and site maintenance worker of Korea.

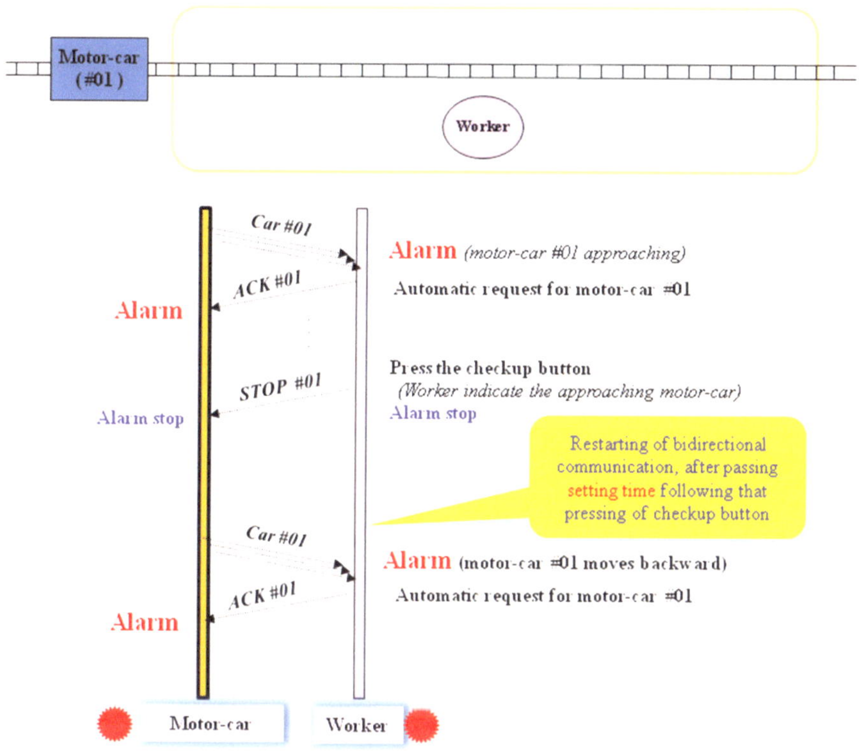

Fig. 7. Alarm mechanism when the motor-car moves backward within the wave transmission area

Actually, motor-cars are being operated for the maintenance of trackside facilities of railway in many railway fields such as the signal, communications, electricity, facility, etc. Generally in case of the railway, the moving location of motor-car can be checked by railway signaling system when the motor-car moves, and accordingly, the control system preventing any clash and rear-end collision between motor-cars by transmitting deceleration and stop signals to the front and rear motor-cars. However, in case of the motor-car, it is impossible to grasp the operation location of motor-car by this signaling system on a real-time basis since it is consisted of a single car or two cars only. Accordingly, it is impossible to check the operation location each other by the system even between the motor-cars, and the operation location each other must be checked by motor-car drivers visually. In addition, because it is impossible to check the location of other motor-cars by eyesights of drivers since operation of these motor-cars are usually accomplished at night, the clash and rear-end collision accidents between each other motor-cars are being frequently occurred currently.

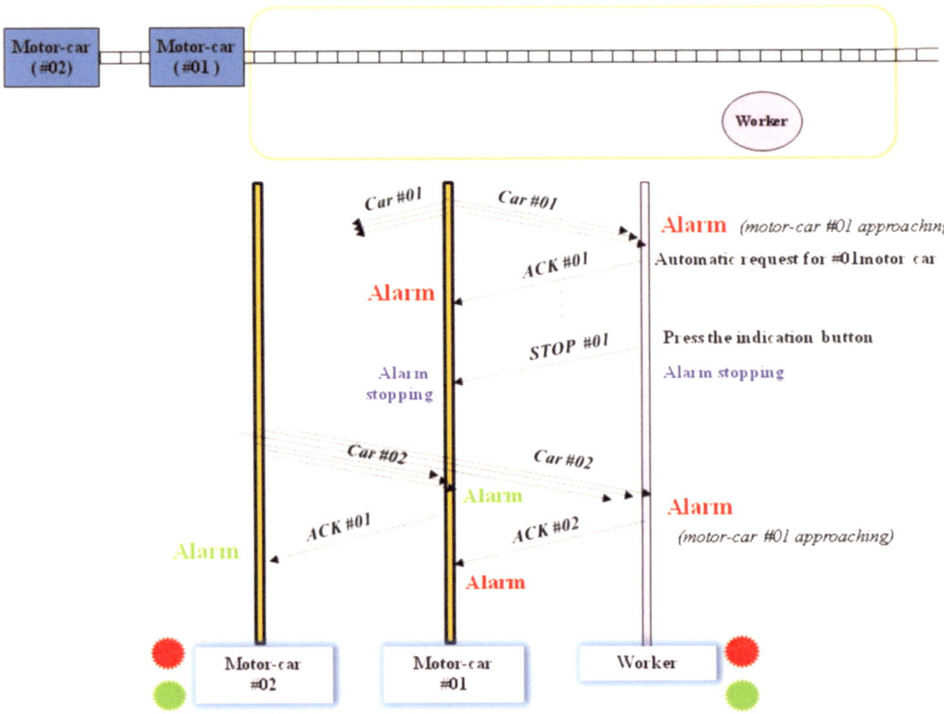

Fig. 8. Alarm operation mechanism the motor-car↔worker and between motor-scars

Figure 8 is the one explaining the mechanism added to prevent clash and rear-end collision accidents between each other motor-cars by making alarm signals occurred in accordance with the approach of each other motor-cars. Although an alarm operation mechanism between the motor-car #01 and the worker is operated in the same manner as several cases explained previously, it is the figure explaining an alarm operation mechanism between each other motor-cars additionally. As shown in the figure, alarm signals between each other will be occurred if the motor-car #01 is approaching to the worker, and the alarm will be stopped by pushing the check button. However, as shown in the figure, the worker terminal makes alarm signals occurred also if the motor-car #02 approaches within the wave transmission area of worker consecutively while moving close to the motor-car #01, and if the motor-car #1 receives a RF signal from the motor-car #02, it makes alarm signals occurred as shown in the figure and makes alarms occurred at the on-board terminal of motor-car #02 by making them fed back to the terminal of motor-car #02. In this case, it was made to have drivers induce safe driving accordingly by making the on-board terminal express alarm signals differently in accordance with whether it is the alarm caused by the worker or by another motor-car. In this prototype, the expression of alarm signal was made to express LED colors differently to classify its recognition on the worker from that on the motor-car.

3. Development and performance testing

3.1 Development of the safety equipment

Safety equipment was manufactured and the test was performed at the railway operation site on the basis of the content designed previously. Figure 9 is the worker terminal of prototype developed through this study, and the Fig. 10 is the picture of terminal for motor-car. In case of the worker terminal, it was made so that the adjacent worker as well as the worker himself/herself can check alarm signals by making alarms output so that the red LED and high-luminance green LED can be turned ON if it receives an approach signal from the motor-car. In addition, we enabled alarm signals to be output in a sound too, and at the same time, we made alarm signals output in various forms such that the vibration is occurred at whole parts of the terminal by operating a vibration motor, etc. Output of the vibration alarm is the same form as that for vibration state of cellular phone. It was manufactured in a slightly smaller size than that of cellular phone so that the worker could carry it conveniently, and it could be attached at the waist of worker or an accessory possible to be hung in the neck through necklace could be attached additionally. By using high-capacity rechargeable batteries, the power supply of worker terminal was made so that the worker could use it conveniently.

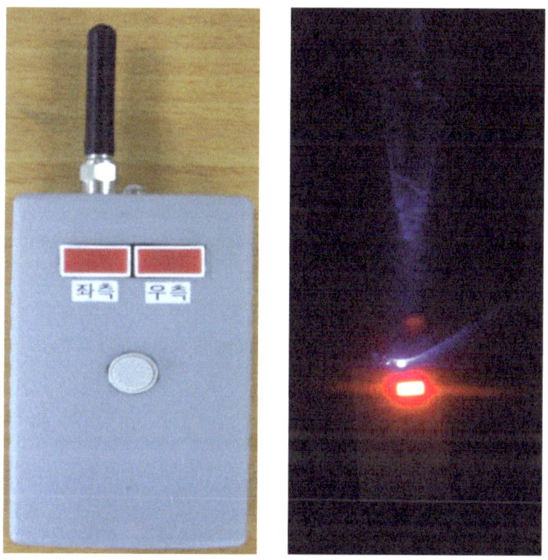

Fig. 9. Prototype of the worker terminal

As for the terminal for motor-car, an alarm LED which will be output in two kinds of color so that whether an adjacent terminal is for the worker or for the motor-car can be distinguished, a setup display button to set the operational direction of corresponding motor-car and the direction display LED according to it, a lever possible to adjust the size of alarm sound, and the check button to stop alarm signals were attached at the front of the terminal. In addition, by attaching a LCD display device, we enabled this LCD display window to be used if the driver of motor-car wanted to obtain more detailed information by making an operation status of his/her own terminal, an unique number, etc. of the terminal for adjacent worker or other motor-car displayed. Unlike the terminal for worker, the output of alarm was limited to LED lights and alarm sounds only without any vibration. Power supply of the motor-car was used as that of the terminal for motor-car, and the power supply of motor-car was used so that the natural role of terminal as the safety equipment could be performed, and we made that the power supply of this safety equipment must be applied during the motor-car operation since no separate power supply switch was designed. This is to prevent the case fundamentally where the driver turns off the power supply of on-board terminal arbitrarily and makes it impossible to be operated as safety equipment.

Fig. 10. Prototype of the motor-car terminal

Figure 11 is the one showing the waveform of signal to be output from the on-board equipment, (a) is the waveform transmitting signals periodically, and (b) is the one showing an output waveform transmitting the transmission frame like Fig. 4. This output signal from on-board equipment outputs various alarm signals by decoding these transmission signals if the portable device for worker receives them within a fixed distance.

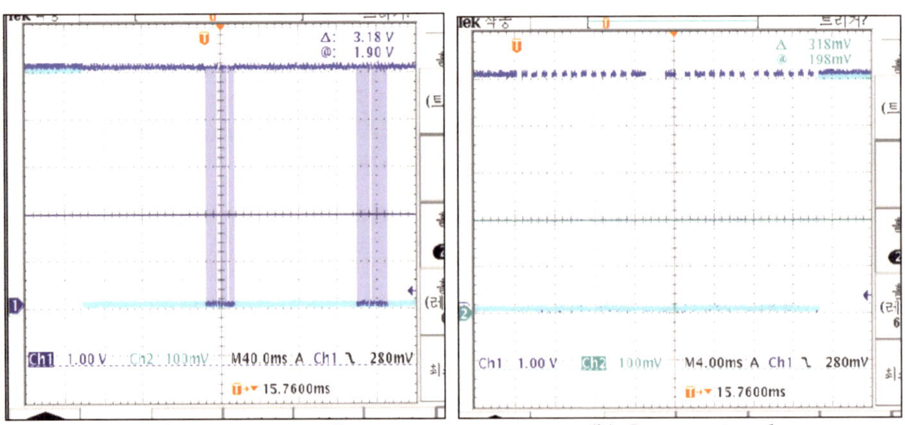

(a) Periodic output waveform (b) Output signal

Fig. 11. Output signal of the on-board safety terminal

(a) On-board terminal installed diverse location

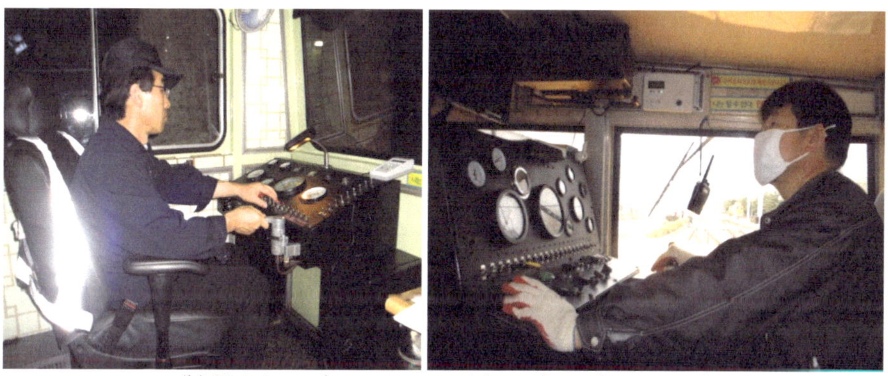

(b) Driving of motor-car with on-board terminal

Fig. 12. Picture of the field test for on-board safety alarm equipment

3.2 Installation and operation as an example at the railway site

For the performance test of developed prototype, we carried out several times of field tests at the track of Seoul Metro, and the functional test to check whether the safety equipment for worker expresses alarm sounds in a form of vibration, buzzer and LED by receiving periodic RF signals from the on-board equipment normally, and whether the mode conversion switch or moving direction of motor-car is expressed normally were carried out in the field test. In addition, the wave transmission distance between the on-board equipment and the equipment for worker was measured to be about 230 ~ 270 m through this field test, and it was verified that this wave transmission distance had satisfied the

requirement of this safety equipment. As for test fields, tests were carried out in accordance with various conditions of those fields such as the underground section, ground section and platform section, etc., and especially, we carried out the test in the section where radius of curvature was 150R for wave transmission distance and performance tests.
Figure 12 is showing the pictures of the installation and operation of manufactured on-board equipment, and like those pictures, it was installed in various ways in accordance with the condition of driver's cab of the motor-car such as the front or side of the driver's control panel or the position at driver's head, etc. since there are various kinds of Korean motor-cars. Figure 13 is the picture of field test through worker terminal, and as can be checked in the figure, the approach of motor-car can be easily checked by the worker himself/herself or a colleague near him/her due to the very bright LED light at the time of its approach. In addition, as shown in the figure, it was manufactured in a small size so that the worker can carry it conveniently, and at the same time, an attaching accessory was added so that it can be attached at the waist belt.

Fig. 13. Picture of the field test for worker terminal

As for the field test, tests were carried out in various railway operation environments such as the platform section, underground tunnel track section, ground track section, etc. As a result of field test in the underground section, the alarm expression mechanism tested in the ground was expressed sufficiently and the minimum wave transmission distance being operated normally was measured to be about 230m. Wave transmission distance of about 230m is the most ideal distance required by the metropolitan rapid transit operating agency, and it was verified that the wave transmission distance of prototype had satisfied the required performance through field tests.

We found optimum output of the on-board and worker's antennae through several tests at the railway sites, and fixed a setup time(2 minutes) of worker terminal. After passing through these field tests, 10 sets of the on-board equipment developed through this study are installed and operated currently as an example in the 4 formation of Seoul Metro motor-cars in Korea. Since lengths of some motor-cars are more than 100m, there are some cases where each of the on-board equipment was installed at the front and rear respectively in case of these motor-cars, and some of the motor-cars have only one on-board equipment per each motor-car also. We are supposed to validate the performance and utility of the developed safety equipment through these actual model operations via this actual railway operation agency, and are planning to make maintenance workers at the trackside site of railway check the utility of this safety equipment.

Fig. 14. Motor-car having a long length where 2 sets of on-board equipment were installed

4. Utilization of the developed safety equipment in the other form

The prototype of safety helmet in this section is the safety equipment to reduce casualties where trackside maintenance workers collide with the motor-car since they did not recognize the approaching motor-car, and whose purpose of utilization is the same as that explained in the previous section. Although its mechanism of transmitting/receiving sides, where wireless signals are transmitted from the approaching motor-car periodically and the safety equipment of worker informs the worker of the alarm on approaching motor-car after receiving them, is the same as that explained in the previous section, but it is different in that the form of safety equipment for worker is the safety helmet using the bone conduction speaker[16-18]. That is, it shows the possibility of utilization in various other forms of safety equipment proposed by the authors by applying the form of safety equipment for worker only to the safety helmet to be worn by the maintenance worker while using the configuration of transmitting/receiving sides developed already in the previous section.

Especially, it is the safety equipment which makes workers evacuate safely by informing them of the alarm to approaching motor-car through bone conduction speaker attached at the safety helmet of trackside maintenance worker not in the general method of alarm expression. Of course, it is identical to the basic operation of safety equipment mentioned in the previous section in that this is the safety equipment to reduce casualties in accordance with the bidirectional RF link by which even the driver of motor-car can check the location of worker by transmitting the location of worker from the safety helmet of maintenance worker to the motor-car. Bone conduction speaker attached at the safety helmet in this section has the characteristics to hear sounds through vibration of the skull, and it was not difficult to prove its utilization because the bone conduction speaker using this principle was commercialized already.

Bone conduction speaker refers to the hearing through vibration of the skull, and the bone conduction speaker using this principle is commercialized. Like Fig. 15, since this bone conduction speaker is attached around the ears, there is no hindrance at all to hear other sounds because the headset does not cover the ears, and it is never unnatural for hearing even when wearing it for a long time, and it is possible to recognize alarm signals to alert an approach of motor-car in any noisy environment.

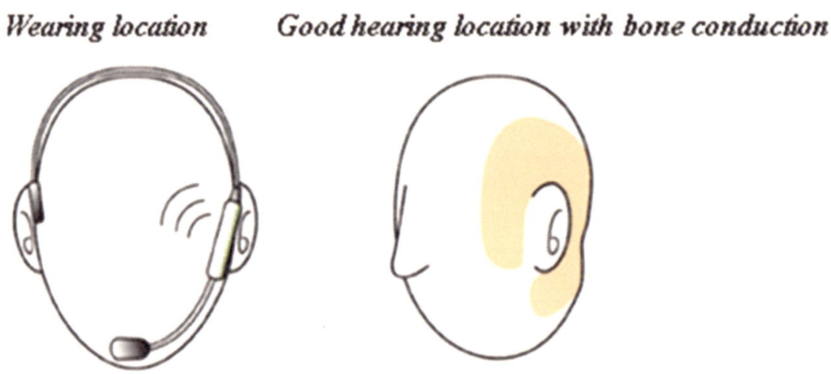

Fig. 15. Wearing location of the bone conduction safety helmet

Since this bone conduction can have the function of speaker only if it is attached around the ears, there is no hindrance at all to hear other sounds even when the headset does not cover the ears. In addition, it is never unnatural for hearing even when wearing it for a long time, and it shows a big advantage that it is possible to recognize alarm sounds to alert an approach of motor-car in any noisy environment.

Therefore, we implemented a bone conduction safety helmet which connects the receiver with bone conduction speaker by using an existing general safety helmet. As explained previously, the function and operation mechanism of safety equipment is identical to that for safety equipment using the wireless proposed in the previous section, and it has the only difference that its method of expressing information on the approach of motor-car is the safety helmet using a bone conduction speaker. The prototype of manufactured safety helmet is divided into the equipment for vehicle and for worker which is identical to the safety equipment proposed in the previous section, and the speaker using a bone conduction vibrator is identical to Fig. 16. Since this bone conduction speaker was attached to the chinning string of safety helmet after being fastened and receives alarm sounds through bone conduction speaker, the worker can recognize hazardous factors immediately and evacuate because he/she can hear the ambient sounds and signal sounds transmitted from the motor-car at the same time since the ears of worker were not covered. All of the workers wearing safety helmets with manufactured bone conduction method and vehicles will communicate on a real-time basis, and the worker can check and grasp alarm sounds immediately through bone conduction and operation of LED if there is any motor-car or person existed when a motor-car approaches within the fixed distance.

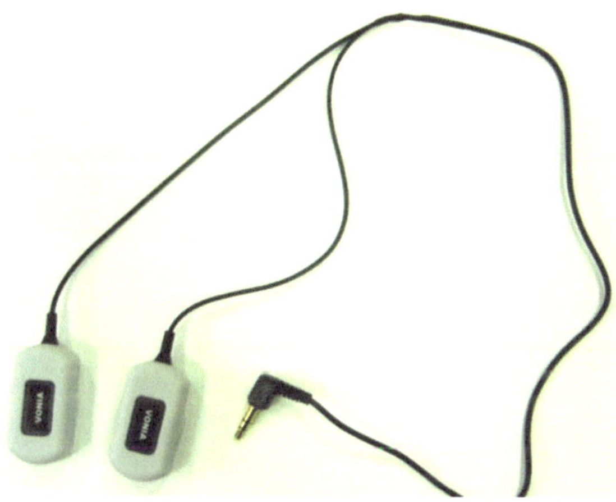

Fig. 16. Developed bone conduction vibrator speaker

The equipment for vehicle sends signals continuously while tracking the location of worker, and the receiver attached at the safety helmet of worker senses them and outputs alarm sounds and alarm signals in LED to the equipment for motor-car simultaneously. Bone conduction receiver attached at the safety helmet receives wireless signals transmitted from the vehicle as a top priority and can recognize that the motor-car is coming by using three stages of wireless signals through bone conduction speaker at the safety helmet of worker while working. Band of wireless signal for developed prototype of the safety helmet with bone conduction speaker is 448.75 Mhz, and used 5mW of output. Figure 17 is picture showing the result of final prototype of the proposed safety equipment which was manufactured in the form of safety helmet using the bone conduction speaker.

Fig. 17. Result of the prototype safety helmet for railways with bone conduction method

5. Conclusion

Since casualties of railway transportation occupy most of the recent railway accidents, it is steadily required to prepare the measure to prevent them. This paper described contents such as the applicability through design, manufacturing and field test of safety equipment developed as a measure to prevent casualties of maintenance worker working at the trackside of railway who corresponds to the employee as the target person of casualties, and the validation on utilization through its implementation in another form called as the safety helmet, etc. The safety equipment being proposed transmits alarm signals bidirectionally to the on-board and worker, and is consisted of the on-board safety equipment to be installed at the driver's cab of motor-car and the safety equipment for worker to be carried by the worker. Each safety equipment outputs information on entering motor-car in the front or information on worker in the form of various alarm signals, and can prevent and reduce casualties of railway transportation by enabling careful driving and evacuation to the safe area.

And, we performed field tests in the tunnel for metropolitan rapid transit which is the actual operation section to prove the effectiveness of developed safety equipment, and as a result of the test, the applicability was validated since requirements as the safety equipment to reduce casualties of worker were satisfied sufficiently. In addition, the possibility of utilizing this technology for safety equipment in various forms was verified by showing the prototype manufactured in the form of safety helmet using the bone conduction speaker by utilizing technologies for safety equipment being proposed. It is expected that the safety equipment having its superior performance and high possibility of utilization like this to prevent casualties of maintenance worker working at the trackside of railway will contribute much to the prevention and reduction of casualties in railway transportation in the future.

6. References

[1] KRRI Research Report, Evaluation on the Safety Performance of Train Control System and the Development of Technology for Prevention against Accidents, Korea Railroad Research Institute (KRRI), July 2009.

[2] Rail Safety and Standard Board, Profile of Safety Risk on the UK Mainline Railway, Issue 5, 2006.

[3] C.W. Park, J.B. Wang, and et al., Development of Accident Scenario Models for the Risk Assessment of Railway Casualty Accidents, *Journal of the Korean Society of Safety*, vol.24, no.3, pp.79-87, 2009.

[4] European Commission, 'Safety Management in Railway, D.2.3: Common Safety Methods', 2004.

[5] Rail Safety and Standard Board, Guidance on the Preparation of Risk Assessments within Railway Safety Cases, Railway Group Guidance Note GE/GN8561, 2002.

[6] FRA Guide for Preparing Accident/Incident Report, 12 U.S. Department of Transportation Federal Railroad Administration, 2003.

[7] C.W. Park, J.B. Wang and et al, Development of Risk Assessment Models for Railway Casualty Accidents, *Journal of the Korean Society for Railway*, vol.12, no.2, pp.190-198, 2009.

[8] Seoul Metro, Practical Business to handle Casualty Accidents in the Subway, Seoul Metro Press, 2004.

[9] Bernard Skar, Digital Communications - Fundamentals and Applications, Prentice Hall, United States of America, 1988.

[10] T.S. Rappaport, Wireless Communications-Principles and Practice, Prentice Hall, pp.110-189, 1996.

[11] Yi-Bing, Imrich Chlamtac, Wireless and Mobile Network Architecture, Wiley Computer Publishing, United States of America, 2001.

[12] Nejikovsky, B. Keller, E, Wireless communications based system to monitor performance of rail vehicles, *Proceedings of the 2000 ASME/IEEE Joint in Newark*, pp.111-124, NJ, USA, June 2000.

[13] G.M. Shafiullah, A. Gyasi-Agyei, P. Wolfs, Survey of Wireless Communications Applications in the Railway Industry, *Proceedings of the 2nd International Conference on Wireless Broadband and Ultra Wideband Communications* (AusWireless 2007), Sydney, Australia, August 2007.

[14] J.G. Hwang, H.J. Jo and Y.G. Kim, Alarm Equipment for Protection of Trackside Maintenance Workers using Bone Conduction Speaker, ITC-CSCC'2009 conference proceeding, Jeju Korea, July 2009.

[15] J.G. Hwang, H.J. Jo, Y.K. Yoon and Y.G. Kim, Development of wireless communication-based safety equipment for protection of trackside maintenance workers, 31st *International Telecommunications Energy Conference* (INTELEC 2009), pp.1-4, October 2009.

[16] Tsuge S., Koizumi D., Fukumi M., and Kuroiwa S., Speaker verification method using bone-conduction and air-conduction speech, *International Symposium on Intelligent Signal Processing and Communication Systems* (ISPACS 2009), pp.449- 452, Issue Date: 7-9, January 2009.

[17] Jack J. Wazen, Jaclyn Spitzer, Results of the Bone-Anchored Hearing Aid in Unilateral Hearing Loss, *The Laryngoscope*, vol.111, Issue 6, pp.955-958, June 2001.
[18] Bance Manohar, Abel Sharon M., Papsin Blake C., Wade Philip, and Vendramini Judy, A Comparison of the Audiometric Performance of Bone Anchored Hearing Aids and Air Conduction Hearing Aids, *Otology & Neurotology*, vol.23, Issue 6, pp.912-919, November 2002.

21

Wireless Communication Protocols for Distributed Computing Environments

Romano Fantacci, Daniele Tarchi and Andrea Tassi
University of Florence
Italy

1. Introduction

The distributed computing is an approach relying on the presence of multiple devices that can interact among them in order to perform a pervasive and parallel computing. This chapter deals with the communication protocol aiming to be used in a distributed computing scenario; in particular the considered computing infrastructure is composed by elements (nodes) able to consider specific application requests for the implementation of a service in a distributed manner according to the pervasive grid computing principle (Priol & Vanneschi, 2008; Vanneschi & Veraldi, 2007).
In the classical grid computing paradigm, the processing nodes are high performance computers or multicore workstations, usually organized in clusters and interconnected through broadband wired communication networks with small delay (e.g., fiber optic, DSL lines). The pervasive grid computing paradigm overcomes these limitations allowing the development of distributed applications that can perform parallel computations using heterogeneous devices interconnected by different types of communication technologies. In this way, we can resort to a computing environment composed by fixed or mobile devices (e.g., smartphones, PDAs, laptops) interconnected through broadband wireless or wired networks where the devices are able to take part to a grid computing process. Suitable techniques for the pervasive grid computing should be able to discover and organize heterogeneous resources, to allow scaling an application according to the computing power, and to guarantee specific QoS profiles (Darby III & Tzeng, 2010; Roy & Das, 2009).
In particular, aim of this chapter is to present the most important challenges for the communication point of view when forming a distributed network for performing parallel and distributed computing. The focus will be mainly on the resource discovery and computation scheduling on wireless not infrastructured networks by considering their capabilities in terms of reliability and adaptation when facing with heterogeneous computing requests.

2. Related works

A particular interest in the literature is towards the interactions between high performance and distributed computing schemes. The main paradigms that allow a wide-area computing in a distributed fashion are represented by the grid (Parashar & Lee, 2005) and the cloud computing (Foster et al., 2008); in the last years these paradigms, originally disjointed, aim to be more overlapped considering the remarkable research efforts regarding communication standards and computing devices. In particular, if we also take into account hardware and

software capabilities of consumer mobile devices (like PDAs or mobile phones) we can realize that they no longer can be considered simply as *service consumers* through which to request a service to an elaboration center, but now they are able to take part to a distributed elaboration process (e.g., the distributed problem solving, etc.).
The pervasive grid and cloud computing paradigms are placed in a scenario characterized by fixed and mobile nodes characterized by different computing power and interconnected by several wired and wireless links relying on different communication technologies with heterogeneous rate and delay profiles.

2.1 Strategies for pervasive grid computing

The pervasive grid paradigm is strictly related to the computational grid concept (Foster & Kesselman, 1999); in this vision a computing architecture is composed by a central computing center made of clusters of fixed nodes that provide a set of services on the outside. An user can exploit these services through a pervasive infrastructure allowing a completely transparent access to the end-user at the computing center. The pervasive infrastructure can be composed by heterogeneous networks, devices with different computing power and equipped by different softwares.
The pervasive grid computing represents a significant innovation because in this case the computing resources are "pervasive" (Parashar & Pierson, 2010); for this reason not only a cluster of workstations can take part to a distributed and parallel computing process, but also a mobile device can be used as a computing node.
The most challenging problems related to a computing infrastructure composed by mobile nodes, interconnected by not reliable communication networks (e.g., P2P networks, etc.) are defined in (Batista & da Fonseca, 2010; Darby III & Tzeng, 2010; Ranjan et al., 2008). The key aspects of a distributed application are: the context-awareness, the self-adaptiveness, the QoS-awareness.
Ref. (Hingne et al., 2003; McKnight et al., 2004; Vanneschi & Veraldi, 2007) present a set of distributed computing models that try to address the context-awareness problem; it is important to note that this aspect is strictly related to the self-adaptiveness problem because if a change in the computing resource set is detected (e.g., a CPU is overloaded or a PDA battery is exhausted) the distributed application should react to this change in order to preserve, e.g., the integrity of a result in a distributed problem solving process. This problem has been addressed in two ways:

- relying on a middleware software layer shared among the computing nodes that globally reconfigures the distributed application (e.g., switching at run-time to different implementation or configuration of a service (Coronato & De Pietro, 2008; Coulson et al., 2005; Emmerich, 2000)) in a way fully invisible to the application itself;
- expressing the self-adaptiveness directly in the distributed application demanding to it the self-configuration problem (Aldinucci et al., 2008; Fantacci et al., 2009; Huebscher & McCann, 2008; Vanneschi & Veraldi, 2007). In particular (Fantacci et al., 2009) describes a pervasive gird application as a set of components interconnected by logical communication channels; a component provides a pool of functionalities and can be deployed in different versions characterized, e.g., by different memory footprints, CPU usages, etc. In this model the self-adaptiveness problem is addressed by switching at run-time between the versions of the same component deployed in the computing nodes.

The QoS problem related to the grid paradigm has been addressed in the literature jointly with the resource discovery problem and the optimal job allocation: a job should be completed according to the SLA between the user and the organization holding the computing

infrastructure. In order to make it possible a job must be mapped in a set of nodes with enough computing power; they can be identified only through an efficient resource discovery technique. In (Al-ali et al., 2003; Sundararaj et al., 2004) all these aspects have been analyzed for networks at "Internet scale"; in particular, the first one proposes an extension of the classical Globus model (Morohoshi & Huang, 2005) adopting a DiffServ (Park, 2006) approach and the second one addresses these problems building a virtual overlay network interconnecting all computing resources in order to route better the network traffic and making the grid infrastructure able to react to bandwidth fluctuations.
In the literature the QoS problems relative to the pervasive grid paradigm have been addressed in the following ways:

- the resource discovery and monitoring is demanded to the middleware layer or to a software service that makes the distributed application aware of the available computing resources (Noble, 2000; Schmidt & Parashar, 2004). The common drawbacks of these techniques are that all the information discovered must be stored in centralized or distributed indexes that can be built only through ad-hoc messages contributing to the network congestion;
- there are other strategies specifically designed for pervasive grid environments, characterized by fixed and mobile devices interconnected through heterogeneous wireless networks where the resource discovery and network routing capabilities are covered by the same service; this happens in (Li et al., 2005) and (Fantacci et al., 2010) where an enhanced version of two routing protocol optimized for mobile and ad-hoc network (MANET) with integrating resource discovery capabilities is described.

Finally, in the literature other aspects has been addressed as the fault tolerance (Agbaria & Sanders, 2005; Bertolli, Vanneschi, Ciciani & Quaglia, 2010; Oliner et al., 2005) or the security (Saadi et al., 2005; The Globus Security Team, 2005) of a pervasive grid application.

2.2 Strategies for cloud computing

Foster et al. in (Foster et al., 2008) define the cloud computing paradigm as a large-scale computing paradigm in which a pool of resources are delivered on demand to external customers over the Internet. In the distributed system scenario a cloud computing system represent a sort of evolution of the classical grid paradigm, like the pervasive grid.
A cloud computing system can provide services at three levels (Zhang et al., 2010):

- Software as a Service (SaaS) making users able to share applications running on a distributed infrastructure;
- Platform as a Service (PaaS) allowing users to access to an integrated environment in order to develop and deploy parallel application;
- Infrastructure as a Service (IaaS) allowing users to share hardware resources (like computing power, storage, etc.).

For these reasons, from the application context-awareness, self-adaptiveness and QoS-awareness point of view, the cloud computing paradigm shares with the pervasive grid one the same problems and solutions (Foster et al., 2008).

3. Implementation model of a parallel and distributed decision support system

In order to introduce the communication protocols definition we introduce now the considered pervasive grid approach proposed in (Aldinucci et al., 2008) and successively adopted in (*CoreGRID Network of Excellence*), where a distributed application can be modeled

as a graph: the vertices are the logical components and the edges are the communication channels. The logical components of the application can be different, performing each one a specific set of operations on the input data. The communication between logical components is achieved through data streams, considered as a set of elements transmitted serially by a component to another one (Bertolli, Buono, Mencagli & Vanneschi, 2010).
A logical component of a distributed application relying on such parallel computing model can be considered as a process running on a device; each node can (virtually) executes all the components forming the distributed application. One of the most important characteristics is that the whole application is able to dynamically reconfigure itself in order to match specific QoS constraints or to react to the context changes (e.g., changes in network topology, or in the computing node load). The adaptivity and the context awareness of the application can be explicitly programmed in every logical component. The two main types of adaptivity are:

- *performance adaptivity* - realized when the parallelism degree of a component changes;
- *functional adaptivity* - realized whenever a different version of the same resolution algorithm (e.g., a reduced memory footprint, etc.) is adopted.

A general purpose model for a parallel computing application should be based on the following set of entities:

- *the data source* - the source generating data; each measure is called *point*. The whole source area can be divided in parts, called *cells*, where the data source is placed;
- *the processing nodes* - in each cell a pervasive computing application relies on a distributed computed infrastructure (DCI) composed by a variable number of mobile users, having a device equipped with a wireless network adapter used to communicate with the data aggregators of the cell and with the other users;
- *the data aggregators* - in each DCI one or more devices are involved, gathering the points produced by the data source operating in the cell where the aggregator is; a user device can also play the role of data aggregator.

A parallel application can be developed according to different models: the two most common paradigms are task farm and data parallel. These two models differ in the type of logical components involved in the model and in the way the logical components cooperate to solve a problem. Other more complex structures can be easily seen as a combination of the two considered models.

3.1 Task farm paradigm

This paradigm, represented in Fig.1, relies on the replication of the same logical components used to perform the same operations on different input data.
A task farm application is composed by the following types of logical components:

- *the emitter (E)* receives an input stream formed by elements of the same type, each of which is transmitted to a worker;
- *the workers (W)* receive a different input stream element but process it with the same function *F*;
- *the collector (C)* gathers the outputs of the workers and forward them on the output channel with the form of an output stream.

In certain cases the emitter role can be played by the data aggregator node; however, we will consider in the following that the two functions are decoupled for a more general case. The main contribution to the computing power comes from the mobile nodes, considering that

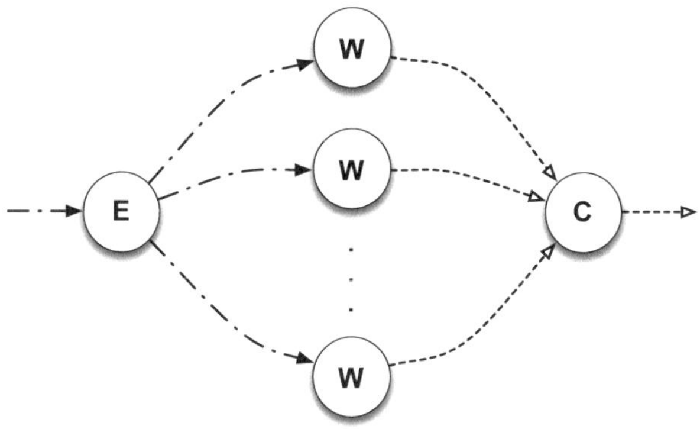

Fig. 1. Task farm model.

each node can execute one or more workers in parallel (e.g., a collector process can run on a single node or in multiple network nodes at the same time).
A task farm application, in a steady state, achieves a five stage pipeline system, where the first stage is composed by the emitter, the second by the communication link between the emitter and the worker node, the third by the workers, the fourth by the communication link between the worker and the collector node and the last by the collector. For this reason the average service time of the application (T_{farm}) can be expressed as:

$$T_{\text{farm}} = \max\left\{T_E, T_{l_1}, \frac{T_W}{N_{farm}}, T_{l_2}, T_C\right\} \tag{1}$$

where T_E is the execution time at the source node (i.e., the time needed to distribute the tasks to be executed at the mobile nodes), T_{l_1} is the communication latency of a stream originating from the source and directed to the worker nodes, T_W is the execution time of W, T_{l_2} is the communication delay between a worker node a the collector, and T_C is the time needed at the collector for re-assemble the output of the workers, and N_{farm} represents the number of workers involved in the parallel computation. Being the third right member of (1) usually the biggest term, we have:

$$T_{farm} = \frac{T_W}{N}. \tag{2}$$

Let T_A the average time elapsed between the consecutive emission of two points (i.e., the average arrival time). We define the optimal parallelism degree ($\hat{N}_{farm}$) as the value that allows to have the average service time of the application equal to the average arrivals time. Hence, we have:

$$\hat{N}_{farm} = \left\lceil \frac{T_W}{T_A} \right\rceil \tag{3}$$

3.2 Data parallel paradigm

In the data parallel paradigm, represented in Fig. 2, the working processes involved in the computation are combined in order to solve one task at a time. As before, we have three types of modules:

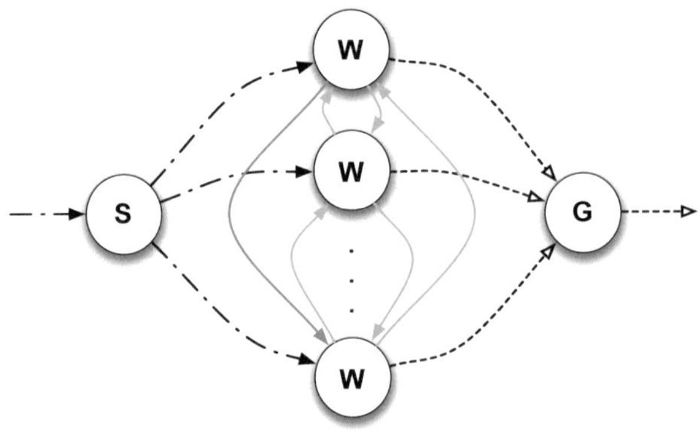

Fig. 2. Data parallel model.

- *the scatter (S)* receives the input stream, and compiles the *input state* (**M**) of the task. **M** is split in a number of parts (called sub-states) identical to the number of workers involved in the computation; each sub-state is transmitted to a worker;
- *the workers (W)* perform the sub-computations initialized with the sub-states received. If we consider **M** as a square matrix of $n \times n$ elements, formed by only a subset of columns of the **M** matrix and that all the sub-states have the same size, the computation can be modeled as an iteratively application of a function $H(\cdot)$, $\hat{S}$ times on each element of the sub-state;
- *the gather (G)* collects and reorders the outputs of the workers. G also builds the solution to be sent on the output line.

It should be noted that a worker involved in the computation can process the sub-state regardless of the other ones (the data parallel application is called *map*) or have some functional dependencies with other workers (in this case the application is called *stencil*). Moreover, we have a functional dependence when a worker needs to know some partial results from one or more workers in order to perform an iteration of $H(\cdot)$ on an element.
Likewise the task farm paradigm, the gather process can run on one or more nodes at the same time, and each node of the local computing cloud can execute in parallel one or more working processes. The node, where the scatter process is executed, is selected time by time through an optimal criteria (see Section 4). Finally, we assume that each worker transmits its output to the data aggregator node that also acts as the gather.
A map application, in a steady state, as in the task farm paradigm, realizes a five stages pipeline paradigm, where the first stage is composed by the scatter, the second by the communication link between the emitter and the worker node, the third by the workers, the fourth by the communication link between the worker and the collector node and the last by the gather. The average service time (T_{map}) can be expressed as:

$$T_{map} = \max\left\{T_S, T_{l_1}, T_W, T_{l_2}, T_G\right\} \quad (4)$$

where T_S and T_G are, respectively, the average service time of S and G, T_{l_1} and T_{l_2} are, respectively, the maximum communication latencies encountered by a communication between the scatter or the gather node and each worker involved in a computation. Also in this type of parallelism, usually, T_W is greater than the other terms. Hence, we have:

$$T_{map} = T_W. \quad (5)$$

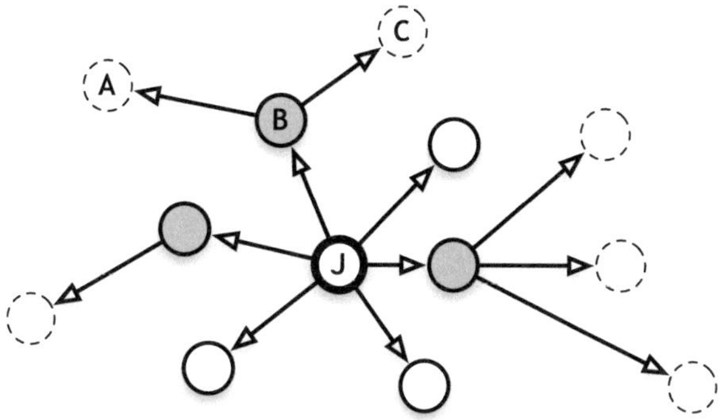

Fig. 3. A flat topology network based on the multi-hop communication paradigm.

Finally, T_W can be expressed as:

$$T_W = \hat{S} \cdot T_H \cdot \frac{n^2}{N_{map}} \tag{6}$$

where T_H is the average time needed by a computing device to apply the H function just one time on a single element coming from the input state, N_{map} is the number of workers involved in the computation and the ratio between the total number of elements of $\mathbf{M}$, n and N_{map} gives the sub-state size (in terms of number of elements).
With this type of parallelism we define the optimal number of workers ($\hat{N}_{map}$) as the amount of computing processes by which it is possible to have an average service time of the whole application equal to the average arrival time, and hence avoiding the saturation of the input queue of the parallel application. In order to have $T_A = T_{map}$ or equivalently, as assumed above, $T_A = T_W$, the workers number, according to (6), results to be:

$$\hat{N}_{map} = \left\lceil \frac{\hat{S} \cdot n^2 \cdot T_H}{T_A} \right\rceil \tag{7}$$

4. Resource discovery and routing

When facing with a heterogeneous network the first challenge to be considered is the discovering of the resources in the network in order to have a more detailed model of the active devices. Herein we assume to be in a flat topology network where each node has the same role. This model allow us to consider the most general case, where no hierarchy is considered within the network.
In such networks (Fig. 3), if the node **A** needs to communicate with **C** (and they are not in the radio connectivity range), it is possible through the relay node **B** according to multi-hop approach.
In order to perform the best selection among the DCI we have to identify the best nodes to be allocated for the execution of a specific distributed application. On the other hand a flat topology network needs to be based on a smart routing algorithm able to find the best route between different nodes; this is even more important in the case mobility becomes an issue: in this case we will refer to the so-called MANET (mobile and ad-hoc networks). The most convenient approach seems to be an exploitation of the routing algorithm in order to fulfill the resource discovery task.

There are several basic routing protocols for ad-hoc networks (Badis & Al Agha, 2005; Clausen & Jacquet, 2003; Haas & Pearlman, 2001; Perkins & Royer, 1999); they can be classified into three families:

- *proactive family* - the routing strategy relies on a periodic update of the routing information stored in each node in order to make a node able to communicate with the rest of the network, the routing table of a node is composed by each possible route. The most popular in this class is the OLSR algorithm (Clausen & Jacquet, 2003) and its QoS-aware extension called QOLSR (Badis & Al Agha, 2005), whose aim is to consider the QoS requirements of the different traffic flows for a better routing decision;
- *reactive family* - differently from the previous routing family, a route from two network nodes is discovered and used in the source and in the intermediate devices of the path only when a source node needs to communicate with the destination node. A well known reactive routing protocol is the AODV (Ad-hoc On-demand Distance Vector (Perkins & Royer, 1999));
- *hybrid family* - these routing algorithms are composed by two parts: the first operate in a proactive way, and the second in a reactive way. The ZRP (Zone Routing Protocol) (Haas & Pearlman, 2001) is one of the most important protocol belonging to this class.

Herein the aim is to identify a routing protocol able to allow a pervasive grid computation in flat topology network. It is well known that reactive protocols require less network traffic than the proactive ones, but the QOLSR principle (Badis & Al Agha, 2005), despite a higher network control traffic with respect to reactive alternatives, can provide the following characteristics:

- the reactive protocols have a not predictable setup time for setting up a route and update the routing tables for the nodes involved in the communication;
- the end-to-end QoS of a path between the source and the destination nodes has to be explicitly monitored in each intermediate node;
- the routing messages cannot be used to periodically broadcast information or as probe messages in order to estimate some QoS indexes.

4.1 An enhanced routing scheme for pervasive grid computing

As highlighted before in the scenario we are considering we have to face with the problem of discovery the resources within the network by exploiting a routing algorithm. The EOLSR protocol (Fantacci et al., 2010), relying on the QOLSR protocol, adds the following characteristics in order to fulfill the requirements of the considered scenario:

- it operates in a distributed way and does not require any supervisor node;
- it does not require a reliable transmission of routing messages;
- it performs an hop-by-hop routing approach, and each network node, belonging to the path connecting the source with the destination device, chooses the next destination to send the traffic;
- it is able to find always the optimal path between every pair of network nodes.

As for the QOLSR case, with the EOLSR protocol each node has to perform the following operations:

1. detecting, through the received HELLO messages, its 1-hop neighbors;
2. performing the MPR (multipoint relay) selection and updating its topology table thought the topology control (TC) messages;

3. computing the routing table.

A node J (Fig. 3) broadcasts the HELLO messages to its 1-hop neighbors with the source address and the list of its 1-hop neighbors. For each element E of the advertised list, the HELLO message carries on also additional informations, as the rate and delay of the links interconnecting J to E. As usual, the HELLO messages are never relayed by the nodes.
The set of 1-hop neighbors of a generic node J is called "neighbor set of J" (N_J^1) and every network device can compute it relying only on the received HELLO messages. The node J, through the advertised list carried on each HELLO message, can also build its 2-hops neighbors set (N_J^2).
According to the QOLSR algorithm (Badis & Al Agha, 2005), every node has to compute its MPR set. The MPR set of the node J (MPR_J) is a subset of N_J^1 and it is composed by those network nodes through which is possible to communicate with every element of the N_J^2 set relying only on two hops paths.
The generic node A, member of the MPR_B, is called "MPR of a node B"; A is informed of its new state through the HELLO messages transmitted by B itself; A keeps a list of nodes (called "MPR selector list", indicated as MPR_{adv}) that have chosen it as MPR node.
All the nodes with a not empty MPR selector list must transmit periodically a Traffic Control (TC) message embedding its MPR selector list; each element of that list stores the IP address of the node that has A in its MPR set, the QoS indexes of the communication link and the context information relative to the that node itself. Differently from the HELLO messages, the TC messages must be received by each node, but they are not broadcast across the network: a TC message of A is processed by only the members of the MPR_A, as well as, A will process only message received by its MPR set. It can be proven that in this way all the network devices receive the TC messages transmitted by a node under the assumptions of an ideal channel and medium access.
Through the received TC messages, each node can build a topology table consisting of entries formed by the IP address of an element coming from the MPR selector list carried by a TC message (called *destination address*), the source address of the TC message itself (called last-hop address), the rate and the delay of the communication link between the last-hop address, and the destination address and the context information relative to the last-hop node.
Aim of the EOLSR protocol is to integrate the resource discovery functionality in the routing procedure. Toward this end, the set of QoS indexes present in the HELLO message has been extended (Fantacci et al., 2010) in order to include the following context information: the remaining battery power, the CPU architecture type (e.g., i386, XScale, MIPS, etc.), the amount of CPU and allocated memory (this one normalized respect to its maximum value) of each 1-hop neighbor advertised by the HELLO message. It is important to note that, even if in the EOLSR the HELLO header size is increased of 32 bits, we have to stress that the size of each element of the advertised list remains of the same dimension.
In order to carry the context aware information it is needed also to extend the TC messages; in particular to make each node able to build an exact snapshot of the network and computing resources, the extended TC messages should be transmitted not only by the node with a not empty MPR selector list but by all network nodes. If the TC messages were transmitted only by the nodes with a non empty MPR selector list, as QOLSR requires for the regular TC messages, only their extended neighbor lists would be propagated all over the network resulting in a partial perception of the real state of the communication and processing capabilities of the network.
The extension of the TC messages does not increase the message header size or the dimensions of the elements of the advertised MPR selector list size whereas the classical QOLSR

dimensions are increased by the extended neighbor list carried within the message; an entry of that list has the same dimension of an element of the MPR selector list (i.e., 12 bytes) and has a number of elements equal to $|E_j^n| - |\mathrm{MPR}_{adv}|$.
When a node has completed the filling (or updating process) of the neighbor and topology tables, it computes (or periodically updates) its own routing table, differently from the QOLSR protocol; the classical entry (destination address, next hop address and, the path length) has been extended (Fantacci et al., 2010) in order to carry also:

- the rate (R) and the delay (d) of the path (not required by the QOLSR protocol) respectively defined as
$$R(r) = \min\{R(A,B), R(B,C), \ldots, R(E,F)\} \tag{8}$$
and
$$d(r) = \sum_{i=1}^{N-1} d(i, i+1), \tag{9}$$
where r is a path through $n-1$ hops from the source A and the destination node F along the $B, C, \ldots, E$ devices.
- the remaining battery life of the path r defined as:
$$P(r) = \min\{P(B), P(C), \ldots, P(F)\} \tag{10}$$
where $P(I)$ is the remaining battery life of the node I normalized respect to its maximum value;
- the processor type, the amount of CPU occupied and memory allocated (this one normalized respect to its maximum value) in the destination node.

The extended version of the routing table can be built (or updated) in the following way:

1. all the entries are removed from the table;
2. each element of the neighbor set is put into a routing table entry, by setting:
   - the destination and the next hop IP equal to the address of the 1 hop neighbors;
   - the information on the network and computing power of the destination node as the same values of those in the neighbor table;
   - the path length to one;
3. for $j = 1$, until at least one is updated, an iteration is performed:
   - for each element (TC_{elem}) of the topology table, with its destination address not matching the destination address of any route (RT_{elem}) and its last hop address corresponding to a destination IP reachable through a route already present in the routing table (with a path length equal to j), the following entry is added: the destination address is the same of that entry, the next hop address is set equal to the next hop address, the path length is set equal to $j+1$, the rate and the remaining battery life of the path are set to the minimum value respectively stored in TC_{elem} e RT_{elem}, the delay equal to the sum of that indexes reported in the same two entries, the indexes describing the computing power of the destination node are the same of those reported in the topology table entry considered;
   - $j = j + 1$;
4. all the not considered entries of the topology table can be erased.

In order to simplify the task scheduling to the nodes, a *cluster table* needs to be defined. In a network of N nodes a cluster table has $N-1$ entries with the following fields:

- *the cluster center (CC)* - it is a data structure storing the IP address of the a certain node; it stores the cluster table, the rate, the delay and the remaining battery power of the path *p* and its computing information (the processor type, the amount of CPU and memory occupied);
- *the list of the cluster members* - given a certain cluster, a network node is one of its cluster member if it is reachable through a path, composed by a number of hops less or equal to *cd* (called "cluster depth"). Each element of that list stores the computing information of the considered cluster member (such as the processor type, the amount of CPU and memory occupied) and the QoS indexes (rate, delay and remaining battery power) related to the path between CC the cluster member itself.

More details regarding the building process of a neighbor, a topology or a cluster table can be found in (Clausen & Jacquet, 2003) and (Fantacci et al., 2010)

5. Lower layers reconfigurability

In the wireless network scenario we are considering, also the lower layers became of great importance. In that sense it will be of particular interest those techniques that foresee the link selection on a reliability base: we will refer to those algorithms that aim to optimize the resource discovery phase by considering the link status among the nodes.
In that sense, we will refer to a scenario where multiple wireless communication technologies co-exist allowing the choice of different paths with different link layer technologies among the nodes. The scenario refers to the wireless networks, often overlapped among them, in presence of multi-interface terminals that can connect to different technologies. Main characteristic of these techniques is to allow to the different technologies to supplement among them and not to compete for the bandwidth.
Typical example is the 3G technology that has a broad coverage, medium bandwidth and not low access cost, and the IEEE 802.11x technologies that are broadband, low cost, but with a low coverage area. This heterogeneity can be an advantage for the mobile devices, thanks to the exploitation of multi-interface solutions, by selecting the best interface for creating a map of the available resources. For this reason the resource discovery techniques defined in the previous can help to map and estimate as best as possible the actual network status, and proceed to its reconfiguration.
At link layer, adaptive techniques for the multiple access management are developed by considering ad-hoc or not infrastructured networks where the QoS respect for certain streams needs to be satisfied; the aim is the definition of a set of adaptive schemes, that can be selected each time in function of the actual network status. In this scenario, also considering the physical layer status, radio resource allocation techniques needs to be considered. In that context, we will refer to the opportunistic scheduling techniques, where the amount of data to be sent depends not only from the priority but also from the wireless channel status.
At physical layer, it is possible to foresee the use of adaptive schemes for the physical parameters for the management of the radio resources. Almost all modern communication systems allow the adaptation of the modulation, coding, and transmission power schemes, and in some cases, also the timing and frequency division. In this scenario, also those schemes that will use multiple antennas for both beamforming and diversity schemes needs to be considered.

6. Computation scheduling

After resource discovery has been performed the computing source needs to schedule the computation to the nodes following the chosen parallelization scheme.

6.1 Mapping for a task farm application

When a new task needs to be scheduled by the emitter, it needs to choose the best network node where mapping the computation. For each network node i we can define a variable and fixed cost (Fantacci et al., 2010), respectively, C_i and B_i, as:

$$C_i = \Delta\widehat{MEM}_i + \Gamma\widehat{CPU}_i \tag{11}$$

$$B_i = \alpha\check{R}_i + \beta d_i + \gamma P_i + \theta MEM_i + \psi CPU_i \tag{12}$$

The first one is a linear combination of the amount of occupied memory ($\widehat{MEM}_i$) and CPU ($\widehat{CPU}_i$) that would be allocated if the computation would be mapped onto the node i, i.e., the "cost to be payed" whenever a computation is mapped on that node; the same computation can allocate a different amount of memory or cause a different CPU load accordingly to the architecture type of the elaboration device where the working process is executed. For this reason it is called variable cost. B_i is a linear combination of:

- the rate margin $\check{R}_i$ (defined as the difference between the maximum applicable rate value and R_i itself), the delay (d_i) and the amount of consumed battery power (P_i) concerning the path between the node E, where the emitter process is executed, and the network node i
- the amount of allocated memory (MEM_i), and the occupied CPU (CPU_i) in the node i at a certain time instant of the network kept by the node E (thanks to its own routing table).

All the QoS and the context information indexes appearing in (11) and (12) are normalized respect to their maximum values. The emitter has to map a computation on the network device i with the minimum *effective cost* K_i, where $K_i = C_i + B_i$. This mapping problem can be expressed as:

$$(\text{TF}) \quad \textit{minimize} \quad \sum_{i \in V} M_i K_i \tag{13}$$

$$\textit{subject to} \quad \sum_{i \in V} M_i = 1 \tag{14}$$

where the set V is the routing table hold by the node where the emitter process is executed, the vector M is the variable of the optimization problem and, M_i (i.e., the i-th component of M with $i \in \{1, 2, \dots, |V|\}$) is the number of computations that will be mapped performed by the node i. By the constraint (14) we will map only one computation at a time as required by the task farm paradigm.
The emitter can solve the optimization problem by performing an exhaustive search in the admissible solution set; for this reason the developed solution is always the optimal mapping regardless the network topology and the distribution of the computing resources in the network nodes. Note that this is not a too computationally expensive approach because a routing table is composed by a number of entries equal to the number of nodes participating to the network, whose value is usually not so high.

Procedure 1 Sub-optimal scheduling scheme for the data parallel paradigm.

```
S ← Ŝ_M
while S ≥ Ŝ_m do
    W ← f(S)
    if W ≥ W_{CT_i} then
        B ← sort(B)
        j ← 1
        while W > 0 do
            if maxWorker(B_i) ≤ W then
                M_{B_j} ← Ŵ_{B_j}
            else
                M_{B_j} ← W
            end if
            W ← W − M_{B_j}
            j ← j + 1
        end while
        return M
    else
        S ← S − 1
    end if
end while
return the sub-computation can't be mapped
```

6.2 Mapping for a data parallel application

The mapping process for a data parallel application should be done in two steps: first of all we choose the optimal cluster of network devices, and then we select the intra-cluster mapping. As described above, in a data parallel application, a set of working processes is globally involved in the solution of one and only one task at time.

Each sub-computation performed by a worker could have a particular stencil relation with other workers; for these reasons all the sub-computations related to a task should be mapped in a set of workers running in a group of network devices interconnected by links with a short delay and high rate (according to the QoS constraints of the computation). The uniform mapping of the sub-computations onto the network devices members of the optimal cluster is not always an optimum solution because they should be mapped preferably on the most powerful or lowest loaded nodes. The cost of the cluster I composted by z network nodes can be defined as:

$$CC_I = \sum_{j=1}^{z} B_j + F(\widehat{W} - W_I) \tag{15}$$

where B_j is the fixed cost of the node j (with $j \in I$), $\widehat{W}$ is the maximum number of sub-computations where a task can be divided, and W_I is the number of the working processes to be executed on the network nodes belonging to the considered cluster. We assume in what follows the optimal cluster, as the one having the lowest cost. The optimal cluster can be selected by performing an exhaustive search in the cluster table of the node where the task dispatcher process is executed. Note that this is a feasible approach because the cluster entries are no more than the routing entries.

The mapping process of the sub-computations, related to nodes belonging to I, is performed by the task dispatcher process itself and can be expressed in terms of the following optimization problem:

$$\text{(DP)} \quad \text{minimize} \quad J \cdot \left[\sum_{i \in I} (M_i C_i + B_i) \right] + K\left(\hat{S}_M - \hat{S}\right) \tag{16}$$

$$\text{subject to} \quad \hat{S}_m \leq \hat{S} \leq \hat{S}_M$$

$$0 \leq M_i \leq \widehat{W}_i, \quad \forall i \in I \tag{17}$$

$$\sum_{i \in I} M_i = W \tag{18}$$

where $\hat{S}_M$ and $\hat{S}_m$ are respectively the maximum and the minimum number of iterations that can be performed by the H function on an element of the input state, $\hat{S}$ are the iterations actually performed, $\widehat{W}_i$ is the maximum number of workers that can be executed in parallel on the node i (where $i \in I$) according to the architecture type of the node itself, W is the number of sub-computations where the task has been divided, J and K are two not negative weights. The variables of that optimization problem are the components of the vector M (M_i with $i \in [1, \ldots, |I|]$) and $\hat{S}$; these variables are all integer and not negative.
The minimization performed in (16) results in a minimization of the mapping cost and in a maximization of the number of iterations performed on each element; the optimization problem is not only bi-objective but also not linear: the number of workers W is function of S (e.g., for a MAP it is given by (7)), C_i is function of W then the fixed cost is function of S. In this case the solution of the mapping problems can not be found through an exhaustive search in the admissible solutions space. This heuristic (reported in Procedure 1 and summarized as follow) can be used to get a sub-optimal solution (Fantacci et al., 2010):

1. compute the fixed cost of all the network devices belonging to the optimal cluster;
2. map in each device a number of sub-computations equal to the number of working processes that can be executed in parallel in the node itself or equal to the remaining sub-computations, starting from the node with a smaller fixed cost;
3. assign the scatter role to the node with the minimum fixed cost.

7. Performance results

In order to have a performance estimation of the distributed computing application in the wireless environment in this section we summarize some numerical results. The following simplified scenario has been considered:

Coefficients	Policy A	Policy B	Policy C
α	2	2	2
β	6	6	6
γ	0	4	4
Δ, θ	0	1500	1500
Γ, ψ	0	1	0
F	100	100	100

Table 1. The weights used to define the policies A, B and, C.

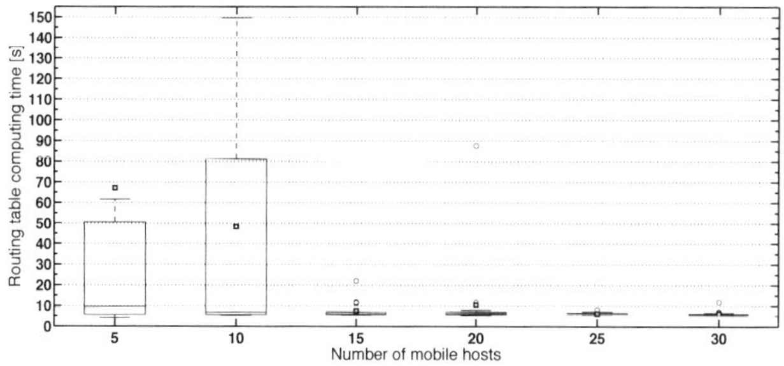

(a) RT_{fill} of the fixed node

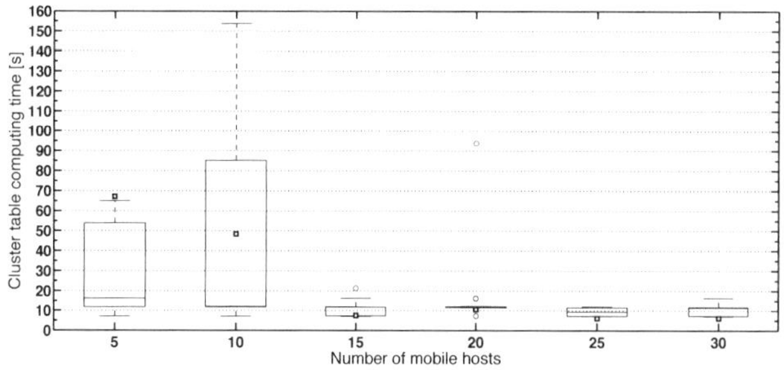

(b) CT_{fill} of the fixed node

Fig. 4. Average time needed to fill-up the routing and the cluster table of the fixed node.

- a fixed node placed in the center of a square of area 0.25 km^2 or 1 km^2;
- a variable number ($5 \div 30$) of mobile nodes randomly placed in the playground, moving according to the random waypoint model (RWP (Bettstetter et al., 2003)), considering a pedestrian model with a speed uniformly distributed within [3 km/h, 5 km/h] and the possibility for each node to remain stationary for a time interval uniformly distributed between 3 s and 30 s;
- communication links using the IEEE 802.11g technology with a radio data rate of 54 Mbit/s.

One of the main performance indicator is the routing tables (RT_{fill}) and the cluster tables (CT_{fill}) filling time, beginning from an empty structure, stored in the node that computes the mapping solution. It can be shown that this values represent the worst case for the updating process because the time interval between two consecutive updates will never be greater than the time required to compute (or refresh) all the items of the routing or cluster table.
Note that it is not possible to identify the globally optimal values for RT_{fill} and CT_{fill} because they depend on the particular application to be implemented according to the pervasive grid computing paradigm. However, for the case of interest here, our analysis has shown that in a low mobility scenario the transmission of the HELLOs at least every 2 s ($T_{\text{HELLO}} = 2$) and the TCs every 5 s ($T_{\text{TC}} = 5$) is the optimal solution. In particular, in Fig.4(a) and 4(b), the RT_{fill} and CT_{fill} are drawn as box-plot[1]. Looking at these results it can be noted that the average values

[1] The top of the rectangle represents the twenty-fifth percentile of the observations, the bottom is the seventy percentile, the horizontal line into the boxes represents the medium value, the whiskers originating from the rectangles connects the minimum and the maximum value not considered as outliers, the circles are the outliers and the little squares represents the mean values of the observations.

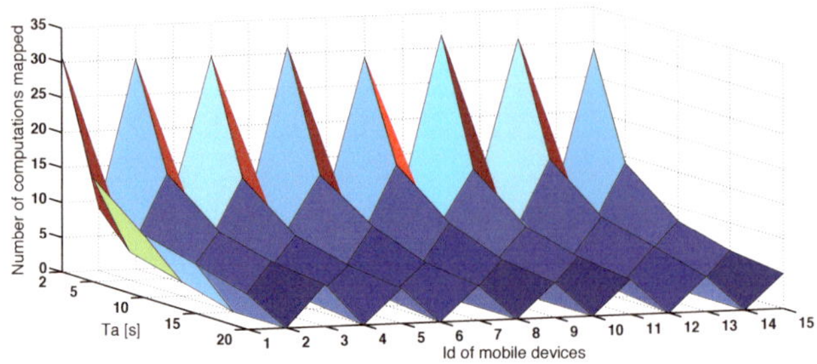

(a) Policy B

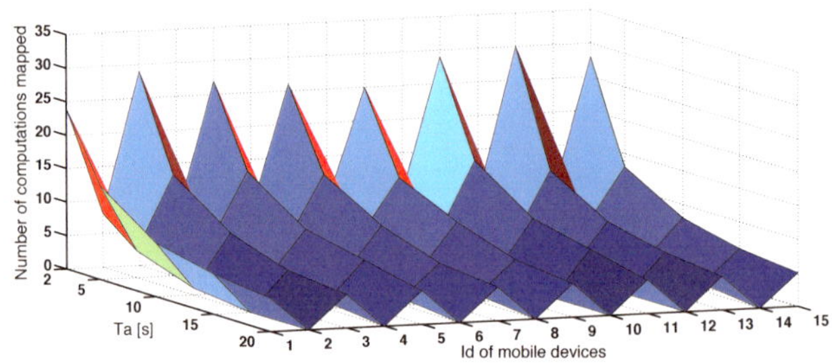

(b) Policy C

Fig. 5. Number of computations mapped on each node relying on a network with nodes with different battery capacity.

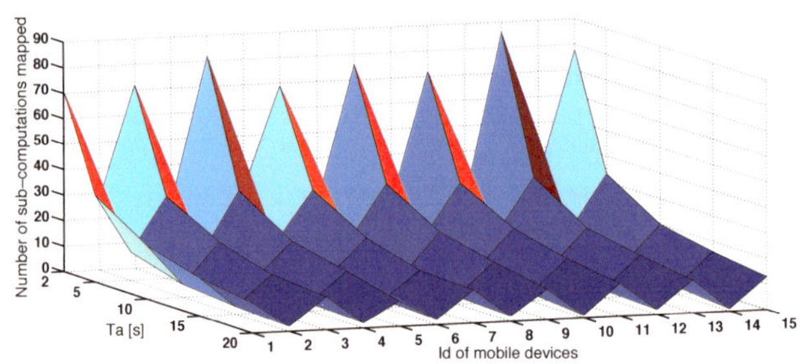

(a) Policy B

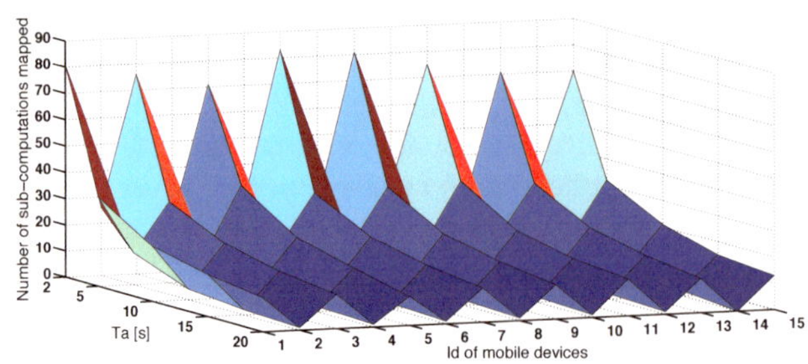

(b) Policy C

Fig. 6. Number of sub-computations mapped on each node relying on a network with nodes having different battery life.

for RT_{fill} and CT_{fill} are always between 5 s and 10 s with networks composed by 15 or more nodes. These values can be reduced or increased changing the maximum transmission period for the HELLOs and TCs In particular, under equal hypothesis, except for the TC messages transmitted every 2 s, it can be noted that the RT_{fill} and CT_{fill} are both less or equal to 10 s.
The other parameter to be taken into account is referred to the scheduling and resource allocation. In particular, we will consider a task farm and a data parallel application characterized by:

- an input and an output state of 1 MB;
- the emission of a new point every 5 s or 10 s.

By properly choosing the weights (see Tab. 1) introduced in (11), (12) and (15), it is possible to compare the results by considering three different policies:

- *Policy A* - the computations or the sub-computations are mapped using only the rate and the delay indexes;
- *Policy B* - the mapping is performed using all the QoS indexes and the context information;
- *Policy C* - it is the same of the policy B while the amount of CPU occupied or that will be occupied in a node i is ignored.

The performance results are expressed in terms of number of computations that can be mapped on each node. We have considered that the nodes are equipped with batteries having a different battery life; in particular, the node with odd id had batteries with an higher battery life than that related to the even ones.
In Figs.5 and6, the performance of the proposed approach is reported in terms of computations (or sub-computations) number mapped on each mobile node for the policies B and C. As for the previous cases, we can see that these policies correctly map more computations on nodes characterized by a greater remaining battery life.
Other two important performance metrics are the average service time and outage probability. The first parameter is the average time needed to finish a task from the emission of a point until than the whole state has not completely received by the node where is running the gather (or the collector) process; the second one can be defined as:

$$\hat{O}_{TF} = 100 - \frac{N_{comp} \cdot 100}{N_{mapped}} \tag{19}$$

for a task farm application, where N_{comp} is the number of output states successfully received by the collector process and N_{mapped} is the number of computations mapped on each working processes in the time interval considered. Likewise, this parameter results to be:

$$\hat{O}_{DP} = 100 - \frac{N_{comp} \cdot 100}{N_{arrived}} \tag{20}$$

for a data parallel application, where $N_{arrived}$ is the number of output states successfully or partially recovered by the gather process in the time interval considered and, in this case, N_{comp} is related to the gather process.
In Fig. 7, the average service time and the outage probability are shown by varying the number of mobile devices, randomly placed in a square of 1 km^2, for the cases of T_a equal to 5 s (Fantacci et al., 2010) and with tasks requiring a computing time T_c equal to 22.65 s. Moreover Figs. 8(a) and 8(b) show, respectively, the average number of pending computations, mapped in a reference working node, that are waiting to be processed and the

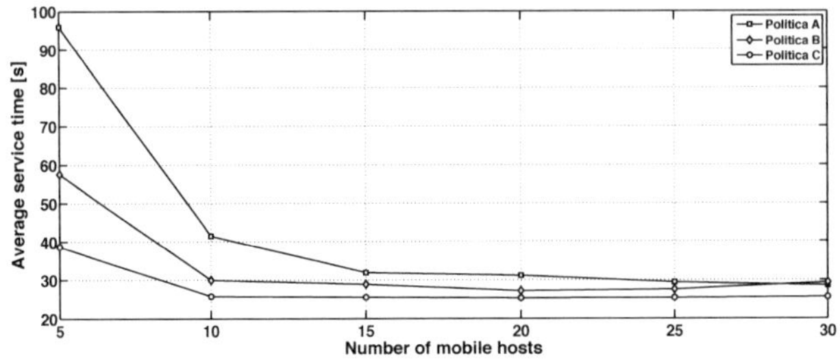

(a) Average service time

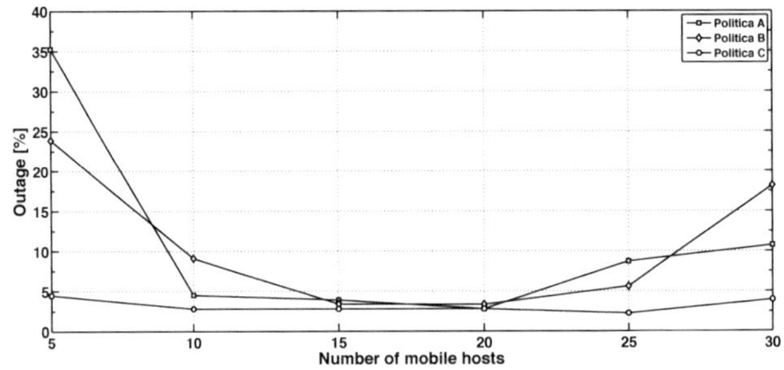

(b) Outage probability

Fig. 7. Computing performances of a task farm application.

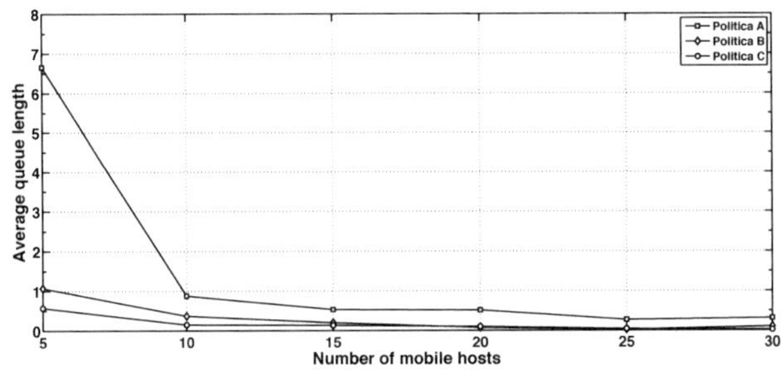

(a) Average input queue length

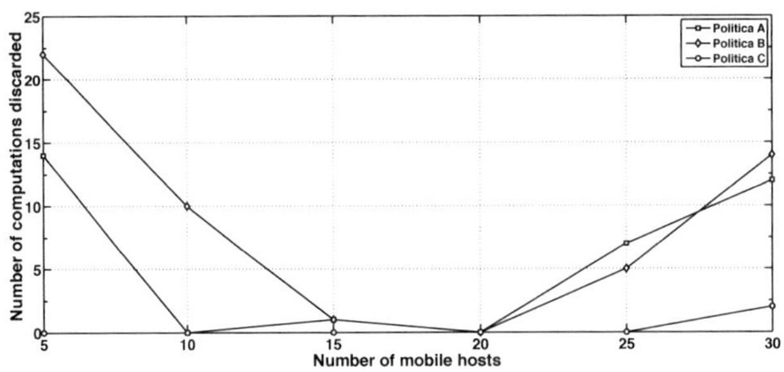

(b) Number of computations discarded

Fig. 8. Average queue length and number of computations discarded for a task farm application.

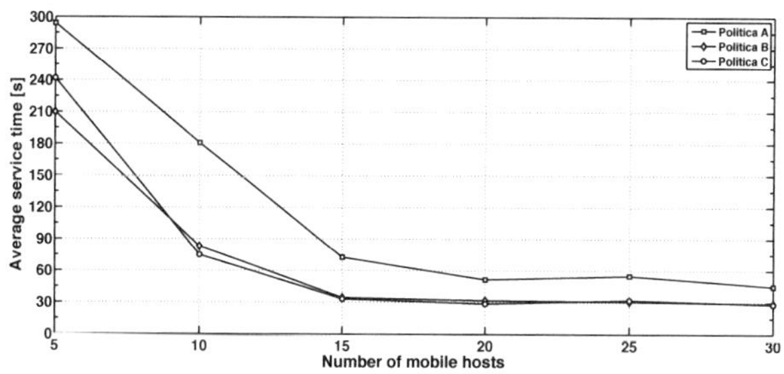

(a) Average service time

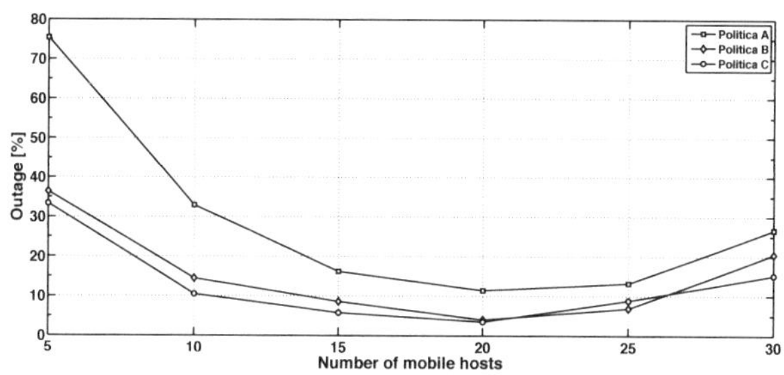

(b) Outage probability

Fig. 9. Computing performances of a data parallel application

number of computations completed but discarded by the working node itself (for the three policies). From Fig. 7, it is possible to note that the policies B and C globally outperforms the policy A. Moreover, it is important to note that:

- the outage events in a network composed up to 15 mobile nodes are mainly caused by a non homogeneous mapping and small number of computing resources present in the network (resulting on a increment of the time spent in the input queue of the device, Fig. 8(a)). The outage events are also caused by the cancellation events of tasks that occurs when the output of a sub computation can not fully be transferred to the collector process due to the output state size and the small spatial density of nodes (as shown in Fig. 8(b));
- in networks composed by 20 or more nodes, as depicted in Fig. 8(b), the outage events are mainly caused by the cancellation events caused by the network interferences that characterize medium/large networks;

In Fig. 9, the computing performance is reported considering a data parallel application characterized by clusters of three network nodes (with one working process running on each one) and using sub computations 15 s long. We can see that with this form of parallelism the policies B and C outperforms A while B and C are characterized mainly by the same performance.

As for a task farm application, Figs. 10(a) and 10(b) depict, respectively, the average number of pending sub computations and the number of the discarded sub computations (for the three policies). In this case the outage events are caused by the non homogeneous mapping in networks composed up to 15 nodes, otherwise, by the cancellation events due to the network interferences.

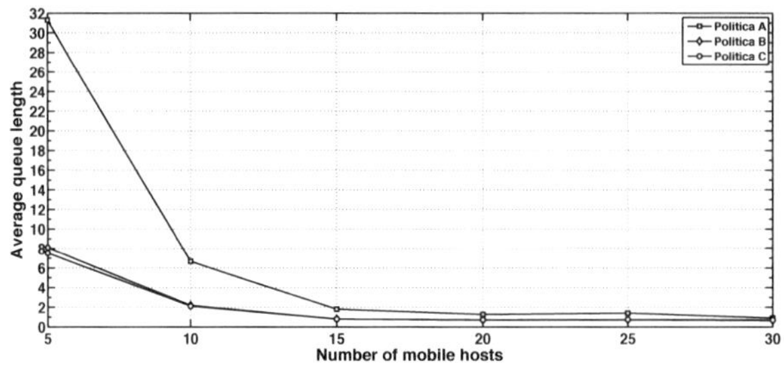

(a) Average input queue length

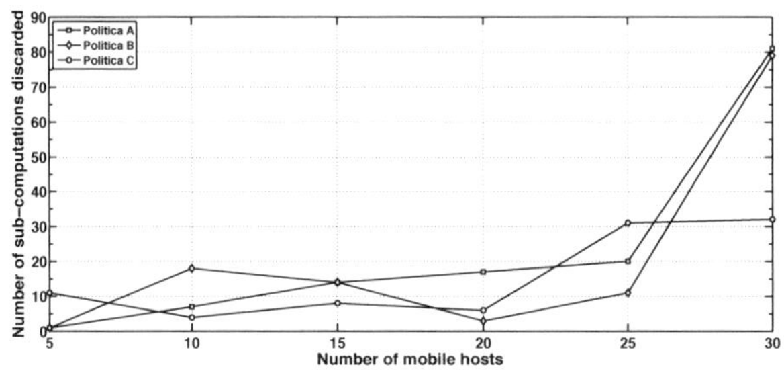

(b) Number of sub-computations discarded

Fig. 10. Average queue length and number of sub-computations discarded for a data parallel application.

8. Conclusion

Distributed computing systems are gaining an even more attention in the world due to their ability in processing great amounts of data. Their importance is even more increased in the recent years due to the introduction of wireless communications protocol able to connect even mobile terminals with broadband connections. Moreover, for the consumer electronics sphere there has been the introduction of small devices with high computations capabilities. This allowed the introduction of the pervasive grid concept aiming to exploit several different devices connected with heterogeneous communication links in order to realize a whole processing system.

In this chapter we have focused our attention on the most important aspects of distributed computing in wireless scenarios. First of all we have to face with the problem of discovering the resources in terms of device and communication link capabilities. This can be realized by exploiting routing algorithms that need to be used within such scenario due to the flat topology of a distributed network. Moreover also lower layer behavior became of importance due to their effect in the communication performance. Finally the scheduling phase is described aiming to find the best nodes in the sense of minimize certain cost functions. The performance results allow to see the importance of a good resource discovery and scheduling algorithm in the distributed computing problems when facing with the wireless environment.

9. References

Agbaria, A. & Sanders, W. H. (2005). Application-driven coordination-free distributed checkpointing, *Proc. of ICDCS 2005*, Columbus, OH, USA, pp. 177–186.

Al-ali, R., Hafid, A., Rana, O. F. & Walker, D. W. (2003). On QoS adaptation in service-oriented grids, *Proc. of MGC2003*, Rio de Janeiro, Brazil.

Aldinucci, M., Campa, S., Danelutto, M., Vanneschi, M., Kilpatrick, P., Dazzi, P., Laforenza, D. & Tonellotto, N. (2008). Behavioural skeletons in GCM: Autonomic management of grid components, *Proc. of PDP 2008*, Toulouse, France, pp. 54–63.

Badis, H. & Al Agha, K. (2005). QoS routing for ad hoc wireless networks using OLSR, *European Transactions on Telecommunications* 16(5): 427–442.

Batista, D. & da Fonseca, N. (2010). A survey of self-adaptive grids, *IEEE Transactions on Communications* 48(7): 94–100.

Bertolli, C., Buono, D., Mencagli, G. & Vanneschi, M. (2010). Expressing adaptivity and context awareness in the ASSISTANT programming model, *Autonomic Computing and Communications Systems*, Vol. 23 of *Lecture Notes of the Institute for Computer Sciences, Social Informatics and Telecommunications Engineering*, Springer Berlin Heidelberg, pp. 32–47.

Bertolli, C., Vanneschi, M., Ciciani, B. & Quaglia, F. (2010). Enabling replication in the ASSISTANT programming model, *Proc. of IWCMC '10*, Caen, France, pp. 509–513.

Bettstetter, C., Resta, G. & Santi, P. (2003). The node distribution of the random waypoint mobility model for wireless ad hoc networks, *IEEE Transactions on Mobile Computing* 2(3): 257–269.

Clausen, T. & Jacquet, P. (2003). Optimized link state routing protocol (OLSR), RFC3626.
URL: *http://www.ietf.org/rfc/rfc3626.txt*

CoreGRID Network of Excellence (n.d.).
URL: *http://www.coregrid.net*

Coronato, A. & De Pietro, G. (2008). MiPeG: A middleware infrastructure for pervasive grids, *Future Generation Computer Systems* 24(1): 17 – 29.

Coulson, G., Grace, P., Blair, G., Duce, D., Cooper, C. & Sagar, M. (2005). A middleware approach for pervasive grid environments, *Proc. of UK-UbiNet/ UK e-Science Programme Workshop on Ubiquitous Computing and e-Research*, Edinburgh, Scotland.

Darby III, P. J. D. & Tzeng, N.-F. (2010). Decentralized QoS-aware checkpointing arrangement in mobile grid computing, *IEEE Transactions on Mobile Computing* 9(8): 1173–1186.

Emmerich, W. (2000). Software engineering and middleware: a roadmap, *Proc. of ICSE '00*, Limerick, Ireland, pp. 117–129.

Fantacci, R., Tarchi, D. & Tassi, A. (2010). A novel routing algorithm for mobile pervasive computing, *Proc. of IEEE Globecom 2010*, Miami, FL, USA

Fantacci, R., Vanneschi, M., Bertolli, C., Mencagli, G. & Tarchi, D. (2009). Next generation grids and wireless communication networks: towards a novel integrated approach, *Wireless Communications and Mobile Computing* 9(4): 445–467.

Foster, I. & Kesselman, C. (1999). *The Globus toolkit*, Morgan Kaufmann Publishers Inc., San Francisco, CA, USA.

Foster, I., Zhao, Y., Raicu, I. & Lu, S. (2008). Cloud computing and grid computing 360-degree compared, *Proc. of GCE '08*, Austin, TX, USA, pp. 1 –10.

Haas, Z. J. & Pearlman, M. R. (2001). ZRP: a hybrid framework for routing in ad hoc networks, *Ad hoc networking*, Addison-Wesley, Boston, MA, USA, pp. 221–253.

Hingne, V., Joshi, A., Finin, T., Kargupta, H. & Houstis, E. (2003). Towards a pervasive grid, *Proc. of IPDPS'03*, Nice, France.

Huebscher, M. C. & McCann, J. A. (2008). A survey of autonomic computing—degrees, models, and applications, *ACM Comput. Surv.* 40(3): 1–28.

Li, Z., Sun, L. & Ifeachor, E. C. (2005). Challenges of mobile ad-hoc grids and their applications in e-healthcare, *Proc. of CIMED 2005*, Lisbon, Portugal.

McKnight, L. W., Howison, J. & Bradner, S. (2004). Guest editors' introduction: Wireless grids–distributed resource sharing by mobile, nomadic, and fixed devices, *IEEE Internet Computing* 8(4): 24– 31.

Morohoshi, H. & Huang, R. (2005). A user-friendly platform for developing grid services over globus toolkit 3, *Proc of ICPADS'05*, Fukuoka, Japan, pp. 668 – 674 Vol. 1.

Noble, B. (2000). System support for mobile, adaptive applications, *IEEE Personal Communications Magazine* 7(1): 44 –49.

Oliner, A. J., Sahoo, R. K., Moreira, J. E. & Gupta, M. (2005). Performance implications of periodic checkpointing on large-scale cluster systems, *Proc. of IPDCS 2005*.

Parashar, M. & Lee, C. A. (2005). Scanning the issue: Special isssue on grid-computing, *Proceedings of the IEEE* 93(3): 479–484.

Parashar, M. & Pierson, J.-M. (2010). Pervasive grids: Challenges and opportunities, *in* K.-C. Li, C.-H. Hsu, L. T. Yang & J. Dongarra (eds), *Handbook of Research on Scalable Computing Technologies*, IGI Global, chapter 2, pp. 14–30.

Park, S. (2006). DiffServ quality of service support for multimedia applications in broadband access networks, *Proc. of ICHIT '06*, Vol. 2, Cheju Island, Korea, pp. 513 –518.

Perkins, C. E. & Royer, E. M. (1999). Ad-hoc on-demand distance vector routing, *Proc. of IEEE WMCSA'99*, New Orleans, LA, USA, pp. 90–100.

Priol, T. & Vanneschi, M. (eds) (2008). *From Grids To Service and Pervasive Computing*, Springer, New York, NY, USA.

Ranjan, R., Harwood, A. & Buyya, R. (2008). Peer-to-peer-based resource discovery in global grids: a tutorial, *IEEE Communications Surveys and Tutorials* 10(2): 6–33.

Roy, N. & Das, S. K. (2009). Enhancing availability of grid computational services to ubiquitous computing applications, *IEEE Transactions on Parallel and Distributed Systems* 20(7): 953–967.

Saadi, R., Pierson, J. M. & Brunie, L. (2005). APC: access pass certificate distrust certification model for large access in pervasive environment, *Proc. of ICPS '05*, pp. 361 – 370.

Schmidt, C. & Parashar, M. (2004). A peer-to-peer approach to web service discovery, *World Wide Web* 7(2): 211–229.

Sundararaj, A. I., Gupta, A. & Dinda, P. A. (2004). Dynamic topology adaptation of virtual networks of virtual machines, *Proc. of LCR'04*, Houston, TX, USA.

The Globus Security Team (2005). Globus toolkit version 4 grid security infrastructure: A standards perspective, *Technical report*, The Globus Alliance.
URL: *http://www.globus.org/toolkit/docs/4.0/security/GT4-GSI-Overview.pdf*

Vanneschi, M. & Veraldi, L. (2007). Dynamicity in distributed applications: issues, problems and the ASSIST approach, *Parallel Computing* 33(12): 822–845.

Zhang, S., Zhang, S., Chen, X. & Huo, X. (2010). Cloud computing research and development trend, *Proc. of ICFN'10*, Sanya, Hainan, China, pp. 93–97.

22

Resume and Starting-Over-Again Retransmission Strategies in Cognitive Radio Networks

Sandra Lirio Castellanos-López[1], Felipe A. Cruz-Pérez[1] and Genaro Hernández-Valdez[2]
[1]*Electrical Engineering Department, CINVESTAV-IPN,*
[2]*Electronics Department, UAM-A*
Mexico

1. Introduction

Cognitive radio has emerged as a promising technology to realize dynamic spectrum access and increase the efficiency of a largely under utilized spectrum (Haykin, 2005). In a cognitive radio network, a cognitive or secondary user (SU) opportunistically makes use of temporary vacant licensed frequency bands (channels) to set up communication links with other devices. The SUs are capable of detecting channels that are unused by the primary users (PUs) and then making use of the idle channels. With respect to the licensed or PUs, such kind of spectrum access is unlicensed and secondary. To avoid interference to the PUs, SUs are forced to vacate the primary channels as soon as PUs return. Those prematurely terminated secondary sessions degrade quality of service. To reduce this adverse impact, interrupted SUs may be allowed to move to other vacant channels. This process is called spectrum handoff (Zhu et al., 2007). Additionally, to further reduce the impact of service interruption, for delay tolerant services, interrupted SUs can be queued in a buffer to wait for the releasing of an occupied channel.

When a SU detects or is informed of an arrival of a PU call/session in its current channel, it immediately leaves the channel and switches to an idle channel, if one is available, to continue its call. These unfinished cognitive transmissions may be simply discarded (Zhu et al., 2007; Zhang, 2008; Ahmed et al., 2008; Pacheco-Paramo et al., 2009). Nonetheless, prematurely terminated secondary sessions degrade quality of service. Alternatively, if at that time all the channels are occupied, the secondary call is queued in a buffer and the call waits until a channel becomes available. Queued secondary calls are served in first-come first-served (FCFS) order. That is, the secondary call at the head of the queue is reconnected to the system when a channel becomes available and transmits its information according to a given retransmission strategy.

In this Chapter, the performance of cognitive radio networks for two different retransmission strategies for interrupted secondary user's calls is mathematically analyzed and evaluated. Resume retransmission and Start Over Again retransmission strategies are considered.

2. Retransmission strategies

Two different retransmission strategies can be used to handle interrupted secondary calls: the Resume (RR) and Start-Over-Again (SOAR) retransmission strategies. In the Resume retransmission strategy, SU transmits its information starting at the point it was preempted. That is, in this strategy the SU does not need to transmit again the information bits transmitted before its previous connection was interrupted. The Resume retransmission strategy can be easily and directly implemented when automatic repeat request-based error control protocols[1] (i.e., Stop-and-wait ARQ, Go-Back-N ARQ, Selective Repeat ARQ, Hybrid ARQ) are used as the receiver must acknowledge received packets. On the other hand, in the Start Over Again retransmission strategy each time a secondary call is interrupted, SU retransmits its information starting at the initial point no matter that some part of its information was transmitted in its previous connection. Contrary to the Resume strategy, the Start Over Again retransmission strategy does not require a control protocol and, therefore, it is simpler.

Under the assumption that service (or call holding) time for SU calls is negative exponentially distributed, authors in (Tang & Mark, 2007; Tang & Mark, 2008), (Tang & Mark a; 2009) have developed system level models for the performance evaluation of cognitive radio networks with the RR strategy. In a related work (Tang & Mark, 2009), the RR strategy is analyzed under the assumption that service time of SUs is phase-type distributed. However, the RR strategy is neither evaluated under different traffic conditions nor the effect of characteristics of the SU service time is investigated. To the best of the authors' knowledge, the performance of cognitive radio networks with the SOAR retransmission strategy has been neither analyzed nor evaluated in the literature. Therefore, the performance of the RR and SOAR strategies has not been compared either. All these important tasks are addressed in this Chapter.

3. System model

The model of (Tang & Mark, 2007; Tang & Mark, 2008; Tang & Mark, 2009) is adopted. It is considered that two types of wireless networks are operating in a given common service area. The one that owns the license for spectrum usage is referred to as the primary system, and the calls generated from this network constitute the primary traffic (PT) stream. The other network in the same service area is referred to as the secondary system, which opportunistically shares the spectrum resource with the primary system. The calls generated from the secondary system constitute the secondary traffic (ST) stream. The system consisting of the primary and secondary systems is called an opportunistic spectrum sharing (OSS) system. A distinct feature of a well-designed OSS system is that the secondary users have the capability to sense channel usage and switch between different channels using appropriate communication mechanisms, while causing negligible interference to the primary users. Such functionality might be realized by cognitive radios (Haykin, 2005).

In the OSS system, the PT calls operate as if there are no ST calls in the system. When a PT call arrives to the system, it occupies a free channel if one is available; otherwise, it will be

[1] Modern wireless communication standards typically consider this type of data transmission protocols (i.e., LTE, WiMax).

blocked. Note that a channel being used by an ST call is still seen as an idle channel by the primary network, since here the primary network and secondary network are supposed not to exchange information. Secondary users detect the presence or absence of signals from primary users and maintain records of the channel occupancy status. The detection mechanism may involve collaboration with other secondary users and/or an exchange with an associated base station (BS) and it is assumed to be error free.

Secondary users opportunistically access the channels that are in idle status. If an initial secondary call finds an idle channel, it can make use of the channel. If all channels are busy, the secondary call is blocked and considered lost from the system. When an ongoing secondary user detects or is informed (by its BS or other secondary users) of an arrival of PT call in its current channel, it immediately leaves the channel and switches to an idle channel, if one is available, to continue the call. (This process is called spectrum handoff.) If at that time all the channels are occupied, the ST call is placed into a buffer located at its BS (for an infrastructured network) or a virtual queue (for an infrastructureless network). The queued ST calls are served in first-come first-served (FCFS) order. That is the ST call at the head of the queue is reconnected to the system when a channel becomes available. It is assumed that ST calls can wait indefinitely to be served. Additionally, to obtain simpler mathematical expressions, it is assumed that there exists no limit in the number of reconnections that an ongoing ST call can perform. Clearly, the maximum number of queued ST calls is M, which corresponds to the limiting case that all the M ongoing calls are ST calls and are eventually preempted to the queue due to the arrivals of PT calls. Thus, a finite queue of length M is considered.

We define the term band as a bandwidth unit in the primary system; and the term sub-band as a bandwidth unit in the secondary system. Accordingly, a PT call needs one band for service and an ST call needs one sub-band for service. The spectrum consists of M bands and each band is divided into N sub-bands. Thus, there exist NM sub-bands (channels) that are shared by the primary and cognitive users. To avoid interference to PU, for a specific band used by a PT call, the underlying N subbands are then unavailable for ST calls. For the sake of clarity and without loss of generality, it is assumed that both types of traffic occupy one channel per call; that is, N=1. Arrivals of the PT and ST calls are assumed to form independent Poisson processes with rates $\lambda^{(P)}$ and $\lambda^{(S)}$, respectively. Service time for primary users is considered exponentially distributed with rate $\mu_s^{(P)}$. The corresponding service time for cognitive users is modeled as a Coxian order 2 distributed random variable. The random variable (RV) used to represent this time is $\mathbf{X}_S^{(S)}$. It is important to remark that the Coxian order 2 distribution includes as particular cases several relevant phase-type distributions (i.e., negative-exponential, Erlang, hypo-exponential). Fig. 1 shows a diagram of phases of a n-th order Coxian distribution. Notice that β_i (for i = 1, 2, ..., n-1) represents the probability that the absorbing state is reached after the i-th phase. For a Coxian order 2 distribution, β_2=1. The i-th phase of this distribution is an independent exponential random variable with parameter $\mu_i^{(S)}$ for (i = 1, 2). The mean service time for secondary users is denoted by $1/\mu_s^{(S)}$. For the Coxian order 2 model, the probability density function (pdf) of secondary service time and its mean value are, respectively, given by

$$f_{X_S^{(S)}}(t) = \beta\mu_1^{(S)}e^{-\mu^{(S)}t} + (1-\beta)\frac{\mu_1^{(S)}\mu_2^{(S)}}{\mu_1^{(S)}-\mu_2^{(S)}}\left(e^{-\mu_2^{(S)}t} - e^{-\mu_1^{(S)}t}\right) \tag{1}$$

$$E\{\mathbf{X}_S^{(S)}\} = \int_0^\infty t f_{\mathbf{X}_S^{(S)}}(t)dt \tag{2}$$

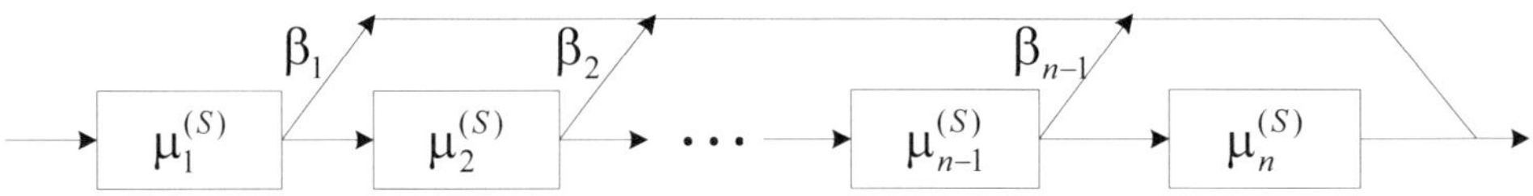

Fig. 1. Diagram of phases of a n-th order Coxian distributed service time

4. Resume retransmission strategy teletraffic analysis

In the RR strategy, when a secondary queued user is reconnected to the system, it transmits its information starting at the point it was preempted. Due to the memory-less property, the probability distribution of the residual permanence time in phase i is also negative-exponential with the same parameter $\mu_i^{(S)}$ of the service time of new secondary calls. Then, it is possible to keep track in a single state variable the number in each phase of the service time of initial and ongoing secondary users.

In this sub-section, the teletraffic analysis for the performance evaluation of cognitive radio networks with RR strategy is developed. A multi-dimensional birth and death process is required for modeling this system. Each state variable is denoted by k_i (for $i = 0, 1, 2, \ldots, n$). k_0 represents the number of ongoing primary users, k_1 the number of ongoing SUs in phase 1, k_2 the number of ongoing and queued SUs in phase 2, and k_3 the number of SU in the queue that were interrupted in phase 1. Fig. 2 shows the transition state diagram. On the basis of the transition state diagram, we develop the set of global balance equations. To simplify mathematical notation the following vectors are defined $\mathbf{k} = (k_0, k_1, \ldots, k_n)$, $\mathbf{e}_i$ is defined as a unit vector of n elements, whose all entries are 0 except the i-th position which is 1 (for $i = 0, 1, 2, \ldots, n$).

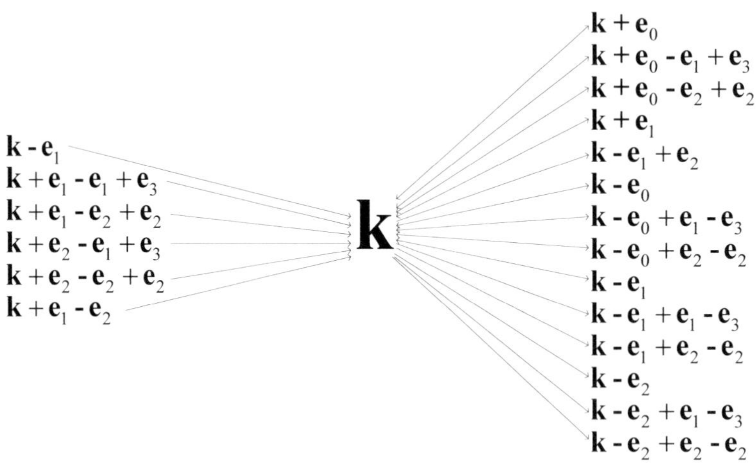

Fig. 2. Transition states diagram

The state space Ω_0 is given by

$$\Omega_0 = \left\{ \mathrm{k} \mid k_i \geq 0, \sum_{i=0}^{3} k_i \leq 2M, \sum_{i=1}^{3} k_i \leq M, \sum_{i=0}^{1} k_i \leq M;\ k_3 = 0 \Big|_{\sum_{i=0}^{2} k_i < M} \quad i = 0,1,2,3 \right\} \tag{3}$$

The steady state probabilities balance equation is given by

$$\begin{aligned}
&\left[\sum_{i=0}^{1} a_i(\mathbf{k}) + \sum_{i=0}^{2} b_i(\mathbf{k}) + c(\mathbf{k}) + \sum_{i=1}^{2} d_i(\mathbf{k}) + \sum_{i=0}^{5} e_i(\mathbf{k}) \right] P(\mathbf{k}) = \\
&= \sum_{i=0}^{1} a_i(\mathbf{k}-\mathbf{e}_i) P(\mathbf{k}-\mathbf{e}_i) + \sum_{i=0}^{2} b_i(\mathbf{k}+\mathbf{e}_i) P(\mathbf{k}+\mathbf{e}_i) + c(\mathbf{k}+\mathbf{e}_1-\mathbf{e}_2) P(\mathbf{k}+\mathbf{e}_1-\mathbf{e}_2) + \\
&+ d_1(\mathbf{k}-\mathbf{e}_0+\mathbf{e}_1-\mathbf{e}_3) P(\mathbf{k}-\mathbf{e}_0+\mathbf{e}_1-\mathbf{e}_3) + d_2(\mathbf{k}-\mathbf{e}_0+\mathbf{e}_2-\mathbf{e}_2) P(\mathbf{k}-\mathbf{e}_0+\mathbf{e}_2-\mathbf{e}_2) + \\
&+ e_0(\mathbf{k}+\mathbf{e}_0-\mathbf{e}_1+\mathbf{e}_3) P(\mathbf{k}+\mathbf{e}_0-\mathbf{e}_1+\mathbf{e}_3) + e_1(\mathbf{k}+\mathbf{e}_0-\mathbf{e}_2+\mathbf{e}_2) P(\mathbf{k}+\mathbf{e}_0-\mathbf{e}_2+\mathbf{e}_2) + \\
&+ e_2(\mathbf{k}+\mathbf{e}_1-\mathbf{e}_1+\mathbf{e}_3) P(\mathbf{k}+\mathbf{e}_1-\mathbf{e}_1+\mathbf{e}_3) + e_3(\mathbf{k}+\mathbf{e}_1-\mathbf{e}_2+\mathbf{e}_2) P(\mathbf{k}+\mathbf{e}_1-\mathbf{e}_2+\mathbf{e}_2) + \\
&+ e_4(\mathbf{k}+\mathbf{e}_2-\mathbf{e}_1+\mathbf{e}_3) P(\mathbf{k}+\mathbf{e}_2-\mathbf{e}_1+\mathbf{e}_3) + e_5(\mathbf{k}+\mathbf{e}_2-\mathbf{e}_2+\mathbf{e}_2) P(\mathbf{k}+\mathbf{e}_2-\mathbf{e}_2+\mathbf{e}_2)
\end{aligned} \tag{4}$$

where $a_i(\cdot)$ represents the call birth rate for cognitive users (for i=1) and primary users (for i=0); $b_i(\cdot)$ represents the call death rate for cognitive users (for i =1, 2) and primary users (for i =0); $c(\cdot)$ represents the transition rate from phase 1 to 2; $d_i(\cdot)$ (for i = 1, 2) represents transition rate of queueing a SU in phase i due to the arrival of a PU; $e_i(\cdot)$ (for i = 0, 1, 2,…, 5) represents the reconnection rate of one cognitive user in phase 1 or 2 due to death of a PU or SU. These coefficient rates are given below.
The call birth rate for PUs or SUs generating a transition from state $\mathbf{k}$ to state $\mathbf{k}+\mathbf{e}_i$ is given by

$$a_i(\mathbf{k}) = \begin{cases} \lambda^{(P)} & \sum_{j=0}^{2} k_j < M;\ k_0 \geq 0;\ k_3 = 0;\ i = 0 \\ \lambda^{(S)} & \sum_{j=0}^{2} k_j < M;\ k_1 \geq 0;\ k_3 = 0;\ i = 1 \\ 0 & ;\text{otherwise} \end{cases} \tag{5}$$

The call death rate for PUs or SUs generating a transition from state $\mathbf{k}$ to state $\mathbf{k}-\mathbf{e}_i$ is given by

$$b_i(\mathbf{k}) = \begin{cases} k_0 \mu_s^{(P)} & \sum_{i=0}^{2} k_i \leq M;\ k_3 = 0;\ i = 0 \\ \beta k_1 \mu_1^{(S)} & \sum_{i=0}^{2} k_i \leq M;\ k_3 = 0;\ i = 1 \\ k_2 \mu_2^{(S)} & \sum_{i=0}^{2} k_i \leq M;\ k_3 = 0;\ i = 2 \\ 0 & ;\text{otherwise} \end{cases} \tag{6}$$

The transition rate of the service time of a SU from phase 1 to phase 2 generating a transition from state $\mathbf{k}$ to state $\mathbf{k}-\mathbf{e}_1+\mathbf{e}_2$ is given by

$$c(\mathbf{k})=\begin{cases}(1-\beta)k_1\mu_1^{(S)} & ;\sum_{i=0}^{1}k_i\le M;\ \sum_{i=0}^{3}k_i\le 2M;\ \sum_{i=1}^{3}k_i\le M;\ k_2\ge 0\\ 0 & ;\text{otherwise}\end{cases} \tag{7}$$

The transition rate of queuing a SU in phase 1 (due to the arrival of a PU at the first stage of its service time) generating a transition from state $\mathbf{k}$ to state $\mathbf{k}+\mathbf{e}_0-\mathbf{e}_1+\mathbf{e}_3$ is given by

$$d_1(\mathbf{k})=\begin{cases}\dfrac{k_1}{M-k_0}\lambda^{(P)} & ;0\le k_0<M;\ \sum_{j=0}^{2}k_j\ge M;\ \sum_{j=0}^{3}k_j<2M;\ k_3\ge 0;\\ & ;\sum_{j=1}^{3}k_j\le M\\ 0 & ;\text{otherwise}\end{cases} \tag{8}$$

The transition rate of queuing a SU in phase 2 (due to the arrival of a PU at the second stage of its service time) generating a transition from state $\mathbf{k}$ to state $\mathbf{k}+\mathbf{e}_0-\mathbf{e}_2+\mathbf{e}_2$ is given by

$$d_2(\mathbf{k})=\begin{cases}\dfrac{M-k_0-k_1}{M-k_0}\lambda^{(P)} & ;0\le k_0<M;\ \sum_{j=0}^{2}k_j\ge M;\ \sum_{j=0}^{3}k_j<2M;\\ & ;\sum_{j=1}^{3}k_j\le M\\ 0 & ;\text{otherwise}\end{cases} \tag{9}$$

The reconnection rate of a SU in phase 1 due to the death of a PU generating a transition from state $\mathbf{k}$ to state $\mathbf{k}-\mathbf{e}_0+\mathbf{e}_1-\mathbf{e}_3$ is given by

$$e_0(\mathbf{k})=\begin{cases}\dfrac{k_3}{k_3+\sum_{j=0}^{2}k_j-M}k_0\mu^{(P)} & ;k_0<M;\ \sum_{j=0}^{2}k_j\ge M;\ \sum_{j=0}^{3}k_j\le 2M;\\ & ;k_1\ge 0;k_3>0;\sum_{j=1}^{3}k_j\le M;i=0\\ 0 & ;\text{otherwise}\end{cases} \tag{10}$$

The reconnection rate of a SU in phase 2 due to the death of a PU generating a transition from state $\mathbf{k}$ to state $\mathbf{k}-\mathbf{e}_0+\mathbf{e}_2-\mathbf{e}_2$ is given by

$$e_1(\mathbf{k}) = \begin{cases} \dfrac{\sum_{j=0}^{2} k_j - M}{k_3 + \sum_{j=0}^{2} k_j - M} k_0 \mu^{(P)} & ; \sum_{j=0}^{1} k_j \le M;\ \sum_{j=0}^{2} k_j \ge M; \\ & ; \sum_{j=0}^{3} k_j \le 2M;\ \sum_{j=1}^{3} k_j \le M;\ i = 1 \\ 0 & ; \text{otherwise} \end{cases} \quad (11)$$

The reconnection rate of a SU in phase 1 due to the death of a SU in phase 1 generating a transition from state $\mathbf{k}$ to state $\mathbf{k} - \mathbf{e}_1 + \mathbf{e}_1 - \mathbf{e}_3$ is given by

$$e_2(\mathbf{k}) = \begin{cases} \dfrac{k_3}{k_3 + \sum_{j=0}^{2} k_j - M} \beta k_1 \mu_1^{(S)} & ; k_0 < M;\ \sum_{j=0}^{2} k_j \ge M;\ \sum_{j=0}^{3} k_j \le 2M; \\ & ; k_3 > 0;\ \sum_{j=1}^{3} k_j \le M;\ i = 2 \\ 0 & ; \text{otherwise} \end{cases} \quad (12)$$

The reconnection rate of a SU in phase 2 due to the death of a SU in phase 1 generating a transition from state $\mathbf{k}$ to state $\mathbf{k} - \mathbf{e}_1 + \mathbf{e}_2 - \mathbf{e}_2$ is given by

$$e_3(\mathbf{k}) = \begin{cases} \dfrac{\sum_{j=0}^{2} k_j - M}{k_3 + \sum_{j=0}^{2} k_j - M} \beta k_1 \mu_1^{(P)} & ; \sum_{j=0}^{1} k_j \le M;\ \sum_{j=0}^{2} k_j > M; \\ & ; \sum_{j=0}^{3} k_j \le 2M;\ \sum_{j=1}^{3} k_j \le M;\ i = 3 \\ 0 & ; \text{otherwise} \end{cases} \quad (13)$$

The reconnection rate of a SU in phase 1 due to the death of a SU in phase 2 generating a transition from state $\mathbf{k}$ to state $\mathbf{k} - \mathbf{e}_2 + \mathbf{e}_1 - \mathbf{e}_3$ is given by

$$e_4(\mathbf{k}) = \begin{cases} \dfrac{k_3}{k_3 + \sum_{j=0}^{2} k_j - M} (M - k_0 - k_1) \mu_2^{(S)} & ; \sum_{j=0}^{2} k_j \ge M;\ \sum_{j=0}^{3} k_j \le 2M \\ & ; k_1 \ge 0;\ k_3 > 0;\ \sum_{j=1}^{3} k_j \le M;\ i = 4 \\ 0 & ; \text{otherwise} \end{cases} \quad (14)$$

The reconnection rate of a SU in phase 2 due to the death of a SU in phase 2 generating a transition from state $\mathbf{k}$ to state $\mathbf{k} - \mathbf{e}_2 + \mathbf{e}_2 - \mathbf{e}_2$ is given by

$$e_5(\mathbf{k}) = \begin{cases} \dfrac{\sum_{j=0}^{2} k_j - M}{k_3 + \sum_{j=0}^{2} k_j - M} (M - k_0 - k_1)\mu_2^{(P)} & ; \sum_{j=0}^{2} k_j > M;\ \sum_{j=0}^{3} k_j \le 2M; \\ & ; \sum_{j=1}^{3} k_j \le M;\ i = 5 \\ 0 & ; \text{otherwise} \end{cases} \tag{15}$$

An arrival of a new cognitive call is blocked when there is not idle sub-bands. That is, new call blocking probability $P_B^{(S)}$ can be computed as follows

$$P_B^{(S)} = \sum_{\substack{k_0=0 \\ \left\{\mathbf{k} \middle| \sum_{i=0}^{2} k_i \ge M\right\}}}^{M} \sum_{k_1=0}^{M-k_0} \sum_{k_2=0}^{M-(k_0+k_1)} P(\mathbf{k}) \tag{16}$$

On the other hand, for the RR strategy is considered, the probability that a SU be interrupted can be computed as follows (Zhang, 2008)

$$P_{Int} = \frac{\sum_{\left\{\mathbf{k}\in\Omega \middle| \sum_{i=0}^{2} k_i \ge NM; k_0 < M\right\}} \dfrac{1}{M - k_0} P(\mathbf{k})}{\sum_{\left\{\mathbf{k}\in\Omega \middle| \sum_{i=0}^{2} k_i \ge NM; k_0 < M\right\}} P(\mathbf{k})} \tag{17}$$

Finally, the forced termination probability for SUs equals zero. This is due to the fact that ST calls are assumed to wait indefinitely to be served.

5. Performance evaluation of SOAR

In the SOAR strategy each time a queued secondary user is reconnected to the system, it retransmits its whole information no matter that some part of this information was transmitted in its previous connection. That is, the service time of a given ongoing secondary call does not change after it experiences an interruption. However, it is evident that SU calls with greater service time are interrupted with higher probability. Then, due to this fact, a bias effect is observed in the distribution of the service time of interrupted SU calls. Specifically, compared with the corresponding parameters of the service time of SU, the mean value of interrupted SUs increases and depends on the number of times a SU in service is interrupted. More important, it is found that, in general, the service time distributions for interrupted SUs are no longer phase-type distributed, and consequently it is not possible to employ a Markovian model. Then, the performance of the SOAR strategy is evaluated through discrete-event computer simulation.

6. Transmission delay

The mean value of the normalized transmission delay, denoted by $E\{\mathbf{X}_{delay}\}$, is computed as follows

$$E\left\{\mathbf{X}_{delay}\right\} = \frac{E\left\{\mathbf{X}_{system}\right\} - E\left\{\mathbf{X}_{S}^{(S)}\right\}}{E\left\{\mathbf{X}_{S}^{(S)}\right\}} \tag{18}$$

where $E\{\mathbf{X}_{system}\}$ represents the mean value of the elapsed time between the epoch the SU arrives to the system to the epoch it finally leaves the system. The numerical results for the mean value of the normalized transmission delay are obtained by a developed discrete event computer simulator. In our simulation, we compute this parameter as follows

$$E\left\{\mathbf{X}_{system}\right\} = \frac{\sum_{i=0}^{n}\left(\mathbf{X}_{arrival(i)} - \mathbf{X}_{death(i)}\right)}{n} \tag{19}$$

where the random variable $\mathbf{X}_{arrival(i)}$ represents the epoch at which the i-th SU enters the system, the random variable $\mathbf{X}_{death(i)}$ represents the epoch at which the i-th SU leaves the system, and n represents the total number of no blocked SU.

7. Numerical results

The goal of the numerical evaluations presented in this section is to investigate the performance of cognitive radio networks with the RR or SOAR strategies considering different phase-type probability distributions for the service time of SU calls. Specifically, numerical results for the following relevant phase-type distributions for modeling service time of SU are presented: negative-exponential, Erlang order 2, and Coxian order 2. System performance is evaluated in terms of both SU new call blocking probability and SU mean normalized transmission delay. Unless otherwise specified, the following values of the system parameters were used in the plots of this section: total number of primary bands M = 3, each primary band is divided into N=1 sub-bands, mean service time for primary users $1/\mu_s^{(P)}$=16.7 s, and mean service time for secondary users $1/\mu_s^{(S)}$=1.22 s. Other system parameters used in this section are summarized in Table 1.

Figs. 3 and 4 (5 and 6) {7 and 8} show, respectively, SU new call blocking probability and SU transmission delay as function of both primary and secondary mean arrival rate for the case when service time for SU is exponentially (Erlang order 2) {Coxian order 2} distributed. As expected, Figs. 3-8 show that blocking probability and transmission delay are monotonically increasing functions of the primary mean arrival rate. This behavior indicates a detrimental effect of the primary arrival rate on the cognitive radio network performance. However, the main conclusion that can be extracted from Figure 3 (5) is that, from the blocking probability point of view and assuming that the service time of SU follows a negative-exponential (Erlang order 2) distribution, the performance of RR and SOAR strategies is very similar irrespective of the values of both primary and secondary mean arrival rates. On the other hand, Fig. 4 shows that, from the point of view of the transmission delay, the RR strategy slightly outperforms the behavior of the SOAR strategy. Specifically, Fig. 4 shows that the difference in performance between this two strategies increases as the mean arrival rate of PUs increases. From Fig. 6, a similar behavior can be observed when service time for SU is modeled as an Erlang order 2 distributed random variable. The reason of this behavior is evident: Contrary to the SOAR strategy, in the RR strategy an interrupted SU does not need to transmit again the information bits transmitted before its previous connection was interrupted. This fact contributes to improve delay transmission.

On the other hand, Figs. 7 and 8 show that, for values of the mean arrival rate of PUs greater than 0.04, the RR strategy significantly outperforms the SOAR strategy when the service time of SU is modeled as a Coxian order 2 distributed random variable. This behavior becomes more evident as the mean arrival rate of PUs increases. The reason of this behavior is due to the bias effect on the service time distribution of preempted SUs. To explain this effect let us considerer Table 2 and Figs. 9-11.

Service time distribution	$\mu_1^{(S)}$	$\mu_2^{(S)}$	β	CV	SK
Negative Exponential	0.82	N/A	1	1	2
Erlang order 2	1.6399	1.6399	0	0.7071	1.4142
Coxian order 2	8.1842	0.018	0.9801	9	15

Table 1. System parameters for the different service time distributions considered in this section

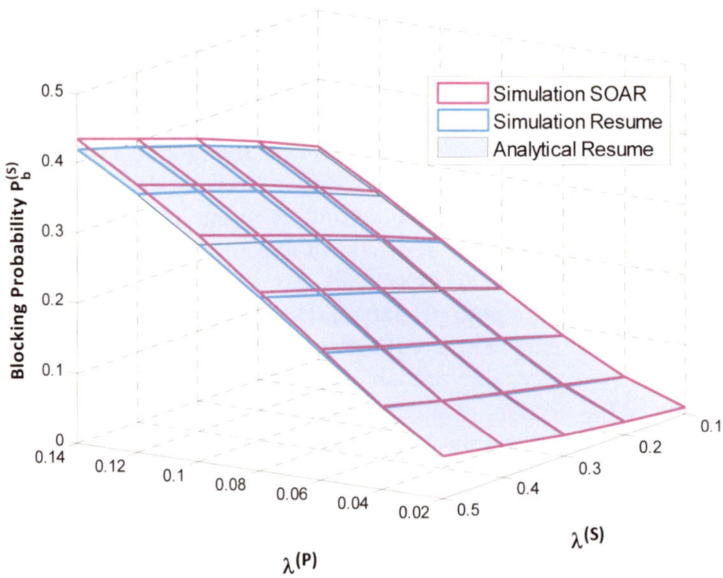

Fig. 3. Analytical and Simulation results for blocking probability for SOAR and Resume retransmission with exponentially distributed service time

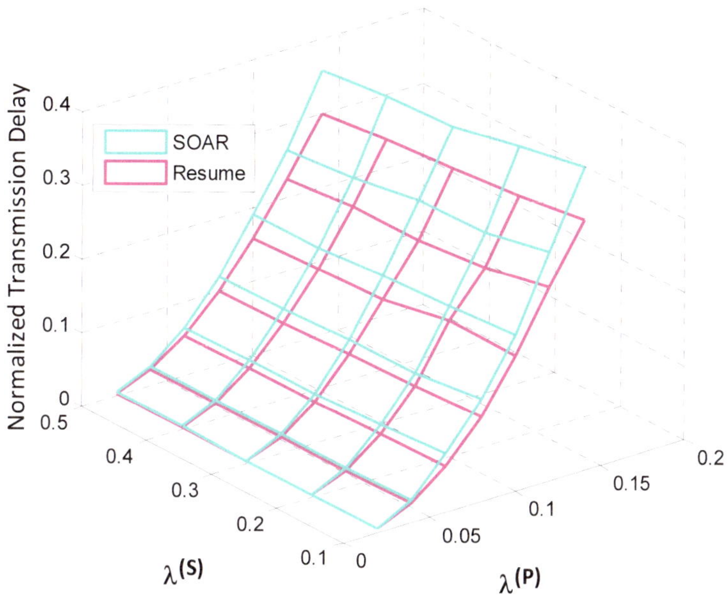

Fig. 4. Simulation results for transmission delay for SOAR and Resume retransmission with exponentially distributed service time

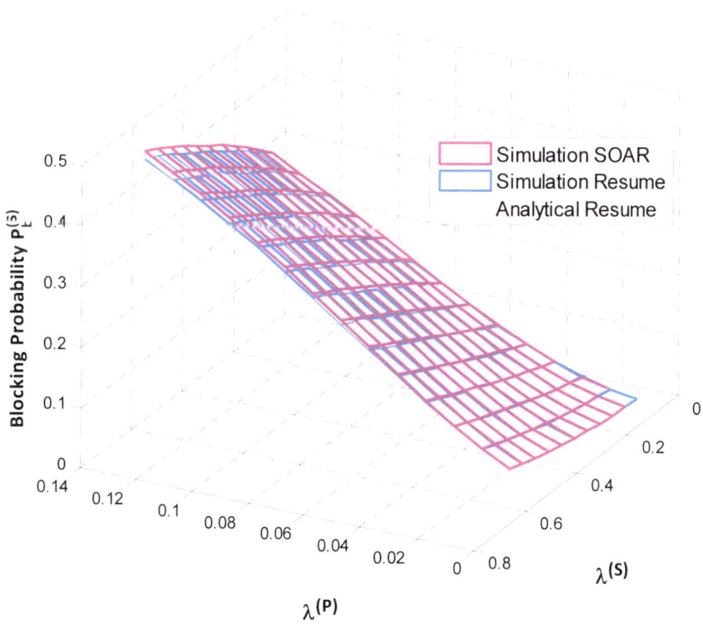

Fig. 5. Analytical and Simulation results for blocking probability for SOAR and Resume retransmission with Erlang order 2 distributed service time

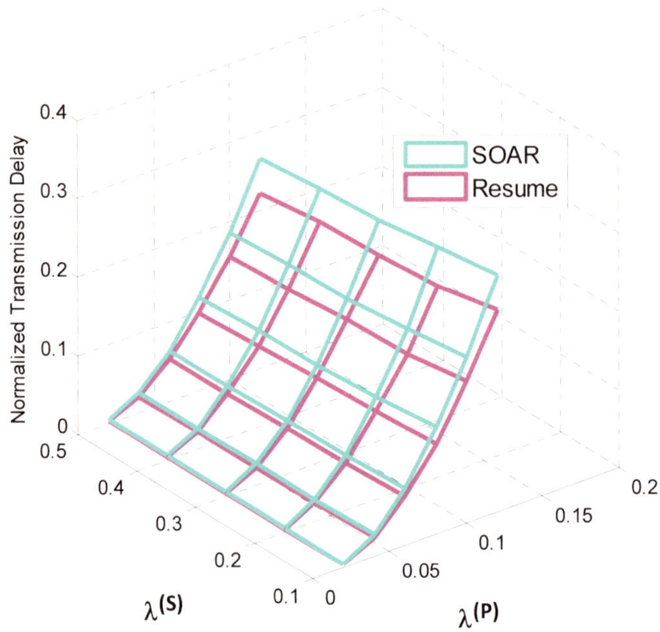

Fig. 6. Simulation results for transmission delay for SOAR and Resume retransmission with Erlang order 2 distributed service time

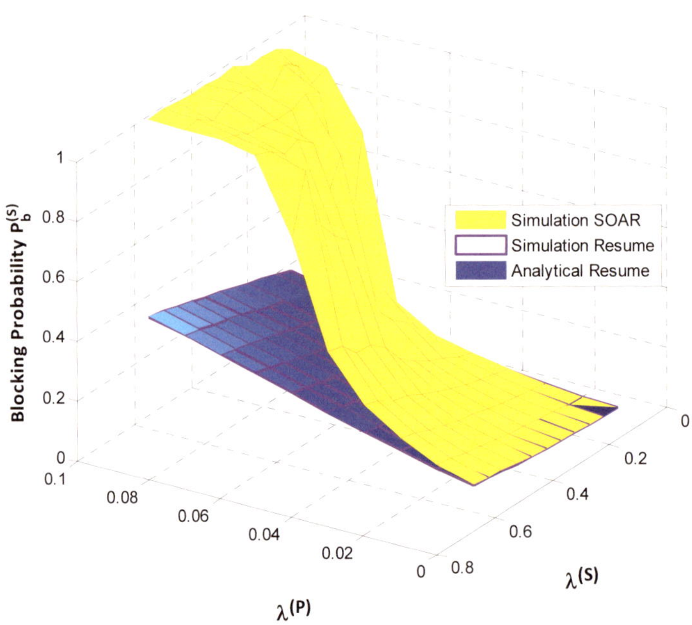

Fig. 7. Analytical and simulation results for blocking probability for SOAR and Resume retransmission with Coxian order 2 distributed service time

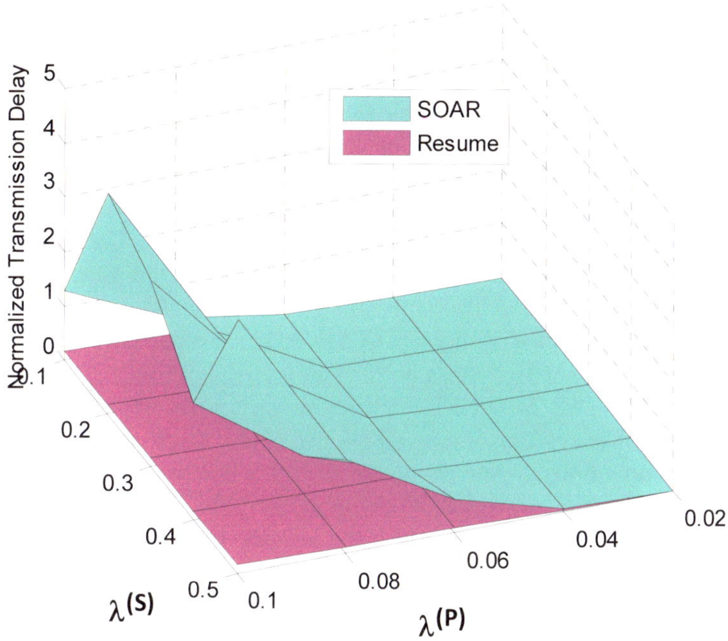

Fig. 8. Simulation results for transmission delay for SOAR and Resume retransmission with Coxian order 2 distributed service time

Moments	EXP-NEG	ERLANG-2	COXIAN-2
$E\{X_S^{(S)}\}$	1.2195	1.2195	1.2195
$E\{X_{S_1}^{(S)}\}$	2.4305	1.8263	89.545
$E\{X_{S_2}^{(S)}\}$	3.4119	2.3472	125.16
$E\{X_{S_3}^{(S)}\}$	4.3038	2.837	147.99
$CV\{X_S^{(S)}\}$	1	0.7071	9
$CV\{X_{S_1}^{(S)}\}$	0.7069	0.5771	0.8443
$CV\{X_{S_2}^{(S)}\}$	0.5818	0.5019	0.6387
$CV\{X_{S_3}^{(S)}\}$	0.505	0.4475	0.5778
$SK\{X_S^{(S)}\}$	2	1.4142	15
$SK\{X_{S_1}^{(S)}\}$	1.4077	1.1471	1.3162
$SK\{X_{S_2}^{(S)}\}$	1.1551	0.9907	1.2768
$SK\{X_{S_3}^{(S)}\}$	0.9976	0.8832	1.1538

Table 2. First three standardized moments of the service time for SU calls interrupted i times (the particular cases for i = 0, 1, 2, 3 are presented in this table)

Table 2 shows the first three standardized moments of the service time for SU calls preempted i times. The particular cases for i = 0, 1, 2, 3 are presented in this table. CV and SK denote the coefficient of variation and skewness operators, respectively. Fig. 9 (10) {11} shows the pdf of the service time for the SU calls preempted 1, 2 and 3 times for SOAR with negative-exponentially (Erlang order 2) {Coxian order 2} distributed service time.
From Figs. 9-11, a bias effect is observed in the distribution of the service time of interrupted SU calls. This behavior is due to the fact that SU calls with greater service time are interrupted with higher probability. Moreover, Table 2, shows that, compared with the corresponding parameters of the service time of SU, we found that the mean value of preempted SUs increases and, at the same time, both skewness and CoV decrease as the number of times a SU in service is interrupted increases. This behavior of the SOAR strategy indicates a detrimental effect on system performance as the number of times an active SU is interrupted increases. This is especially true in situations where high values of the coefficient of variation of service time of SU are presented. Thus, numerical results reported in Table 2 clearly show that, in general, as the CoV of the service time of SU increases, the system performance improvement becomes significantly for the RR strategy relative to the SOAR strategy. On the other hand, when the service time of SUs is considered either exponentially (i.e., CV = 1) or Erlang order 2 (i.e., $CV = 1/\sqrt{2}$) distributed, numerical results show that similar system performance is obtained with both retransmission strategies.

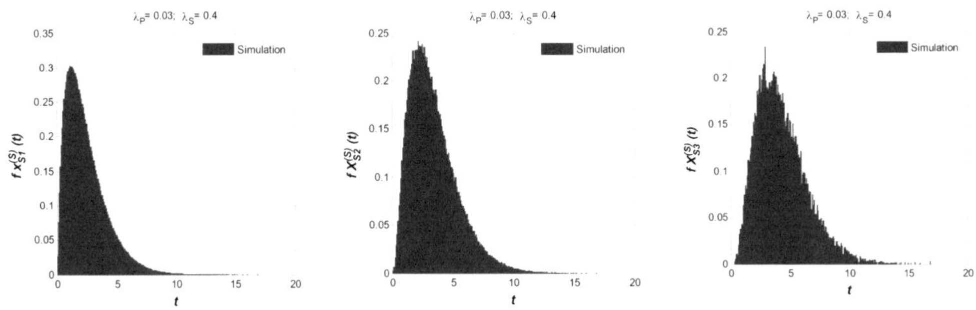

Fig. 9. Service time distribution for the SU calls preempted 1, 2 and 3 times for SOAR with exponentially distributed service time

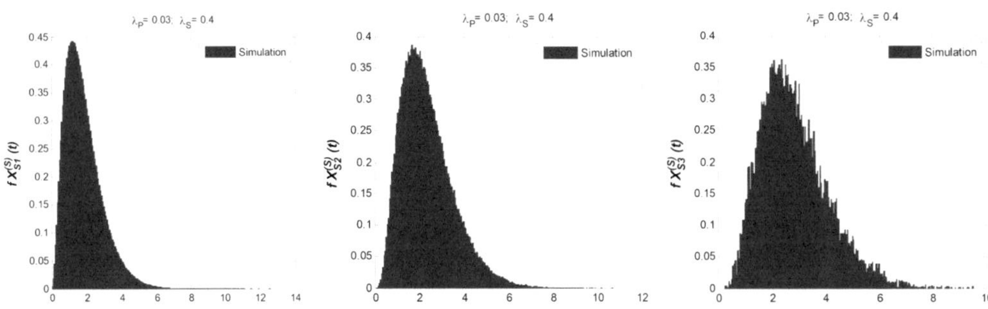

Fig. 10. Service time distribution for the SU calls preempted 1, 2 and 3 times for SOAR with Erlang order 2 distributed service time

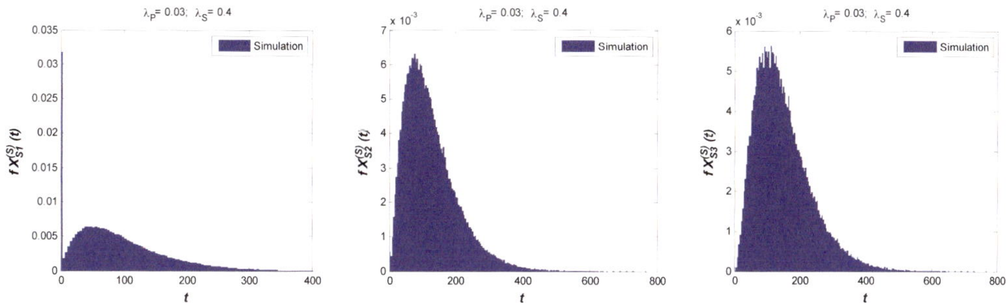

Fig. 11. Service time distribution for the SU calls preempted 1, 2 and 3 times for SOAR with Coxian order 2 distributed service time

8. Conclusions

Performance comparison between the RR and SOAR strategies were performed for different traffic conditions and characteristics of the SU service time. Numerical results show relevant system implications. We found that the value of the coefficient of variation (CoV) of service time of SUs plays a major role in the system performance of cognitive radio networks when RR or SOAR strategies are considered. For instance, we found that as the (CoV) of the service time of SU increases, the system capacity improvement becomes significantly greater for the RR strategy relative to the SOAR strategy. On the other hand, when the service time of SUs is considered either exponentially or Erlang order 2 distributed (i.e., CoV $\leq$ 1), numerical results show that similar system performance is obtained with both retransmission strategies. Thus, we conclude that for scenarios where the coefficient of variation of service time for SU has values around 1, the SOAR strategy is preferred over the more complicated RR strategy. On the contrary for scenarios where the CoV has high values, the RR strategy is preferred over the SOAR one due to its much better performance.

9. References

Ahmed W., Gao J., and Faulkner M., Performance evaluation of a cognitive radio network with exponential and truncated usage models, in *Proc. IEEE International Symposium on Wireless and Pervasive Computing* (*ISWPC'*09), Melbourne, Australia, Feb. 2009.

Haykin S., Cognitive Radio: Brain-Empowered Wireless Communications, *IEEE J. Selected Areas in Comm.*, vol. 23, pp. 201–220, Feb. 2005.

Pacheco-Paramo D., Pla V., and Martinez-Bauset J., Optimal admission control in cognitive radio networks, in *Proc. IEEE 4th International Conference on Cognitive Radio Oriented Wireless Networks and Communications* (CROWNCOM'09), Hannover, Germany, Jun. 2009.

Tang S. and Mark B.L., Performance Analysis of a Wireless Network with Opportunistic Spectrum Sharing, in *Proc. IEEE Global Communications Conference* (*Globecom'*2007), Washington, DC, USA, Nov. 2007.

Tang S. and Mark B.L., An Analytical Performance Model of Opportunistic Spectrum Access in a Military Environment, in *Proc. IEEE Wireless Communications and Networking Conference* (*WCNC'*2008), Las Vegas, NV, Mar.-Apr. 2008, pp. 2681-2686.

Tang S. and Mark B.L., Analysis of Opportunistic Spectrum Sharing with Markovian Arrivals and Phase-Type Service, *IEEE Trans. Wireless Commun.*, Vol. 8, No. 6, pp. 3142-3150, June 2009.

Tang S. and Mark B. L., a, Modeling and analysis of opportunistic spectrum sharing with unreliable spectrum sensing, *IEEE Trans. on Wireless Communications*, vol. 8, pp. 1934–1943, Apr. 2009.

Zhang Y., Dynamic spectrum access in cognitive radio wireless networks, in *Proc. IEEE International Conference on Communications* (*ICC'*2008), Beijing, China, May 2008, pp. 4927–4932.

Zhu X., Shen L., and Yum T.-S. P., Analysis of cognitive radio spectrum access with optimal channel reservation, *IEEE Commun. Lett.*, vol. 11, no. 4, pp. 1-3, Apr. 2007.

Part 8

System Fabrication

23

Fabrication and Characterizations of Multi-Layer Thin Film Internal Antenna for Wireless Communication

Book-Sung Park, Hyun-Sang Lee and Soren Pedersen
Nokia, MS Symbian Smartphones Device R&D
Republic of Korea
United States of America
Denmark

1. Introduction

In 1990s, mobile communications were developed based on the Code Division Multiple Access (CDMA) which is used in Korea, USA, and Japan and Global System for Mobile communications (GSM) which is used in Europe and other countries. Beginning in 2000s, global roaming was required for unifying these two communication methods, but the different frequency allocations in various countries impeded the unification. Therefore, the complexities of mobile handsets were increased to support 2G, 2.5G, and 3G at the same time. The development of semiconductor technique makes it necessary to upgrade the electronic components which are smaller and more powerful than those used in the multimedia and frequency bands of the early 1990s(F. Adachi et al., 1998). This kind of growth of electronic components means that handsets have more complex functions and a reduced size. And the antenna which is used for the mobile communicating set has been changed from an external one to an internal one thing. The internal antenna allows the handset to be small and easily portable (K. Hirasawa & M. Haneishi, 1991). For that reason, most of handset has the internal antenna these days. The internal antennas of several kinds of design techniques such as monopole antenna, Planar Inverted-F Antenna (PIFA) antenna, and high dielectric internal antenna are used and studied in many companies and research labs (W. L. Stutzman & G. A. Thiele, 1998). The monopole antenna has one feeding point basis on dipole antenna topology and the advantage is small size and wide frequency bandwidth on the other hand the disadvantage is that its radiation characteristic is more affected by its surroundings such as ground, user's body, hand, and head than the others. The PIFA has both of the feeding and shorting point and the advantage is that the radiation performance cannot be affected by human and ground condition, impedance matching and the Total Radiated Power (TRP), Total Isotropic Sensitivity (TIS) and Special Absorption Rate (SAR) performance is better than that of monopole antenna, but the frequency bandwidth is narrower than monopole antenna. The high dielectric antenna is consisted of high dielectric materials and metal antenna patterns. This technique is the best solution pertaining to the size, but the cost is the worst. So, the PIFA type internal antenna is the most interested solution and is studied in labs and companies.

The proposed sputter-deposited multilayer thin film internal antenna solution is a technological revolution. Thus, the sputter-deposited multilayer thin film internal antenna solution is better off compare with the current carrier-based internal antenna method. This new manufacturing technology on internal antenna can achieve the advanced antenna development. For realization of this method, antenna meander pattern is sputtered on the cover of handset material which is polycarbonate substrate by DC sputter-deposited method(D. Yuepeng, 2005). Especially, the sputter-deposited internal antenna performance is better than the ink print method antenna that was recently proposed. Because the ink print method is can't get a good uniformity of antenna meander line with the ink print method. For this reason, ink print method cannot get the uniformity of molecule density and this will make some degradation on the antenna performance. Owing to the sputter-deposited internal antenna method on polycarbonate is vastly attractive to the next generation 4G Multiple-Input Multiple-Output (MIMO) system.

2. Experiment results and discuss of the multilayer thin film

2.1 Multilayer thin film fabrication

The multilayer thin film internal antenna solutions are presented based on the precursor with the Ni/Ag thin film solution. The overall size is 43.0 × 24.0 × 0.0015mm^3 (height: 1.5um). Figure 1 illustrates a flow diagram of fabrication processes with the Ni/Ag/Ni thin film. The sputtering parameters and co-sputtering techniques of the experiments are listed in Table 1(G. C. Stutzin et al., 1993). This section describes co-techniques and fabrication processes.

To begin with, the proposed multilayer thin films fabricate of the tri-structural layer with the Ni and Ag material. Actually, the multilayer thin film solution needs a previous work, spray-coating with 80um spray-coating process on the polycarbonate substrate at 80°C for 90 minutes used WP100 material. This is the reason why the polycarbonate surface is seriously rough to be adapted to wireless mobile propagation application. Therefore, the multilayer (Ni/Ag/Ni) thin film radiators need for the compensate material as well as WP100 materials can compensate for surface flatness.

Second, the multilayer internal antenna is composed of three stacked layer(Ni/Ag/Ni). The first layer is called the adhesion layer, the adhesion layer is made by growth of Ni material with 3,000Å thickness on poly carbonate substrate and the sputtering condition was 7 KW per 180 seconds in plasma circumstances. The second layer is defined as the conducted layer, conducted layer is manufactured by growth of Ag material on the Ni layer, total experimental sputtering thickness is approximately 8,000Åwith 7 KW per 1,500 seconds conditions. And the last layer is defined as the safeguard layer, safeguard layer is manufactured by growth of Ni material with 4,000Å thickness with 7 KW per 240 seconds conditions.

Last, the multilayer thin film radiator is characterized by Energy-dispersive X-ray spectroscopy (EDX) and analysis of cross-sectional structures is observed by field-emission scanning electron microscopy (FE-SEM). The standing wave ratio characteristic is measured with Agilent E5071B Network Analyzer and Agilent ADS simulation system was used for getting the optimum standing wave ratio. The quad-band TRP and TIS characteristics are measured in an anechoic chamber with CTIA (CTIA Certification, 2005).

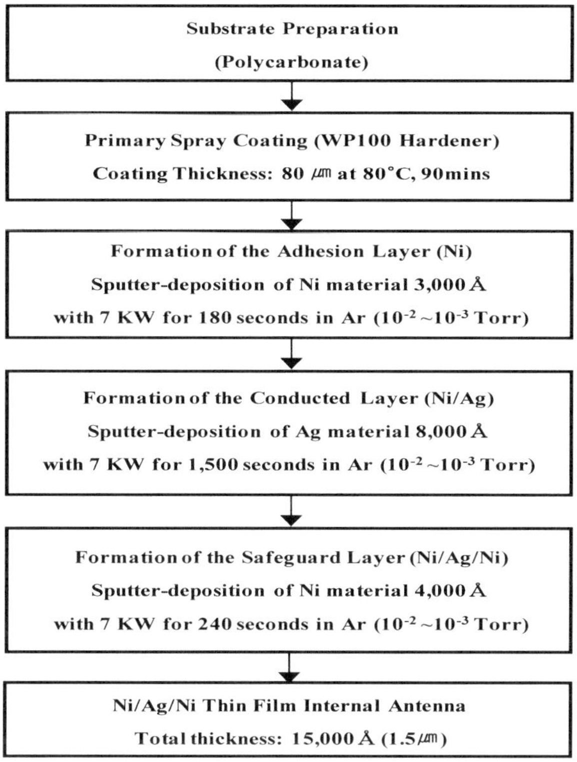

Fig. 1. Fabrication flow for multilayer (Ni/Ag/Ni) thin film process solution; Total thickness target 15,000Å (1.5um)

Target material	Power	Ar flow	Distance (target to substrate)	Time
Ni	7 KW	70 sccm	70mm	180 s
Ag	7 KW	70 sccm	70mm	1500 s
Ni	7 KW	70 sccm	70mm	240 s

Table 1. Experiments sputtering parameters and co-sputtering technique (Ni/Ag/Ni thin film)

2.2 Geometry of the multilayer thin film internal antenna

The configurations of quad-band planar inverted-F antennas have either modified L-shaped slots on the radiating patch in Figure 2. The geometry of quad-band PIFA antenna is shown in Figure 2 (C. T. P. Song et al., 2000).

Figure 2 (a) shows geometry configuration with PCB (RCC $\varepsilon_r = 3.40$, CCL $\varepsilon_r = 4.20$ at under 3GHz) and rear side view of sputter-deposit internal antenna in Figure 2 (b), and Figure 2 (c) is front side view of sputter-deposit internal antenna. To understand the operation of our design with a conventional PIFA using air dielectric with dimensions (l, w) = (43.0, 24.0)mm, height h = 0.0015mm in which the shorting and feeding are located at center of the plate as shown in Figure 2 (b).

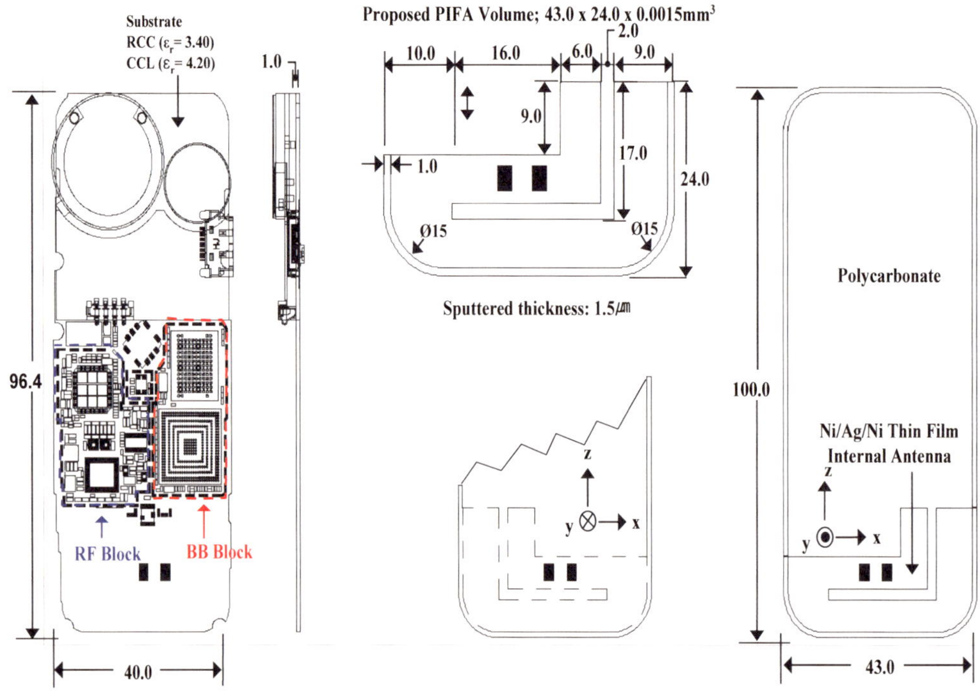

Fig. 2. Geometry configuration of the multilayer thin film internal antenna by sputter-deposited; (a) Geometry configuration of the PCB and quad-band part placement, (b) Rear side view of the sputter-deposit planar inverted-F antenna, (c) Front side view of the sputter-deposit planar inverted-F antenna

2.3 Fabrication of the Ni/Ag/Ni thin film internal antenna

Figure 3 shows an investigated scheme for the Ni/Ag/Ni thin film based on Ni layer. The sputter-deposit Ni/Ag/Ni thin film radiators are composed of primary incident ions, reflect ions, secondary electrons and sputtered atoms on polycarbonate substrate with Ar^+ ion in plasma circumstances. Currently, there are many materials that are characterized for frequency versus skin depth effect. Along with the analysis data, the sputtered thickness should be decreased as the frequency goes high. Figure 4 shows estimated sputtering target thickness on frequency plane. The experimental total target thickness is 1.5um. As the experimental results, the Ni material has best performance in the skin depth aspect. However, characteristics of the Ni resistivity is poor than Ag or Cu materials. I got results of the novel typed Ni/Ag/Ni thin film through many times of trial and error, also in this research suggested the best way to solve the problem. The proposed Ni/Ag/Ni thin film combinations are composed of three stack layer. Figure 4 shows the experiment condition of target thickness and frequency range for Ni/Ag/Ni thin film. The growth of Ni/Ag/Ni thin films are each 3.0×10^3Å, 8.0×10^3Å and 4.0×10^3Å.

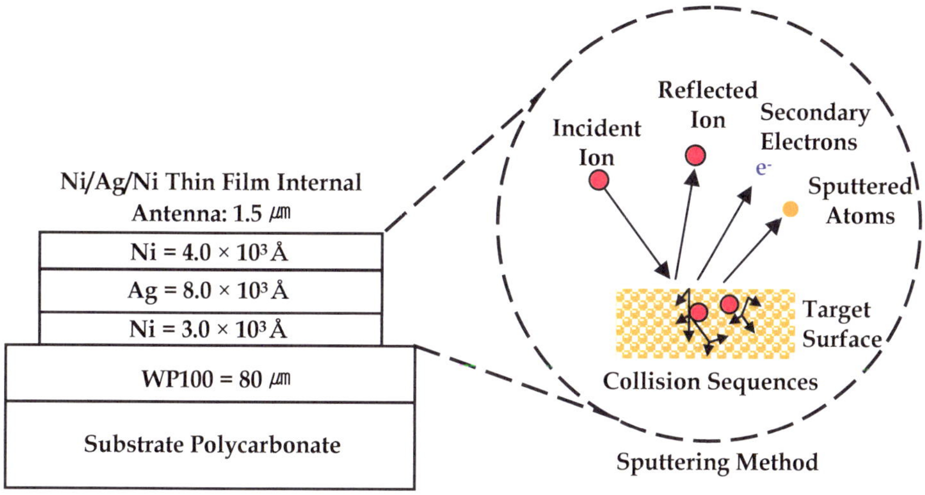

Fig. 3. Cross-section of the experimental procedure for the Ni/Ag/Ni thin film

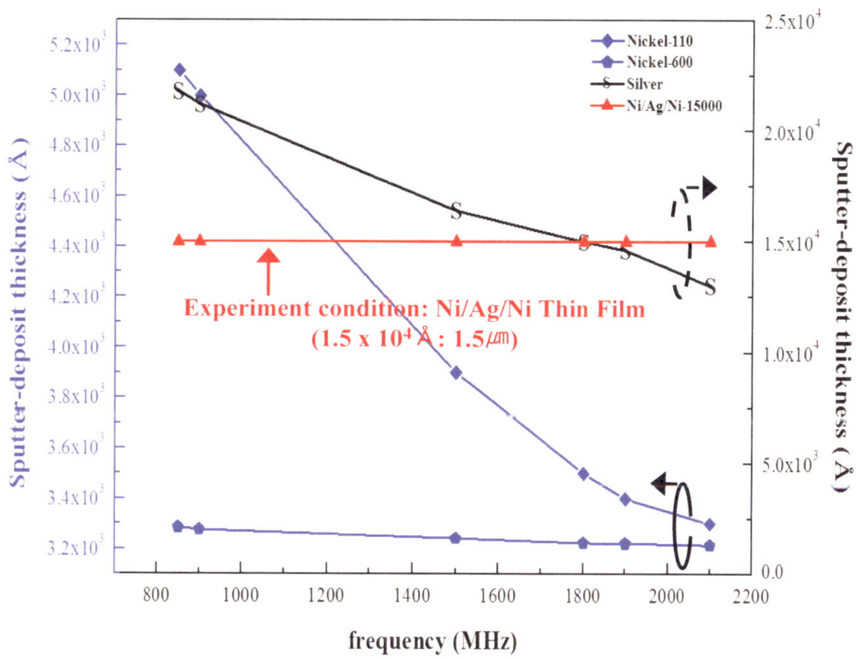

Fig. 4. Experiment conditions of target thickness and frequency range (Ni/Ag/Ni)

Figure 5 shows fabrication process of three stacked Ni/Ag/Ni thin film radiator. This research studied the Ni/Ag/Ni thin film radiator with growth of Ni and Ag. The estimated and measured total radiator thickness is 1.5um. Measurement of the adhesion layer thickness is 3.0×10^3Å by growth of Ni material on poly carbonate substrate. The Sputter-deposition condition is 7 KW per 180 seconds in plasma circumstances. And then, the measurement of the conducted layer thickness is 8.0 × 10^3Å by the growth of Ag material on the adhesive layer. The Sputter-deposition condition is 7 KW per 1,500seconds. The last measurement of safeguard layer thickness is 4.0 × 10^3Å by Ni material on Ni/Ag stack layer with thickness with 7 KW per 240 seconds.

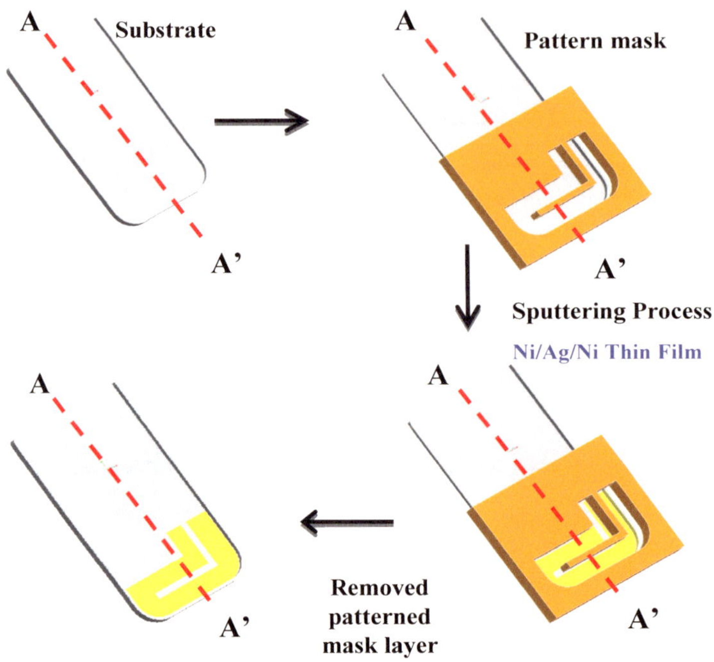

Fig. 5. Fabrication processes of the Ni/Ag/Ni thin film radiator on polycarbonate substrate

Figure 6 shows the pilot sample photo image of the Ni/Ag/Ni thin film, the measurement of the total cavity of sputter-deposited antenna is 43.0 × 24.0 × 0.0015mm^3(sputter-deposit thickness: 1.5um). This work has an enormous benefit for the height between ground plane and antenna height. The actual measured height is 9.5mm from PCB ground to Ni/Ag/Ni thin film internal antenna. Also, this research used contact feeding method for mobile application. Figure 6 shows photo image and geometry information for the Ni/Ag/Ni thin film radiator having resonant frequencies available for quad-band. The electrical length of each associated radiating element closely corresponds to each quarter-wavelength ($\lambda_g/4$) from the feed point A to B and C and D. Next, this research designed radiator pattern for GSM 850 and E-GSM band from A to B also estimated the GSM 1800/GSM 1900 band radiated pattern from C to D at 1710 MHz to 1990 MHz. Actually, A to B meander pattern and C to D meander pattern are significant to characterized of S_{11} and SWR also width and gap distance are key element. Figure 7 shows SEM images of the sputter-deposited Ni/Ag/Ni thin film. It shows surface is uniform magnifying view. Figure 7 (a) shows primary growth image of Ni surface with × 25,000, 30.0kV and 6.0um conditions, Figure 7 (b) shows redundancy layer image for Ag surface (× 10,000, 30.0kV and 8.8um), Figure 7 SEM photo image shows last layer for Ni surface (× 1,000, 30.0kV and 8.8um), and Figure 7 (d) shows interfacial tension image of the sputter-deposit Ni/Ag/Ni thin film. The total thickness of Ni/Ag/Ni thin film seemed to be 100um.

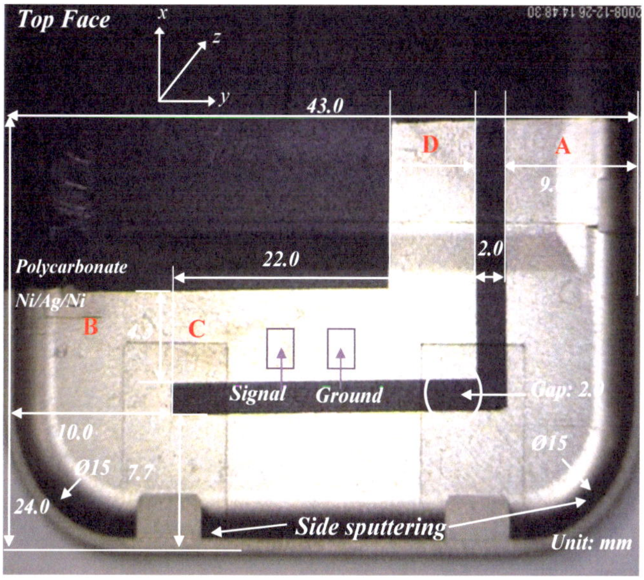

Fig. 6. Prototype photo image of the Ni/Ag/Ni thin film internal antenna by sputter - deposited

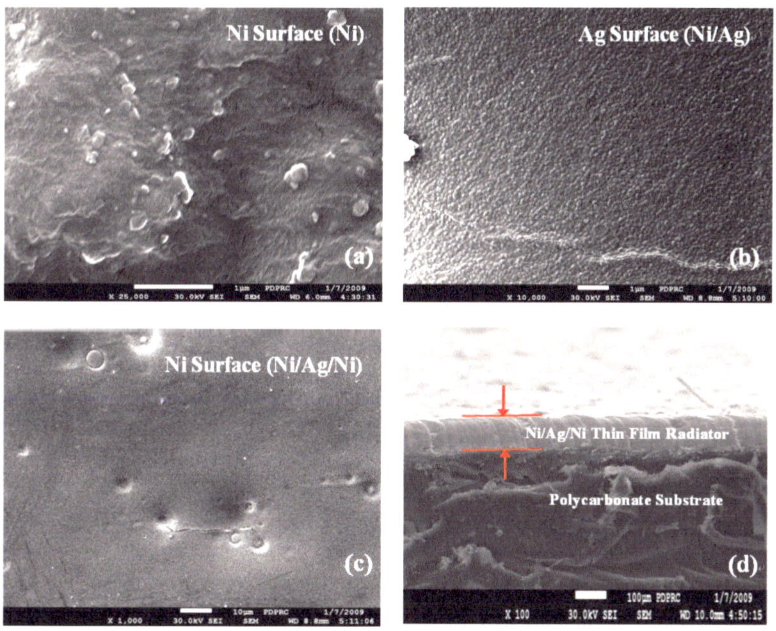

Fig. 7. SEM images of the Ni/Ag/Ni thin films by sputter-deposited. (a) primary growth image of the Ni surface with × 25,000, 30.0kV and 6.0um, (b) redundancy growth image of the Ag surface with × 10,000, 30.0kV and 8.8um, (c) last growth image of the Ni surface with × 1,000, 30.0kV and 8.8um, (d) Interfacial tension image of the Ni/Ag/Ni thin film by sputter-deposited

Figure 8 shows of the material spectrums distribution image for the Ni/Ag/Ni thin film radiator. Figure 8 (a) shows the properties of materials distribution result at Ni surface layer from 0keV to 12keV, the Ni material spread distributions are each 0.743 keV, 0.762 keV, 0.851 keV, 7.478 keV, and 8.265 keV. Figure 8 (b) shows of the Ag material distribution properties curve on Ni material surface also the Ag material spread distributions are each 2.643 keV, 2.806 keV, 2.984 keV, and 3.151 keV. The Ni material characteristic of peak-to-peak is 0.743 keV and the Ag material peak-to-peak is 2.634 keV. Figure 8 (c) shows of the Ni surface (Ni/Ag/Ni) spectra image and of material properties spread spectrum for both materials (Ag and Ni).

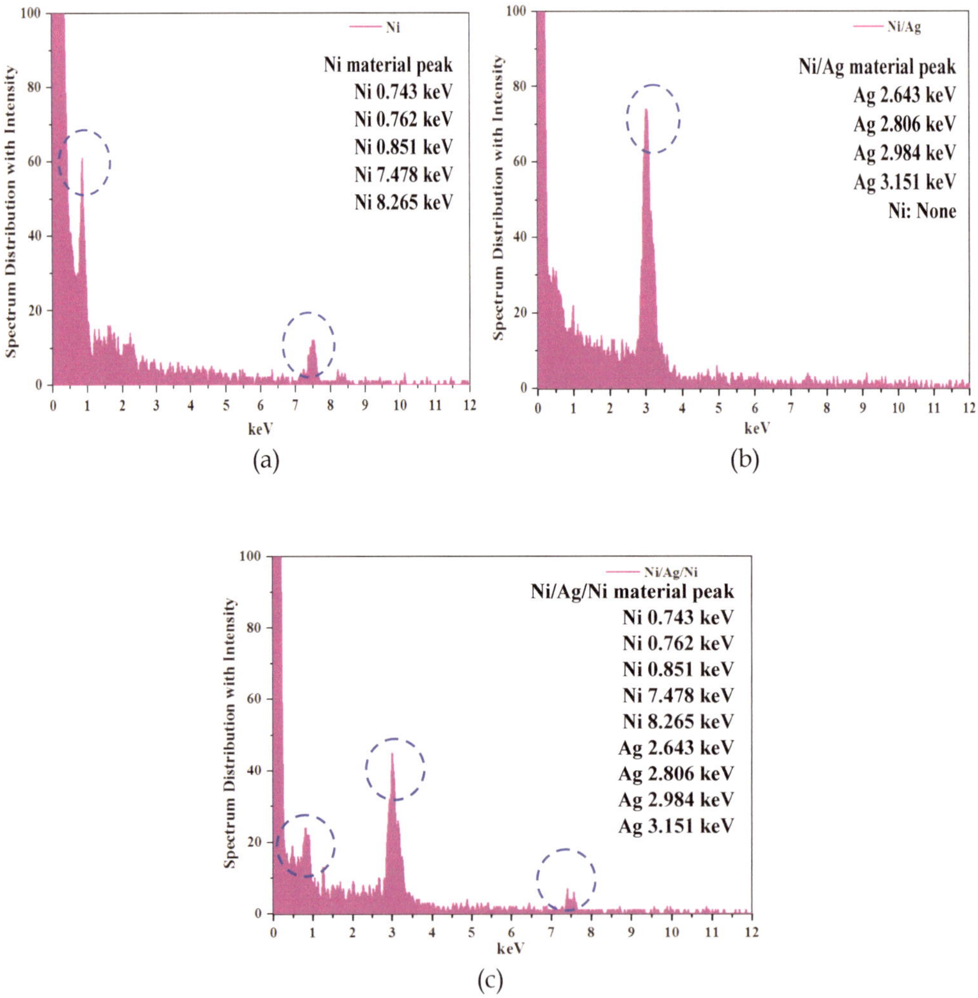

Fig. 8. The Energy-dispersive X-ray spectroscopy pattern images for Ni surface and Ag surface on Ni/Ag/Ni thin film. (a) Spectra image of Ni surface, (b) spectra image of Ni/Ag, (c) spectra image of Ni/Ag/Ni surface

2.4 Characteristics of SWR for the Ni/Ag/Ni thin film internal antenna by sputter-deposited

Figure 9 shows the measurement results of the SWR for prototyped sputter-deposit internal antenna versus optimized with the Ni/Ag/Ni thin film. The operated frequency range is 800 MHz to 2.0 GHz measurement used by Agilent Network Analyzer (E5071B). Figure 9 shows SWR characteristics of the prototyped Ni/Ag/Ni thin film internal antenna and optimized one. The SWR results of prototyped one are indicates each 3.13, 3.17, 3.09 and 2.22 at 824 MHz, 960 MHz, 1710 MHz and 1990 MHz. On the contrary, the case of the optimized Ni/Ag/Ni thin film radiator's SWRs are each 2.18, 2.52, 3.55, and 2.27 at 824 MHz, 960 MHz, 1710 MHz and 1990 MHz, respectively which is fine-tuned with phi type matching network through Agilent ADS simulation. Figure 10 shows of the prototyped Ni/Ag/Ni thin film internal antenna and optimized Ni/Ag/Ni thin film internal antennas S_{11} characteristics. In Figure 10 show prototyped thin film S_{11} result. The measured of S_{11} are each -5.74 dB and -5.67 dB at 824 MHz and 960 MHz also -5.82 dB and -8.44 dB at 1710 MHz to 1990 MHz. On the contrary, optimized internal antenna results marks -8.60 dB, -7.26 dB, -5.01 dB, and -8.22 dB at 824 MHz, 960 MHz, 1710 MHz and 1990 MHz, respectively.

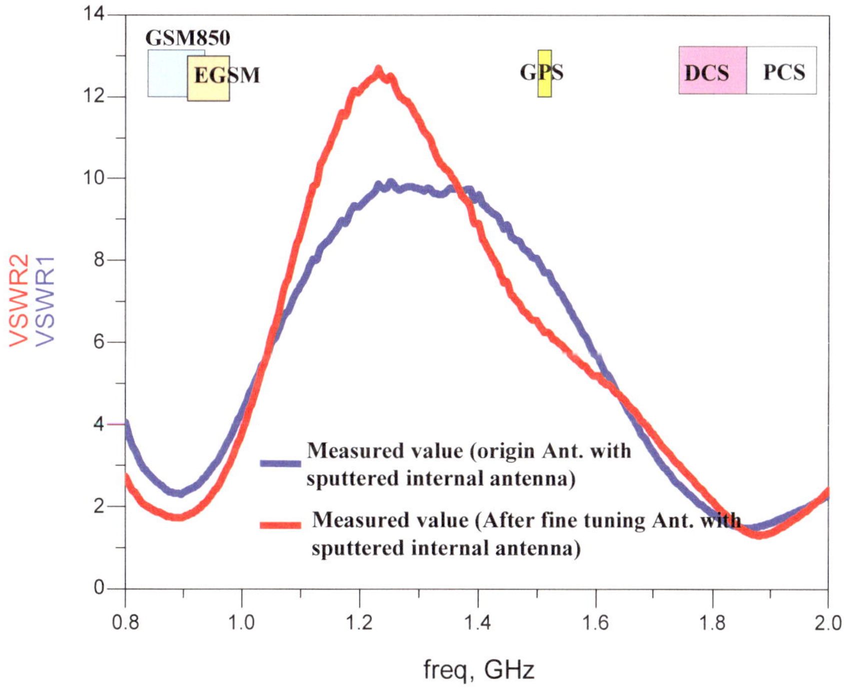

Fig. 9. Measured SWR result comparison the sputter-deposit internal antenna versus after fine tuning the Ni/Ag/Ni thin film internal antenna

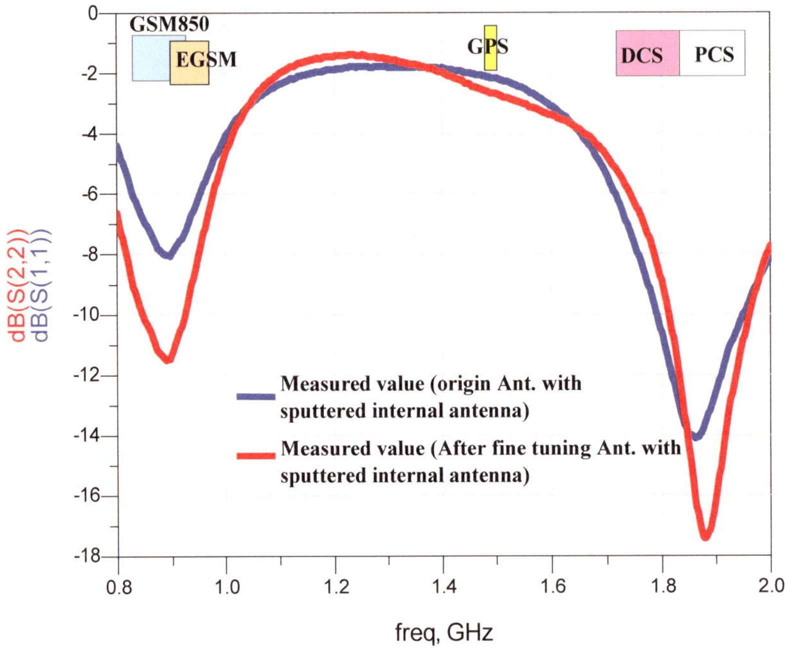

Fig. 10. Measured S_{11} result comparison the sputter-deposit internal antenna versus after fine tuning the Ni/Ag/Ni thin film internal antenna

2.5 Characteristics of current distribution for the Ni/Ag/Ni thin film internal antenna by sputter-deposited

In this experiment describes effect of current distribution for the Ni/Ag/Ni thin film internal antenna. The Ni/Ag/Ni thin film internal antenna solution is efficient rate in each frequency ranges. The prototyped Ni/Ag/Ni thin film internal antenna's overall size is 43.0 × 24.0 × 0.0015mm³. The simulation result shows 131A/m and 44.5A/m at 870MHz and 1990MHz. Figure 11 and Figure 12 shows the optimized current distribution results for the Ni/Ag/Ni sputter-deposit internal antenna. The measured current distribution ratio of optimized Ni/Ag/Ni sputter-deposit internal antenna is better off than prototype internal antenna. Figure 13 and Figure 14 shows efficiency distribution image for the optimized Ni/Ag/Ni sputter-deposit internal antenna at 870MHz and 1990MHz, total efficiency result are 47% and 55% in par field condition, respectively.

Figure 15 through Figure 18 shows of the 3D far-field (theta and phi) simulated radiation pattern results for the optimized sputter-deposit internal antenna in free space and SAM condition. The simulated frequency range is 870MHz and 1990MHz used by SEMCAD computing program. The results of measured 3D far-field TRP and TIS shows good performance in free space and SAM condition also measured directivity and gains as well as total efficiency rate are agreed well at 870MHz to 1990MHz. The measured of TRP simulation results are each 28.84dBm and 28.30dBm at 870MHz and 1990MHz with SAM condition. Also, measured of TIS simulation results are -101.85dBm and -101.31dBm at 870MHz and 1990MHz with SAM condition. The simulated results listed in Table 2 at free space and SAM condition. The measured two kinds of the experiment is significant meaning which is consumer related aspect.

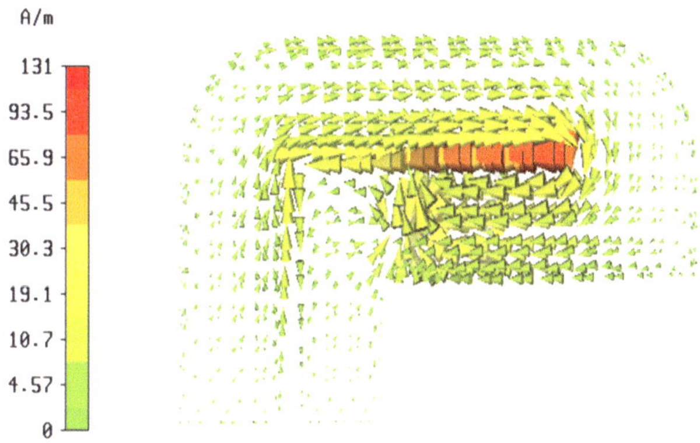

Fig. 11. Optimized current distribution image of the pilot radiator with Ni/Ag/Ni thin film internal antenna handset at 870MHz with CST program (Computer Simulation Technology)

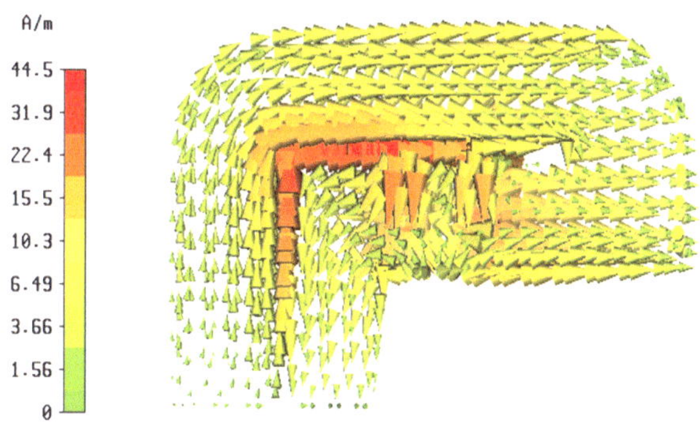

Fig. 12. Optimized current distribution image of the pilot radiator with Ni/Ag/Ni thin film internal antenna handset at 1990MHz with CST program

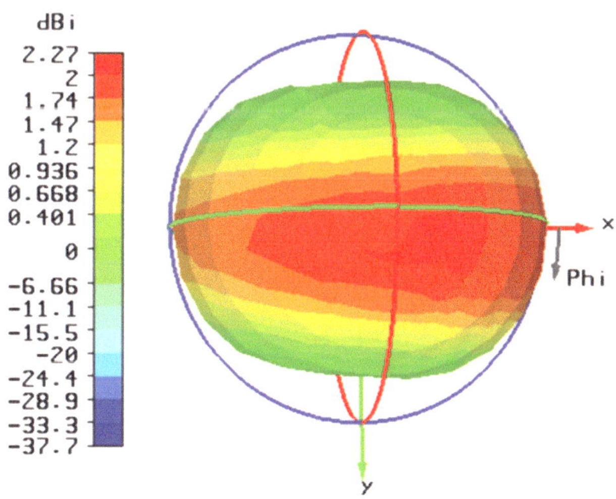

Fig. 13. Optimized total power distribute efficiency image of the pilot radiator with Ni/Ag/Ni thin film internal antenna handset at 870MHz (with CST program)

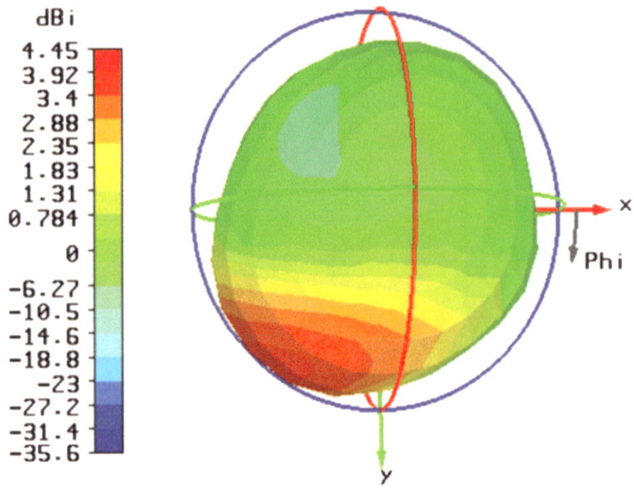

Fig. 14. Optimized total power distribute efficiency image of the pilot radiator with Ni/Ag/Ni thin film internal antenna handset at 1990MHz (with CST program)

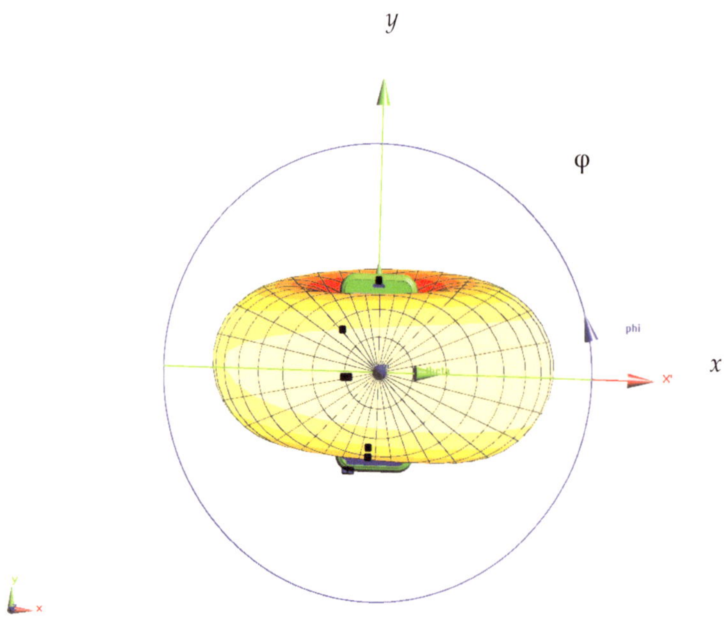

Fig. 15. Optimized 3D Far-field (θ , φ) radiation pattern image of the pilot radiator with Ni/Ag/Ni thin film internal antenna handset at 870MHz free space condition (with SEMCAD program)

Obviously say, the simulated and measured results of the proposed Ni/Ag/Ni sputter-deposit internal antenna show good agreement with each other in free space and SAM condition.

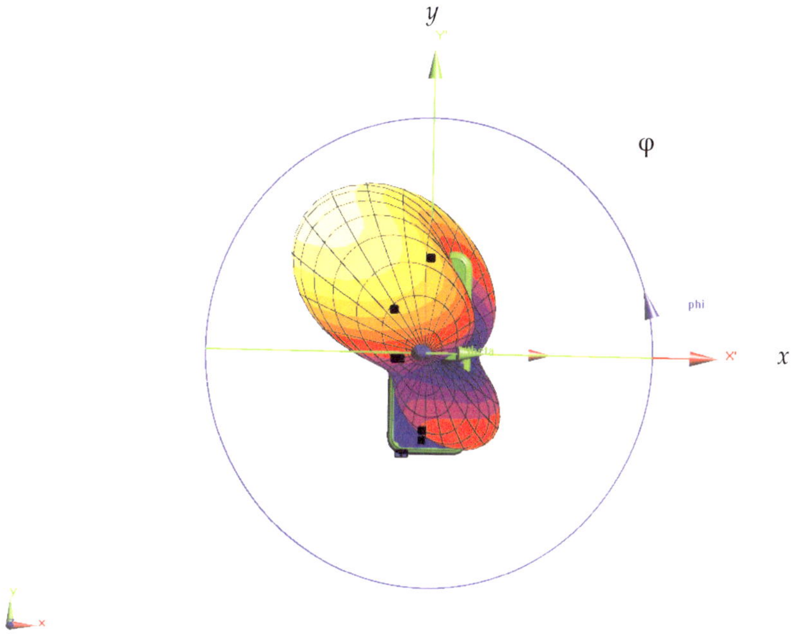

Fig. 16. Optimized 3D Far-field (θ , φ) radiation pattern image of the pilot radiator with Ni/Ag/Ni thin film internal antenna handset at 1990MHz free space condition (with SEMCAD program)

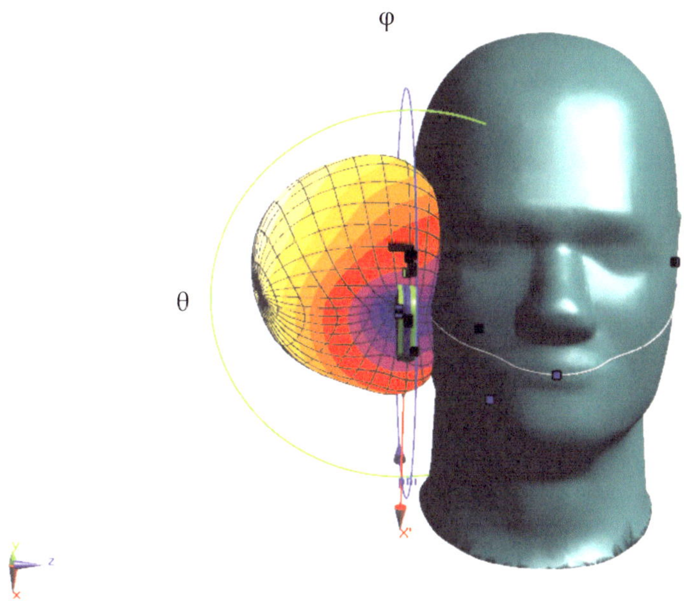

Fig. 17. Optimized 3D Far-field (θ , φ) radiation pattern image of the pilot radiator with Ni/Ag/Ni thin film internal antenna handset at 870MHz SAM condition (with SEMCAD program)

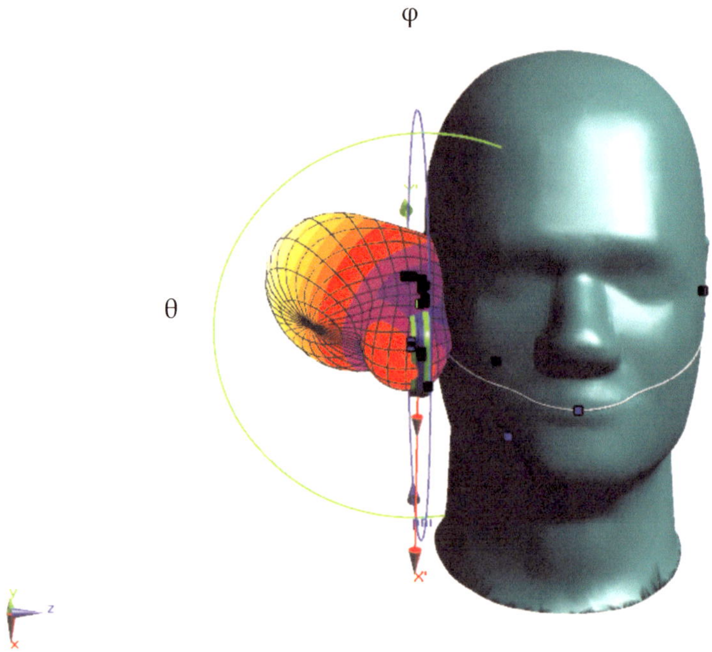

Fig. 18. Optimized 3D Far-field (θ , φ) radiation pattern image of the pilot radiator with Ni/Ag/Ni thin film internal antenna handset at 1990MHz SAM condition (with SEMCAD program)

3-D Far Field (θ , φ)	Free space		SAM	
	870MHz	1990MHz	870MHz	1990MHz
Total Radiated Power (P_{rad})	1.687W (32.27dBm)	0.853W (29.31dBm)	0.767W (28.84dBm)	0.676W (28.30dBm)
Total Isotropic Sensitivity (P_{TIS})	-105.28 dBm	-102.32dBm	-101.85dBm	-101.31dBm
Directivity (dB_i)	2.12	4.90	3.96	6.88
Gain (dB_i)	1.54	1.29	-0.17	2.20
Total Efficiency (η_{total})	0.84	0.42	0.38	0.34

Table 2. Comparisons of 3D Far-field (θ , φ) radiation pattern for the Ni/Ag/Ni sputter-deposit internal antenna handset at free space and SAM condition each frequencies (f = 870 MHz, 1990 MHz)

2.5 Characteristics of antenna performance with SAM condition

This section describes the radiation pattern characteristics of the carrier-based internal antenna and the sputter-deposit internal antenna. Figure 19 shows of radiation pattern results in SAM condition. The measured radiation pattern experiment is very significant for antenna performance aspects. At the same times this method can verify the close to real human effect. Figure 19 shows of the measured data of peak and average gain for carrier-based internal antenna radiation patterns, Figure 19 (a) shows the E1-plane (y-z plane) measured result, Figure 19 (b) shows E2-plane (x-z plane) and Figure 19 (c) shows H-plane (x-y plane) characteristics at 869MHz and 1930MHz, the carrier-based internal antennas same to measured in an anechoic chamber complied with CTIA (CTIA Certification, 2005).

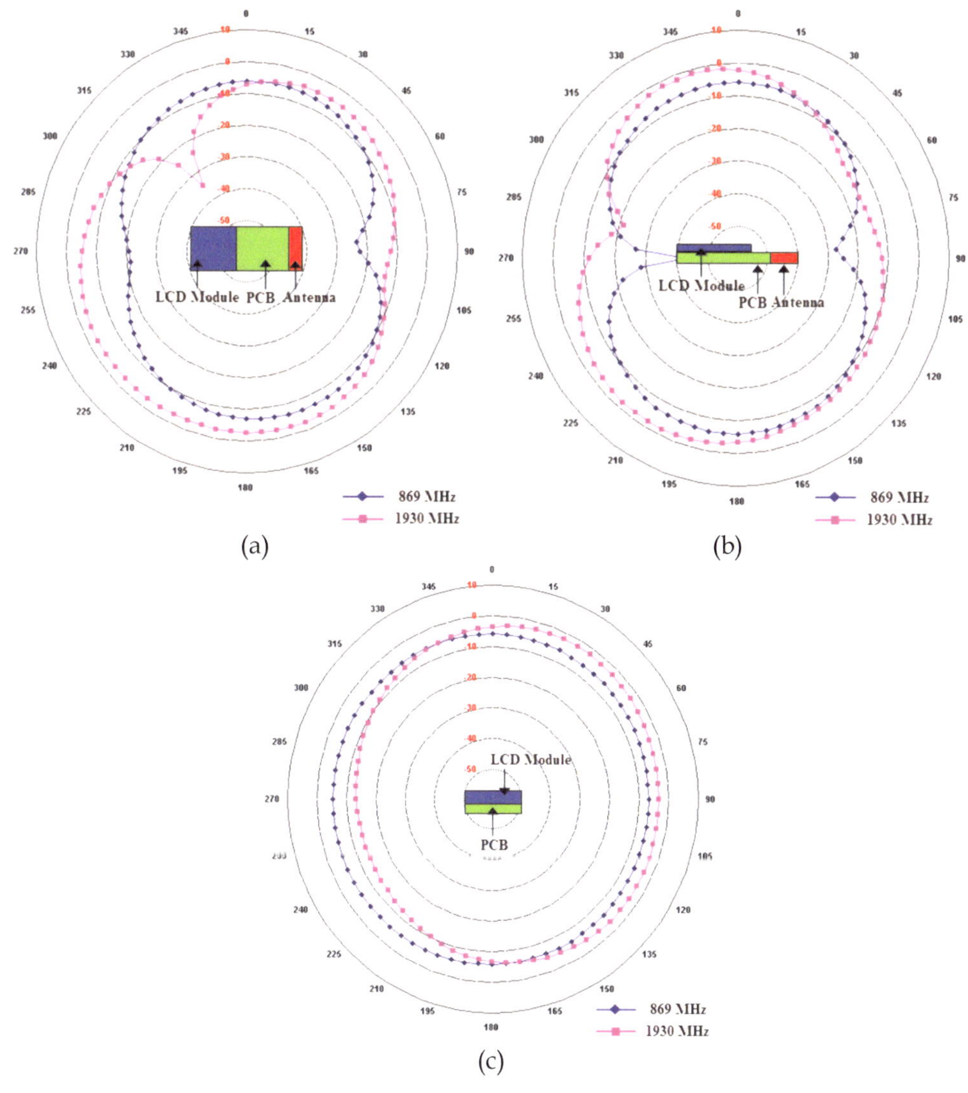

Fig. 19. Measured radiation pattern of E-plane and H-plane for the sputter-deposit Ni/Ag/Ni internal antenna handset at resonance (f = 869 MHz, 1930 MHz) (a) E1-plane, (b) E2-plane, (c) H-plane

The measured results of peak gain each E1, E2, and H-plane are listed in Table 3. Shows of the experiment result, the measured E1-plane (y-z) average radiation gains are each -6.05dBi and -5.55dBi at 869MHz and 1990MHz and then measured E2-planes (x-z) average radiation gains indicates -9.20dBi and -5.45dBi at 869MHz and 1930MHz also, the measured H-plane (x-y) average radiation gains are each -9.20dBi and -5.34dBi at 869MHz and 1930MHz, respectively. Furthermore, measured E1-plane (y-z) peak radiation gain results are -5.92dBi (165 degree) and -2.49dBi (335 degree) at 869MHz and 1990MHz and then the measured E2-planes (x-z) peak radiation gains are -5.89dBi (355 degree) and -1.44dBi (345 degree) at 869MHz and 1930MHz also, the measured H-plane (x-y) peak radiation gains indicates -5.37dBi (250 degree) and -2.36dBi (30 degree) at 869MHz and 1930MHz, respectively.

Consequently, two kinds of internal antenna radiation pattern show good agreement as well as meet for CTIA regulation. Especially, the proposed Ni/Ag/Ni thin film internal antenna result shows come to good basis on experiment. Therefore, in this research is enormous benefit such as extended to antenna carrier volume and adapted diversity topology for next generation wireless mobile antenna solution also cost effective.

Frequency	E1-plane (y-z)	E2-plane (x-z)	H-plane (x-y)
Gain Average			
869 MHz	-6.05 dBi	-9.20 dBi	-5.97 dBi
1930 MHz	-5.55 dBi	-5.45 dBi	-5.34 dBi
Gain Peak			
869 MHz	-5.92 dBi, 5 deg	-5.89 dBi, 355 deg	-5.37 dBi, 250 deg
1930 MHz	-2.49 dBi, 165 deg	-1.44 dBi, 345 deg	-2.36 dBi, 30 deg
Gain min			
869 MHz	-23.61 dBi, 85 deg	-42.88 dBi, 270 deg	-6.87 dBi, 85 deg
1930 MHz	-35.00 dBi, 325 deg	-21.54 dBi, 285 deg	-13.70 dBi,245 deg

Table 3. Measured E-plane and H-plane radiation pattern for the Ni/Ag/Ni sputter-deposit PIFA antenna handset at resonance (f = 869 MHz, 1930 MHz), E1-plane (y-z plane), E2-plane (x-z plane), and H-plane (x-y plane)

2.6 Characteristics of field test

In this section, outlines evaluating for wireless handset performance through the analysis of voice quality and handset sensitivity measurements. In particular, this experiment is considered collected voice quality measurements in live-network test beds. This method is close to user experience. In this experiment discusses the collected voice quality measurement, handset sensitivity, and field trial performance. Figure 20 describes a sound source of speak British English and portion of speak British English with metrico field trial system. It means that measurements made using non-speech signals, such as tones or white noise, are unrepresentative and misleading. Metrico field experiments operate with 5 sec for each of two talkers (one male, one female), 10 sec in total (Metrico Muse system). Therefore, these sections discuss the field trial results between the carrier-based internal antenna handset and the proposed sputter-deposit internal antenna handset.

The experiments methods for data generation consist of the usage of mobile phones while make a call inside cars. On the contrary, communicated base station located in possible to make a connection. The metrico field trial system can verify the communication error and data generation interact with mobile phone, which is uplink and downlink paths. This experiment test bed is used on country lanes in Figure 21. To figure out how many times disconnect a call and the variation of electric field strength in worst GSM field area is the purpose of this experiment

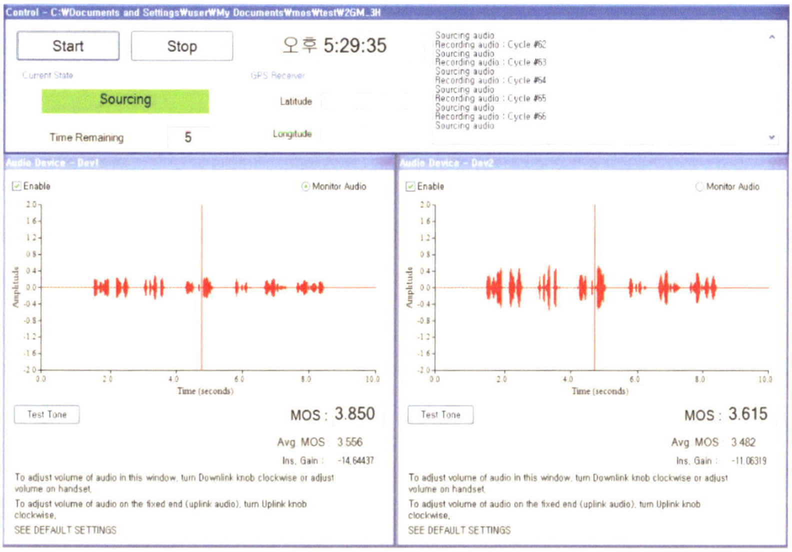

Fig. 20. Portion of the speak British English with metrico field trial system; 5 sec for each of two talkers (one male, one female), 10 sec in total

	Downlink MOS		Uplink MOS	
	Carrier-based Internal Antenna Handset	Sputter-deposit Internal Antenna Handset	Carrier-based Internal Antenna Handset	Sputter-deposit Internal Antenna Handset
Average	3.64	3.62	3.49	3.51
Standard Deviation	0.40	0.41	0.28	0.32
Maximum Score	4.10	4.07	3.92	3.94
Count	202	202	202	202
% MOS gather than 3.2	88%	87%	88%	85%
% MOS less than 3	9%	9%	7%	10%
% MOS less than 2.3	2%	1%	0%	1%

Table 4. Comparison of MOS distribution result the carrier-based internal antenna handset and the sputter-deposit based internal antenna handset at Maryland Baltimore Howard area (2G GSM network)

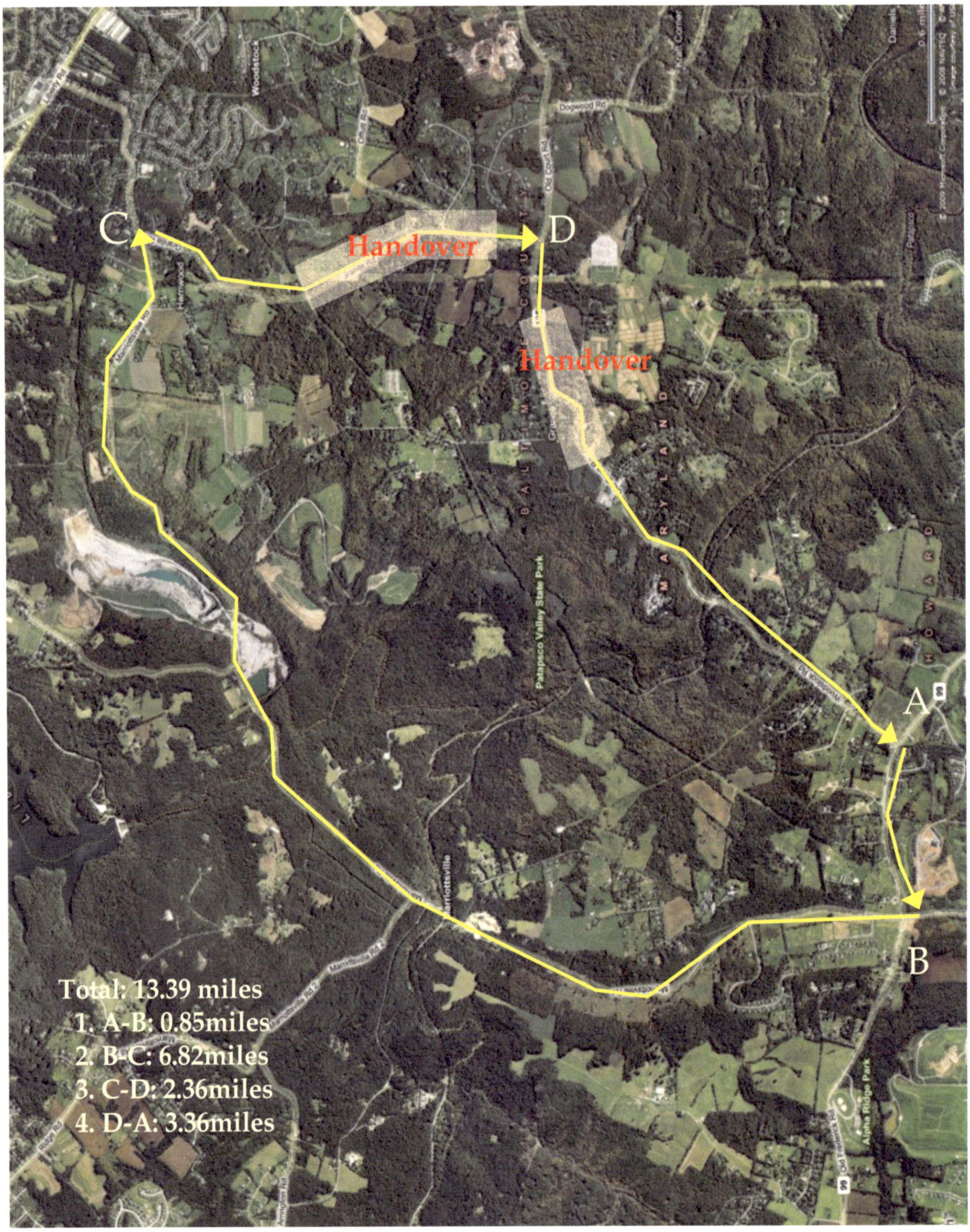

Fig. 21. Photo image of the 2G (GSM network) field trial route and the handover area information in USA (Microsoft Virtual Earth)

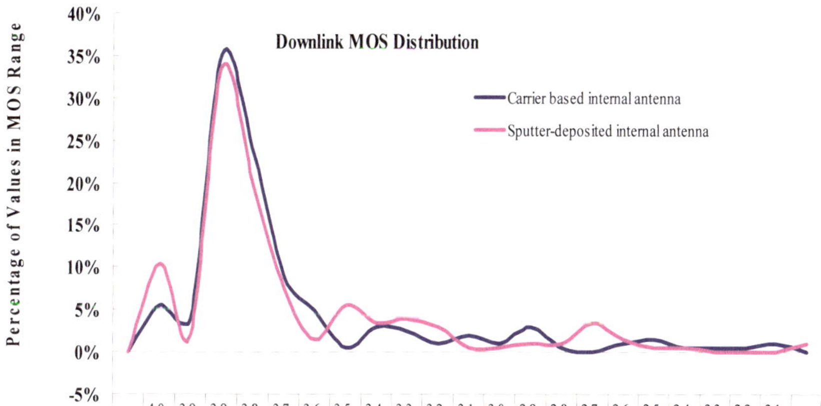

	>4.1	4.0-4.1	3.9-4.0	3.9-3.8	3.8-3.7	3.7-3.6	3.6-3.5	3.5-3.4	3.4-3.3	3.3-3.2	3.2-3.1	3.1-3.0	3.0-2.9	2.9-2.8	2.8-2.7	2.7-2.6	2.6-2.5	2.5-2.4	2.4-2.3	2.3-2.2	2.2-2.1	2.1-2.0	<2.0
Carrier based internal antenna	0%	5%	4%	35%	23%	9%	5%	0%	3%	2%	1%	2%	1%	3%	0%	0%	1%	1%	0%	0%	0%	1%	0%
Sputter-deposited internal antenna	0%	10%	2%	34%	19%	7%	1%	5%	3%	4%	3%	0%	0%	1%	1%	3%	1%	0%	0%	0%	0%	0%	1%

MOS Range

(a)

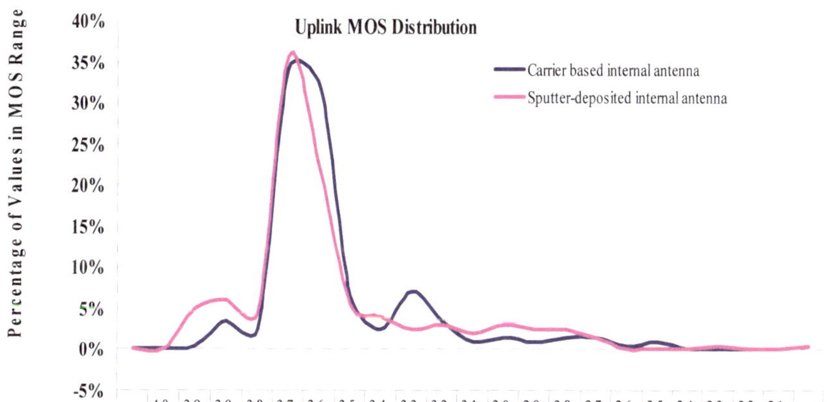

	>4.1	4.0-4.1	3.9-4.0	3.9-3.8	3.8-3.7	3.7-3.6	3.6-3.5	3.5-3.4	3.4-3.3	3.3-3.2	3.2-3.1	3.1-3.0	3.0-2.9	2.9-2.8	2.8-2.7	2.7-2.6	2.6-2.5	2.5-2.4	2.4-2.3	2.3-2.2	2.2-2.1	2.1-2.0	<2.0
Carrier based internal antenna	0%	0%	0%	3%	2%	34%	32%	6%	2%	7%	3%	1%	1%	1%	1%	1%	0%	1%	0%	0%	0%	0%	0%
Sputter-deposited internal antenna	0%	0%	5%	6%	4%	36%	22%	5%	4%	2%	3%	2%	3%	2%	2%	1%	0%	0%	0%	0%	0%	0%	0%

MOS Range

(b)

Fig. 22. Comparison of MOS distribution result the carrier-based internal antenna handset with sputter-deposit based internal antenna handset at Maryland Baltimore in USA (2G GSM network)

Figure 22 shows MOS distribution profile between the carrier-based internal antenna handset and the proposed sputter-deposit internal antenna handset in Maryland Baltimore Howard area. Computed the total distance is 13.39miles, Serving cell and neighbor cell network indicates each 133, 142, 145, 146 channel in GSM850 band also indicates 636, 630, 670 channel in GSM 1900 at start place, until now measured Rx sensitivity range is -80dBm to -103dBm around A boundary. Also bring about network handover at C to D area and D to A area in Figure 21. Figure 23 shows the real-log data about D to A handover area. Table 4 shows MOS distribution result comparison between the carrier-based internal antenna handset and the proposed sputter-deposit internal antenna handset. As a result, two kinds of handsets average MOS score marks over 3.0. Namely, carrier-based internal antenna handset and the sputter-deposit internal antenna handset is "fair" and "Good" performance in Uplink and Downlink paths. Because of Metrico field trial system basis on ITU defined theory, in other words, ITU defined voice quality ratio at five-point scale each called the mean opinion score (MOS) step, where 1 is poor and 5 is excellent quality. Therefore, the proposed sputter-deposit internal antenna handset shows good performance in the GSM network (ITU-T Rec., 2001).

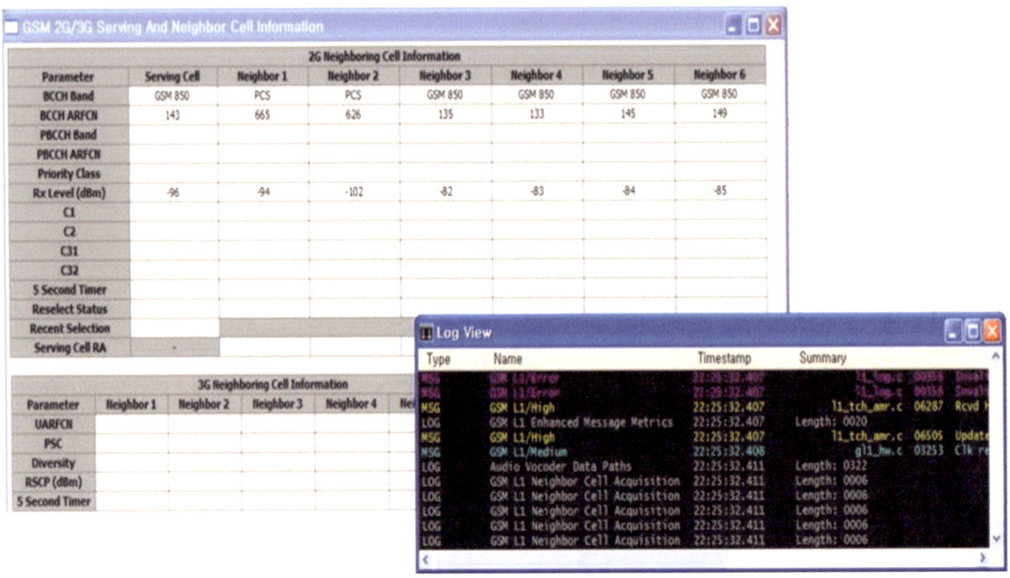

Fig. 23. Field trial log information of the GSM 2G network serving and Neighbor cell nearby Old Frederick Rd 99 and Woodstock Rd subway 125 junctions

3. Conclusion

This chapter fabricated and estimated of the novel Ni/Ag/Ni thin film internal antenna. Also, experiment characteristics of SWR and efficiency aspect for the proposed Ni/Ag/Ni thin film solution. The experiment Ni/Ag/Ni thin film internal antennas overall size is 43.0 × 24.0 × 0.0015mm^3 without feeding mechanism. As the demonstrated results, the proposed Ni/Ag/Ni thin film internal antenna has dual resonances in frequency which is suitable for a quad-band mobile communication system. Furthermore, the proposed Ni/Ag/Ni sputter-deposit planar inverted-F antenna occupies attractive size in volume. Briefly speaking of the

this experiment results, in this chapter reviewed fabrication process and characteristics for the Ni/Ag/Ni thin film internal antenna by sputter-deposited on polycarbonate substrate with 1.5um thickness, which is layers sputtered each 3,000Å, 8,000Å and 4,000Å, respectively. As a result, this solution is proven out last layer has characteristics of both materials Ag and Ni in distribution material spread spectrum. Moreover, the optimized SWRs and gain characteristics of radiation patterns are suitable for quad-band antenna. Also, this experiment verified comparison with carrier-based internal antenna having 40.4 × 19.2 × 6.25mm^3 volumes as well as this research performed current distribution and efficiency simulation used by CST and SEMCAD computing program.
The objective of this research is to perform an interaction with human head and field experiments used the carrier-based internal antenna and the sputter-deposit Ni/Ag/Ni thin film internal antenna. This research has the previous test result of radiation pattern characteristics with SAM condition from 824MHz to 1990MHz each E1, E2 and H plane on both side antennas. Also, this research is investigated for field trial effect comparing with reference handset including carrier-based internal antenna handset and the proposed sputter-deposit internal antenna handset having the Ni/Ag/Ni thin films at each 2G, 3G, and DOOC live-network test beds. As a consequence, the proposed sputter-deposit internal antenna handset obtained over 3.0 MOS score in the GSM network also, over 3.5 MOS score at WCDMA live-network at Baltimore Maryland in USA. The real field test result shows that the performance of the proposed Ni/Ag/Ni sputter-deposit internal antenna is almost same as carrier-based internal antenna, and especially at the 3G field, the strength of electric field is very stable. And then, this study found that the evidence converging to support the experiments from interaction with human head effect and field trial results (2G, 3G and DOOC field trial)
To conclude, this research is very attractive for adapting to wireless applications such as portable antenna, MediaFLO antenna, and so on. Furthermore, the Ni/Ag/Ni thin film internal antenna radiation performances show good agreement as well as meet for CTIA regulation and field test performances. Therefore, I firmly hold a view that the sputter-deposit internal antennas exercise is a far-reaching positive influence upon wireless mobile systems and embed modem or device application having several GHz for next generation mobile solution that is also cost effective.

4. References

F. Adachi, M. Sawahashi, and H. Suda, Wideband DS-CDMA for Next Generation Mobile Communications Systems, *IEEE Communications Magazine*, Vol. 36, pp. 56-69, 1998.

K. Hirasawa and M. Haneishi, Analysis, Design, and Measurement of Small and Low Profile Antennas, Artech House, ISBN 0-89006-486-5, 1991.

W. L. Stutzman and G. A. Thiele, Antenna Theory and Design, *John Willy & Sons Inc. press*, 1998.

D. Yuepeng, The Film Sputtering of Gadolinium and Chromium-doped Yttrium Aluminum Garnet, Ph.D Dissertation, *The University of Tennessee*, Knoxville, pp.1-14, 2005.

G. C. Stutzin, K. Rozsa, and A. Gallangher, Vacuum, Surface, and Films, *Journal of Vacuum* Science *& Technology*, Vol. 11, p 647, 1993.

CTIA Certification, Test Plan for Mobile Station over the Air Performance, Revision 2.1, *CTIA*, p.142, 2005.

C. T. P. Song, P. S. Hall, P. S. Ghafouri-Shiraz, and D. Wake, Triple Band Planar Inverted F Antennas for Handheld Devices, *Electronics Lett.*, Vol.36, p.112, 2000.

ITU-T Rec., An Objective Method for End-to-end Speech Quality Assessment of Narrowband Telephone Networks and Speech Codecs, *International Telecommunication Union*, Geneva, Switzland, P.862, 2001.

Metrico Muse system, http://www.metricowireless.com/

Microsoft Virtual Earth, http://maps.msn.com/

24

Design of CMOS Integrated Q-enhanced RF Filters for Multi-Band/Mode Wireless Applications

Gao Zhiqiang, Associate Professor
Department of microelectronics of Harbin Institute of Technology
China

Section I: Wideband reconfigurable CMOS Gm-C filter for wireless applications

1. Introduction

Recent developments in portable applications and systems have lead to a significant in wireless standards. Therefore, cost efficiency of CMOS technology implementation has been greatly enhanced with the emergence of multi-mode wireless applications. Now multi-mode/multi-band receivers are designed based on the scheme of reuse[1]-[3]. They avoid using multiple chipsets and can be made tunable which makes them more efficient in term of area and power consumptions. In a flexible receiver front-end, analog baseband filtering is a key task as it is used to select the required information under desired channel bandwidth. A large tuning range of the band-pass filter should be required for various wireless applications.

To meet different specifications for the desired channel in multimode receivers, there has been a tremendous amount of research [1-6] effort aimed at improving the performance of integrated reconfigurable continuous-time (CT) filters in recent years. However, due to the open-loop operation nature, Gm-C filters generally use operational transconductance amplifier (OTA) driving a capacitor load at the cost of moderate linearity, sensitivity to parasitics. Moreover, the major disadvantage of OTA is the large distortion caused by the nonlinear behavior of the transistors involved. To enhance the linearity of the OTA and avoid potential stability problems, an approach to linear Gm-C integrators with inherent CMFB is developed based on the techniques of the cross-coupled differential pairs and source degeneration with passive resistors. In Section 2, the high linear transconductor Gm is presented. The design of the Chebyshev bandpass filter is discussed, as such the simulated results of the bandpass filter are given in Section 3. The conclusion is given in Section 4.

2. The linearized techniques of transconductors

The transconductor in CMOS process is required for wideband reconfigurable Gm-C filter. Thus, the following section discusses the reported basic linearity technique in CMOS process. The transconductor linearity techniques can be broadly classified into three types: (a) source degeneration (b) cross coupling (c) active biasing.

2.1 Source degeneration

Figure 1 shows circuit implementation of the source degeneration technology. The feedback equivalent resistance R (or M3, M4) is called source degeneration resistor, and differential pair M1, M2 and source degeneration resistors consist of the structure of source degeneration. The output current of the structure is related to the input voltage by the following equation

$$I_O = I_{D1} - I_{D2} = (V_d - I_O R)\sqrt{2KI_{SS}}\sqrt{1 - \frac{K(V_d - I_O R)^2}{2I_{SS}}} \tag{2.1}$$

Where $K = \frac{1}{2}\mu_0 C_{ox}\frac{W}{L}$, I_{SS} is tail current source of the transconductor as shown in Figure 1, and the nonlinearity term of (2.2) is $V_d - I_O R$.

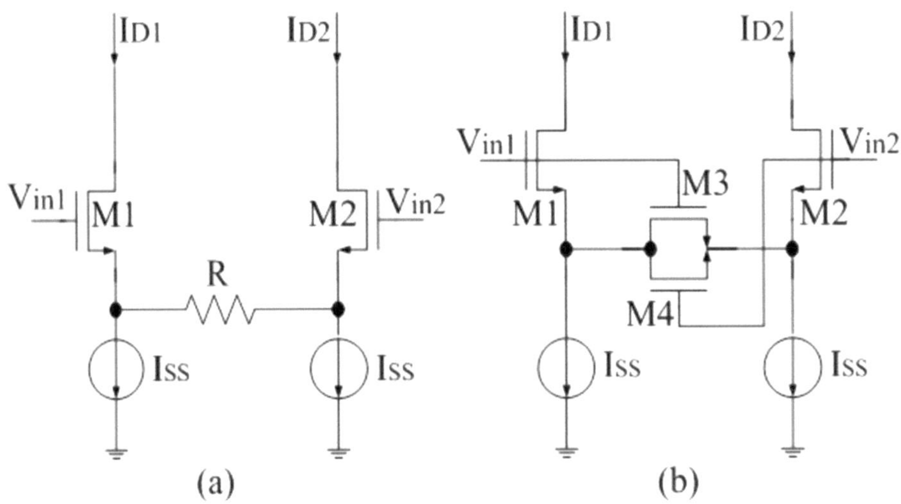

Fig. 1. The typical source-degeneration structure of transconductor

The transconductance Gm of source–degeneration structure can be about expressed as

$$Gm \approx \frac{g_m}{1 + g_m R} \tag{2.2}$$

When the resistance is much greater than 1/gm, the transconductance Gm≈1/R. However, this is traded-off with the noise and power consumption. In CMOS process, high quality passive resistance is achieved difficultly.

2.2 Cross coupling

A simple differential pair can cancel out the even order harmonics of distortion of transconductor output current. The remaining odd order harmonics can be cancelled out by two cross-coupling differential pairs with the same distortion but with different gm values. The circuit is shown in Figure 2.

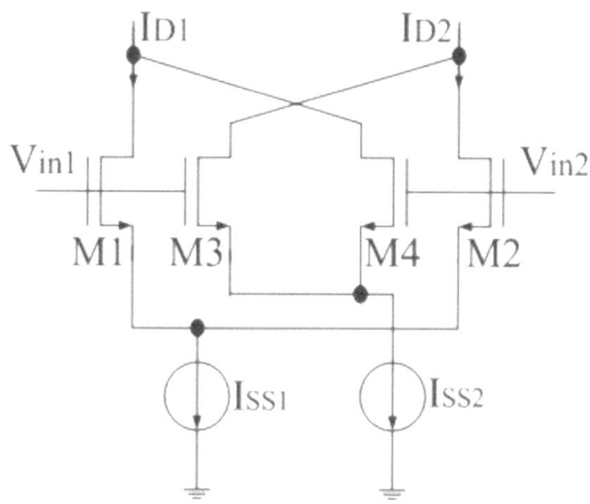

Fig. 2. The transconductor with differential cross-coupled pairs

The 3rd order harmonic is the main concern since it is now the most significant distortion. From Eq. (2-3), the 3rd order harmonic distortion (HD3) of output current can be obtained as:

$$HD_3 = \frac{K^{3/2}}{2\sqrt{2I_{SS}}} V_d^3 \tag{2.3}$$

Since HD3 depends on the ratio of $K^{3/2}$ and $Iss^{1/2}$ only, the distortion can be cancelled by connecting two differential pairs M1, M2 in parallel with M3, M4 as shown in Figure 2. The transconductor parameter $K_{3,4}$ and $K_{1,2}$ are related to I_{SS2} and I_{SS1} as follows:

$$\left(\frac{K_{3,4}}{K_{1,2}}\right)^3 = \left(\frac{(W/L)_{3,4}}{(W/L)_{1,2}}\right)^3 = \frac{I_{SS2}}{I_{SS1}} \tag{2.4}$$

The corresponding effective gm is then given by:

$$g_{meff} = g_{m1,2}[1 - \left(\frac{K_{3,4}}{K_{1,2}}\right)^2] = g_{m1,2}[1 - \left(\frac{I_{SS2}}{I_{SS1}}\right)^{2/3}] \tag{2.5}$$

According to equation (2.5), when $I_{SS2} \ll I_{SS1}$, the transconductance is approximated as linearity. But the noise performance is worse than that of a simple differential pair because 2 differential pairs are connected. However, the noise is not doubled because $K_{3,4} < K_{1,2}$.

2.3 Active biasing

The idea of active biasing is to make the biasing current compensate for the non-linear term:

$$I_{SS} = I_{DC} + \frac{KV_d^2}{2} \tag{2.6}$$

Where I_{DC} is the DC bias current, and V_d is input differential signal. Now the bias Iss supplies I_{DC} when $V_d = 0$ for the static bias. When there is a signal, an additional bias current $KV_d/2$ will compensate for the drop of the gm. This can be verified by inserting the new Iss into Eq. (2.7):

$$I_{D1} + I_{D2} = 2K(V_{gs} - V_{th})^2 \tag{2.7}$$

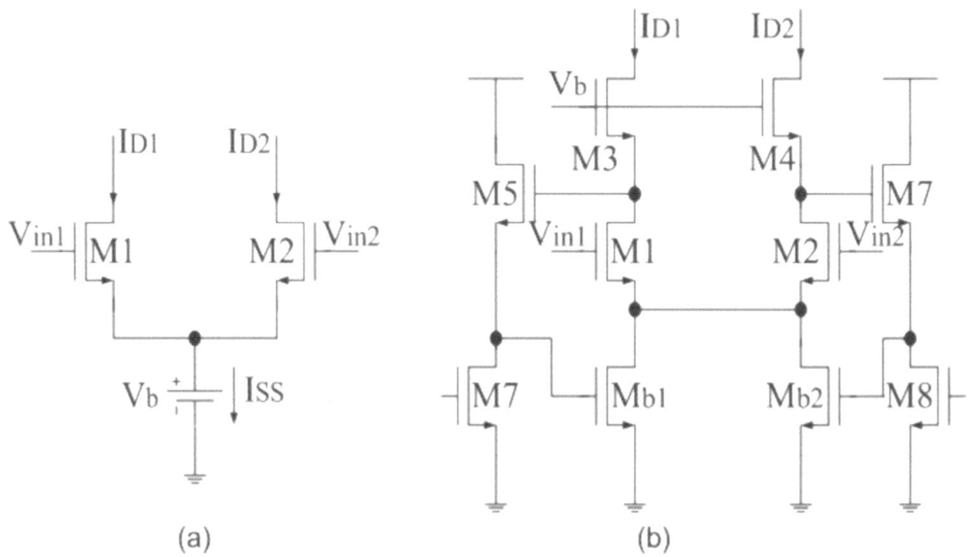

Fig. 3. The transconductor with active-biasing differential pair

In this design, all transistors are matched except M5-M8. For this cascode circuit, when there is an input signal, the same amplitude appears at the drains of M1 and M2 because the loading is $1/gm_{3,4}$ and $gm_{3,4}=gm_{1,2}$. The capacitance at that node and the loss of the level shifter M5-M8 are ignored. Both gates of M_{b1} and M_{b2} sense the differential voltage. Because the drains of M_{b1} and M_{b2} are connected together, a bias current is obtained as in Eqs. (2-26). The required active biasing is then established. But in the common-mode sense, now the conductance of M_{b1} and M_{b2} increases in phase with the input signal. This is a kind of feed-forward and thus causes a boost-up of the common-mode gain. As a result, CMRR drops and common-mode instability will be resulted.

2.4 The design of high linear transcoductor

The OTA is based on the Gilbert multiplier, which uses the two cross-coupled differential pairs (M1 - M2, M3-M4) as the input stage to reduce the nonlinearities as shown in Figure 6. Thank to mismatching of passive resistor in CMOS process, active source-degeneration resistor M_{R1} and M_{R2} is perfect choice. For this OTA structure, all transistors operate in the saturation region except for the transistors M_{R1} and M_{R2}. The MOS transistor is approximated as

$$\frac{1}{R_{eq}} \approx K_R(V_R - V_{th} - V_{CMS}) \tag{2.8}$$

Where K_R is relative to MOS process parameter, $V_{R1,\ 2}$ is control voltage of source degeneration resistor, and V_{CMS} is common-mode voltage of tail current source. The output current of the transconductance is

$$I_O = I_{O1} - I_{O2} = (I_{d1} - I_{d3}) - (I_{d2} - I_{d4}) = (I_{d1} + I_{d4}) - (I_{d2} + I_{d3})$$
$$= \sqrt{2KI_{DC1}}V_d\sqrt{1-\left(\frac{V_d}{2V_{dsat1}}\right)^2} - \sqrt{2KI_{DC2}}V_d\sqrt{1-\left(\frac{V_d}{2V_{dsat2}}\right)^2} \quad (2.9)$$

Where V_d is input differential voltage, I_{DC1}, I_{DC2} is drain terminal current M_{b1}-M_{b4} respectively. V_{dsat1}, V_{dsat2} is source-drain overdrive voltage M_{b1}-M_{b4} respectively. Expanding (2.9) in the Taylor series and considering the first three terms only, the even terms for differential is neglected, and (2.10) becomes

$$I_O = I_{O1} - I_{O2} \approx (g_{m1} - g_{m2})V_d - \frac{1}{8}\left(\frac{g_{m1}}{V_{dsat1}^2} - \frac{g_{m2}}{V_{dsat2}^2}\right)V_d^3 \quad (2.10)$$

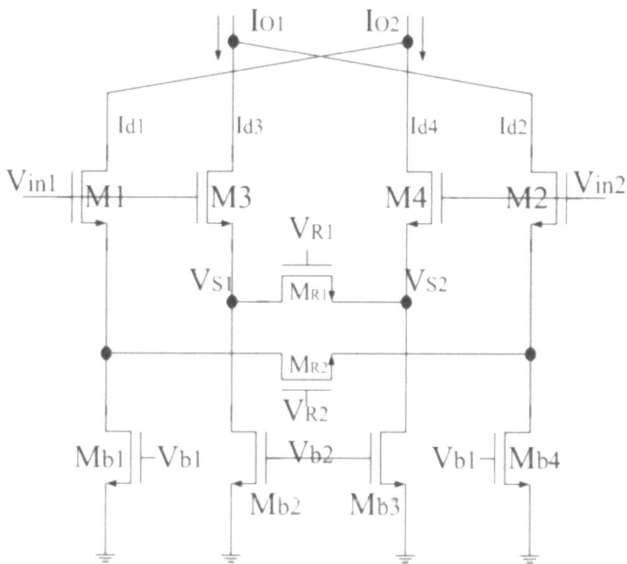

Fig. 4. The Gilbert OTA with source degeneration

Taking into account the mobility degradation, equation (2.10) is expressed as

$$I_O = I_{O1} - I_{O2} \approx \left(\frac{g_{m1}}{1+g_{m1}R_1'} - \frac{g_{m2}}{1+g_{m2}R_2'}\right)V_d$$
$$-\frac{1}{8}\left(\frac{g_{m1}}{V_{dsat1}^2(1+g_{m1}R_1')^3} - \frac{g_{m2}}{V_{dsat2}^2(1+g_{m2}R_2')^3}\right)V_d^3 \quad (2.11)$$

where $R_1' = R_1 + R_{\theta 1}$, $R_2' = R_2 + R_{\theta 2}$, $R_{\theta 1}$, $R_{\theta 2}$ are source series resistance of the mobility degradation, $R_\theta = \frac{2\theta}{K}$, and θ is the mobility reduction coefficient.

In equation (2.11), if the nonlinearity third-order term satisfies

$$\frac{g_{m1}}{V_{dsat1}^2(1+g_{m1}R_1')^3} - \frac{g_{m2}}{V_{dsat2}^2(1+g_{m2}R_2')^3} = 0 \tag{2.12}$$

Then the transconductance is expressed as

$$Gm = \frac{g_{m1}}{1+g_{m1}R_1'} - \frac{g_{m2}}{1+g_{m2}R_2'} \tag{2.13}$$

If the condition $R/\gg 1/g_m$ is satisfied, the transconductance can be obtained by

$$G_m \approx \frac{1}{R_1'} - \frac{1}{R_2'} \tag{2.14}$$

Figure 5 is overall structure of the high linear transconductor. Figure 6 shows the simulation of step response of the transconductance. When the dc common-mode voltage is about 1.67V, the transient-time response is less than 60ns, and the variation of common-mode voltage is less than 15mV. We use 5pF as the loading capacitance to verify the AC response of the transconductor. The bandwidth of unit gain is about 98MHz, and the phase margin is about 76 degree as shown in Figure 7.

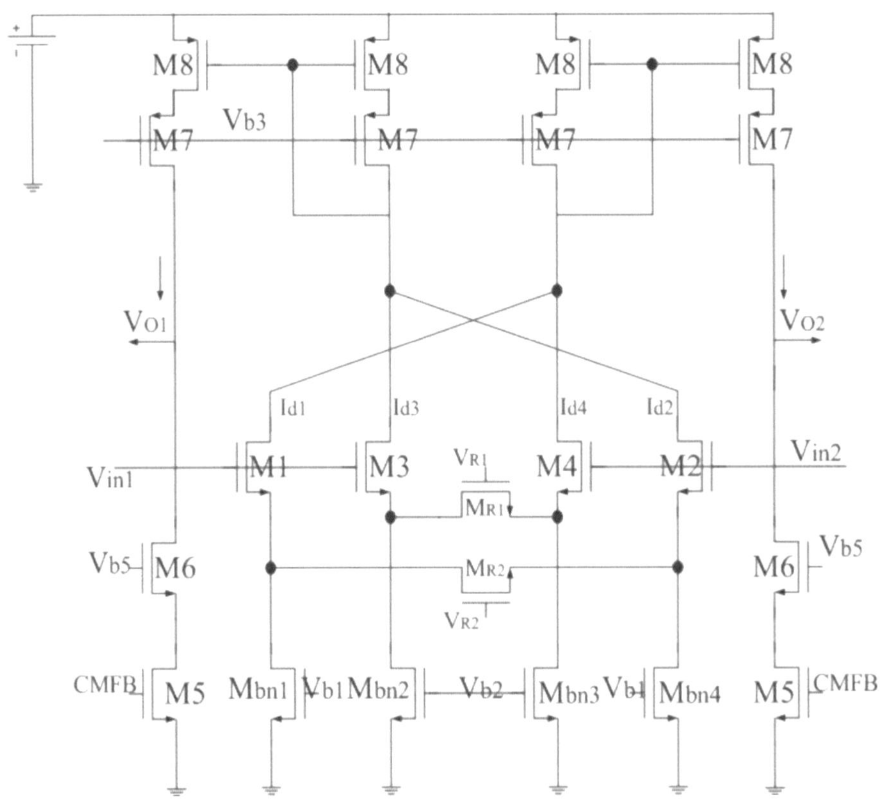

Fig. 5. The overall structure of high linear transconductor

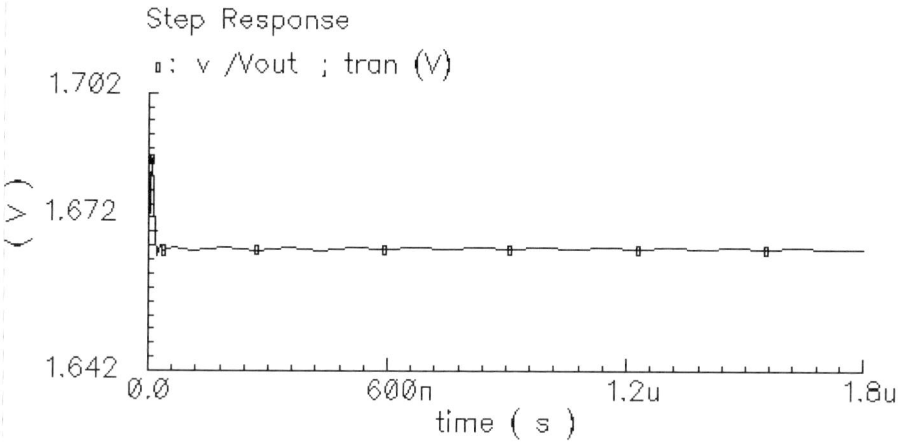

Fig. 6. Step response of the proposed transconductor

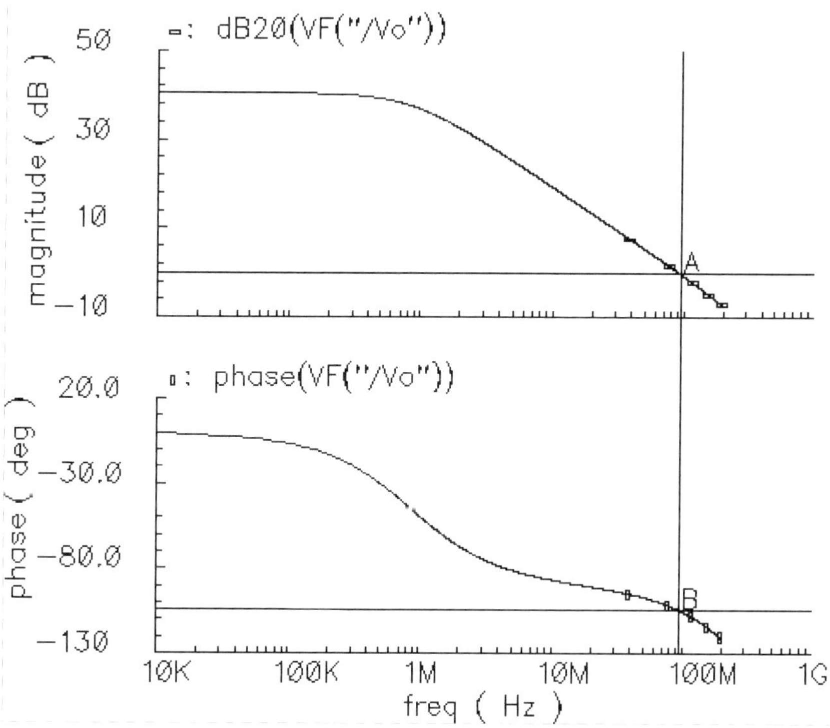

Fig. 7. The response of amplitude and phase for the transconductor

Figure 8 shows the simulated Gm plot with the input voltage. The linear range of the proposed active degenerative resistance (ADR) Gm of cross-couple differential pair is about ±1V. The linear range is higher than the other Gm of differential cross-coupled pair without ADR and differential pair with ADR (source degeneration structure as shown in Figure 2). When the operating frequency is 4MHz, the third-order intermodulation IM3 is -72dB as shown in Figure 9.

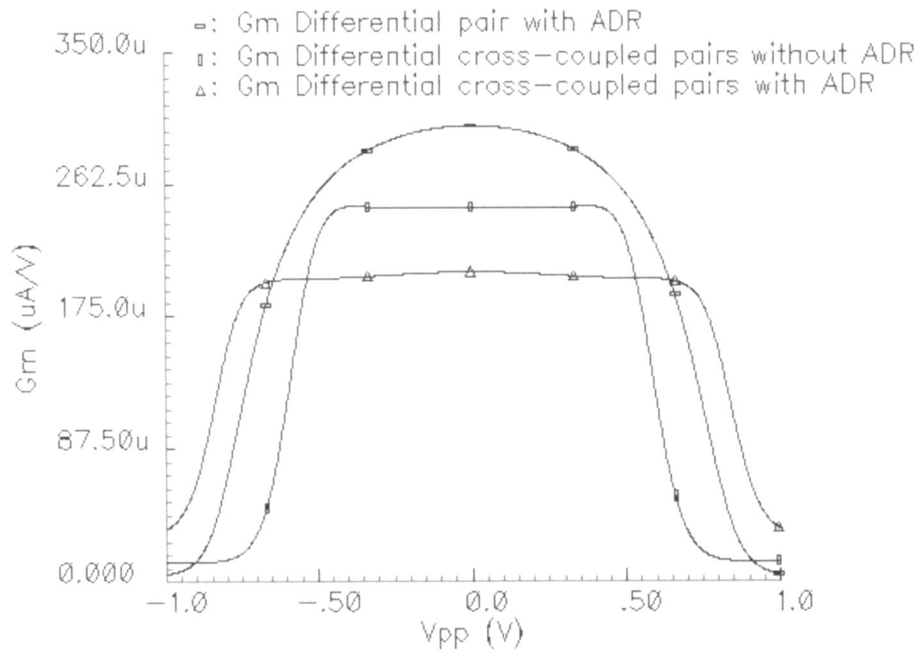

Fig. 8. Simulation of linearity for the three differential linearized transconductor

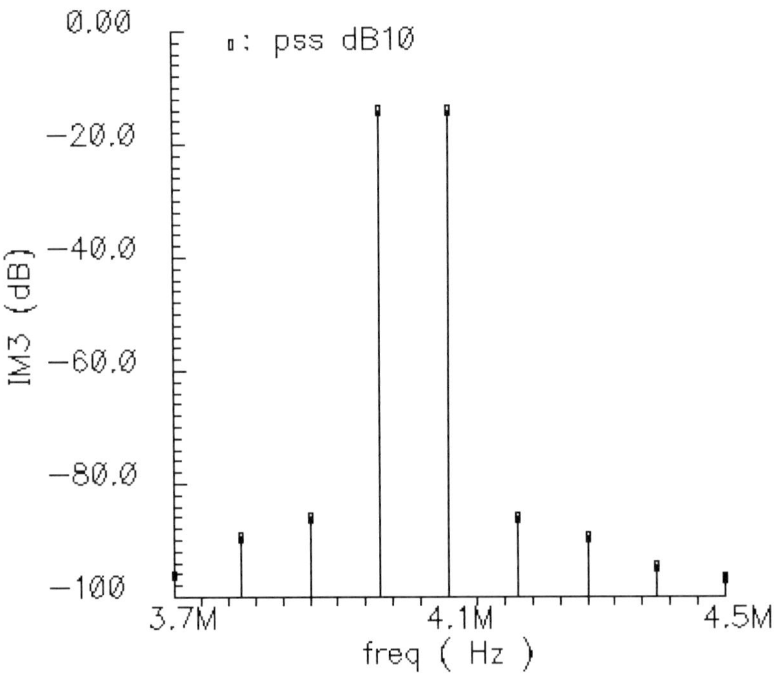

Fig. 9. Response of third-order intermodulation distortion of the OTA at 4MHz

3. Circuit design of Gm-C filter

Using the proposed high linear OTA, a six-order Chebyshev bandpass filter is designed. To obtain a passband frequency with minimal sensitivites to individual component values, the filter topology is derived from a doubly terminated passive RLC lowpass prototype as shown in Figure 10. The associated signal flow graph (SFG), shown in Figure 11 is obtained by writing down the state equations for six reactive components. Notice that the SFG contains only integrators and summers. The bandpass filter topology is derived by applying the well-known lowpass to bandpass transformation

$$S_L = \frac{s^2 + \omega_0^2}{s\omega_C} \tag{2.15}$$

Where S_L is the normalized lowpass Laplace variable, ω_0 is the center frequency, and ω_C is the bandwidth of the bandpass filter to be designed.

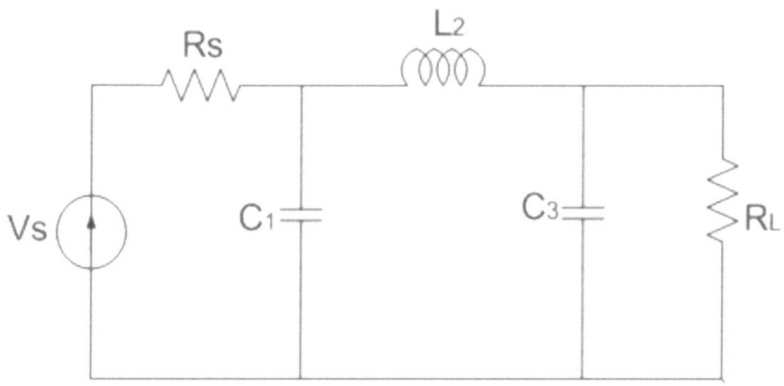

Fig. 10. The passive RLC lowpass prototype of low-pass filter

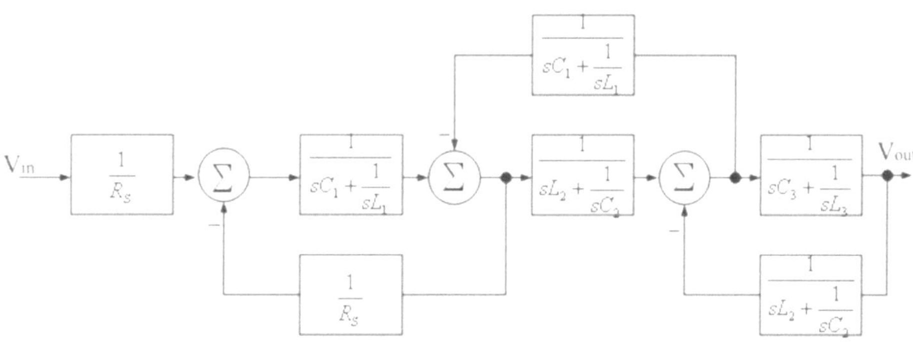

Fig. 11. The signal flow of the transfer function from passive low-pass filter to bandpass filter

The design method is based on component substitution. A ground inductor produces two transconductors and one capacitor, while a floating inductor need four transconductors and one capacitor as shown in Figure 12(a),(b). Figure 12(c) shows the use of a differential transconductor connected as a pseudo-resistor. The bandpass filter topology is obtained by replacing six integrators with six coupled resonators.

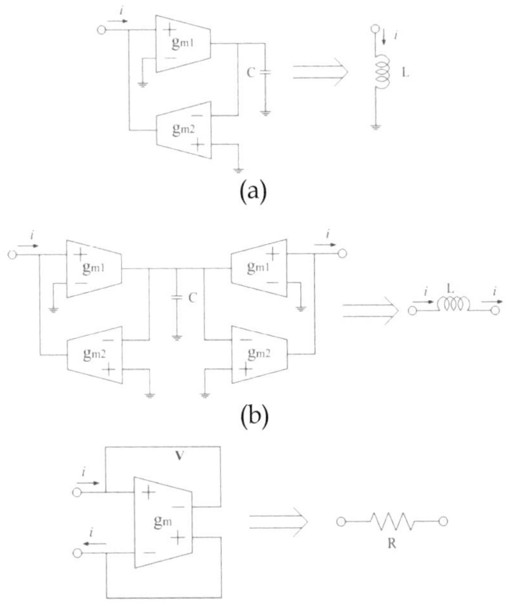

Fig. 12. Methods of passice component substitution

The complete filter is shown in Figure 13. The resonator is composed of two Gm-C integrators with feedback loop.

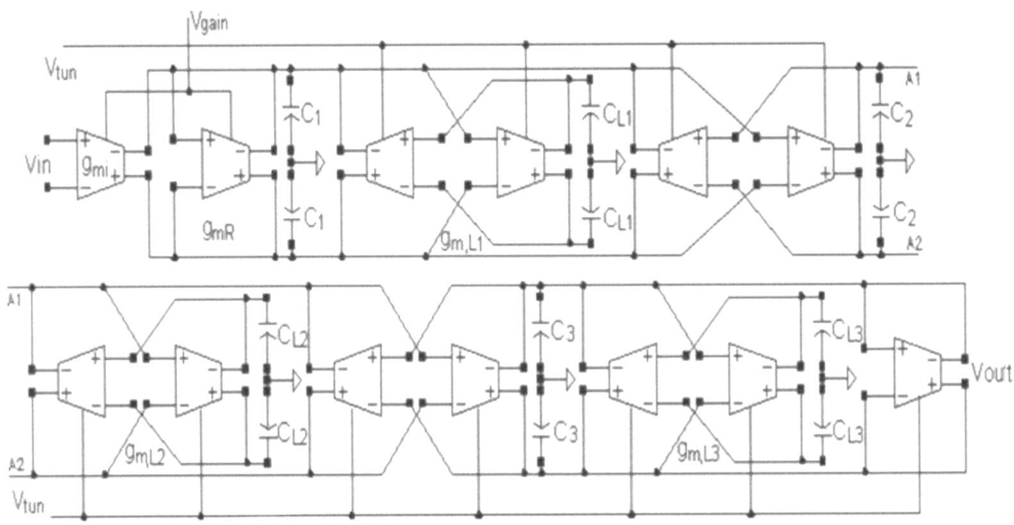

Fig. 13. The sixth-order Chebshev OTA-C bandpass filter

The proposed filter is simulated with Cadence's Spectre softwares using TSMC 0.25um standard CMOS process models. Simulation results in Figure 14 and Figure 15. Figure 13 shows the AC tuning-Q response of the filter when the tuning center frequency is about 2MHz. The center frequency tuning range is about 0.5MHz to 10MHz as shown in Figure 14.

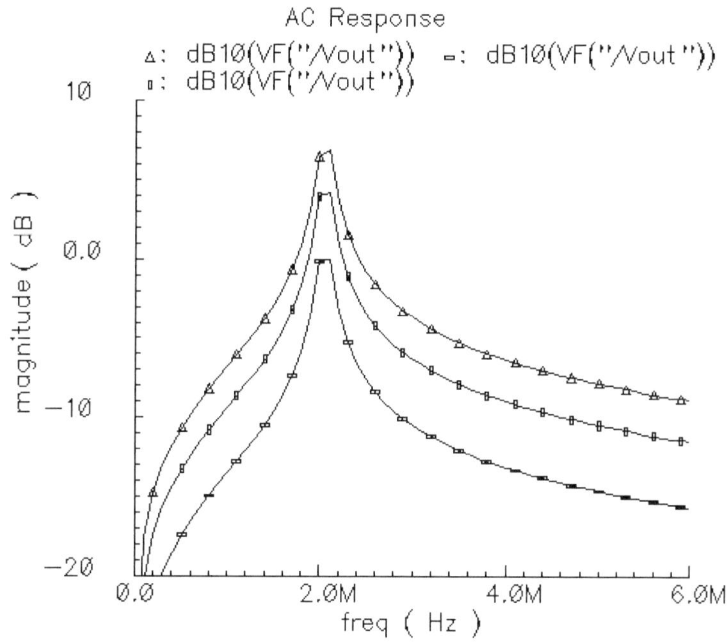

Fig. 14. The tuning-Q response of the Gm-C bandpass filter at f_c≈2MHz

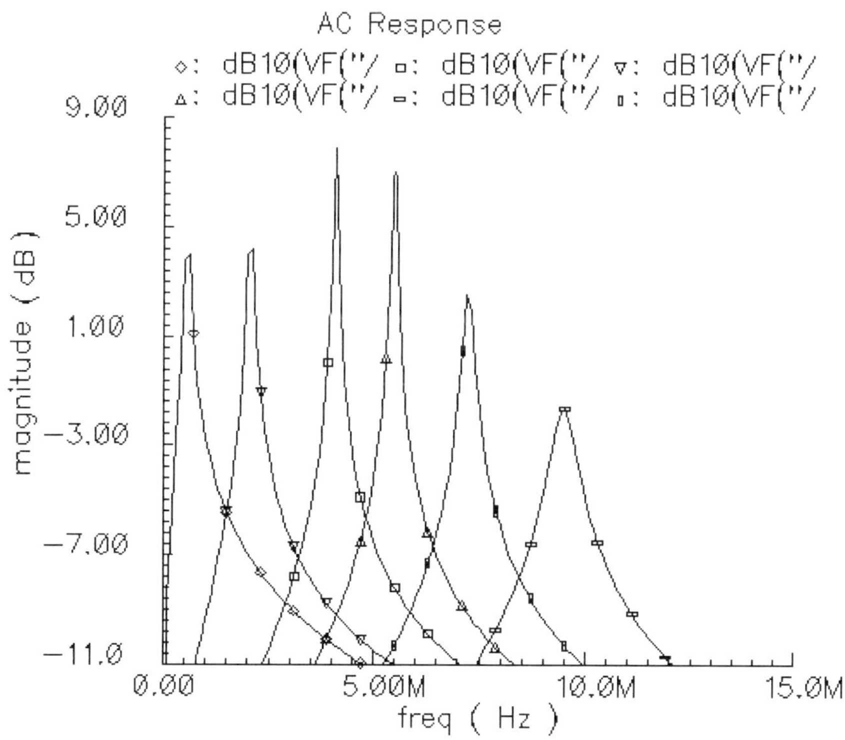

Fig. 15. Tuning center frequency of the OTA-C bandpass filter

4. Conclusion

A full CMOS six-order Gm-C Chebyshev filter based on passive LC-ladder synthesis is designed in TSMC standard 0.25um CMOS process, which uses a highly linear operational transconductance amplifier (OTA) based on cross-coupled differential pairs with source-degeneration structure, which exhibits a wide product of gain-bandwidth, and high linearity. The simulated results show the center frequency tuning range of the filter is from about 0.5MHz to 10MHz and the maximum quality factor of 150 at the center frequency 4.3MHz. The filter is suitable for multi-band wireless applications.

5. References

[1] J. Ryynäen, S. Lindfors, et al. Integrated Circuits for Multi-Band Multi-Mode Receivers. *IEEE Circuits and System Magazine*. 2006, 6(2): 5-16.

[2] Ahmed N. M.,Edgar S. S., Jose S. M., A fully balancedpseudo-differential OTA with common-Mode Feedforward and Inherent common-mode feedback detector *IEEE J.Of Solid-State Circuits*, vol.38,No.4, p.663-668 2003.

[3] L. E. Aguado, K. K. Wong, et al. Coexistence Issues for 2.4 GHz OFDM WLANs. *3G Mobile Communication Technologies*, London, 2002: 400–404.

[4] D. Chamla, A. Kaiser. A Gm-C Low-pass Filter for Zero-IF Mobile Applications with a Very Wide Tuning Range. *IEEE Journal of Solid-State Circuits*. 2005, 40(7): 1443-1450.

[5] A. D. Sanchez, R. Anglulo, J., et al. A CMOS Four Quadrant Current/ Transconductance Multiplier, *Analog Integrated Circuits Signal Process*. 1999, 19(2): 163-168.

[6] R. G. Carvajal, et al. The Flipped Voltage Follower: A Useful Cell for Low-Voltage Low-Power Circuit Design, *IEEE Transactions on Circuits and System*-I: Regular Paper. 2005, 52(7): 1276-1289.

Section II: A RF LC Q-enhanced CMOS filter for wireless receivers

1. Introduction

Despite decades of research in developing "single-chip" radio transceivers, most designs continue to rely on off-chip components for RF bandpass filtering. Implementing these filters on-chip remains nearly as challenging today due to problems in meeting system requirements. Recent advances in silicon-on-chip IC processes targeted at RF designs, however, offer the possibility of producing on-chip filters in the coming years using Q-enhancement techniques.

CMOS technology is an attractive solution due to the low cost, high-level integration. One of prevalent off-chip component required in wireless receiver circuits is RF bandpass filter, usually realized with a surface acoustic wave (SAW) or ceramic device. If on-chip high frequency filters with acceptable electrical characteristics can be realized, this would eliminate or reduce the need for these currently required off-chip filters. This implementation of integrated filters could lead to complete communications system design solutions on monolithic chip that would decrease the complexity, reduce the size, lower the power and cost of wireless transceiver circuits. However, the use of on-chip RF bandpass filters in commercial radio transceivers has been limited so far by inferior performance relative to system requirements. Such requirements include: narrow bandwidths, high linearity, low insertion and noise figure, and the need for low-power consumption in wireless system of aerospace applications. This fact has made the acceptance of on-chip designs much more difficult than it would be if the system specifications were more relaxed, pushing radio designers to embrace modified, and generally problematic, radio architectures such as the direct-conversion, or zero-IF schemes. If on-chip bandpass filters are accepted into commercial products, they must at least compete with the performance of products designed around these architectures.

In this section, we outline the alternatives for building on-chip bandpass filters practical considerations in section 2. The design of the integrated on-chip 1.8V 2.14GHz Q-enhanced LC filter using silicon CMOS process is presented in section 3. The simulated results of the filter presented are provided in section 4. Finally in section 5, conclusion is drawn.

2. Filter technology

A wide range of technologies exists for implementing RF bandpass filters, as illustrated in Figure 16.

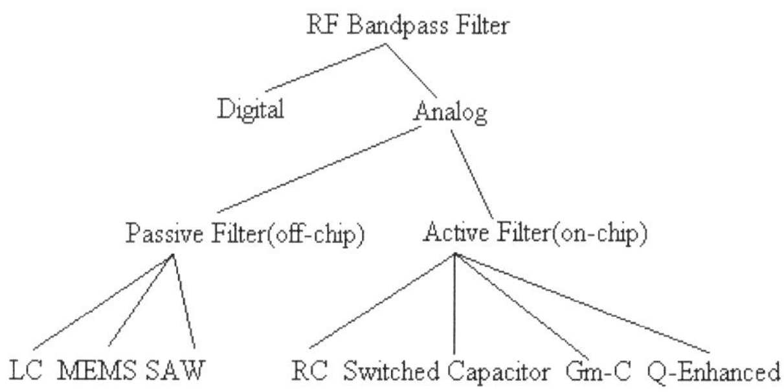

Fig. 16. Taxonomy of RF bandpass filter implementations

In theory, digital filters could implement any filter desired, and achieve true "software-radio" realizations. However, their applications are still generally limited to baseband frequency due to problems with power consumption and noise at high frequencies. To illustrate these problems, bounds on power consumption were developed in based on CV^2f considerations, because the scale of the digital filter has at least thousands of transistors and each of the transistors is considered as source of the noise. If the digital filter is operated at RF band, the power consumption and noise of the filter is large enough to beyond imagination.

Currently, however, on-chip RF bandpass filtering remains an analog endeavor. Here, the choices involve passive or active designs, each with several implementation possibilities including LC, and fully active architectures. In these active architectures, RC filter and switched capacitor filter isn't suited for high frequencies application. Although Gm-C filter can be operated at high frequencies, it poses its own drawbacks, namely, large power consumption and high noise contribution. A promising solution is to implement a active LC filter using on-chip passive elements with loss compensation circuitry to improve the effective quality factor [1, 3-7, 10].

3. Q-enhanced filter design

3.1 On-chip spiral inductor

The design and characterization of on-chip inductors is central to the implementation of high performance Q-enhanced LC filters. In a typical two-metal silicon IC process, these inductors are fabricated using planar spiral geometries as illustrated in Fig. 17. Top layer metallization usually provides the lowest resistivity and capacitance to the underlying substrate and is therefore used for the spiral turns, while the lower metallization layer is used for connection to the spiral center.

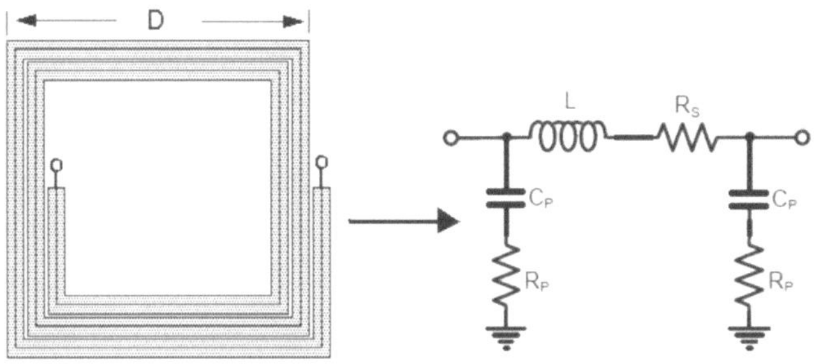

Fig. 17. Top view of an on-chip spiral inductor and its electrical model

In practice, electrical characteristics of the integrated inductor are generally frequency dependent and are more precisely described with a lumped-element model of greater complexity. A commonly used square-spiral IC layout and a more accurate electrical model for the inductor, the п-model, are shown in Figure 2. In this model, Rs represents the resistive losses in the metal traces of the inductor, any contact losses, and losses attributable to eddy currents in the substrate. Note that the top branch of Figure 2, which is composed of series resistor R_S, along with the inductance L represents the simplified series resistance model for the inductor shown in Figure 2. The substrate capacitance is modeled by Cp, and R_p represents loss caused by substrate conductance. With the help of a patterned ground shield, the electric field from the lossy substrate [3][10]. Thus, the only dominant loss due to the serious resistance R_S, and to cancel it, it is necessary to implement a loss compensation mechanism that effectively introduces a negative resistance of the same magnitude in series with R_S.

3.2 Q enhancement

A primary method for increasing the Q of non-ideal on-chip resonators is through the use of active devices to create negative resistance. Although methods that include phase-shifted current feedback via coupled inductors [21] have been investigated, the direct use of active devices as negative resistors is the prevalent Q enhancement technique. Single-ended negative resistance methods have been documented [23-25], while the more common differential method using a cross-coupled transistor pair is presented in Figure 18. The voltage to current ratio indicates the effective negative resistance at the terminals of the cross-coupled MOSFET shown in the figure and is described by

$$R = -\frac{2}{g_{mQ}} \tag{2.16}$$

It is clear from Figure 18 and Equation (2.16) that the effective negative resistance can be adjusted by changing the bias source, I_Q, and thereby the transconductance, g_{mQ}, of the differential pair MQ1, MQ2. This facilitates electronic tuning of this loss-canceling mechanism.

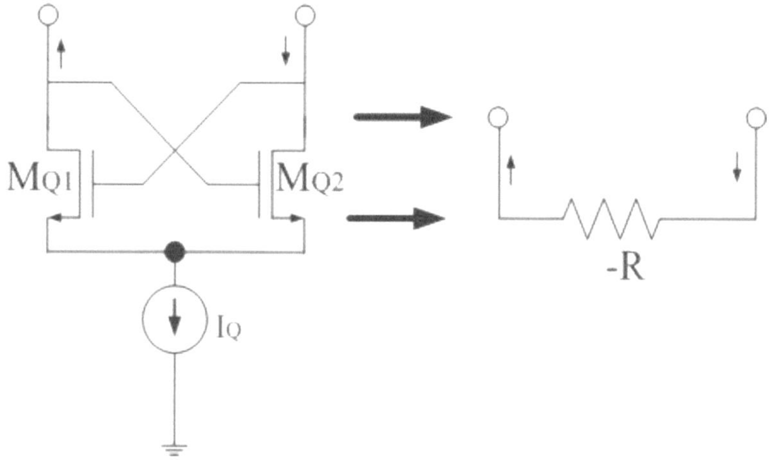

Fig. 18. Cross-coupled MOSFET negative transconductance

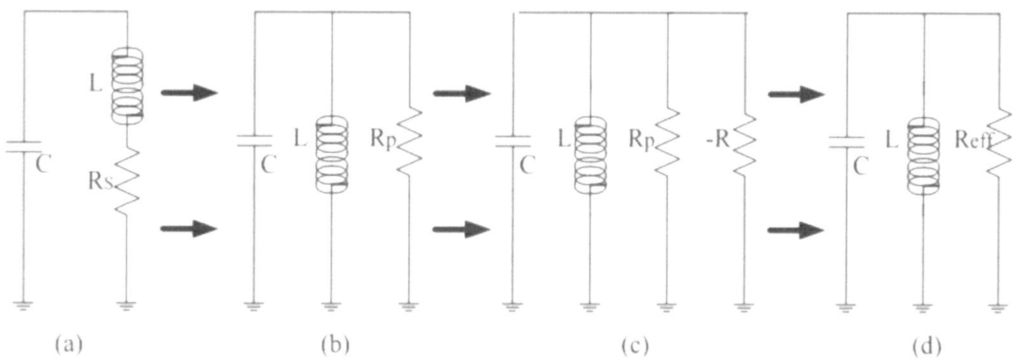

Fig. 19. Q-enhanced LC circuit

The concept of Q-enhancement for an LC tank circuit with parallel-connected negative resistance is illustrated in Figure 18-19, with the series resistance inductor model utilized to simplify the analysis. We assume for now that a lossy inductor and a capacitor can be simplistically modeled as shown in Figure 19(a), in which R_S represent the losses in the inductor. We can compensate the losses by connecting negative resistor in parallel with the LC tank as shown in Figure 19(c). In this approach, the negative resistance has been implemented negative resistance –R as shown in Figure 17 to cancel the loss represented by R_p. The effective parallel resistance R_{eff} and the effective quality factor Q_{enh} of the LC resonator as shown in Figure 19(d) is given by

$$R_{eff} = R_p // \frac{-1}{g_m} = \frac{1}{1-g_m R_p} R_p \tag{2.17}$$

and

$$Q_{enh} = \frac{R_{eq}}{X_L} = \frac{1}{1-g_m R_p} Q_0 \tag{2.18}$$

Where Q_0 is the self-tuning quality factor of the circuit as illustrated in Figure 19(a). It should be noted that as $g_m R_p$ continues to increase and approaches the unit, the value of Q_{enh} is infinite and the circuit (theoretically and practically) become an oscillator.
The prototype circuit of the second-order RF Q-enhanced bandpass filter based on the above negative-resistance techniques is shown in figure 20. Common-source transistor M1 and M2 are employed for the input buffer stage. They are large devices and biased to have low-input impedance and small distortion. Two pair of PMOS transistors M_C are varactors which are used to tune the center frequency of the filter and also adjust the quality factor of the filter through DC voltage V_{con}. The PMOS M_C capacitors are operated in depletion and inversion regions within the tuning range. The negative-resistance circuit can be realized by cross-coupled differential pair M_{Q1} and M_{Q2}. The negative resistance is $-2/g_m$ if we assume that the two transistors have the same size. As such, the negative resistance can be adjusted by current source I_Q.

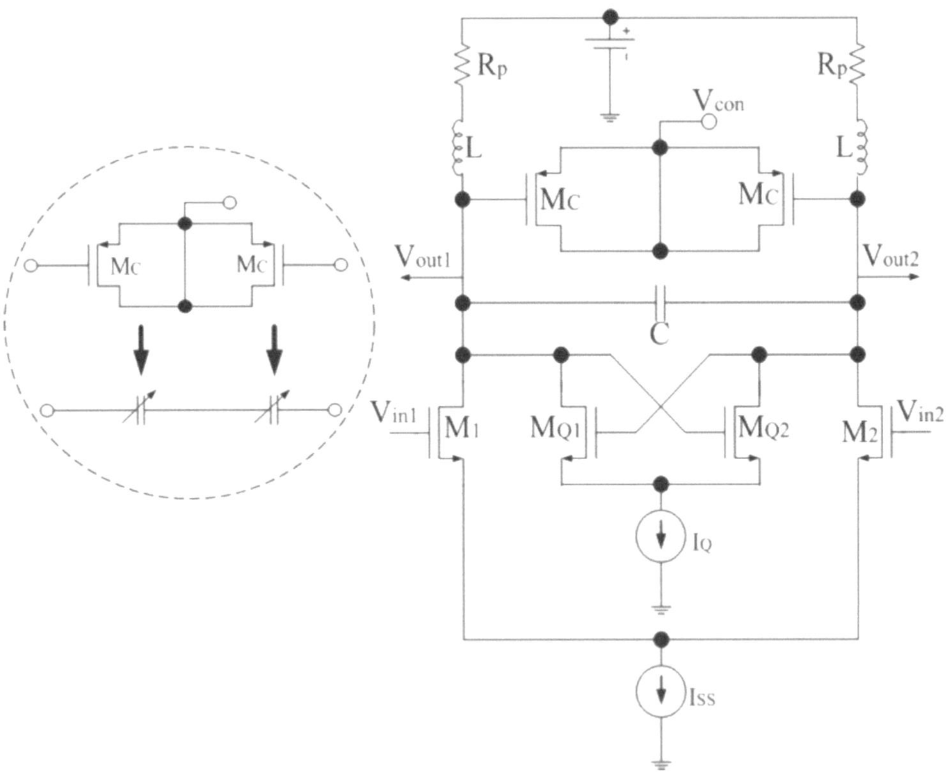

Fig. 20. A 2nd Q-enhanced on-chip LC bandpass filter

The transfer function, quality factor Q, and center frequency ω_0 of the biquad Q-enhanced filter can be expressed as

$$H(s) = \frac{\frac{g_{m,in}}{C_{tot}}(s + \frac{R_p}{L})}{s^2 + (\frac{R_p}{L} - \frac{g_{mQ}}{C_{tot}})s + \frac{1}{LC_{tot}}(1 - g_{mQ}R_p)} \tag{2.19}$$

$$Q = \frac{R_p C_{tot}}{\sqrt{LC_{tot}}(1 - g_{mQ} R_P)} \qquad (2.20)$$

$$\omega_0 = \frac{1}{\sqrt{LC_{tot}}} \qquad (2.21)$$

Where $C_{tot}=C+2C_{gmc}+2C_{gm,in}+2C_{gmQ}$, C_{gmc} is the parasitic capacitance of transistor Mc, $C_{gm,in}$ is the parasitic capacitance of input buffer M_1, M_2, C_{gmQ} is the parasitic capacitance of transistor M_{Q1}, M_{Q2}. $g_{m,in}$ and g_{mQ} are the transconductance values of the input buffer M_1, M_2 and Q-enhanced cross-coupled differential pair M_{Q1} and M_{Q2}, respectively.
To facilitate a theoretical noise analysis of the circuit, an appropriate noise model for the MOSFET and passive components is required. For noise modeling, passive L and C components will be considered noiseless. The accepted expression is used for passive resistors and transistors. As shown in Figure 19, the mean square noise contributions of each component at the center frequency are given by

$$NF = 1 + \frac{8kT\gamma(g_{mQ} + g_{m\blacklozenge in}) + 8kTR_p}{4kTR_S g_{m,in\blacklozenge}^2} \qquad (2.22)$$

4. Simulation results

To verify the design of the Q-enhanced RF bandpass filter, the filter was simulated with TSMC 0.18μm CMOS technology. At the same time, in order to test the circuit, the external wideband transformers are employed to serve as the impedance matching. The quality factor Q, gain S21, and noise performance is simulated with Cadence Spectre tools as shown in Figure 21-23. The input reflection coefficient S_{11} is about –23dB when the center frequency is about 2.14GHz and bandwidth is about 36MHz in Figure 24. The effect of Q-tuning controls on the filter's response is shown in Figure 21 when the bias current I_Q and I_{SS} is from 200uA to 500uA. The maximal value of the quality factor for the filter can be attained 60. Noise figure is about 15dB at center frequency of 2.14GHz in Figure 22. Figure 23 shows the gain of the filter at center frequency of 2.14GHz and Q=60, S_{21} is about 15dB.
The linearity performance of the filter for f_C=2.14GHz and input power -60dBm is tested by IIP3 as shown in Figure 25. Two-tone signal at 2.14 and 2.144GHz is presented at the filter input through an RF power combiner, the input power at the filter input is -30dBm, which is small (the amplitude of the input voltage is about equals to 7mV) when the input load is 50Ohm. The third-order intercept point(IP3) is about -7.63dBm with SpectreRF PSS tools. The input noise floor is also measured by Cadence tools and the RMS value N_{out} is measured to be about -90.5dBm. Thus, the spurious-free dynamic range (SFDR)[2] can be calculated as

$$SFDR = \frac{2}{3}(IIP3 - N_{out}) \approx 56dB \qquad (2.23)$$

The relation between the dynamic range and the quality factor of the filter is simulated as shown in Figure 26 for the center frequency of 2.14GHz. The simulation in Figure 25 shows that the dynamic range is lower when the Q is increased. The main reason for the degradation in the dynamic range is quality factor and the output noise voltage is increased, it leads to deteriorating the linearity of the filter. The performance of the filter is summarized in Table 1.

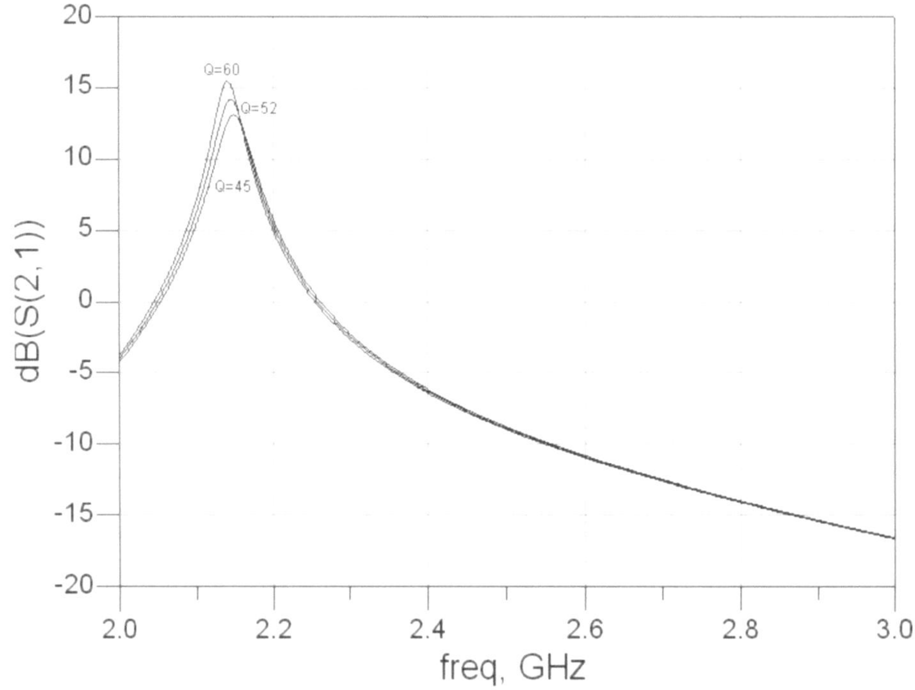

Fig. 21. Quality factor tuning of the RF LC Q-enhanced filter

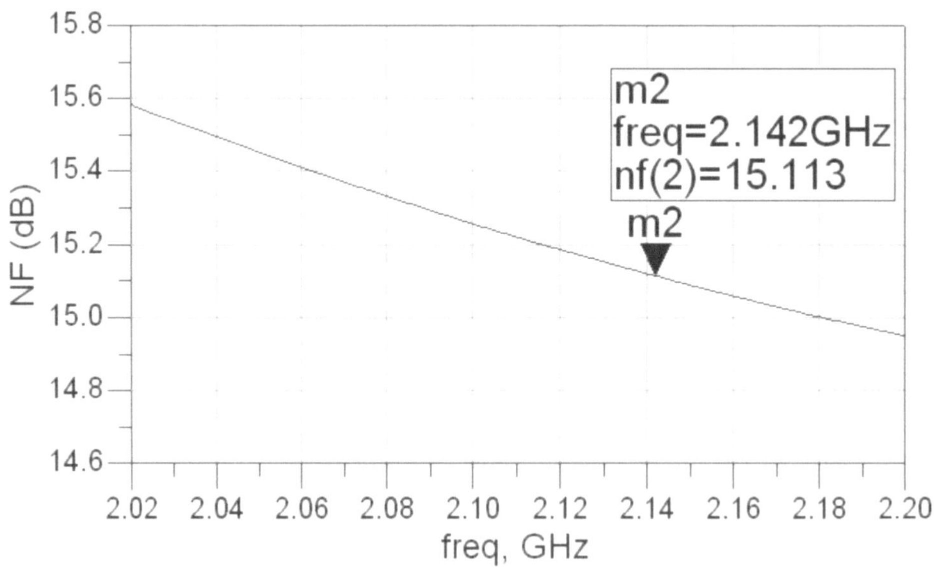

Fig. 22. Noise figure of the RF LC Q-enhanced filter

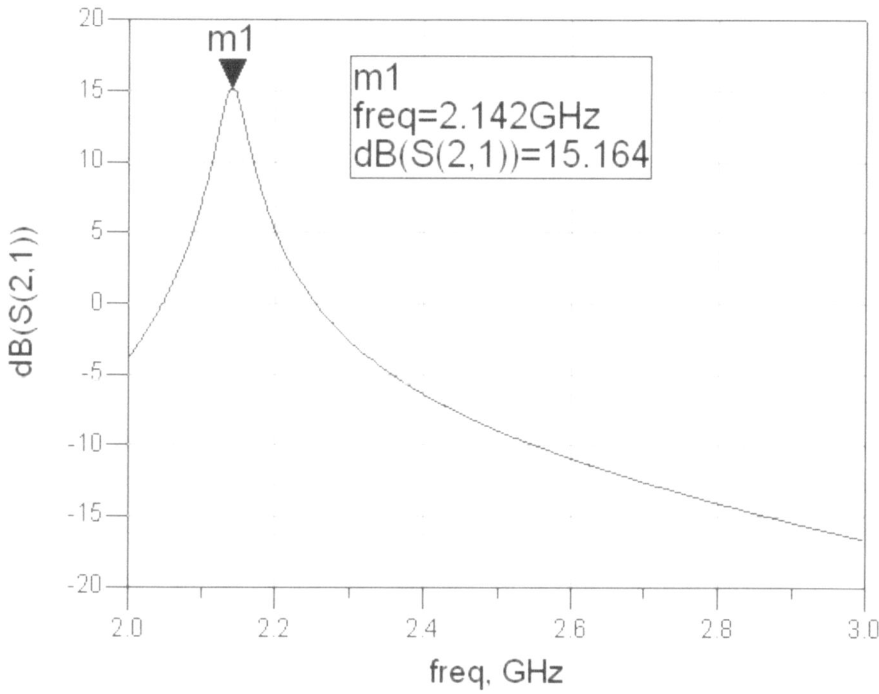

Fig. 23. S21 response of the RF LC Q-enhanced filter

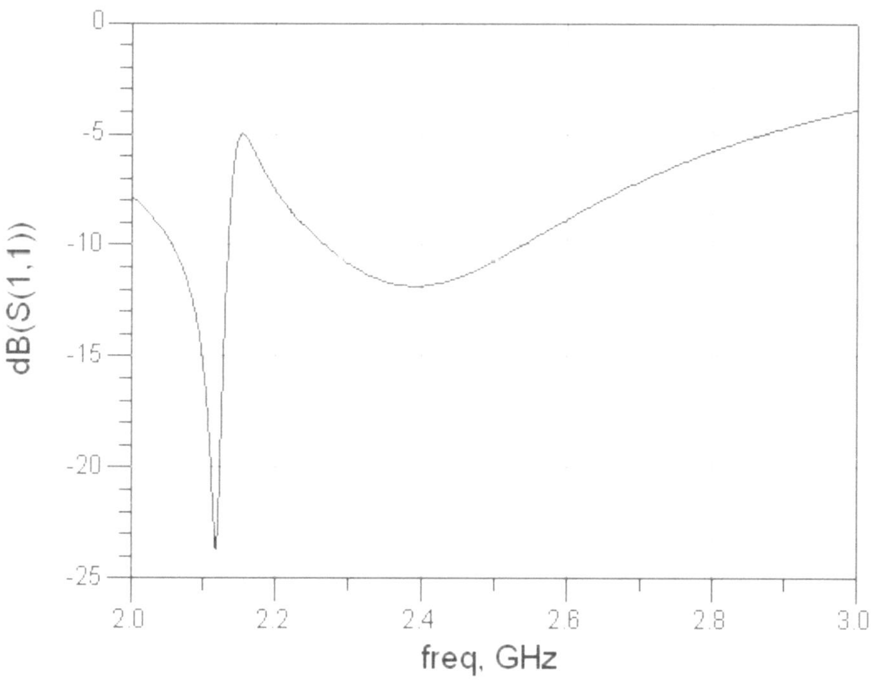

Fig. 24. Input reflected loss response S11 of the RF filter

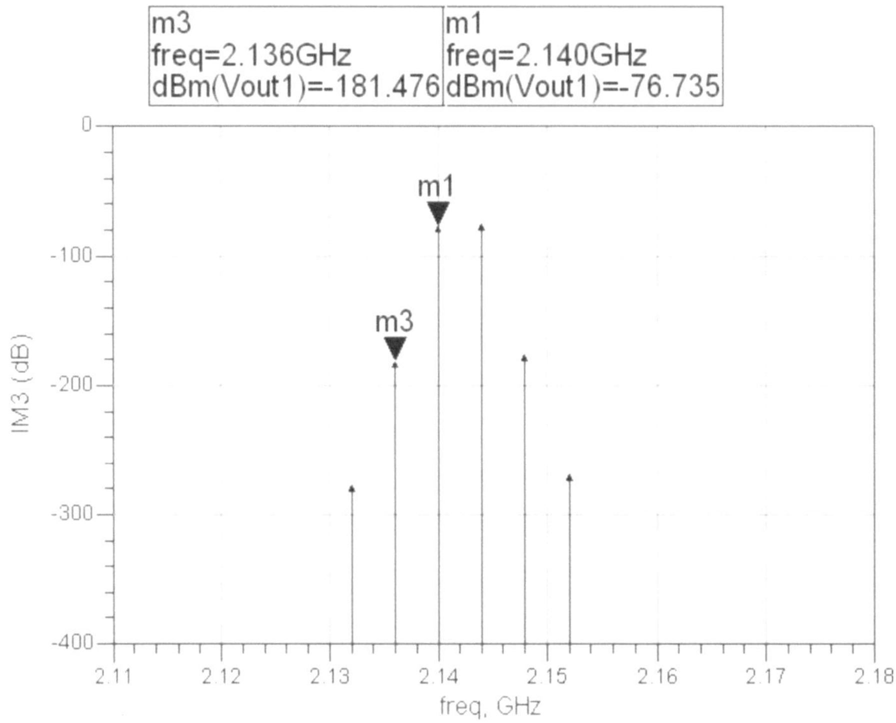

Fig. 25. The 3rd order intercept point response of the RF filter

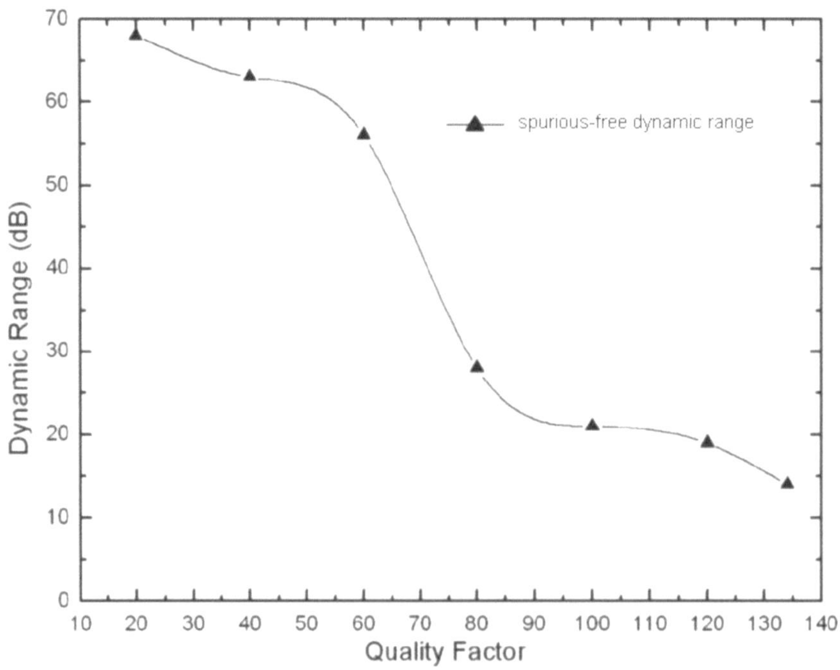

Fig. 26. The related curve of the dynamic range and quality factor

Performance Parameters	[11]	[12]	This work
Technology	0.25μm CMOS	0.5-Si-SOI	0.18μm CMOS
Center frequency	2.14GHz	2.5GHz	2.142GHz
3-dB Bandwidth	60MHz	70MHz	36MHz
Maximum Gain in passband	0dB	14dB	15dB
Noise Figure	19dB	6dB	15dB
Supply voltage	2.5V	3V	1.8V
DC consumption	17.5mW	15mW	15mW

Table 1. The performance comparision of RF active integrated LC filter

Table 1 shows the comparison for published CMOS, and bipolar RF integrated bandpass filters in the literature. The comparison table demonstrates that the proposed RF filter has lower power-supply, the highest selectivity, and the largest gain.

5. Conclusion

A 2.14GHz CMOS fully integrated second-order Q-enhanced LC bandpass filter with tunable center frequency is presented. The filter uses a resonator built with spiral inductors and inversion-mode MOS capacitors which provide frequency tuning. The simulated results are shown that the filtering Q and gain can be attained 60 and at 2.14GHz, and the spurious-free dynamic range (SFDR) is about 56dB with Q=60 and power consumption is about 15mW. The presented filter is suitable for S-band wireless applications.

6. References

[1] B. Georgescu, H. Pekau, J. Haslett and J. Mcrory, Tunable coupled inductor Q-enhancement for parallel resonant LC tanks, *IEEE Trans. Circuit and System*-II: analog and digital signal processing, vol. 50, pp705-713, Oct. 2003.

[2] T.H. Lee, The design of CMOS radio-frequency integrated circuits, U.K.: Cambridge Univ. Press, pp.390-399, 2004.

[3] W.B.Kuhn, F. W. Stephenson, and A. Elshabini-Riad, A 200MHz CMOS Q-enhanced LC bandpass filter, *IEEE J. Solid-State Circuits*, vol. 31, pp.1112-1122, Oct. 1996.

[4] W. B. Kuhn, D. Nobbe, D. Kelly, A. W. Orsborn, Dynamic range performance of on-chip RF bandpass filters, *IEEE Trans. Circuit and Systems*-II:analog and digital signal processing, vol. 50, pp. 685-694, Oct. 2003.

[5] S. Bantas, Y. Koutsoyannopoulos, CMOS active-LC bandpass filters with coupled inductor Q-enhancement and center frequency tuning, *IEEE Trans. Circuits and Systems*-II: express briefs, vol. 51, pp.69-77 Feb. 2004.

[6] S.Pipilos, Y.P. Tsividis, J. Fenk, and Y. Papanaos, A Si 1.8 GHz RLC filter with tunable center frequency and quality factor, *IEEE J. Solid-State Circuits*, vol. 31, pp. 1517-1525, Oct. 1996.

[7] F. Dulger E. S. Sinencio and J. Silva-Martinez, A 1.3V 5mW fully integrated tunable bandpass filter at 2.1GHz in 0.35um CMOS, *IEEE J. Solid-State Circuits*, vol. 38 pp. 918-927, June 2003.

[8] W.B. Kuhn, A. Elshabini-Riad, and F. W. Stephenson, Center-tapped spiral inductors for monolithic bandpass filters, *Electron. Lett.*, vol. 31, pp.625-626, Apr. 1995.
[9] F. Krummenacher, G. V. Ruymbeke, Integrated selectivity for narrow-band FM IF systems, *IEEE J. Solid-State Circuits*, vol. SC-25, pp.757-760, June 1990.
[10] T. Soorapanth, S. S. Wong, A 0dB IL 2140 ± 30 MHz bandpass filter utilizing Q-enhanced spiral inductors in standard CMOS, *IEEE J. Solid-State Circuits* vol.37, pp. 579-586, may, 2002.

Section III: A fully integrated CMOS active bandpass filter for multi-band RF front-ends

1. Introduction

Now, the fast-growing market in wireless communications has led to the development of multi-standard mobile -terminals [1-3]. This creates a strong interest toward the highly integrated RF transceivers in a compact and low-cost way. So, it is becoming more and more attractive to have a single chip of the complete CMOS multi-band transceiver in the industrial, scientific, and medical (ISM) bands. However, the integrated high-performance filters working at RF frequency still remain the one of the most difficult parts in the integrated RF front-ends. The existence of large interference, spurious tones, unwanted image and carrier frequencies, as well as their harmonics in the wireless communication environment demands the use of RF filters with high selectivity in the RF front-ends as shown in Figure 27.

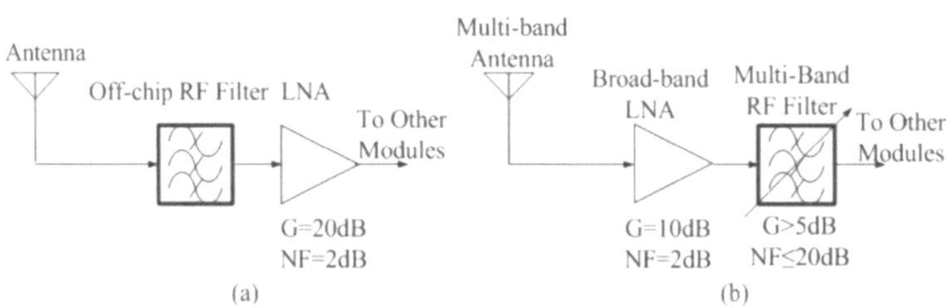

Fig. 27. Multi-Band RF front-end designs

In fact, in current gigahertz-range transceivers, the bulky and expensive off-chip bandpass filters [2] are still required to handle the existence of large out-of-band interference as shown in Figure 1(a). Furthermore, it increases the size, power consumption, and cost of multi-standard transceivers significantly by adding different copies of discrete filters for different bands. Great efforts have been made to use an on-chip tunable Q-enhanced filter to replace such off-chip preselect filter.

To this extent, recent researches on integrated filter design have fallen into the active-LC category [5]-[11]. Filters of this category are built around on–chip spiral inductors and capacitors used as LC resonant tanks, whereas an important cause for the limited integration of RF filters is the low quality factor of monolithic spiral inductors. These inductors are inherently lossy due to ohmic losses in the metal traces and due to substrate resistance and eddy currents. This problem has been addressed by using various methods such as patterned ground shields and geometry improvements, but the Q factor of integrated inductors is still generally limited to a value less than 20 [12] in standard RF CMOS process.

For multi-band RF front-end designs, a suitable on-chip tunable filter is available, but the tunable nature of the on-chip passive inductors is hard.

Compared with the passive inductors, the RF bandpass filter using active inductors can not only achieve wide frequency tuning range and high quality factor, but also occupy the small chip areas. However, it also pays for the higher noise and the worse linearity. In commercial designs as shown in Fig. 1 (a), an LNA combined with a 3dB insertion loss discrete filter typically achieves a net 5dB noise figure, 17dB gain, and 1dB input compression point about -17dBm if the input P1dB of LNA is about -20dBm, while consuming 15mW [4]. If the filter using active inductors is located in the RF front-end as shown in Fig. 1(b), and the input P1dB of LNA is about 20dBm, the proposed RF filter and the LNA can achieve a net less than 4dB, and a net more than or equal to -20dBm input compression point with 15dB gain, so the proposed RF filter combined with other RF modules will satisfy the performance of the moderate noise figure and linearity of RF system requirements such as Bluetooth, 802.11b and so on.

The section is organized as follows. Section 2 presents the novel Q-enhanced active inductor topology, as well as the analysis of the noise figure linearity and stability. Section 3 describes the RF bandpass filter based on the active inductors and the measured results of the filter are demonstrated. Finally, conclusion is given in section 4.

2. Circuit principle

2.1 Proposed active inductor

An often-used way for making active inductors is through the combination of a gyrator and capacitor, but designing high-Q active inductors at GHz with opamps or standard transconductance-C techniques is very difficult due to relatively significant power consumption and noise. The active inductor based on the principle of gyration, consisting of minimum-count transistors can be operated at GHz easily because f_T of single transistor is so high as hundreds of GHz. A class of active inductors have been proposed by researchers [14][19][20] in Figure 27. A common feature of these active inductor topologies is that they all employ some kind of shunt feedback to emulate the inductive impedance in Figure 28.

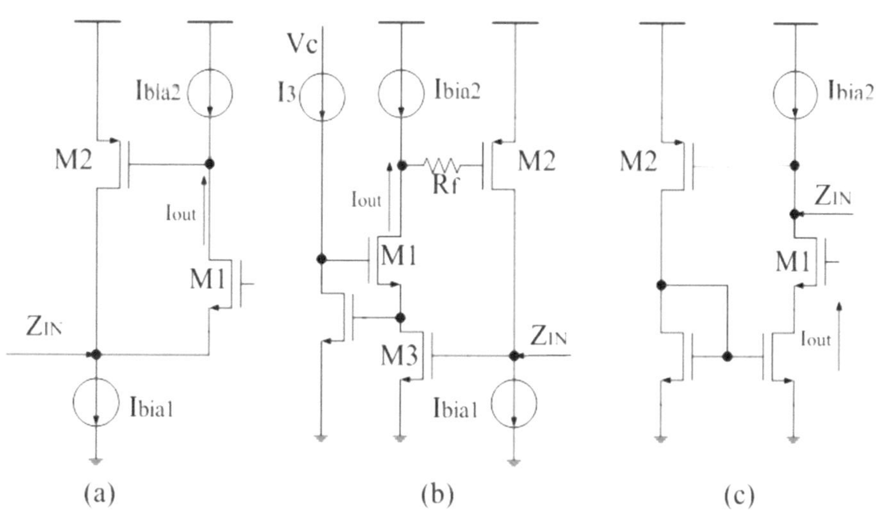

Fig. 28. The proposed CMOS active inductor topology

Intuitively, the circuits can be explained as follows: the input signal at the source of M2 will generate a current $g_{m2}V_i$ at the drain of M2, this current will be integrated on the gate-source capacitance C_{gs1}. The voltage at the gate of M1 will then generate the input current, thus generating the inductive loading effect. Compared with the active inductor proposed in Figure 28(a) and improved (b) or (c), we found the active inductor in Fig. 28(a) has some advantages over the active inductor in Figure 28(b) or (c). As can be seen from the circuit figure, the minimum voltage for the active inductor itself is only max($V_{gs1}+V_{ds1}+V_{in}$, $V_{gs2}+V_{ds2}+V_{gs1}+V_{in}$). Therefore, the circuit in Fig 28(a) is better than the circuit in (b) or (c), and it has two transistors contributing noise directly to the input. In our design, the current-reused active inductor based on (a) is chosen.

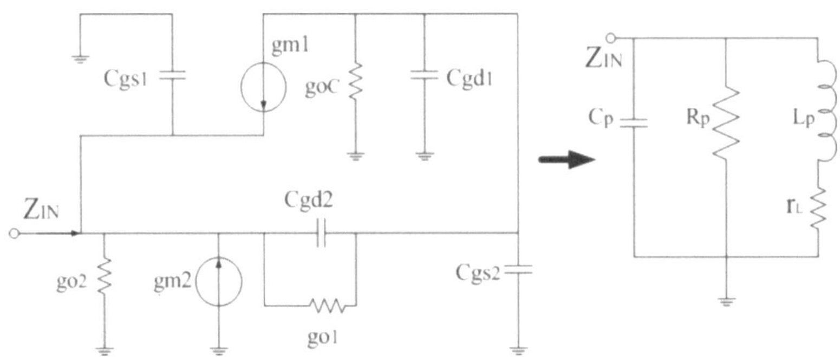

Fig. 29. The small-signal equivalent circuit of the proposed active inductor

A conceptual illustration of the proposed active inductor is shown in Figure 27. A more detailed small- signal representation of Figure 28(a) is shown in Figure 29, where g_O is the drain-source conductance and g_{OC} represents the loading effect of the nonideal biasing current source Z_{load}. The impedance of Z_{in} can be expressed as

$$Z_{in} \equiv \frac{V_{in}}{I_{in}} = R_p \,//\, C_p \,//\, Z_L \tag{2.24}$$

where the inductive impedance of Z_{in} is

$$Z_L = \frac{g_{oc} + g_{o1} + s(C_{gs2} + C_{gd2} + C_{gd1})}{g_{m1}g_{m2} + [g_{m2} - g_{m1} + g_{oc} + s(C_{gs2} + C_{gd1})](g_{o2} + sC_{gd2})} \tag{2.25}$$

The small-signal analysis of the circuit in Figure 28(a) shows that Z_{in} is a parallel RLC resonant tank with the following values:

$$Rp = \frac{1}{g_{o2}} \,||\, \frac{1}{g_{m1}} \approx 1/g_{m1} \quad C_p = C_{gs1} \quad L_p \approx \frac{C_{gs2}}{g_{m1}g_{m2}} \quad r_L \approx \frac{g_{oc} + g_{o1}}{g_{m1}g_{m2}} \tag{2.26}$$

where r_L is the intrinsic resistor of the active inductor. The self-resonant frequency ω_0 and intrinsic quality-factor of the inductor is

$$\omega_0 \approx \sqrt{\frac{g_{m1}g_{m2}}{C_{gs1}C_{gs2}}} = \sqrt{\omega_{t1}\omega_{t2}} \tag{2.27}$$

and

$$Q_0 = \frac{R_p}{\omega_0 L_p} \approx \sqrt{\frac{g_{m2} c_{gs1}}{g_{m1} c_{gs2}}} \tag{2.28}$$

where ω_{t1} and ω_{t2} are the unity-gain frequency of M1 and M2, respectively.

2.2 Noise analysis

Unlike the passive inductor where the damping resistor rL is the main noise contributor, the noise in active inductor originates from the thermal noise of MOS transistor channel [14], [15]. By referring to the transistor noise sources to the terminals of the active inductor in Figure 28(a), the noise figure of the circuit will be computed considering, for simplicity, only three main noise sources, i.e., the thermal noise of the two transistors (M1 and M2) and the noise of the load impedance Rp (i.e. $\frac{1}{g_O} || Z_{load}$). where $\overline{v_{n1}^2} = 4kT\gamma\Delta f / g_{m1}$, and $\overline{i_{n2}^2} = 4kT\gamma\Delta f g_{m2}$, kT is Boltzmann's constant times temperature in Kelvin, and γ is chosen empirically to match the observed thermal noise behavior of a given fabrication process. Computing the transfer functions from all noise sources to the output node, the following expression for the NF (at the resonance frequency) can be obtained

$$NF = 1 + \frac{\gamma}{g_{m1} R_S} + \gamma g_{m2} R_S + \frac{(1 + g_{m1} R_S)^2}{g_{m1}^2 R_S \cdot R_P} \tag{2.29}$$

Where R_S is the source impedance. The second term in the right-hand side of (6) represents the noise contributed by transistor M1 and it has the same expression as for a common-gate amplifier. However, in this case, due to the feedback in the gyrator, g_{m1} can be made larger than $1/R_S$ while still ensuring matching conditions. The third term represents the noise introduced by the feedback transistor M2. Consistently with the intuition, transistor M2 injects noise directly at the input, and its transconductance has to be small to have a low noise. The fourth term in the equation represents the noise contributed by the load. If $g_{m1}R_S >> 1$, this term becomes approximately equal to R_S/R_P. Notice that increasing R_P (i.e., increasing the quality factor of the resonant load) reduces the noise contributed by the load but also the noise of M2, since it results in a reduction of g_{m2}.

2.3 Nonlinear distortion

As shown in Fig. 27, the distortion is mainly influenced by two factors: the additional current path provided by M2 and the effect of negative feedback on both the gate-source voltage swing across M1 and its DC bias point. The analytical expression for the circuit input P1dB can be found from Sansen's theory [13]. Considering the transistor in strong inversion, the input P1dB for the circuit as a function of the transconductance of transistors becomes

$$V_{in,1dB} = 2\sqrt{\left|\frac{0.244 V_{in}^2}{1 - 2 g_{m1} g_{m2} R_S R_p}\right|} \cdot (1 + g_{m1} g_{m2} R_S R_p)^2 \tag{2.30}$$

Where V_{in} is the input voltage, and the loop gain of the circuit is given by $g_{m1}g_{m2}R_SR_p$. According to (2.30), the distortion of the circuit can cancel completely for specific values of the loop gain. This causes the large difficulty to maintain over a wide range of transistor variables.

2.4 Q-enhanced technique and stability analysis

Since the basic concept in the Q-enhanced LC filter is to use lossy LC tank, it is necessary to implement a loss compensation to boost the filter quality factor incorporating negative-conductance. Negative conductance g_{mF} realizes the required negative resistance to compensate for the loss in the tank. The effective quality factor [6] of the filter at the resonant frequency can be shown to be

$$Q_{en} = \frac{Q_0}{1 - g_{mF} R_p} \tag{2.31}$$

Where Q_0 is the base quality factor of the LC tank, which is dominated by the equivalent inductor. Theoretically it can be set as high as desired with appropriate g_{mF}. Indeed, the filter core can be tuned to oscillate if negative transconductance is sufficiently large, i.e., greater than $1/R_P$.

Additionally, the main problem is that the use of shunt feedback by M2 to compensate the loss resistance of the active inductor can result in potential instability depending on the filter terminating impedances yet. In order to make sure that the circuit is stable, the poles of the circuit must be in the left half-plane [16], [17]. In this condition, according to (1), using closed-loop analysis, the circuit will be stable provided that

$$g_{m1} < \frac{(C_{gs2} + C_{gd1}) g_{o2}}{C_{gd2}} + g_{m2} + g_{oc} \tag{2.32}$$

Simultaneously it must be ensured that the magnitude of the input reflection coefficient is less than unity i.e. $|S_{11}| < 1$. Due to the stability problem, we should determine the reasonable transconductance g_{m1} and g_{m2} in order that the trade-offs between noise, Q enhancement and stability will satisfy the requirements of the communication systems.

3. Design of the RF filter and its measured results

3.1 Circuit design

The complete prototype circuit of the proposed second-order RF bandpass filter based on the active inductor topology is shown in Figure 30. This circuit consists of three different stages, including two differential high Q-enhancement active inductors, negative impedance and buffers. Common-drain transistors M11, M13 and M12, M14 are employed for the output buffer stages. This common drain configuration can offer to minimize the loading effect and output impedance matching.

M1, M3, M5 and M2, M4, M6 construct LC-resonant circuit which is made up of the active inductor respectively. Note that the transistor M5 and M6 are respectively used to amplify the signal of shunt feedback in the active inductor topology in order to boost the impedance of active inductors. M7, M8 and M9, M10 consisting of unbalanced cross-coupled pairs are employed not only to produce negative resistance for canceling the inductor loss, but also increase linearity of the filter when the signal is large. The transistors and capacitors are sized to optimize gain in the passband, noise figure, and linearity. Transistors M1, M2 have a length/width ratio of 2um/0.18um, M3, M4 have 4um/0.18um, M5, M6 have

20um/0.18um, and M7, M8 have 0.4um/0.2um and M9, M10 have 0.3um/0.18um. For the output buffers, transistors M11, M12 have a length/width ratio of 3um/0.18um, and M13, M14 have 2um/0.18um. The input capacitance is about 120ff. The DC bias current I_{Q1} and I_{Q2} can be used to tune the Q of the active inductors and the transconductance of the cross-coupled pairs. V_b and V_c are bias voltages which are used for DC operating state of the filter. The DC bias currents I_{bia1} and/or I_{bia2} can be adjusted to tune the center frequency of the circuit and also change the Q of the inductance in Fig. 3.

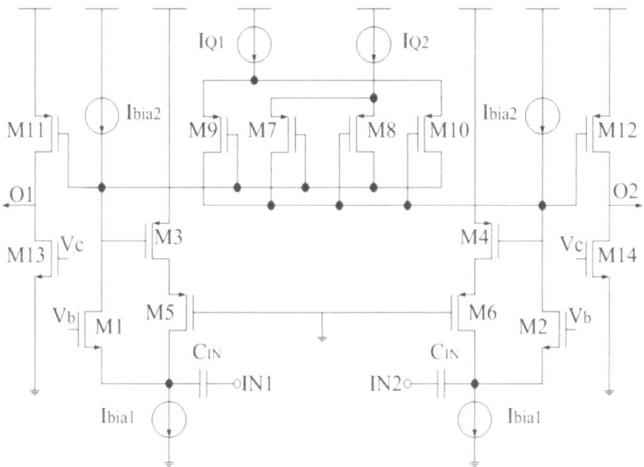

Fig. 30. The fully Q-enhancement bandpass filter

3.2 Measured results

The circuit is fabricated in 0.18-um UMC-HJTC CMOS process through the educational service. The die photograph of the fabricated circuit is shown in Figure 31. To ensure the fully differential operation, a symmetrical layout is used for the design. The total chip area is $0.7\times0.75mm^2$ including the pads, where the active area occupies only $0.15\times0.2mm^2$.

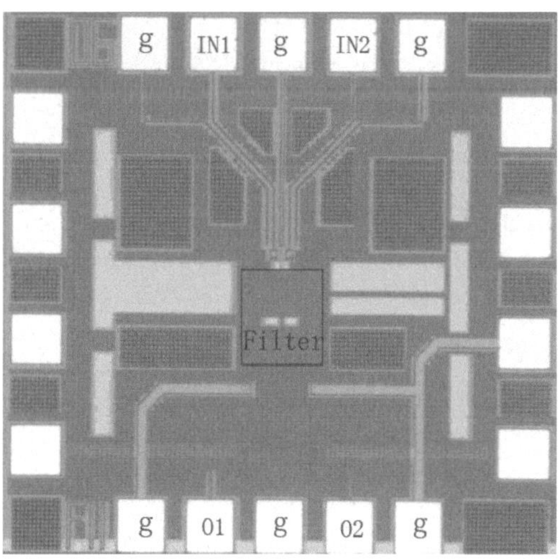

Fig. 31. Photomicrograph of the Q-enhanced RF bandpass filter

The two-port S-parameter measurements were made with the vector network analyzer Agilent E8363B. Noise measurements were made with a spectrum analyzer equipped with power measurement software and a noise source. The 1-dB compression point measurements were made with a spectrum analyzer and a power meter. The measured RF bandpass filter forward transmission response, S21, is shown in Figure 32, Figure 33 and Figure 34, respectively. Figure 32 shows the passband center frequency is 1.92GHz and 3-dB bandwidth is about 28MHz. The maximum gain in the passband is about 11.64dB and the input return loss, S11 is -14.67dB in Figure 32. In Figure 33, the center frequency is about 2.44GHz and 3-dB bandwidth is about 60MHz. The maximum gain in the passband is about 5.99dB. Moreover, the S21 at about center frequency 3.82GHz is about 12dB and return loss S11 is about -29dB as shown in Figure 34.

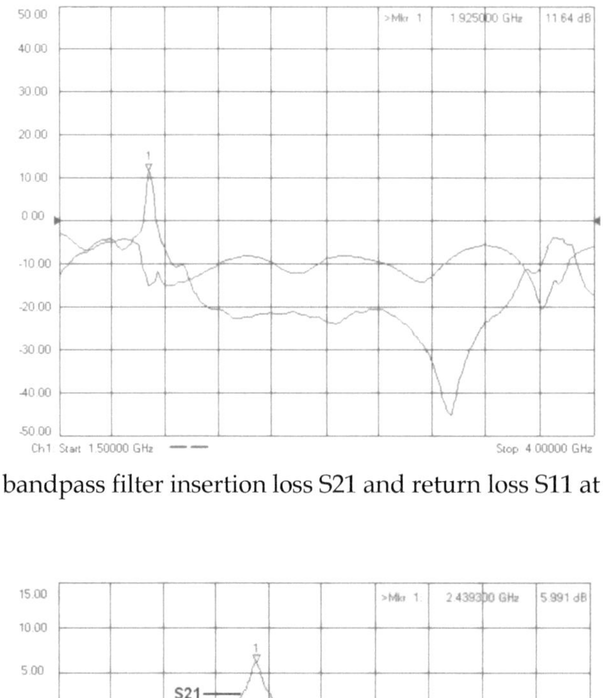

Fig. 32. Measured bandpass filter insertion loss S21 and return loss S11 at center frequency about 1.92GHz

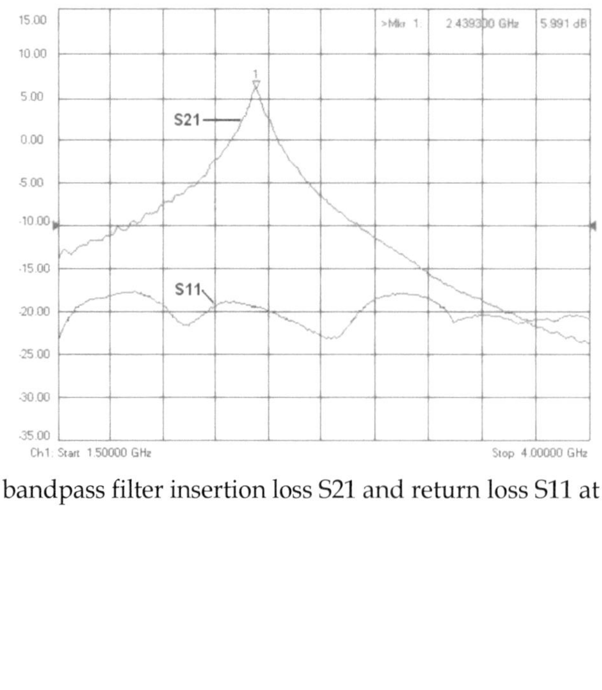

Fig. 33. Measured bandpass filter insertion loss S21 and return loss S11 at center frequency about 2.44GHz

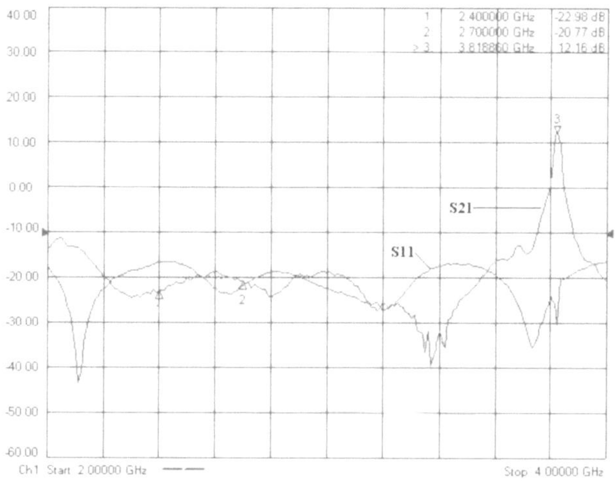

Fig. 34. Measured bandpass filter insertion loss S21 and return loss S11 at the center frequency about 3.82GHz

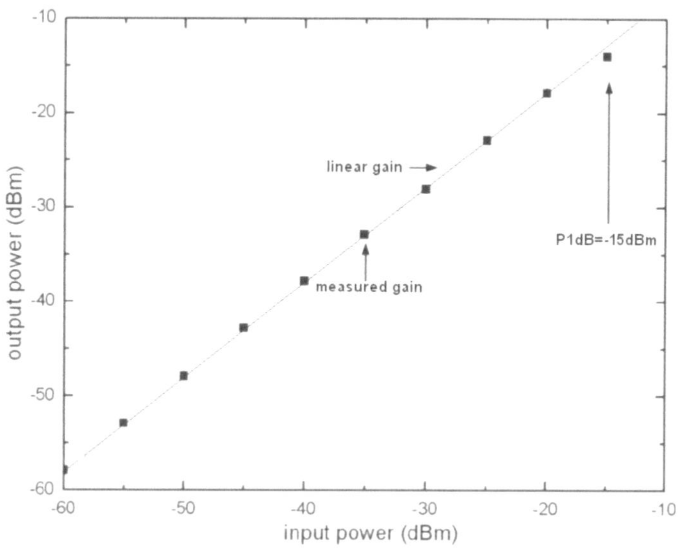

Fig. 35. P1dB measurement at center frequency about 2.44GHz

A measurement to the input 1dB compression point of the circuit can be obtained by sweeping the input power to the tank and measuring the output power. As the input power is increased, the input impedance presented by the Q-enhanced active inductor tanks begins to drop due to nonlinear effects, which can be observed when the output power no longer depends on the input power in a linear fashion as shown in Figure 35. The measured bandpass filter P1dB input power compression point is -15dBm at the center frequency about 2.44GHz passband. The noise figure of 18dB was also measured by disconnecting the input signal. The RF filter has wide-tuning range from the center frequency about 1.92GHz to 3.82GHz when the DC voltage sources of the controlled bias currents Ibia1 and/or Ibia2 are adjusted from 0.5 to 1.5V or vice versa. The noise figure evaluated in each band gives the following results: 15dB for center frequency 1.92GHz, 18dB for center frequency about 2.44GHz, 20dB for center frequency about 3.82GHz. Furthermore, 1-dB compress point is about -17dBm, -15dBm, -18dBm respectively.

Ref.	[8]	[9]	[10]	[11]	This work
Process	0.25um-CMOS	0.5-Si-SOI	0.18um-CMOS	0.18um-CMOS	0.18um-CMOS
Die area	3.5mm^2	2.5mm^2	2.25mm^2	0.81mm^2	0.53mm^2
N-orders	6	2	3	4	2
f_{center}	2.14GHz	2.5GHz	2.36GHz	2.03GHz	2.44GHz
-3dB Bandwidth	60MHz	70MHz	60MHz	130MHz	60MHz
Tuning range	-	250MHz	-	60.9MHz	1900MHz
Noise figure	19dB	6dB	18 dB	15 dB	18 dB
Mid-band gain	0dB	14dB	-1.8dB	0dB	6dB
Supply voltage	2.5V	3V	1.8V	1.8V	1.8V
FOM	72	82	78	77	81

Table 2. Comparison of the RF bandpass filters Performance

The summary of the measured performance and the comparisons of the performance among the fabricated RF filters in CMOS and other process is given in Table 2. A figure of merit [18] (FOM) which allows comparison between other RF filters in silicon is given as

$$FOM = \frac{N \cdot P_{1dBW} \cdot f_{center} \cdot Q_{filter}}{P_{DC} \cdot NF} \tag{2.33}$$

where N is the number of poles, P_{1dBW} is the inband 1-dB compression point in Watt, f_{center} is the center frequency, Q_{filter} is the ratio of the center frequency and the 3-dB bandwidth, P_{DC} is the DC power dissipation in Watt, and NF is the noise figure (not in dB). It has shown from Table II that the filter presented in this work achieves a good FOM with higher quality factor and gain in the passband, and the tuning range is the largest, and the chip area is the smallest.

4. Conclusion

The design and implementation of tunable RF bandpass filter in 0.18um CMOS process have been introduced and verified, which demonstrate that the RF bandpass filter can achieve high quality factor and large tuning range from 1.92GHz to 3.82GHz. Although the noise and linearity of the proposed active inductors are inferior to passive ones, the smallest chip area, and the largest tenability make them apply to the multi-band on-chip wireless systems in future.

5. References

[1] A. Tasic, W.A. Serdijn, J.R. Long. Adaptive multi-standard circuits and systems for wireless communications. *IEEE Magazine On Circuits and Systems*, vol. 6, no. 1, pp. 29-37, Quarter, 2006.

[2] Y. Satoh, O. Ikata, T. Miyashita, and H. Ohmori, RF SAW filters Chiba Univ., Japan, 2001 [Online]. Available:
http://www.usl.chiba-u.ac.jp/ken /Symp2001/PAPER/SATOH.PDF.

[3] A. Tasic, S. Lim, W.A. Serdijn, J.R. Long. Design of adaptive multi- mode RF front-end circuits. *IEEE J. of Solid-State Circuits*, vol. 42, pp. 313-322, Feb. 2007.

[4] MBC13916 General purpose SiGe: C RF Cascade Amplifier. Motorola, Data Sheet.

[5] S. Li, N. Stanic, Y. Tsividis. A VCF loss-control tuning loop for Q- enhanced LC filters. *IEEE Trans. On Circuits and Systems*-II: express briefs, vol. 53, pp. 906-910, Sep. 2006.

[6] W. B. Kuhn, D. Nobe, N. Kely, A.W. Orsborn. Dynamic range performance of on-chip RF bandpass filters. *IEEE Trans. On Microwave Theory and Techniques*, vol. 50, pp. 685-694, Oct. 2003.

[7] B. Bantas,Y. Koutsoyannopoulos. CMOS active-LC bandpass filters with coupled-inductor Q-enhancement and center frequency tuning. *IEEE Trans. Circuits and Systems*-II: express briefs, vol. 51, pp. 69-76, Feb. 2004.

[8] T. Soorapanth S. S. Wong. A 0-dB IL, 2140±30MHz bandpass filter utilizing Q-enhanced spiral inductors in standard CMOS. *IEEE J. of Solid-State Circuits*, vol. 37, 579-586, May 2002.

[9] X. He, W. B. Kuhn. A 2.5GHz low-power, high dynamic range, self-tuned Q-enhanced LC filter in SOI. *IEEE J. of Solid-State Circuits*, vol. 40, pp.1618-1628, Aug. 2005.

[10] J. Kulyk, J. Haslett. A monolithic CMOS 2368±30MHz transformer based Q-enhanced series-C coupled resonator bandpass filter. *IEEE J. of Solid-State Circuits*, vol. 41, 362-374, Feb. 2006.

[11] B. Georgescu, I. G. Finvers, F. Ghannouchi. 2 GHz Q-enhanced active filter with low passband distortion and high dynamic range. *IEEE J. of Solid-State Circuits*, vol. 41, pp.2029-2039, Sep. 2006.

[12] Y.Cao, R. A. Groves, X. Huang et. al. Frequency-independent equivalent-circuit model for on-chip spiral inductors. *IEEE J. of Solid-State Circuits*, vol. 38, 419-426, Mar. 2003.

[13] W. Sansen. Distortion in elementary transistor circuits. *IEEE Trans. On Circuits and Systems*-II: express briefs, vol. 46, 315-325, Mar. 1999.

[14] Z. Gao, M. Yu, Y. Ye, and J. Ma. A CMOS RF tuning wide-band bandpass filter for wireless applications. In *Proc. IEEE Int'l Conf.* SOC, pages 79–80, Spet. 2005.

[15] G. Groenewold. Noise and group delay in active filters. *IEEE Trans. On Circuits and Systems*-I: regular papers, vol. 54, pp. 1471-1480, July, 2007.

[16] P. R. Gray and R. G. Meyer, Analysis and Design of Analog Integrated Circuits, 3rd ed. New York: Wiley, 1993.

[17] Robert W. Jackson. Rollett Proviso in the stability of linear Microwave circuits-A tutorial. *IEEE Trans. on Microwave Theory and Techniques*, vol. 54, pp. 993-1000, Mar. 2006.
[18] K.T. Christensen, T. H. Lee, E. Bruun. A high dynamic range programm- able CMOS Front-end filter with tuning range from 1850-2400 MHz. Norwell, MA: Kluwer, 2005.
[19] A.Karsilayan and R. Schaumann A High-Frequency High-Q CMOS Active Inductor with DC Bias Control, *Proc. IEEE Midwest Symp. Circ. Syst.* (MWSCAS), Aug. 2000.
[20] Y. Wu, M. Ismail, and H. Olsson, A novel fully differential inductorless RF bandpass filter in *Proc. IEEE Int. Symp. Circuit and System* (ISCAS), Geneva, Switzerland, May 2000, pp. 149-152.

25

High-frequency Millimeter Wave Absorber Composed of a New Series of Iron Oxide Nanomagnets

Asuka Namai and Shin-ichi Ohkoshi
Department of Chemistry, School of Science, the University of Tokyo, Japan

1. Introduction

High-speed wireless communications using millimeter waves (30–300 GHz) have received much attention as a next-generation communication system capable of transmitting vast quantities of data such as high-definition video images. Due to the recent development of transistors composed of complementary metal-oxide semiconductors or double heterojunction bipolar transistors,[1-5] electromagnetic (EM) waves in the millimeter wave range are beginning to be used in high-speed wireless communication.[6-8] Especially, for 60 GHz-band wireless communication, Wigig alliance was established in December 2009, and televisions and local area network (LAN) using 60 GHz millimeter wave have been extensively researched and developed. Millimeter wave wireless communication is anticipated to realize a transmission rate that is several handred times greater than current wireless communication. On the other hand, in a wireless communication, electromagnetic interference (EMI) is a problem. In addition, the unnecessary EM waves should be eliminated to protect the human body, although the potential health effects due to the millimeter wave have not yet been understood.[9] To solve these problems, millimeter wave absorbers need to be equipped with electronic devices such as isolators or be painted on a wall of building, etc. However, currently materials that effectively restrain EMI in the region of millimeter waves almost do not exist. Thus, finding a suitable material has received much attention. Insulating magnetic materials absorb EM waves owing to natural resonance. Particularly, a magnetic material with a large coercive field (H_c) is expected to show a high-frequency resonance. In recent years, we firstly succeeded to obtain a single phase of ε-Fe_2O_3 nanomagnet (Figure 1), and found that ε-Fe_2O_3 nanomagnet exhibited an extremely large H_c value of 20 kOe at room temperature, which is the highest H_c value for insulating magnetic materials.[10-19] In this paper, we report a new millimeter wave absorber composed of ε-$Ga_xFe_{2-x}O_3$ ($0.10 \leq x \leq 0.67$) nanomagnets, which shows a natural resonance in the range of 35–147 GHz at room temperature.[20] This is the first example of a magnetic material which shows a natural resonance above 80 GHz. In addition, the study of the magnetic permeability of ε-$Ga_xFe_{2-x}O_3$ was performed in 60 GHz region (V-band). By analyzing electromagnetic wave absorption properties, the magnetic permeability (μ'-$j\mu''$) and dielectric constant (ε'-$j\varepsilon''$) of ε-$Ga_xFe_{2-x}O_3$ were evaluated.[21]

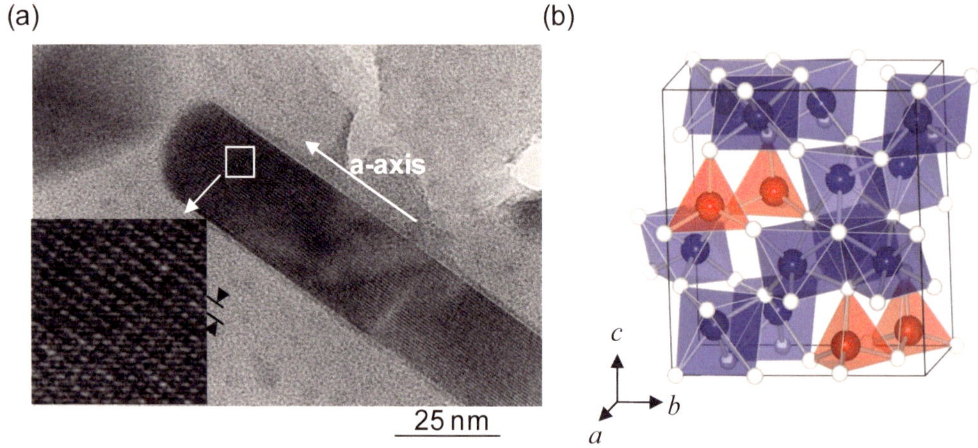

Fig. 1. (a) TEM image of ε-Fe_2O_3 at high magnification. The inset is the high resolution image. (b) Crystal structure of ε-Fe_2O_3.

2. Synthesis, crystal structures and magnetic properties

In this section, we show the synthesis, crystal structures and magnetic properties of a new millimeter-wave absorber composed of ε-$Ga_xFe_{2-x}O_3$ ($0.10 \leq x \leq 0.67$) nanoparticles.

2.1 Synthesis of ε-$Ga_xFe_{2-x}O_3$ nanomagnets

A new series of ε-$Ga_xFe_{2-x}O_3$ ($0.10 \leq x \leq 0.67$) nanoparticles was synthesized by the combination of reverse micelle and sol–gel techniques or only the sol–gel method. Figure 2 describes the flowchart of the synthetic procedure for ε-$Ga_xFe_{2-x}O_3$ nanoparticles. In the combination method between the reverse-micelle and sol-gel techniques, microemulsion systems were formed by cetyl trimethyl ammonium bromide (CTAB) and 1-butanol in n-octane. The microemulsion containing an aqueous solution of $Fe(NO_3)_3$ and $Ga(NO_3)_3$ was mixed with another microemulsion containing NH_3 aqueous solution while rapidly stirring. Then tetraethoxysilane was added into the solution. This mixture was stirred for 20 hours and the materials were subsequently sintered at 1100 °C for 4 hours in air. The SiO_2 matrices were etched by a NaOH solution for 24 hours at 60 °C.

2.2 Morphology and crystal structure

In the transmission electron microscope (TEM) image, sphere-type particles with an average particle size between 20-40 nm are observed as shown in the inset of Figure 2. Rietveld analyses of X-ray diffraction (XRD) patterns indicate that materials of this series have an orthorhombic crystal structure in the $Pna2_1$ space group (Figure 3). This crystal structure has four nonequivalent Fe sites (A-D), i.e., the coordination geometries of the A-C sites are octahedral [FeO_6] and that of the D site is tetrahedral [FeO_4]. For example, in the case of x= 0.61, 92% of the D sites and 20% of the C sites are substituted by Ga^{3+} ions, but the A and B sites are not substituted because Ga^{3+} (0.620 Å), which has a smaller ionic radius than Fe^{3+} (0.645 Å),[22] prefers the tetrahedral sites. The shade of blue in Figure 3 depicts the degree of Ga substitution.

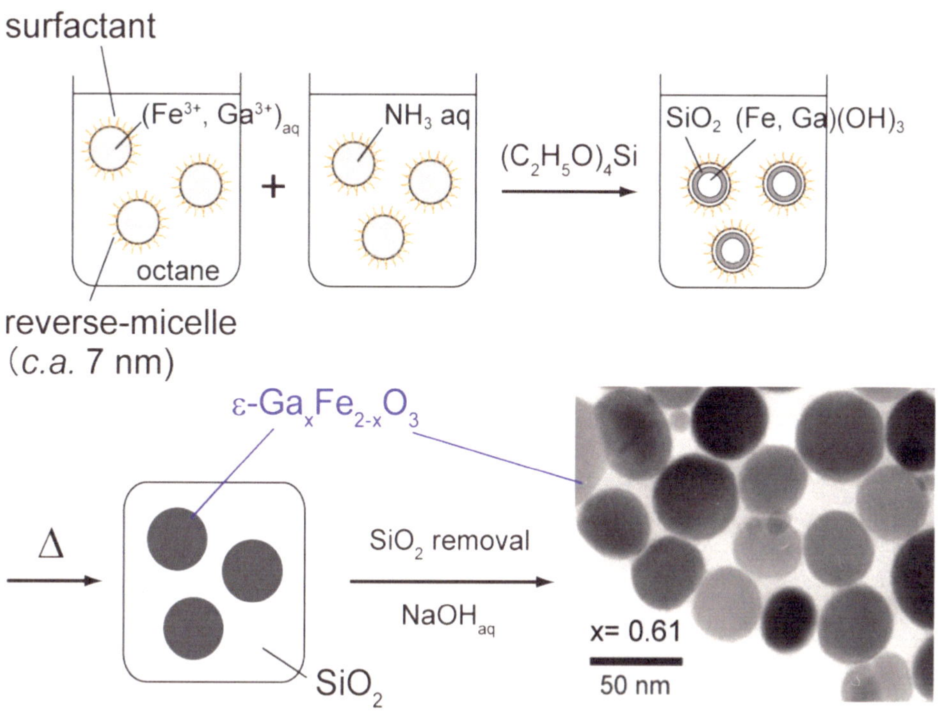

Fig. 2. Schematic illustration of the synthetic procedure of ε-$Ga_xFe_{2-x}O_3$ nanocrystal using combination method between reverse-micelle and sol-gel techniques. The inset is TEM image of ε-$Ga_xFe_{2-x}O_3$ particles.

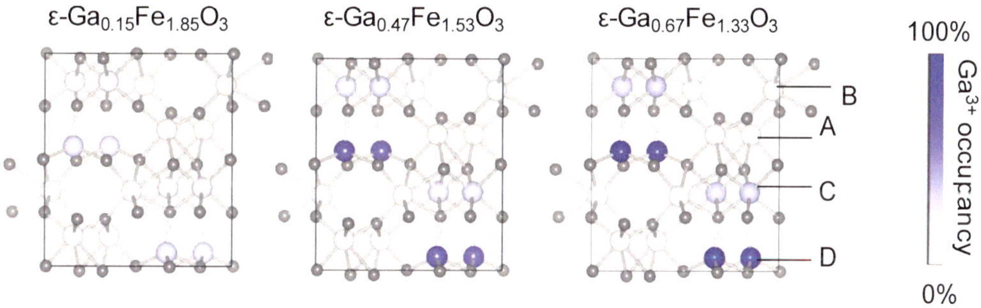

Fig. 3. Crystal structure of ε-$Ga_xFe_{2-x}O_3$. Degrees of Ga substitution at each Fe site (A–D) described by the shade of blue.

2.3 Magnetic properties

The magnetic properties of this series are listed in Table 1. The field-cooled magnetization curves in an external magnetic field of 10 Oe show that the T_C value monotonously decreases from 492 K (x= 0.10) to 324 K (x= 0.67) as x increases (Figure 4a). Figure 4b shows the magnetization vs. external magnetic field plots at 300 K. The H_c value decreases from 15.9 kOe (x= 0.10) to 2.1 kOe (x= 0.67). The saturation magnetization (M_s) value at 90 kOe increases from 14.9 emu g^{-1} (x= 0.10) to 30.1 (x= 0.40) and then decreases to 17.0 (x= 0.67).

		x= 0.10	x= 0.22	x= 0.29	x= 0.35	x= 0.40	x= 0.47	x= 0.54	x= 0.61	x= 0.67
T_C (K)		492	470	453	441	432	407	385	355	324
M_s (emu/g)	300 K	14.9	24.7	27.4	28.7	30.1	28.5	25.4	23.3	17.0
	2 K	19.2	36.1	42.1	47.5	52.0	52.7	51.0	51.6	42.8
H_c (kOe)	300 K	15.9	11.6	10.0	9.3	8.8	6.8	5.5	4.7	2.1
	2 K	15.5	15.7	14.1	13.7	13.4	12.8	13.1	13.7	14.2

Table 1. Magnetic properties of ε-$Ga_xFe_{2-x}O_3$.

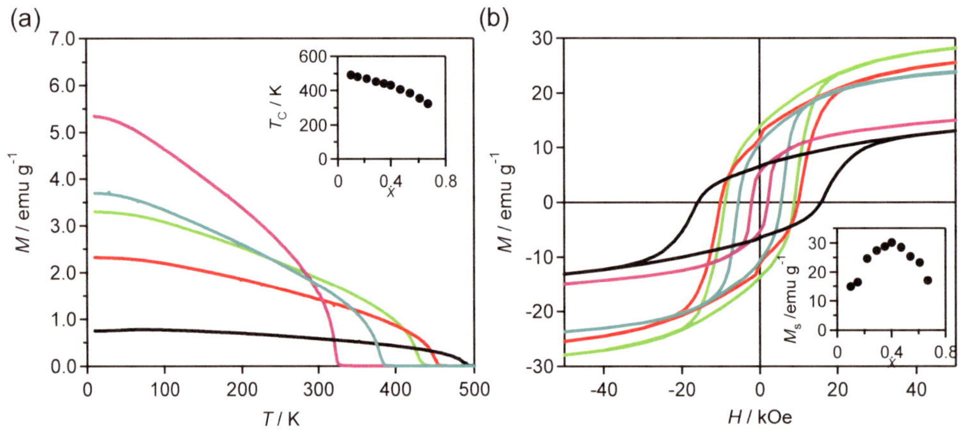

Fig. 4. Magnetic properties of ε-$Ga_xFe_{2-x}O_3$. (a) FCM curves for x= 0.10 (black), 0.22 (red), 0.40 (green), 0.54 (light blue), and 0.67 (magenta) in the external magnetic field of 10 Oe. (b) Magnetization vs. external field plots for x= 0.10 (black), 0.22 (red), 0.40 (green), 0.54 (light blue), and 0.67 (magenta).

The changes in magnetic properties were understood by the replacement of magnetic Fe^{3+} (S= 5/2) by non-magnetic Ga^{3+} ($3d^{10}$, S= 0). ε-Fe_2O_3 is a collinear ferrimagnet at room temperature where the magnetic moments at the B and C sites (M_B and M_C sublattice magnetization) are antiparallel to the A and D sites (M_A and M_D sublattice magnetization), i.e., $M_{total} = M_B + M_C - M_A - M_D$.[15,23] In addition, M_D sublattice magnetization is smaller than the other three sublattice magnetization. Ga^{3+} substitution reduces the M_D sublattice magnetization value due to selective substitution at the D sites in the region of $0.10 \le x \le 0.40$. Hence, M_{total} values of ε-$Ga_xFe_{2-x}O_3$ system increase as the x values increase. On the other hand, the decrease of M_{total} at $0.47 \le x$ is caused by Ga replacement at the C, B, and A sites.

3. Millimeter wave absorption of ε-$Ga_xFe_{2-x}O_3$ nanomagnets

In this section, we deal with the millimeter wave absorption due to the natural resonance in ε-$Ga_xFe_{2-x}O_3$ nanoparticles.

3.1 Natural resonance

In general, when an EM wave is irradiated into a ferromagnet, the gyromagnetic effect leads to resonance, which is called a "natural resonance" (Figure 5a). In a ferromagnetic material with a magnetic anisotropy, the direction of magnetization is restricted around the magnetic easy-axis. Once an external magnetic field tilts the magnetization, then the magnetization starts to precesses around the easy-axis due to the gyromagnetic effect. When this precession of magnetization resonates with an applied EM wave, a natural resonance occurs and EM wave absorption is observed.[24] The natural resonance frequency (f_r) is proportional to the magnetocrystalline anisotropy (H_a), which is expressed by $f_r = (\nu/2\pi)H_a$, where ν is the gyromagnetic ratio. Common magnetic materials such as spinel ferrite show EM wave absorption in a few GHz region, and even a f_r value of metal-substituted barium ferrite is 80 GHz or less.

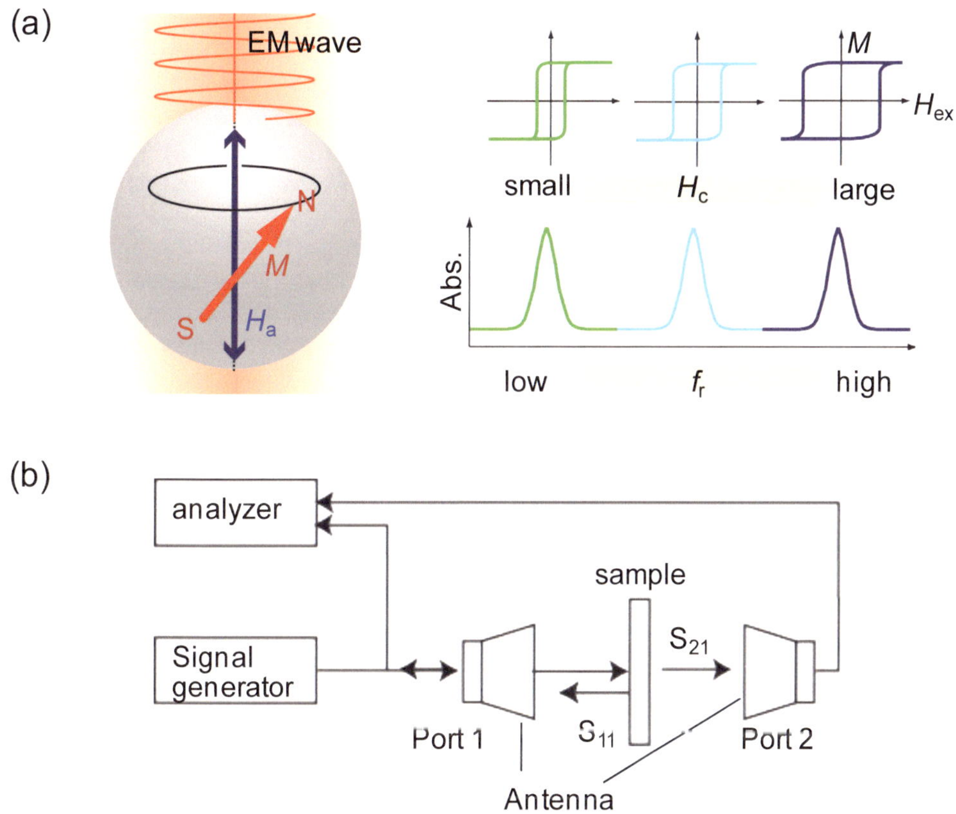

Fig. 5. (a) Schematic illustration of the natural resonance due to the gyromagnetic effect. Precession of magnetization (M) around an anisotropy field (H_a) causes electromagnetic wave absorption. Resonance frequency (f_r) is expressed as $f_r = (\nu/2\pi) H_a$. In magnets of a uniaxial magnetic anisotropy, f_r is proportional to magnetic coercive field (H_c). (b) Diagram of the free space millimeter wave absorption measurement system.

3.2 Millimeter wave absorption properties

The EM absorption properties (V-band; 50-75 GHz, and W-band; 75-110 GHz) were measured at room temperature using a free space EM wave absorption measurement system (Figure 5b). The powder-form samples were filled in a 30 mmϕ × 10 mm quartz cell with the fill ratios of *ca.* 40%. The reflection coefficient (S_{11}) and permeability coefficient (S_{21}) were obtained, and the absorption of the EM waves was calculated by the following equation: (Absorption) = $-10\log[|S_{21}|^2/(1-|S_{11}|^2)]$ (dB). An absorption of 20 dB indicates that 99% of the introduced EM waves are absorbed, which is the target value for EM absorbers from an industrial point of view.

The center of Figure 6 shows millimeter wave absorption spectra of the samples between x= 0.61 and 0.29 in the frequency region of 50–110 GHz. The sample for x= 0.61 shows a strong absorption at 54 GHz. As x decreases, the frequency of the absorption peak shifts to a higher one, i.e., 64 GHz (x= 0.54), 73 GHz (x= 0.47), 84 GHz (x= 0.40), 88 GHz (x= 0.35), and 97 GHz (x= 0.29). In the case of samples for x= 0.67, 0.22, 0.15 and 0.10, the absorption peaks exceed the measurement range (50–110 GHz). To confirm the frequency of these materials, hand-made apparatuses for the range of 27–40 GHz and 105–142 GHz were prepared. As a result, the sample for x= 0.67 showed the absorption peak at 35 GHz (Figure 6, left). In the frequency range of 105–142 GHz, the peak frequencies for x= 0.22 and 0.15 are observed at 115 and 126 GHz, respectively, and that for x= 0.10 is estimated to be observed at 147 GHz by supplementation of the spectrum using the Lorentzian function (Figure 6, right). The absorption intensities of this series are strong (for example, the absorption intensity for x= 0.40 reaches 57 dB (99.9998%)).

As mentioned above, the f_r value is proportional to the magnetocrystalline anisotropy field (H_a), which is expressed by $f_r = (\nu/2\pi)H_a$ where ν is the gyromagnetic ratio. When the sample consists of randomly oriented magnetic particles with a uniaxial magnetic anisotropy, the H_a value is proportional to the H_c value. Figure 7 shows the relationship between f_r and the H_c values in the present series.

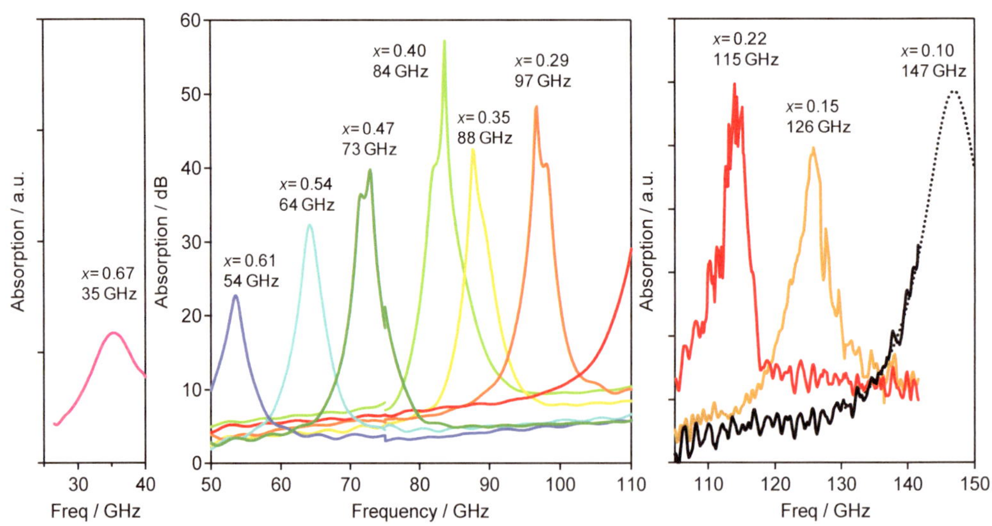

Fig. 6. Millimeter wave absorption properties of ε-$Ga_xFe_{2-x}O_3$. (left) Millimeter wave absorption spectra for x= 0.67 (gray) in the range of 27–40 GHz. (center) Millimeter wave absorption spectra for x= 0.61 (blue), 0.54 (light blue), 0.47 (green), 0.40 (light green), 0.35 (yellow), 0.29 (orange), and 0.22 (red) in the range of 50–110 GHz. (right) Millimeter wave absorption spectra for x= 0.22 (red), 0.15 (ocher) and 0.10 (black) using a hand-made apparatus in the range of 105–142 GHz. The peak of the spectrum for x= 0.10 is supplemented by the line fitted by the Lorentzian function (dotted black line).

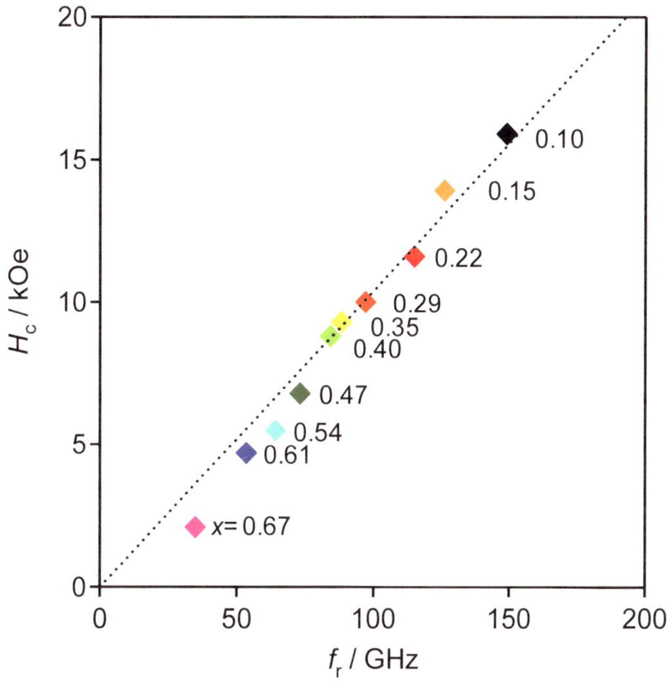

Fig. 7. Relationship between f_r and H_c of ε-$Ga_xFe_{2-x}O_3$.

4. Magnetic permeability (μ) and dielectric constant (ε) of ε-$Ga_xFe_{2-x}O_3$ nanomagnets

The metal substituted ε-Fe_2O_3 has attracted much attention as a potential stable EMI suppression material for millimeter wave electronics such as isolators and circulators.[20,25] The magnetic permeability of such millimeter wave absorbers is important to determine the attenuation and reflection properties, for the purpose of designing a millimeter wave absorber painted on a wall. Here we describe the reflectance and transmittance data of a series of ε-$Ga_xFe_{2-x}O_3$ (x= 0.51, 0.56, 0.61) in the region of 60 GHz band (V-band) and the evaluation of the magnetic permeability.

4.1 Theoretical background – Magnetic permeability near the natural resonance

The motion of magnetization can be described by the Landau-Lifshitz equations as follows:[26,27]

$$\frac{d\boldsymbol{M}}{dt} = -\nu\left(\boldsymbol{M} \times \boldsymbol{H}\right) - \frac{4\pi\mu_0\lambda}{M^2}\left(\boldsymbol{M} \times \left(\boldsymbol{M} \times \boldsymbol{H}\right)\right), \tag{1}$$

where $\boldsymbol{M}$ is a vector of magnetization, $\boldsymbol{H}$ is a vector of magnetic field, μ_0 is the vacuum magnetic permeability, and ν is the gyromagnetic coefficient. The first term describes magnetization precessing toward the direction of -($\boldsymbol{M} \times \boldsymbol{H}$), whereas the second term is for the case where braking acts on the precession and magnetization receives force in the direction of ($\boldsymbol{M} \times$ ($\boldsymbol{M} \times \boldsymbol{H}$)). λ is the coefficient called the relaxation frequency, which represents the degree of braking with a unit of Hz. By solving Eq. (1), the magnetic permeability at frequency of f is obtained as:

$$\mu'(f) = \frac{\nu M^2}{4\pi\mu_0 \lambda H_a} \sin\varphi(f)\cos\varphi(f) + 1, \tag{2}$$

$$\mu''(f) = \frac{\nu M^2}{4\pi\mu_0 \lambda H_a} \sin^2\varphi(f), \tag{3}$$

where H_a is the anisotropy field and $\varphi(f)$ is described by:

$$\varphi(f) = \tan^{-1}\left(\frac{4\pi\mu_0\lambda}{\nu M}\frac{H_a}{H_a - 2\pi f/\nu}\right). \tag{4}$$

As shown in Figure 8, $\mu'(f)$ shows dispersive-shaped lines around the natural resonance frequency f_r, while $\mu''(f)$ shows absorption peaks at f_r, where f_r is described by $f_r = \nu H_a/2\pi$.

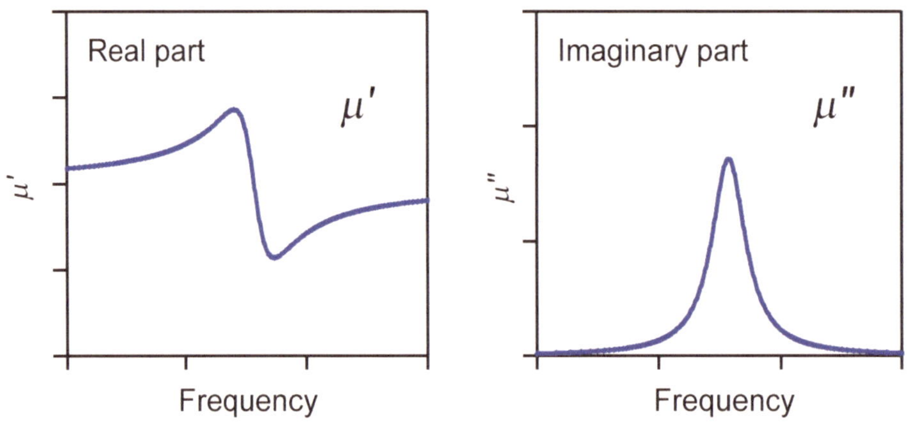

Fig. 8. Theoretical behavior of magnetic permeability around natural resonance.

4.2 Determination of magnetic permeability (μ) and dielectric constant (ε)

The reflectance (S_{11}) and transmittance (S_{21}) were measured by a free space EM wave absorption measurement system. Powder form samples were filled on a foam polystyrene holder with a 0.5 mm gap (filling ratio was *ca.* 20 vol. %). EM waves in the V-band (50-75 GHz) were irradiated vertically into the sample, and the transmitted and reflected waves were analyzed using waveguides and vector network analyzer. Figure 9a shows the measured S_{11} and S_{21} values in V-band. The absorption peaks of the transmitted waves were observed around 65 GHz (x= 0.51), 59 GHz (x= 0.56), and 55 GHz (x= 0.61). The reflected waves exhibited similar absorptions.

Using the measured S_{11} and S_{21} values, the magnetic permeability and dielectric constant were determined via the following procedure. When EM waves are irradiated vertically into a material, the reflection coefficient (Γ) and transmission coefficient (T) are represented as follows:

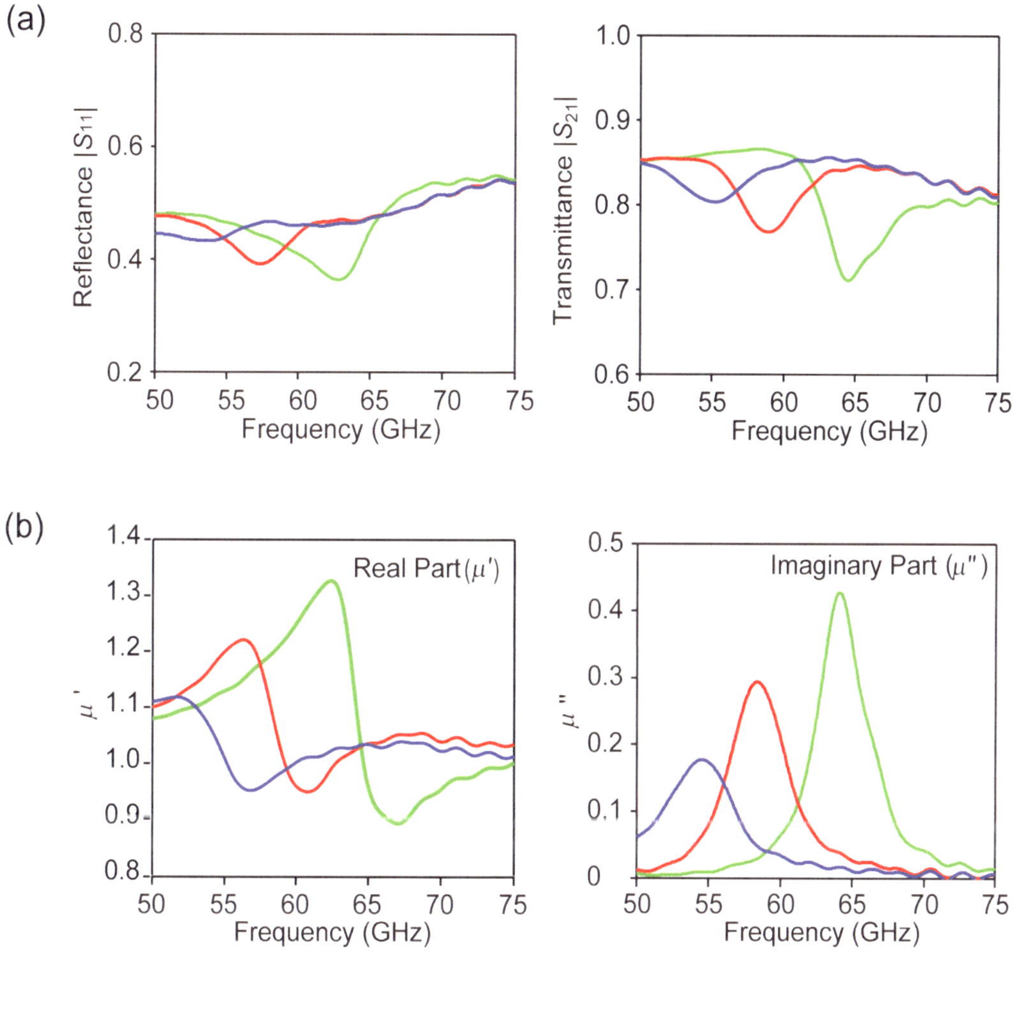

Fig. 9. (a) Reflectance and transmittance of ε-$Ga_xFe_{2-x}O_3$ for x= 0.51 (green), 0.56 (red), and 0.61 (blue). (b) the magnetic permeability of ε-$Ga_xFe_{2-x}O_3$ for x= 0.51 (green), 0.56 (red), and 0.61 (blue).

$$\Gamma = \frac{\sqrt{\mu_r/\varepsilon_r} - 1}{\sqrt{\mu_r/\varepsilon_r} + 1}, \tag{5}$$

$$\mathrm{T} = \exp\left(-jd\omega\sqrt{\varepsilon_0\varepsilon_r\mu_0\mu_r}\right), \tag{6}$$

where μ_0 is the vacuum magnetic permeability, ε_0 is the vacuum dielectric constant, μ_r is the relative magnetic permeability of the materials, ε_r is the relative dielectric constant, d is the thickness of the material, and j is the imaginary unit. Considering the effect of multiple reflections using the Nicolson-Ross Weir model,[28,29] the reflectance (S_{11}) and transmission (S_{21}) are represented by Γ and T as follows:

$$S_{11} = \frac{\Gamma\left(1 - T^2\right)}{1 - \Gamma^2 T^2}, \tag{7}$$

$$S_{21} = \frac{\left(1 - \Gamma^2\right)T}{1 - \Gamma^2 T^2}, \tag{8}$$

Using Eqs. (5)–(8), ε_r and μ_r of ε-$Ga_xFe_{2-x}O_3$ (x= 0.51, 0.56, 0.61) were determined from the measured S_{11} and S_{21} values. Figure 9b shows the determined magnetic permeability and dielectric constant of ε-$Ga_xFe_{2-x}O_3$. The μ'' values reached a maximum around 60 GHz; μ''_{max}= 0.43 (64 GHz), μ''_{max}= 0.29 (58 GHz), and μ''_{max}= 0.18 (55 GHz) for x= 0.51, 0.56, and 0.61, respectively. On the other hand, the real part of magnetic permeability showed dispersive-shaped lines at 65 GHz (x= 0.51), 59 GHz (x= 0.56), and 54 GHz (x= 0.61). Regarding dielectric constant, all samples did not show any significant variation. The sample for x= 0.51 exhibited μ''_{max} of 0.43 at 64 GHz, which is the highest μ''_{max} value among reported millimeter wave absorber in V-band region.[30]

5. Summary and prospective

In this article, we reported a millimeter wave absorber composed of ε-$Ga_xFe_{2-x}O_3$. This absorber can absorb millimeter waves in a wide range between 35–147 GHz. In addition, the μ'' values of ε-$Ga_xFe_{2-x}O_3$ are the highest values among reported magnetic millimeter wave absorbers in the V-band region, which means this series of materials can absorb millimeter waves with high efficiency. These new materials will be suitable for an absorber to restrain the EMI (for example, a millimeter wave absorber painted on the wall of office, private and medical room, or the body of car, train, and airplane), and an optoelectronic device to stabilize the EM sending (for example, a circulator and an isolator for millimeter waves of needless magnetic field).

6. References

[1] C. H. Doan, S. Emami, A. M. Niknejad and R. W. Brodersen, IEEE J. Solid-State Circuits 40, 144 (2005).

[2] M. J. W. Rodwell, *High Speed Integrated Circuit Technology, towards 100 GHz Logic* (World Scientific, Singapore, 2001).
[3] C. Cao, E. Seok and K. K. O, IEE Electronics Lett. 42, 208 (2006).
[4] B. R. Wu, W. Snodgrass, M. Feng and K. Y. Cheng, J. Crystal Growth 301-302, 1005 (2007).
[5] W. Snodgrass, B. R. Wu, W. Hafez, K. Y. Cheng and M. Feng, Appl. Phys. Lett. 88, 222101.
[6] K. J. Vinoy and R. M. Jha, *Radar Absorbing* (Kluwer, Boston, 1996).
[7] A. Vilcot, B. Cabon and J. Chazelas, *Microwave Photonics* (Kluwer, Boston, 1996).
[8] Y. Naito and K. Suetake, IEEE Trans. Microwave Theory Tech. 19, 65 (1971).
[9] Committee on identification of research needs relating to potential biological or adverse health effects of wireless communications devices, National Research Council *Identification of Research Needs Relating to Potential Biological or Adverse Health Effects of Wireless Communication* (National Academies Press, Washington, 2008).
[10] J. Jin, S. Ohkoshi and K. Hashimoto, Adv. Mater. 16, 48 (2004).
[11] S. Ohkoshi, S. Sakurai, J. Jin and K. Hashimoto, J. Appl. Phys. 97, 10K312 (2005).
[12] S. Sakurai, J. Jin, K. Hashimoto and S. Ohkoshi, J. Phys. Soc. Jpn. 74, 1946 (2005).
[13] E. Tronc, C. Chanéac and J. P. Jolivet, J. Solid State Chem. 139, 93 (1998).
[14] E. Tronc, C. Chanéac and J. P. Jolivet, J. M. Grenèche, J. Appl. Phys. 98, 053901 (2005).
[15] M. Gich, C. Frontera, A. Roig, E. Taboada, E. Molins, H. R. Rechenberg, J. D. Ardisson, W. A. A. Macedo, C. Ritter, V. Hardy, J. Sort, V. Skumryev and J. Nogues, Chem. Mater. 18, 3889 (2006).
[16] M. Popovici, M. Gich, D. Niznansky, A. Roig, C. Savii, L. Casas, E. Molins, K. Zaveta, C. Emache, J. Sort, S. Brion, G. Chouteau and J. Nogues, Chem. Mater. 16, 5542 (2004).
[17] M. Kurmoo, J. Rehspringer, A. Hutlova, C. D'Orleans, S. Vilminot, C. Estournes and D. Niznansky, Chem. Mater. 17, 1106 (2005).
[18] S. Sakurai, A. Namai, K. Hashimoto and S. Ohkoshi, J. Am. Chem. Soc., 131, 18299 (2009).
[19] S. Sakurai, K. Tomita, H.Yashiro, K. Hashimoto and S. Ohkoshi, J. Phys. Chem. C., 112, 20212 (2008).
[20] S. Ohkoshi, S. Kuroki, S. Sakurai, K. Matsumoto, K. Sato and S. Sasaki, Angew. Chem. Int. Ed. 46, 8392 (2007).
[21] A. Namai, S. Kurahashi, H. Hachiya, K. Tomita, S. Sakurai, K. Matsumoto, T. Goto and S. Ohkoshi, J. Appl. Phys., 107, 09A955 (2010).
[22] R. D. Shannon, Acta Cryst. A 32, 751 (1976).
[23] S. Ohkoshi, A. Namai and S. Sakurai, J. Phys. Chem. C 113, 11235 (2009).
[24] S. Chikazumi, *Physics of Ferromagnetism* (Oxford University Press, New York, 1997).
[25] A. Namai, S. Sakurai, M. Nakajima, T. Suemoto, K. Matsumoto, M. Goto, S. Sasaki and S. Ohkoshi J. Am. Chem. Soc. 131, 1170 (2009).
[26] L. Landau and E. Lifshitz, Phys. Z. Sowjet-union 8, 153 (1935).
[27] A. Herpin, *Théorie du Magnétism* (Presses Universitaires de France, Paris, 1968).

[28] A. M. Nicolson and G. F. Ross, IEEE Transactions on instrumentation and measurement 19, 377 (1970).
[29] W. B. Weir, Proceedings of the IEEE, 62, 33 (1974).
[30] K. A. Korolev, L. Subramanian and M. N. Afsar, J. Appl. Phys. 99, 08F504 (2006).

26

Trends and Challenges in CMOS Design for Emerging 60 GHz WPAN Applications

Ahmed El Oualkadi
Abdelmalek Essaadi University,
National school of applied sciences of Tangier,
Laboratoire des Technologies de l'Information et de la Communication,
Morocco

1. Introduction

The extensive growth of wireless communications industry is creating a big market opportunity. Wireless operators are currently searching for new solutions which would be implemented into the existing wireless communication networks to provide the broader bandwidth, the better quality and new value-added services. In the last decade, most commercial efforts were focused on the 1-10 GHz spectrum for voice and data applications for mobile phones and portable computers (Niknejad & Hashemi, 2008). Nowadays, the interest is growing in applications that use high rate wireless communications. Multi-gigabit-per-second communication requires a very large bandwidth. The Ultra-Wide Band (UWB) technology was basically used for this issue. However, this technology has some shortcomings including problems with interference and a limited data rate. Furthermore, the 3-5 GHz spectrum is relatively crowded with many interferers appearing in the WiFi bands (Niknejad & Hashemi, 2008).

The use of millimeter wave frequency band is considered the most promising technology for broadband wireless. In 2001, the Federal Communications Commission (FCC) released a set of rules governing the use of spectrum between 57 and 66 GHz (Baldwin, 2007). Hence, a large bandwidth coupled with high allowable transmit power equals high possible data rates. Traditionally the implementation of 60 GHz radio technology required expensive technologies based on III-V compound semiconductors such as InP and GaAs (Smulders et al., 2007). The rapid progress of CMOS technology has enabled its application in millimeter wave applications. Currently, the transistors became small enough, consequently fast enough. As a result, the CMOS technology has become one of the most attractive choices in implementing 60 GHz radio due to its low cost and high level of integration (Doan et al., 2005). Despite the advantages of CMOS technology, the design of 60 GHz CMOS transceiver exhibits several challenges and difficulties that the designers must overcome.

This chapter aims to explore the potential of the 60 GHz band in the use for emergent generation multi-gigabit wireless applications. The chapter presents a quick overview of the state-of-the-art of 60 GHz radio technology and its potentials to provide for high data rate and short range wireless communications. The chapter is organized as follows. Section 2 presents an overview about 60 GHz band. The advantages are presented to highlight the performance characteristics of this band. The opportunities of the physical layer of the IEEE

802.15.3c standard for emerging WPAN applications are discussed in section 3. The tremendous opportunities available with CMOS technology in the design of 60 GHz radio is discussed in section 4. Section 5 shows an example of 60 GHz radio system link. Some challenges and trade-offs on the design issues of circuits and systems for 60 GHz band are reported in section 6. Finally, section 7 presents the conclusion and some perspectives on future directions.

2. Overview of the 60 GHz band characteristics

The quest for higher data rates and the spectrum scarcity makes designers of wireless communication systems explore higher frequency bands, such as the millimeter wave frequency band (30-300 GHz).

In 1995, the FCC has decided to open the largest contiguous bandwidth in history, 59-64 GHz for non-government unlicensed wireless communications (Van Tuy, 1996). Subsequently, this bandwidth was extended to 7 GHz, in United States in 2001, providing 5 GHz of overlap with unlicensed spectrum in Japan (59–66 GHz) and other geographical regions over the world. Table 1 shows the allocation of the international unlicensed spectrum around 60 GHz. This available spectrum can enable a huge channel bandwidth (2500 MHz) compared to other wireless communication standards.

Based on Shannon's theorem (Shannon, 1948), the maximum possible date rate of a communication channel is given by:

$$C = BW \log_2\left(1 + \frac{S}{N}\right) \qquad (1)$$

where C is the channel capacity, BW is the bandwidth of the channel, S is the total received power over the bandwidth, and N is the total noise power over the bandwidth.

The maximum possible data rate, known as channel capacity, increases with increasing channel bandwidth. Consequently, the 60 GHz band can be considered an attractive solution for high date rate wireless communications.

Region	Low frequency (GHz)	High frequency (GHz)	Bandwidth (GHz)
USA	57 GHz	64 GHz	7
Canada	57 GHz	64 GHz	7
Europe	57 GHz	66 GHz	9
Korea	57 GHz	64 GHz	7
Japan	59 GHz	66 GHz	7
Australia	59.4 GHz	62.5 GHz	3,1

Table 1. The allocation of the international unlicensed spectrum around 60 GHz in various region over the world

However, the 60 GHz spectrum is characterized by high levels of atmospheric radiofrequency (RF) energy absorption. Figure 1 shows the variation of oxygen attenuation versus frequency (FCC, 1997).

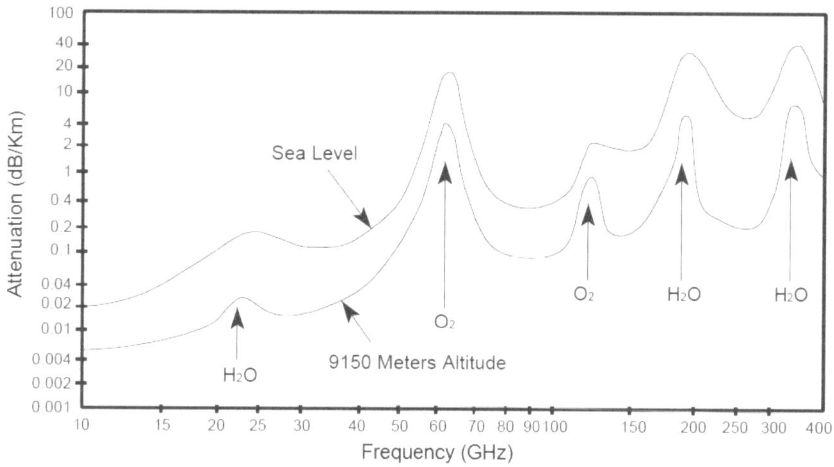

Fig. 1. The oxygen attenuation versus frequency (FCC, 1997)

The oxygen absorption has its maximum (10–15 dB/km) in the 60 GHz band. This makes the transmitted energy quickly absorbed by oxygen molecules in the atmosphere over long distances (Daniels & Heath, 2007). So that signals cannot travel far beyond their intended recipient. While this limits distances that they can cover, it also offers interference and security advantages which can make the 60 GHz band becomes an attractive alternative for high security, short-range and high-speed wireless communications (Guo et al., 2007).

In this context, the Ultra-Wide Band (UWB) technology has a long been used for short range and high date rate applications. However, this technology suffers from the immunity to interference (Guo et al., 2007). In the millimeter wave band, the oxygen absorption enables the benefit of reduced co-channel interference. Therefore, the transmitted signal from one 60 GHz transmitter is rapidly reduced in a manner that will not interfere with other links operating in the same geographic vicinity (Smulders et al., 2007). This enables dense wireless communication due to shorter frequency reuse distance.

Besides oxygen absorption, they have other parameters that degrade the performance of a 60 GHz transmission link which due to:

- Losses due to transmission channel
- Attenuation by rain
- Refraction
- Depolarization of signal

According to the Friis transmission equation (Friss, 1944), the free-space path loss (FSPL) formula is given by the following equation:

$$FSPL = \left(\frac{4\pi R}{\lambda}\right)^2 \tag{2}$$

where λ is the wavelength, and R is the distance between terminals.

Figure 2 shows the variation of FSPL versus distance with and without oxygen absorption at 60 GHz frequency. The FSPL is proportional to the square of the distance between the transmitter and receiver, as a result, the increase of this distance raises the FSPL.

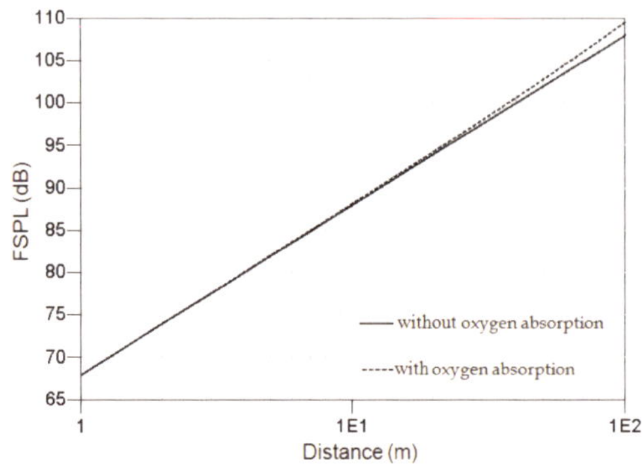

Fig. 2. The FSPL versus distance at 60 GHz

The FCC and various regulators over the world have allowed the limits on transmit power and the Equivalent Isotropic Radiated Power (EIRP) to ensure the wireless transmission in the 60 GHz band. Thus, the large unlicensed bandwidth associated with a high allowable transmit power can enable multi-gigabit wireless communications (Yong & Chong, 2007).

Actually, the millimeter wave band has several other advantages. In addition to the large spectral capacity, it can offer small antennas, and compact and light equipment (Daniels & Heath, 2007). Moreover, at 60 GHz operating frequency, the beamwidth is only equal to a fewdegrees and for WPAN applications an omnidirectional antenna pattern is usually desired (Lee et al., 2010).

A whole range of new applications in the area of consumer electronics devices can exploit this band for high data rate wireless applications. From uncompressed video distribution in the home, fast downloads of Gbytes of data at video kiosks, to Gbit/s wireless connections between laptops and printers (Fig. 3).

Fig. 3. Short range and high data rate millimeter wave communications with several devices

However, the design of 60 GHz wireless systems is not straightforward, and it exhibits several challenges. Indeed, the imperfections related to the blocks of a 60 GHz radio system (imperfect components, phase noise, non-linearity, etc...) can cause degradation in the overall-performance. The interior of buildings is also a multipath channel. Many obstacles (walls, partitions, ceilings, furnishings) are reflective surfaces for the waves. The existence of multiple paths is the cause of channel fading which requires a high-performance signal processing in reception (synchronization, equalization, correction of errors) especially when the date rate is significant (Daniels & Heath, 2007).

3. IEEE 802.15.3c standard for emerging WPAN applications

The IEEE 802.15.3 Task Group 3c (TG3c) was formed in March 2005. The TG3c developed a millimeter wave based alternative physical layer (PHY) for the existing 802.15.3 Wireless Personal Area Network (WPAN) Standard 802.15.3-2003. The 802.15.3c-2009 was published on September 11, 2009. This is the first standard that addresses multi-gigabit short-range wireless systems. It is aimed to support a minimum data rate of 2 Gbps over a few meters with optional data rates in excess of 3 Gbps. The 802.15.3c-2009 employs a channel plan that divides the 60 GHz spectrum into channels of approximately 2.16 GHz each. Such wide channels make it easy to achieve gigabit data rate even with relatively simple modulation and coding schemes (Yang, 2008). Three PHY modes are specified in the standard: single carrier (SC) PHY, high speed interface (HSI) orthogonal frequency division multiplexing (OFDM) PHY and audio video (AV) OFDM PHY. Table 2 shows some characteristics of these PHY modes. The existence of three PHY modes, with different characteristics, is due mainly to the possibility for supporting various applications.

	SC	HSI OFDM	AV OFDM
Modulation	BPSK, (G)MSK, QPSK, 8PSK, 16QAM	QPSK, 16QAM, 64QAM	QPSK, 16QAM
Data rate	25.3Mbps-5.1 Gbps	31.5Mbps-5.67Gbps	0.95-3.8 Gbps

Table 2. Some characteristics of the PHY modes

Actually, the SC PHY mode provides three classes of modulation and coding schemes targeting different wireless connectivity applications. Class 1 is specified to address the low-power low-cost mobile market while maintaining a relatively high data rate of up to 1.5 Gbps. Class 2 is specified to achieve data rates up to 3 Gbps. Class 3 is specified to support high performance applications with data rates in excess of 5 Gbps. However, the HSI PHY mode is designed for devices with low-latency, bidirectional high-speed data and uses OFDM. HSI PHY supports a variety of modulation and coding schemes using different frequency-domain spreading factors, modulations, and LDPC block codes. Finally, the AV PHY is implemented with two PHY modes, the high-rate PHY (HRP) and low-rate PHY (LRP), both of which use OFDM. A Common mode signaling is defined which is an SC-based $\pi/2$ binary phase shift key (BPSK) with low data rate (25 Mbps) in order to promote coexistence among these PHY modes.

4. CMOS technology for 60 GHz radio design

It is commonly believed that the promising 60 GHz radio technology has introduced new opportunities and perspectives for several wireless applications. Thus, the design of millimeter wave circuits is achieving growing interest in modem communication systems (Winkler et al., 2004). Traditionally, technologies based on III-V compound semiconductor, which achieve frequency transitions of several tens of gigahertz, were exclusively used for the implementation of millimeter wave circuits due to their superior noise characteristics and power handling at higher frequencies (Reynolds, 2004). Such technologies were mainly intended for military applications for which the cost is not very relevant (Floyd et al., 2005). Moreover, these technologies show low power efficiency and limited the digital integration.

The intensive investigations in the design of millimeter wave circuits and systems are characterized by a deep research of maximum performances with minimum costs following the targeted wireless communication standards (Hajimiri, 2007). Reducing costs come through high level integration of a maximum functions within the radio communication system. In this context, the complementary metal-oxide semiconductor (CMOS) technology based on silicon is generally the most suitable for implementing on-chip radios since the silicon remains incomparable both in terms of digital integration, production capacity and overall reliability of design and performance.

Nowadays, thanks to the large progress of lithography, CMOS processes below 130 nm, led to maximum frequency of operation (f_{max}) comparable to those of the best processes in bipolar silicon and AsGa. Actually, the continuous progress of silicon CMOS technology has enabled its application in millimeter wave applications. The scaling of the dimensions of transistors, following the Moore's law (Moore, 1965), has the peculiar property of improving cost, performance, and power consumption. Currently, the transistors became small enough, consequently fast enough and show a very high transition frequency (more than 400 GHz) (Fig. 4). Therefore, the CMOS technology is becoming the future technology of choice in implementing millimeter wave integrated circuits due to low cost manufacturing and feasibility of the integration with digital circuits (Doan et al., 2004).

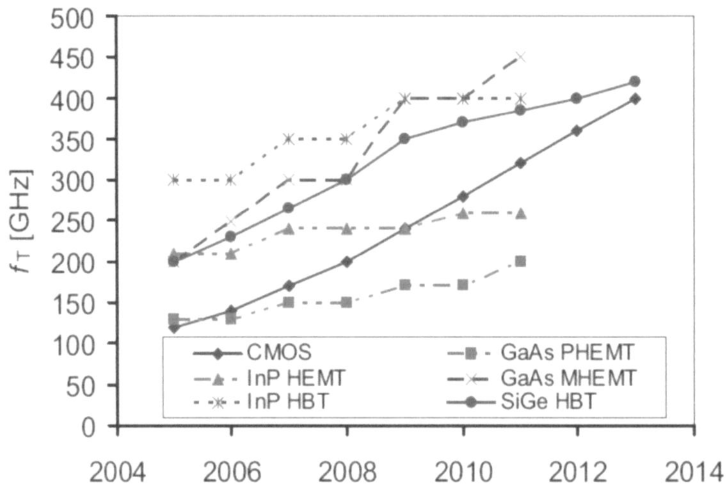

Fig. 4. The evolution of f_T by year of production comparing silicon and III-V compound semiconductor devices (Niknejad et al., 2008)

5. 60 GHz radio system link

The aim of this section is to test the performance of a 60 GHz link for WPAN applications. In order to do that, a case study of a transceiver is implemented based on performances, at 60 GHz, of its building blocks in the literature (Barakat, 2008).

Fig. 5 shows the transceiver setup with characteristics of different building blocks at 60 GHz. The used filters are ideal filters with quality factors depend on the specified frequency. This simulation schematic allows to study the link budget by given the power at each point of a link. The received power after demodulation is considered in this simulation.

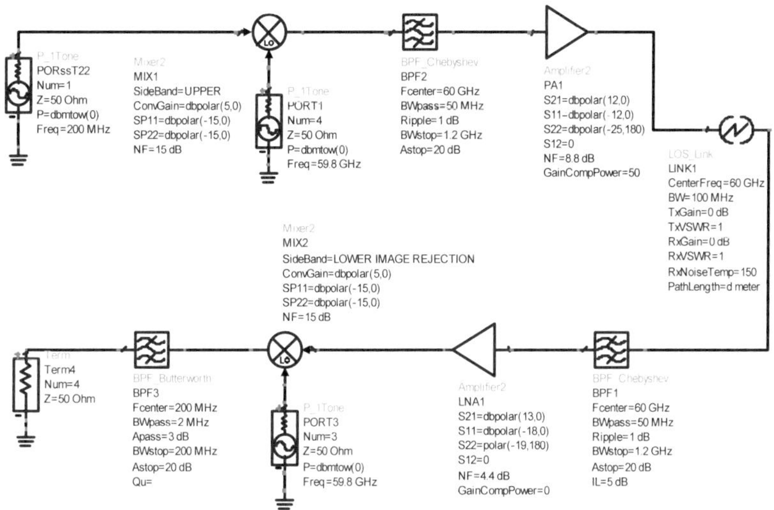

Fig. 5. The simulation setup with the characteristics of different building blocks

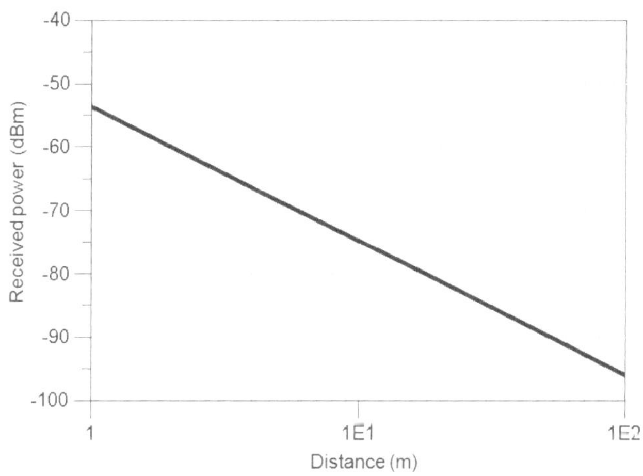

Fig. 6. The received power after demodulation at 60 GHz for a transmit power of 0 dBm vs. distance

Fig .6 shows the variation of the received power, after demodulation at 60 GHz, in function of distance when the transmit power is equal to 0 dBm. Since, the WAPN applications in the 60 GHz band require short-range distance (10 to 100 meters); it is possible to ensure 60 GHz multi-gigabit wireless communications (Yong & Chong, 2007).

The design of 60 GHz wireless system is not straightforward and exhibits several challenges (Emami et al., 2007). In the literature, several transceiver architectures have been proposed for millimeter frequency band. Actually, the Low IF architecture requires stringent image rejection, as an adjacent channel becomes its image (Razavi, 2006). The Zero IF is referred to as "no image" but it is susceptible to flicker noise, DC offset and also suffers from impairments of even order distortion, LO pulling and LO leakage (Reynolds et al., 2006). Therefore heterodyne structure with two down-conversion steps can be considered as interesting solution of implementing 60 GHz radio transceivers for WPAN applications (Parsa & Razavi, 2009).

6. Trends and challenges in designing 60 GHz building blocks in CMOS

The design and modeling of 60 GHz building blocks of a transceiver requires several challenges and trends. Actually, the CMOS design at millimeter wave can be characterized by two different approaches which depend on the simulation environments and the related techniques. As an example, analog RF designers prefer to use inductors rather than transmission lines which are used by microwave designers (Leenaerts et al., 2001). Indeed, these choices can have an impact on the layout since transmission lines consume a large area while spiral inductors generally occupy a smaller area (Scheir et al., 2007).
Furthermore, at millimeter wave frequencies, the design of active and passive devices and interconnects becomes more complicated, since the effects of layout parasitic elements cannot be neglected, otherwise a strong frequency down-shift will occur between simulation and measurement results (Majek et al., 2009). Consequently, the accurate modeling of active and passive devices is normally considered as the premise of the design success in millimeter wave circuits (Liang et al., 2009).
This section outlines the various design trade-offs of millimeter wave CMOS integrated circuits based on the review of the state-of-the-art. The study will focus in three of the most critical building blocks in the radio front-end: LNA (Low-Noise Amplifier), Mixer and VCO (Voltage-Controlled-Oscillator) used as a LO (Local Oscillator).

6.1 Low-Noise Amplifiers

The Low Noise Amplifier (LNA) is the most critical building blocks in transceiver since it bears the receiver noise performance according to Friis formula (Friis, 1944):

$$F = F_1 + \frac{F_2 - 1}{G_1} + \frac{F_3 - 1}{G_1 G_2} + \ldots + \frac{F_N - 1}{G_1 G_2 \ldots G_{N-1}} \tag{3}$$

where F is the noise figure of the recevier, F_i is the noise figure of the stage number i and the G_i is the gain of the stage number i.
Indeed, the first stage of the LNA supports the noise figure of the receiver. Besides the low noise figure, high gain, good isolation, large bandwidth and low power consumption are the main parameters of a high performance LNA.
The common gate and common source topologies have a long been employed in the design of LNAs for RF, microwave and millimeter wave applications. While these simple architectures can exhibit a low noise figure, they cannot achieve the good isolation and high gain compared to a classical cascade topology (Maruhashi et al. 2008).
In the literature, several references have been reported the design of CMOS LNA in the 60 GHz band. The design reported in (Doan et al., 2005) is the first tentative 60 GHz amplifier on CMOS; this design is more a general purpose amplifier than a LNA.
A three-stage common source LNA is reported in (Kai Kang al., 2010). Fig. 7 shows the schematic of this LNA. The size of the MOSFETs is 32x1μmx90nm. The width of the microstrip lines is either 5 μm or 9 μm and V_D=1.2 V (Kai Kang al., 2010).

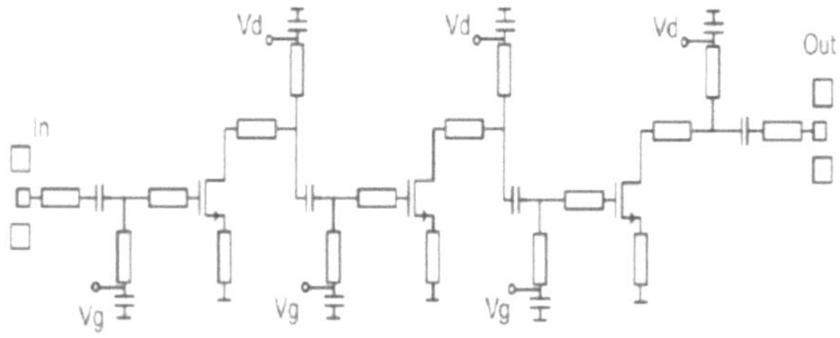

Fig. 7. The three-stage common source LNA (Kai Kang al., 2010)

This design is implemented in 90 nm CMOS process and it achieves a gain of 18.6 dB and a noise figure of 5.7 at 57 GHz. However, it consumes 24 mA from a 1.2 V supply voltage (Kai Kang al., 2010).

The cascode topology represents the most widespread circuit solution for realizing high-gain and stable low-noise amplifiers (Razavi, 2005). However, the cascode LNA needs new circuit technique to achieve good performances. One solution is the interstage matching topology. A serie inductor inserted between the common gate and the common source stages as proposed in (Tao et al., 2009). Fig. 8 shows this single-stage cascode low noise amplifier operating in the range of 57 to 64 GHz. The co-simulation performances of the LNA at 60 GHz are reported in (Tao et al., 2009). The voltage gain and noise figure are equal to 18.7 dB and 4.2 dB respectively while the DC power is equal to 4.9 mW.

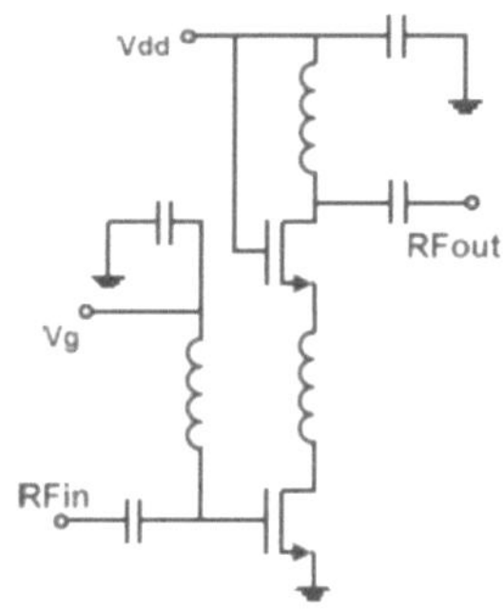

Fig. 8. The single-stage cascode LNA (Tao et al., 2009)

6.2 Mixers

The mixer is an essential component in wireless transceivers for frequency translation, which requires high conversion gain, low noise figure, and high linearity. In the literature several mixer architectures, which are suitable for operating in the millimeter wave frequencies, has been studied for WPAN Applications.

The resistive mixers show a high linearity, superior intermodulation properties and virtually zero dc power consumption. Indeed, the performance of the resistive mixers remains unaffected by the low supply voltage allowed in the deep submicron CMOS-technologies (Motlagh et al., 2006). However, these resistive mixers have a conversion loss instead of gain (Motlagh et al., 2006). The bulk-driven architecture that uses the transistor as a four terminal device can provide low voltage and low power operation for mixer design (Wang & Tsai, 2009). A bulk-driven mixer has been designed using 130 nm CMOS technology (Wang & Tsai, 2009). In spite of having a high noise figure which is equal to 23 dB, this bulk-driven mixer exhibits a conversion gain of 1 dB and a power consumption of 3 mW at 60 GHz. The millimeter wave passive mixer followed by an IF amplifier can reach roughly the same noise figure and conversion gain as an active topology does (Razavi, 2009). However, the passive mixer suffers from a lower input impedance than does the active mixer, heavily loading the LNA (Razavi, 2008). The Gilbert-cell down-conversion mixer operating at 60 GHz has been reported in (Tsai et al. 2007). These mixers showed good isolation between RF and LO ports associated with high power consumption which make these Gilbert-cell mixers not suitable for low power and low-voltage applications (Wang & Tsai, 2009). In contrast, the double-balanced gate mixers exhibit low supply voltage and low dc consumption (Lien et al., 2010). Compared to other double-balanced mixers, these mixers show low LO power, low noise figure and high conversion gain, and they have better isolations than the single-balanced gate mixers (Lien et al., 2010). The design in (Emami et al., 2005) shows a 60-GHz quadrature balanced single-gate mixer implemented in 130 nm CMOS technology. This design can be considered as the first mixer realization in the 60 GHz range. This mixer shows a conversion loss less than 2 dB and the return loss at the RF and LO ports higher than 15 dB while consuming 2.4 mW. The input-referred 1-dB compression point is -3.5 dBm.

The dual-gate MOSFET mixer can be considered as alternative choice compared to the previous topologies (El Oualkadi et al., 2009). Fig. 9 shows the architecture of this mixer. The RF signal signal is applied to the gate of the transistor M_RF and the LO signal is applied to the gate of the second transistor M_LO.

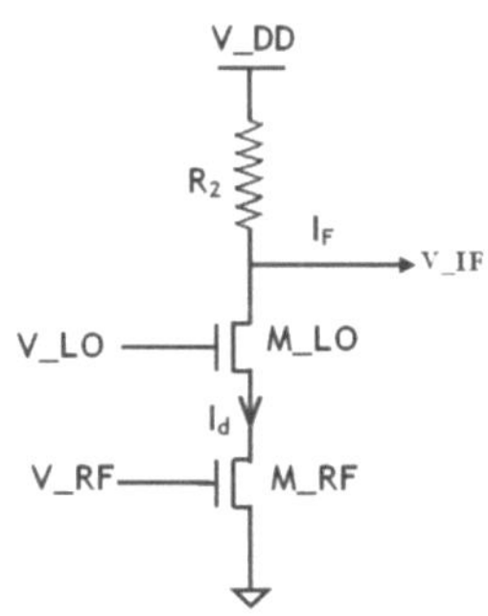

Fig. 9. The architecture of the dual-gate MOSFET mixer

The mixer architecture is composed by two transistors in cascade. The advantage of using a cascode topology is that it allows the RF input and the LO signal to be fed into two different MOSFET gates, avoiding the need for area-consuming power combiners. Since the RF and LO rejections at the IF output are not so critical due to the large spectral differences, this topology can be employed instead of Gilbert mixers and thus avoiding the use of lossy baluns (Maas, 1986). The M_RF transistor operates in the saturation region and provides a transconductance g_m, which is a function of the drain voltage of M_RF transistor controlled by the LO signal. However, the M_LO transistor operates in the linear region and used for commutation as a switch according to the LO signal.

The 60 GHz dual-gate MOSFET mixer was designed and optimized in CMOS 65 nm technology (El Oualkadi et al., 2009). The mixer shows a suitable conversion gain when considering that the supply voltage does not exceed 1.2 V with a power consumption of 8.5

mW. Table 3 shows the performance of this mixer compared to the previous published 60 GHz mixers. This dual-gate mixer shows a good compromise between simplicity and good performances.

	(Emami et al., 2005)	(Lai et al., 2006)	(Wang & Tsai, 2009)	(El Oualkadi et al, 2009)	(Lien et al., 2010)
Approach	Single-gate	Cascode	Bulk-driven	Dual-gate	Double-balanced
Process	130nm CMOS	90nm CMOS	130nm CMOS	65nm CMOS	130nm CMOS
Freq (GHz)	54-61	60	51-61	60	
Conversion Gain (dB)	-1 @ 60 GHz	-1.2	1 @ 60 GHz	0.4	-3~0
Input P_{1dB} (dBm)	-3.5	0.2	-19	1.264	-8
Supply Voltage (V)	1.2	-	1	1.2	-
Power consumption (mW)	2.4	29.4	3	8.5	14

Table 3. Performance comparisons of some millimeter wave mixers reported in the state-of-the-art

6.3 Oscillators

A key building block in radio transceiver is the VCO which is employed as a LO for assuring the modulation/demodulation. The implementation of VCOs in CMOS technology is justly felt as one of the major challenges that must be overcome in the design of integrated 60 GHz WPAN transceivers (Regimbal et al., 2009). Indeed, the limited transistor speeds and long interconnects causes some critical issues related to the generation of I and Q phases of the LO at 60 GHz. The quadrature operation typically degrades the phase noise considerably (Razavi, 2005). While, the division of LO frequency poses a problem, since; the design of high-speed dividers requires many challenges at 60 GHz (Razavi, 2009). Besides these challenges, a number of performance requirements have to be met to make a VCO suitable for 60 GHz WPAN applications . Most importantly, low phase noise is required to avoid corrupting the mixer-converted signal by close interfering tones. Low power consumption and tenability are also two important aspects that define the performance of a VCO (Razavi, 2000).

The ring oscillators and passive RC-CR networks are two of the most commonly used solutions for quadrature generation. While ring oscillators are widely used for digital-based applications, passive networks suffer from high loss and inaccuracy. The LC cross-coupled oscillators and Colpitts oscillators are the most suitable for RF and millimeter applications due to their excellent phase noise performance (Kim et al., 2008). However, the use of several inductors in the LC VCOs leads to difficulties in the layout. Indeed, the substrate loss affects directly the quality factors of inductors and varactors in the millimeter wave range (Liang et al., 2009). Therefore, the trade-offs between the phase noise, the tuning range, and the power dissipation become much more severe (Razavi, 2009).

The millimeter wave CMOS oscillators proposed in the literature commonly used a cross coupled transistor pair with different resonator structures (Farahabadi et al., 2009).
An example of a LC VCO based on cross coupled topology is proposed in (Borremans et al., 2008). This design implemented in 130 nm CMOS shows interesting performances at 60 GHz. The measured phase noise is below -90 dBc/Hz at 1 MHz offset with a power consumption of 3.9 mW at 1 V. The tuning range exceeds 10 %, for a tuning voltage restricted from ground to the supply (Borremans et al., 2008). Such performances can allow this VCO to be an interesting solution for WPAN applications.
To realize the direct dowconversion operation, a 60 GHz receiver requires a VCO with quadrature phase generation. A VCO using an injection-coupled topology is used in (Sakian et al. 2009) to generate quadrature 60 GHz outputs. Fig. 10 shows the schematic of this VCO.

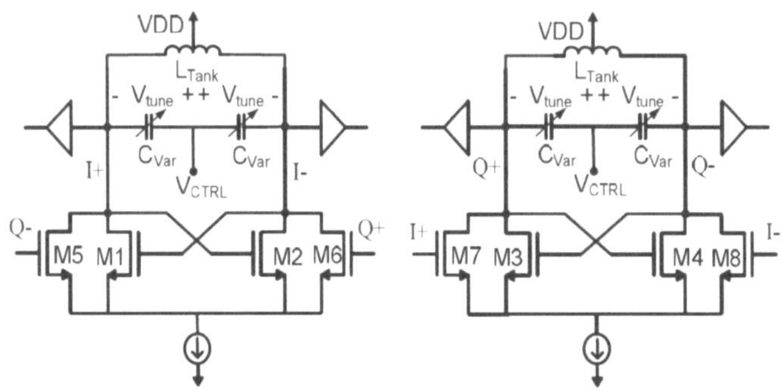

Fig. 10. The two LC-VCOs coupled in anti-phase to provide I-Q outputs (Sakian et al. 2009)

The required negative conductance is generated by the cross-coupled pairs M1-M2 and M3-M4. The coupling transistors M5-M8 inject the output signals of one cross-coupled pair to the input of the other to produce anti-phase coupling required for quadrature generation (Sakian et al. 2009).
The measurements show a tuning range of 5.6 GHz (57.5 to 63.1 GHz), a phase noise of -95.3 dBc/Hz at 1 MHz offset and a power consumption of 36 mW. Despite the additional challenges and limitations imposed by the quadrature topology, the obtained performances are comparable to state of the art single-phase VCOs, (Sakian et al. 2009).

7. Conclusion

During the recent years, the 60 GHz band has gained increased academic and commercial interest mainly due to the availability of a large unlicensed spectrum in the vicinity of 60 GHz. Nowadays, thanks to the development of the IEEE 802.15.3c standard for WPAN, various commercial applications have been emerged. Thus, the 60 GHz band is considered as an attracting solution for broadband wireless in particularly for short range and high data rate applications.
The implementation of new 60 GHz wireless applications is strictly related to the development of high performance 60 GHz radio transceivers. This implies that the designers of circuits and systems must overcome several challenges and trade-offs which occurring when working in the millimeter wave spectrum (Hajimiri, 2007).
The CMOS technology which is the dominating technology for most wireless products below 10 GHz, is characterized by reliability, maturity, low manufacturing cost and low

power consumption compared to traditional semiconductor technologies based on III-V compound materials such as SiGe and GaAs. In addition, CMOS is the most suitable technology for designing system-on-chip, since it enables integration of the analog RF circuits with the digital signal processing and baseband circuits in the lowest possible chip area, which leads to a lower cost and more compact solution. With the enormous world-wide effort to scale to lower gate-lengths, CMOS technology is pushing further into the millimeter wave region with maximum frequency of oscillation exciding 300 GHz promising increasing performance in the future (Niknejad, 2008).

Today, the interest on designing millimeter wave CMOS circuits and systems is growing rapidly offering a fertile ground for innovation. CMOS technology is becoming the strong candidate for implementing low cost and less power consuming 60 GHz WPAN transceivers which are expected to boost wireless communication data rates to the order of multi-gigabit-per-second.

Actually, if several efforts have been done that ameliorate the challenges in millimeter wave design many questions still remain (Razavi, 2009). Therefore, various areas of investigation will certainly be the subject of deep research in the next coming years. For example:

- At the device level, several efforts should be done in the accurately modeling of both active and passive devices in the millimeter wave band. The objective is to have scalable models which would allow an efficient design of the building blocks.
- At the circuit level, some building blocks require new design techniques in order to improve the targeted performance at 60 GHz, like power amplifiers and switches. The integration of antennas still remains as a big challenge to promote the single on-chip transceivers.
- At the system level, new methodologies for simulation of large transceivers and their layouts should be developed. Issues related to packaging must be solved to facilitate coupling among various building blocks through the power lines and the substrate.

8. References

Baldwin, G. L. (2007). Background on development of 60 GHz for commercial use. SiBEAM.com, white paper

Barakat, M. H. (2008). Dispositif Radiofréquence Millimétrique Pour Objets Communicants de Type Smart Dust. PhD Thesis. University of Joseph Fourier, Grenoble, France.

Borremans, J.; Dehan, M.; Scheir, K.; Kuijk, M. and Wambacq, P. (2008). VCO design for 60 GHz applications using differential shielded inductors in 0.13um CMOS. *Proceedings of IEEE Radio Frequency integrated Circuits Symposium (RFIC 2008)*, pp. 135-138, ISBN 0-7803-8983-2, Atlanta, Georgia, USA, June 2005, IEEE, Piscataway

Daniels, R. C. & Heath, R. W. (2007). 60 GHz Wireless Communications: Emerging Requirements and Design Recommendations. IEEE Vehicular Technology Magazine, Vol. 2, N. 3, pp. 41-50, ISSN 1556-6072

Doan C. H.; Emami, S.; Niknejad, A.M. and Brodersen, R.W. (2004). Design of CMOS for 60 GHz applications, *Proceedings of IEEE International Solid-State Circuits Conference (ISSCC '04)*, pp. 440-538, ISBN 0-7803-8267-6, San Francisco, California, USA, Feb. 2004, IEEE, Piscataway

Doan, C. H.; Emami, S.; Niknejad, A. M & Brodersen R. W. (2005). Millimeter-wave CMOS design. *IEEE J. Solid-State Circuits*, Vol. 40, No. 1, pp. 144–155, ISSN 0018-9200

El Oualkadi, A. ; Faitah, K. & Ouahman, A. A. (2009). mm-Wave CMOS Mixer Design in 65 nm Technology for 60 GHz Wireless Communications, *Proceedings of IEEE Mediterranean Microwave Symposium (MMS'09)*, pp. 1-4, ISBN 978-1-4244-4664-3, Tangier, Morocco, Nov. 2009, IEEE, Piscataway

Emami, S.; Doan, C.H.; Niknejad, A.M. and Brodersen, R.W. (2005). A 60-GHz down-converting CMOS single-gate mixer. *Proceedings of IEEE Radio Frequency integrated Circuits Symposium (RFIC 2005)*, pp. 163-166, ISBN 0-7803-8983-2, Long Beach, California, USA, June 2005, IEEE, Piscataway

Emami, S.; Doan, C.H.; Niknejad, A.M. and Brodersen, R.W. (2007). A Highly Integrated 60GHz CMOS Front End Receiver. *Proceedings of IEEE Solid-Sate Circuits Conference (ISSCC2007), Digest of technical papers*, pp. 190-191, ISBN 1-4244-0853-9, San Francisco, California, USA, Feb. 2007, IEEE, Piscataway

Farahabadi, P. M.; Naimi, H. M. & Zabihi, M. (2009). An enhanced low phase noise VCO in 130 nm CMOS for 60 GHz applications, *Proceedings of 2nd International Conference on Power Electronics and Intelligent Transportation System (PEITS)*, pp. 40-43, ISBN 978-1-4244-4544-8, Shenzhen, China, Fev. 2009, IEEE, Piscataway

FCC. (1997). Millimeter Wave Propagation: Spectrum Management Implications. *Federal Communications Commission – Office of Engineering and Technology*, Bulletin N 70, Washington, DC 20554.

Floyd, B.A.; Reynolds, S.K.; Pfeiffer, U.R.; Zwick, T.; Beukema, T. & Gaucher, B. (2005). SiGe bipolar transceiver circuits operating at 60 GHz. *IEEE J. Solid-State Circuits*, Vol. 40, No. 1, pp. 156–167, ISSN 0018-9200

Friis, H. T. (1944). Noise figures of radio receivers. *Proceedings of the IRE*, Vol. 32, No. 7, pp. 419–422, ISSN 0096-8390

Guo, N.; Qiu, R. C.; Mo, S. S. & Takahashi, K. (2007). 60-GHz Millimeter-Wave Radio: Principle, Technology, and New Results. *EURASIP Journal on Wireless Communications and Networking*, Vol. 2007, Article ID 68253, pp. 1-8, ISSN 1687-1499

Hajimiri, A. (2007). mm-Wave Silicon ICs: Challenges and Opportunities. *Proceedings of IEEE Custom Intergrated Circuits Conference (CICC 2007)*, pp. 741-748, ISBN 978-1-4244-1623-3, San Jose, California, USA, Sep. 2007, IEEE, Piscataway

Kang, K.; Brinkhoff, J. and Lin, F. (2010). A 60 GHz LNA with 18.6 dB gain and 5.7 dB NF in 90nm CMOS. *Proceedings of IEEE International Conference on Microwave and Millimeter Wave Technology (ICMMT 2010)*, pp. 164-167, ISBN 978-1-4244-5705-2, Chengdu, China, May 2010, IEEE, Piscataway

Kim, N.; Lee, S. and Rieh, J-S. (2008). A Millimeter-Wave LC Cross-Coupled VCO for 60 GHz WPAN Application in a 0.13-µm Si RF CMOS Technology. *IEEE Journal of Semiconductor Technology and Science*, Vol. 8, No. 4, pp. 295–301, ISSN 1598-1657

Lai, I.C.H.; Kambayashi, Y. and Fujishima, M. (2006). 60-GHz CMOS Down-Conversion Mixer with Slow-Wave Matching Transmission Lines, *Proceedings of IEEE Asian Solid-State Circuits Conference (ASSCC 2006)*, pp. 195-198, ISBN 0-7803-9734-7, Hangzhou, China, Nov. 2006, IEEE, Piscataway

Lee, W.; Kim, J.; Cho, C. S & Yoon, Y. J. (2010). Beamforming Lens Antenna on a High Resistivity Silicon Wafer for 60 GHz WPAN. *IEEE Transactions on Antennas and Propagation*, Vol. 58, No. 3, pp. 706–713, ISSN 0018-926X

Leenaerts, D.; Van der Tang, J.; Vaucher C. S. (2001). *Circuit Design for RF Transceivers*, pp. 1-344, Kluwer Academic Publishers, ISBN 978-0792375517, USA

Liang, C. and Razavi, B. (2009). Systematic transistor and inductor modeling for millimeter wave design. *IEEE J. Solid-State Circuits,* Vol. 44, No. 2, pp. 450-457, ISSN 0018-9200

Lien, C-H.; Huang, P-C. ; Kao, K-Y.; Lin, K-Y. and Wang, H. (2010). 60 GHz Double-Balanced Gate-Pumped Down-Conversion Mixers With a Combined Hybrid on 130 nm CMOS Processes. *IEEE Microw. Wireless Compon. Lett.,* Vol. 20, No. 3, pp. 160-162, ISSN 1531-1309

Majek, C.; Severino, R.R.; Taris, T.; Deval, Y.; Mariano, A.; Begueret, J.-B. and Belot, D. (2009). 60 GHz cascode LNA with interstage matching: performance comparison between 130nm BiCMOS and 65nm CMOS-SOI technologies. *Proceedings of 3rd IEEE International Signals, Circuits and Systems (SCS 2009),* pp. 1-5, ISBN 978-1-4244-4397-0, Medenine, Tunisia, Nov. 2009, IEEE, Piscataway

Maruhashi, K.; Tanomura, M.; Hamada, Y.; Ito, M.; Orihashi, N. and Kishimoto, S. (2008). 60-GHz-Band CMOS MMIC Technology for High-Speed Wireless Personal Area Networks. *Proceedings of IEEE Compound Semiconductor Integrated Circuits Symposium (CSIC '08),* pp. 1-4, ISBN 978-1-4244-1939-5, Monterey, California, USA, Oct. 2008, IEEE, Piscataway

Moore, G. E. (1965). Cramming more components onto integrated circuits. *IEEE Proceedings,* Vol. 38, No. 8, pp. 82–85, ISSN 0018-9219

Motlagh, B.M.; Gunnarsson, S.E.; Ferndahl, M. and Zirath, H. (2006). Fully integrated 60-GHz single-ended resistive mixer in 90-nm CMOS technology. *IEEE Microw. Wireless Compon. Lett.,* Vol. 16, No. 1, pp. 25–27, ISSN 1531-1309

Niknejad, A. M. & Hashemi, H. (2008). *mm-Wave Silicon Technology 60 GHz and Beyond,* pp. 1-302, Springer, ISBN 978-0-387-76558-7, USA

Parsa, A. and Razavi, B. (2009). A new transceiver architecture for the 60-GHz band. *IEEE J. Solid-State Circuits,* Vol. 44, No. 3, pp. 751–762, ISSN 0018-9200

Razavi, B. (2000). *Design of Analog CMOS Integrated* Circuits, pp. 1-684, McGraw-Hill, ISBN 978-0072380323, New York, USA

Razavi, B. (2006). CMOS transceivers for the 60-GHz band. *Proceedings of IEEE Radio Frequency integrated Circuits Symposium (RFIC 2006),* pp. 231–234, ISBN 0-7803-9572-7 San Francisco, California, USA, June 2006, IEEE, Piscataway

Razavi, B. (2008). A millimeter-wave circuit technique. *IEEE J. Solid-State Circuits,* Vol. 43, No. 9, pp. 2090–2098, ISSN 0018-9200

Razavi, B. (2009). Design of Millimeter-Wave CMOS Radios: A Tutorial. *IEEE Transactions on Circuits and Systems I: Regular Papers,* Vol. 56, No. 1, pp. 4-16, ISSN 1549-8328

Regimbal, N.; Deval, Y.; Badets, F. & Begueret, J-B. (2009). Limitations of fractional synthesizers for 60 GHz WPANs: A survey, *Proceedings of IEEE North-East Workshop on Circuits and Systems and TAISA Conference,* pp. 1-4, ISBN 978-1-4244-4573-8, Toulouse, France, July 2009, IEEE, Piscataway

Reynolds, S.K. (2004). A 60-GHz superheterodyne downconversion mixer in silicon-germanium bipolar technology. *IEEE J. Solid-State Circuits,* Vol. 39, No. 11, pp. 2065–2068, ISSN 0018-9200

Reynolds, S. K.; Floyd, B. A.; Pfeiffer, U. R.; Beukema, T.; Grzyb, J.; Haymes, C.; Gaucher, B. and Soyuer, M. (2006). A silicon 60-GHz receiver and transmitter chipset for broadband communications. *IEEE J. Solid-State Circuits,* Vol. 41, No. 12, pp. 2820–2831, ISSN 0018-9200

Sakian, P. v. d.; Heijden, E.; Cheema, H.M.; Mahmoudi, R. and van Roermund, A. (2009). A 57–63 GHz quadrature VCO in CMOS 65 nm. *Proceedings of European Microwave Integrated Circuits Conference (EuMIC 2009)*, pp. 120-123, ISBN 978-1-4244-4749-7, Rome, Italy, Sep. 2009, IEEE, Piscataway

Scheir, K.; Wamback, P.; Rolain, Y. and Vandersteen, G. (2007). Design and analysis of inductors for 60 GHz applications in a digital CMOS technology. *Proceedings of IEEE* 69th ARFTG Conference, pp. 1-4, ISBN 978-0-7803-9762-0, Honolulu, Hawaii, USA, June 2007, IEEE, Piscataway

Shannon, C. (1948). A Mathematical Theory of Communication. *The Bell System Technical Journal*, Vol. 27, No., pp. 379-423, 623-656, ISSN 1089-7089

Smulders, P.; Haibing Yang & Akkermans, I. (2007). On the design of low-cost 60-GHz radios for multigigabit-per-second transmission over short distances. *IEEE Communications Magazine*, Vol. 45, No. 12, pp. 44 - 51, ISSN 0163-6804

Tao, S.; Rodriguez, S. ; Rusu, A. and Ismail, M. (2009). Device modelling for 60 GHz radio front-ends in 65 nm CMOS. *Proceedings of IEEE NORCHIP*, pp. 1-4, ISBN 978-1-4244-4310-9, Trondheim, Norway, Nov. 2009, IEEE, Piscataway

Tsai, J.-H. ; Wu, P.-S.; Lin, C.-S.; Huang, T.-W.; Chern, J. G. J.; Huang, W.-C. and Wang, H. (2007). A 25–75 GHz broadband Gilbert-cell mixer using 90-nm CMOS technology. *IEEE Microw. Wireless Compon. Lett.*, Vol. 17, No. 4, pp. 247–249, ISSN 1531-1309

Van Tuy, R. L. (1996). Unlicensed millimeter wave communications. A new opportunity for MMIC technology at 60 GHz, *Proceedings of* IEEE GaAs IC Symp. Dig., pp. 3-5, ISBN 0-7803-3504-X, Orlando, Florida, USA, Nov. 1996, IEEE, Piscataway

Wang, C-Y. and Tsai, J-H. (2009). A 51 to 65 GHz Low-Power Bulk-Driven Mixer Using 0.13um CMOS Technology. *IEEE Microw. Wireless Compon. Lett.*, Vol. 19, No. 8, pp. 521–523, ISSN 1531-1309

Winkler, W.; Borngraber, J.; Gustat, H. & Korndorfer, F. (2004). Design of CMOS for 60 GHz applications, *Proceedings of the 30th European Solid-State Circuits Conference (ESSCIRC)*, pp. 83-86, ISBN 0-7803-8480-6, Leuven, Belgium, Sep. 2004, IEEE, Piscataway

Yang, L.L. (2008). 60GHz: opportunity for gigabit WPAN and WLAN convergence. ACM SIGCOMM Computer Communication Review, Vol. 39, N. 1, pp. 56-61, ISSN 0146-4833

Yong, S. K. & Chong, C-C. (2007). An Overview of Multigigabit Wireless through Millimeter Wave. *EURASIP Journal on Wireless Communications and Networking*, Vol. 2007, Article ID 78907, pp. 1-10, ISSN 1687-1499